MW01181843

Reforming the Civil Justice System

Justice and Judicial Administration

A series sponsored by
The Institute of Judicial Administration
New York University School of Law

Volume I
Reforming the Civil Justice System
Edited by Larry Kramer

Reforming the Civil Justice System

Edited by
Larry Kramer

NEW YORK UNIVERSITY PRESS
New York and London

NEW YORK UNIVERSITY PRESS
New York and London

Library of Congress Cataloging-in-Publication Data
Reforming the civil justice system / edited by Larry Kramer.
p. cm.
"Papers . . . presented as part of the Institute of Judicial Administration's 'Research Conference on Civil Justice Reform in the 1990s', held in New York on October 05–16, 1993" – Preface
Includes bibliographical references and index
ISBN 0-8147-4665-9 (alk. paper)
1. Justice, Administration of – United States. 2. Courts – United States. 3. Civil procedure – United States. 4. Law reform – United States. I. Kramer, Larry
KF8700.A75R44 1996
347.73 – dc20
[347.307] 96-10869
CIP

New York University Press books are printed on acid-free paper, and their binding materials are chosen for strength and durability.

Manufactured in the United States of America

10 9 8 7 6 5 4 3 2

Contents

A. Valuation Difficulties

The standard economic model views the value of a claim in litigation, net of litigation costs, as the product of the expected judgment if the plaintiff prevails (usually denoted by "J") and the probability *ex ante* that the plaintiff will win (usually denoted by "P"). Both items, P and J, are often difficult to quantify.[8]

Consider the expected judgment, J. This will be determined, in most cases, by the fact finder's view of the extent to which the plaintiff has been injured by the defendant's wrongful conduct. Some elements of the plaintiff's injury—for example, out-of-pocket medical expenses—will be relatively easy to quantify. But many others will not. In a personal injury suit, for example, the plaintiff is likely to seek damages for items such as lost future income or pain and suffering, both of which are difficult to appraise even by a trier of fact with access to all the relevant information.

The probability of success, P, is often subject to even greater uncertainty. The applicable legal standard may be unsettled, so that the value of the claim turns, in part, on predictions of how the courts will interpret the law. Even if the law is clear, the application of the law to the facts rarely is. In a personal injury case, for example, whether the actions which the defendant undertook, or failed to undertake, amounted to negligence sufficient to establish the defendant's liability is often a difficult question. The plaintiff's actions are also relevant if the defendant raises a defense of comparative or contributory negligence. Difficult questions of causality may also complicate the application of the applicable legal standard.

All these problems exist even if the underlying facts—what actually happened—are clear. But the underlying facts typically are not clear, because the relevant actions occurred in the past and the record of these actions will often be imperfectly preserved. How fast was the defendant driving at the time of the accident? There is no black box or flight recorder in an automobile to answer such questions reliably; the trier of fact must rely on inferences drawn from testimonial and other evidence. And because the case is in litigation, the witnesses will often have an interest in the outcome that is likely to bias their accounts. Even if the witnesses have no personal interest in the outcome, their testimony will be adduced by attorneys working in an adversary system, who will attempt to present the testimony to the trier of fact in the light most favorable to their own clients.

Additional uncertainties are introduced when we allow litigation costs to enter the picture. The value of the claim to the plaintiff *ex ante* the litigation is less than the expected judgment weighted by its probability (PJ) since the plaintiff must expend resources to prosecute the claim (call these costs "Cp"). The value of the claim to the plaintiff, under the standard model, is thus PJ – Cp. It will often be difficult for the plaintiff to determine the expected litigation costs because the plaintiff will not know when the case will terminate at the time the case is brought. The plaintiff and defendant might agree to settle the case almost immediately, in which case the plaintiff's litigation costs would be minimal. On the other hand, in the worst case, the litigation might progress all the way through trial, and may result in a judgment which is then reversed and remanded for a new trial by an appellate court. There is an enormous range of litigation costs between these outcomes, and the plaintiff has little ability *ex ante* to predict what the ultimate costs will be. The plaintiff can reduce or eliminate this uncertainty by arranging for the attorney to take the case on a contingency fee basis, but such an arrangement does not eliminate the uncertainty about litigation costs on the plaintiff's side; rather it transfers risk about the costs to the plaintiff's attorney who will often be a superior risk-bearer.

Uncertainty about litigation costs also affects the defendant's calculus. From the standpoint of the defendant, the value of the case—that is, the value of obtaining legal protection against further litigation on the same claim—is not simply PJ, but includes also the defendant's expected litigation costs (call these "Cd"): the defendant expects to pay PJ + Cd in order to obtain protection against further litigation. The defendant's litigation costs, are just as uncertain as the plaintiff's costs, and for many of the same reasons. The defendant may avoid litigation costs if the suit is defended by a liability insurer, but this simply transfers risk to the insurance company and away from the defendant, and does not eliminate the uncertainty built into appraisal of the case.[9]

These problems of uncertainty are aggravated, moreover, by informational asymmetries that characterize many litigation settings. It will usually be the case that the plaintiff has superior information about the value of J—the expected judgment if plaintiff prevails—because the plaintiff is in a better position to know the extent of his or her injuries or other losses stemming from the defendant's actions.[10] The defendant, on the other hand, will usually know much more about the value of P—the probability of success of the litigation *ex ante*—because the defendant has superior information about matters such as what the defendant did, his or her knowledge about the dangerousness of the condition that caused the plaintiff's injury, the precautions that the defendant took or did not take, and so on.

These information asymmetries increase the uncertainty associated with valuing claims in litigation. Similar problems occur, of course, in many economic settings. It will often be the case, for example, that the seller of an asset has superior information about the value of the asset. In other settings the problem is typically handled through warranties: the party with superior information provides a warranty, and thus reliably informs the other party to the transaction of matters within the specialized knowledge of the warrantor. If the party providing the warranty is a seller, and the information turns out to be false, the buyer can proceed against the seller or the seller's bond for breach of warranty.

Devices analogous to warranties are used in litigation settings as well, but they are not particularly effective as means of transferring information. Plaintiffs and defendants do have an incentive voluntarily to inform each other of facts within their knowledge, both before and after suit is filed, but the incentive works best when the information provided is unexpectedly beneficial for the party providing the information.[11] For example, the defendant is likely to offer a warranty of facts that establish the defendant's non-liability, but will obviously be less inclined to warrant facts that establish the plaintiff's right to recover. Similarly, the plaintiff in a personal injury suit has an incentive to warrant that his or her injuries are more severe than would ordinarily be expected from the accident, but not to warrant that the injuries are less severe. This structure of incentives occurs as well outside the litigation setting—for example, the seller of a business is likely to volunteer the information that profits are greater than expected, but not that they are lower—but the problem appears to be particularly severe in litigation where the parties do not meet in a cooperative framework for negotiation.

There are, moreover, other difficulties with the use of warranties in litigation that are unlikely to be present in the sale of an ordinary economic asset. In the sale of an ordinary asset, such as an ongoing business, the buyer can confirm the truthfulness of most of the seller's representations after purchase, since the buyer takes possession of the asset about which the warranties are made. This is not usually the case in litigation. The defendant does not take possession of the plaintiff in order to check whether the plaintiff's asserted disabilities are truly permanent or not. Thus, the plaintiff's superior information about the value of J may not be overcome with a warranty because the defendant may lack a reliable method for confirming the plaintiff's representations on which the defendant relied. The same problem occurs when it is the defendant making the representations. The defendant may warrant to the plaintiff that the defendant took due precautions in order to avoid the incident in question; but the plaintiff may have little reason to rely on these warranties because the plaintiff is not in a good position to check after settlement to determine whether or not the defendant's representations were true.

The legal system attempts to remedy some of these defects in the information flow between plaintiff and defendant. The rules governing civil discovery can be conceptualized as a system of mandatory warranties backed by relatively severe sanctions for noncompliance. Parties in litigation do not have the option of refusing to respond to bona fide discovery requests from the other side. If they fail to comply, they will be hit with an order compelling discovery,[12] and if they remain recalcitrant they risk having the court impose severe sanctions up to and including the rendering of a default judgment.[13]

Although the discovery system corrects some of the problems inherent in voluntary warranties in the litigation setting, it is far from a panacea. As has often been observed, the mandatory feature of discovery allows parties opportunistically to impose costs on their adversaries.[14] Further, problems with checking the accuracy of warranties in the litigation setting are only partially overcome by discovery. A plaintiff or defendant might be more careful about misrepresenting or distorting the facts in response to discovery requests, but it remains difficult in many cases to check the accuracy of responses to discovery requests, and any experienced trial lawyer will confirm that accuracy cannot be presumed.

All these problems with valuing claims are aggravated by a selection effect. There are hundreds of billions of potential legal disputes extant in American society at any given time. Every executory contract, every extension of credit, every purchase and sale, and much else besides can potentially generate disputes. It distorts the problem of settlement to see it in terms of disputes not settling once a lawsuit is filed. The vast—indeed, overwhelming—majority of potential disputes are resolved without any lawsuit being filed. Most of these are never conceptualized as disputes because there is no misunderstanding as to rights and duties. People usually pay their bills simply because they do not dispute the validity of the claim being asserted on them by their creditors.

A lawsuit arises only when there is a disagreement among parties over the validity or amount of a claim. The claims that are observed in litigation are a tiny, and biased, sample of the total set of claims that exist in society at any given time; the claims that are selected for litigation tend to be those in which the problems of valuation are severe enough to induce substantial disagreement among the parties.[15] Thus, the selection effect sorts for claims which are difficult to appraise.[16]

B. Bilateral Monopoly

Aggravating these problems of valuation is the fact that the transaction in question occurs in a setting of bilateral monopoly. The assets involved are claims, and as such they can be liquidated only by a transaction between the holder of the claim and the party against whom the claim is asserted.

In most sales transactions, there is a ready resolution to the problem if the parties are unable to agree on a price. The parties simply walk away from the bargaining table and the seller seeks another buyer.[17] When, as in the litigation setting, the asset being sold is a claim by one party against another, the option of walking away from the negotiation is not present. A transaction is going to occur between the parties even if they cannot settle their dispute by agreeing on a price. If the parties do not agree, the court will force a sale at a price determined by the trier of fact.

The looming presence of a forced sale at the close of the day does not necessarily deter settlement. Quite the contrary, because the parties do not have the option to walk away, they are more likely to settle with one another through bargaining "in the shadow of the law" than they would be otherwise.[18] The point here is simply that the existence of bilateral monopoly in the litigation setting exercises a profound effect on the incentives facing the parties when they bargain with one another for the settlement of a lawsuit.

II. Reasons for Non-Settlement

The economic model of litigation suggests that it is ordinarily in the interest of both parties to a lawsuit to settle the case prior to trial, since by doing so they can avoid the litigation costs that will be expended to obtain a judicial valuation of the claim. The model thus implies that when cases do not settle, it is because the savings in litigation costs do not provide a sufficient incentive to induce settlement. There are four principal reasons, consistent with the standard model, why this may be so.

A. Mutual Optimism

The most obvious reason why a case might not settle, despite the cost savings that can be achieved through settlement, is mutual optimism by the parties.[19] If both parties are highly optimistic about their own chances, the costs saved by settling the dispute prior to trial may not be sufficient to induce a settlement.[20] The condition for trial is that the difference between the plaintiff's estimate of the value of the case net of litigation costs (call this PpJp) and the defendant's estimate of the same figure (PdJd) must exceed the sum of their trial costs. Otherwise they can make themselves mutually better off by settling and avoiding the costs; settlement will not occur if $Cd + Cp < PpJp - PdJd$.[21]

The optimism hypothesis for trials has considerable intuitive appeal given the analysis presented above of the difficulties in valuing a lawsuit.[22] Where PJ is difficult to value, there is inevitably going to be a wide dispersal of estimates of value among different parties. A diffuse distribution of possible trial outcomes is more likely to generate mutual optimism than a tight one. Moreover, there may be bargaining effects that make it difficult for the parties reliably to share information and thereby reduce excessive optimism.[23] Cases where the plaintiff assigns a much higher value to PJ than the defendant does are the ones which are likely, other things equal, to go to trial rather than settle.[24]

B. Agency Costs

A different economic reason why cases may not settle is the agency costs of litigation. Parties ordinarily do not represent themselves in court, but hire attorneys to do so. The attorney in this setting is the client's agent, and like all agents has an incentive to serve his or her own interests rather than those of the client where the two conflict.[25] The nature of the agency conflict between attorney and client is heavily dependent on the compensation arrangement. If the attorney is compensated on an hourly fee basis, the attorney has an obvious incentive to discourage settlement of litigation, since settlement will terminate the attorney's (profitable) work on the case.[26] Other compensation schemes have different settlement effects: for example, an attorney working on a contingent fee basis may have an incentive to settle the case early for too low a figure in order to obtain a high hourly return on his or her efforts.[27]

C. Strategic Effects

Another set of problems, not fully analyzed to date, concerns the strategic effects of settlement negotiations.[28] When strategic effects are considered, it turns out not to be necessarily true that a case will settle whenever the combined litigation costs exceed the difference between the parties' appraisals of the case net of litigation costs.[29] Because litigation is a bilateral monopoly, there is no market price which can allocate the gains from settlement between a producer and a consumer surplus. The percent of the settlement "pie" which the parties appropriate for themselves will depend, in each individual case, on how favorable a settlement they are able to obtain. To obtain a bigger share of the surplus, a party might adopt an intransigent bargaining posture, in hopes that the other side will capitulate. But this strategy may backfire: the other side may decide to behave equally stubbornly, keeping the parties' settlement offers far apart and maybe precluding the possibility of settlement altogether.[30] Similarly strategic factors may impede the process by which accurate and credible information is transferred between the parties, and thus may reduce the probability of settlement by leaving the parties in an overly optimistic frame of mind about the value of the case.[31] These sort of game-theoretic considerations suggest that a favorable outcome is not always to be expected, or may not always occur early in the litigation, even when the conditions for settlement are present.[32]

A somewhat different strategic problem may impair the settlement process as well. Practicing attorneys often say that it is unwise to come forward too early in the litigation process with realistic settlement proposals. Some go so far as to recommend that their clients ought not in general to be the first to suggest settlement. The reason is concern for the signaling effect of settlement offers. If the plaintiff comes to the defendant early in a lawsuit with a surprisingly low settlement offer, the defendant may well take this as a signal by the plaintiff that the suit is weak. Otherwise the plaintiff would insist on a higher amount or would not come forward with a settlement proposal at all. But, having drawn this inference, the defendant might proceed to revise his or her own estimate of the value of the lawsuit. Even if the plaintiff's offer was within the range where the defendant would have been willing to accept a settlement *ex ante*, the fact that the offer was made may drive the defendant's reservation price down even lower, thus inducing the defendant to reject the settlement offer and, potentially, discouraging settlement altogether.[33]

D. Nonmonetary Relief

Special problems arise when the parties seek nonmonetary relief, either exclusively or as an important element of the overall package. If the parties value the nonmonetary part of the relief highly, and if the nonmonetary item is not easily divisible (for example, it may be that only one of two divorcing parents can have custody), there may be a wide range of cases where the parties will go to trial even if they have similar estimates of *ex ante* probabilities and are able to save litigation costs by settling.[34] It may simply be impossible for one party to pay the other party enough money to obtain the nonmonetary relief in question.

III. Arguments for and against Settlement

It might seem that settlement of litigation is obviously a social benefit without significant costs. Except for professional litigants, few people get much utility from being party to a lawsuit. The resources spent on lawyers, transcripts, transportation, photocopying and all the incidental costs of litigating could seemingly be better spent on nearly any other activity. Litigation, moreover, seems to stir up animosity and hatred in a particularly unpalatable way. Settlement avoids some or all of these costs; as such, what objection could there be to social policies that encourage parties to settle their disputes out of court?

Essentially two varieties of argument have been made against settlement, one grounded in concerns for justice, the other in terms of economic wealth-maximization. I discuss these in turn.

A. Justice Concerns

In an often-cited article, *Against Settlement*,[35] Owen Fiss argues that settlement should not generally be preferred to judgment, and that it should not be institutionalized on a wholesale or institutional basis. Fiss argues, among other things, that settlements do not reflect substantive justice: the party in the weaker bargaining position will often have to accept a settlement proposal which is less favorable than the party could obtain in judgment simply because the party does not have the resources to pursue the matter. Settlement favors the strong and wealthy over the weak and poor, and thus tends to embed, rather than to rectify, conditions of social disparity and injustice.

Other concerns are raised by Jules Coleman and Charles Silver in their article, *Justice in Settlements*.[36] Coleman and Silver argue that settlements are problematic because they may not achieve substantive justice—the agreement of the parties is substituted for the judgment of a court or jury on the fundamental question. The quality of justice in the society is thereby strained.

Albert Alschuler argues that parties settle disputes to avoid the excessive expense, risk, and delay incident to civil litigation, or to comply with the blandishments of judges who aggressively encourage settlement.[37] In Alschuler's view, there is nothing particularly desirable about settlement if it is largely used as a means to avoid the even less desirable dispute resolution mechanism of trial. Alshuler's objection to settlement is largely based on the idea that the heavy focus on settlement detracts from the need to reform the trial process.

Common to these critiques of settlement is a sense—sometimes vaguely expressed—that trials are, or should be, more "just" or "fair" than the private resolution of disputes. As Alschuler puts it, "[i]n a more civilized society, the extensive rationing of adjudication by price and queue would not assure wrongdoers that they always could 'settle' and profit from their wrongs."[38] The notion is that settlement undermines justice in particular cases.

Why this should be so is not clear, however. The proposition that judges are better able than individual litigants to determine the "just" result is supported by no evidence. While judges may have a better sense of the law, they may also act arbitrarily or irrationally. And the parties surely will have a greater command of the facts. The idea that there is a "just" result that differs systematically from the outcomes voluntarily agreed to by the parties requires greater support than has been offered to date by the opponents of settlement.

It may well be that certain aspects of the trial process tend to disadvantage one type of party over another in a way that is not obviously related to substantive outcomes. The high cost of litigation may, as Fiss and others argue, work against the interests of poorly financed litigants who may not be able to pay their attorneys. Delay in the courts may, as Alschuler asserts, work against the interests of plaintiffs.[39] But viewing these features as problematic is premised, in part, on the notion that the substantive right in question is necessarily separate from the procedural mechanism used to vindicate that right. These authors do not consider the possibility that substantive rights of recovery might be set at a level that corrects for imbalances introduced by the procedural system.

Moreover, it is incorrect to view the procedural system as "only" disadvantaging plaintiffs or poorly financed parties. Poorly financed parties may suffer a disadvantage in litigation as *plaintiffs* (although the degree of disadvantage is reduced by devices such as contingency fees and class actions). But they have a major advantage as *defendants* when compared with deep pocket litigants. Rich defendants are routinely sued even when they have only a tangential relationship to the litigation, whereas poor persons are unlikely to be sued even if they are the principal culprits on the theory that "you can't get blood out of a stone." Further, rich defendants probably suffer more at the hands of civil juries than do poor defendants. Is it completely clear that the disadvantages poor people suffer in litigation as plaintiffs outweigh the advantages they enjoy as defendants?

By the same token, the advantage defendants enjoy stemming from delay—a principal focus of Professor Alschuler's attack—is offset to a substantial degree by advantages that our procedural system gives to plaintiffs as compared with defendants: for example, the liberal notice pleading rules that allow plaintiffs to come to court with only the vaguest specification of their grievances; and rules relating to civil discovery, which tend systematically to benefit plaintiffs because the typical plaintiff is able to impose greater discovery burdens on defendants than the typical defendant can impose on plaintiffs. It simply is not clear that, taken as a whole, the litigation system favors defendants over plaintiffs, rich over poor, or any other broad-based class of persons.

B. Economic Considerations

In addition to objections based on concepts of justice, a number of economic arguments are made against settlement. The most significant of these is that settlement prevents the creation of a judicial precedent, and judicial precedents are public goods with significant external benefits.[40] Parties settling a dispute "in the shadow of the law," are able to do so because there exists a relatively well-defined body of law against which the parties can judge their particular controversy. Much of that prior law is in the form of judicial cases that are generated by lawsuits. Thus, settling parties in essence free ride on the precedents created by others. Because precedents are a public good, too few of them will be generated in an unregulated market since the parties to a lawsuit cannot capture the full economic benefit of their activities.

This argument has some cogency, but it is not convincing as a systematic objection to settlement. The public good aspect of settlements is counteracted by the fact that litigation in the United States is subsidized; indeed, a standard economic justification of subsidizing the court system is the public goods aspect of judicial precedents. The courts are free to litigants, or nearly so, despite the fact that taxpayers pay for them. Other things being equal, subsidized litigation will induce a higher level of litigation than would be socially optimal, not the reverse.[41] Thus we have a tradeoff between the inadequate demand for litigation predicted to result from the fact that judicial precedents are a form of public good, and the excessive demand for litigation generated by the fact that the court systems are subsidized. There is no way in theory to predict which effect will dominate—or whether they might even cancel each other out, resulting in a rough social optimality in the demand for litigation.

Some of the arguments put forward by the justice theorists can also be elaborated in economic terms, although the policy prescriptions generated by the economic form of these arguments are more ambiguous than the opponents of settlement on justice grounds would admit. A socially optimal system of regulation would include a cost-benefit analysis, not only of the effects of the substantive rights being enforced, but also of the procedures utilized to enforce those rights. For example, if procedural considerations are ignored, it might be the case that a particular negligence rule, perfectly enforced, would achieve the optimal level of deterrence and would induce the socially efficient level of expenditures on precautionary measures. But if it is costly to enforce these rights, the rule may not be fully enforced. Potential defendants may find it possible to expend fewer resources on precaution than would be socially desirable because they know that the probability of being sued and forced to pay damages for harms caused by their negligent activities is significantly less than one. The general point is that optimal social regulation must endogenize the enforcement process itself.[42]

If it turns out that the opportunity to settle cases induces a level of enforcement below the optimal level, then settlement might be seen as imposing real social costs. This argument might potentially counsel against settlement of cases if the social value of the added deterrence obtained by taking cases to trial exceeded the social costs incurred by not settling.[43] However, if settlement does lead to underdeterrence, raising the substantive penalty might be a simpler and more effective means for correcting the problem as compared with placing restraints on settlement.

However, there is little reason to believe that settlement does systematically result in economically inefficient under- enforcement of legal norms. While defendants may pay too little in some cases as a result of settlement, in others—nuisance suits are an example[44]—defendants pay too much. In some settings, such as plea-bargaining, the possibility of settlement may increase deterrence, not reduce it, by allowing for a more effective application of prosecutorial resources than would be possible without plea bargaining.[45] Moreover, the deterrent effect of litigation includes not only the amounts the defendant must pay in judgment or settlement on the merits, but also the defendant's cost of litigation itself. This added cost may correct for problems of under-enforcement. And the law may contain other correctives for the costs of litigation to plaintiffs. There is no reason why the substantive law must be set at a level reflecting an assumption of perfect enforcement. More likely, the substantive law is crafted, at least in a rough way, so as to correct for the under-enforcement that might occur because some good cases will not be brought. For example, the defendant may face potential punitive damages or damages for "soft" items such as pain and suffering, items that on balance bring the level of deterrence up toward the socially appropriate level notwithstanding the fact that litigation costs may deter some cases from being filed or may induce the plaintiff to settle for an amount below what the plaintiff can expect to receive at trial. Alternatively, plaintiffs may be given benefits in terms of burdens of proof or underlying standards of liability that make it easier for plaintiffs to recover than would be socially optimal under an assumption of perfect enforcement.

This discussion of the pros and cons of settlement must end on an inconclusive note. The various considerations involved are too complicated to generate intuitively persuasive arguments that the level of settlement is too high, too low, or about right. Nevertheless, it seems plausible to entertain, at least as a working hypothesis, the proposition that if there are mechanisms that the law can provide at little or no cost, which the parties can choose at their option in order to facilitate the private settlement of litigation, those measures probably ought to be made available. Devices for encouraging settlement that override the wishes of one or both parties are more controversial, and require stronger justification to recommend them as appropriate social policy. The next section of this paper discusses some of the leading devices for encouraging settlement, as well as some interesting proposals for reform.

IV. Devices to Induce Settlement

The perceived benefits of settlement over litigation have sparked enormous enthusiasm—cheerleading even—for a variety of devices that allegedly encourage settlement of litigation and are referred to collectively as Alternative Dispute Resolution (ADR).[46] Because these devices operate quite differently, and have quite different effects on the settlement process, they are discussed separately. It should be emphasized that the issues raised by the various forms of ADR are enormously complex and only a summary treatment is possible here. There is an extensive literature on most of these settlement devices, to which the reader is directed for further discussion.

The various devices to encourage settlement can be sorted by their economic function, and they can be understood as means to overcome some of the impediments to settlement identified above.[47]

A. Devices to Combat Optimism

As we have noted, the principal reason given in the economic literature for why cases don't settle is optimism by the parties. When both sides feel their case is strong, they are unlikely to settle even if they can save substantial litigation costs by doing so. Excessive optimism is an information problem: one or both parties are misinformed about the strength of their case. The solution, then, would appear to be to provide mechanisms for informing the parties about the true condition of the facts or law. A wide variety of procedural devices—not all of them traditionally recognized as settlement-inducing mechanisms—attempt to fulfill this goal.

Civil discovery is a most obvious means for inducing settlement by informing the parties.[48] The purpose of discovery is to provide both parties with information relevant to the outcome of the case. As discovery progresses, it will often be the case that one or both parties realize that their initial optimism was misguided. Witnesses they hoped would testify unambiguously in their favor hedge their stories, documents they hoped would substantiate their position cannot be located or do not exist, and so on. Enough disappointment of this sort will eventually induce the party to revise his or her estimate of the value of the lawsuit—in some cases with the result that settlement becomes possible after discovery when it was not possible before.

Pretrial motions can also reduce party optimism early in the litigation. The parties' view of applicable law can be tested through motions to dismiss, motions for judgment on the pleadings, and motions for summary judgment. The court's ruling on such motions often provides preliminary information about how a judge evaluates the applicable law—information that is all the more relevant in jurisdictions in which the judge ruling on preliminary motions also has responsibility for conducting the trial. Probably equally important, pretrial motions force the parties to engage in legal research and subject that research to adversarial testing. The generous notice pleading requirements of most U.S. systems allows the filing of complaints with only minimal legal research, even when the possibility of sanctions under Rule 11 or analogous state rules is considered. When conducting research on preliminary motions, a party may discover—or have called to his or her attention by the other side—previously unknown precedents or other legal materials unfavorable to the party's case. The result may be to correct for the party's initial excessive optimism about the value of the case.[49]

Motions for preliminary relief—temporary restraining orders or preliminary injunctions—have a similar function. Because one element of preliminary relief is typically that the party seeking the relief must demonstrate a probability of success on the merits, the court's rulings on motions for such relief provide relevant information about the ultimate outcome. Motions for preliminary relief address both facts and law, and may do so in a trial-type hearing that provides a good test of the parties' predictions as to the strengths of their cases. Further, the demeanor and attitude of the trial judge, which provide important information about the ultimate outcome, may be evaluated during the hearing for preliminary relief.

Federal Rule of Civil Procedure 16, and similar mechanisms at the state level, encourage an active stance by judges in encouraging settlement prior to trial.[50] Part of the function of the pretrial conference is to give the parties a candid view of the judge, and of the judge's view of the case, outside the formal procedures of rulings on motions or formal in-court hearings on requests for preliminary relief.

Beyond these, there is a panoply of "new age" forms of alternative dispute resolution procedures which serve the function of increasing the information available to the parties to combat excessive optimism. The function of settlement conferences may be partly contracted out, as it were, through devices such as neutral evaluation programs,[51] special settlement masters,[52] private "rent-a-judge" programs,[53] and court-annexed arbitration.[54] The summary jury trial, which has received considerable attention in recent years, is another such device: it offers an early—and allegedly low-cost—trial run that permits the parties to revise their prior estimates of the value of the case based on the conduct and outcome of the summary trial.[55]

A final important regulation in this area is the applicable rule for compensating attorneys. Under the "American Rule," each side pays his or her own attorney, win or lose, whereas under the "British Rule," the loser pays his or her own attorney and also the winner's fees as determined by a judicial official.[56]

The rule on attorney compensation will not affect the information set available to the litigants and so will not tend to deter unjustified optimism. However, the attorney compensation rule can significantly alter the risk, costs, and expected return of litigation. Because different characteristics of risk and return may influence the settlement rate, the choice between the English and American rules has a potentially significant impact on the parties' propensity to go to trial.

The literature on which rule induces a higher level of settlements is as vigorous as it is inconclusive, with scholars divided between those who claim that the English Rule is more likely to lead to settlement than the American Rule,[57] those who believe the American Rule is better,[58] and those who see the question as ambiguous.[59]

B. Overcoming Agency Costs

In contrast with the large number of devices used or proposed to overcome the problem of excessive optimism, there are few devices set forth in the litigation system itself which are intended to, or have the effect of, overcoming the agency costs of the attorney-client relationship. The reason, presumably, is that judges in an adversary system do not ordinarily insert themselves between lawyer and client. The lawyer is presumed, in general, to act as a good agent of the client, and evidence to the contrary is not ordinarily within the judicial purview. The judge may often think privately that the attorney is directing a client away from an advantageous settlement, but it would be inappropriate for the judge in most settings to say so publicly. The most important regulations designed to control agency costs of settlement, accordingly, are not judicially enforceable rules of procedure, but rather are attorney disciplinary rules which apply to the relation of lawyer and client.[60]

There are, however, a number of procedural rules which can be understood as operating to combat extreme forms of agency costs. One is Federal Rule of Civil Procedure 11, which prohibits the filing of pleadings that are not reasonably grounded in fact and law. Sanctions under the rule can, depending on the circumstances, be imposed either on the client, the attorney, or both. One potential function of the rule is to police against litigation strategies by attorneys that do not serve their client's best interests. The rule deters the filing of frivolous claims and arguments that suggest to the client that the litigation should be continued rather than settled, in cases where the attorney would benefit by continuing the litigation and the client would be better off if the litigation were either settled or dropped. In this respect Rule 11 helps encourage settlement by controlling agency costs.

More explicit control of agency costs in settlement is found in the class action and shareholders' derivative suit contexts. Because the named plaintiff in such litigation is likely to be no more than a cipher or "key to the courthouse door," the plaintiffs' attorneys in such cases often act as private entrepreneurs free of any form of extensive client monitoring.[61] These agency costs are particularly problematic in the area of settlement of litigation, where the law requires judicial scrutiny of settlement proposals to ensure that they are substantively fair to the class or corporation.[62] The efficacy of judicial scrutiny of such settlement proposals is much in doubt, however.[63] One possible mechanism for controlling agency costs in the settlement of class and derivative actions is for the court to conduct an auction of the action to the highest bidder, thus eliminating agency costs and directing the proceeds of the auction to the represented party.[64] The auction would also allow the defendant itself to bid, thus settling the case if the defendant turns out to be the high bidder.[65]

C. Overcoming Strategic Effects

Although procedural rules and programs are rarely explicitly justified on the ground that they control strategic problems that may impair settlement, several procedural rules do, in fact, have this effect. The scholarly community is beginning to recognize the potential value and utility of devices to overcome strategic impediments to settlement.[66]

One of the most important strategic rules now on the books is Rule 68, the federal offer-of-judgment rule.[67] Rule 68 provides that defendants may serve formal offers of judgment on plaintiffs, which if rejected result in the offeree being required to pay the offeror's post-offer costs if the judgment finally obtained by the offeree is not more favorable than the offer. The advantage of the rule, from the standpoint of strategic impediments to settlement, is that it provides a reason for parties to disclose information about their case by making bona fide settlement offers that do not necessarily trigger adverse inferences by the other party. Because Rule 68 provides the defendant with an incentive to come forward with a realistic offer of settlement early in the litigation, plaintiffs will not necessarily conclude that such offers reflect weakness in the defendant's case.

Recent work on Rule 68 suggests that the rule can have potential benefits for settlement. Kathryn Spier finds that Rule 68 encourages settlement when the parties disagree about a continuous variable by deterring them from making exaggerated claims, but that the rule does not encourage settlement when the outcome is a dichotomous variable (such as "win" or "lose").[68] More generally, Spier concludes that a two-sided version of an offer-of-judgment rule—under which either side could make an offer of judgment under the rule rather than only the defendant as under current law—can minimize the total cost of litigation.[69]

David A. Anderson suggests two interesting modifications to an offer of judgment rule.[70] First, Anderson explores what he calls the "sincerity rule," which permits either side to make an offer of judgment, with the offeror paying the offeree's post-offer fees if the offer is rejected. A possible advantage of the sincerity offer is that the party making the offer bonds himself or herself to the fairness of the offer by voluntarily agreeing to accept a substantial penalty if the offer is rejected. Second, Anderson discusses a final offer auction, under which either party can bid for the right to make the final offer, with the revenue from the top bid being granted to the opposing party. The high bidder is then allowed to make a final offer, which, if refused, results in the case proceeding to trial with no further bargaining. Anderson argues that, under certain assumptions, a final offer auction yields a settlement midway between the parties' estimates of the expected verdicts.[71]

Robert Gertner and I propose an unusual but apparently practical remedy for the problem of signaling in settlement negotiations.[72] The signaling problems could potentially be overcome if there existed some legal device through which parties could make settlement offers without the other side knowing they are doing so. We call this device a settlement escrow, which would simply be an arrangement with an officer of the court to accept settlement offers from either side. The device would be limited to cash offers to settle the entire case. Collateral matters such as court costs would be established by convention—for example, the rule could be that costs would be divided equally among the parties for any case settled out of the escrow. The escrow agent's sole function would be to examine the offers and to hold them. The agent would be specifically barred from disclosing to anyone—including the judge—the amount of the offers, or even the fact that an offer has been made. This information would be disclosed only if the two sides submit offers that cross—if, for example, the plaintiff puts an offer into the escrow that proposes to settle the case for less than the defendant has offered in the escrow. When offers cross, the escrow agent announces that a settlement has concluded. Under the rules of the escrow, the settlement would be at the midpoint between the two offers.

Settlement escrows address the signaling problem by disguising from either party the fact that the other has made an offer. A party sends at most only a weak signal of weakness in his or her case by making a realistic, bottom-line offer into the escrow, since the other side will be made aware of the offer if and only if that side submits a crossing offer. Accordingly, parties ought not to be deterred from making realistic settlement offers into the escrow early in the case. At the same time, both parties are perfectly free to continue the litigation and to engage in the full range of settlement negotiations outside of the escrow.

Conclusion

This review of the current state of the literature on the settlement of litigation necessarily has left many issues unexplored and others ambiguous. It is impossible to identify a consistent scholarly consensus across a wide range of issues. Even the justification for settlement itself is in dispute.

From the standpoint of economic analysis of law, however, it would appear that at least some tentative judgments are possible:

1. Settlement presents the enormous advantage of avoiding trial costs. Those who argue against settlement must make the case that the benefits of trial exceed the benefits of avoiding trial costs. While coherent arguments can be constructed to the effect that settlement represents a form of socially inefficient free riding on the public good of judicial precedent, or that settlement reduces the enforcement of the law below socially optimum levels, these arguments are neither supported by much evidence nor intuitively compelling. In the absence of relatively strong reasons to believe that the costs of settlement exceed the benefits, the case against settlement is not persuasive. Thus, private, voluntarily negotiated settlements should ordinarily be enforced by the judicial system.[73]

2. Devices to encourage extrajudicial resolution of disputes appear socially desirable when they are freely agreed to and paid for by the parties.[74] For example, if contracting parties agree to submit future conflicts to binding arbitration, there is little reason in public policy for concern. Similarly, if parties to litigation voluntarily submit their dispute to arbitration or neutral evaluation, or otherwise agree to some type of alternative dispute resolution procedure, the law has no real cause for concern.[75]

3. On the other hand, devices that *compel* parties to participate in procedures to which they have not assented are more problematic—even when the procedures in question are non-binding in the sense that either party is free to reject the result and proceed to trial.[76] If either party does not wish to participate, it requires a relatively strong reason of social policy to override his or her preference. The strength of the justification needed to support compulsory alternative dispute resolution would appear to be a function, among other things, of the costs of the particular procedure in question.

Most economic analysts, in other words, would probably opt for a middle ground between the naysayers about settlement, who see it as a means for perpetuating social inequality or substantive injustice, and the cheerleaders, who favor settlement devices that can be forced on the parties even when they do not desire them. Economic analysis, in general, sees social welfare being served when autonomous parties are allowed to make rational choices. Most economic analysts would probably view the decision to litigate or settle in similar terms.

Notes

1. This review is limited to work analyzing the settlement of litigation. For an excellent general survey of the economic literature on litigation through

1989, see Robert D. Cooter & Daniel L. Rubinfeld, *Economic Analysis of Legal Disputes and Their Resolution*, 27 J. Econ. Literature 1067 (1989).

2. John Gould, *The Economics of Legal Conflicts*, 2 J. Legal Stud. 279 (1973).
3. William Landes, *An Economic Analysis of the Courts*, 14 J. L. & Econ. 61 (1971).
4. Richard A. Posner, *An Economic Approach to Legal Procedure and Judicial Administration*, 2 J. Legal Stud. 399 (1973).
5. Stephen Shavell, *Suit, Settlement, and Trial: A Theoretical Analysis Under Alternative Methods for the Allocation of Legal Costs*, 11 J. Legal Stud. 55 (1982).
6. For an interesting analysis of the consequences of the doctrine of *res judicata* for settlement of disputes, finding that *res judicata* and its related doctrine, collateral estoppel, tend to induce settlements related to the merits of the litigation, see Bruce L. Hay, *Some Settlement Effects of Preclusion*, 1993 U. Ill. L. Rev. 21.
7. For a treatment of the value of a claim in litigation as an option, see Bradford Cornell, *The Incentive to Sue: An Option Pricing Approach*, 19 J. Legal Stud. 173 (1990).
8. For discussion of empirical work documenting the difficulty in quantifying the value of claims in litigation, see Herbert M. Kritzer, Let's Make a Deal: Understanding the Negotiation Process in Ordinary Litigation 58–59 (1991).
9. A defense contingent fee is theoretically possible—the defendant's law firm could, for example, agree to indemnify the defendant for the amount of any judgment in the case in exchange for a substantial up-front fee—but such arrangements are rarely observed.
10. In some cases, however, the defendant may have superior information about the value of J—for example, copyright, patent and trademark cases in which the plaintiff can recover the defendant's profits or gain from the infringement.
11. See Steven Shavell, *Sharing of Information Prior to Settlement or Litigation*, 20 Rand J. Econ. 193 (1989); Louis Kaplow, *The Value of Accuracy in Adjudication*, 23 J. Legal Stud. 307 (1994); Douglas G. Baird, Robert Gertner, and Randal Picker, Game Theory and the Law, ch. 9 (1993).
12. See Fed. R. Civ. Proc. 37(a).
13. See Fed. R. Civ. Proc. 37(b).
14. See, e.g., Robert Cooter & Daniel Rubinfeld, *An Economic Model of Legal Discovery*, 23 J. Legal Stud. 435 (1994); John K. Setear, *The Barrister and the Bomb: The Dynamics of Cooperation, Nuclear Deterrence, and Discovery Abuse*, 69 B.U.L. Rev. 569 (1989).
15. See George L. Priest & Benjamin Klein, *The Selection of Disputes for Litigation*, 13 J. Legal Stud. 1 (1984).
16. Selection effects have generated a substantial economic literature. In addition to the foundational work of Priest & Klein cited in note 15, studies include Theodore Eisenberg, *Testing the Selection Effect: A New Theoretical Framework with Empirical Tests*, 19 J. Legal Stud. 297 (1990); Samuel Gross & Kent Syverud, *Getting to No: A Study of Settlement Negotiations and the Selection of Cases for Trial*, 90 Mich. L. Rev. 319 (1991); Keith N. Hylton, *Asymmetric Information and the Selection of Disputes for Litigation*, 22 J. Legal Stud. 187 (1993); George L. Priest, *Selective Characteristics of Litigation*, 90 J. Legal Stud. 399 (1980); George L. Priest, *Reexamining the Selection Hypothesis*, 14

J. Legal Stud. 215 (1985); Linda R. Stanley & Don L. Coursey, *Empirical Evidence on the Selection Hypothesis and the Decision to Litigate or Settle*, 19 J. Legal Stud. 145 (1990); Donald Wittman, *Is the Selection of Cases for Trial Biased?*, 14 J. Legal Stud. 185 (1985); Donald Wittman, *Dispute Resolution, Bargaining, and the Selection of Cases for Trial: A Study of the Generation of Biased and Unbiased Data*, 17 J. Legal Stud. 313 (1988).

17. The distinctive features of litigation in this regard should not be overstressed, however, since elements of bilateral monopoly exist in many standard commercial settings as well.
18. See Robert Cooter, Stephen Marks & Robert Mnookin, *Bargaining in the Shadow of the Law*, 11 J. Legal Stud. 225 (1982).
19. For an experimental study supporting the proposition that parties tend to go to litigation when they are mutually optimistic, see Stanley & Coursey, *supra* note 16.
20. See, e.g., Stephen Shavell, *Alternative Dispute Resolution: An Economic Analysis*, 24 J. Legal Stud. 1, 11 (1995); Stephen McG. Bundy, *The Policy in Favor of Settlement in an Adversary System*, 44 Hastings L.J. 1, 13 (1992).
21. Shavell, *supra* note 20, at 11.
22. In addition, psychological pressures may induce parties to estimate their own chances overly optimistically. See George Lowenstein, Samuel Isacharoff, Colin Camerer & Linda Babcock, *Self-Serving Assessments of Fairness and Pretrial Bargaining*, 22 J. Legal Stud. 135 (1993)(finding that parties tend systematically to overestimate their chances of success in litigation); Daniel Kahneman & Amos Tversky, *Conflict Resolution: A Cognitive Perspective*, in Barriers to Conflict Resolution (Arrow, ed.) (forthcoming). There may also be an endowment effect present in this context. Many studies have demonstrated that people tend to demand more to give up an entitlement they have than to obtain one which they do not have. See, e.g., Herbert Hovenkamp, *Legal Policy and the Endowment Effect*, 20 J. Legal Stud. 225 (1991). Litigation can be seen as a situation in which both parties believe they are being asked to relinquish an entitlement. In such a case, both parties are likely to demand more to give up the endowment than they would be willing to pay for it if they did not already possess it—resulting in higher plaintiff demands, and lower defendant offers, than might otherwise be the case.
23. See, e.g., Lucian Bebchuk, *Litigation and Settlement Under Imperfect Information*, 15 Rand J. Econ. 404 (1984); Ivan P'ng, *Strategic Behavior of Suit, Settlement, and Trial*, 14 Bell J. Econ. 539 (1983); J. Reiganum & L. Wilde, *Settlement, Litigation and the Allocation of Litigation Costs*, 17 Rand J. Econ. 557 (1986); Barry Nalebuff, *Credible Pretrial Negotiation*, 18 Rand J. Econ. 198 (1987); J. Ordover & A. Rubinstein, *A Sequential Concession Game with Asymmetric Information*, 101 Q.J. Econ. 879 (1986); Katheryn E. Spier, *The Dynamics of Pretrial Negotiation*, 59 Rev. Econ. Stud. 93 (1992).
24. A countervailing consideration, however, is that cases presenting severe valuation difficulties will also tend to require higher litigation expenses by the parties—providing an additional inducement to settlement in order to avoid these costs. William Landes has demonstrated that bifurcated trials and similar devices for coping with high litigation costs when valuation is uncertain will also tend to reduce the settlement rate simply because they

save litigation expenses for the parties. William M. Landes, *Sequential versus Unitary Trials: An Economic Analysis*, 22 J. Legal Stud. 99 (1993); see also Baird, Gertner, & Picker, *supra* note 11, at ch. 9.

25. See Geoffrey Miller, *Some Agency Problems in Settlement*, 16 J. Legal Stud. 189 (1987).
26. See *id.* These problems are particularly acute in the class action context, where members of the plaintiff class have virtually no ability to monitor the behavior of class counsel. See, e.g., Jonathan Macey & Geoffrey Miller, *The Plaintiffs' Attorney's Role in Class Action and Derivative Litigation: Economic Analysis and Recommendations for Reform*, 58 U. Chi. L. Rev. 1 (1991).
27. See Miller, *supra* note 25. For an empirical study providing support for this hypothesis, see Terry Thomason, *Are Attorneys Paid What They're Worth? Contingent Fees and the Settlement Process*, 20 J. Legal Stud. 187 (1991). For an attempt to devise a contingency fee that avoids this problem, see Kevin M. Clermont & John D. Currivan, *Improving on the Contingent Fee*, 63 Cornell L. Rev. 529 (1978).
28. For one book-length treatment, however, see Kritzer, *supra* note 8.
29. See, e.g., Robert Cooter, Stephen Marks & Robert Mnookin, *Bargaining in the Shadow of the Law: A Testable Model of Strategic Behavior*, 11 J. Legal Stud. 225, 246 (1982); Bundy, *supra* note 20, at 13.
30. See Cooter, Marks & Mnookin, *supra* note 18.
31. See sources cited *supra* note 23.
32. For an interesting empirical study of strategic behavior in settlement bargaining, see Samuel and Syverud, *supra* note 16.
33. This problem is discussed in Robert Gertner & Geoffrey Miller, *Settlement Escrows*, 24 J. Legal Stud. 87, 95–97 (1995).
34. See Steven Shavell, *Suit Versus Settlement When Parties Seek Nonmonetary Judgments*, 22 J. Legal Stud. 1 (1993).
35. Owen Fiss, *Against Settlement*, 93 Yale L.J. 1073 (1984). A recent LEXIS search disclosed 164 citations to this article in the Law Review data base through September, 1993.
36. Jules Coleman & Charles Silver, *Justice in Settlements*, Soc. Phil. & Pol'y. 103 (Autumn 1986).
37. Albert Alschuler, *Mediation with a Mugger: The Shortage of Adjudicative Services and the Need for a Two-Tier System in Civil Cases*, 99 Harv. L. Rev. 1808 (1991).
38. *Id.* at 1859.
39. For systematic exposition, see George L. Priest, *Private Litigants and the Court Congestion Problem*, 69 B.U.L. Rev. 527 (1989); Geoffrey P. Miller, *Some Thoughts on the Equilibrium Hypothesis*, 69 B.U.L. Rev. 561 (1989).
40. This point is made by a number of writers in the economic school. See, e.g., Richard A. Posner, The Federal Courts: Crisis and Reform 11 (1985).
41. See *id.* at 10–11.
42. See Kaplow, *supra* note 11.
43. For a paper which treats the settlement-trial decision as endogenous within a general theory of deterrence, see A. Mitchell Polinsky & Daniel L. Rubinfeld, *The Deterrent Effects of Settlement and Trials*, 8 Int'l. Rev. L. and Econ. 109 (1988). For interesting discussion of the interplay between litigation costs and the design of damage awards, see Kathryn Spier, *Settlement Bargaining*

and the Design of Damage Awards, Harvard Law School Program in Law and Economics, Discussion Paper No. 126 (1993).

44. There is a sizable literature on whether the litigation system is likely to generate nuisance suits. Posner argues that such suits are likely to be rare because defendants will call plaintiffs' bluff, see Posner, *supra* note 4, at 433. Others have devised models in which nuisance suits are possible. See, e.g., Lucian Bebchuk, *Suing Solely to Extract a Settlement Offer*, 17 J. Legal Stud. 437 (1988); Avery Katz, *The Effect of Frivolous Lawsuits on the Settlement of Litigation*, 8 Int'l. Rev. L. & Econ. 3 (1990); Rosenberg & Shavell, *A Model in Which Suits are Brought for Their Nuisance Value*, 5 Int'l. Rev. L. & Econ. 3 (1985). For an analysis of the economic effects of rules permitting judges to sanction frivolous suits, see A. Mitchell Polinsky & Daniel L. Rubinfeld, *Sanctioning Frivolous Suits: An Economic Analysis*, Stanford Law School John M. Olin Program in Law and Economics, Working Paper No. 103 (1993).
45. See Landes, *supra* note 3.
46. For a sampling of the vast literature on ADR, see, e.g., Stephen B. Goldberg, Eric D. Green, and Frank A. Sanders, Dispute Resolution (1985); National Institute of Dispute Resolution, Paths to Justice: Major Public Policy Issues for Dispute Resolution (1983); Wayne Brazil, *A Close Look at Three Court-Sponsored ADR Programs: Why They Exist, How They Operate, What They Deliver, and Whether They Threaten Important Values*, 1990 U. Chi. Legal Forum 303; Harry Edwards, *Alternative Dispute Resolution, Panacea or Anathema?*, 99 Harv. L. Rev. 668 (1986); Jethro K. Lieberman & James F. Henry, *Lessons from the Alternative Dispute Resolution Movement*, 53 U. Chi. L. Rev. 424 (1986); Roger J. Patterson, *Dispute Resolution in a World of Alternatives*, 37 Catholic U.L. Rev. 591 (1988). There is also a major law school casebook on ADR, Stephen Goldberg, Frank Sander, and Nancy Rogers, Dispute Resolution: Negotiation, Mediation, and Other Processes (2d ed. 1992).
47. See *supra* notes 19–34 and accompanying text.
48. The settlement-inducing effect of discovery in organizing the transfer of information among the parties is offset, however, by the tendency of discovery to mandate the disclosure by parties of information unfavorable to their case, which can reduce the probability of settlement by correcting for false pessimism by the other side. See Cooter & Rubinfeld, *supra* note 14.
49. See William Landes, *Sequential versus Unitary Trials: An Economic Analysis*, 22 J. Legal Stud. 99 (1993).
50. For discussion, see, e.g., David L. Shapiro, *Federal Rule 16: A New Look at the Theory and Practice of Rulemaking*, 137 U. Penn. L. Rev. 1969 (1989); Carrie Menkel-Meadow, *Pursuing Settlement in an Adversary Culture: A Tale of Innovation Co-Opted or "The Law of ADR,"* 19 Fla. St. U.L. Rev. 1 (1991); Carrie Menkel-Meadow, *For and Against Settlement: Uses and Abuses of the Mandatory Settlement Conference*, 33 U.C.L.A. L. Rev. 485 (1985); Leonard L. Riskin, *The Represented Client in a Settlement Conference: The Lessons of* G. Heileman Brewing Co. v. Joseph Oat Corp., 69 Wash. U.L.Q. 1059 (1991). The activist role of some federal judges in settlement negotiations is part of a broader trend of greater judicial involvement in case management, especially in institutional reform litigation. See Judith Resnik, *Managerial Judges*, 96 Harv. L. Rev. 376 (1982).

51. See, e.g., Donald L. Levine, *Early Neutral Evaluation: The Second Phase*, 1989 J. Dispute Resolution 1.
52. See, e.g., Wayne Brazil, *Special Masters in Complex Cases: Extending the Judiciary or Reshaping Adjudication?*, 53 U. Chi. L. Rev. 394 (1986).
53. See Lisa Bernstein, *Understanding the Limits of Court-Connected ADR: A Critique of Federal Court–Annexed Arbitration Programs*, 141 U. Penn. L. Rev. 2249, 2251 n.1 (1993).
54. See, e.g., Patricia A. Beener & Donnar R. Betancourt, Court-Annexed Arbitration: The National Picture (1985).
55. See, e.g., Thomas D. Lambros, *The Summary Jury Trial and Other Alternative Methods of Dispute Resolution*, 103 F.R.D. 461 (1984); Richard A. Posner, *The Summary Jury Trial and Other Methods of Alternative Dispute Resolution: Some Cautionary Observations*, 53 U. Chi. L. Rev. 366 (1986).
56. For background on the American Rule, see John Leubsdorf, *Toward a History of the American Rule on Attorney Fee Recovery*, 47 L. & Contemp. Probs. 9 (1984).
57. See, e.g., John C. Hause, *Indemnity, Settlement, and Litigation, or I'll Be Suing You*, 18 J. Legal Stud. 157 (1989).
58. See, e.g., Posner, *supra* note 4, at 417–420; Shavell, *supra* note 5.
59. E.g., John Donohue, *The Effects of Fee Shifting on the Settlement Rate: Theoretical Observations on Costs, Conflicts, and Contingency Fees*, 54 L. & Contemp. Probs. 195 (1991); Avery Katz, *Measuring the Demand for Litigation: Is the English Rule Really Cheaper?*, 3 J.L. Econ. & Org. 143 (1987).
60. For discussion, see Miller, *supra* note 25, at 210.
61. The leading scholar to explore systematically the implications of this fact is John C. Coffee, Jr. See John C. Coffee, Jr., *The Regulation of Entrepreneurial Litigation: Balancing Fairness and Efficiency in the Large Class Action*, 54 U. Chi. L. Rev. 877 (1987); John C. Coffee, Jr., *Understanding the Plaintiff's Attorney: The Implications of Economic Theory for Private Enforcement of Law Through Class and Derivative Actions*, 86 Colum. L. Rev. 669, 676 (1986); John C. Coffee, Jr., *The Unfaithful Champion: The Plaintiff as Monitor in Shareholder Litigation*, 48 L. & Contemp. Probs. 5 (Summer 1985); John C. Coffee, Jr., *Rescuing the Private Attorney General: Why the Model of the Lawyer as Bounty Hunter is Not Working*, 42 Maryland L. Rev. 215 (1983).
62. Fed. R. Civ. Proc. 23(e) (class actions), 23.1 (derivative litigation).
63. See Macey & Miller, *supra* note 26.
64. This proposal is found in *id.* at 105–116.
65. The advantages of defendant bidding in litigation auctions have been questioned, however. See Randall S. Thomas & Robert G. Hansen, *Auctioning Class Action and Derivative Lawsuits: A Critical Analysis*, 87 Nw. U. L. Rev. 423 (1993). For a response, see Jonathan R. Macey & Geoffrey P. Miller, *Auctioning Class Action and Derivative Suits: A Rejoinder*, 87 Nw. U. L. Rev. 458 (1993).
66. See, e.g., Bundy, *supra* note 20, at 61–63 (favoring judicial intervention to overcome strategic problems but not for other purposes).
67. For discussion, see, e.g., David A. Anderson, *Improving Settlement Devices: Rule 68 And Beyond*, 23 J. Legal Stud. 225 (1994); Geoffrey Miller, *An Economic Analysis of Rule 68*, 15 J. Legal Stud. 93 (1986); George Priest, *Regulating the Content and Volume of Litigation: An Economic Analysis*, 1

Sup. Ct. Econ. Rev. 163 (1982); Roy D. Simon, Jr., *The Riddle of Rule 68*, 54 Geo. Wash. L. Rev. 1 (1985); Kathryn E. Spier, Pretrial Bargaining and Fee-Shifting Mechanisms: A Theoretical Foundation for Rule 68 (1992); Jay N. Varon, *Promoting Settlements and Limiting Litigation Costs by Means of the Offer of Judgment: Some Suggestions for Using and Revising Rule 68*, 33 Am. U.L. Rev. 813 (1984). For a preliminary empirical study, see Thomas D. Rowe, Jr., *Empirical Research on Offers of Settlement: A Preliminary Report*, 51 L. & Contemp. Probs. 13 (1988).

68. Spier, *supra* note 67.
69. *Id.*
70. Anderson, *supra* note 67.
71. *Id.*
72. Gertner & Miller, *supra* note 33.
73. By the same token, the law should ordinarily defer to long-standing informal mechanisms for dispute resolution outside the litigation system. Cf. Lisa Bernstein, *Opting Out of the Legal System: Extralegal Contractual Relations in the Diamond Industry*, 21 J. Legal Stud. 115 (1992) (analyzing private mechanisms for resolving disputes in the wholesale diamond industry).
74. See Shavell, *supra* note 20 (concluding that *ex ante* ADR agreements made by knowledgeable parties raise social welfare, absent external effects, and should generally be enforced).
75. The social welfare implications of voluntary *ex post* ADR procedures are not as clear-cut as those of *ex ante* agreements, however. See *id.*
76. See Bernstein, *supra* note 53; Shavell, *supra* note 20.

Settlements Under Joint and Several Liability*

Lewis A. Kornhauser
Richard L. Revesz**

Introduction

Last Term, in *Musick, Peeler & Garrett v. Employers Insurance*,[1] the Supreme Court granted certiorari to decide whether defendants held jointly and severally liable in actions under section 10(b) of the Securities Exchange Act of 1934 and Rule 10b-5 of the Securities and Exchange Commission have the right to seek contribution from other liable defendants.[2] The briefs submitted by the parties and by several amici representing powerful trade associations disagreed vigorously about which sets of rules regarding a right of contribution would better

---

*This article was previously published at 68 N. Y. U. L. Rev. 427 (1993). We are grateful to the author and publishers for their permission to reprint it.
**Professors of Law, New York University School of Law.
We acknowledge the generous financial support of the Filomen D'Agostino and Max E. Greenberg Research Fund at the New York University School of Law. We are grateful for the comments of Vicki Been, Samuel Estreicher, Mark Geistfeld, Marcel Kahan, and A. Mitchell Polinsky, and for the research assistance of Munish Rametra. A prior version of this Article was presented at the Institute of Judicial Administration's Research Conference on Civil Justice Reform in the 1990s at the New York University School of Law, and at law and economics workshops at the University of Michigan Law School and the University of Pennsylvania Law School.

promote settlements.[3] Ultimately, the Court declined to consider these arguments.[4] Focusing instead on the structure of the statutory scheme, it held that contribution was available.[5]

In many other contexts, however, common law courts are choosing among alternative rules governing the litigation of claims involving multiple defendants based on the courts' views about the relative settlement-inducing properties of these rules. This practice is by no means limited to the state courts.[6] Federal courts routinely make such decisions, invoking their common law powers under such disparate statutes as the Securities Exchange Act,[7] the Comprehensive Environmental Response, Compensation and Liability Act (CERCLA),[8] the Civil Rights Act,[9] the Employee Retirement Income Security Act (ERISA),[10] the Federal Deposit Insurance Act,[11] as well as under the federal law of admiralty.[12]

The federal common law governing litigation involving multiple defendants is rife with conflicts among the circuits. Under the securities laws,[13] ERISA,[14] and admiralty,[15] the circuits differ on the set-off to be applied, as a matter of federal common law, to a plaintiff's claim against a non-settling defendant following a settlement with another defendant.[16]

This Term, the Supreme Court granted certiorari to resolve the conflict among the circuits on the appropriate set-off rule under the law of admiralty.[17] Unlike the situation in the Musick, Peeler & Garrett case, statutory guidance is simply unavailable in this case.[18] The Court will therefore have no alternative but to invoke its power to fashion federal common law.[19] Given the strong and oft-repeated interest in promoting the settlement of disputes, particularly in multi-defendant cases,[20] the relative impact of the competing rules on the choice between settlement and litigation is likely to play an important role in the resolution of these disputes.

The purpose of this Article is to guide the choice of an appropriate legal regime—at both the federal and state levels—to govern litigation involving joint tortfeasors. Our analysis focuses solely on the impact of the competing legal rules on the choice between settlement and litigation: the plaintiff has already suffered the harm, and the question is whether it will have to litigate in order to recover.[21] We do not consider which rules are better from the perspective of inducing the socially desirable amount of deterrence.[22]

Part I categorizes legal rules in this area by reference to eight relevant elements: (1) whether there is joint and several liability; (2) whether there is a right of contribution; (3) whether the right of contribution is pro rata or by reference to comparative fault; (4) whether, when the plaintiff settles with one defendant and litigates against the other, its claim against the non-settling defendant is reduced by the amount of the settlement (a pro tanto set-off rule), or, instead, by the settling defendant's share of the liability (an apportioned share set-off rule); (5) whether settling defendants are protected from contribution actions; (6)

whether settling defendants have a right to bring contribution actions; (7) whether there is judicial supervision of the substantive adequacy of settlements; and (8) whether the claims involving all the joint tortfeasors are joined together in a single proceeding. This scheme, rather than the truncated taxonomy generally used by the courts, significantly aids the analysis of the relative merits of the competing rules.

Part II provides a comprehensive analysis of the settlement-inducing property of a rule containing the following elements: (1) joint and several liability; (2) a right of contribution; (3) contribution determined by reference to comparative fault; (4) a pro tanto set-off rule; (5) contribution protection for settling defendants; (6) no right of contribution for settling defendants; (7) no judicial supervision of the substantive adequacy of settlements; and (8) joinder of the claims against all the joint tortfeasors. It shows that the impact of this rule on the choice between settlement and litigation depends centrally on the correlation of the plaintiff's probabilities of success against both defendants.[23]

Because the correlation of the plaintiff's probabilities of success plays such a central role in our analysis and yet has been overlooked in the prior works, it is important at this point to elucidate the concept. These probabilities are independent if the outcome of the plaintiff's claim against one defendant does not depend upon whether the plaintiff prevails against, loses to, or settles with the other defendant. For example, suppose that the plaintiff seeks to recover the costs of cleaning up a hazardous waste site, and each of two unrelated defendants argues that it did not send hazardous substances to the site. The outcome of the plaintiff's case against one defendant is then independent of the outcome of its case against the other. Or, consider a "hub and spoke" conspiracy in which several parties are alleged to have conspired with the "hub." The fact that one party did so says nothing about whether others did so as well; thus the plaintiff's probabilities of prevailing against the various "spokes" are independent.

In contrast, the plaintiff's probabilities are perfectly correlated if, when the plaintiff litigates against both defendants, it either prevails against both or loses to both. In the previous example, suppose that the defendants argue, instead, that the plaintiff's cleanup was inappropriately expensive; there is then no scenario under which one would prevail if the other does not. The plaintiff's probabilities of success are also perfectly correlated in a case in which only two defendants are alleged to have engaged in a conspiracy; because it is not possible for a party to conspire with itself, if one defendant prevails, the other will do so as well. Respondeat superior cases in which the agent's authority is conceded also have this feature.

Part II establishes that if the plaintiff's probabilities of success are independent, the plaintiff litigates against both defendants unless the costs of litigation are sufficiently high; this result also holds if the probabilities are sufficiently, though not wholly, independent. In contrast, if these probabilities are perfectly correlated, the plaintiff settles with at least one defendant regardless of the magnitude of the litigation costs; this result also holds if the probabilities are sufficiently, though not perfectly, correlated. Part II concludes with an analysis of the relevance of the model's assumptions.

Part III studies the settlement-inducing properties of some alternative legal rules. It reaches three principal conclusions. First, the pro tanto set-off rule generally promotes more settlements than the apportioned share set-off rule when the costs of litigation are low, but can promote fewer settlements when these costs are high. Second, a regime with no right of contribution has identical effects on the choice between settlement and litigation as one with contribution. Third, joint and several liability discourages settlement when the plaintiff's probabilities of success are independent; in contrast, when these probabilities are perfectly correlated, joint and several liability generally promotes settlement when it is coupled with the pro tanto set-off rule, and has no effect on settlement when it is coupled with the apportioned share set-off rule.

Part IV turns its attention to the work of common law courts in the area in which the courts are most deeply divided: the choice of set-off rules. It shows that essentially all the arguments raised by the courts about the relative settlement-inducing properties of the competing set-off rules are based on an incomplete or incorrect understanding of the incentives faced by the respective parties. In particular, the courts fail to account for the strategic nature of the interaction among the parties.

This Article presents the first comprehensive analysis of the problem of settlement in cases involving joint tortfeasors. The two most serious prior efforts in this area both focused on only a subset of the problem—the case of perfectly correlated probabilities—and studied only a limited subset of the legal rules.[24] Because they did not understand the way in which their analyses were limited, they couched their conclusions—most importantly, that joint and several liability promotes settlement—in general terms. We show, by focusing on the impact of the correlation of the plaintiff's probabilities of success, that what the prior works took to be a general result is in fact a special case, and that the problem is far more complex than the prior commentators had acknowledged.

I. Categorizing the Legal Regime

In order to analyze properly the impact of joint and several liability on settlement, one must specify with care each of the components of the competing legal rules. We first categorize such rules by reference to eight elements. We then show why our taxonomy eliminates some of the confusion reflected in judicial decisions.

A. A Taxonomy

For each of the eight elements that we use to define the legal regime governing the litigation of claims involving joint tortfeasors, we discuss the major alternatives. We focus principally on the approaches of the Restatement (Second) of Torts (Restatement),[25] the Uniform Contribution Among Tortfeasors Act (UCATA),[26] and the Uniform Comparative Fault Act (UCFA).[27] In the margin, we consider federal common law rules developed under some important federal statutes.

1. Joint and Several Liability Versus Non-Joint (Several Only) Liability

Under joint and several liability, if the plaintiff litigates against two defendants and prevails against only one, it can recover its full damages from that defendant. In contrast, under non-joint (several only) liability, the plaintiff would only recover the portion of the damages attributable to the actions of the losing defendant.

The Restatement calls for the application of joint and several liability where damages "cannot be apportioned among two or more causes."[28] The comments add that "where two or more causes combine to produce . . . a single result, incapable of division on any logical or reasonable basis, and each is a substantial factor in bringing about the harm, the courts have refused to make an arbitrary apportionment for its own sake, and each of the causes is charged with responsibility for the entire harm."[29] As an example, the Restatement provides the case of two automobiles driven negligently that hit a bystander; the two drivers would be jointly and severally liable to the bystander.[30]

The Restatement has been influential in the development of federal common law. For example, under CERCLA, relying explicitly on the Restatement's provisions, the courts have fashioned a rule of joint and several liability where the harm caused by the presence of hazardous substances at a site is "indivisible."[31]

The remaining elements set forth in this Section are relevant only for joint and several liability. Under non-joint liability, the plaintiff essentially has independent claims against the defendants, and the questions discussed below do not arise.

2. The Right of Contribution

A right of contribution permits a defendant that has paid a disproportionately large share of the plaintiff's liability to obtain compensation from a defendant that has paid a disproportionately small share of this liability.[32] Under the Restatement, there is a right of contribution among defendants found jointly and severally liable for a single harm.[33] Both the UCATA and UCFA also recognize such a right.[34]

The Restatement, the UCATA, and the UCFA thus reject the traditional common law rule, generally traced to *Merryweather v. Nixan,*[35] barring contribution among defendants found jointly and severally liable for a harm. This common law rule has been rejected by the federal courts under their common law powers,[36] as well as by the vast majority of states.[37]

3. The Nature of the Right of Contribution

Under the UCATA, contribution is determined by reference to pro rata shares of the liability.[38] Contribution is available only to a tortfeasor that has paid more than its pro rata share of the liability.[39] In turn, contribution is not available from a tortfeasor that has paid at least its pro rata share of the liability.[40] Thus, if two defendants are jointly and severally liable, contribution is available only to a defendant that has paid more than half of the liability, and the comparative levels of fault play no role in the determination of whether contribution is available.[41]

In contrast, under the UCFA and the Restatement, contribution is determined by reference to comparative fault.[42] The Restatement further provides that a defendant can avail itself of this right only if it has paid more than its equitable share of the liability. Moreover, no defendant can be required to contribute beyond its equitable share.[43] The comparative fault approach is the rule generally adopted under federal common law[44] and in most state jurisdictions.

4. The Choice of Set-Off Rule

The question of an appropriate set-off rule arises when the plaintiff settles with one defendant and litigates against the other. The UCATA provides that in the event of a settlement with one defendant, the plaintiff's claim against the non-settling defendant is reduced "to the extent of any amount stipulated by the release or the covenant, or in the amount of the consideration paid for it, whichever is greater."[45] This rule is commonly referred to as a pro tanto set-off rule.

In contrast, under the UCFA, the plaintiff's claim is reduced by the settling defendant's "equitable share of the obligation."[46] We refer to this rule as the apportioned share set-off rule. Note that while under the UCFA the apportioned share set-off rule is coupled with contribution by reference to comparative fault, one could have an apportioned share set-off rule in a legal regime in which contribution was determined pro rata. Then, the plaintiff's claim against a non-settling defendant would be reduced by the pro rata share attributable to the settling defendant. In both cases, the plaintiff's claim is reduced by the amount that would have been attributable to the settling defendant if both defendants had litigated and lost. For this reason, we find the term "apportioned share set-off rule" more revealing than the terms "proportional" set-off rule[47] or "comparative fault" set-off rule,[48] which are generally employed by the courts.[49]

The Restatement addresses the issue of set-off rules in two separate places. Section 885(3) provides that "a payment by any person made in compensation of a claim for a harm for which others are liable as tortfeasors diminishes the claim against the tortfeasors, at least to the extent of the payment made."[50] This section thus provides that the set-off would be no less than that provided under the pro tanto set-off rule. The Restatement's comments to section 886A, however, describe both the pro tanto and apportioned share set-off rules, but do not endorse either rule.[51]

As indicated above, the federal courts are deeply divided on the choice between these two set-off rules. This split exists not only across statutory schemes, but also within a single scheme.[52]

The two set-off rules differ in their effect on the plaintiff's recovery when it settles with one defendant and prevails in litigation against the other. Under the pro tanto set-off rule, the plaintiff recovers its full damages regardless of the amount of the settlement. Under the apportioned share set-off rule, if the settlement is for less than the settling defendant's apportioned share of the liability, the plaintiff does not recover its full damages even if it prevails against the other defendant.

Consider an example in which contribution is determined by reference to comparative fault, the two defendants are each equally at fault, and the plaintiff's damages are $100. If the plaintiff settles with one defendant for $20, under the apportioned share set-off rule it can recover only $50 from the other defendant, thus suffering a shortfall of $30. What happens, however, if the settlement is for $70? Can the plaintiff nonetheless recover $50 from the non-settling defendant? Most jurisdictions allow such recovery,[53] as do the federal courts under the securities laws.[54] The reasoning is that because under the apportioned share set-off rule the plaintiff bears the risk of a low settlement, it should obtain the benefit of a high settlement.[55] In contrast, New York follows a constrained version of the apportioned set-off rule—limiting the plaintiff's total recovery to its damages in the event that it settles with one defendant and litigates against the other.[56]

The preceding discussion assumes that there is a right of contribution. In the absence of such a right, there also is a question about how a settlement with one defendant should affect the plaintiff's claim against the non-settling defendant.[57] The most logical approach in that instance is to use a pro tanto set-off rule.[58] Without a right of contribution, if the plaintiff litigates and prevails against both defendants, it can choose to obtain its full damages from one of the defendants, despite the resulting unfairness. It is not clear why one should be more concerned about this unfairness when the plaintiff settles with one defendant and litigates against the other.[59] We are not aware of any jurisdiction that has coupled a rule of no contribution with an apportioned share set-off rule.

5. Contribution Protection for Settling Defendants

Of course, in the absence of a general right of contribution, settling defendants, like all other defendants, are protected from contribution actions. In contrast, regimes that recognize the right of contribution between defendants found jointly and severally liable at trial must answer the further question whether a contribution action can be maintained against a settling defendant.

When one defendant settles, and the other litigates and ultimately loses, the question whether the settling defendant is protected from contribution actions arises only for the pro tanto set-off rule, under which it is possible that the litigating defendant will be liable for more than its equitable share of the liability. Under the apportioned share set-off rule, the litigating defendant never has to pay more than its equitable share of the liability and therefore never has the right to maintain a contribution action.

In contrast, when the plaintiff settles with both defendants, and one of them pays more than its equitable share of the liability while the other pays less than its share, the question whether the former defendant can bring a contribution action against the latter arises under both set-off rules.[60] The resolution depends both on whether settling defendants are protected from contribution actions, which is the focus of this Subsection, and on whether settling defendants have the right to bring contribution actions, to which we turn in the next Subsection.

The Restatement presents examples of legal rules with and without contribution protection for settling defendants, but it does not endorse either option.[61] The UCATA provides that if a settlement is entered in good faith, "it discharges the tortfeasor to whom it is given from all liability for contribution to any other tortfeasor."[62] The UCFA provides that a settlement discharges that defendant "from all liability for contribution."[63] Thus, while the Restatement neither approves nor disapproves of it, both model laws provide for contribution protection, though the UCATA qualifies this protection by limiting it to settlements entered in good faith.[64]

6. Contribution Rights for Settling Defendants

The existence of a right of contribution among defendants found jointly and severally liable does not necessarily imply that settling defendants also will enjoy such a right. The question of the contribution rights of settling defendants can arise in three instances. First, as indicated above, if both defendants settle, a defendant that has paid more than its equitable share can bring an action against one that has paid less than its equitable share only if the legal regime allows a right of contribution for settling defendants and does not protect settling defendants from such actions. This problem can arise under either set-off rule.

Second, if the legal regime gives settling defendants a right of contribution, a defendant that settles for more than its apportioned share of the liability can bring a contribution action against a defendant that litigates, loses, and is liable for a judgment that is less than its equitable share of the liability. This situation arises only under the pro tanto set-off rule, because under the apportioned share set-off rule, a defendant that litigates and loses would pay its equitable share of the liability.

Third, current rules of collateral estoppel allow a defendant that settles for more than its apportioned share of the liability to bring a contribution action against a defendant that prevailed in its litigation against the plaintiff. Such an action may be brought under either set-off rule.[65]

Under the Restatement, the UCATA, and the UCFA, a settling defendant can seek such contribution only to the extent that the plaintiff's claim against the other defendants is extinguished by the settlement.[66] Thus, a settling defendant cannot avail itself of the right of contribution in cases in which the plaintiff settles with it and litigates against the other defendant, or where the plaintiff settles with both. Such a right is available only when the settlement with one defendant provides that the plaintiff will drop its claim against the other.[67]

7. The Nature of "Good Faith" Hearings on the Adequacy of Settlements

Under the pro tanto set-off rule, if the plaintiff enters into an inadequately low settlement with one defendant and that defendant obtains contribution protection as a result of the settlement, the other defendant is responsible for the shortfall if it litigates and loses. To protect the interests of non-settling defendants, courts typically require "good faith" or "fairness" hearings on the adequacy of settlements.[68]

The Restatement, UCATA, and UCFA are all silent on the nature of good faith hearings. The courts are divided on whether this hearing should involve only a procedural inquiry about the absence of collusion between the plaintiff and the settling defendant,[69] or whether it should also scrutinize the substantive adequacy of the settlement.[70] This split is well illustrated by *Tech-Bilt, Inc. v. Woodward-Clyde & Associates.*[71] In *Tech-Bilt,* the California Supreme Court held that the good faith inquiry "would enable the trial court to inquire, among other things, whether the amount of the settlement is within the reasonable range of the settling tortfeasor's proportional share of comparative liability for the plaintiff's injuries."[72] In a strong dissent, Chief

Justice Bird argued that "a settlement satisfies the good faith requirement if it is free of corrupt intent, that is, free of intent to injure the interests of the nonsettling tortfeasors. A settlement is made in bad faith only if it is collusive, fraudulent, dishonest, or involves tortious conduct."[73] Under her approach the inquiry is solely procedural; she would not inquire into the substantive adequacy of the settlement.[74]

The preceding discussion was limited to regimes of contribution, contribution protection, and pro tanto set-off. There is no reason to have good faith hearings in the absence of a right of contribution. If the plaintiff can collect its damages in any way that it wants when it litigates and prevails against both defendants, it is not logical to be concerned about fairness when the plaintiff settles with one defendant and litigates against the other.[75] Also, there is no reason for such hearings under contribution regimes that do not provide contribution protection to a settling defendant. Then, the remedy for a non-settling defendant that pays more than its apportioned share of the liability is to seek contribution from the settling defendant. Finally, good faith hearings are not necessary under the apportioned share set-off rule because there the plaintiff, rather than the non-settling defendant, suffers the loss from a low settlement.

8. Joinder Rules

If the plaintiff joins all the joint tortfeasors in a single suit, its claims against all of them will be adjudicated in the same proceeding. If the plaintiff chooses not to join all the tortfeasors as defendants, the question arises whether a named defendant can join another tortfeasor as a third-party defendant. Otherwise, the named defendant would have to file a separate action for contribution after the adjudication of its liability to the plaintiff.

Both the Restatement and the UCATA state in their comments that this matter is governed by the procedural rules of the state in which the action is brought.[76] The UCFA states that the right of contribution "may be enforced either in the original action or in a separate action brought for that purpose,"[77] but does not specify how this determination should be made.

In federal court, this question is determined by reference to Rules 14(a) and 42 of the Federal Rules of Civil Procedure, which govern third-party practice. Rule 14(a) provides that a defendant, acting as a third-party plaintiff, may bring an action for contribution, as of right within ten days of the filing of its answer, and with leave of the court thereafter.[78] Rule 42 gives the court discretion either to order a single trial or to sever the actions for separate trial.[79] In general, courts have been reluctant to sever contribution or indemnification claims from the primary action.[80]

B. Competing Taxonomies

Some recent cases provide different ways to categorize the legal regimes governing the litigation of claims against joint tortfeasors.[81] This Section explains how our taxonomy removes many ambiguities and makes possible a clearer analysis of the relative merits of the different legal rules.

In re Oil Spill by the Amoco Cadiz[82] provides the most comprehensive categorization of the legal regime that we have found in the case law. There, the Seventh Circuit observes that there are four potential rules: (1) no contribution, (2) contribution, (3) contribution plus settlement bar, and (4) claim reduction.[83] Under all four rules, each defendant is jointly and severally liable for the full damages if the plaintiff prevails against both.[84]

Under a rule of no contribution, the plaintiff can collect any part of its award from any of the defendants and no defendant can obtain contribution from another. Under a rule of contribution, the plaintiff can collect any part of the award from any of the defendants, and a party that pays more than its share of the award can get contribution from a party that pays less than its share. A rule of contribution plus settlement bar differs from the former in that a defendant cannot obtain contribution from a settling defendant. The settlement bar is thus equivalent to what we call contribution protection for settling defendants.[85] Finally, under a rule of claim reduction, if the plaintiff settles with one defendant, its claim against the other defendant is reduced by the share attributable to the settling defendant; the non-settling defendant cannot obtain contribution from the settling defendant because it does not pay more than its share of the liability.[86] Claim reduction is thus equivalent to what we call the apportioned share set-off rule.[87]

These categories are confusing for several reasons. First, the rules of contribution and contribution plus settlement bar implicitly assume that a settling defendant has the right to bring contribution actions. Indeed, under the former there is no limit to the reach of the contribution right, and under the latter the only limit is that a settling defendant cannot be sued. The assumption that a settling defendant can bring a contribution action is inconsistent with the approaches of the two model acts.[88] More importantly, by conflating three elements—whether defendants found jointly and severally liable have a right to contribution, whether settling defendants have a right to contribution, and whether settling defendants are protected from contribution actions—into two categories, the Seventh Circuit's approach diverts attention from the important question whether settling defendants can bring contribution actions.

Second, the claim reduction rule does not specify whether defendants can bring contribution actions (or be exposed to such actions) in the event that they both settle.[89] If one of these defendants were to litigate, it could not be held liable for more than its apportioned share of the liability, since its liability would be reduced by the apportioned share of the settling defendant. At first glance, it might appear odd that this defendant would pay more in settlement. But if the plaintiff's probability of prevailing is sufficiently high, litigation costs are sufficiently high, and the plaintiff has sufficient bargaining power to capture a great deal of the surplus produced by settlement, such a result could well ensue. A defendant that paid more than its apportioned share of the liability would then have a contribution claim, if the legal regime allowed such claims.[90] Here, the Seventh Circuit's approach conflates two elements—the set-off rule, and the contribution rights and obligations of the settling defendants.[91]

Third, the nomenclature is confusing with respect to the effects of a rule of contribution. As we have discussed, contribution among defendants found jointly and severally liable is consistent with using either the pro tanto set-off rule or the apportioned share set-off rule in the event that one of them settles. What the Seventh Circuit calls "contribution" is in fact a contribution rule with a pro tanto set-off rule and no contribution protection for settling defendants. What the Seventh Circuit calls "contribution plus settlement bar" is a contribution rule with a pro tanto set-off rule and contribution protection for settling defendants.[92] What the Seventh Circuit calls "claim reduction" is a contribution rule with an apportioned share set-off rule. Here, the court's typology conflates two elements—whether there is a right of contribution and the nature of the set-off rule.

Fourth, the rule of no contribution is ambiguous as to what happens if the plaintiff settles with one defendant and litigates against the other. The implicit assumption seems to be that a pro tanto set-off rule would apply, so that the plaintiff could in sum recover its full damages if it prevails against the non-settling defendant.[93] While this assumption is justified,[94] the lack of explicit attention to this question detracts from the analytical clarity of the Seventh Circuit's approach.

Fifth, the Seventh Circuit's categories do not purport to deal with the manner in which contribution is determined (pro rata or on the basis of comparative fault), the nature of a good faith hearing under the pro tanto set-off rules, or joinder rules. These elements are all relevant to the analysis of the choice between settlement and litigation and therefore should be included in a taxonomy of possible legal rules.[95]

II. The Choice Between Settlement and Litigation

In this Part, we analyze the settlement-inducing properties of one particular rule, which has the following eight components. First, joint and several liability applies. Second, there is a right of contribution among defendants held jointly and severally liable. Third, the contribution of each defendant is determined by reference to its comparative fault. Fourth, if the plaintiff settles with some defendants and litigates against others, its claim against the non-settling defendants is reduced by the amount of the settlement—a pro tanto set-off rule. Fifth, settling defendants are protected from contribution actions. Sixth, settling defendants are barred from bringing contribution actions. Seventh, there is no substantive judicial supervision of the settlement offers made by the plaintiff. Eighth, the plaintiff's claims against all of the defendants are joined together in a single proceeding.

We first specify the model that will guide our inquiry. We then analyze each party's choice between settlement and litigation when the plaintiff's probabilities of success against the defendants are independent. We next turn to the case of perfectly correlated probabilities. Then, we move away from these polar cases and consider the continuum between independent and perfectly correlated probabilities. Finally, we consider the extent to which the results depend upon the particular specifications in our model.

A. The Model

We consider an example in which a single plaintiff has a claim of $100 against two defendants, Row and Column, each equally at fault. All the parties are risk neutral, and the defendants are infinitely solvent.[96] The probability that the plaintiff will prevail against each defendant is fifty percent.[97] All the parties have accurate information about this value. We assume initially that the costs of litigation are zero.[98]

The parties may either litigate or settle the claim. Settlement negotiations have the following structure. The plaintiff makes settlement offers to the two defendants; each knows the offer made to the other. Row and Column decide simultaneously whether to accept these offers. We assume that costs of coordinating their actions are sufficiently high that they act non-cooperatively.[99] The plaintiff then litigates against the non-settling defendants, if any. We adopt the convention that if a party is indifferent between settlement and litigation, it settles.[100] To keep the exposition comprehensible to readers without technical training, we proceed here by first providing a numerical example and then explaining the intuition for why the example is illustrative of some general propositions.[101]

B. The Case of Independent Probabilities

Consider first the case of independent probabilities: the plaintiff's probability of success against one defendant is the same regardless of whether the plaintiff has prevailed against, lost to, or settled with the other defendant. Recall that the plaintiff has a fifty percent probability of prevailing against each of the defendants and that the plaintiff's damages are $100. As a consequence of joint and several liability, the plaintiff recovers its full damages not only if it prevails against both defendants but also if it prevails against one and loses to the other. Because the plaintiff's probabilities of success against the two defendants are independent, each of four different scenarios carries a probability of twenty-five percent: (1) that the plaintiff prevails against both defendants, (2) that the plaintiff prevails against Row and loses against Column, (3) that the plaintiff prevails against Column and loses against Row, and (4) that the plaintiff loses against both defendants. In the first three cases, carrying an aggregate probability of seventy-five percent, the plaintiff recovers its full damages of $100. Thus, its expected recovery from litigating against both defendants is $75.[102]

In turn, each defendant's expected loss is $37.50. Row has a fifty percent probability of prevailing and, therefore, of not having to pay anything. There is a probability of twenty-five percent that Row will lose and Column will win. In this case, Row has to pay the plaintiff's full damages of $100. Finally, there is a probability of twenty-five percent that Row and Column will both lose. Row then has to pay its share, $50, with Column paying the rest.[103]

A risk-neutral plaintiff will not accept a settlement with both defendants that yields less than $75, but it would find acceptable an aggregate settlement for $75 or more. What would happen if the plaintiff made settlement offers to the two defendants for $37.50 each, so that its aggregate recovery, if they accepted, would be equal to the expected recovery of litigating against both defendants? If one defendant, say Row, accepted the offer, would the other defendant accept it as well? Column would accept the settlement only if the expected loss from litigating is at least $37.50. Under the pro tanto set-off rule, Column's exposure in the event of litigation is reduced to $62.50: the plaintiff's damages of $100 minus Row's settlement of $37.50. But Column faces only a fifty percent probability of losing the litigation. Thus, in light of Row's settlement, Column's expected loss from litigation is only $31.25.

It therefore follows that if the plaintiff were to make offers of $37.50 to each defendant, at least one of them would reject the offer. If one defendant settles, the plaintiff's expected recovery would then be $68.75 (Row's settlement of $37.50 plus an expected recovery of $31.25 from litigating against Column). This amount is lower than the plaintiff's expected recovery from litigating against both defendants. Thus, the plaintiff would never make offers of $37.50 to each defendant.[104]

More generally, there is no pair of settlement offers that would be acceptable to the plaintiff and both defendants. There are three relevant classes of offers. First, the plaintiff could make an offer of $37.50 to one defendant and a lower offer to the other, make offers of less than $37.50 to both defendants, or make an offer of less than $37.50 to one defendant and more than $37.50 to the other, with these two offers adding to less than $75. If both defendants then accepted the offers, the plaintiff's recovery would be less than its expected recovery from litigating against both defendants.

Second, the plaintiff could make an offer of \$37.50 to one defendant and a higher offer to the other, or it could make higher offers to both. Since at least one defendant preferred to litigate when they both received offers of \$37.50, it follows that higher offers will make settlement even less attractive.[105]

Third, the plaintiff could make an offer of less than \$37.50 to one defendant and an offer of more than \$37.50 to the other, with the two offers adding to at least \$75. Say that the plaintiff makes an offer of a to Row and (\$75 - a) to Column, with the offers thus adding to \$75.[106] Assume initially that a is less than \$37.50. What would Column do if Row accepted the offer of a? If Column litigated, it would face a fifty percent probability of having to pay the plaintiff's full damages of \$100 minus Row's settlement of a; its expected loss would therefore be 0.5 times (\$100 - a). This expected loss is lower than the settlement offer of (\$75 - a) for any value of a that is less than \$50. It thus follows that offers of a and (\$75 - a), where a is less than \$37.50, would not induce settlements with both defendants. Moreover, if a is greater than \$37.50, then (\$75 - a) is less than \$37.50. As a result, if Column accepted the offer of (\$75 - a), Row would not.

In summary, for the plaintiff to settle with both defendants, settlement must be advantageous to all three parties. There is no set of circumstances under which this would be the case. In the face of offers that are sufficiently attractive to the plaintiff, at least one defendant would prefer to litigate, and offers that the defendants would both be willing to accept are undesirable for the plaintiff.

A simple extension of the preceding discussion also establishes that the plaintiff would not settle with one defendant. Assume that the plaintiff settles with Row and litigates against Column. Given that Column litigates, Row would be willing to settle as long as the offer is no greater than \$37.50—its expected loss in the event of litigation. What happens if the plaintiff makes Row an offer of b? Its expected recovery from litigating against Column is then 0.5 times (\$100 - b), or (\$50 - 0.5b). Its total expected recovery (the settlement with Row of b plus its expected recovery from Column of (\$50 - 0.5b)) is then (\$50 + 0.5b). For the plaintiff's expected recovery from settling with Row and litigating against Column to be equal to at least \$75 (the plaintiff's expected recovery from litigating against both defendants), b (the settlement paid by Row) must be at least \$50. But, as already noted, given that Column litigates, Row will settle only if b is no greater than \$37.50. Here, too, no offer acceptable to one defendant would give the plaintiff an expected recovery as high as its expected recovery from litigating against both defendants. As a result, the plaintiff will litigate against both defendants.

So far, we have provided only an example of this phenomenon. The skeptical reader might wonder what would happen if the defendants were not equally at fault, or if the plaintiff's probability of success against each of the defendants were not fifty percent. It is still the case that the plaintiff would litigate rather than settle. This phenomenon has two sources: (1) the surplus that the plaintiff obtains from litigation as a result of joint and several liability when its probabilities of success against the defendants are independent and (2) the benefit that a non-settling defendant receives from the set-off created by the plaintiff's settlement with the other defendant.

If the plaintiff were litigating against only one defendant rather than two, its expected recovery from litigation would be $50 rather than $75: it would have a fifty percent probability of recovering from that defendant its full damages of $100. Similarly, if the plaintiff were litigating against two defendants under non-joint (several only) liability, its expected recovery would also be $50: it would have a fifty percent probability of recovering $50 from each of the defendants. The lower recovery stems from the fact that if the plaintiff prevails against only one defendant, it does not recover its full damages of $100 but only the losing defendant's share of $50. Finally, if the plaintiff were litigating against two defendants under joint and several liability, but its probabilities of success against the defendants were perfectly correlated, it would also have an expected recovery of only $50. The perfect correlation of the probabilities implies that the plaintiff either prevails against both defendants or loses against both; in the former case, which carries a probability of fifty percent, it recovers its full damages of $100, whereas in the latter case it gets nothing.

As a result of the surplus that the plaintiff obtains from litigating against both defendants under joint and several liability when its probabilities of prevailing are independent, the plaintiff will not accept from one defendant a settlement that is too low even if the plaintiff intends to litigate against the other. Say, for example, that the plaintiff accepted a settlement of $0 from Row and litigated against Column. Its expected recovery would then be only $50 (a fifty percent probability of recovering $100); the settlement with Row will have reduced its expected recovery by $25. If the plaintiff accepted a settlement of $10 from Row, its expected recovery from litigating against Column would be $45 (a fifty percent probability of recovering $90), for a total expected recovery of $55; the loss from the low settlement with Row is $20.

So as not to lose its surplus, the plaintiff would thus have to demand a sufficiently high settlement from Row. But a settlement that is sufficiently desirable for the plaintiff to accept confers a benefit upon Column. If, for example, the plaintiff were to settle with Row for $25, Column's expected loss from litigation would be $37.50 – the same expected loss as if Row litigated. Any higher settlement with Row reduces Column's expected loss. We have already shown that a settlement with Row for $37.50 reduces Column's expected loss from $37.50 to $31.25, giving it a benefit of $6.25. In order to recover $75, the plaintiff would have to obtain from Row a settlement of $50 (which would leave an expected recovery from Column of $25 and thus confer upon Column a benefit of $12.50). Row, however, would not agree to such a settlement because, given that Column litigates, it is better off litigating as well and facing an expected loss of only $37.50.

We have thus illustrated why the plaintiff cannot capture the full benefit of Row's settlement if its probabilities of success are independent. Part of this settlement confers an external benefit upon Column. It is this externality that stands in the way of settlement. Indeed, the only way that the plaintiff can obtain the full benefit of a defendant's payment is by litigating, because if it settles, part of the benefit accrues to the other defendant.

C. The Case of Perfectly Correlated Probabilities

The problem changes considerably if the plaintiff's probabilities of success against both defendants are perfectly correlated:[107] if the plaintiff litigates against both defendants, it either prevails against both (with a probability of fifty percent) or loses against both (also with a probability of fifty percent). Its expected recovery from litigation is $50 rather than $75; each defendant's expected loss is then $25.

In the case of perfectly correlated probabilities, the plaintiff will settle with both defendants. It is easy to see that the plaintiff will settle with at least one of the defendants. Say that the plaintiff settles with Row for $10, it faces a fifty percent probability of recovering $90 from Column, and thus its total expected recovery is $55 – $5 higher than its recovery from litigating against both defendants. The effect of this settlement is to give the plaintiff $10 with certainty but reduce its expected recovery from litigation by $5. As a result, the plaintiff's settlement with one defendant and litigation against the other is always more attractive to the plaintiff than litigation against both.

In fact, in this example, the plaintiff will settle with both defendants, obtaining $25 from one, say Row, and $37.50 from the other. In the face of a settlement of $25 with Row, Column faces an expected loss from litigation of $37.50 and is therefore willing to pay that amount in settlement. In turn, in the face of a settlement of $37.50 with Column, Row faces an expected loss from litigation of $31.25[108] and therefore prefers to pay $25 in settlement. The plaintiff's total recovery of $62.50 is $12.50 higher than its expected recovery from litigating against both defendants.

Two questions might arise at this point. First, why is it not possible for the plaintiff to extract more than $25 out of Row, given that Row's expected loss from litigation is higher? Second, why does the plaintiff settle for different amounts with the two defendants, even though they have responsibility for equal shares of the liability?

If the plaintiff were to make equal offers to both defendants, the largest amount that it could extract in settlement is $33.33 from each defendant. If Row accepted this offer, Column would face an expected loss in litigation of $33.33 (a fifty percent probability of losing $66.67) and would therefore choose to settle. The same logic shows that if Column accepted the offer, Row would accept it as well. Thus, the pair of $33.33 offers produces an outcome in which settlement with both defendants, yielding the plaintiff a recovery of $66.66, is an equilibrium solution.[109] This recovery is the largest that the plaintiff can obtain if it settles with both defendants.[110]

Consider now what would happen if Row rejected the offer of $33.33 and chose to litigate. Column's expected loss through litigation would be only $25 (a fifty percent probability of splitting with Row the plaintiff's damages of $100); Column would therefore reject the offer as well. The same logic shows that if Column rejected the offer, Row would also reject it. Thus, the pair of $33.33 offers produces an outcome in which litigation with both defendants, yielding the plaintiff an expected recovery of only $50, is also an equilibrium solution.[111] To avoid the possibility that both defendants would reject its offers, the plaintiff makes the offers of $25 and $37.50 to Row and Column, respectively. Litigation with both defendants would then not ensue because if Column were to litigate, Row, which would face an expected loss of $25 if it litigated, would choose to settle. Thus, offering one of the defendants a settlement of $25 is necessary to eliminate the possibility of an equilibrium in which both defendants litigate.

The result that perfectly correlated probabilities induce the parties to settle is not dependent on the particular value of the plaintiff's probability of success that we used in the example. For any value of this probability, the plaintiff is always better off by settling with at least one defendant. Moreover, the reasoning presented above for why the plaintiff settles with both defendants extends to any value of the plaintiff's probability of success.

With respect to the defendants' shares of the liability, the result derived in this Section also extends to instances in which the defendants are not equally at fault. It is easy to make small changes in the defendants' relative faults and still show that both settle.

If the defendants' shares of the liability were sufficiently different, however, the plaintiff would settle with the defendant that had the greater fault, say Column, and litigate against the other. Consider a case in which Row's share of the liability is twenty-five percent and Column's is seventy-five percent. The plaintiff would then settle with Column for $37.50 and litigate against Row with an expected recovery of $31.25 (a fifty percent probability of recovering its damages of $100 minus Column's settlement of $37.50);[112] its total expected recovery would therefore be $68.75. Given that Row litigates, if Column were to litigate as well, its expected loss would be $37.50 (a fifty percent probability of having to pay seventy-five percent of $100). Column would settle as long as the settlement offer is no greater than this amount.[113] Note that if instead of litigating against Row, the plaintiff settled with it for $31.25, Column would face an expected loss of $34.37 (a fifty percent probability of paying the plaintiff's damages of $100 minus Row's settlement of $31.25) if it litigates, and would thus not be willing to settle for $37.50. As a result, the plaintiff is better off litigating against Row.

In summary, when the plaintiff's probabilities of success are perfectly correlated, the problem is quite different than when the probabilities are independent. Whereas in the latter case, the plaintiff litigates against both defendants, in the former case it does not. Instead, the plaintiff settles with both defendants if their shares of the liability are sufficiently similar, and it settles with one defendant—the one with the larger share of the liability—and litigates against the other if the defendants' shares of the liability are sufficiently different.

D. The Continuum Between Independent and Perfectly Correlated Probabilities

While the cases of independent and perfectly correlated probabilities are paradigmatic, generally litigation will fall somewhere in the continuum between these two extremes. The hazardous waste example discussed above might raise two issues: whether each of two defendants sent hazardous substances to the site, and whether the plaintiff's clean-up was appropriate. For the first issue the plaintiff's probabilities of success are independent, whereas for the second issue they are perfectly correlated. To obtain relief, the plaintiff must prevail on the second issue, and it must also prevail on the first issue against at least one defendant. For the case as a whole, its probabilities of success are neither independent (because of the second issue) nor perfectly correlated (because of the first issue).

Our conclusion that for independent probabilities the plaintiff litigates against both defendants also applies when these probabilities are somewhat correlated. The effect of some correlation is to reduce the surplus that the plaintiff obtains from litigating against both defendants. (Recall that when the probabilities are perfectly correlated, this surplus disappears altogether.[114]) As the surplus gets smaller, the plaintiff is willing to accept lower settlements. In turn, a lower settlement on the part of one defendant results in a smaller external benefit for the other defendant. At some threshold, the externality disappears, and the result that the plaintiff litigates against both defendants no longer holds. But for correlations lower than this threshold, the results are identical to those that arise in the case of independent probabilities.[115]

Similarly, our conclusion that the plaintiff settles with at least one defendant when its probabilities of success are perfectly correlated also applies when the correlation is less than perfect. The effect of a lower correlation is that the plaintiff's expected recovery from litigating against one defendant is no longer identical to its expected recovery from litigating against both defendants. Thus, by settling with one defendant, the plaintiff pays a price. At some point, this price is high enough that the settlement becomes unattractive.[116]

E. The Relevance of the Model's Assumptions

The central conclusions of Part II.B and C are that for independent probabilities the plaintiff litigates against both defendants, and for perfectly correlated probabilities the plaintiff settles with at least one defendant. The model that we used to establish these results made several assumptions. We discuss in this Section whether any of these results would be different if those assumptions were relaxed.

1. Litigation Costs

To simplify the exposition, we assumed that the costs of litigation were zero. In the real world, of course, litigation is expensive. Litigation costs have the effect of inducing settlement because the plaintiff and defendants can save these outlays, and divide them among each other in some fashion, if they decide not to litigate. Take a simple one-defendant case in which the plaintiff has a fifty percent probability of obtaining $100 in damages.[117] In the absence of litigation costs, the parties are indifferent between litigating and settling for $50; no other settlement amount would be mutually acceptable. If instead each party faced litigation costs of $10, the plaintiff would be willing to accept $40 or more in settlement, and the defendant would be willing to pay $60 or less. Thus, both parties will prefer a settlement of between $40 and $60 to litigation. Litigation costs create a surplus that the parties can divide among themselves if they settle.

Our result that under independent probabilities the plaintiff litigates against both defendants holds when the costs of litigation are zero as well as when they are positive but sufficiently small. When litigation costs exceed a certain threshold, however, the plaintiff settles with both defendants. In the case of perfectly correlated probabilities, to the extent that settlement is the chosen option in the absence of litigation costs, it is even more desirable when such costs are present.

2. Risk Aversion

We also assumed that the parties are risk neutral. Risk aversion promotes settlement because it makes the certainty of a settlement relatively more desirable than the expected value of litigation. Return to the simple one-defendant case. If the plaintiff is risk averse, it prefers the certainty of a settlement of $50 to a fifty percent probability of obtaining $100 in litigation. The higher the plaintiff's degree of risk aversion, the lower the amount that it would be willing to accept to forgo litigation. Similarly, if the defendant is risk averse, it prefers the certainty of a settlement of $50 to a fifty percent probability of having to pay $100. The higher the defendant's degree of risk aversion, the higher the amount that it would be willing to pay to forgo litigation. Risk aversion, like litigation costs, creates a surplus that the parties can divide among themselves if they settle.

Our conclusion that under independent probabilities the plaintiff litigates against both defendants holds for risk-neutral parties and also for some range of risk aversion. When the level of risk aversion exceeds a certain threshold, however, the plaintiff settles with both defendants. In the case of perfectly correlated probabilities, to the extent that settlement is the chosen option for risk-neutral parties, it is even more desirable for risk-averse parties.

3. Informational Inaccuracies

We have assumed throughout that all the parties have accurate information about the plaintiff's probabilities of success. There are two other relevant scenarios. The beliefs of a plaintiff and a defendant are pessimistic when a plaintiff's estimate of its probability of success is lower than the defendant's estimate of the plaintiff's probability of success. Conversely, the beliefs of the parties are optimistic when a plaintiff's estimate of its probability of success is higher than the defendant's estimate of the plaintiff's probability of success. As we illustrate below, pessimism promotes settlement, whereas optimism discourages settlement.[118]

Return now to the one-defendant example, in which the plaintiff's true probability of prevailing is fifty percent, its damages are $100, and there are no litigation costs. Assume that the parties are pessimistic: the plaintiff believes that its probability of success is forty percent, and the defendant believes that the plaintiff's probability of success is sixty percent. The plaintiff would then be willing to accept any settlement of at least $40, and the defendant would be willing to pay up to $60. Conversely, it is easy to see that if the parties were optimistic there would be no settlement.

Our result that under independent probabilities the plaintiff litigates against both defendants holds for parties with accurate information as well as for parties that are somewhat pessimistic. When the level of pessimism exceeds a certain threshold, however, the plaintiff settles with both defendants. In the case of perfectly correlated probabilities, to the extent that settlement is the chosen option for parties with accurate information, it is even more desirable for pessimistic parties.

Conversely, a sufficiently high degree of optimism would lead to litigation with both defendants even in the case of perfectly correlated probabilities.

4. Structure of the Settlement Negotiations

We assumed that the plaintiff makes take-it-or-leave-it offers to the defendants. As a result of this assumption, the plaintiff captures the full surplus, if any, from settlement. For example, in the one-defendant case in which each party faces $10 in litigation costs, if the plaintiff is able to make a take-it-or-leave-it offer, it would ask, and obtain, $60. In contrast, if the defendant is able to make such an offer, it would settle for only $40. If neither party is able to make a take-it-or-leave-it offer, the settlement will be somewhere between $40 and $60. In the absence of litigation costs, however, the structure of the settlement negotiations is not material. Regardless of who makes a take-it-or-leave-it offer in this example, the plaintiff will not settle for less than $50 and the defendant will not pay more than $50.

More generally, the assumption that one party can make a take-it-or-leave-it offer does not affect the existence or size of a settlement range: it affects only the manner in which the surplus is divided among the parties. Thus, neither of our central conclusions are affected by the assumption that the plaintiff can make take-it-or-leave-it offers.

5. Timing of the Plaintiff's Offers

We also assumed that the defendants decide simultaneously whether to accept the plaintiff's offer. Neither of our central conclusions turns on this assumption. Recall that, in the case of independent probabilities, for a settlement with one defendant to be advantageous to the plaintiff, it must be for at least $50; then, the expected value of the plaintiff's claim against the other defendant is $25 (a fifty percent probability of recovering $50).[119] Say that the plaintiff makes Row an offer of $50, and, if Row rejects it, the plaintiff then makes Column an offer of $50. Row would reject the offer because its expected loss if Column accepts the offer is $25, and its expected loss if Column rejects the offer is $37.50 (half of the plaintiff's expected recovery of $75); both these expected losses are less than the settlement offer. In turn, Column rejects the offer as well because the resulting expected loss of litigating, given that Row also litigates, is only $37.50.

The case of perfectly correlated probabilities is also straightforward. Say that the plaintiff first makes Row a settlement offer. If Row rejects it, the plaintiff will want to settle with Column for whatever Column is willing to pay because, when its probabilities of success are perfectly correlated, its expected recovery from litigation is the same regardless of whether it litigates against both Row and Column or only against Row.

Thus, if Row rejects the initial offer, the plaintiff will make Column a settlement offer of $25 – its expected value of litigation given that Row also litigates. When Column accepts this offer, the plaintiff's expected recovery from Row is $37.50 (a fifty percent probability of recovering its full damages of $100 minus Column's settlement of $25). Because Row knows at the outset that this will be its fate if it rejects a settlement offer, it will be willing to settle for $37.50. Thus, as in the case of simultaneous offers, the plaintiff settles with one defendant for $37.50; the other defendant faces a fifty percent probability of being liable for $62.50 and settles for $31.25.

6. Knowledge of the Offers

We assumed that both defendants know the amounts of the plaintiff's offers. Even if they did not,[120] the plaintiff would litigate against both defendants if its probabilities of success are independent. How would a defendant, say Row, react to an offer of $37.50 if it did not know the amount of the other offer? It could surmise that the other offer would be for no less than $37.50, because it would be irrational for the plaintiff to make offers that summed to less than its expected value of litigation. Thus, it would reject the offer because if Column also rejected the offer its expected loss would be $37.50; but if Column accepted the offer its expected loss would be less as a result of the external benefit provided by the settlement. Because the defendants would reject offers of $37.50, it follows that they would reject higher offers as well.[121]

In the case of perfectly correlated probabilities, the plaintiff can always extract a settlement of at least $25 from one of the defendants, say Row. Indeed, if Column does not settle, Row's expected loss from litigation is $25 (a fifty percent probability of paying $50). If Column does settle, Row's expected loss from litigation is more than $25 unless Column's settlement is for at least $50; Row's expected loss would then be $25 (a fifty percent probability of paying the plaintiff's damages of $100 minus Column's settlement of $50). Column, however, would not accept a settlement offer of $50. This amount is greater than its expected loss from litigation regardless of whether Row litigates or settles; in the latter case, Column's expected loss is $50 only in the implausible case that Row's settlement is for $0. As a result, regardless of what Column does, it is in Row's interest to accept a settlement offer of $25. Thus, even if the defendants do not know each other's offers, at least one of them will settle when the plaintiff's probabilities of success are perfectly correlated.

7. Solvency

We assumed that the defendants are fully solvent. In the context of joint and several liability, a defendant's solvency is limited if it has insufficient resources to pay the plaintiff's full damages. When the plaintiff's probabilities of success are independent, if Row has solvency of less than $100, it will not be able to pay the plaintiff's full damages in the event that it loses and Column prevails.[122] As a result, limited solvency reduces the plaintiff's expected recovery in the event that it litigates against both defendants. We showed, however, that in the case of independent probabilities, the plaintiff receives a surplus from litigating against both defendants: if it settles with both, the maximum settlements that the defendants would pay are smaller than the plaintiff's expected recovery from litigating against both defendants. The effect of a defendant's limited solvency is to reduce this surplus, but, unless the defendant's solvency is sufficiently low, it will not eliminate the surplus altogether. Thus, our conclusion that the plaintiff litigates against both defendants when its probabilities of success are independent holds not only when the defendants are fully solvent but also when their solvencies, though limited, are above a given threshold.[123]

The effects of limited solvency are less straightforward when the plaintiff's probabilities of success are perfectly correlated. We show elsewhere that limited solvency on the part of the defendants can either induce settlements that otherwise would not occur or deter settlements that otherwise would occur.[124] Nonetheless, when the solvency of the defendants is above a threshold, the plaintiff settles with at least one defendant, just as it does when the defendants are fully solvent.[125]

The plaintiff's insolvency can also have important effects. Limited solvency on the part of the plaintiff plays no role if litigation costs are zero. The plaintiff then does not need to advance any money to pay for the litigation, and the level of its solvency therefore does not affect its strategy. Typically, however, litigation costs must be expended before the plaintiff recovers a judgment. If these costs are positive, the plaintiff might not have sufficient money to undertake the litigation, even though its expected recovery from litigating could exceed by a great deal its costs of bringing the actions. If capital markets operated efficiently, for example through the existence of contingency fee arrangements, the plaintiff could simply borrow the money necessary to finance the litigation. Otherwise, however, the plaintiff would face an incentive to enter into an otherwise undesirable settlement with one defendant in order to finance its litigation against the other.[126]

8. Non-Cooperative Action by the Defendants

We assumed that the defendants act non-cooperatively in responding to the plaintiff's offers. Consider what would happen if the defendants were able to enter into agreements to coordinate their actions in a situation in which the plaintiff makes take-it-or-leave-it offers. In the case of independent probabilities, if the plaintiff made offers of $37.50

to each defendant, they could agree to have one of them accept the offer and the other reject it: as indicated above,[127] the plaintiff's expected recovery would then be $68.75. So, the plaintiff would not make these offers even if the defendants could coordinate their action. In contrast, if the defendants could both coordinate their actions and make take-it-or-leave-it offers, and they each offered the plaintiff $37.50, the plaintiff's recovery from this settlement would be equal to its expected recovery from litigation and it would therefore settle. The plaintiff, of course, would not accept less than $75—its expected recovery from litigating.[128]

In the case of perfectly correlated probabilities, if the defendants could coordinate their actions, they would each reject any offer of more than $25—their expected liability at trial. The plaintiff would make offers of $25 to each, which would yield it the same expected recovery as litigating against both.

9. Number of Defendants

So far, our analysis has been restricted to two defendants. Our central conclusions hold as well for more defendants, however. Consider, first, the situation in which the plaintiff's probabilities of success are independent. When there are three defendants, the plaintiff recovers its full damages of $100 except when it loses against all of the defendants. The probability of this occurrence is 12.5 percent. Thus, the plaintiff's expected recovery is $87.50.[129] What would happen if the plaintiff offered each of the defendants a settlement of $29.17 (one-third of $87.50)? Assume that the first two defendants accept the offers. If the third litigated, it would face a fifty percent probability of paying $41.66 (the plaintiff's full damages of $100 minus the two settlements for $29.17 each). Its expected loss of $20.83 therefore is less than the settlement offer. Thus, this defendant would reject the offer. As a result, as in the case of two defendants, the plaintiff would not make such offers because they lead to a smaller expected recovery than it can obtain by litigating.[130]

In the case of perfectly correlated probabilities, the plaintiff always settles with at least one defendant. Such a settlement does not reduce its expected recovery from litigation and thus is always in its interest.[131]

10. Summary

The central results of our model are that the plaintiff will litigate against both defendants if its probabilities of success are independent, and that the plaintiff will settle with at least one defendant if its probabilities of success are perfectly correlated.[132] These results are not dependent on many of the assumptions that we made in order to simplify the exposition. They apply not only when litigation costs are zero but also when they are positive, not only when the parties are risk neutral but also when they are risk averse, not only when the parties have accurate information but also when they are pessimistic and optimistic, not only when the plaintiff makes take-it-or-leave-it offers but also when the defendants do so, not only when the defendants decide simultaneously whether to accept the plaintiff's offers but also when they decide sequentially, not only when the settlement offers are known by the two defendants but also when they are not, not only when the defendants are fully solvent but also when their solvencies are limited, and not only when there are two defendants but also when there are more.

Significantly, however, our conclusions do depend on the assumption that the defendants act non-cooperatively. Otherwise, regardless of the correlation of the plaintiff's probabilities of success, in the absence of litigation costs the parties would be indifferent between settlement and litigation, and for any level of litigation costs they will prefer to settle.[133] We believe that non-cooperative action is common. Indeed, although defendants in multi-party cases sometimes retain joint representation, they typically do not relinquish to the joint representative the authority to accept offers on their behalf. Moreover, in order for cooperation agreements to work, the defendants must enter into detailed contracts.[134] These contracts must specify not only what joint offers the defendants would make but also how they would respond to any counteroffers by the plaintiff. Casual observation suggests that such agreements are not common, indicating that the costs of drafting them must be very high.[135]

III. Extending the Analysis to Different Legal Regimes

So far, we have analyzed the problem under one particular legal rule: joint and several liability, a right of contribution, contribution being determined by reference to comparative fault, pro tanto set-off, contribution protection for settling defendants, no contribution rights for settling defendants, no substantive judicial supervision of the settlement offers, and joinder. In this Part, we study the effects of varying each of these components.

We perform this analysis by changing the components one at a time, so that the effect of each choice can be properly isolated. Our analysis also makes possible the comparison of any two legal regimes, and we make explicit many comparisons that vary more than one component at any time.[136] Thus, for example, in Part II we studied a rule of joint and several liability, with contribution and pro tanto set-off. Here we compare non-joint liability both to that rule and to joint and several liability, with contribution and apportioned share set-off.

A. The Set-Off Rule

Under the pro tanto set-off rule, if the plaintiff settles with one defendant and litigates against the other, its claim against the non-settling defendant is reduced by the amount of the settlement. Under the apportioned share set-off rule, in contrast, the plaintiff's claim is reduced by the settling defendant's apportioned share of the liability.[137]

The difference between these two set-off rules does not affect either the plaintiff's expected recovery or the defendants' expected loss in the event that the plaintiff litigates against both defendants. It does, however, affect the plaintiff's recovery not only when it settles with one defendant and litigates against the other, but also when it settles with both, since the maximum settlement that one defendant will be willing to pay is equal to its expected loss in litigation, and the expected loss is a function of the set-off rule.

Consider once again the simple example developed in Part II,[138] first when the plaintiff's probabilities of success are independent. What happens under the apportioned share set-off rule when the plaintiff makes offers of $37.50 to Row and to Column? If Row accepted the offer, the plaintiff's expected recovery from Column would be only $25: in the event that it prevails—an outcome carrying a probability of fifty percent—it recovers its full damage of $100 minus Row's apportioned share of $50. The plaintiff's total expected recovery would then be $62.50. This amount is less than both its expected recovery of $68.75 from settling with one defendant and litigating against the other under the pro tanto set-off rule, and its expected recovery of $75 from litigating against both defendants under either set-off rule.

As a result, under the apportioned share set-off rule, as under the pro tanto set-off rule, the plaintiff would not make offers of $37.50 to each defendant when its probabilities of success are independent. Instead, it would litigate. The explanation for this result is the same for the apportioned share set-off rule as for the pro tanto set-off rule. For both set-off rules, the plaintiff obtains a surplus from litigating against both defendants under joint and several liability when its probabilities of success are independent, as compared to its recovery in the one-defendant case, in the two-defendant case under non-joint liability, or in the two-defendant case under joint and several liability when its probabilities of success are perfectly correlated.

Moreover, under the apportioned share set-off rule, any settlement with Row, regardless of the amount, reduces Column's expected liability from $37.50 (its expected loss from litigation if Row also litigates) to $25 (its expected loss from litigation if Row settles, which consists of a fifty percent probability of being liable for the plaintiff's damages of $100 minus Row's apportioned share of $50). As a result, Row's settlement confers an external benefit on Column. Once again, it is this externality that induces the plaintiff to litigate against both defendants.[139]

In fact, when Row settles for its expected loss from litigation in the event that both defendants litigate, it confers a larger benefit upon Column under the apportioned share set-off rule. Recall that under the pro tanto set-off rule, a settlement with Row for $37.50 reduced Column's expected loss from $37.50 to $31.25, conferring upon it a benefit of $6.25. Under the apportioned share set-off rule, Column's expected loss is reduced from $37.50 to $25—Row's settlement thereby confers upon Column a benefit of $12.50.

As a result, the maximum settlement that the plaintiff could extract from both defendants is lower under the apportioned share set-off rule. This difference implies that, when the plaintiff's probabilities of success are independent and litigation costs are zero, the apportioned share set-off rule discourages settlement. It is true that for risk-neutral parties with accurate information, both rules will lead the plaintiff to litigate against both defendants. Moreover, for sufficiently risk-averse parties, or sufficiently pessimistic parties, both rules will lead the plaintiff to settle with both defendants. There is, however, an intermediate range of risk aversion and pessimism for which the pro tanto set-off rule would lead the plaintiff to settle with both defendants, whereas the apportioned share set-off rule would lead the plaintiff to litigate against both defendants.

The results are different when litigation costs are sufficiently high.[140] One feature of the pro tanto set-off rule is that when the plaintiff settles with one defendant and litigates against the other, it cannot recover more than its full damages. Under the apportioned share set-off rule, in contrast, if the plaintiff is able to extract from one defendant more than that defendant's apportioned share, its claim against the other defendant is reduced only by that defendant's apportioned share. Thus, if the plaintiff prevails in the litigation, its recovery from the litigating defendant and its settlement with the other defendant sum to more than its damages.[141]

When litigation costs are sufficiently high, the plaintiff can extract in settlement more than a defendant's apportioned share because, by settling, the defendant saves its litigation costs. In turn, given that one defendant settles for more than its apportioned share, the other defendant would be prepared to settle for more under the apportioned share set-off rule than under the pro tanto set-off rule, because it is exposed to higher damages under the former if it litigates and loses.

Thus, for sufficiently high litigation costs, the plaintiff gets a larger surplus from settlement under the apportioned share set-off rule than under the pro tanto set-off rule. Under this condition, the apportioned share set-off rule encourages settlement. Both rules would lead the plaintiff to settle with the two defendants when all the parties have accurate information. Moreover, if the parties are sufficiently optimistic, both rules would lead the plaintiff to litigate against the two defendants. There is, however, an intermediate range of optimism for which the apportioned share set-off rule would lead the plaintiff to settle with both defendants, whereas the pro tanto set-off rule would lead the plaintiff to litigate against both defendants. In summary, when the plaintiff's probabilities of success are independent, the pro tanto set-off rule has a settlement-inducing effect when litigation costs are low, but a settlement-deterring effect when litigation costs are high.

To prevent confusion, it is important to clarify the conditions under which this latter conclusion holds. The apportioned share set-off rule has better settlement-inducing properties only when the plaintiff can settle for more than the defendant's apportioned share. If the plaintiff can make take-it-or-leave-it offers, sufficiently high transaction costs will guarantee this result, for then the plaintiff will be able to capture the full surplus produced by the settlement.[142] The result also holds even if the plaintiff cannot make take-it-or-leave-it offers, as long as its bargaining power is great enough that it can capture a sufficiently large portion of the surplus.

We turn now to the case in which the plaintiff's probabilities of success against the defendants are perfectly correlated. Recall that under the pro tanto set-off rule, in the absence of litigation costs, the plaintiff settles with the two defendants for $25 and $37.50, respectively, as compared with an expected recovery of $50 from litigating against both.[143] In contrast, under the apportioned share set-off rule, if one defendant settles, regardless of the amount, the other defendant's expected loss through litigation is $25.[144] Thus, the highest settlement that the plaintiff could extract is $25 from each defendant, for a total recovery of $50.[145] The parties are therefore indifferent between settling and litigating.

Moreover, whereas under the pro tanto set-off rule the plaintiff settles with both defendants not only if the parties have accurate information but also if they are somewhat optimistic, under the apportioned share set-off rule any degree of optimism would frustrate the settlement. Thus, when litigation costs are zero and the plaintiff's probabilities of success are perfectly correlated, choosing the apportioned share set-off rule over the pro tanto set-off rule deters settlement.

The preceding discussion assumed that the defendants' shares of the fault are equal. Recall, however, that if these shares are sufficiently different, the pro tanto set-off rule leads to settlement with only one defendant and to litigation with the other.[146] Then, it follows that the apportioned share set-off rule, by making the parties indifferent between settling and litigating, has the effect of encouraging settlement with respect to one defendant and discouraging settlement with respect to the other.

In the case of high litigation costs, for perfectly correlated probabilities of success as for independent probabilities, the plaintiff can extract higher settlements under the apportioned share set-off rule. This is because, in the event that it settles with one defendant and litigates against the other, its recovery is not constrained by its damages. Thus, for sufficiently high litigation costs, choosing the apportioned share set-off rule over the pro tanto set-off rule promotes settlements.

Interestingly, then, regardless of the correlation of probabilities, the pro tanto set-off rule has better settlement-inducing properties than the apportioned share set-off rule for low litigation costs and worse settlement-inducing properties for high litigation costs in cases in which the plaintiff has sufficient bargaining power.

B. The Nature of the Right of Contribution

Before the introduction of comparative fault, contribution shares were determined pro rata. Thus, if the plaintiff prevailed against both defendants, each would pay half the damages regardless of their degrees of fault. The example that we analyzed in detail in Part II,[147] in which contribution was determined by reference to the defendants' relative shares of the liability, involved two defendants that were each fifty percent at fault. Thus, that example is equivalent to the case of pro rata contribution.

The question, then, is how pro rata contribution compares to contribution determined by reference to comparative fault when the defendants' shares of the liability are different. We have already identified one situation—perfectly correlated probabilities and low litigation costs under the pro tanto set-off rule—in which the plaintiff settles with both defendants only if their shares of the fault are relatively similar. In that case, pro rata contribution has better settlement-inducing properties.[148]

C. The Right of Contribution

Absent a right of contribution between the defendants, they are stuck with the plaintiff's distribution of the damages. If the plaintiff prevails against both defendants, it can collect its full damages from either of them, or it can divide the amount that it seeks from each defendant in whatever way it chooses, subject only to the constraint that it cannot recover more than its damages. To keep the discussion simple, we focus on situations in which the plaintiff collects its full damages from only one defendant.

Say that Row believes that the probability that the plaintiff will collect the judgment from it is q_R, and Column believes that this probability is q_C. Assume, initially, that both these probabilities are fifty percent. The problem then is exactly analogous to the one discussed in Part II.[149] If the plaintiff litigates against both defendants and its probabilities of success are independent, each defendant faces an expected loss of $37.50. Row, for example, would have to pay the plaintiff's full damages of $100 if it loses and Column prevails—an outcome that carries a probability of twenty-five percent. If both defendants lose—an outcome that also carries a probability of twenty-five percent—there is a fifty percent probability that the plaintiff would collect its judgment of $100 from Row. Thus, the expected loss of each defendant is not affected by the absence of a right of contribution.[150]

In the case of perfectly correlated probabilities, if the plaintiff litigates against both defendants, each faces an expected loss of $25: there is a fifty percent probability that both defendants lose, and if they do, each faces a fifty percent probability of having to pay the whole judgment. Here, too, each defendant faces the same expected loss as when a right of contribution exists.[151]

Thus, for this example at least, the absence of a right of contribution does not affect the choices between settlement and litigation. The equivalence between the two problems, in fact, is even more general. For both problems, if the plaintiff prevails against only one defendant, it collects its full damages from that defendant. If the plaintiff prevails against both defendants under a right of contribution, Row and Column each pay proportions r and $(1 - r)$, respectively, of the plaintiff's damages. If the plaintiff prevails against both defendants in the absence of a right of contribution, each defendant's proportion of the expected loss is q_R and q_C, respectively. Clearly, if each defendant's assessment of the probability that the plaintiff will collect the judgment against it in the case of no contribution is equal to its share of the liability—that is, if $q_R = r$ and $q_C = (1 - r)$—then the two problems are identical.

More generally, if q_R and q_C sum to one—in which case the defendants are neither pessimistic nor optimistic about their aggregate expected losses in litigation—then the contribution and no contribution problems have the same structure: joint and several liability discourages settlement when the plaintiff's probabilities of success are independent and encourages settlement with at least one defendant when these probabilities are perfectly correlated.[152]

Alternatively, if q_R and q_C sum to less than one, the defendants are optimistic about their aggregate expected losses and litigation. This optimism has an anti-settlement effect. In contrast, if q_R and q_C sum to more than one, the defendants are pessimistic about their aggregate expected losses and litigation. This pessimism has a pro-settlement effect.[153]

D. Joint and Several Liability Versus Non-Joint Liability

Under non-joint liability, the plaintiff could not recover its full damages of $100 if it prevailed against only one defendant. Instead, it could recover only that defendant's apportioned share of the liability, or $50. Thus, the plaintiff's expected recovery from litigating against both defendants is only $50 (a fifty percent probability of recovering $50 from each of the defendants), regardless of the correlation of the plaintiff's probabilities of success. Each defendant therefore faces an expected loss of $25 (a fifty percent probability of having to pay $50). Under non-joint liability, the plaintiff would simply make offers of $25 to each defendant and they would accept the offers.

We can now compare non-joint liability, and joint and several liability, initially under a pro tanto set-off rule. As before, we start by considering a situation in which litigation costs are zero.

When the plaintiff's probabilities of success are independent, joint and several liability discourages settlements. Whereas non-joint liability induces the plaintiff to settle with both defendants, joint and several liability induces it to litigate against both defendants because joint and several liability gives the plaintiff a surplus that it would lose, at least in part, if it settled.[154]

In contrast, when the plaintiff's probabilities of success are perfectly correlated, joint and several liability has a less straightforward effect. Consider first the case in which the defendants' relative degrees of fault are sufficiently similar. Under joint and several liability, as under non-joint liability, the plaintiff settles with both defendants. Under joint and several liability, however, the plaintiff's recovery from settling is higher than its expected recovery from litigating,[155] whereas under non-joint liability the recoveries are identical. Thus, under joint and several liability settlement takes place not only when the parties have accurate information but also when they are optimistic, whereas under non-joint liability optimistic parties will litigate. In this case, joint and several liability promotes settlements.

Second, recall that under joint and several liability, when the defendants' shares of the liability are sufficiently different, the plaintiff settles with the defendant that is responsible for the larger share of the liability, and litigates against the other.[156] The plaintiff's expected recovery from this outcome is higher than its expected recovery from litigating against both defendants or settling with both defendants. Thus, joint and several liability has the effect of promoting settlements with the defendant responsible for the larger share of the liability and discouraging settlements with the defendant responsible for the smaller share of the liability.

These conclusions assume that litigation costs are zero or sufficiently low. When litigation costs are high, however, the analysis is different for two reasons.

First, one feature of the pro tanto set-off rule, as we have already explained,[157] is that when the plaintiff settles with one defendant and litigates against the other, it cannot recover more than its full damages. Under non-joint liability, in contrast, the plaintiff's recovery is not constrained in this manner.[158] When the plaintiff makes a take-it-or-leave-it offer and litigation costs are sufficiently high, a defendant under non-joint liability will be willing to pay more than its apportioned share of the liability in order to avoid litigation. For litigation costs in this range, the plaintiff obtains larger settlements under non-joint liability than under joint and several liability coupled with the pro tanto set-off rule.

At the same time, however, when the plaintiff's probabilities of success are independent, its recovery from litigating against both defendants is higher under joint and several liability than under non-joint liability, and is equal under both rules when the probabilities are perfectly correlated. If a defendant were able to make take-it-or-leave-it offers, it would offer the plaintiff the smallest amount that would make the plaintiff indifferent between settling and litigating. The amount thus offered is higher under joint and several liability than under non-joint liability when the plaintiff's probabilities of success are independent, and is equal under both rules when the probabilities are perfectly correlated.

In the real world, none of the parties can make take-it-or-leave-it offers; instead, the parties must engage in bargaining. The case in which the plaintiff makes a take-it-or-leave-it offer defines the upper bound of the settlement range: the plaintiff captures the full surplus of settlement. Similarly, the case in which one of the defendants makes a take-it-or-leave-it offer defines the lower bound of the settlement range: here, the defendant captures the full surplus of settlement. For sufficiently high litigation costs, the settlement range is greater under non-joint liability if the plaintiff has sufficient bargaining power (because, compared to joint and several liability, it recovers more in settlement and less in litigation). For sufficiently high litigation costs, risk-neutral parties with accurate information will settle under both joint and several liability (coupled with a pro tanto set-off rule) and non-joint liability. In contrast, sufficiently optimistic parties will litigate under both rules. The higher settlement range for non-joint liability implies that for an intermediate range of optimism, there will be settlements under non-joint liability but not under joint and several liability.

We now compare the settlement-inducing properties of non-joint liability with those of joint and several liability coupled with an apportioned share set-off rule. Several differences between the set-off rules are significant to this comparison. First, the apportioned share set-off rule, unlike the pro tanto set-off rule, does not constrain the plaintiff's recovery when it settles with one defendant and litigates with the other.[159] Second, when the plaintiff settles with both defendants, its recovery is equal to its recovery from settling with both defendants under non-joint liability. Indeed, given that one defendant settles, the other will settle as long as the amount of the settlement is no greater than its expected loss through litigation. In the event that it loses the litigation, under the apportioned share set-off rule the defendant must pay the plaintiff's full damages reduced by the share of the settling party. This amount is identical to its apportioned share of the liability, which is what it would pay under non-joint liability.

With these differences in mind, consider first the case of independent probabilities. For low litigation costs, joint and several liability coupled with an apportioned share set-off rule deters settlements as compared to non-joint liability. Under non-joint liability the parties settle over the whole range of litigation costs, but for sufficiently low litigation costs they do not settle under joint and several liability. For high litigation costs, the settlement range is larger under non-joint liability because the plaintiff's recovery from litigation is lower; here, too, joint and several liability deters settlements.

Recall that in the case of perfectly correlated probabilities, the plaintiff's recovery from litigation under joint and several liability is identical to its recovery under non-joint liability.[160] We have shown above that both joint and several liability with an apportioned share set-off rule and non-joint liability produce identical settlements when the plaintiff can make take-it-or-leave-it offers.[161] Thus, for perfectly correlated probabilities, joint and several liability with an apportioned share set-off rule has the same settlement-inducing effects as non-joint liability.

E. Contribution Protection for Settling Defendants

The rule modeled in Part II granted settling defendants protection from contribution actions brought either by non-settling defendants or by other settling defendants. Here, we consider the effect of allowing non-settling defendants to bring contribution actions against settling defendants.[162]

Exposing settling defendants to contribution actions has the unambiguous effect of discouraging settlements. Consider the example in which the plaintiff makes offers of $37.50 to each defendant when litigation costs are zero and the plaintiff's probabilities of success are independent. Recall that under a rule of contribution protection, if one defendant, say Row, accepts the settlement, it confers a benefit of $6.25 on Column, reducing Column's expected loss, in the event that both defendants litigate, from $37.50 to $31.25 (a fifty percent probability of recovering $100 minus $37.50), and that, as a result of this externality, settlement does not occur.[163]

Removing contribution protection increases the magnitude of this externality. Indeed, the plaintiff has a fifty percent probability of recovering $62.50 from Column ($100 minus Row's settlement of $37.50). Column's expected loss to the plaintiff is therefore $31.25. If the plaintiff prevails (a probability of fifty percent), Column, in turn, has a fifty percent probability of recovering from Row the $12.50 representing the excess that Column paid above its apportioned share of the liability, which is $50. The probability that Column will recover this $12.50 is twenty-five percent: for recovery to occur, the plaintiff must prevail against Column and Column must prevail against Row. Column's expected recovery in the contribution action is thus $3.12 (twenty-five percent of $12.50), and its expected loss if it chooses to litigate in light of Row's settlement of $37.50 is $28.13 (its expected loss of $31.25 under a rule of contribution protection minus its expected recovery of $3.12 in the contribution action).[164] Thus, removing contribution protection increased the size of the externality by $3.12.

F. Contribution Rights for Settling Defendants

In Part II, we modeled a rule in which settling defendants were denied contribution rights but granted contribution protection. Maintaining the regime of contribution protection but granting settling defendants contribution rights promotes settlements. This change in the legal regime, however, has an effect only when the settlement is for more than the defendant's apportioned share of the liability, because otherwise the defendant would not be entitled to exercise its right.

If one defendant chooses to litigate, there will be situations in which the other defendant, say Row, would be willing to pay a higher settlement when settling defendants have the right to bring contribution actions. This result occurs in cases in which the costs of litigation are sufficiently high, and in which the plaintiff has sufficient bargaining power, that the settling defendant pays more than its apportioned share of the liability. Thus, Row will accept certain offers by the plaintiff that it would have rejected absent a right of contribution for settling defendants. In turn, given that Row settles, Column is more likely to settle as well when doing so shields it, as a result of the rule of contribution protection for settling defendants, from a contribution action that Row could otherwise bring.

G. "Good Faith" Hearings

In Part II, we analyzed a legal regime in which the amounts of the plaintiff's settlement offers were not scrutinized by the courts. Expanding the nature of a "good faith" hearing beyond a procedural determination of lack of collusion to include substantive judicial scrutiny of the amount of the settlement has the simple effect of discouraging settlements.

Consider a case in which the plaintiff's probabilities of success are independent. Recall that, for sufficiently low litigation costs, no settlement with both defendants is as attractive to the plaintiff as litigation against both. It follows a fortiori that settlement would be comparatively less attractive if the plaintiff were constrained by the courts from making certain settlement offers.

Next, consider cases in which the plaintiff chooses to settle with both defendants in a legal regime under which the good faith hearing is solely procedural. If this hearing also had a substantive component, it might invalidate the settlement offers that maximized the plaintiff's recovery.

As a result, the settlement offers permitted under an expanded good faith hearing might be less desirable than litigating against either one or both defendants.

Thus, adding a substantive component to the good faith hearing makes the pro tanto set-off rule relatively less desirable from the perspective of inducing settlements than the apportioned share set-off rule: there will be some cases in which the former has better settlement-inducing properties when the good faith hearing is solely procedural, but worse properties when this hearing also has a substantive component. For similar reasons, an expanded good faith hearing makes joint and several liability coupled with a pro tanto set-off rule relatively less desirable than non-joint liability.

This undesirable result is magnified when the costs of litigation are not zero. One of the advantages of settlement is that it saves litigation costs, creating a surplus for the parties to divide. To the extent that this surplus is reduced as a result of the litigation costs expended in the good faith hearing, the incentives for settlement are diminished.

H. Joinder Rules

In Part II, the plaintiff either sued both defendants in a single action, or, if it sued only one, that defendant impleaded the other. We consider here a situation in which the plaintiff initially sues only one defendant and impleader is not allowed, so that the adjudication of the right of contribution must await a separate proceeding.

Consider, first, the case in which the plaintiff's probabilities of success are independent. If the plaintiff sues only one defendant, say Row, and prevails, it collects its full damages from that defendant. In turn, Row can file a contribution action against Column. In order to recover, it will have to show that Column was liable to the plaintiff. Because the plaintiff's probabilities of success would have been independent if it had sued both defendants, the plaintiff's probability of prevailing in the first action and Row's probability of prevailing in the contribution action are also independent.

In this case (independent probabilities), if the plaintiff loses to Row, the rules of collateral estoppel do not preclude it from bringing a subsequent action against Column.[165] Consider, for example, the case where the plaintiff is a pedestrian who was hit by two cars that jumped onto the sidewalk, and the issue is whether each of the drivers was negligent. The fact that the plaintiff was unable to show Row's negligence in no way precludes it from attempting to show that Column was negligent.[166]

Moreover, if the plaintiff prevails against Column after having lost to Row, Column can bring a contribution action against Row. In order to prevail in that action, Column would have to show that Row was liable to the plaintiff. While this issue was decided in favor of Row in the first proceeding, the current rules on collateral estoppel permit Column to relitigate it because it was not a party to that proceeding.[167] This feature creates a difference between joinder and non-joinder. Whereas under the former a losing defendant cannot obtain contribution from a co-defendant that prevailed against the plaintiff, under the latter such contribution is possible.

Turn now to the example developed in Part II.[168] If the plaintiff litigates first against Row, and, in the event that it loses, then litigates against Column, its expected recovery, as in the case in which it litigates against both defendants together, is $75. Indeed, with a probability of fifty percent, it recovers $100 from Row, and with a probability of twenty-five percent (if it loses against Row and then prevails against Column), it recovers $100 from Column.

The allocation of this burden between the defendants is different than in the case in which the actions are joined, where each defendant faces an expected loss of $37.50. In the absence of joinder, Row's expected loss from litigating against Column has the following components. First, with a probability of fifty percent, Row loses and must pay the plaintiff $100 (an expected loss of $50); in this event, however, its expected recovery from Column in a contribution action is $12.50 (with a probability of fifty percent, the plaintiff prevails against Row; in that event, with a probability of fifty percent, Row prevails against Column in the contribution action and recovers Column's share of $50). Second, with a probability of fifty percent, Row prevails against the plaintiff but may be subject to a contribution action from Column. Its expected loss from this action is $6.25 (with a probability of fifty percent, the plaintiff loses to Row; in that event, with a probability of fifty percent, the plaintiff prevails against Column; in that event, with a probability of fifty percent Column prevails in the contribution action and recovers Row's share of $50). Thus, Row's expected loss is not $37.50, as it is under joinder, but $43.75 ($37.50 plus $6.25). Since, as we noted in the prior paragraph, the plaintiff's expected recovery is not affected by the lack of joinder, it follows that Column's expected loss is $31.25 ($37.50 minus $6.25).

Row would be willing to settle for an amount equal to its expected loss in litigation—$43.75. But if Row settles for this amount, Column faces an expected loss of $28.12 under the pro tanto set-off rule (a fifty percent probability of losing $100 minus Row's settlement of $43.75) and $25 under the apportioned share set-off rule (a fifty percent probability of losing $100 minus Row's apportioned share of $50). As a result of the benefit conferred on Column by Row's settlement, the plaintiff's maximum recovery from settling with both defendants is less than its expected recovery from litigating against both defendants.[169]

Now, turn to the case in which the plaintiff's probabilities of success are perfectly correlated. If the plaintiff sues only one defendant, say Row, and prevails, it collects its full damages from that defendant. In turn, Row can file a contribution action against Column. Because Column was not a party to the initial litigation, Row cannot prevail simply on the basis of collateral estoppel.[170]

Moreover, even though the plaintiff would have prevailed against both defendants if it had sued them both together, it does not follow that because the plaintiff prevailed against Row in the first action, Row will necessarily prevail in its contribution action against Column. For example, assume that the litigation is whether Row and Column conspired against the plaintiff. Because a single party cannot conspire with itself, in a single proceeding against the two defendants, the plaintiff would have either prevailed against both or lost against both. Row's contribution action against Column, however, takes place at a different time, before a different trier of fact, and with different parties. Therefore, it may well come out differently.

In contrast, in this case (perfectly correlated probabilities), if the plaintiff loses against Row, the rules of non-mutual collateral estoppel preclude it from bringing a subsequent action against Column. If the plaintiff was unable to convince one court that Row conspired with Column, it cannot attempt to convince another court that Column conspired with Row.[171] In turn, if the plaintiff cannot bring an action against Column after it has lost against Row, Column will have no occasion to bring a contribution action. Thus, in the case of perfectly correlated probabilities, there is no scenario under which Row could prevail against the plaintiff but still face contribution from Column.

Returning to the example developed in Part II, the plaintiff's expected recovery in litigation when its probabilities of success are perfectly correlated is $50, regardless of whether it sues one defendant or both. Under the pro tanto set-off rule, recall that when the plaintiff sues both defendants offers of $33.33 to each can produce either an equilibrium solution in which they both settle or an equilibrium solution in which they both litigate, and that, to be assured a settlement, the plaintiff instead makes offers of $37.50 and $25.[172]

What happens if the plaintiff sues Row and then offers it a settlement of $33.33? If Row rejects the settlement, it faces an expected loss in its litigation against the plaintiff of $50 (a fifty percent probability of losing $100). If it was assured victory in its contribution action, its expected recovery from Column would be $25: in the event that Row loses to the plaintiff (a fifty percent probability), it would recover $50 from Column. Thus, Row's aggregate expected loss if it litigates against the plaintiff is only $25, and Row would reject any larger settlement.[173] If Row settles for $25, the plaintiff's expected recovery from Column is $37.50 (a fifty percent probability of recovering $75), the amount it could obtain in settlement. Thus, the lack of joinder does not change the outcome: the plaintiff still settles with one defendant for $25 and with the other for $37.50.

Finally, under the apportioned share set-off rule, recall that when the plaintiff sues both defendants, it settles for $25 with each.[174] In the case of non-joined defendants, Row, once again, would be willing to settle for $25 – its expected loss in litigation. The plaintiff's expected recovery from Column is then $25 (a fifty percent probability of recovering $50), the amount it could obtain in settlement. As under the pro tanto set-off rule, the lack of joinder does not change the outcome.

The preceding analysis shows that none of our major qualitative results are driven by the joinder of the actions. We have identified, however, two ways in which the lack of joinder might make a difference: when the plaintiff's probabilities of success are independent, a defendant that prevails against the plaintiff might nonetheless be subjected to a contribution action; and when the plaintiff's probabilities of success are perfectly correlated, the fact that the plaintiff prevails against one defendant does not imply that this defendant will prevail in the contribution action.

In addition, the litigation costs expended by the parties might depend on whether the actions are joined. For example, there may be economies of scale in litigation, so that it may be cheaper for the plaintiff to litigate against both defendants in a single action than to litigate against them separately. To the extent that the settlement-inducing properties of the different legal rules depend on the levels of litigation costs,[175] joinder would have an effect on whether cases are settled or litigated. A full exploration of this question is beyond the scope of this Article.

I. Summary of the Major Results

The preceding discussion establishes three major results. First, we showed that as between the pro tanto set-off rule and the apportioned share set-off rule, the former is generally more likely to induce settlements for low litigation costs and less likely to do so for high litigation costs.[176] The one exception concerns the case in which the plaintiff's probabilities of success are perfectly correlated and the defendants' shares of the liability are sufficiently different. In that case, while the pro tanto set-off rule encourages settlements with one of the defendants, it discourages settlements with the other.

Second, we showed that a regime of contribution has the identical effects on the choice between settlement and litigation as one of no contribution. This result is independent of the set-off rule, the level of litigation costs, and the correlation of the plaintiff's probabilities of success.

The third set of results, which concerns the choice between joint and several liability and non-joint liability, is somewhat less straightforward. These results are summarized in Tables I and II. When the plaintiff's probabilities of success are independent, joint and several liability always

	Low Litigation Costs	High Litigation Costs
Pro Tanto Set-Off	Discourages settlement	Discourages settlement
Apportioned Share Set-Off	Discourages settlement	Discourages settlement

Table I. Effects of Joint and Several Liability on Settlement When the Plaintiff's Probabilities of Success Are Independent.

discourages settlement. In contrast, when the plaintiff's probabilities of success are perfectly correlated, joint and several liability has no effect on the choice of settlement and litigation when it is coupled with the apportioned share set-off rule. Under the pro tanto set-off rule, joint and several liability discourages settlements for sufficiently high litigation costs; for sufficiently low litigation costs, joint and several liability encourages settlements with both defendants when their shares of the liability are sufficiently similar, and it encourages settlements with one defendant and discourages settlements with the other when these shares are sufficiently different.

	Low Litigation Costs	High Litigation Costs
Pro Tanto Set-Off	Encourages settlement with at least one defendant	Discourages settlement
Apportioned Share Set-Off	No effect	No effect

Table II. Effects of Joint and Several Liability on Settlement When the Plaintiff's Probabilities of Success Are Perfectly Correlated.

IV. The Judicial Choice Between Set-Off Rules

The courts are deeply divided over the choice between set-off rules. The courts typically justify their choice between the pro tanto and apportioned share set-off rules at least in part on the basis of their assessments of the relative settlement-inducing properties of these competing rules.[177] We show that practically all of the judicial decisions stem from basic conceptual misunderstandings of the dynamics of the settlement process. Section A examines judicial arguments in favor of the settlement-inducing properties of the pro tanto set-off rule. Section B analyzes decisions maintaining that the apportioned share set-off rule encourages more settlements. Section C looks at cases preferring the apportioned share set-off rule on the ground that the pro tanto set-off rule induces undesirable settlements.

A. Decisions Maintaining That the Pro Tanto Set-Off Rule Encourages More Settlements

Courts maintaining that the pro tanto set-off rule is better from the perspective of inducing settlement advance essentially three distinct arguments for this proposition: (1) that the plaintiff does not bear the risk of a low settlement, (2) that a non-settling defendant bears the risk of a larger share of the liability, and (3) that the level of uncertainty is reduced.[178]

1. The Plaintiff Does Not Bear the Risk of a Low Settlement

Some courts argue that the pro tanto set-off rule encourages settlement because the plaintiff does not bear the risk of a low settlement with one defendant since it can recover the shortfall through litigation against the other defendants.[179] It is true, as we have explained above,[180] that a plaintiff that settles with one defendant for less than that defendant's apportioned share and then prevails in litigation against the other defendant can recover its full damages under the pro tanto set-off rule but not under the apportioned share set-off rule.

The courts, however, overlook the fact that even under the pro tanto set-off rule, if the plaintiff settles with one defendant for an amount that is too low, it compromises its expected recovery. The reason is that if the plaintiff loses the subsequent litigation, its only recovery will have come from the settling defendant.[181]

Moreover, in the case of independent probabilities of success, a low settlement poses an additional risk to the plaintiff. Settlement with one defendant deprives the plaintiff of the "insurance" that results from its ability to recover its full damages when it litigates against two defendants even if it prevails only against one. So, if the plaintiff settles with one defendant, say Row, and litigates and loses against Column, the settlement with Row deprives it of the possibility of having litigated against Row and won. This "insurance," however, is unavailable when the probabilities of success are perfectly correlated, because then the plaintiff's loss against Column implies that if Row had not settled, the plaintiff would have lost against Row as well.

In addition, under the apportioned share set-off rule, unlike under the pro tanto set-off rule, the plaintiff is not precluded from recovering more than its damages if it settles with one defendant and litigates against the other: this result will ensue whenever the settlement is for more than the defendant's apportioned share of the liability.[182] Thus, while the courts focus on one of the effects of the pro tanto set-off rule in cases in which the plaintiff settles with one defendant and litigates against the other—that it leads to a higher total recovery when the settlement is low—they overlook the mirror image of that effect—that it leads to a lower total recovery when the settlement is high.

Also, the fact that under one set-off rule the plaintiff might be willing to accept a lower settlement does not, by itself, make settlement more likely. The question one must ask, but which the courts do not, is whether the defendant contemplating settlement would be willing to pay as much under that rule. If the set-off rule also resulted in lower offers on the part of such a defendant, it would not follow that the plaintiff's willingness to accept a lower settlement would make settlement more likely.[183] We now proceed to show, moreover, that even this inquiry would not take us very far.

Fundamentally, the courts overlook the strategic nature of the problem. Even if the plaintiff's settlement with one defendant under the pro tanto set-off rule would not compromise its recovery against the other, it does not follow that the pro tanto set-off rule would encourage settlements. The plaintiff will settle with one defendant, say Row, and litigate against the other, rather than litigating against both, only if the following conditions are met. First, the plaintiff's expected recovery from settling with one defendant and litigating against the other must be greater than its expected recovery from litigating against both defendants. Second, given that Column litigates, Row must prefer to settle rather than litigate. Third, given that Row settles, Column must prefer to litigate rather than settle.

One must then determine the effects of the two set-off rules on each of these conditions. The plaintiff's expected recovery in the event that it litigates against both defendants is unaffected by the choice of set-off rule: in the absence of litigation costs, it depends only upon its probabilities of success against the defendants, the correlation of these probabilities, and its damages. In contrast, the plaintiff's expected recovery from Column in the event that it settles with Row and litigates against Column is affected by the choice of set-off rule: for a given settlement with Row, the plaintiff's expected recovery under the pro tanto set-off rule is higher if the settlement is for less than Row's apportioned share of the liability, and lower if the settlement is for more than Row's apportioned share of the liability. Thus, settling with one defendant appears relatively more attractive to the plaintiff (compared with litigating against both) under the pro tanto set-off rule when the settlement with Row is for less than Row's apportioned share of the liability, and relatively less attractive when this settlement is for more than Row's apportioned share of the liability. Because the plaintiff is potentially able to extract higher settlements from Row when litigation costs are high,[184] the plaintiff's relative recoveries under the two scenarios depend upon the level of litigation costs.

With respect to the second condition, given that Column litigates, the highest amount that Row would be willing to pay in settlement is unaffected by the choice of set-off rule: in the absence of litigation costs, it is simply the expected value of litigating given that Column also litigates—a value which depends upon Row's share of the liability, as well as upon the plaintiff's probabilities of success against the defendants, the correlation of these probabilities, and its damages.

With respect to the third condition, given that Row settles, the smallest settlement offer that would induce Column to litigate rather than settle is affected by the set-off rule. If Row settles for less than its apportioned share of the liability, as it would when litigation costs are low,[185] Column's expected loss through litigation (and thus the smallest settlement that would induce it to litigate rather than settle) is higher under the pro tanto set-off rule.[186] The opposite is true when Row's settlement is for more than its apportioned share.

So far, the discussion of the strategic nature of the problem focused only on the plaintiff's choice of litigation against both defendants as opposed to settlement with one defendant and litigation against the other—the choice that was the implicit focus of the courts. The full analysis of the problem also requires us to consider the effects of the set-off rules on the conditions necessary for settlement with both defendants. First, the plaintiff's expected recovery from settling with both defendants must be greater than its expected recovery from litigating against both defendants or from settling with one and litigating against the other. Second, given that Column settles, Row must prefer to settle rather than litigate. Third, given that Row settles, Column must prefer to settle rather than litigate. As the preceding discussion should make clear, the first condition is unaffected by the choice of the set-off rule, but the second and third conditions are affected by this choice. Given that Row settles, the highest settlement that Column would pay rather than litigate, which is equal to its expected loss through litigation, is higher under the pro tanto set-off rule if Row settled for less than its apportioned share of the liability. If, in contrast, Row settled for more than its apportioned share of the liability, the highest settlement that Column would pay rather than litigate is lower under the pro tanto set-off rule. This discussion shows that, from the perspective of inducing settlements with both defendants, the relative desirability of the set-off rules depends on the level of litigation costs.

2. A Non-Settling Defendant Bears the Risk of a Larger Share of the Liability

A second argument advanced by courts in favor of the settlement-inducing properties of the pro tanto set-off rule is that this rule encourages settlements because a non-settling defendant bears the risk that by not settling it will end up paying more than its apportioned share of the liability.[187] These courts focus implicitly on whether, given that one defendant settles, the other would settle as well. They maintain that, in light of a plaintiff's settlement with one defendant, not settling would be relatively more costly to the other defendant under the pro tanto set-off rule, and that this higher cost would create incentives for the defendant to settle.

This argument stems from the same conceptual misunderstandings as the prior one. The pro tanto set-off rule leaves a non-settling defendant worse off only if the plaintiff's settlement with the other defendant is for less than that defendant's apportioned share of the liability. Moreover, the question is not simply whether litigation would be relatively more expensive for one defendant. One must also ask how the choice of set-off rule affects the amount that the plaintiff demands in settlement—a question that one cannot answer without considering, as we did in criticizing the previous argument, the full strategic nature of the problem.

3. The Level of Uncertainty Is Reduced

Some courts state that the pro tanto set-off rule promotes settlements by reducing the level of uncertainty faced by litigating parties.[188] Under both rules, the litigating parties face uncertainty about the level of damages that will be assessed by the finder of fact. Under the apportioned share set-off rule, however, the plaintiff faces the additional uncertainty about the degree of fault that will be attributed to the settling defendant.[189] Indeed, whereas under the pro tanto set-off rule, when the plaintiff settles with one defendant and litigates against the other, its recovery if it prevails is reduced by the amount of the settlement regardless of the settling defendant's share of the liability, under the apportioned share set-off rule, its recovery is reduced by that share.

Thus, following the plaintiff's settlement with one defendant, the pro tanto set-off rule does, in fact, reduce the uncertainty faced by the plaintiff and the non-settling defendant. But there is no reason to equate less uncertainty with a higher probability of settlements. If, under the apportioned share set-off rule, the parties have the same estimate of the settling defendant's share of the liability, the fact that they are not certain that their estimate is correct does not affect the probability of settlement as long as the parties are risk neutral. If, in contrast, they are risk averse, less uncertainty leads to a *lower* probability of settlement.

Alternatively, the uncertainty over the settling defendant's share of the liability could result in different estimates of this share on the part of the plaintiff and the non-settling defendant. In this situation there are two relevant scenarios: the plaintiff and the non-settling defendant could be either optimistic or pessimistic. They are optimistic if the plaintiff's assessment of the settling defendant's share is lower than the estimate of the non-settling defendant; then, under the apportioned share set-off rule, the plaintiff would expect to recover more than the non-settling defendant would expect to pay. In contrast, the parties are pessimistic if the plaintiff's assessment of the settling defendant's share is higher than the estimate of the non-settling defendant; then, under the apportioned share set-off rule, the plaintiff would expect to recover more than the non-settling defendant would expect to pay.

As we indicated above,[190] pessimism encourages settlement, whereas optimism discourages settlement. Thus, if the parties are pessimistic, the pro tanto set-off rule discourages settlement relative to the apportioned share set-off rule: by eliminating one source of the uncertainty over the plaintiff's recovery, it makes settlement less likely. In contrast, if the parties are optimistic, the pro tanto set-off rule encourages settlement relative to the apportioned share set-off rule.

B. Decisions Maintaining That the Apportioned Share Set-Off Rule Induces More Settlements

Courts that claim that the apportioned share set-off rule induces more settlements advance two different arguments: that a non-settling defendant may gamble on a verdict rather than settle, and that the need for a "good faith" hearing under the pro tanto set-off rule discourages settlements.

1. A Non-Settling Defendant May Gamble on a Verdict

Some courts claim that the pro tanto set-off rule "may act as an impediment to total settlement as a nonsettling defendant may count on the guaranteed credit and then gamble on the verdict rather than settle."[191] In contrast, the argument goes, under the apportioned share set-off rule, "total settlement is encouraged after partial settlement as a culpable nonsettlor cannot escape responsibility when a settling defendant pays more than his fair share and cannot gamble on a jury verdict in view of a guaranteed credit."[192]

The reasoning of these courts is far from clear. They could be focusing on the relative sizes of the plaintiff's credit under the two set-off rules. In that case, they overlook that, under either set-off rule, a non-settling defendant gets a credit when the plaintiff settles with the other defendant: this credit is larger under the apportioned share set-off rule when the settling defendant pays less than its apportioned share, but if the settling defendant pays more than its apportioned share, the pro tanto set-off rule produces the larger credit. In the event of a settlement with one defendant, the size of the credit ought to have no effect on the likelihood of settlement. The plaintiff would demand more, and the non-settling defendant would be willing to pay more, if the credit is smaller. Of course, this argument does not answer the question of which rule would induce one of the defendants to settle in the first place—an inquiry that cannot be undertaken without considering the strategic relationships among the parties.[193]

Alternatively, the courts could be focusing on the "guaranteed" nature of the credit under the pro tanto set-off rule, which is known as soon as the plaintiff settles with one defendant. In contrast, under the apportioned share set-off rule, the credit is not determined until the trial with the non-settling defendant. The argument that the guaranteed nature of the credit under the pro tanto set-off rule makes settlement less likely is equivalent to the argument that the pro tanto set-off discourages settlement because it eliminates one source of uncertainty from the plaintiff's case against the non-settling defendant—an argument which, as we explained above, holds only in the case of pessimistic parties.[194]

2. Litigation Costs Associated with a "Good Faith" Hearing Under the Pro Tanto Set-Off Rule

Some courts complain that the pro tanto set-off rule requires a cumbersome "good faith" hearing to determine the adequacy of the settlement.[195] By making settlement relatively more costly, the need for this hearing removes some of the incentives to settle.[196] This argument rests on an implicit empirical claim that is difficult to test. It is true that, in instances in which the plaintiff settles with one defendant and litigates against the other, the pro tanto set-off rule requires some sort of "good faith" hearing to determine the adequacy of the settlement. In contrast, however, the apportioned share set-off rule requires that, if the plaintiff prevails against the non-settling defendant, the courts determine, retrospectively, the apportioned share of the settling defendant. Thus, each of the set-off rules requires a judicial inquiry that the other does not.[197] Unless the inquiry required by one of the rules is systematically more cumbersome, no general claim about the relative desirability of the rules can be made on this basis.

Even if the costs associated with the good faith hearing under the pro tanto set-off rule were higher, it would not necessarily follow that this set-off rule would discourage settlement. To the extent that such a hearing imposes high costs on the non-settling defendant, which must attempt to persuade the court to set aside the settlement, it makes settlement appear relatively more attractive to that defendant.

C. Decisions Maintaining That the Pro Tanto Set-Off Rule Induces Undesirable Settlements

Other courts focus on the relative desirability of the settlements under the two set-off rules and maintain that the apportioned share set-off rule performs better.[198] They claim that the pro tanto set-off rule promotes collusive settlements, that it permits guiltier parties to settle early for less than their equitable share of the liability, that it forces wealthy defendants to bear a disproportionate share of the liability, and that it unfairly penalizes a non-settling defendant.

1. The Pro Tanto Set-Off Rule Promotes Collusive Settlements

Some courts claim the pro tanto set-off rule promotes collusive settlements: "By accepting a low partial settlement, plaintiffs would be able to fund further litigation with no diminution of the total amount eventually received."[199] As explained above, these courts overlook the fact that this strategy would compromise the plaintiff's expected recovery: there is no diminution in the amount received only if the plaintiff prevails in the subsequent litigation.[200]

2. Under the Pro Tanto Set-Off Rule, Guiltier Parties Would Settle Early for Less Than Their Equitable Share of the Liability

Courts have suggested that the pro tanto set-off rule "would allow guiltier defendants to get off cheaply by settling first."[201] This argument stems from the same misconception as stated previously. In the event that the plaintiff settles with one defendant and litigates against the other, if it fails to maximize its recovery in settlement, it will compromise its expected recovery because it is not guaranteed success in the litigation. The plaintiff faces this penalty regardless of whether the settlement is with the guiltier or less guilty defendant.[202]

3. The Pro Tanto Set-Off Rule Forces Wealthy Defendants to Bear a Disproportionate Share of the Liability

Some courts claim that the pro tanto set-off rule is undesirable because "plaintiffs could effect low settlements with defendants who had limited resources, and thereby *force* wealthier defendants to pay more than if all parties proceeded to trial."[203] In contrast, under the apportioned share set-off rule, the plaintiff would bear the whole shortfall if it settled for a small amount with a defendant that had limited solvency.

The courts, however, fail to consider what would happen if such a settlement did not take place. If the plaintiff litigated against both defendants and prevailed against both at trial, the wealthier defendant would have to make up for the shortfall under either set-off rule if the share of the defendant with limited resources was greater than its solvency.

It is true that in this case, the defendant with limited solvency would pay its full solvency to satisfy the judgment, whereas in the event of a settlement it would pay a lower amount, reflecting the probability that it would prevail at trial. At the same time, however, litigating the case would consume some, perhaps even all, of that defendant's assets, so it is possible that the amount remaining, if any, to satisfy the judgment would be lower than what the defendant would have been willing to pay in settlement. In this scenario, by discouraging the plaintiff from settling with the defendant that has limited solvency, the apportioned share set-off rule produces a *less* equitable share of the burdens.

4. The Pro Tanto Set-Off Rule Unfairly Penalizes a Non-Settling Defendant

Courts also maintain that the pro tanto set-off rule unfairly penalizes the non-settling defendant. The argument is that as a result of the saving of litigation costs that comes from settlement, a plaintiff will be willing to settle for a lesser amount than what it might recover through litigation, leaving the other defendant responsible for a larger proportion of the plaintiff's damages.[204] This problem, the courts maintain, is not corrected by a "good faith" hearing because courts allow this type of discounting in determining whether the settlement was appropriate.[205]

These courts fail to consider two relevant elements of this problem. While the plaintiff saves litigation costs by settling with one defendant, it does not necessarily follow that the settling defendant would get the benefit from this saving in the form of a lower settlement. In fact, it is equally likely that high litigation costs would increase the amount of the settlement because of the resulting saving to the settling defendant.

Consider this issue in the context of a single-defendant problem in which the plaintiff has a probability of fifty percent of recovering damages of $100. In the absence of litigation costs, risk-neutral parties with accurate information would settle for $50. If litigation costs are $10, the range of settlement is between $40 and $60. If the plaintiff's bargaining power is greater, the settlement is likely to be for more than $50; if the defendant's bargaining is greater, it is likely to be for less than $50. It is the relative bargaining power of the parties, rather than the amount of the litigation costs, that determines whether the settlement is for more than the plaintiff's expected recovery through litigation.[206]

Conclusion

This Article generates some strong conclusions. For example, it shows that settlements are promoted both by contribution protection rules and by rules giving contribution rights to settling defendants. The latter conclusion is significant because the legal regime has generally denied settling defendants such rights.[207]

However, the reader who was hoping to learn from this Article whether, from the perspective of inducing settlements, joint and several liability is generally preferable to non-joint liability, or whether a pro tanto set-off rule is generally preferable to an apportioned share set-off rule might be disappointed. This Article identifies conditions under which joint and several liability performs better than non-joint liability, but shows that neither rule is consistently better than the other.[208] We reach a similar conclusion with respect to the choice between set-off rules.[209]

Despite the lack of easy answers in this area, our analysis has important implications for judges and policymakers. First, we show why any simplistic choice of one rule stems from a lack of appreciation of the complexity of the problem. Our approach improves upon the current understanding of the choice between settlement and litigation in cases involving joint tortfeasors. The courts reach different conclusions from the ones we present in this Article not because they are engaged in a different enterprise. Like us, they choose among the competing legal rules based, at least in part, on their predictions of which rule creates better incentives for the settlement of multi-defendant claims. Nor are the behavioral models employed by the courts more sophisticated than ours. Like us, the courts assume, at least implicitly, that plaintiffs seek to maximize their recoveries and defendants seek to minimize their losses.

In trying to answer the same questions, however, the courts systematically fail to focus on the complex, strategic relationships among the plaintiff and the various defendants under schemes of joint and several liability. As a result, their predictions concerning which rules perform better are the product, quite simply, of logical flaws. By forcing us to think systematically about the nature of the problem, the tools of economic analysis make possible a much deeper understanding of the incentives for the settlement of multi-defendant cases.

Second, we define conditions under which one set of rules performs better than others. For example, joint and several liability generally deters settlements when the plaintiff's probabilities of success are independent.[210] Similarly, the pro tanto set-off rule performs better when litigation costs are low compared to the level of damages.[211]

These insights might permit a decisionmaker to choose the best rules for different categories of problems. For example, as noted above, in a case in which the plaintiff charges that two defendants engaged in a conspiracy, the plaintiff's probabilities of success are perfectly correlated.[212] In those cases, the choice of joint and several liability would be comparatively more desirable than in cases in which the plaintiff's probabilities of success are likely to be independent. Similarly, some types of litigation involve relatively more litigation costs than others. When litigation costs are higher, the choice of the apportioned share set-off rule would be relatively more desirable.

Third, our analysis suggests that the choice among the competing legal rules might be better made by administrative agencies than by common law judges. When presented with a particular case, judges are unlikely to be able to collect the data necessary to determine whether, for the bulk of cases in that category, the plaintiff's probabilities of success are highly correlated, or whether litigation costs are high. These determinations are easier for administrative officials, who have better means of obtaining empirical information and easier access to the types of expertise necessary to analyze this information.

Notes

1. 113 S. Ct. 2085 (1993).
2. *Id.* at 2086. For the order granting certiorari, see *Musick, Peeler & Garrett v. Employers Ins.*, 113 S. Ct. 54 (1992).
3. Amicus briefs were filed by the American Institute of Certified Public Accountants, the Securities Industry Association, the National Association of Securities and Commercial Law Attorneys, and several investment banks. See *Musick, Peeler & Garrett*, 113 S. Ct. at 54 (granting motion to file). These briefs, as well as those filed by the parties, uncritically present many of the judicial arguments that we criticize in Part IV. For further discussion, see notes 24, 152 *infra*.
4. See 113 S. Ct. at 2089.
5. See *id.* at 2089-92.
6. For influential decisions at the state level, see, e.g., *American Motorcycle Ass'n v. Superior Court,* 578 P.2d 899, 915-16 (Cal. 1978); *Dole v. Dow Chem. Co.,* 282 N.E.2d 288 (N.Y. 1972).
7. See, e.g., *Franklin v. Kaypro Corp.,* 884 F.2d 1222, 1229-32 (9th Cir. 1989), cert. denied, 498 U.S. 890 (1990); *Singer v. Olympia Brewing Co.,* 878 F.2d 596, 599-601 (2d Cir. 1989), cert. denied, 493 U.S. 1024 (1990); *TBG Inc. v. Bendis,* 811 F. Supp. 596, 602-05 (D. Kan. 1992); *Alvarado Partners, L.P. v. Mehta,* 723 F. Supp. 540, 549-53 (D. Colo. 1989). For academic commentary, see, e.g., M. Patricia Adamski, *Contribution and Settlement in Multiparty Actions Under Rule 10b-5*, 66 Iowa L. Rev. 533 (1981); W. Bruce Davis, Comment, *Multiple Defendant Settlements in 10b-5: Good Faith Contribution Bar*, 40 Hastings L.J. 1253 (1989).

8. CERCLA contains statutory provisions that govern settlements in cases in which the plaintiff is the federal government or the states. See 42 U.S.C. §§9613(f)(1)-(2), 9622 (1988). These provisions, however, do not apply when the plaintiff is a private party, and the courts in such cases have developed federal common law. See, e.g., *United States v. SCA Servs., Inc.*, No. F89-29, 1993 U.S. Dist. LEXIS 10175, at *20-29 (N.D. Ind. June 28, 1993); *Comerica Bank-Detroit v. Allen Indus., Inc.*, 769 F. Supp. 1408, 1413-15 (E.D. Mich. 1991); *United States v. Western Processing Co.*, 756 F. Supp. 1424, 1429-32 (W.D. Wash. 1991); *Lyncott Corp. v. Chemical Waste Management, Inc.*, 690 F. Supp. 1409, 1416-20 (E.D. Pa. 1988); *Edward Hines Lumber Co. v. Vulcan Materials Co.*, No. 85-C1142, 1987 WL 27368, at *1-2 (N.D. Ill. Dec. 4, 1987). For academic discussion of CERCLA's settlement provisions, see, e.g., Lynnette Boomgaarden & Charles Breer, *Surveying the Superfund Settlement Dilemma*, 27 Land & Water L. Rev. 83 (1992); Frank B. Cross,*Settlement Under the 1986 Superfund Amendments*, 66 Or. L. Rev. 517 (1987); Elizabeth F. Mason, *Contribution, Contribution Protection, and Nonsettlor Liability Under CERCLA: Following Laskin's Lead*, 19 B.C. Envtl. Aff. L. Rev. 73 (1991); Note, *Superfund Settlements: The Failed Promise of the 1986 Amendments*, 74 Va. L. Rev. 123 (1988).
9. See, e.g., *Dobson v. Camden*, 705 F.2d 759, 768-71 (5th Cir. 1983), rev'd on other grounds, 725 F.2d 1003 (5th Cir. 1984); *Miller v. Apartments & Homes, Inc.*, 646 F.2d 101, 105-10 (3d Cir. 1981).
10. See, e.g., *In re Masters Mates & Pilots Pension Plan & IRAP Litig.*, 957 F.2d 1020, 1026-32 (2d Cir. 1992); *Donovan v. Robbins*, 752 F.2d 1170, 1180-81 (7th Cir. 1984) (Posner, J.). For academic commentary, see Elizabeth A. Di Cola, *Fairness and Efficiency: Allowing Contribution Under ERISA*, 80 Cal. L. Rev. 1543, 1548-53 (1992).
11. See, e.g., *FDIC v. Geldermann, Inc.*, 975 F.2d 695 (10th Cir. 1992); *Resolution Trust Corp. v. Gallagher*, 815 F. Supp. 1107, 1110-12 (N.D. Ill. 1993).
12. See, e.g., In re Oil Spill by the Amoco Cadiz, 954 F.2d 1279, 1315-18 (7th Cir. 1992) (per curiam); *Hernandez v. M/V RAJAAN*, 841 F.2d 582, 591 (5th Cir.), cert. denied, 488 U.S. 981 (1988); *Leger v. Drilling Well Control, Inc.*, 592 F.2d 1246, 1248-51 (5th Cir. 1979).
13. Compare *Franklin v. Kaypro Corp.*, 884 F.2d 1222, 1231 (9th Cir. 1989) (adopting apportioned share set-off rule), cert. denied, 498 U.S. 890 (1990) with *Singer v. Olympia Brewing Co.*, 878 F.2d 596, 600 (2d Cir. 1989) (adopting pro tanto set-off rule), cert. denied, 493 U.S. 1024 (1990). For district court decisions outside the Ninth Circuit that are consistent with *Kaypro*, see, e.g., *United States Fidelity & Guar. Co. v. Patriot's Point Dev. Auth.*, 772 F. Supp. 1565, 1577 (D.S.C. 1991); *Alvarado Partners, L.P. v. Mehta*, 723 F. Supp. 540, 552-53 (D. Colo. 1989); *In re Sunrise Sec. Litig.*, 698 F. Supp. 1256, 1261 (E.D. Pa. 1988). For district court decisions outside the Second Circuit that are consistent with *Singer*, see, e.g., *TBG Inc. v. Bendis*, 811 F. Supp. 596, 604-05 (D. Kan. 1992); *Biben v. Card*, Nos. 84-0844-CV-W-6, 84-0846-CV-W-6, and 84-0978-CV-W-6, 1991 WL 272848, at *3 (W.D. Mo. Dec. 10, 1991); *MFS Mun. Income Trust v. American Medical Int'l, Inc.*, 751 F. Supp. 279, 281-87 (D. Mass. 1990); *Dalton v. Alston & Bird*, 741 F. Supp. 157, 159-60 (S.D. Ill. 1990); *In re Terra-Drill Partnerships Sec. Litig.*, 726 F. Supp. 655, 656-57 (S.D. Texas 1989). The rules adopted in these cases are defined at Part I.A.4 infra.

14. Compare *In re Masters Mates & Pilots Pension Plan & IRAP Litig.*, 957 F.2d at 1029-31 (holding that set-off should be no less than under pro tanto set-off rule) with *Lumpkin v. Envirodyne Indus.*, 933 F.2d 449, 464 (7th Cir.) (adopting apportioned share set-off rule), cert. denied, 112 S. Ct. 373 (1991).
15. The courts have identified three different approaches: (1) reducing the plaintiff's claim against the non-settling defendant using a pro tanto set-off rule and allowing a non-settling defendant that pays more than its apportioned share of the liability to bring an action for contribution against the settling defendant; (2) reducing the plaintiff's claim against the non-settling defendant by a pro tanto set-off rule and protecting the settling defendant from contribution actions; and (3) reducing the plaintiff's claim against the non-settling defendant using an apportioned share set-off rule. See *Miller v. Christopher*, 887 F.2d 902, 905 (9th Cir. 1989). The Eighth Circuit has adopted the third approach. See *Associated Elec. Coop. v. Mid-America Transp. Co.*, 931 F.2d 1266, 1269-71 (8th Cir. 1991). The Seventh Circuit has rejected the third approach but has not chosen between the first two. See *Amoco Cadiz*, 954 F.2d at 1315-18. The Eleventh Circuit has adopted the first approach. See *Boca Grande Club, Inc. v. Polackwich*, 990 F.2d 606 (11th Cir.), cert. granted sub nom. *Boca Grande Club, Inc. v. Florida Power & Light Co.*, 114 S. Ct. 39 (1993); *Great Lakes Dredge & Dock Co. v. Tanker Robert Watt Miller*, 957 F.2d 1575, 1581 (11th Cir.), cert. denied, 113 S. Ct. 484 (1992). The Ninth Circuit has rejected the first approach but has not chosen between the second and third. See *Miller*, 887 F.2d at 906-07. For a discussion of the conflict, see *Great Lakes Dredge & Dock Co.*, 957 F.2d at 1581-83.
16. Throughout most of this Article, we focus specifically on the problem of two tortfeasors. In Part II.E.9, however, we show how our central conclusions hold when there are more than two defendants.
17. See *Boca Grande Club*, 990 F.2d at 606; see also *McDermott, Inc. v. Clyde Iron*, 979 F.2d 1068 (5th Cir. 1992), cert. granted sub nom. *McDermott, Inc. v. AmClyde & River Don Castings Ltd.*, 113 S. Ct. 3033 (1993).
18. In particular, a great deal of admiralty law is judge-made. See, e.g., *Edmonds v. Compagnie Generale Transatlantique*, 443 U.S. 256, 259 (1979); *United States v. Reliable Transfer Co.*, 421 U.S. 397, 409 (1975).
19. For discussions of this power, see, e.g., Martha A. Field, *Sources of Law: The Scope of Federal Common Law*, 99 Harv. L. Rev. 883 (1986); Thomas W. Merrill, *The Common Law Powers of Federal Courts*, 52 U. Chi. L. Rev. 1 (1985).
20. See, e.g., *Franklin v. Kaypro Corp.*, 884 F.2d 1222, 1225 (9th Cir. 1989), cert. denied, 498 U.S. 890 (1990); *Sears v. Atchison, Topeka & Santa Fe Ry.*, 749 F.2d 1451, 1455 (10th Cir. 1984), cert. denied, 471 U.S. 1099 (1985); Fed. R. Civ. P. 16(c) advisory committee's note; Fed. R. Evid. 408 advisory committee's note.
21. In prior works, we studied the impact of regimes of joint and several liability on deterrence. See Lewis A. Kornhauser & Richard L. Revesz, *Apportioning Damages Among Potentially Insolvent Actors*, 19 J. Legal Stud. 617 (1990); Lewis A. Kornhauser & Richard L. Revesz, *Sharing Damages Among Multiple Tortfeasors*, 98 Yale L.J. 831 (1989).
22. For discussion of this issue in the context of a single defendant, see A.

Mitchell Polinsky & Daniel L. Rubinfeld, *The Deterrent Effects of Settlements and Trials*, 8 Int'l Rev. L. & Econ. 109 (1988).

23. Compare Part II.B (independent probabilities) with Part II.C (perfectly correlated probabilities).
24. See generally Frank H. Easterbrook, William M. Landes & Richard A. Posner, *Contribution Among Antitrust Defendants: A Legal and Economic Analysis*, 23 J.L. & Econ. 331 (1980); A. Mitchell Polinsky & Steven Shavell, *Contribution and Claim Reduction Among Antitrust Defendants: An Economic Analysis*, 33 Stan. L. Rev. 447 (1981); see also Jong Goo Yi, Litigations with Multiple Defendants: How to Settle Under Different Apportionment Rules 73-82 (1991) (unpublished Ph.D. dissertation, Stanford University) (on file with the New York University Law Review) (analyzing same limited set of rules and assuming implicitly that plaintiff's probabilities of success are perfectly correlated). For an analysis of these works, see notes 83, 95, 99, 100, 107, 111, 135, 152, 212 *infra*. Most of the briefs in *Musick, Peeler & Garrett v. Employers Ins.*, 113 S. Ct. 2085 (1993), rely on the Easterbrook, Landes and Posner article for some of their arguments but do not recognize its limitations.
25. Restatement (Second) of Torts (1965) [hereinafter Restatement].
26. Unif. Contribution Among Tortfeasors Act, 12 U.L.A. 57 (1975) [hereinafter UCATA].
27. Unif. Comparative Fault Act, 12 U.L.A. 43 (Supp. 1993) [hereinafter UCFA].
28. Restatement §433A.
29. *Id*. cmt. i.
30. See *id*. illus. 12.
31. See, e.g., *United States v. Alcan Aluminum Corp.*, 964 F.2d 252, 268-70 (3d Cir. 1992); *O'Neil v. Picillo,* 883 F.2d 176, 178-83 (1st Cir. 1989), cert. denied, 493 U.S. 1071 (1990); *United States v. Monsanto Co.*, 858 F.2d 160, 171-73 (4th Cir. 1988), cert. denied, 490 U.S. 1106 (1989); *United States v. Chem-Dyne Corp.*, 572 F. Supp. 802, 810-11 (S.D. Ohio 1983). A federal common law rule of joint and several liability has also been fashioned in admiralty actions. See *Edmonds v. Compagnie Generale Transatlantique,* 443 U.S. 256, 259-60 (1979).
32. The computation of these shares is discussed in Part I.A.3 *infra*.
33. See Restatement §886A(1).
34. UCATA §1, 12 U.L.A. at 63; UCFA §4, 12 U.L.A. at 54.
35. 101 Eng. Rep. 1337 (K.B. 1799).
36. See, e.g., *Musick, Peeler & Garrett v. Employers Ins.*, 113 S. Ct. 2085 (1993) (securities laws); *Cooper Stevedoring Co. v. Fritz Kopke, Inc.,* 417 U.S. 106 (1974) (admiralty). Under ERISA, the circuits differ on whether the federal courts have the power to fashion a common law right of contribution. Compare *Chemung Canal Trust Co. v. Sovran Bank/Maryland,* 939 F.2d 12, 16-18 (2d Cir. 1991) (fashioning such a right), cert. denied, 112 S. Ct. 3014 (1992) with *Kim v. Fujikawa,* 871 F.2d 1427, 1432-33 (9th Cir. 1989) (refusing to fashion such a right). The 1986 amendments to CERCLA provide an express right of contribution. See 42 U.S.C. §9613(f)(1) (1988). Prior to these amendments, the courts had fashioned a federal common law right of contribution. See, e.g., *United States v. New Castle County,* 642 F. Supp. 1258, 1265-69 (D. Del. 1986); *United States v. Conservation Chem. Co.,* 619

F. Supp. 162, 228-29 (W.D. Mo. 1985); *Colorado v. ASARCO, Inc.*, 608 F. Supp. 1484, 1486-92 (D. Colo. 1985). But see *United States v. Westinghouse Elec. Co.*, 22 Env't Rep. Cas. (BNA) 1230, 1234 (S.D. Ind. 1983) (refusing to fashion a federal common law rule). The Supreme Court, however, refused to fashion a federal common law right of contribution under the antitrust laws, see *Texas Indus., Inc. v. Radcliff Materials, Inc.*, 451 U.S. 630 (1981), and under the Equal Pay Act and Title VII of the Civil Rights Act, see *Northwest Airlines, Inc. v. Transport Workers*, 451 U.S. 77 (1981). In those cases, it reasoned that Congress, in those statutes, had not "intended courts to have the power to alter or supplement the remedies enacted." *Texas Indus.*, 451 U.S. at 638; see also *Northwest Airlines*, 451 U.S. at 91; *Musick, Peeler & Garrett*, 113 S. Ct. at 2088 (discussing *Texas Indus.* and *Northwest Airlines*).

37. See *Northwest Airlines*, 451 U.S. at 86-88 & n.17.
38. See UCATA §1(a), 12 U.L.A. at 63.
39. See *id.* §1(b).
40. See *id.*
41. The UCATA provides, however, that "if equity requires[,] the collective liability of some as a group shall constitute a single share." *Id.* §2(b), 12 U.L.A. at 87.
42. See Restatement §886A(2); UCFA §4(a), 12 U.L.A. at 54.
43. See Restatement §886A(2).
44. See, e.g., *United States v. Reliable Transfer Co.*, 421 U.S. 397 (1975) (admiralty); *Environmental Transp. Sys., Inc. v. Ensco, Inc.*, 969 F.2d 503, 507-10 (7th Cir. 1992) (CERCLA); *Weyerhaeuser Co. v. Koppers Co.*, 771 F. Supp. 1420, 1426-27 (D. Md. 1991) (same).
45. UCATA §4(a), 12 U.L.A. at 98.
46. UCFA §6, 12 U.L.A. at 57.
47. See, e.g., *TBG Inc. v. Bendis*, 811 F. Supp. 596, 603 (D. Kan. 1992); *United States v. Western Processing Co.*, 756 F. Supp. 1424, 1430 (W.D. Wash. 1990).
48. See, e.g., *Donovan v. Robbins*, 752 F.2d 1170, 1181 (7th Cir. 1984) (Posner, J.); *MFS Mun. Income Trust v. American Medical Int'l, Inc.* 751 F. Supp. 279, 282 & n.3 (D. Mass. 1990).
49. Other courts refer to this rule as a claim reduction rule. See text accompanying notes 83-87 *infra*.
50. Restatement §885(3).
51. See *id.* §886A caveat & cmt. m.
52. See notes 13-15 *supra* (setting forth conflict among circuits under federal securities laws, ERISA, and admiralty). Interestingly, CERCLA adopts a statutory pro tanto set-off rule in cases brought by the federal government or the states. See 42 U.S.C. §§9613(f)(2), 9622(g)(5), (h)(4) (1988). But see *United States v. Laskin*, No. C84-2035Y, 1989 U.S. Dist. LEXIS 4900, at *18-20 (N.D. Ohio Feb. 27, 1989) (adopting apportioned share set-off rule despite explicit statutory mandate to the contrary). In cases brought by private parties, however, the courts have adopted an apportioned share set-off rule under their common law powers. See, e.g., *United States v. SCA Servs., Inc.*, No. F89-29, 1993 U.S. Dist. LEXIS 10175, at *33-42 (N.D. Ind. June 28, 1993); *American Cyanamid Co. v. King Indus., Inc.*, 814 F. Supp. 215, 217-19 (D.R.I. 1993); *Comerica Bank-Detroit v. Allen Indus., Inc.*, 769 F.

Supp. 1408, 1415 (E.D. Mich. 1991); *United States v. Western Processing Co.*, 756 F. Supp. 1424, 1429-32 (W.D. Wash. 1991); *Edward Hines Lumber Co. v. Vulcan Materials Co.*, No. 85-C1142, 1987 WL 27368, at *2 (N.D. Ill. Dec. 4, 1987).

53. See, e.g., *Austin v. Raymark Indus.*, 841 F.2d 1184, 1190-91 (1st Cir. 1988) (applying Maine law); *Kussman v. City & County of Denver,* 706 P.2d 776, 779-82 (Colo. 1985); *Thomas v. Solberg,* 442 N.W.2d 73, 76-78 (Iowa 1989); *Rambaum v. Swisher,* 435 N.W.2d 19, 22-23 (Minn. 1989); *Duncan v. Cessna Aircraft Co.*, 665 S.W.2d 414, 429-32 (Tex. 1984).
54. See, e.g., *Franklin v. Kaypro Corp.*, 884 F.2d 1222, 1231-32 (9th Cir. 1989), cert. denied, 498 U.S. 890 (1990); *MFS Mun. Income Trust v. American Medical Int'l, Inc.*, 751 F. Supp. 279, 284-85 (D. Mass. 1990).
55. See, e.g., *Austin*, 841 F.2d at 1190-91; *MFS Mun. Income Trust*, 751 F. Supp. at 285; *Duncan*, 665 S.W.2d at 430.
56. N.Y. Gen. Oblig. Law §15-108 (McKinney 1992); see also *First Fed. Sav. & Loan Ass'n v. Oppenheim, Appel, Dixon & Co.*, 631 F. Supp. 1029, 1032-37 (S.D.N.Y. 1986) (applying New York rule in federal securities action).
57. In *Sears v. Atchison, Topeka & Santa Fe Ry.*, 749 F.2d 1451, 1454-55 (10th Cir. 1984), cert. denied, 471 U.S. 1009 (1985), the court considered what set-off rule to apply under Title VII, under which contribution is unavailable. See note 36 *supra*. The Tenth Circuit deferred to the district court's choice of a pro tanto set-off rule on the ground that this rule would encourage settlements. 749 F.2d at 1455.
58. This approach is followed under the antitrust laws, where, as we discussed in note 36 *supra*, contribution is barred. See, e.g., *Gulfstream III Assocs. v. Gulfstream Aerospace Corp.*, 995 F.2d 425, 434 (3d Cir. 1993).
59. Note, however, that if the plaintiff settles for more than the settling defendant's apportioned share of the liability, it would be better off under the apportioned share set-off rule, which would allow it to recover more than its damages. See text accompanying notes 53-54 *supra*.
60. Thus, under the federal securities laws, courts adopting the apportioned share set-off rule have nonetheless faced the question of whether settling defendants are protected from contribution actions, and have approved settlements containing provisions specifying such protection. See, e.g., *Franklin v. Kaypro Corp.*, 884 F.2d 1222, 1229 (9th Cir. 1989), cert. denied, 498 U.S. 890 (1990); *Alvarado Partners, L.P. v. Mehta,* 723 F. Supp. 540, 550-51 (D. Colo. 1989).
61. See Restatement §886A caveat & cmt. m(1)-(2).
62. UCATA §4(b), 12 U.L.A. at 98. The 1939 version of the UCATA had not provided contribution protection. The Commissioners' Comment indicates that the lack of such protection "has been one of the chief causes for complaint where the Act has been adopted, and one of the main objections to its adoption." Id. cmt. on subsection (b), 12 U.L.A. at 99.
63. UCFA §6, 12 U.L.A. at 57.
64. As noted in note 15 *supra*, the circuits are split on the question of contribution protection in admiralty actions. Compare *Miller v. Christopher,* 887 F.2d 902, 906 (9th Cir. 1989) (providing contribution protection) with *Boca Grande Club, Inc. v. Polackwich,* 990 F.2d 606 (11th Cir.) (declining to provide contribution protection), cert. granted sub nom. *Boca Grande Club, Inc. v.*

Florida Power & Light Co., Inc., 114 S. Ct. 39 (1993); *Great Lakes Dredge & Dock Co. v. Tanker Robert Watt Miller,* 957 F.2d 1575, 1581 (11th Cir.) (same), cert. denied, 113 S. Ct. 484 (1992). Under the federal securities laws, courts have routinely approved settlements that include contribution protection provisions. See, e.g., *TBG Inc. v. Bendis,* 811 F. Supp. 596, 602 (D. Kan. 1992); *MFS Mun. Income Trust v. American Medical Int'l, Inc.*, 751 F. Supp. 279, 287 (D. Mass. 1990); cases cited in note 60 *supra*. For differing approaches under ERISA, see *In re Masters Mates & Pilots Pension Plan & IRAP Litig.*, 957 F.2d 1020, 1031-32 (2d Cir. 1992) (noting that contribution protection provisions in settlements are valid only for "fair" settlements); *Donovan v. Robbins,* 752 F.2d 1170, 1181 (7th Cir. 1984) (Posner, J.) (declining to adopt rule of contribution protection where settlement agreement does not call for such protection). CERCLA includes a statutory provision of contribution protection for settlements with the federal government or the states. See 42 U.S.C. §§9613(f)(2), 9622(g)(5), (h)(4) (1988). In cases brought by private parties, however, the courts have fashioned such a rule under their common law powers. See, e.g., *United States v. SCA Servs., Inc.*, No. F8-29, 1993 U.S. Dist. LEXIS 10175, at *23-30 (N.D. Ind. June 28, 1993); *Comerica Bank-Detroit v. Allen Indus., Inc.*, 769 F. Supp. 1408, 1414 (E.D. Mich. 1991); *Lyncott Corp. v. Chemical Waste Management, Inc.*, 690 F. Supp. 1409, 1416-19 (E.D. Pa. 1988); *Edward Hines Lumber Co. v. Vulcan Materials Co.*, No. 85-C1142, 1987 WL 27368, at *2 (N.D. Ill. Dec. 4, 1987).

65. See text accompanying notes 167-74 *infra*.
66. See Restatement §886A cmt. f; UCATA §1(d), 12 U.L.A. at 63; UCFA §4(b), 12 U.L.A. at 54.
67. CERCLA contains a statutory provision giving defendants that settle with the federal government or with a state the right to bring contribution actions against non-settling defendants, regardless of whether the settlement extinguishes the plaintiff's rights against those defendants. See 42 U.S.C. §9613(f)(3)(B) (1988). The courts have held that this statutory provision does not extend to settlements with private parties, and they have fashioned a common law rule that, consistent with the UCATA and UCFA, precludes contribution except where the settlement extinguishes the liability of the party from whom contribution is sought. See, e.g., *American Cyanamid Co. v. King Indus., Inc.*, 814 F. Supp. 215, 217-18 (D.R.I. 1993); *Amland Properties Corp. v. Aluminum Co.*, 808 F. Supp. 1187, 1197-99 (D.N.J. 1992).
68. See notes 69-74 *infra*.
69. CERCLA has no statutory requirement for a "good faith" hearing. In the case of settlements with the government, the courts have inquired whether the settling parties acted in bad faith. In the absence of malfeasance, the courts have given a great deal of deference to the government's decision to settle and have not engaged in a detailed analysis of the substantive adequacy of the settlement. See, e.g., *Comerica Bank-Detroit v. Allen Indus., Inc.*, 769 F. Supp. 1408, 1411-12 (E.D. Mich. 1991); *Kelley v. Thomas Solvent Co.*, 717 F. Supp. 507 (W.D. Mich. 1989). For commentary, see Mason, *supra* note 8, at 112-14.
70. Under the federal securities laws, the inquiry has both procedural and substantive components. See, e.g., *TBG Inc. v. Bendis,* 811 F. Supp. 596, 605 (D. Kan. 1992); *In re Jiffy Lube Sec. Litig.*, 772 F. Supp. 890, 892-93 (D. Md.

1991); *MFS Mun. Income Trust v. American Medical Int'l, Inc.*, 751 F. Supp. 279, 287-89 (D. Mass. 1990). The same approach is followed under ERISA, see *In re Masters Mates & Pilots Pension Plan & IRAP Litig.*, 957 F.2d 1020, 1031 (2d Cir. 1992), and under the law of admiralty, see *Miller v. Christopher*, 887 F.2d 902, 907-08 (9th Cir. 1989).

71. 698 P.2d 159 (Cal. 1985).
72. *Id.* at 166.
73. *Id.* at 169 (Bird, C.J., dissenting).
74. Approaches similar to that of *Tech-Bilt* have been adopted in other jurisdictions. See, e.g., *International Action Sports, Inc. v. Sabellico*, 573 So. 2d 928, 929-30 (Fla. Ct. App.), review denied, 583 So. 2d 1036 (Fla. 1991); *Pickett v. Stephens-Nelsen, Inc.*, 717 P.2d 277, 282 (Wash. Ct. App. 1986). Several jurisdictions, however, have rejected the *Tech-Bilt* approach and have sided with Chief Justice Bird. See, e.g., *Noyes v. Raymond*, 548 N.E.2d 196, 199-200 (Mass. App. Ct. 1990). Other courts have held that the *Tech-Bilt* inquiry is not required and have given the trial courts broad discretion to determine what factors are relevant to the good faith inquiry. See, e.g., *Velsicol Chem. Corp. v. Davidson*, 811 P.2d 561 (Nev. 1991).
75. See text accompanying notes 58-59 *supra*.
76. Restatement §886A cmt. i; UCATA §3(b) Commissioners' cmt., 12 U.L.A. at 89.
77. UCFA §4(a), 12 U.L.A. at 54.
78. Fed. R. Civ. P. 14(a).
79. Fed. R. Civ. P. 42.
80. See, e.g., *FDIC v. Loube*, 134 F.R.D. 270, 274 (N.D. Cal. 1991); *State Mut. Life Assur. Co. v. Arthur Anderson & Co.*, 63 F.R.D. 389, 392-94 (S.D.N.Y. 1974).
81. See text accompanying notes 82-95 *infra*.
82. 954 F.2d 1279 (7th Cir. 1992) (per curiam).
83. *Id.* at 1315. Easterbrook, Landes, and Posner use a similar typology, perhaps not surprisingly since Judge Easterbrook was a member of the panel in *Amoco Cadiz*. See Easterbrook, Landes & Posner, *supra* note 24, at 356-64. Polinsky and Shavell define only three rules–no contribution, contribution, and claim reduction. See Polinsky & Shavell, *supra* note 24, at 448. Their contribution rule assumes that a settling defendant is not protected from contribution actions. See *id.* at 458.
84. In an earlier Seventh Circuit decision, *Donovan v. Robbins*, 752 F.2d 1170 (7th Cir. 1984), Judge Posner defines three rules: (1) the traditional rule, (2) the traditional rule modified by not allowing contribution from a settling defendant, and (3) the comparative fault rule. *Id.* at 1180-81; see also *Miller v. Christopher*, 887 F.2d 902, 905 (9th Cir. 1989) (defining similar categories). Comparing these rules to those in the *Amoco Cadiz* case, the first corresponds to the contribution rule, the second corresponds to the contribution plus settlement bar rule, and the third corresponds to the claim reduction rule. Thus, even within a single circuit, there are serious inconsistencies in the nomenclature used to describe the various legal rules.
85. See Part I.A.5 *supra*.
86. See text accompanying notes 59-60 *supra*.
87. See text accompanying notes 46-49 *supra*.

88. See text accompanying notes 66-67 *supra* (describing UCATA's and UCFA's denial of contribution to settling defendants).
89. Obviously, this question is not trivial, since the UCFA, which adopts an apportioned share set-off rule, specifies that settling defendants are protected from contribution actions and can maintain contribution actions only if the plaintiff's claim against the other defendants is extinguished by the settlement. See text accompanying notes 66-67 *supra*. If the question of contribution actions between settling defendants under the apportioned share set-off rule never arises, it is unlikely that the UCFA would address it.
90. For a discussion of this problem, see Part I.A.6 *supra*; text accompanying notes 141-42 *infra*.
91. Because the question of contribution under the apportioned share set-off rule arises only if both defendants settle, a contribution action may be maintained only if two conditions hold: (1) the defendants have the right to bring such actions, and (2) they are not protected against such actions.
92. Not surprisingly, the courts are confused by all these terms. One court has stated that "the pro tanto rule is also known as the settlement bar rule." *MFS Mun. Income Trust v. American Medical Int'l, Inc.*, 751 F. Supp. 279, 282 n.2 (D. Mass. 1990). As indicated in the text, the fact that the plaintiff's claim against the non-settling defendant is reduced by the amount of the settlement says nothing about whether the settling defendant is protected from contribution actions.
93. See text accompanying notes 52-53 *supra*.
94. See text accompanying notes 57-59 *supra*.
95. The analyses in Easterbrook, Landes & Posner, *supra* note 24, and Polinsky & Shavell, *supra* note 24, which have the same limitations, therefore do not capture the richness of the legal regime.
96. A person i' risk neutral if she is indifferent between a lottery and its expected value. So, for example, she would be indifferent between bearing a risk herself and buying an insurance policy with a fair premium (equal to the expected value of the loss). A careful discussion of decisionmaking under risk is presented in David M. Kreps, A Course in Microeconomic Theory 71-132 (1990). For a definition of risk neutrality, see *id.* at 82.
97. Under our model, there is uncertainty about the defendant's liability (the plaintiff is not certain to prevail) but not about the defendant's shares of the fault or the plaintiff's damages. We deal briefly with uncertainty over shares at text accompanying notes 189-90 *infra*. Uncertainty over damages should not affect the analysis in the case of risk-neutral parties. Assume that there was a 50% probability that the plaintiff's damages were \$150 and a 50% probability that they were \$50; the expected value of the plaintiff's damages is \$100. Risk-neutral parties will respond to this problem in the same way as to the problem described in the text, in which there is certainty that the damages are \$100: they will be affected solely by the expected value of the damages and not by the probability distribution over the possible values. For a definition of risk neutrality, see note 96 *supra*; for a definition of expected recovery, see note 102 *infra*.
98. Later, we relax this assumption. See Part II.E.1 *infra*.
99. Both Easterbrook, Landes & Posner, *supra* note 24, at 359-60, 365-66, and Polinsky & Shavell, *supra* note 24, at 458-59, make similar assumptions.

100. The model in Polinsky & Shavell, *supra* note 24, at 469, also assumes take-it-or-leave-it offers, but there the defendants, rather than the plaintiff, make such offers. In Easterbrook, Landes & Posner, *supra* note 24, the bargaining model is not fully specified. It is not clear, for example, which parties make the initial offers or how many offers each party can make.

101. In Lewis A. Kornhauser & Richard L. Revesz, *Multidefendant Settlements: The Impact of Joint and Several Liability*, 23 J. Legal Stud. 41 (1994), we provide formal proofs for the propositions discussed in Parts II.B and II.C. In this Article, in addition to presenting that argument in an accessible manner, in Part I we provide a typology to guide judicial thinking, in Part III we apply the conclusions of Part II to make comparisons about the settlement-inducing properties of the competing rules, and in Part IV we provide a critique of the judicial arguments concerning the choice of set-off rules.

102. The expected recovery from a litigation weighs each possible outcome of the litigation by the likelihood of that outcome and then sums these weighted recoveries. The expected recovery is thus the mathematical expectation of the distribution of outcomes presented by the litigation. On a frequency interpretation of probability, the expectation is simply the average payoff from a large number of (independent) repetitions of the risk (here, the litigation). For a philosophically informed discussion of the emergence of the concept of a mathematical expectation, see Ian Hacking, The Emergence of Probability 92-101 (paperback ed. 1984).

103. Under joint and several liability, if the plaintiff prevails against both Row and Column, it could satisfy its full judgment from one of the defendants. This defendant would then have to seek contribution from the other. In the absence of litigation costs, it does not matter whether the plaintiff seeks $50 from Row and $50 from Column, or whether, for example, it seeks $100 from Row, which then recovers $50 from Column in a contribution action, as long as the plaintiff's action and the contribution action are joined. We discuss the relevance of joinder in Part III.H *infra*.

104. Given that one defendant rejects the offer, the other would be indifferent between accepting it and rejecting it, since under both scenarios its expected loss is $37.50. Under our convention, the indifferent party would settle. Our convention, however, is here slightly at odds with the strategic structure of the situation. Though it is a Nash equilibrium for one party to settle and the other party to litigate, this equilibrium is somewhat implausible because, when transaction costs are zero, litigation is a weakly dominant strategy for each defendant–each defendant does at least as well by litigating, and sometimes it does better. Consequently, the Nash equilibrium in which both parties litigate is more plausible. Thus, litigation assures Row of an expected loss of no more than $37.50 regardless of Column's decision; if Column settles, Row's expected loss declines to $31.25. The fact that, in response to offers of $37.50, both defendants might litigate is not inconsistent with the argument in the text: the plaintiff would not make offers of $37.50 to each defendant if it believed that they would choose one of the equilibria in which one party settles. It is, therefore, weakly dominant for the plaintiff to make offers greater than $37.50 to each party. Such offers will present defendants with a game in which the unique equilibrium is for each to litigate. The

concept of the Nash equilibrium is discussed in note 109 *infra*.

105. See note 106 *infra*.

106. If offers that add up to $75 do not induce acceptable settlements, offers that add up to a larger sum will not do so either. For example, if the pair of offers a and $(75 - a)$ does not induce a settlement, neither would offers of a and $(80 - a)$, which add up to $80. Settlement is relatively less desirable for Column and no more desirable for Row.

107. Easterbrook, Landes & Posner, *supra* note 24, at 356-57, and Polinsky & Shavell, *supra* note 24, at 451-52, 470, assume implicitly that the plaintiff's probabilities of success are perfectly correlated. Thus, they overlook the central importance of the correlation of the plaintiff's probabilities of success.

108. See text accompanying notes 103-04 *supra*.

109. The Nash equilibrium is the primary solution concept used in the theory of non-cooperative games in normal form. In this context, each player selects a strategy from her set of possible strategies. (In our game, there are two players, Row and Column, and each has available two strategies–settle and litigate.) In a Nash equilibrium, no player in the game has a (unilateral) incentive to change her strategy choice. Put differently, each player is doing the best she can, given that all other players continue to follow their equilibrium strategies. For a lucid, non-technical discussion of Nash equilibria, see David M. Kreps, Game Theory and Economic Modelling 28-36 (1990).

110. See Kornhauser & Revesz, *supra* note 101.

111. Easterbrook, Landes & Posner, *supra* note 24, overlooks the existence of these multiple equilibria and assumes, incorrectly, that the defendants would necessarily settle for the same amounts. See *id.* at 356-58. Polinsky & Shavell, *supra* note 24, at 470-71, considers the possibility of multiple equilibria.

112. Our model assumes that the plaintiff makes simultaneous offers to both defendants. Here, it would make Row an offer of more than $31.25 so that Row would refuse it.

113. If, in contrast, the plaintiff litigated against Column, Row's expected loss from litigation would be $12.50 (a 50% probability of having to pay 25% of the plaintiff's damages of $100); Row would pay no more than this amount in settlement. Column's expected liability would then be $43.75 (a 50% probability of having to pay $87.50). Thus, if the plaintiff settled with Row and litigated against Column, its total expected recovery would be only $56.25. If the plaintiff settled with both defendants, the best it could do would be to obtain $33.33 from each, for a total recovery of $66.66–less than its recovery from settling with Column and litigating against Row. As indicated above, if one defendant, say Row, accepts an offer of $33.33, the other defendant's expected loss from litigation is $33.33 (a 50% probability of having to pay $66.67). Column would thus be willing to accept a settlement of $33.33. Note that in this instance the plaintiff does not face the risk that offers of $33.33 to Row and Column, respectively, would induce both defendants to litigate rather than settle. See text accompanying notes 107-13 supra. If Row litigated, Column's expected loss from litigation would be $37.50 (a 50% probability of having to pay 75% of the plaintiff's damages of $100).

114. See text accompanying notes 107-08 *supra*.

115. See Kornhauser & Revesz, *supra* note 101.
116. See *id*. The plaintiff's probabilities of success can also be negatively correlated: perfect negative correlation means that the plaintiff either wins against Row and loses to Column or vice versa. The plaintiff's expected recovery from litigation is then $100–it recovers its full damages with certainty. Could the plaintiff settle with each of the defendants for $50? If one of the defendants, say Row, accepted the offer, the other would have an expected loss through litigation of only $25 (a 50% probability of paying the plaintiff's full damages of $100 minus the settlement of $50). As a result, the plaintiff would never make offers of $50 to each of the defendants. Row's settlement confers an external benefit of $25 on Column. Like in the case of independent probabilities, this externality precludes settlements. Note, moreover, that the externality is larger for negatively correlated probabilities than it is for independent probabilities. See text accompanying notes 103-04 *supra* (for independent probabilities, the corresponding benefit is only $6.25).
117. Our discussion in Part II.E of the one-defendant case is informed by Richard A. Posner, Economic Analysis of Law 434-41 (2d ed. 1977); John P. Gould, *The Economics of Legal Conflicts*, 2 J. Legal Stud. 279, 284-93 (1973); William M. Landes, *An Economic Analysis of the Courts*, 14 J.L. & Econ. 61, 66-69 (1971).
118. In all these situations, each party knows the other party's assessment of the plaintiff's probabilities of success. For an economic analysis of the effects of informational asymmetries when a plaintiff litigates against a single defendant (asymmetries that generally increase the likelihood of litigation), see Lucian A. Bebchuk, *Litigation and Settlement Under Imperfect Information*, 15 RAND J. Econ. 404 (1984); Barry Nalebuff, *Credible Pretrial Negotiation*, 18 RAND J. Econ. 198 (1987).
119. See text accompanying notes 106-07 *supra*.
120. In the case of sequential offers, however, the first settlement must be made public since, under the pro tanto set-off rule, it affects the plaintiff's claim against the other defendant.
121. See note 106 *supra*.
122. If Row's solvency is less than $50, it will not be able to pay its full share of the damages in the event that the plaintiff prevails against both defendants.
123. For a technical analysis of the effects of a defendant's insolvency on settlements, see generally Lewis A. Kornhauser & Richard L. Revesz, *Multidefendant Settlements Under Joint and Several Liability: The Problem of Insolvency*, 23 J. Legal Stud. (forthcoming 1994).
124. See *id*.
125. See *id*.
126. For further discussion of the costs of this course of action, see Part IV.A.1 *infra*.
127. See text accompanying notes 103-04 *supra*.
128. Settlement would also occur if the plaintiff could make its settlement offers contingent on both defendants accepting them; if either defendant rejected the offer, both would be deemed rejected. Offers of $37.50 would then be accepted by both defendants. As a practical matter, however, this result is dependent upon cooperation between the defendants. In the event that neither party is able to make take-it-or-leave-it offers, offers from the plaintiff

produce counteroffers from the defendants, which would need, at this stage, to coordinate their actions.

129. The surplus that the plaintiff obtains from litigating under joint and several liability when its probabilities of prevailing are independent is thus larger when there are three defendants than when there are two. See text accompanying notes 106-07 *supra* (analyzing two-defendant case).
130. A full analysis of this problem is beyond the scope of this Article.
131. See text accompanying notes 107-08 *supra*; see also Easterbrook, Landes & Posner, *supra* note 24, at 358-63.
132. See Part II.C *supra*.
133. See Part II.E.8 *supra*.
134. The proposition that any level of litigation costs will cause the defendants to settle relies on the assumption that the defendants can cooperate without expending coordination costs. Otherwise, the defendants will settle only if the litigation costs are sufficiently high compared to the coordination costs.
135. For a discussion of how the plaintiff could defeat attempts on the part of the defendants to cooperate, see Easterbrook, Landes & Posner, *supra* note 24, at 360, 365-66.
136. The legal regime we model is characterized by eight elements, and each has at least two alternatives. It would therefore appear that there are more than 2^8–that is, 256–different rules. In fact, the number is somewhat smaller. For example, the need for a "good faith" hearing arises only if there is a right of contribution, with pro tanto set-off and contribution protection for settling defendants. See text accompanying notes 74-75 *supra*.
137. See text accompanying notes 45-49 *supra*.
138. See text accompanying notes 96-101 *supra*.
139. See Part II.B *supra*.
140. We do not consider the possibility that litigation costs would be different under the two set-off rules. If one rule had higher litigation costs this factor would push in the direction of settlements, because it would create an additional incentive for the parties to settle rather than litigate, but this factor could be outweighed by other factors.
141. See text accompanying notes 53-55 *supra*. But see text accompanying note 56 *supra* (discussing constrained version of apportioned share set-off rule).
142. See Part II.E.4 *supra*.
143. See Part II.C *supra*.
144. See text accompanying notes 138-39 *supra*.
145. When litigation costs are positive, this lower recovery from settlement under the apportioned share set-off rule will reduce the number of lawsuits, with a consequent savings in litigation costs. One cannot determine whether such a result is desirable without studying its impact on deterrence. See text accompanying notes 21-22 *supra*.
146. See text accompanying notes 112-13 *supra*.
147. See text accompanying notes 96-101 *supra*.
148. A full analysis of this question is beyond the scope of this Article.
149. See text accompanying notes 96-101 *supra*.
150. See text accompanying notes 102-03 *supra*.
151. See text accompanying note 107 *supra*.

152. In the context of their more limited inquiry, Easterbrook, Landes & Posner, *supra* note 24, find, like we do, that a rule of no contribution has the same settlement-inducing properties as a rule of contribution, as long as the latter is coupled with contribution protection for settling defendants. See *id.* at 363. In the conclusion to their article, however, they state, referring to the choice "between contribution and no contribution," that "[a] rule of no contribution creates competition among defendants to settle rather than litigate." See *id.* at 365. While it is obvious from the context, see *id.* at 360-63, that the comparison they are making is between a rule of no contribution and a rule of contribution *without* contribution protection, their claim can be easily misunderstood. For example, one of the briefs in *Musick, Peeler & Garrett v. Employers Ins.,* 113 S. Ct. 2085 (1993), relied on the Easterbrook, Landes & Posner article for the general proposition that "[a] judicially created cause of action for contribution is contrary to public policy because it discourages settlement of litigation." See Brief of Amicus Curiae National Association of Securities and Commercial Law Attorneys in Support of Petitioners at 18, *Musick, Peeler & Garrett* (No. 92-34).
153. The general impacts on settlement of optimism and pessimism are discussed in Part II.E.3 *supra*.
154. See Part II.B *supra*.
155. Recall that if it litigates, the plaintiff's expected recovery from each defendant is $25, but if it settles, it can obtain $25 from one and $37.50 from the other. See Part II.C *supra*.
156. See text accompanying notes 107-12 *supra*.
157. See text accompanying notes 52-53 *supra*.
158. See, e.g., *Roland v. Bernstein,* 828 P.2d 1237, 1239 (Ariz. Ct. App. 1991); *Glenn v. Fleming,* 732 P.2d 750, 755-56 (Kan. 1987); *Stratton v. Parker,* 793 S.W.2d 817, 820 (Ky. 1990); *Wilson v. Galt,* 668 P.2d 1104, 1107-10 (N.M. Ct. App.), cert. quashed, 668 P.2d 308 (N.M. 1983).
159. See text accompanying notes 53-55 *supra*.
160. See text accompanying note 107 *supra*.
161. See text accompanying note 159 *supra*.
162. As indicated above, to allow settling defendants to bring contribution actions against each other requires not only eliminating the rule of contribution protection for settling defendants but also granting settling defendants the right of contribution. See text accompanying notes 60-61 *supra*.
163. See Part II.B *supra*.
164. See text accompanying notes 103-04 *supra*.
165. For an economic analysis of these rules, see Note, *Exposing the Extortion Gap: An Economic Analysis of the Rules of Collateral Estoppel,* 105 Harv. L. Rev. 1940, 1944-60 (1992).
166. See Restatement (Second) of Judgments §27 (1982).
167. See *id.* §29.
168. See text accompanying notes 96-101 *supra*.
169. The full comparison of the impact of joinder and non-joinder rules is beyond the scope of this Article.
170. See Restatement (Second) of Judgments §29.
171. Non-mutual collateral estoppel applies to this situation. See *Parklane Hosiery Co. v. Shore,* 439 U.S. 322, 326-33 (1979); *Blonder-Tongue Labs. v. University of*

Ill. Found., 402 U.S. 313, 328-50 (1971); Restatement (Second) of Judgments §29.

172. See text accompanying notes 109-13 *supra*.
173. Unless Row settled for more than $50, it could not maintain a contribution even if the legal regime allowed settling defendants to bring such actions, because it would not have paid more than its apportioned share of the liability.
174. See text accompanying notes 144-45 *supra*.
175. See note 140 *supra*.
176. The latter result holds only if the plaintiff's bargaining power is sufficiently great. See text accompanying notes 140-42 *supra*.
177. For partial lists of the various reasons given by the courts, see *United States v. Western Processing Co.,* 756 F. Supp. 1424, 1430-31 (W.D. Wash. 1990); Thomas V. Harris, *Washington's Unique Approach to Partial Tort Settlements: The Modified Pro Tanto Credit and the Reasonableness Hearing Requirements*, 20 Gonz. L. Rev. 69, 88-90 (1984/85).
178. Some courts merely refer to the better settlement-inducing properties of the pro tanto set-off rule without explaining their reasoning. See, e.g., *Sears v. Atchison, Topeka & Santa Fe Ry.,* 749 F.2d 1451, 1454-55 (10th Cir. 1984); *American Motorcycle Ass'n v. Superior Court,* 578 P.2d 899, 915-16 (Cal. 1978).
179. See, e.g., *United States v. Western Processing Co.,* 756 F. Supp. 1424, 1430 (W.D. Wash. 1990); *MFS Mun. Income Trust v. American Medical Int'l, Inc.,* 751 F. Supp. 279, 284 (D. Mass. 1990); *Alvarado Partners, L.P. v. Mehta,* 723 F. Supp. 540, 552-53 (D. Colo. 1989).
180. See text accompanying notes 52-53 *supra*.
181. If the plaintiff wins, but the losing defendant is insolvent, or the costs of collecting from this defendant are high, the plaintiff's recovery will also be compromised.
182. See text accompanying notes 53-55 *supra*.
183. Cf. Geoffrey P. Miller, *An Economic Analysis of Rule 68*, 15 J. Legal Stud. 93, 111-12 (1986) (making similar argument with respect to effects of Fed. R. Civ. P. 68).
184. See note 185 *infra*.
185. For example, under the pro tanto set-off rule, for perfectly correlated probabilities, when litigation costs are zero the defendants settle for $37.50 and $25, respectively. See text accompanying notes 107-12 supra. The apportioned share of each defendant's liability is $50. The reason that the settlement is lower than the apportioned share of the liability is that the settlement reflects the probability that the defendants would win the litigation. When litigation costs are high, however, the defendants might be willing to settle for more than their apportioned share in order to avoid having to expend these costs.
186. The fact that, for a particular set of offers, Column might choose to settle in light of Row's settlements does not guarantee that those offers would in fact lead to settlement with both defendants. It may be that, given that Column settles, Row would prefer to litigate.
187. See, e.g., *TBG Inc. v. Bendis,* 811 F. Supp. 596, 603 (D. Kan. 1992); *Dalton v. Alston & Bird,* 741 F. Supp. 157, 160 (S.D. Ill. 1990); *In re Sunrise Sec.*

Litig., 698 F. Supp. 1256, 1259 (E.D. Pa. 1988). For commentary supporting this position, see Boomgaarden & Breer, *supra* note 8, at 110.

188. See, e.g., *Gomes v. Brodhurst,* 394 F.2d 465, 468-69 (3d Cir. 1968); *TBG*, 811 F. Supp. at 604; *United States v. Western Processing Co.*, 756 F. Supp. 1424, 1431 (W.D. Wash. 1990). One court has the opposite intuition on both scores: that the pro tanto set-off rule gives rise to more uncertainty and that increased uncertainty promotes settlements. See *Dalton*, 741 F. Supp. at 160.
189. See *TBG*, 811 F. Supp. at 604; *Western Processing*, 756 F. Supp. at 1431.
190. See Part II.E.3 *supra*.
191. *Western Processing*, 756 F. Supp. at 1430.
192. *Id*. at 1431.
193. See text accompanying notes 182-87 *supra*.
194. See Part IV.A.3 *supra*.
195. See, e.g., *Donovan v. Robbins,* 752 F.2d 1170, 1181 (7th Cir. 1984) (Posner, J.); *Resolution Trust Corp. v. Gallagher,* 815 F. Supp. 1107, 1111 (N.D. Ill. 1993); *Western Processing*, 756 F. Supp. at 1431.
196. See *Donovan*, 752 F.2d at 1181 ("The fairness hearing makes the settlement process more costly; and as the costs of settlement rise closer to those of trial, the likelihood of settlement falls–maybe far enough to offset the incentive that a defendant has who knows that settling will enable him to avoid all liability to the other tortfeasors.").
197. See *In re Atlantic Fin. Management, Inc. Sec. Litig.*, 718 F. Supp. 1012, 1018 (D. Mass. 1988).
198. One court has gone so far as to argue that "the only settlements that the pro tanto set-off rule promotes, beyond those promoted by [an apportioned share set-off rule], are bad ones." *MFS Mun. Income Trust v. American Medical Int'l, Inc.*, 751 F. Supp. 279, 284 (D. Mass. 1990) (citing *In re Sunrise Sec. Litig.*, 698 F. Supp. 1256, 1259 n.5 (E.D. Pa. 1988)).
199. *Franklin v. Kaypro Corp.*, 884 F.2d 1222, 1230 (9th Cir. 1989), cert. denied, 498 U.S. 890 (1990); see also *In re Masters Mates & Pilots Pension Plan & IRAP Litig.*, 957 F.2d 1020, 1029 (2d Cir. 1992); *Dobson v. Camden,* 705 F.2d 759, 768 (5th Cir. 1983), rev'd on other grounds, 725 F.2d 1003 (5th Cir. 1984).
200. See text accompanying notes 179-82 *supra*.
201. See *Donovan v. Robbins,* 752 F.2d 1170, 1181 (7th Cir. 1984) (Posner, J.); see also *Sunrise Sec. Litig.*, 698 F. Supp. at 1259 (citing *Donovan*, 752 F.2d at 1181).
202. The relative effects of the set-off rules in allocating expected losses between the defendants is a complex question. We discuss some of the technical issues in Lewis A. Kornhauser & Richard L. Revesz, *Multi-Defendant Settlements: The Choice Among Set-Off Rules* (unpublished manuscript, Oct. 1992) (on file with the New York University Law Review).
203. *Kaypro*, 884 F.2d at 1230; see also *United States Fidelity & Guar. Co. v. Patriot's Point Dev. Auth.*, 772 F. Supp. 1565, 1575 (D.S.C. 1991) (stating pro tanto set-off rule "allows plaintiffs to target deep-pocket defendants, and fund . . . litigation through 'war chests' created by settlements with more culpable parties purportedly unable to pay their fair share of damages"); cf. *Dobson*, 705 F.2d at 768 ("Certainly, nothing prevents a collusive, low settlement with a less solvent tortfeasor, who might even be largely responsible for the harm,

in exchange for that tortfeasor's assistance in prosecuting a claim against the less responsible, more solvent joint tortfeasors."). For further discussion, see text accompanying notes 125-26 *supra*. The *Kaypro* court also adds that the apportioned share set-off rule promotes settlements. See *Kaypro*, 884 F.2d at 1231. The only justification it gives for this pronouncement is that "[d]efendants that are inclined to settle may do so without penalty or risk." *Id*. The court seems to be comparing the apportioned share set-off rule to the pro tanto set-off rule without contribution protection for settling defendants. With contribution protection, settling defendants under the pro tanto set-off rule are protected against further liability in the same manner as settling defendants under the apportioned share set-off rule.

204. See *Kaypro*, 884 F.2d at 1230.
205. See *id*.
206. As one court perceptively noted, "both the plaintiff and the settlor save litigation expenses by settling. Consequently, the litigation savings provide a range on either side of that figure in which the parties may compromise." *MFS Mun. Income Trust v. American Medical Int'l, Inc.*, 751 F. Supp. 279, 284 (D. Mass. 1990).
207. See Part I.A.6 *supra*.
208. See Part III.D *supra*.
209. See Part III.A *supra*.
210. See text accompanying note 154 *supra*.
211. See text accompanying notes 137-40 *supra*.
212. See text accompanying notes 23-24 *supra*. Therefore, it is not surprising that Easterbrook, Landes & Posner, *supra* note 24, and Polinsky & Shavell, *supra* note 24, who were primarily interested in antitrust conspiracies, assumed implicitly that the plaintiff's probabilities of success would be perfectly correlated. See note 107 *supra*.

Settlement Incentives and Joint Tortfeasors: A Comment on Kornhauser and Revesz

Patrick E. Higginbotham*

Professors Kornhauser and Revesz shed light upon liability rules and their effect upon settlements. Their explanation of pro tanto versus apportioned share set-off rules is persuasive and I find myself commenting upon work with which I am in substantial agreement. I am not so convinced, however, that the incentives operate as Kornhauser and Revesz suggest. Ultimately our differences mirror the occasional collision of theoretically and highly analytical methods with the hardened instincts of the street. There is a large caveat. Experience is not always a powerful teacher. It is easily confused with ignorance masking force of habit.

I

Under the pro tanto rule, a plaintiff who reaches a small settlement with one defendant may pick up the balance from another. Under this rule, a plaintiff has a relatively greater incentive to settle with a defendant for less than that defendant's share of liability. But even under a pro tanto rule, a plaintiff still has some incentive not to settle cheaply with one defendant, because he must account for the risk of not recovering the remainder from the other defendant.

We could also say that the apportioned share rule gives a plaintiff greater incentives to settle when a defendant is willing to settle for more than his share of liability. That is because the apportioned share

*Circuit Judge, United States Court of Appeals for the Fifth Circuit.

rule gives a plaintiff a shot at a double recovery, once from a generous settlement and a second time at trial.

Kornhauser and Revesz reason that when litigation costs are low, defendants will settle for less than their share of liability. Otherwise, they would have no incentive to settle. The contention continues that when litigation costs are high, defendants are likely to settle for more than their share of liability to avoid litigation costs. Thus, they conclude, the pro tanto rule is better at inducing settlements than the apportioned share rule when litigation costs are low, because it makes small settlements more attractive. By the same reasoning, the pro tanto rule is weaker with high costs because it makes large settlements less attractive.

I am not so sure. When litigation costs are high, they tend to be high for both parties. If anything, they may be higher for a plaintiff than for one of two codefendants, as codefendants may be able to share costs. Thus, a plaintiff stands to gain from settlement at least as much as a defendant. The litigation costs on both sides create potential gains from cooperation that both parties can split, and the parties are likely to share these gains. There is no a priori way to determine how the parties will allocate these gains. Particularly if parties are risk averse, high litigation costs encourage settlement because settlement limits a defendant's maximum exposure and guarantees a plaintiff a minimum recovery. Plaintiffs want a floor and defendants want a ceiling.

II

Kornhauser and Revesz rightly note that a plaintiff has some incentive not to settle cheaply, because he cannot be certain of recovering the remainder from the other defendant. But in relative terms, this incentive is smaller under the pro tanto rule than under the apportioned share rule, because the pro tanto rule gives a plaintiff a chance to recoup the damages bargained away in the process of reaching a small settlement.

Obviously multiple forces in complex cases chew away at any reluctance to settle cheaply; if I am correct that this reluctance is relatively less under the pro tanto rule, it produces more settlements. The first impetus is risk aversion. A plaintiff wants to be guaranteed at least enough money to pay his medical bills and legal fees, and he would much prefer to have that money now rather than later. Because a plaintiff often needs immediate cash to pay accident-related bills, it stands to reason that he may be more risk averse than a defendant and more willing to settle, even at the price of a bad bargain.

Kornhauser and Revesz assume that both parties are likely to be equally risk averse; they also assume that risk aversion is constant over a range of expected results. But this is unrealistic. A plaintiff with $25,000 in medical bills, $25,000 in lost wages, $50,000 in pain-and-suffering damages, and claiming $100,000 in punitive damages is most desperate to get the first $25,000, needed to cover medical bills, and the next $25,000, needed to provide for his family and pay legal fees. He is more willing to gamble with the $50,000 damages for pain and suffering, because he has no pressing need for them and can afford to drive a hard bargain or go to trial. He is least risk averse with respect to the final $100,000 in damages, because the previous three items of recovery provide him with a cushion. If risk aversion declines in this way, plaintiffs have powerful incentives to first create a cushion by settling against one defendant, then roll the dice against the other one. The pro tanto set-off rule makes this strategy more attractive because it does not penalize low settlements as much as the apportioned share rule would.

Moreover, the cushion provided by an early settlement can fuel later litigation. One case quoted by Kornhauser and Revesz notes: "By accepting a low partial settlement, plaintiffs would be able to fund further litigation with no diminution of the total amount eventually received."[1] Kornhauser and Revesz are correct to note that a low settlement might diminish "the total amount eventually received," because a plaintiff might lose at trial. But this misses the quoted language dealing with a plaintiff's incentive to settle in order to fund litigation against the remaining defendant. As Justice Stevens put it in *AmClyd*: "[T]he settlement figure is likely to be significantly less than the settling defendant's equitable share of the loss, because settlement reflects the uncertainty of trial and provides the plaintiff with a 'war chest' with which to finance the litigation against the remaining defendants."[2]

There is an element of perversity afoot: while the pro tanto rule encourages settlement against one defendant, it makes it more likely that the case will go to trial against the remaining defendant. That is hardly a cheering prospect—a trial against one defendant costs almost as much and takes almost as much time as a trial against both of them. Instead of celebrating a lone settlement, we should pick rules that encourage all parties to settle before trial—rules that settle cases not claims.

III

Our preoccupation with settlement sees trial as a failure of the system. Much of the current popularity with alternative dispute resolution shares the same dismal view of trial. Yet trials, and a steady stream of them, are essential. The assessment of risk and assumption of consequence flowing from risk assume sufficient expertise of the actors to access it; more fundamentally risk management assumes a level of predictability of result. Take away the steady flow of trials and you erode the impact of the rules we adopt. These are *trial* courts. That is their business, and it is the trial that sustains the settlement. If nine of ten cases are settled, it is because the tenth was tried.

There are also countervailing considerations of fairness that should give us pause. By making one defendant's liability dependent on the other's settlement, the pro tanto rule can make equally culpable defendants unequally liable; a good settlement for the first defendant translates into a raw deal for the remaining one.[3] The unfairness is even more pronounced when defendants are not equally at fault. The pro tanto rule leads a plaintiff to settle with the defendant who is more at fault—even at the price of a small settlement—and to litigate against the one less at fault. In other words, the pro tanto rule can reduce the liability of the tortfeasor who most deserves it.

This discussion underscores a broader point about law and economics reasoning: it is a tool, and no more. It does not tell us how to account for moral blame or distributive justice. It tells us about the likelihood of settlement, but we must supply the missing premise about whether settlement is good or bad. But within these limits, law and economics deserves the influence that it has earned. We must use all the analytical tools at hand—while listening to the steady drum of experience, history, and tradition. Justice Cardozo put it well: "Often a liberal antidote of experience supplies a sovereign cure for a paralyzing abstraction built upon theory."[4] The Supreme Court acknowledged as much in *McDermott v. AmClyde*, which relied heavily on Kornhauser and Revesz in choosing between pro tanto and apportioned share set-off rules in maritime law.[5] Citation, not imitation, is the sincerest form of flattery. Theirs is an impressive work, undeniably influential.

Notes

1. *Franklin v. Kaypro Corp.*, 884 F.2d 1222, 1230 (9th Cir. 1989), cert. denied, 498 U.S. 890 (1990).
2. *McDermott, Inc. v. AmClyde,* 114 S. Ct. 1461, 1467 (1994).
3. See *id.* at 1468 (noting that pro tanto rule puts pressure on defendents to settle because of disadvantage that rule inflicts on holdouts).
4. Benjamin N. Cardozo; Paradoxes of Legal Science 125 (1928).
5. See 114 S. Ct. at 1467-69 & nn. 13, 14, 20, 24.

Rule 68, Fee Shifting, and the Rulemaking Process

Edward H. Cooper*

I. Introduction

This is the story of a first exposure to the offer-of-judgment procedure of Federal Rule of Civil Procedure 68. The context is the workaday setting of the rulemaking process. Rule 68 has been viewed by many, including me, as an uninteresting provision that remains on the fringe of procedure because it has been little used to scant effect. Past efforts to make it more effective were abandoned. Now a carefully worked-out proposal for revision has brought the subject back for renewed attention.[1] The proposal is in the early stages of consideration by the Civil Rules Advisory Committee. My own thinking is at an equally early stage. As I go about learning something of Rule 68, the prospect of revision seems to present remarkably complex questions. More than anything else, this review of the puzzlements is a catalogue of questions that must be considered. If in the warm light of collective examination they stand revealed as ghosts easily put to rest, so much the better.

A. The Simple Purpose of Rule 68

Figures vary from one survey to another, but fewer than ten percent of the civil actions filed in federal court survive to trial. A large portion of

*Thomas M. Cooley Professor of Law, University of Michigan School of Law; Reporter, Civil Rules Advisory Committee.

those that disappear are settled. Notwithstanding the high disappearance rate, Civil Rule 68 has once again attracted interest as a potential means of improving the settlement process. Two forms of improvement are contemplated. One is to increase the total number of cases that settle. Another is to accelerate the time of settlement for cases that now settle later than need be.

The benefits from increasing the number of cases that settle could be dramatic. A seemingly small increase in the total fraction of cases that disappear before trial could yield a large decrease in the number of cases that are tried. If 92% of all cases are now resolved without trial, an increase to 94% would effect a 25% reduction—from 8% to 6%—in the number of trials. The benefits from accelerating the time of settlement might not be as easily observed, but could be even more important. If earlier settlements reduced the total volume of pretrial activity, particularly through disclosure and discovery, the savings would be obvious and valuable. Even if earlier settlements resulted from accelerating a constant level of pretrial activity, there would be real benefits from achieving earlier repose.

The case for amending Rule 68 rests on the belief that traditional unregulated settlement processes are not as effective as should be. A formal offer-of-judgment or offer-of-settlement process, on this view, enhances the overall process. The proposals that have been considered in the rulemaking process have assumed that such a formal process should supplement the traditional process, not supplant it. The formal process is made available to facilitate settlement when an offering party believes that added incentives are useful. Negotiations outside the Rule 68 framework can continue unimpeded, and perhaps enhanced, by one or more Rule 68 offers.

These simple hopes may be attainable. They do not rest on detailed knowledge of present settlement processes. Not enough is known about the factors that cause cases to settle or not. They do not rest on uncontested theory; at least for the moment, too much is known about the complications of theory, and no means is available to cut through the competing complications. The following discussion will focus on a specific model based on a proposal of Judge William Schwarzer to amend Rule 68.[2] The proposal is a thoughtful one that addresses many of the concerns that surrounded earlier efforts to amend Rule 68. After sketching the proposal and one version of the highest hopes that might be advanced for its success, I will concentrate on the doubts that beset this and any other proposal to strengthen Rule 68. This focus reflects caution, not a judgment that the doubts are right.

B. The Current Proposal

A first draft of an amended Rule 68 is set out as an appendix. This proposal raises the stakes of Rule 68 offers by a limited shift of an adversary's attorney fees to a party who fails to improve on a Rule 68 offer at trial. It also authorizes offers by all parties, whether advancing or resisting claims, and allows successive offers by a single party that do not cancel the potential consequences of earlier offers.

Shifting attorney fees is a constant feature of Rule 68 proposals. At least two distinct reasons account for this interest. One is the view that settlement, and ideally early settlement, is an important means of reducing litigation expenditures. Attorney fees are a substantial part of litigation expenditures. A party who has offered a settlement that accurately forecasts the result of trial should not have to bear the expense of proving the accuracy of the forecast. Instead, the party who has failed to accept the trial-vindicated offer should compensate for the harm caused by its rejection. This reason in effect posits a duty to engage in reasonable settlement behavior. The other reason is the pragmatic judgment that substantial consequences are required to make Rule 68 work. Attorney fee shifting is a familiar and natural enforcing device.

Shifting attorney fees is also a lightning rod for controversy. The "American Rule" that each party bears its own attorney fees–win, lose, or draw–continues to have strong emotional support notwithstanding legions of statutes and occasional common law rules that provide for fee shifting. Any proposal that may require a plaintiff to bear defense attorney fees stirs immediate and hostile reaction.

The proposal limits the introduction of fee shifting by two major features that seek an accommodation to achieve the advantages of fee shifting while assuaging the potential disadvantages. First, reasonable fees incurred after the offer expires are reduced by the benefit that results from the difference between offer and judgment. If a defendant's $50,000 offer is followed by reasonable attorney fees of $15,000 and a $40,000 judgment, for example, the first $10,000 of post-offer fees is discarded. The fee award is $5,000. This puts the offering party in the same position as if the offer had been accepted. (There may be some connection between the fee expenditure and the difference between the offer and the judgment, but this possibility does not provide any significant additional support for subtracting the benefit of the judgment. The efforts of defendant's counsel may have been so inept as to have increased the amount of the judgment; more effective counsel might have won a defense verdict, a verdict for less than $40,000, or a $40,000 verdict after a $5,000 fee expenditure. No one proposes that these possibilities should be investigated in setting the amount of a fee award.)

Next, the fee award is capped. An award to the defendant cannot exceed the amount of the judgment: if the defendant had incurred reasonable post-offer fees of $60,000, the award would be not $50,000 but $40,000. This feature protects the plaintiff against out-of-pocket losses greater than the costs that also are shifted under Rule 68. A symmetrical provision equalizes the fee-shifting stakes by limiting a fee award against a defendant to the amount of the judgment.

The questions that must be addressed in considering this proposal do not flow along any obvious linear path. They include the simple predictive question whether it would increase the number of cases that settle or at least advance the time of settlement in cases that eventually would settle in any event, and the more contentious question whether an increase or acceleration of settlement is necessarily desirable. At quite a different level, they invoke unanswerable questions of responsibility for attorney fees, questions that go deeper than the familiar debate over the virtues of the "American" and "British" rules. Another set of problems arises from the constraints and habits of the rulemaking process: a single rule is proposed for all federal civil actions, without regard to the nature of the dispute or the character of the uncertainties that may make settlement difficult; concerns for administration invite compromises that may seem of doubtful intrinsic merit; and fair questions may be raised whether feeshifting in this setting is authorized by the Rules Enabling Act. Still different problems arise from the details of implementation: as pedestrian as these problems may seem in the realm of lofty discourse, they reflect constraints that must be considered in attempting to move from theory to practice. The many interdependencies among these problems foreclose neat exposition, but at least some rough order is possible in the thoughts that follow.

II. Promoting [Early] Settlement

A. The Optimistic View

There are many ways to describe the hope that offer-of-judgment procedure can be made more effective by adding limited fee-shifting consequences and allowing any party to make an offer. The common element is a belief that there are cases that should but do not settle, or that settle later than should be. Beyond that point, the reasons for deferred or failed settlements must be set out.

Strategic calculation may be a major obstacle that prevents mutually beneficial settlements. Although all parties understand that settlement is more rational than litigation, settlement fails because each party holds out for a larger share of the potential settlement benefits. An effective offer-of-judgment rule may disarm self-defeating strategies, and might even foster strategies that facilitate settlement. Enhanced Rule 68 consequences may help by changing an opening offer from an implicit confession of weakness to an aggressive adversarial act. (Of course this may also reduce the usefulness of a settlement offer as a signal of a party's real evaluation of a case.) Incentives may be reduced for advancing ill-founded claims or defenses that exploit an imbalance between the costs and prospective benefits of litigation.[3] Bargaining over division of the potential gains from settlement may be placed on a more even footing that facilitates agreement.

Another obstacle may be simple failure to think rationally about settlement as early as should be, or perhaps ever. The failure may occur because the parties have not gathered sufficient information to think rationally about probable outcomes. A rule that encourages early settlement offers may encourage early gathering of information to support or respond to meaningful offers. A failure to settle that occurs for reasons other than lack of information may be cured directly whenever enhanced incentives induce offers that are considered and responded to.

This optimistic description of the process must include an element that runs parallel to the emphasis on settlement. Allowing plaintiffs to shift fee responsibility by making offers close to the expected result at trial should encourage plaintiffs to file strong small claims. When the defendant shares the plaintiff's estimate, settlement should follow. When the defendant has a significantly lower estimate of the plaintiff's success, however, the result may be a trial.

In addition to improving the settlement process, Rule 68 fee shifting may seem intrinsically desirable. A party who offers to settle for a figure at least equal to the eventual judgment may seem to deserve compensation for wasteful fee expenditures caused by failure to accept. The judgment proves that failure to accept was unreasonable, at least to the extent that justice requires protecting the offering party. Fee shifting both deters improvident refusals to settle and compensates the provident offer.

B. The Doubting View

1. Predicted Behavior

One range of questions arises from doubts as to the number of cases in which the present incentives to settle will be enhanced by a limited fee-shifting scheme. There is a large and growing body of literature devoted to economic exploration of the general effects of fee-shifting rules and the more particular effects of fee-shifting inducements in offer-of-judgment rules. Even without accounting for strategic behavior, it is possible to identify many plausible situations in which settlement behavior is not likely to be affected by Rule 68 and some situations in which a fee-shifting rule may make settlement more difficult.[4] When game theory is invoked, matters become ever so much more complicated.[5]

Moving from abstract theory to more pedestrian terrain, similar concerns may be voiced. Whatever purposes the rulemakers may have, adversary lawyers will seek to use Rule 68 to maximum adversary advantage. Offers will be made not only in hopes that acceptance will end the litigation, but also in hopes that rejection will pave the way for strategic advantage. The opportunity to make multiple offers may be seized by opening offers close to the extremes of plausible outcomes, generating risks and corresponding adjustments in later offers that are further complicated if fee shifting is limited in the ways currently proposed. Sheer complexity and confusion may deter settlement.[6]

Much effort has been devoted to the process of settling complex litigation involving large stakes. The amendments proposed for Federal Rule of Civil Procedure 16 regularly include provisions aimed at enhancing the prospects of early settlement in such cases, and it is unlikely that limited fee shifting under Rule 68 will contribute much to these efforts. The stakes, both direct and often indirect, are likely to dwarf the prospective benefits of fee shifting, and the resources of the parties often will further diminish any potential incentive effect. For many such cases, it seems likely that settlement will occur when the parties believe they know enough to assess probable results, or it will not occur at all. If so, a major potential benefit from Rule 68 will disappear. Greater hope may be held out for encouraging early settlement of litigation for smaller stakes, involving one or more parties of modest means. Such cases, however, raise the question whether even a limited fee-shifting incentive involves encouragement or coercion.

The concern with coercion arises from the potential effect of fee shifting on risk-averse litigants. Most concern is directed toward individual plaintiffs who have something to lose and who face well-endowed institutional litigants. Even under the limited fee shifting currently proposed, a plaintiff can lose all the value of an important and valid claim. Particularly in cases in which there is a realistic prospect that the defendant may win at trial or in which there is a wide range of reasonably predicted awards, the pressure to accept a relatively modest Rule 68 offer may be far greater than the pressure to accept an identical offer made outside Rule 68. The fear is not that an enhanced Rule 68 will fail to increase the number of settlements, but that it will increase the number of settlements in undesirable ways.

2. Desirability of settlement

The premise that it is useful to encourage earlier settlement of cases that settle now has not drawn much dissent beyond fear for the impact on risk-averse plaintiffs. If early settlement means curtailment rather than acceleration of discovery, however, it may be based on relatively greater ignorance–either mutual or one-sided–and involvc distortions that must be weighed against the savings of discovery costs. Even if earlier settlement were based on the same full knowledge as later settlement, the terms of settlement are not likely to be the same. The time horizons are different, strategic behavior may be different, and the anticipated costs and benefits of settlement are likely to be different.

The premise that it is useful to encourage settlement of cases that now do not settle is more controversial. There are many reasons why a reasonable settlement may not satisfy the needs of one or more parties. Familiar illustrations involve stakes beyond the prospective money judgment. Putting aside specific relief as a matter of obvious difficulty, an action for money alone may involve reputation, a desire to vindicate principles of public importance, or a test case. Both the plaintiff and the defendant in a newspaper defamation action, for example, may fight for interests more precious than any predictable judgment. Attaching sanctions to Rule 68 offers in this setting may occasionally deter any litigation at all. It may occasionally facilitate a settlement that otherwise would not occur. It may occasionally–perhaps often–simply shift attorney fees based on comparative strategic skill or luck in picking the offer figure.

Equally familiar but less discussed concerns may be involved in an action in which money is the only stake. A simple version is provided by a case in which damages are uncontested at $1,000,000. The plaintiff believes there is a 50% probability of winning $1,000,000, with predicted future fee expenditures of $200,000. The plaintiff's expected value is thus $300,000. The defendant may believe the plaintiff has a 30% probability of winning $1,000,000, with predicted future defense fees of $250,000. The defendant's expected cost is thus $550,000. A settlement anywhere in a range from $300,000 to $550,000 would be "better" for both parties. The plaintiff, however, may need $800,000 to restore the business that was destroyed by the defendant; anything less is futile. The defendant may barely be able to manage the costs of defense before diverting assets from equally important needs. A rule that increases the pressure to settle often will have no effect in such circumstances, apart from adding the possibility of fee shifting to the $0 or $1,000,000 judgment after the defendant's $250,000 offer and the plaintiff's $800,000 offer both fail.

This last example raises the broader question whether litigation can properly be viewed as a matter of probabalistic money equivalencies alone. Quite apart from the suggested special needs that may establish sharp discontinuities in the marginal value of money to a particular party, there may be legitimate desires for vindication or even vindictiveness. There is no demonstrably right answer to the plaintiff who protests that the defendant should not be allowed to buy off a million dollar liability for half that price merely because we are dissatisfied with a system that will not compensate the costs of defense should the plaintiff in fact lose.

Perhaps we have not yet reached the pass in which our system is forced to operate as nothing for principle, all for money.[7]

3. Risk-Averse Plaintiffs

By far the most vehement criticism of efforts to give more bite to Rule 68 has come from those who fear coercion of risk-averse plaintiffs. This criticism will not be much muted by the limited form of fee shifting currently proposed. The common illustration is the plaintiff of modest means pursuing a single claim that is personally important and confronting a relatively wealthy defendant who repeatedly engages in litigation. The illustration describes many cases. Even with a cap set at the amount of the judgment, such a plaintiff can win a valid claim and lose all that has been gained because of a wrong guess in response to a Rule 68 offer. The resulting pressure to accept an offer increases in the many cases in which damages are subject to fair dispute over a relatively wide range, and in which there is a prospect that a court may mimic the settlement process by compromising the determination of liability with the computation of damages. The response that such plaintiffs should not be more free than any others to impose unnecessary fee expenditures on such defendants is not fully satisfying.

The problem of the risk-averse plaintiff may be matched by a potential conflict of interest generated by the offer. The conflict arises because the prospect that the plaintiff will have the means to pay attorney fees, whether on a contingent-fee agreement or otherwise, is affected by Rule 68. The spirit of the cap implies that counsel cannot contract to recover a share of the judgment before accounting for Rule 68 consequences. The theory that contingent-fee counsel should have a portfolio of cases, and should be able to rely on realistic assessments of settlement offers across them all, may not respond to all facets of reality.

4. Fee Statutes and Conflict of Interest

The potential for conflicting interests just described is acute if Rule 68 offers can cut off the right to recover statutory fee entitlements, as happens now.[8] Some plaintiffs may be represented by counsel who have a wide portfolio of statutory fee cases and who are unmoved by the prospect that denial of fees in any particular case under Rule 68 will defeat any compensation for pursuing that case. It is difficult to believe that all will fall into that category.

III. Fee-Shifting Rationale

Rule 68 fee-shifting proposals are most reasonably considered against the background of the "American Rule" that ordinarily each party bears its own attorney fees. The proponents do not seem moved by a secret desire to use Rule 68 as a step toward general adoption of a rule imposing the winner's reasonable fees on the loser. Perhaps more important, the rulemaking process is not an appropriate means of adopting a general fee-shifting system. Whether fee-shifting is regarded as "procedural" or "substantive" for purposes of the Rules Enabling Act,[9] the topic is far too sensitive and bound up with political concerns to be addressed in this process.

Scant comfort is afforded by the conclusion that Rule 68 must be considered in the framework of the American Rule unchanged. Any effort to impose liability on one party for an adversary's attorney fees, whoever has prevailed on the merits, must be supported by a theory that justifies the imposition in defiance of the American Rule. That task, in turn, requires a coherent theory that justifies the American Rule in comparison to at least two alternatives. The obvious alternative is a rule that makes the prevailing party whole, so that nominally complete relief for a plaintiff or vindication for a defendant is not diluted by liability for the expense of suit. At best it is very difficult to explain adherence to the American Rule in the face of these concerns. The alternative less often considered is a system that provides public representation for any party who wishes, leaving private representation as an affair properly financed by any party who prefers it. If we fear that the risk of bearing all attorney fees will deter just claims and force the surrender of just defenses, that fear can be addressed by offering free lawyers just as we offer free judges. The question is not whether we should force public representation on all parties, a system most of us would readily reject; it is only whether access to public justice should be rationed by ability to pay or to find contingent-fee representation. An answer is not even started by speaking of the inherent character of an adversary system in which each adversary sportingly bears the costs of the contest, nor by protesting that we need some means of rationing access to justice lest we be swamped by grossly inefficient levels of litigation that impose social costs far out of proportion to the tangible private stakes.

The lack of any coherent theory to explain the general refusal to shift attorney fees might seem to justify reliance on purely pragmatic concerns in approaching Rule 68. If we have no theory against which to test changes, why bother with theory at all? All that need concern us is actual effects, as well as we can predict them. Unfortunately, the matter is not so simple.

The first complication arises from the multiple statutes and occasional judicial doctrines that provide for attorney fee shifting, most frequently in favor of plaintiffs. As Rule 68 is now interpreted, a plaintiff's statutory fee right is cut off as to fees incurred after an offer that is as at least as good as the judgment, so long as the statute characterizes the fees as "costs."[10] There is no reason whatever for distinguishing between fee statutes that happen to have been expressed in terms of costs and other statutes that characterize fees as fees. If nothing else is done to Rule 68, it should be amended to eliminate this unintended linguistic consequence. It is far more important to consider the question whether Rule 68 should cut off statutory fee rights in any case. So long as fee-shifting statutes are exceptions to a general rule, they are most easily understood as attempts to support and encourage litigation of particularly favored types of claims. Such purposes can be overcome by offer-of-judgment policies only if those policies are clearly understood.

The second complication, stemming from the desire to compensate for costs incurred after a provident offer, is far more pervasive. So long as the American rule stands, it represents a determination that the cost of advancing or resisting judicial claims should be borne by each party, not by the adversary and not by the public. Failure to accept a formal offer of judgment seems much less serious conduct in that light. The innocence of such behavior is most apparent when the offer and judgment are close together; indeed both Rule 68 and the proposed amendment impose consequences when offer and judgment are the same. Adhering to the American Rule when a plaintiff has lost utterly or has been vindicated completely stands in stark contrast to a rule that shifts attorney fees if plaintiff or defendant guesses wrong by rejecting an offer that–in the extreme example–happens to match the judgment perfectly. The proposed "benefit of the judgment" adjustment and cap may even seem perverse in this light, since the result shifts a larger portion of the offeror's fees as the offer and judgment converge. Thus a defendant whose $100,000 offer is rejected may, after a $100,000 judgment, recover up to $100,000 of fees reasonably incurred; but after judgment for the defendant will recover nothing. In either case, the plaintiff gets nothing. We accept the null award as right when it is a judgment on the merits. To accept it as a departure from the American Rule when the plaintiff was $100,000 right on the merits but wrong in predicting the actual judgment is more difficult.

The difficulty may be underscored by considering two extreme examples in which the defendant spent all $100,000 of post-offer fees either in seeking to contest liability or in seeking to contest damages. If the expenditure was all for liability and the defendant lost on liability, it might fairly be asked why failure to accept the offer should impose on the plaintiff the cost of defense fees that proved a waste. If the expenditure was all for damages and was well-advised, it may well have cost the plaintiff more than a $100,000 reduction of the judgment. Again, it might fairly be asked why the plaintiff should pay twice for this "benefit." The response that the plaintiff should make the defendant whole in relation to the position that would have resulted from accepting the offer assumes that the duty to accept the offer imposes greater obligations, in relation to the general rule against fee shifting, than the decision to file suit.

Consideration of this second complication may be advanced by focusing on the implied duty to settle. By far the most satisfactory explanation for imposing Rule 68 consequences is that litigants have a duty to behave reasonably in settlement. It is unfair to focus criticism on the extreme illustrations in which one party makes a better prediction of the outcome in the face of massive uncertainties as to liability and amount of damages, whether as a matter of better luck or greater sophistication. What is called for is realistic, reasonable, accommodating settlement behavior. Litigation is a gamble. The more uncertain the outcome, the less reasonable it is to insist on pursuing any outcome on the merits. It is reasonable to persist to final judgment if all parties want to gamble, and to make all parties to the gamble carry their own costs. If a party prefers the more rational course of a certain settlement, and offers to settle on terms at least as favorable to the adversary as the final judgment, the offer should shield against the costs of continuing the gamble.

There is much to commend a duty to behave reasonably in settlement. The argument is strongest to those whose faith in litigation is weakest. It may seem overwhelming to those who reject pursuit of litigation as a means of vindicating substantive rights, either because of intrinsic doubts about the rationality of litigation results or because of the costs of litigation. Even if a duty of reasonable settlement is recognized, however, it remains necessary to implement it reasonably.

If Rule 68 is to be explained as implementing a duty of reasonable settlement behavior, the means of implementation are questionable. One dimension of doubt is set out above: great consequences may hinge on very small differences between offer and judgment. There is no reason to draw inferences of unreasonable behavior from the bare fact that an offer was, by whatever margin, more favorable than the judgment. This problem could be reduced by adding a margin-of-difference element; the wider the margin, the weaker the objection. If Rule 68 imposed consequences only if the offer were at least 50% more favorable than the judgment, for example, it would be more plausible to infer that it was unreasonable to reject the offer. In some cases the inference would be strong or even overwhelming.

A margin-of-difference feature would not abate all of the difficulties in using actual outcome to assess the reasonableness of settlement behavior. Reasonableness is affected by the character of uncertainty and confidence in assessing uncertainty. It is easy to illustrate the purely economic reasonableness of settling cases in which all parties agree on the probability of liability and the range of damages and have equal stakes and like risk aversion. It is much more difficult to define reasonable settlement behavior, even in purely economic terms, when the picture is more complicated. Some cases do present genuine uncertainty as to liability, and the parties may reasonably evaluate the uncertainty at different levels. Some cases do present genuine uncertainty as to damages over relatively wide ranges, and, again, the parties may reasonably evaluate the uncertainty at different levels. These complications alone mean that it may be entirely reasonable for two parties to adhere to settlement figures that cannot be brought together. If it is reasonable to consider matters other than the expected dollar results of the instant litigation, the problem is even worse.

The simple illustration offered above described a range of mutually beneficial settlement between $300,000 and $550,000. Somehow the parties must divide the expected benefits of settlement. It seems difficult to say that it is unreasonable for the plaintiff to ask for more than $300,000 and for the defendant to offer less than $550,000. We expect them to divide the difference by bargaining. And the bargaining process may reasonably go astray. The very precise figures used for purposes of illustration, moreover, disguise the fact that the parties may lack confidence in their best efforts to predict the outcome. It seems reasonable to prefer litigation to settlement based on guesses that are known to be unreliable.

The difficulty of predicting outcomes is entrenched by jury trial. Views about the predictability of jury verdicts may vary, but it seems likely that juries do the unexpected often enough to add a wild element to reasonable predictions.

Enough has been said to support a simple assertion: A duty of reasonable settlement behavior cannot support fee shifting based on simple differences between offer and judgment. Reasonable behavior often will lead to rejection of an offer that proves better than the eventual judgment.

If a duty of reasonable settlement behavior cannot support the present Rule 68 proposal, some other theory must be found. Fee shifting is serious business, and deserves a serious theory. The theory cannot be found in analogies to the attorney fee sanctions imposed for violation of various procedural rules. Such procedures as discovery have been adopted for clear procedural purposes, often wisely, and we have a clear theory of procedural duty to comply. Fee sanctions are a natural means of enforcement. This theory would support imposition of sanctions, including fee shifting, for refusal to participate in good faith in court-ordered settlement processes. It does not support sanctions for refusal to reach settlement until we have a theory of duty to reach settlement.

IV. Limits of Rulemaking

The full course of the rulemaking process may show that these doubts mean much or little, but they do deserve at least some consideration as part of that process. They also suggest the value of reflecting on the process itself. Several features of the rule making process may suggest caution in approaching fee shifting by rule. The Civil Rules ordinarily apply to all litigation, or at least to very broad categories of litigation. Abstract theoretical goals must be compromised to meet the needs of workaday administration. And the rules are not to abridge, enlarge, or modify substantive rights.

A. Universalizing Tendencies

The universalizing tendency of the Civil Rules is frequently described by the ugly adjective "transsubstantive." The rules characteristically are written in broad terms and rely on trial court discretion to fit general procedures to the more specific needs of individual litigation. There are many reasons for this approach. Among them are limits on the rulemaking process; it is not possible to understand all the needs of the full range of present litigation, much less future litigation, and craft detailed rules carefully adapted to each particular setting. Attempts to define specific rules for specific categories of litigation, moreover, might eventually raise questions whether the rules were intended to affect specific substantive rights. Perhaps the most important set of reasons involves faith in the ability of district courts to exercise discretion wisely. Although it would be easy for anyone to identify instances of inept procedural decisions, the results often seem better than might be expected from a more detailed code of procedure.

An offer-of-judgment rule must be addressed in this light. It is not enough to suggest situations in which fee shifting may be a desirable means of encouraging settlement. Instead it must be shown that the overall result is desirable, either across the full range of federal court litigation or across narrower categories of cases that can be described in a rule limited to those cases. The earlier discussion suggests the nature of the problem. There are cases in which it seems inappropriate to impose fee-shifting consequences merely because of a difference between offer and judgment. Such cases exist even if settlement is approached solely as a matter of economic rationality defined in expected net present dollars. Wide divergences in expected outcomes not only occur, but occur for good reasons. Nothing can be said with confidence about the frequency of such cases, but that of itself is reason for caution. If account is also taken of other factors that properly affect settlement decisions, the number of cases that legitimately are not settled increases. The increase is greater as additional weight is assigned to such elusive factors as the desire for vindication, protection of public interests, and the like. Any sensible accounting also must reckon with the prospect that revisions of Rule 68 may affect the very character of the cases that are brought into the system–indeed some skeptical opponents of the 1983 and 1984 proposals believed that the primary purpose was to deter risk-averse plaintiffs from filing in federal court.

It may prove possible to draft a rule identifying categories of cases that justify a fee-shifting offer-of-judgment rule. That possibility has yet to be explored.[11] A more common response to such difficulties is to draft a rule that relies on district court discretion to distinguish cases that merit fee shifting from those that do not. That alternative also is questionable, unless some clear guidance can be given on the factors that merit fee shifting.

B. Reasonable Refusal

If the purpose of Rule 68 is to encourage reasonable settlement behavior, the obvious approach would be to draft the rule in those terms. That ploy in fact was adopted in the 1984 proposal, which authorized imposition of "an appropriate sanction" if "an offer was rejected unreasonably, resulting in unnecessary delay and needless increase in the cost of the litigation." The attempt to guide this decision deserves quotation in full:

> In making this determination the court shall consider all of the relevant circumstances at the time of the rejection, including (1) the then apparent merit or lack of merit in the claim that was the subject of the offer, (2) the closeness of the questions of fact and law at issue, (3) whether the offeror had unreasonably refused to furnish information necessary to evaluate the reasonableness of the offer, (4) whether the suit was in the nature of a "test case," presenting questions of far-reaching importance affecting non-parties, (5) the relief that might reasonably have been expected if the claimant should prevail, and (6) the amount of the additional delay, cost, and expense that the offeror reasonably would be expected to incur if the litigation should be prolonged.[12]

Determination of the appropriateness of the sanction was to consider, among other factors, the costs, expenses, and attorney fees incurred "as a result" of the rejection, and the burden of the sanction on the offeree.

The open-ended list of illustrative factors in this proposal covers many of the most important elements bearing on the reasonableness of settlement behavior. The implication that only "questions of far-reaching importance" justify consideration of abstract stakes may seem begrudging; the suggestion that the offeree should be sympathetically concerned with the impact on an adversary offeror is somewhat puzzling. Nonetheless, the list provides a rich illustration of the costs of implementing a rule geared to reasonable settlement behavior. A judge who has tried a case without a jury would have to disentangle the process of decision, however clear or difficult it was, from the retrospective attempt to evaluate the case as a party might reasonably have seen it at the time of the offer–or offers, since successive offers were allowed. A judge who has tried a case to a jury might have to disentangle from the retrospective evaluation speculation about a process of decision that the judge may think led to a wrong result. Gathering full information and assessing it from the perspective of the offeree would be difficult. An attempt to make the assessment in the context of actual or potential counter-offers would be all the more difficult.

The difficulty courts would face in evaluating the reasonableness of settlement behavior would feed back to affect behavior in the offer-of-judgment process. The need to predict the outcome in relation to the offer would be compounded by the need to predict potential fee-shifting consequences. Strategic behavior would be complicated even more if courts came to assess the "fairness" of bargaining behavior as well as more tangible factors.

If Rule 68 consequences are to be justified by a duty of reasonable settlement, those consequences should be measured by a rule that resembles the 1984 proposal much more than an automatic comparison of offer and judgment. The manifest burden of implementing such a rule however, must weigh heavily against pursuing it.

C. Enabling Act Concerns

Rule 68 does not now refer to "sanctions." The 1984 proposal did refer to sanctions. Reliance on the sanction concept may seem to alleviate Enabling Act concerns that liability for an adversary's attorney fees is too much a matter of substantive right to be addressed through the rulemaking process. The analogy to discovery sanctions falls ready to hand: the rules create a procedural duty to respond to discovery, and provide sanctions that compensate for the cost of enforcing proper demands. The framework of the 1984 proposal was calculated to rely on this analogy. The rules create a duty to behave reasonably in response to settlement offers and impose a sanction that compensates for the cost caused by failure to fulfill this duty.[13] Early reactions to the 1993 draft, however, have expressed concern that reliance on the sanctions concept creates untoward collateral consequences. Assuming that Rule 68 sanctions are imposed on the party alone, the fact remains that advice on settlement is provided by counsel. If counsel is tainted by sanctions imposed on a party–who may indeed have rejected advice to accept a Rule 68 offer–the potential distortions of attorney-client relationships threatened by Rule 68 may be exacerbated. Attribution of the sanction to counsel seems increasingly unfair, moreover, as the failure to settle seems increasingly reasonable. The unfairness of tarring counsel with the sanctions brush may be no greater than the unfairness of forcing the client to pay adversary counsel fees, a question that can be answered only with a sound theory of the American Rule. That question, however, remains the main point of inquiry. It is easy enough to draft a rule that shifts counsel fees without referring to sanctions. Reliance on the sanctions concept, indeed, simply papers over the real question: is a duty to accept a reasonable settlement a matter of procedure akin to a duty to cooperate in authorized discovery? At this point it may be important to insist on that definition of the issue; to the extent that consequences are measured by actual results, it is not a matter of a duty to engage in reasonable settlement behavior, but of a duty to accept a settlement. It might be a duty to accept a settlement offer that is reasonable in light of all the things that are known, predictable, and unpredictable. It might be a duty to accept a settlement offer that in the event proves at least as favorable as the judgment. But it is a duty to accept a settlement. And if there is a duty to accept a settlement offer, why should there not also be a duty to make a settlement offer? With a little ingenuity, a system could be devised that requires all parties to make settlement offers and rewards the party whose offer comes closest to the final judgment.

Although the nature of the question is not directly changed by invoking or discarding the sanctions label, the sanctions characterization is useful because it suggests that the procedural character of a regulation cannot be assessed apart from its consequences. A rule that requires a party to accept a settlement offer found reasonable by the court without a decision on the merits, on pain of contempt or dismissal, will not do. A rule that requires a party to pay costs, including forfeiture of post-offer statutory attorney fees otherwise allowable as "costs," will do. We have it now. A rule that shifts attorney fees, requiring one party to bear fees incurred by another, occupies an uncertain middle ground. It can be argued that if present Rule 68 does not abridge, enlarge, or modify a substantive right when it defeats a statutory right to recover attorney fees as costs, an amended Rule 68 would no more abridge, enlarge, or modify a substantive right by requiring one party to compensate another for expenses incident to rejection of an offer more favorable than the judgment. It can be argued in response that defeating a statutory qualification of the basic rule that each party bears its own expenses is not as fundamental (substantive?) as changing the basic rule.

Confronting a question of Enabling Act authority in the course of the rulemaking process is different from the finest point of academic analysis. Even a clear answer to an initially troubling question of authority may not justify pushing ahead. It is responsible to promulgate a clearly desirable rule if close examination justifies rejection of cogent doubts. Greater caution is appropriate if the justification for a proposed rule is less certain, particularly if prediction of its consequences also is uncertain. The American Rule remains a venerable part of our tradition, qualified much more often by one-way pro-plaintiff exceptions than by equal opportunity two-way shifting. Even if it is purely procedural, and even if–indeed perhaps because–it is difficult to identify and articulate its premises, it deserves deep respect in the rulemaking process. We should be quite sure of what we are doing before adopting the current proposal.

V. Difficulties of Implementation

One of the most enduring lessons of drafting exercises is that a promising idea is throughly tested by translation into detailed implementation. The simple illustrations used above involved a single offer on a single claim between two parties. Many lawsuits involve only one claim and two parties. Even then suits may involve a complicating series of offers, particularly if Rule 68 is extended to both parties. Greater complications ensue from a proliferation of parties, particularly if the substantive law has abolished joint and several liability. These and other problems must be weighed in deciding whether to press ahead with revision of Rule 68. The problems described below have been chosen in the hope of viewing Rule 68 from a variety of perspectives.

A. Successive Offers

The proposal expressly permits all parties to make successive offers. The most obvious reasons for allowing repeated resort to Rule 68 spring from its conjoint purpose to encourage settlement and to encourage early settlement. Early offers–and thus early settlements–are encouraged if an early offer does not cut off further use of Rule 68. Later offers, moreover, can readily promote settlement as the parties' expectations are brought closer together by continuing preparation for trial and even external events. Another reason may be that allowing only one offer per party, or even requiring the parties to bid for the right to make the only offer, would so confuse Rule 68 strategy as to discourage frequent use.

1. Calculating the Comparison

Permitting successive offers requires careful attention to the grounds for comparing each offer to the final judgment. The problem is more than a drafting challenge alone. A series of three related examples illuminates the complexities.

The plaintiff offers $50,000. After the plaintiff's offer expires, the plaintiff incurs $20,000 in attorney fees. The defendant then offers $60,000. Each party incurs an additional $15,000 in attorney fees after the defendant's offer expires. Judgment is for $55,000. If the plaintiff had won a litigated judgment of $55,000 at the time of the defendant's $60,000 offer, the plaintiff would have received $15,000 toward its $20,000 fees after deducting the $5,000 benefit of the judgment, and netted the same $50,000 it would have won had the defendant accepted the plaintiff's offer. In this sense, the judgment is better than the defendant's $60,000 offer. There is much to be said for writing Rule 68 to reach this result. There will be some proper resistance, however, arising from two facts. First, the defendant's $60,000 offer was greater than the actual judgment, and–apart from fee-shifting possibilities–much more favorable to the plaintiff than the $40,000 the plaintiff netted by persisting to a $55,000 judgment after expending an additional $15,000 on fees. There is a strong argument that the defendant should be entitled to shift its fees to the plaintiff under Rule 68. Perhaps both views are sound, so that plaintiff and defendant each win Rule 68 fee awards that are offset against each other. Second, and raising a quite different concern illustrated by the next example, the defendant's offer likely was made without knowing the amount of attorney fees incurred by the plaintiff after the plaintiff's $50,000 offer expired.

The second example is the same as the first, except that the plaintiff incurred only $5,000 in attorney fees before the defendant made the $60,000 offer. Now the $55,000 judgment, together with the attorney fees incurred by the plaintiff between expiration of the plaintiff's $50,000 offer and the defendant's offer, is not better than the defendant's offer. The plaintiff is not entitled to attorney fees on the basis of its offer unless the effects of the offer persist beyond the plaintiff's rejection of the defendant's offer: although the $50,000 offer was more favorable to the defendant than the $55,000 judgment, the $5,000 benefit of the judgment eliminates the $5,000 in fees incurred by the time of the defendant's offer. It would seem strange indeed, however, to allow the plaintiff to recover fees incurred after it rejected the $60,000 offer that would have netted $55,000 after deducting the interim fees. The defendant's offer supersedes the plaintiff's offer. The defendant is entitled to $10,000 in attorney fees after deducting the $5,000 benefit of the judgment from the $15,000 incurred after expiration of the defendant's offer.

The second example is intended to underscore the importance of the attorney fees incurred by one party during the period between expiration of its own offer and an offer made by another party. The consequences to the defendant in these two examples are remarkably different because of the different figures used for interim fee expenses. To be intelligent, a second offer must account for these expenses. Each of the three most obvious strategies for making the calculation is questionable. One is to guess, based on an estimate of visible attorney time and the closeness of trial. The estimate depends on the work habits and other commitments of opposing counsel, often difficult to guess. Another is to make an offer that allows the court to determine attorney fees—in a case that has not been tried, that may be won by either party, that may not include a statutory fee right, and in which the amount of the fee may affect the attraction of the offer drastically. Yet another is to ask the other party—at best, that would lead to informal negotiations with an eye to formulating the formal Rule 68 offer.

The third example simply increases the defendant's offer to $80,000. The defendant gets no award because its post-offer fees are wiped out by the $25,000 benefit of the judgment. Although the defendant was willing to pay $80,000 to get out of the further proceedings and guessed better than the plaintiff, it may be argued that this and countless additional variations simply demonstrate the sporting character of the proposed system in cases that include substantial uncertainty as to liability, damages, or both. In addition, a somewhat inconsistent argument may be made that when the outcome of litigation is as uncertain as it often is, the reasonableness of settlement behavior should be tested by some measure more rational than the perhaps compromised outcome.

2. Offer Strategy

A more important concern can be stated in shorter compass. A system that allows successive offers that do not negate the consequences of failing to accept an earlier offer invites strategic offers. Initial offers will be made, not for the purpose of winning early settlement but for the purpose of generating consequences that will affect subsequent bargaining. Defendants and plaintiffs alike should make routine offers barely less favorable than the best result to be hoped for. A plaintiff should demand everything. A defendant who offers next to nothing has little to gain if fee recovery is capped by the amount of the judgment, but may gain powerful bargaining leverage by offering a significant amount, but less than the expected judgment, in cases that seem likely to impose at least a significant liability. The greater the incentives for early settlement that are created by a revised Rule 68, indeed, the greater effect the incentives should have on bargaining both within and without the Rule 68 framework. At times settlement will be impeded, not promoted, by adding this element to the strategic calculation.

It seems difficult to predict the courses of behavior that experienced litigators would be able to develop with years of practice in manipulating a revised Rule 68. If we cannot be confident in predicting the strategic behavior that will develop, revision must be supported by stronger justifications than would suffice with more certain prediction.

B. Multiple Parties

Multiparty litigation can complicate Rule 68. A defendant, for example, may much prefer a global settlement that establishes the full limits of liability. A plaintiff may prefer, for a variety of reasons, to settle separately with some defendants. More complex combinations can easily emerge. These complexities must be overcome in private bargaining. The Rule 68 question is whether formal account should be taken of multiparty complications in drafting the rule.

Multiple plaintiffs provide an easy illustration. The defendant, as master of its offer, should be free to offer terms that require acceptance by all plaintiffs. Suppose all but one accept, the offer expires, and the judgment is less favorable to all? Can those who sought to accept be held to pay post-offer fees to the defendant? Should all of the burden be imposed on the one who held out? If only those who reject are subject to Rule 68 consequences, what happens if those who reject do better by the judgment and those who would have accepted do worse, as should happen whenever each made an accurate prediction of the judgment? Comparative fault can provide a simple illustration of the problems that may arise from multiple-defendant cases. The plaintiff in an automobile accident case offers to settle with the two defendants for $50,000 each, then wins judgment allocating $100,000 damages 60% to one defendant and 40% to the other. Should the rule be written so that one defendant pays a portion of the plaintiff's post-offer fees, but not the other, when the outcome depends on a matter as elusive as the allocation of fault?

Multiple defendants provide a more complicated illustration if the case arises under a law that has rejected joint-and-several liability. One defendant wishes to settle with the only plaintiff. The plaintiff must evaluate the offer not only for its direct impact, but also for its uncertain impact on the other defendants. An offer that seems acceptable if the defendant is held liable for 20% of total damages may not be acceptable if, following settlement, trial allocates 30% of the total to that defendant.

The Supreme Court of Arizona recently considered and rejected a Rule 68 amendment that would allow the plaintiff to tender a conditional acceptance to the defendants who do not join in the offer. If all defendants accept, no fault is apportioned to the defendant who settled; the amount of the settlement is subtracted from the plaintiff's full damages, and the remainder is allocated among the remaining defendants in proportion to their shares of fault. If one or more defendants reject the conditional acceptance, the rejecting defendants share equally "any Rule 68 sanctions which would otherwise be assessed against the plaintiff in favor of the offering defendant."[14] At best, this system complicates the process of calculating the offer, and imposes a difficult prediction on defendants faced with a plaintiff's conditional acceptance. If Rule 68 sanctions actually generate significant settlement incentives, a defendant would, among other things, have to predict how other defendants would react.

Different complications would arise from alternative approaches. If, for example, it were decided to allow acceptance by one or more defendants, so that some were entitled to a reduction of damages according to fault calculated without regard to the settling defendant, while others were involved in litigating the fault of the settling defendant, trial would be complicated still further. The current Rule 68 proposal does not account for this problem. Silence presumably would mean that Rule 68 consequences flow without accommodation to the circumstances of several liability, or for that matter, the various ways in which settlement affects joint-and-several liability. A plausible argument can be made, however, that the *Erie* doctrine[15] commands adherence to a state offer-of-judgment rule specifically adapted to state rules allocating shares of liability.

C. Fee-Shifting Statutes

Any project to revise Rule 68 must consider the decision in *Marek v. Chesny*.[16] After the plaintiff in an action under 42 U.S.C. §1983 had incurred $32,000 in attorney fees, the defendant offered $100,000 to settle the claim and attorney fee liability under 42 U.S.C. §1988. The plaintiff persisted to trial and won $60,000. The Court ruled that Rule 68 cut off the §1988 claim for $139,692 in fees incurred after the offer, observing that this expenditure "resulted in a recovery $8,000 less than petitioners' settlement offer."[17] Rule 68 provides that if the judgment is not more favorable than the offer, "the offeree must pay the costs incurred after the making of the offer." Section 1988 provides for an award of attorney fees "as part of the costs." The meaning of the two provisions together was said to be "plain": "Since Congress expressly included attorney's fees as 'costs' available to a plaintiff in a §1983 suit, such fees are subject to the cost-shifting provision of Rule 68."[18] Justice Brennan dissented, arguing first that it is foolish to hinge application of Rule 68 on the accident whether a particular fee-shifting statute refers to fees as "costs." He went on to argue that the Court's decision "will lead to a number of skewed settlement incentives that squarely conflict with Congress' intent" in providing attorney fee recovery. This argument was extended to the conclusion that application of Rule 68 to defeat a statutory right to attorney fees modifies a substantive right in violation of the Rules Enabling Act.[19]

If nothing else, any revision of Rule 68 should correct the dependence on the frequently happenstance statutory choice whether to refer to attorney fees as costs. There is no apparent reason for distinguishing among fee statutes this way. And matters may become still more confused if an occasional sophisticated attempt is made to take advantage of the current rule in drafting new legislation.[20]

The question whether to perpetuate *Marek v. Chesny* will prove far more contentious. The arguments for overruling it are forceful. Cutting off statutory fee rights seems inconsistent with the probable purpose of one-way fee-shifting statutes to encourage enforcement of particularly favored rights. Even if Rule 68 is amended to provide for offers by plaintiffs, the prospect of losing statutory fees as well as limited liability to pay defense fees makes the effects of Rule 68 more pressing as to these seemingly favored plaintiffs. So long as the plaintiff need only "prevail" to be entitled to statutory attorney fees, moreover, there is little apparent benefit to the plaintiff in making a Rule 68 offer; the only obvious advantage would be to curtail the discretion to deny costs to the plaintiff even though successful. And the risk of losing statutory fees may create a painful conflict of interest for counsel advising on the attractiveness of an offer. Occasional benefits nonetheless might result from the rule in *Marek v. Chesny*. There is a risk that litigation will be pursued for the purpose of augmenting attorney fees after an offer that, intrinsically, is fully satisfactory. The potential use of Rule 68 to eliminate such fee-driven litigation is attractive.

Rule 68 could be written to exclude fee-shifting, or to exclude both fee-shifting and costs liability, as to any claim that entails statutory fee-shifting. That leaves the problem of cases that combine fee-shifting claims with other claims. A modest variation on *Marek v. Chesny* illustrates the problem. A plaintiff advancing constitutional and state-law claims arising from an assault by a police official is offered $20,000 to settle all claims and wins $19,000 on each theory at trial. Should the defendant be allowed to recover post-offer reasonable attorney fees in excess of $1,000 up to the amount of the state-law judgment because the state-law claim does not invoke a fee-shifting statute? If so, exemption of the §1983 claim alone does not fully protect the pro-plaintiff policies that may underlie the fee-shifting scheme. One undesirable consequence might be failure to advance state-law claims in order to remain outside Rule 68. The protection would be diluted further still in cases with different state and federal law awards if the Rule 68 consequences were considered in determining the extent of the plaintiff's recovery of statutory fees as "prevailing party." If not, the exemption would be extended at least to the fee-shifting claim and any other theory that is part of the same "claim" as defined by the claim preclusion branch of res judicata.

Exclusion of claims governed by fee-shifting statutes would raise other, perhaps minor, questions. One is whether so many cases would be affected as to dilute the potential benefits of providing fee shifting under Rule 68. Another is whether it is backward to provide fee shifting under Rule 68 only as to claims that have been left outside the apparently growing number of statutory fee-shifting provisions.

D. Determining Reasonable Fees

Fee sanctions entail responsibility for determining reasonable fees. The 1993 amendments to Rule 11 are designed in part to subordinate the role of private sanctions, including attorney-fee sanctions. Determining reasonable fees in other settings has generated lengthy litigation. A rule that blandly calls for determination of reasonable fees is not very helpful. An attempt to devise a helpful formula for determining reasonable fees, however, is not to be undertaken lightly. It is appropriate to ask that Rule 68 be expanded to include fee-shifting only if there are solid grounds for expecting that the benefits will more than compensate the added labors. Perhaps this will happen because so many cases settle, and because actual fees will so far outstrip any possible shift after reduction for the benefit of the judgment and capping at the amount of the judgment that reasonableness is not an issue.[21] Perhaps not.

E. Other Implementation Questions

1. Forgiveness

There are attractive reasons for allowing discretionary exemption from Rule 68 consequences. Only the most obvious examples are needed. An offer may be made in a state of legal uncertainty that is resolved after the offer expires. Facts that seemed clear at the time of the offer may later become uncertain or worse, and unknown facts may appear. A low defense offer may be followed by an even lower compromise verdict that would be swallowed up even after recognizing the benefit of the judgment. If discretion is recognized, however, it must be kept narrow lest it undermine the possible benefits of fee shifting by diminishing the incentive to accept an offer and increasing the occasions for collateral litigation.

2. Bilateral Cap

The proposal limits fee sanctions to the amount of the judgment. Beginning from the desire to ensure that a claimant not be out-of-pocket, this feature appears to achieve rough equality between claimants and defendants. In some cases, however, the equality may prove illusory. Suit on a $100,000 life insurance policy, for example, could turn entirely on the question of fraud by the insured. The insurer is liable for $100,000 or nothing. The plaintiff offers $100,000 and the defendant offers nothing. If the plaintiff wins $100,000 the defendant is liable for reasonable attorney fees up to $100,000. If the plaintiff wins nothing, the defendant receives no attorney fees. Occasional consequences such as these need not defeat the proposal. They do, however, illustrate that it is not entirely simple.

3. Specific Relief

The draft proposal caps any fee award at the amount of the judgment. If only specific relief is involved, fees are not shifted because the "amount" of the judgment is zero. This approach has at least two benefits. One is that it enables plaintiffs in "public interest" litigation to reduce or eliminate exposure to fee-shifting under Rule 68 by reducing or eliminating demands for money damages. The other is that it avoids any need to find an alternative cap for cases that involve only specific relief.

Cases that involve both monetary and specific relief raise the question of comparing the specific relief terms of offer and judgment. The most easily managed approach would be to set the threshold at a judgment that includes every term of the offer. Rule 68 benefits flow to a plaintiff who offered to settle for the same or less relief and to a defendant who offered to settle for the same or greater relief. The draft proposal sets a lower threshold, looking to "substantially all the nonmonetary relief offered." This approach rests on the belief that it would be remarkable to develop an offer that included all the elements of a litigated decree in complex institutional reform litigation. It also might reflect concern that choices in shaping the decree should not be subject to the pressure of Rule 68 consequences. Administration of the more flexible test, however, may require more effort than it is worth.

VI. Alternative Approaches

Any number of different approaches could be taken to encourage settlement, either through offer-of-judgment rules or through other means. A few may be noted briefly.

The strategic calculus of Rule 68 would be changed greatly if each party could make only one offer, and even more if only one party could make an offer.

The stakes of Rule 68 would be reduced if it were limited to an award of post-offer costs. To make the rule a meaningful tool for plaintiffs, it would be accompanied by a change in the rule that ordinarily the prevailing party recovers its costs.[22] The stakes could be increased, but ordinarily not to the level of attorney fee shifting, by including expert witness fees in the costs.

Concern that Rule 68 may entail serious consequences for a close miss in predicting the judgment could be reduced by introducing a margin of error. The extent of the margin would be based on perception of the average for reasonable error across a wide range of cases. If fees were shifted only when the judgment falls more than 50% beyond the offer, for example, objections to the proposal might be softened substantially.

The other means of encouraging settlement most prominent today are a host of devices grouped together under such labels as "court-annexed arbitration." Refusal to accept the recommended judgment can carry whatever consequences might be attributed to Rule 68. The advantage of these procedures is that they rely on an impartial assessment of the case as seen by an outsider, and ideally should lead to a recommendation based on that assessment without strategic calculation of what is likely to prove acceptable to whom. This feature may suggest that it is better to rely on such procedures to expedite settlement than to tinker with Rule 68. The disadvantage of these procedures is that ordinarily they are curtailed; the parties may arrive and leave with a much better understanding of the case than can be communicated at a brief hearing or even a "mini-trial." This characteristic may make Rule 68 seem more attractive after all.

Although no alternative is obviously better than "capped benefit-of-the-judgment" fee shifting under Rule 68, alternative versions of Rule 68 and other procedures should be considered before adopting the proposed version with the improvements that inevitably will occur in the drafting process.

VII. The Nature of Settlement

Instinctive reactions to the nature of settlement may account for some part of my uneasiness with Rule 68 fee shifting. Let me provide a preliminary sketch without undertaking rigorous development.

There are many reasons for welcoming settlements voluntarily reached by the parties in face of the uncertainties and costs of further litigation. To be sure, settlements are seldom voluntary in any pure sense. The prospect of official decision and public enforcement of an official judgment often is an indispensable incentive. The motives that influence settlement are shaped by both the strengths and weaknesses of the adversary system we have chosen as our means of official enforcement. Settlement, for example, may be encouraged by knowledge that litigation will produce the right result, or by fear that litigation will produce a wrong result. Rules as to attorney fee shifting are among the characteristics of the system that influence settlement. Changing those rules solely because of a formal offer of judgment changes the influences that affect settlement. The question may be as simple as the choice between two perspectives. On one view, we have an existing set of rules about fee shifting that we accept as the best compromise between competing needs. Because these rules are ordinary, they influence settlement in a natural way. Any change created by a formal offer-of-judgment rule is a distortion. From another perspective, we have a set of rules about fee shifting that defeat full compensation for deserving claimants or impose unjustified costs on prevailing defendants. These rules at best represent an unhappy compromise of irreconcilable needs. Departure from these rules is justified when a party has spurned an offer better than the eventual judgment.

Choosing between these perspectives may be influenced by the reasons for favoring settlement. Half a dozen reasons may be suggested in short compass.

The parties often know the facts of their dispute more truly than they can be known to a court. The traditions of adversary presentation, augmented in some measure by restrictive rules of evidence, ensure that. Settlement is affected by predicted ability to persuade the court of inaccurate factual propositions, but may rest on the hope or fear that the court will find the facts correctly. A settlement based on tacit recognition of the facts may be truer than a litigated judgment.

Litigation of most civil disputes is in form, and often in fact, an all-or-nothing affair even in close cases resolved at the midpoint of the often broad range of residual doubt referred to as the preponderance of the evidence. Settlements that compromise remedy and liability together may be intrinsically more fair.

The parties may be attracted or even bound to each other in relationships they hope to maintain. Settlement on mutually acceptable terms may be better even for a party who knows it would win more by trial.

The very substantive rules underlying the litigation may not be as wise as the rules the parties can create for themselves. This feature is particularly prominent with respect to forward-looking remedies. The parties may be able to work out terms of operation or gradual shutdown of a nuisance that accommodate all needs better than the decree that would result from adversary litigation.

Settlement also accommodates risk aversion. Quite apart from the virtues just noted, each party may be able to bear partial but not total defeat. Mutual avoidance of unilateral disaster is obviously desirable.

The cost savings from settlement, finally, tie directly to the offer-of-judgment rationale. Paying and receiving a $500,000 settlement is far more attractive than paying and receiving a $500,000 judgment after each side has spent $150,000 on attorney fees.

For these advantages and others, we treasure settlement. Party autonomy is viewed as so important in this respect that judges have no power to prevent settlement of ordinary civil litigation. Settlement, indeed, moots the litigation, depriving the court of power to continue.

These advantages depend on settlements that represent the free choices of the parties whether to pursue litigation further. An incentive aimed specifically at settlement behavior exerts an influence that does not depend on any other entrenched feature of the adversary system, the strength of the parties' positions, or the identity and resources of the parties. We should insist on a clear statement of the reasons for increasing settlement pressures before concluding that this pressure will improve, not distort, the process.

VIII. Conclusion

This exercise in doubt is more a quest for reassurance than a dissent. Much of it can be assigned to two categories: doubts about the duty to settle and its relationship to fee shifting; and doubts about difficulties of implementation.

Fundamental doubts arise from questions about the imperative of settlement and the American Rule that ordinarily litigants bear their own attorney fees, win, lose, or draw. Even a carefully regulated fee-shifting revision of Rule 68 seems to rest on two assumptions. One is that a party who makes a formal Rule 68 offer that proves at least as favorable to the offeree as the eventual judgment deserves to be made whole for attorney fee expenditures "caused" by rejection of the offer. The implicit duty to settle is not measured by reasonable litigation behavior, nor by reasonable settlement behavior, but primarily by the actual result. The other assumption is that we can redress this attorney-fee injury, at least within limits, without intruding too far on the values served by the American Rule. Neither assumption can be accepted uncritically. No theory has yet been advanced to clearly justify the proposition that although attorney fees should not be shifted merely because a party has brought an action and lost, or has defended an action and lost, shifing is proper because a party has made a wrong prediction in response to a formal offer of judgment.

The doubts that arise from implementing a fee-shifting approach have been detailed in ways that at times may seem unfair. It is easy to emphasize particularly troubling situations, no one of which may arise with any frequency. The cumulative impact of these situations, however, deserves some attention in approaching revision of Rule 68. Occasional untoward results may be reduced by recognizing discretion to excuse Rule 68 consequences. The untoward results that remain can be tolerated if there is a clear prospect of substantial redeeming advantage. Those who doubt the rationale and impact of the proposal, however, may fairly suggest that the costs of bearing some untoward results and the administrative costs of avoiding others bear on the decision.

With all of this, the current proposal demands attention. It offers a carefully thought-out attempt to establish an effective offer-of-judgment procedure. It avoids many of the objections that can be made to unlimited fee shifting, as well as the great administrative costs that attend an effort to enforce directly a duty of reasonable settlement behavior. Practical judgment about actual impact may be more important than abstract dithering. Help will be found in surveying practicing attorneys to learn about their experiences with settlement and their predictions of the impact of limited fee shifting, a project now underway at the Federal Judicial Center.[23] Much help will be found in the public comment process if the rulemaking process moves forward to that stage. Perhaps in ten or fifteen years we will have so much favorable experience with a limited fee-shifting version of Rule 68 that these early doubts will seem captious.

Appendix: Proposed Rule 68. Offer of Settlement

(a) Offers. A party may make an offer of settlement to another party.

(1) The offer must:

(A) be in writing and state that it is a Rule 68 offer;

(B) be served at least 30 days after the summons and complaint if the offer is made to a defendant;

(C) [not be filed with the court] {be filed with the court only as provided in (b)(2) or (c)(2)};

(D) remain open for [a stated period of] at least 21 days unless the court orders a different period; and

(E) specify the relief offered.

(2) The offer may be withdrawn by writing served on the offeree before the offer is accepted. [Withdrawal nullifies the offer for all purposes.]

(b) Acceptance; Disposition.

(1) An offer made under (a) may be accepted by a written notice served [on the offeror] while the offer remains open.

(2) A party may file {the} [an accepted] offer, notice of acceptance, and proof of service. The clerk or court must then enter the judgment specified in the offer. [But the court may refuse to enter judgment if it finds that the judgment is unfair to another party or contrary to the public interest.]

(c) Expiration.

(1) An offer expires if it is not withrawn or accepted before the end of the period set under (a)(1)(D).

(2) Evidence of an expired offer is admissible only in a proceeding to determine costs and attorney fees under Rule 54(d).

(d) Successive Offers. A party may make an offer of settlement after making[, rejecting,] or failing to accept an earlier offer. A successive offer that expires does not deprive a party of {remedies} [sanctions] based on an earlier offer.

(e) {Remedies} [Sanctions]. Unless the final judgment is more favorable to the offeree than an expired offer the offeree must pay a remedy [sanction] to the offeror.

(1) If the offeree is not entitled to a statutory award of attorney fees, the remedy [sanction] must include:

(A) costs incurred by the offeror after the offer expired; and

(B) reasonable attorney fees incurred by the offeror after the offer expired, limited as follows:

(i) the monetary difference between the offer and judgment must be subtracted from the fees; and

(ii) the fee award must not exceed the money amount of the judgment.

(2) If the offeree is entitled to a statutory award of attorney fees, the remedy [sanction] must include:

(A) costs incurred by the offeror after the offer expired; and

(B) denial of attorney fees incurred by the offeree after the offer expired.

(3) (A) The court may reduce the {remedy} [sanction] to avoid undue hardship [or because the judgment could not reasonably have been expected at the time the offer expired].

(B) No remedy may be given [sanction may be imposed] on disposition of an action by acceptance of an offer under this rule or other settlement.

(4) (A) A judgment for a party demanding relief is more favorable than an offer to it:

(i) if the amount awarded—including the costs, attorney fees, and other amounts awarded for the period before the offer {was served} [expired]—exceeds the monetary award that would have resulted from the offer; and

(ii) if nonmonetary relief is demanded and the judgment includes all the nonmonetary relief offered, or substantially all the nonmonetary relief offered and additional relief.

(B) A judgment is more favorable to a party opposing relief than an offer to it:

(i) if the amount awarded—including the costs, attorney fees, and other amounts awarded for the period before the offer {was served} [expired]—is less than the monetary award that would have resulted from the offer; and

(ii) if nonmonetary relief is demanded and the judgment does not include [substantially] all the nonmonetary relief offered.

(f) Nonapplicability. This rule does not apply to an offer made in an action certified as a class or derivative action under Rule 23, 23.1, or 23.2.

* * *

Fee statute alternative

(e) Remedies [Sanctions]. Unless the final judgment is more favorable to

the offeree than an expired offer the offeree must pay a {remedy} [sanction] to the offeror.

(1) The {remedy} [sanction] must include:

(A) costs incurred by the offeror after the offer expired; and

(B) reasonable attorney fees incurred by the offeror after the offer expired, limited as follows:

(i) the monetary difference between the offer and judgment must be subtracted from the fees; and

(ii) the fee award must not exceed the money amount of the judgment.

(2) (A) The court may reduce the remedy[sanction] to avoid undue hardship [or because the judgment could not reasonably have been expected at the time the offer expired].

(B) No remedy may be given[sanction may be imposed]:

(i) against a party that otherwise is entitled to a statutory award of attorney fees;

(ii) on disposition of an action by acceptance of an offer under this rule or other settlement.

* * *

(e) (2)(B)(i) might take less protective forms: No remedy may be given:

Costs but not fee shifting

(i) that requires payment of attorney fees by a party that is entitled to a statutory award of attorney fees; or

Statutory fees not affected

(i) that affects the statutory right of a party to an award of attorney fees;

Committee Note

Former Rule 68 has been properly criticized as one-sided and largely ineffectual. It was available only to parties defending against a claim, not to parties making a claim. It provided little inducement to make or accept an offer since in most cases the only penalty suffered by declining an offer was the imposition of the typically insubstantial taxable costs subsequently incurred by the offering party. Greater incentives existed after the decision in *Marek v. Chesny*, 473 U.S. 1 (1985), which ruled that a plaintiff who obtains a positive judgment less than a defendant's Rule 68 offer loses the right to collect post-offer attorney fees provided by a statute as "costs" to a prevailing plaintiff. The decision in the Marek case, however, was limited to cases affected by such fee-shifting statutes. It also provoked criticism on the ground that it was inconsistent with the statutory policies that favor special categories of claims with the right to recover fees.

Earlier proposals were made to make Rule 68 available to all parties and to increase its effects by authorizing attorney fee sanctions. These proposals met with vigorous criticism. Opponents stressed the policy considerations involved in the "American Rule" on attorney fees. They emphasized that the opportunity of all parties to attempt to shift fees through Rule 68 offers could produce inappropriate windfalls and would create unequal pressures and coerce unfair settlements because parties often have different levels of knowledge, risk-averseness, and resources.

The basis for many of the changes made in the amended Rule 68 is provided in an article by Judge William W. Schwarzer, *Fee-Shifting Offers of Judgment—An Approach to Reducing the Cost of Litigation*, 76 Judicature 147 (1992).

The amended rule allows any party to make a Rule 68 offer. The incentives for early settlement are increased by increasing the consequences of failure to win a judgment more favorable than an expired offer. A plaintiff is liable for post-offer costs even if the plaintiff takes nothing, a result accomplished by removing the language that supported the contrary ruling in *Delta Air Lines, Inc. v. August*, 450 U.S. 346 (1981). Post-offer attorney fees are shifted, subject to two limits. The amount of post-offer attorney fees is reduced by the difference between the offer and the judgment. In addition, the attorney fee award cannot exceed the amount of the judgment. A plaintiff who wins nothing pays no attorney fees. A defendant pays no more in fees than the amount of the judgment.

A plaintiff's incentive to accept a defendant's Rule 68 offer includes the incentive that applies to all offers—the risk that trial will produce no more, and perhaps less. It also includes the fear of Rule 68 consequences; the defendant's post-offer attorney fees may reduce or obliterate whatever judgment is won, leaving the plaintiff with all of its own expenses and the defendant's post-offer costs. A defendant's incentive to accept a plaintiff's Rule 68 offer is similar: not only must it pay a larger judgment, but it can be held to pay post-offer costs and the plaintiff's post-offer attorney fees up to the amount of the judgment.

Attorney fee shifting is limited to reflect the difference between the offer and the judgment. The difference is treated as a benefit accruing to the fee expenditure. If fees of $40,000 are incurred after the offer and the judgment is $15,000 more favorable than the offer, for example, the maximum fee award is reduced to $25,000.

Subdivision (a). Several formal requirements are imposed on the Rule 68 offer process. Offers may be made outside of Rule 68 at any time before or after an action is commenced. The requirement that the Rule 68 offer be in writing and state that it is made under Rule 68 is designed to avoid claims for awards based on less formal offers that may not have been recognized as paving the way for an award.

A Rule 68 offer is not to be filed with the court until it is accepted. The offeror should not be influenced by concern that an unaccepted offer may work to its disadvantage in later proceedings.

The requirement that an offer remain open for at least 21 days is intended to allow a reasonable period for evaluation by the recipient. Consquences cannot fairly be imposed if inadequate time is allowed for evaluation. Fees and costs are shifted only from the time the offer expires; see subdivision (e)(1) and (2). A party who wishes to increase the prospect of acceptance may set a longer period. The court may order a different period. As one example, it may not be fair to require a defendant to act on an offer early in the proceedings, under threat of Rule 68 consequences, without more time to gather information. If the court orders that the period for accepting be extended, the offer can be withdrawn under paragraph (2). The opportunity to withdraw is important for the same reasons as the power to extend—developing information may make the offer seem less attractive to the plaintiff just as it may make the offer seem more attractive to the defendant. As another example, the 21-day period may foreclose offers close to trial; the court can grant permission to shorten the period to make an offer possible.

Paragraph (2) establishes power to withdraw the offer before acceptance. This power reflects the fact that the apparent worth of a case can change as further information is developed. It also enables a party to retain control of its own offer in face of an order extending the time for acceptance. Withdrawal nullifies the offer—consequences cannot be based upon a withdrawn offer.

Subdivision (b). An offer can be accepted only during the period it remains open and is not withdrawn. Acceptance requires service on the offeror. An acceptance is effective notwithstanding an attempt to withdraw the offer if the acceptance is served on the offeror before the withdrawal is served on the offeree. If it is uncertain whether acceptance or withdrawal was served first, the doubt should be resolved by giving effect to the withdrawal, since the parties remain free to make successive Rule 68 offers or to settle outside the Rule 68 process.

Once an offer is accepted, judgment may be entered by the clerk or court according to the nature of the offer. Ordinarily the clerk should enter judgment for money or recovery of clearly identified property. Action by the court is more likely to be required for entry of an injunction or declaratory relief.

The court has the same power to refuse to enter judgment under Rule 68 as it has to refuse judgment on agreement of the parties in other settings. An injunction may be found contrary to the public interest, for example, if it requires the court to enforce terms that the court feels unable to supervise. A settled decree may affect public interests in broader terms, particularly in actions such as those to control the conduct of public institutions, protect the environment, or regulate employment practices. The parties cannot force the court to adopt and enforce a decree that defeats important interests of nonparties. A Rule 68 judgment also might be unfair to other parties in a multiparty action. An extreme illustration of unfairness would be an agreement to allocate all of a limited fund to one party, excluding others. Less extreme settings also might justify refusal to enter judgment.

Subdivision (c). An offer expires if it is not withdrawn or accepted.

An expired offer may be used only for the purpose of providing remedies under subdivision (e). The procedures of Rule 54(d) govern requests for costs or attorney fees.

Subdivision (d). Successive offers may be made by any party without losing the opportunity to win remedies based on an earlier expired offer, and without defeating exposure to remedies based on failure to accept an offer from another party. This system encourages the parties to make early Rule 68 offers, which may promote early settlement, without losing the opportunity to make later Rule 68 offers as developing familiarity with the case helps bring together estimates of probable value. It also encourages later Rule 68 offers following expiration of earlier offers by preserving the possibility of winning remedies based on an earlier offer.

The operation of the successive offers provision is illustrated by Example 4 in the discussion of subdivision (e).

Subdivision (e). Remedies are mandatory, unless reduced or excused under paragraph (3).

Final judgment. The time for determining remedies is controlled by entry of final judgment. In most settings finality for this purpose will be determined by the tests that determine finality for purposes of appeal. Complications may emerge, however, in actions that involve several parties and claims. A final judgment may be entered under Rule 54(b) that disposes of one or more claims between the offeror and offeree but leaves open other claims between them. Such a judgment can be the occasion for invoking Rule 68 remedies if it finally disposes of all matters involved in the Rule 68 offer. It also is possible that a Rule 54(b) judgment may support Rule 68 remedies even though it does not dispose of all matters involved in the offer. A plaintiff's $50,000 offer to settle all claims, for example, might be followed by a $75,000 judgment for the plaintiff on two claims, leaving two other claims to be resolved. Usually it will be better to defer the determination of remedies to a single proceeding upon completion of the entire action. If there is a special need to determine remedies promptly, however, an interim award may be made as soon as it is inescapably clear that the final judgment will be more favorable than the offer.

Costs and fees. Remedies are limited to costs and attorney fees. Other expenses are excluded for a variety of reasons. In part, the limitation reflects the policies that underlie the limits of attorney fee awards discussed below. In addition, the limitation reflects the great variability of other expenses and the difficulty of determining whether particular expenses are reasonable.

Costs for the present purpose include all costs routinely taxable under Rule 54(d). Attorney fees are treated separately. This provision supersedes the construction of Rule 68 adopted in *Marek v. Chesny*, 473 U.S. 1 (1985), under which statutory attorney fees are treated as costs for purposes of Rule 68 if, but only if, the statute treats them as costs.

Several limits are placed on remedies based on attorney fees incurred after a Rule 68 offer expired. The fees must be reasonable. The award is reduced by deducting from the amount of reasonable fees the monetary difference between the offer and the judgment. To the extent that the judgment is more favorable to the offeror than the offer, it is fair to attribute the difference to the fee expenditure. This reduction is limited to monetary differences. Differences in specific relief are excluded from this reduction because the policy underlying the benefit-of-the-judgment rule is not so strong as to support the difficulties frequently encountered in setting a monetary value on specific relief.

The attorney fee award also is limited to the amount of the judgment. A claimant's money judgment can be reduced to nothing by a fee award, but out-of-pocket liability is limited to costs. A defending party's exposure to fee shifting is made symmetrical by limiting the stakes to the money amount of the judgment. If no monetary relief is awarded, attorney fee remedies are not available to either party. This result not only avoids the difficulties of setting a monetary value on specific relief but also diminishes the risk of deterring litigation involving matters of public interest.

Several examples illustrate the working of this "capped benefit-of-the-judgment" attorney fee provision.

Example 1. (No shifting) After its offer to settle for $50,000 is not accepted, the plaintiff ultimately recovers a $25,000 judgment. Rejection of this offer would not result in any award because the judgment is more favorable to the offeree than the offer. Similarly, there would be no award based on an offer of $50,000 by the defendant and a $75,000 judgment for the plaintiff.

Example 2. (Shifting on rejection of plaintiff's offer) After the defendant rejects the plaintiff's $50,000 offer, the plaintiff wins a $75,000 judgment. (a) The plaintiff incurred $40,000 of reasonable post-offer attorney fees. The $25,000 benefit of the judgment is deducted from the fee expenditure, leaving an award of $15,000. (b) If reasonable post-offer attorney fees were $25,000 or less, no fee award would be made. (c) If reasonable post-offer fees were $110,000, deduction of the $25,000 benefit of the judgment would leave $85,000; the cap that limits the award to the amount of the judgment would reduce the attorney fee award to $75,000.

Example 3. (Shifting on rejection of defendant's offer) After the plaintiff rejects the defendant's $75,000 offer, the plaintiff wins a $50,000 judgment. (a) The defendant incurred $40,000 of reasonable post-offer attorney fees. The $25,000 benefit of the judgment is deducted from the fee expenditure, leaving a fee award of $15,000. (b) If reasonable post-offer attorney fees were $25,000 or less, no fee award would be made. (c) If reasonable post-offer fees were $110,000, deduction of the $25,000 benefit of the judgment would leave $85,000; the cap that limits the fee award to the amount of the judgment would reduce the attorney fee award to $50,000. The plaintiff's judgment would be completely offset by the fee award, and the plaintiff would remain liable for post-offer costs.

Example 4. (Successive offers) After a defendant's $50,000 offer lapses, the defendant makes a new $60,000 offer that also lapses. (a) A judgment of $50,000 or less requires an award based on the amount and time of the $50,000 offer. (b) A judgment more than $50,000 but not more than $60,000 requires an award based on the amount and time of the $60,000 offer. This approach preserves the incentive to make a successive offer by preserving the potential effect of the first offer.

Example 5. (Counteroffers) The effect of each offer is determined independently of any other offer. Counteroffers are likely to be followed by judgments that entail no award or an award against only one party. The plaintiff, for example, might make an early $25,000 offer, followed by $20,000 of fee expenditures before a $40,000 offer by the defendant, additional $15,000 fee expenditures by each party, and judgment for $42,000. The plaintiff's $25,000 offer is more favorable to the defendant than the judgment, so the plaintiff is entitled to a fee award. The $35,000 of post-offer fees is reduced by the $17,000 benefit of the judgment, netting an award of $18,000. The defendant is not entitled to any award.

In some circumstances, however, counteroffers can entitle both parties to awards. Offers made and not accepted at different stages in the litigation may fall on both sides of the eventual judgment. Each party receives the benefit of its offer and pays the consequences for failing to accept the offer of the other party. The awards are offset, resulting in a net award to the party entitled to the greater amount. As an example, a plaintiff might make an early $25,000 offer, then incur reasonable attorney fees of $5,000 before the defendant's $60,000 offer, after which each party incurred reasonable attorney fees of $25,000. A judgment for $50,000 would support a fee award for each party. The $50,000 judgment is more favorable to the plaintiff than the plaintiff's expired offer. The $50,000 is less favorable to the plaintiff than the defendant's expired offer. The attorney fee award to the plaintiff would be reduced to $5,000 by subtracting the $25,000 benefit of the judgment from the $30,000 of post-offer fees. The attorney fee award to the defendant would be reduced first to $15,000 by subtracting the $10,000 benefit of the judgment from the $25,000 of post-offer fees. The $15,000 award to the defendant would be set off against the $5,000 award to the plaintiff, leaving a $10,000 net award to the defendant.

Example 6. (Counterclaims) Cases involving claims and counterclaims for money alone fall within the earlier examples. Each party controls the terms of any offer it makes. If no offer is accepted, the final judgment is compared to the terms of each offer. (a) The defendant's offer to pay $10,000 to the plaintiff to settle both claim and counterclaim is followed by a $25,000 award to the plaintiff on its claim and a $40,000 award to the defendant on its counterclaim. The result is treated as a net award of $15,000 to the defendant. This net is $25,000 more favorable to the defendant than its offer. If the defendant's reasonable post-offer attorney fees were $35,000, the attorney fee award payable to the defendant is $10,000. (b) If the defendant's reasonable post-offer attorney fees in example (a) had been $45,000, the attorney fee award payable to the defendant would be limited to the $15,000 amount of the net award on the merits. (c) The defendant's offer to accept $10,000 from the plaintiff to settle both claim and counterclaim is followed by an award of nothing to the plaintiff on its claim and a $40,000 award to the defendant on its counterclaim. The result is treated as a net award of $40,000 to the defendant, which is $30,000 more favorable to the defendant than its offer.

Contingent Fees. The fee award to a successful plaintiff represented on a contingent fee basis should be calculated on a reasonable hourly rate for reasonable post-offer services, not by prorating the contingent fee. The attorney should keep time records from the beginning of the representation, not for the post-offer period alone, as a means of ensuring the reasonable time required for the post-offer period.

Hardship or surprise. Rule 68 awards may be reduced to avoid undue hardship or reasonable surprise. Reduction may, as a matter of discretion, extend to denial of any award. As an extreme illustration of hardship, a severely injured plaintiff might fail to accept a $100,000 offer and win a $100,000 judgment following a reasonable attorney fee expenditure of $100,000 by the defendant. A fee award to the defendant that would wipe out any recovery by the plaintiff could be found unfair. Surprise is most likely to be found when the law has changed between the time an offer expired and the time of judgment. Later discovery of vitally important factual information also may establish that the judgment could not reasonably have been expected at the time the offer expired.

Statutory Fee Entitlement. Rule 68 consequences for a party entitled to statutory attorney fees have been governed by the decision in *Marek v. Chesny*, 473 U.S. 1 (1985). Revised Rule 68 continues to provide that an otherwise existing right to a statutory fee award is cut off as to fees incurred after expiration of an offer more favorable than the judgment. The only additional Rule 68 consequence for a party entitled to statutory fees is liability for costs incurred by the offeror after the offer expired. The fee award provided by subdivision (e)(1)(B) for other cases is not available. These rules establish a balance between the policies underlying Rule 68 and statutory attorney fee provisions. It is desirable to encourage early settlement in cases governed by statutory attorney fee provisions just as in other cases. Effective incentives remain important. The award of an attorney fee against a party entitled to recover statutory fees, however, could interfere with the legislative determination that the underlying claim deserves special protection. The balance struck by Rule 68 does not address the question whether failure to win a judgment more favorable than an expired offer should be taken into account in determining whether any particular statute supports an award for fees incurred before expiration of the offer.

Settlement. All potential effects of a Rule 68 offer expire upon acceptance of a successive Rule 68 offer or other settlement. This rule makes it easier to reach a final settlement, free of uncertainty as to the prospect of Rule 68 consequences. The prospect of Rule 68 consequences remains, however, as one of the elements to be considered by the parties in determining the terms of settlement.

Judgment more favorable. Many complications surround the determination whether a judgment is more favorable than an offer, even in a case that involves only monetary relief. The difficulties are illustrated by the provisions governing offers to a party demanding relief. The comparison should begin with the exclusion of costs, attorney fees, and other items incurred after expiration of the offer. The purpose of the offer process is to avoid such costs. Costs, attorney fees, and other items that would be awarded by a judgment entered at the expiration of the offer, on the other hand, should be included. An offer that matches only the award of damages is not as favorable as a judgment that includes additional money awards. Beyond that point, comparison of a money judgment with a money offer depends on the details of the offer, which are controlled by the offeror. An offer may specify separate amounts for compensation, costs, attorney fees, and other items. The total amount of the offer controls the comparison. There is little point in denying a Rule 68 award because the offer was greater than the final judgment in one dimension and smaller—although to no greater extent—in another dimension. If the offer does not specify separate amounts for each element of the final judgment and award, the same comparison is made by matching any specified amounts and treating the unspecified portion of the offer as covering all other amounts. For example, a defendant's lump-sum offer of $50,000 might be followed by a $45,000 judgment for the plaintiff. The judgment is more favorable to the plaintiff than the offer if costs, attorney fees, and other items awarded for the period before the offer expired total more than $5,000.

Comparison of the final judgment to successive offers requires that the judgment be treated as if entered at the time of each offer and adjusted to reflect any Rule 68 award that would have been made had judgment been entered at that time. To illustrate, a plaintiff's $25,000 offer might be followed by reasonable attorney fees of $15,000 before a defendant's $35,000 offer, followed by a $30,000 judgment. The judgment is more favorable to the plaintiff than the offer because a $30,000 judgment at the time of the offer would have supported a $10,000 fee award to the plaintiff. The judgment and fee award together would have been $40,000, $5,000 more than the offer.

Nonmonetary relief further complicates the comparison between offer and judgment. A judgment can be more favorable to the offeree even though it fails to include every item of nonmonetary relief specified in the offer. In an action to enforce a covenant not to compete, for example, the defendant might offer to submit to a judgment enjoining sale of 30 specified items in a two-state area for 15 months. A judgment enjoining sale of 29 of the 30 specified items in a five-state area for 24 months is more favorable to the plaintiff if the omitted item has little importance to the plaintiff. Any attempt to undertake a careful evaluation of significant differences between offer and judgment, on the other hand, would impose substantial burdens and often would prove fruitless. The standard of comparison adopted by subdivision (e)(4)(A)(ii) reduces these difficulties by requiring that the judgment include substantially all the nonmonetary relief in the offer and additional relief as well. The determination whether a judgment awards substantially all the offered nonmonetary relief is a matter of trial court discretion entitled to substantial deference on appeal.

The tests comparing the money component of an offer with the money component of the judgment and comparing the nonmonetary component of the offer with the nonmonetary component of the judgment both must be satisfied to support awards in actions for both monetary and nonmonetary relief. Gains in one dimension cannot be compared to losses in another dimension.

The same process is followed, in converse fashion, to determine whether a judgment is more favorable to a party opposing relief.

There is no separate provision for offers for structured judgments that spread monetary relief over a period of time, perhaps including conditions subsequent that discharge further liability. The potential difficulties can be reduced by framing an offer in alternative terms, specifying a single sum and allowing the option of converting the sum into a structured judgment. If only a structured judgment is offered, however, the task of comparing a single-sum judgment with a structured offer is not justified by the purposes of Rule 68, even when a reasonable actuarial value can be attached to the offer. If applicable law permits a structured judgment after adjudication, however, it may be possible to compare the judgment with a single sum offer. Should a structured judgment offer be followed by a structured judgment, it seems likely that ordinarily the comparison should be made under the principles that apply to nonmonetary relief, since the elements of the structure are not likely to coincide directly.

Multiparty offers. No separate provision is made for offers that require acceptance by more than one party. Rule 68 can be applied in straightforward fashion if there is a true joint right or joint liability. An award should be made against all joint offerees without excusing any who urged the others to accept the offer; this result is justified by the complications entailed by a different approach and by the relationships that establish the joint right or liability. Rule 68 should not apply in other cases in which an offer requires acceptance by more than one party. The only situation that would support easy administration would involve failure of any offeree to accept, and a judgment no more favorable to any offeree. Even in that setting, a rule permitting an award could easily complicate beyond reason the already complex strategic calculations of Rule 68. Offers would be made in the expectation that unanimous acceptance would prove impossible. Acceptances would be tendered in the same expectation. Apportioning an award among the offerees also could entail complications beyond any probable benefits.

Subdivision (f). Rule 68 does not apply to actions certified as class or derivative actions under Rules 23, 23.1, or 23.2. This exclusion reflects several concerns. Rule 68 consequences do not seem appropriate if the offeree accepts the offer but the court refuses to approve settlement on that basis. It may be unfair to make an award against representative parties, and even more unfair to seek to reach nonparticipating class members. The risk of an award, moreover, may create a conflict of interest that chills efforts to represent the interests of others.

The subdivision (f) exclusions apply even to offers made by class representatives or derivative plaintiffs. Although the risk of conflicting interests may disappear in this setting, the need to secure judicial approval of a settlement remains. In addition, there is no reason to perpetuate a situation in which Rule 68 offers can be made by one adversary camp but not by the other.

Notes

1. The impetus for consideration by the Civil Rules Advisory committee came from an article by Judge William W. Schwarzer, *Fee-Shifting Offers of Judgment—An Approach to Reducing the Cost of Litigation*, 76 Judicature 147 (1992). The draft Rule 68 appended at the end departs from Judge Schwarzer's proposal in some ways. The discussion in text likewise ranges beyond Judge Schwarzer's proposal. The core, however, is taken straight from it.

   The central provisions of Judge Schwarzer's proposal are adopted in S. 585, 103d Cong. 1st Sess., §3 (1993).
2. See *supra* note 1.
3. Both nuisance claims and "stonewalling" defenses may be reduced. Bringing suit on an unfounded claim is more likely to scare a profitable settlement if the plaintiff can impose greater costs on the defendant than the plaintiff must bear. An offer procedure that promises to transfer some of the defense costs to the plaintiff reduces this potential divergence of costs. Resistance to a valid claim based on knowledge that the costs of winning a judgment exceed the value of the judgment can be undermined by the same process.
4. There are too many articles to list. Among the good articles are Cooter & Rubinfeld, *Economic Analysis of Legal Disputes and Their Resolution*, 27 J. Econ. Literature 1067 (1989); Donohue, *Opting for the British Rule, or if Posner and Shavell Can't Remember the Coase Theorem, Who Will?*, 104 Harv. L. Rev. 1093 (1991); Donohue, *The Effects of Fee Shifting on the Settlement Rate: Theoretical Observations on Costs, Conflicts, and Contingency Fees*, 54 L. & Contemp. Probs. 195 (1991); Hause,*Indemnity, Settlement, and Litigation, or I'll be Suing You*, 18 J. Legal Stud. 157 (1989); Katz, *Measuring the Demand for Litigation: Is the English Rule Really Cheaper?*, 3 J.L. Econ. & Org. 143 (1987); Miller, *An Economic Analysis of Rule 68*, 15 J. Legal Stud. 93 (1986); Rowe, *Predicting the Effects of Attorney Fee Shifting*, 47 L. & Contemp. Probs. 139 (1984); Rowe & Vidmar, *Empirical Research on Offers of Settlement: A Preliminary Report*, 51 L. & Contemp. Probs. 13 (1988); Shavell, *Suit, Settlement, and Trial: A Theoretical Analysis Under Alternative Methods for the Allocation of Legal Costs*, 11 J. Legal Stud. 55 (1982); Snyder & Hughes, *The English Rule for Allocating Legal Costs: Evidence Confronts Theory*, 6 J.L. Econ. & Org. 345 (1990); and Toran, *Settlement, Sanctions, and Attorney Fees: Comparing English Payment Into Court and Proposed Rule 68*, 35 Am. U.L. Rev. 301 (1986).

   Articles focusing on earlier efforts to revise Civil Rule 68 include Simon, *The Riddle of Rule 68*, 54 Geo. Wash. L. Rev. 1 (1985); and Woods, *For Every Weapon, a Counterweapon: The Revival of Rule 68*, 14 Fordham Urb. L.J. 283 (1986).

5. Game theory is touched upon in several of the articles cited in note 4 above. Good examples of recent work in progress include David A. Anderson, *Improving Settlement Devices: Rule 68 and Beyond* (1993 ms.); Kathryn E. Spier, *Pretrial Bargaining and the Design of Fee-Shifting Rules* (1993 ms.)
6. Many experienced lawyers who have reviewed the draft of Rule 68 set out in the appendix have thought the scheme too complicated to administer. Although regular litigators would come to understand the complications, others might remain perplexed.
7. Of course official decision may be sought not to vindicate but to humiliate or intimidate. The value of establishing precedent by a test case may be tarnished by the ability of institutional litigants to select favorable cases and tribunals by settling less favorable cases. These facts diminish, but do not defeat, the value of public adjudication.
8. See *Marek v. Chesny*, 473 U.S. 1 (1985).
9. 28 U.S.C. §2072.
10. *Marek v. Chesny*, 473 U.S. 1 (1985).
11. One set of abstract distinctions comes readily to mind. Cases arise in which liability is clear and even conceded, but the amount of damages is uncertain over a wide range. In other cases the amount of damages is fixed but liability is quite uncertain. Yet other cases may present little uncertainty in either dimension, while still others defy rational prediction of the outcome in either dimension. It may be possible to reason through to a rule that applies only to cases with appropriate levels of predictability. Actual application of such a rule by determining the ranges of reasonable prediction in each case–presumably at the time of each potentially relevant offer–is likely to be difficult or impossible in many cases.
12. The 1984 proposal is reprinted at 102 F.R.D. 432.
13. The virtue of the sanctions approach in assuaging Enabling Act concerns is explored in Burbank, *Proposals To Amend Rule 68–Time To Abandon Ship*, 19 Mich. L. Rev. 425 (1986).
14. The proposal was advanced by petition of the State Bar of Arizona on August 19, 1993, *In re Rule 68, Arizona Rules of Civil Procedure,* Supreme Court No. R-93-0031. The petition was denied by Order, March 17, 1994. A summary of the proposal by Daniel J. McAuliffe is set out in Arizona Assn. of Defense Counsel, Winter 1993, p. 1.
15. *Erie R.R. v. Tompkins,* 304 U.S. 64 (1938).
16. 473 U.S. 1 (1985).
17. *Id.* at 11.
18. *Id.* at 9.
19. *Id.* at 28-38. The shortest statement was that: "The Court's interpretation of Rule 68 * * * clearly collides with the congressionally prescribed substantive standards of §1988, and the Rules Enabling Act requires that the Court's interpretation give way." *Id.* at 37.
20. The attempt to overrule *Marek v. Chesny* for claims arising under Title VII of the Civil Rights Act of 1964 is a good illustration. Section 9 of H.R. 1, 102d Cong., 1st Sess. (1991), would have amended §706(k), 42 U.S.C. §2000e-5(k), by deleting "as part of the," so that the statute would allow recovery of a "reasonable attorney's fee (*including expert fees*) *and* as part of the costs." The reasons for overruling *Marek v. Chesny* in this setting were

described in H.R. Rep. No. 102-40(I), Educ. & Labor Comm., 102d Cong., 1st Sess., p. 82 (1991), and H.R. Rep. No. 102-40(II), Judiciary Comm., p. 30 (1991). In the end, the Civil Rights Act of 1991 did not adopt the proposed amendment. New §706(g)(2)(B), 42 U.S.C. §2000e-5(g)(2)(B), however, does allow "attorney's fees and costs" to be recovered upon proof of a violation of §703(m), 42 U.S.C. §2000e-2(m). This is, to say the least, a subtle method of drafting.

21. See Schwarzer, *supra* note 1, at 152.
22. See Miller, *supra* note 4.
23. John Shappard of the Federal Judicial Center, who has worked for years with Rule 68 proposals, has designed a survey that should be completed soon.

Settling Cases: The Lawyer's Perspective

Robert N. Sayler*

I like this commentator role. It's fun; you get to pick on others. It also affords the perfect opportunity to plagiarize. A writer named Clarence Kellen once served as a commentator at a session just like this, with several presenters and a large distinguished audience. Kellen rose to his feet and said, "Now, ladies and gentlemen, the job of the commentator, I've been told, is to be so infernally dull that the presenters sound brilliant by contrast." And, Kellen went on, "Yet I've read the speakers' papers and now I've heard them. I can't do it." That, of course, only half applies. I promise I will be dull. I always am. But these characters don't need my help to appear brilliant. Their papers and their words speak for themselves.

I come here with a confession that I used to be a rule freak. I wholeheartedly subscribed to the notion that rules would assist the settlement process, would induce torrents of amicable accords from Maine to California. But now I'm a recovering rule freak. At the risk of some overstatement, I no longer think that judicial rules have anything to do with the settlement process–or at least not very much. Our session is entitled "The Dynamics of the Settlement Process." And there are dynamics to the settlement process. I just do not think they have much to do with rules. Here, instead, are Sayler's six simple-minded requirements for settlement. These are things that I think about when I'm trying to settle a case. I never look at the rules.

---

*Partner, Covington & Burling, Washington, D.C.

I should confess right off that I find the settlement process very taxing and difficult. I love to try cases, but I didn't lose my hair trying cases. I lost it trying to settle cases. Anyway, this is what I think it takes to get to "yes," to settlement. If you don't have these what I call "predictive indicators" in place, you usually will not get a settlement.

Requirement one: The parties must be anxious about the litigation process, either because they fear its cost, its time demands, the prospect of destroying future business relationships by fighting with natural friends, or because they fear the publicity, the fish bowl problem of going to war in public. If they don't feel anxiety, if the time isn't ripe yet, you have to devise a way to make them feel that stress. And it has to be perceived on both sides.

Requirement two: On both sides the real decisionmakers must be open to learning to trust the settlement process. That means the lawyer has to educate the client on his or her choices in a non-litigated settlement—anything from private settlement to binding arbitration—and to convince the client that there is an amicable resolution mechanism that makes sense. So there is a positive education process at work. But there is also a "dis-education" process. You have to "dis-educate" the knee-jerk reaction that many parties have that settlement, or any form of ADR, is for wimps. That feeling only gets worse once the litigation process has started: "they called me a name, this is too wimpy, I'm not going to do any of this settlement stuff because now I'm mad." So that's requirement two—an educable client.

Requirement three is that the process should be sought by both sides. Ideally, it should be *voluntarily* sought, but I have occasionally seen mandatory ADR work too. It surprises me when it does, but it does. Within the last three weeks, for example, $300 million dollars has changed hands in two cases I was involved in. In one my client paid, and in one my client received. In both cases, the parties did not want to mediate, but the judge ordered them to do so. And by the time we got to check-signing (the mediation only lasted two days in each case), the parties had come to trust the process.

It is far preferable if the trust is developed *ahead* of time; yet here the parties, the principals, the people with the checks, came to trust it by the second day. And, by golly, unsolvable, unsettleable cases, were resolved because the parties came to trust the process.

Requirement four is that lawyers are absolutely crucial to the process and dynamics of settlement. If the lawyers are constructive, settlement is often achieved. If the lawyers are *destructive*, you have to organize the settlement process so that each lawyer can get his message through to the *opposing* principal–for instance, forcing the principal to listen to a preview of the closing argument, to hear how the opponent's case will sound in court. If the opponent's lawyer has been filtering out the strong points of your case, it does a world of good to have the principal hear from the trial lawyer on the other side: "This is what this baby's going to sound like in court. It's going to be painful for you. There will be a lot of discovery. And here's what my closing argument is going to sound like."

You've now squeezed his lawyer out of the filtering process. At some point you may have to go a step further and take *all* of the lawyers out of the process. This may happen, for example, when the principals get together and really start talking dollars. Lawyers should not be in that room unless they're *both* constructive settlement facilitators.

The *fifth requirement* is a capable, experienced neutral–whether he or she is serving as a mediator (privately hired or court appointed), a non-binding arbitrator, or an early evaluator. That should, perhaps, be number one on the list: a respected, revered, experienced neutral, one who'll cause both sides to cock their heads and listen because they know that he or she brings objectivity and talent to the table. Remember this is the first neutral either side will see. Previously, the parties have just been listening to their lawyers. Now, finally, they get an unvarnished view.

And my *sixth requirement* is that the settlement process must be affordable. Much of middle income and poor America is involved in disputes that could be better resolved without war in court. Yet often these folks have to pay for the neutral–which means that often they don't have meaningful access to settlement services. I am presently head of the Litigation Section of the ABA, and we are about to announce a major pro bono project to make arbitration and mediation services available for free to those who cannot afford them. That should provide a useful push in the direction of promoting settlements.

Thus ends my sermon. I wish I could say that I support all the proposed changes to Rule 68. I support many of them in concept. Yet I am virtually certain that the plaintiff's bar and the public interest bar will not welcome them. They see changes of this sort as letting a camel's nose under the tent in the direction of the English rule. And most of the versions I have seen have problems. How in the world would the proposed rule work with contingency fees? How is it going to work in cases with multiple parties? How do you stop a defendant in the product liability context with 10,000 lawn mower cases from offering $10 in every case? Statistically, it knows it prevails on liability, say, 50 percent of the time. If so, doesn't the new rule produce the English rule half the time? In most formulations it would.

One could make a long list of problems like this that need to be solved. And when you've addressed them all, I fear that you have just engendered more satellite litigation.

Rule 68 and Settlement Dynamics

Larry Kramer*

The discussion began with consideration of some particular reform proposals offered by panel members. Professor Cooper was asked about the extent to which should judges would or should have power under Rule 68 to reject a settlement. Cooper answered that the Advisory Committee is considering a provision to amend Rule 68 and give the judge power in certain instances to reject a settlement. He offered the example of a settlement in institutional litigation that called for equitable relief that the court did not want to get involved in or thought was otherwise inappropriate. Cooper added that the Committee had not yet discussed whether to allow judges to reject an offer on the ground that the attorney's fees seem excessively large or extortionate.

Another audience member criticized Rule 68 for failing to address "cultural" factors involved in the practice of law today. We should, he urged, consider the fact that lawyers are comfortable engaging in brinkmanship and settling on the day of trial. And we need to worry more about the conflicts that arise between attorneys and clients when fee shifting becomes an important factor in litigation. More generally, the fee structure matters enormously and may impede the settlement process. Whether a client is paying by the hour or has a contingency arrangement makes a difference. A lawyer who is getting paid by the hour has a disincentive to settle early, because he needs to put some time in to make money from the case. This is true, moreover, for plaintiffs as well as defendants. In civil rights cases, for example, the plaintiff's

*Professor of Law, New York University School of Law

attorney wants to bill some hours and generate a fee before talking settlement seriously. Such factors have not adequately been taken into account in current proposals to amend Rule 68.

A third audience member questioned Professor Miller's proposal to appoint an "escrow agent" to take blind settlement offers. On the one hand, if (as Miller suggests) the parties are reluctant to make settlement offers because these have a signalling effect, and (as Sayler suggests) lawyers do not want to seem like "wimps," won't litigants be reluctant to make this kind of silent offer? On the other hand, to the extent that settlement offers are useful in providing information about the strength of a case, won't encouraging uncommunicated offers decrease their usefulness as a signalling device? Professor Miller responded by observing that, even if the lawyer *feels* like a wimp making an offer to the escrow agent, because no one else will know that an offer has been made, he or she won't *look* like one—which should eliminate this problem. As for the signalling effect of settlement offers, this should be unaffected: the existence of the escrow agent doesn't limit or affect the ordinary settlement process; parties can still communicate and make whatever offers they want through the usual mechanisms. The proposal to create escrow agent simply adds another route to settlement.

At this point, the discussion turned to the broader question of whether a provision like Rule 68 is desirable at all. Much of the audience seemed uncomfortable with the focus on fee shifting as the best way to encourage settlement. The real problems, they suggested, lay outside the fee system and should be dealt with directly. Three comments are illustrative. One of the judges in the audience noted—to considerable applause—that "most of the reform proposals and academic suggestions don't speak to the real issues facing judges, and they often have unforseen consequences that make things harder." While judges are of course concerned about the relation between litigation costs and settlement, this speaker explained, when and how a case settles is affected by when it will otherwise go to trial. Hence, adoption of the Speedy Trial Act had tremendous effects on civil settlements, since implementing the Act made it nearly impossible to hear any civil cases for almost a year. The general point, he concluded (deliberately overstating the case), is that nothing will happen in settlement unless and until we can give people a firm trial date; the process won't even begin in earnest until the lawyers and the parties know when they might have to go to trial. Yet the reform proposals do not deal with this problem at all.

A second comment from another of the judges identified two important factors in settlement that "haven't received enough attention." First, there is the risk and imminence of loss: "someone who is going to be hanged in the morning is more concerned about settling a case than someone who isn't." Second, there is the problem of assuring that someone with authority is present to negotiate: settlement discussions will go nowhere unless someone who can write checks is present to make decisions. The speaker described an experiment undertaken by the judges of his court. They required insurance companies to send someone who could make binding commitments to negotiate, and they instructed this representative to make the same offer he or she would make on the day of trial—with the promise that (if reasonable) this offer would cap recovery. Within a year, the court eliminated the glut of tort cases on its docket, settling 82% of the outstanding cases. The court went from one of the most backlogged in the state to second best. The key, according to this speaker, is to approach settlement pragmatically by adopting rules that force parties to take settlement seriously and insure that persons with real authority are present to talk settlement. Proposals like Rule 68 don't do this.

Robert Conason, a practicing lawyer who participated as a member of the panel, replied that a system based on active judicial participation won't work in the federal courts because federal judges don't know tort law and don't like tort cases. As a result, federal judges are reluctant to get heavily involved in common law tort litigation and make poor mediators. Given this attitude, Conason concluded, the proposal to provide a firm and early trial date may be the best change we can make in the federal system. A different audience member responded that Conason must be thinking mostly about older judges and that more recent appointees are a lot more willing to get involved in the settlement process. (He might have added that state tort cases are hardly the cause of any backlog in the federal system and that the problems associated with settlement should be approached in light of the general run of cases.)

Pointing in a somewhat different direction, a third audience member observed that the real solution to the litigation problem is in substantive reform. "Unfortunately," this speaker noted, "the whole process is impeded by the irrationality of Congress." Consequently, efforts at substantive reform in the product area have been futile. Damages caps and fee-shifting alternatives came up against powerful opposition and so went nowhere. A recent proposal—the Rockefeller/Danforth proposal—may do better because it has features that appeal to both plaintiff's bar and industry. But there's no particular reason to think that this proposal—which provides, among other things, that defendants can't be liable for more than $50,000 in attorney's fees—constitutes a substantive improvement. If the proposal is politically palatable, "it is not for fancy theoretic reasons," but just because it seems to be happening that way. "We've got to remember that any substantive reform proposals must pass through the world's biggest sausage factory: the U.S. Congress." These comments are, of course, all the more telling in light of the 1994 midterm elections and the torrent of reform proposals currently under consideration in Congress.

For the most part, these criticisms of Rule 68 seem correct. Making this formerly modest litigation tool an important factor in the litigation and settlement process (by turning it into a conditional fee shifting device) is a mistake. The goal seems less to encourage settlement than to encourage *early* settlement, or at least earli*er* settlement. I doubt that this is or should be an important objective. But even if it is, Rule 68 is a poor means to that end. For in the rush to make the parties reach agreement sooner, we have created another tactical device that encourages gamesmanship with no reason to believe that we are getting more or better settlements. Presumably both parties are willing to settle when they feel that they have enough information to do so. Rule 68 simply alters the strategic playing field, shifting the advantage to whichever party is in a better position to make an early evaluation. We should allow each party independently to gather enough information to make a comfortable decision about settlement before holding a gun to its head (or worse, before holding a gun to the lawyer's head and creating a conflict between lawyer and client). If the problem is discovery abuse, we should address it directly and as such.

Part II
Trial:
Science in the Courts

The Age of Science may have begun a very long time ago, but it only recently became a problem for courts. Most new developments in science did not bear much on the trial process, and the discoveries or inventions that did were carefully regulated under the *Frye* rule – the requirement, announced in 1923 by the D.C. Circuit in *United States v. Frye*,[1] that scientific evidence be admitted in court only if "generally accepted" by the relevant scientific community. This grudging test assured a long lag time between new science and its use in adjudication. Equally important, *Frye* shifted responsibility for determining admissibility (through a kind of virtual representation) to the scientific community itself. Judges were not asked to make judgments about scientific validity, but merely to listen passively to the "relevant scientific community." Hence, polygraphs were out, fingerprints in, spectrographs out (in most courts), ballistics evidence in. And it all seemed easy.

A number of developments conspired to undermine *Frye*. Science grew more complex and less self-confident. It lost the sure sense of objectivity that it had carried into the 20th century, and it splintered into a myriad of sub-disciplines and sub-specialties. No longer could one easily say what the relevant scientific community was, much less whether that community had "generally accepted" a given technique or methodology. These developments, in turn, complicated the judge's task by forcing him or her to look more closely at evidence and make judgments about whose views counted, and why. At the same time, there was a veritable flowering of scientific techniques that could be used in court: blood group testing, *in vitro* and *in vivo* studies, epidemiology, cell structure comparisons, DNA fingerprinting, statistics, and so on. The amount of science used in courtrooms today is vastly greater, and more complex, than it was, say, in 1975.

Why 1975? Because that's when the most important development took place: enactment of the Federal Rules of Evidence. Under these rules, "all relevant evidence is admissible" (Rule 402), including scientific knowledge "[i]f it will assist the trier of fact to understand the evidence or to determine a fact in issue" (Rule 702). Nothing here about "general acceptance" or deferring to the "relevant scientific community." On the contrary, the conspicuous absence of such language appeared to call *Frye*'s continuing viability into question, at least in federal courts. Lower courts were soon divided on the question.[2]

The Supreme Court, in the meantime, stayed silent for nearly 20 years. Then, finally, in 1993, the Court stepped forward to announce that *Frye* is indeed dead, that it did not survive adoption of the Federal Rules. The timing of *Daubert v. Merrell Dow Pharmaceuticals, Inc.*[3] is particularly significant. The increasing use of scientific evidence in courts has given rise to a chorus of complaints about how much of it is "junk" and how greater judicial vigilance is required.[4] One might have expected such concerns to generate calls for a reinvigorated version of *Frye*, telling judges to make sure there really *is* general acceptance. Instead, commentators urged courts to be less passive in evaluating experts called by the parties, to step in and exercise independent judgment.

Whether motivated by the language of the Federal Rules of Evidence, by a perceived need to increase judicial scrutiny, or by both, the Court responded, replacing *Frye* with a new test. To decide whether a proffer of scientific evidence meets the requirement of Rule 702, the trial judge must now make "a preliminary assessment of whether the reasoning or methodology underlying the testimony is scientifically valid and of whether that reasoning or methodology properly can be applied to the facts in issue."[5] Speaking through Justice Blackmun, the Court elaborated (solely by way of illustration) and recommended that trial judges look at such considerations as whether a technique is falsifiable, whether it has been subjected to peer review, whether its error rate is known, and (an old friend) whether it has achieved general acceptance in the scientific community. The critical shift, of course, is the shift from having judges examine whether scientists accept a technique to having judges examine the technique's validity themselves.

Daubert is thus a very important decision—the first (and, for a time at least, probably the last) word we have from the Supreme Court about how science should be treated in the courtroom. In this Part, therefore, we explore the meaning and implications of *Daubert* for trial and appellate practice.

We begin with a general discussion of the case. Professor Rochelle Dreyfuss organizes and introduces the issues. As she points out, these cover a very broad range. Some are mundane: Who really won? Others are interpretive and procedural: How broad is the holding? Is it more restrictive or more liberal than *Frye*? How should courts apply its factors? What kind of procedures should be used to determine admissibility? Will these be costly and time consuming? Still other questions are institutional or epistemological: How much deference should judges give to scientists? Can we keep questions of scientific validity separate from substantive questions, like the allocation of responsibility? Who is better able to determine the meaning and usefulness of science? Do science and law even share a sense of meaning or utility? Do they share a sense of truth and objectivity?

Professor Dreyfuss's introduction is followed by the transcript of a roundtable discussion of these issues, moderated by Professor Arthur Miller (a veteran of such discussions and master of the format). The participants include a mix of judges, both state and federal, trial and appellate; lawyers from both sides of *Daubert*; leading practitioners from the plaintiff and defense bars; legal academics in the fields of procedure, evidence, and science and the law; and scientists. Skillfully led by Professor Miller, they engage in a lengthy debate of the questions posed by Professor Dreyfuss, together with some others that came up in the course of their deliberations. The conversation is lively and engaging, and remarkably candid— including some heated exchanges on issues like how judges should handle scientific evidence in the future and what this is likely to mean for the parties.

Because it is an unplanned conversation, the roundtable discussion is not perfectly linear. Accordingly, Professor Margaret Farrell, who served as reporter for this portion of the Conference, has added a piece that synthesizes and organizes the major themes and conclusions of the session. In addition to providing a concise description of the positions taken, Professor Farrell includes additional citations to the relevant literature and offers her own observations to help broaden the readers' perspectives.

While the roundtable discussion is fascinating and informative, its format precludes the participants from demonstrating their points in detail or offering substantial support. Accordingly, we have rounded out this Part with articles from two of the nation's leading scholars on evidence and the use of experts.

Professor Sam Gross analyzes the intricate, often deceptive, relationship between rules of evidence and rules of substance. This was a topic that came up repeatedly in the panel discussion. While generally approving of *Daubert*, Professor Gross argues that the Court failed to address the structural problem that caused the difficulty in the first place. The rules of evidence governing expert testimony, he explains, must be understood against a background of procedural rules that disfavor overturning a verdict on grounds of insufficient evidence: so long as some evidence was admitted on both sides of an issue, judges are reluctant to take the case away from the jury.

This rule of deferential review does not prevent judges from making substantive decisions about the merits of science-based claims. Rather, it drives them to disguise these decisions as questions about the admissibility of evidence: by excluding evidence on the ground that it lacks scientific merit, they render one side's case unsupported, which makes dismissal easy. Nowhere is this tendency more evident than in mass toxic tort cases, like *Daubert*, where the same scientific issue may be litigated time and again in different courts on the basis of similar or identical evidence. In an appendix to his article, Professor Gross canvasses the post-*Daubert* decisions to show the persistence of this problem and to identify emerging patterns in the case law.

Professor Gross argues that judges should make substantive decisions on science-based claims—at least in cases like *Daubert*, where the scientific proof points strongly toward one conclusion. They should do so, moreover, openly and directly as a form of common lawmaking or "legislative fact finding." Unfortunately, many cases are not easy, and this method cannot be used in all cases where scientific issues are in dispute. In these harder cases, Gross concludes, the only general method for courts to use in improving their treatment of scientific evidence is to obtain reliable expert information from non-partisan sources outside the normal adversary process, e.g., to use court appointed experts under Rule 706.

Professor Joseph Sanders, known in this field for his superb work on the Bendectic litigation, looks at a different set of questions. Scrutinizing the new test articulated in *Daubert*, Professor Sanders addresses two questions that will face judges attempting to apply the decision: (1) What approach should courts employ in assessing the admissibility of expert scientific opinion? (2) Given this approach, how restrictive should courts be in allowing expert opinion into evidence? In the course of answering these questions, Professor Sanders offers useful guidance on some of the difficult issues that lie ahead.

With respect to the first question, Sanders notes that the heart of *Daubert*'s approach to admissibility is its understanding of scientific validity. Unfortunately, Sanders explains, the Court fails to recognize that scientific validity has multiple meanings and is always a matter of degree. Sanders elaborates by describing four dimensions of scientific validity recognized among scientists: statistical conclusion validity, internal validity, construct validity, and external validity. He illustrates different ways in which each of these types of validity may be threatened.

With respect to the question of how restrictive courts should be in keeping evidence from juries, Sanders criticizes *Daubert* for providing too little guidance and no realistic examples of how to apply its new standard. He explores this question himself, using the evidence on Bendectin to test what *Daubert* actually implies. Some of the most restrictive admissibility determinations in recent years, including *Daubert* itself, have occurred in cases involving Bendectin. Sanders re-examines several of these cases, in which the court excluded the plaintiff's expert testimony, under the scientific validity standard that seems appropriate after *Daubert*. He concludes that most of the rulings are questionable under that standard.

Finally, Sanders considers two explanations for the judicial propensity to exclude scientific evidence: achieving judicial efficiency, and improving jury decisionmaking. The former explanation is especially salient in the mass tort context, where the same expert evidence is repeatedly presented. The latter explanation, in contrast, is relevant in all cases that involve complex scientific data.

Although these are reasonable objectives, Professor Sanders (like Professor Gross) concludes that restrictive evidentiary rulings should not be a primary means for achieving them. Excluding evidence is particularly ill-suited to control the flow of information to juries in this context. First, it is difficult, if not impossible, to achieve consistency across cases. More important, marginal science is not the primary reason juries have trouble with scientific evidence anyway. The real problem, as common sense and a number of studies show, is the way in which the evidence is presented. Adversarial litigation is a poor method for presenting intricate and complex ideas. By the time an opponent has finished deconstructing whatever conclusions an expert offered, the jury may or may not be persuaded, but it will almost certainly be confused and/or bored to distraction. Professor Sanders thus concludes by proposing some modest alternatives to assist the fact finder in understanding and weighing the testimony in complex cases. These, he suggests, may serve better than overly restrictive evidentiary rulings.

Notes

1. 293 F. 1013 (D.C. Cir. 1923).
2. Compare, e.g., *United States v. Shorter,* 809 F.2d 54 (D.C. Cir. 1987)(applying *Frye*) with *DeLuca v. Merrell Dow Pharmaceuticals, Inc.*, 911 F.2d 941 (3d Cir. 1990)(rejecting *Frye*).
3. 113 S. Ct. 879 (1993).
4. See, e.g., Peter Huber, *Galileo's Revenge: Junk Science in the Courtroom* (1991).
5. 113 S. Ct. at 2796.

Implications of *Daubert v. Merrell Dow*

Rochelle C. Dreyfuss*

Through its 1993 decision in *Daubert v. Merrell Dow Pharmaceuticals, Inc.*,[1] the Supreme Court set the stage for considerable controversy in cases involving technologically complicated issues. Although *Daubert* formally presented a fairly narrow question concerning the extent to which the Federal Rules of Evidence displaced common law, the case touched on broader concerns: the relationship between science and law, and the influence of scientists in society. Thus, the effect of the Court's decision will surely extend beyond the tort dispute in which it arose and the confines of federal court. What follows is a short discussion of *Daubert* followed by a survey of the broader questions it raises, focusing in particular on the role that scientists ought to play in determining how courts utilize their input.

I. The *Daubert* Case

Daubert began with the birth of two children with limb reductions. The mothers, who had taken Bendectin to control nausea during their otherwise-uneventful pregnancies, sued Merrell Dow Pharmaceuticals, Bendectin's manufacturer, claiming that the birth defects were caused by the drug. Bendectin had been the target of similar litigation since 1977, which was also the year the first of at least 30 epidemiological studies of its teratogenicity was published. None of the published studies found

*Professor of Law, New York University School of Law.

a relationship between Bendectin and birth defects. Accordingly, earlier cases were generally won by the manufacturer.[2]

The *Daubert* plaintiffs persisted nonetheless. In response to a motion for summary judgment, they offered, through the testimony of cxpert witnesses, three proofs of causation: (1) in vitro and in vivo animal studies which tended to show a correlation between Bendectin and malformations; (2) a structural analysis of Bendectin demonstrating its physical similarities to substances known to produce birth defects, and (3) a statistical study conducted by Dr. Shanna Helen Swan, a biostatistician employed by the California Department of Health and Services as chief of the section that determincs causes of birth defects. Dr. Swan had reanalyzed prior epidemiological studies with a new methodology and had reached conclusions at odds with the earlier studies.

The trial court granted the defendant's motion, and the Ninth Circuit affirmed in a terse opinion by Judge Alex Kozinski.[3] The court reasoned that the plaintiffs could not succeed without some epidemiological evidence demonstrating a connection between Bendectin and birth defects. Such a study is admissible only if it meets the standard of *Frye v. United States*:[4] its scientific basis must "be sufficiently established to have gained general acceptance in the particular field in which it belongs."[5] Although the Ninth Circuit agreed that reanalysis is a generally accepted technique, it considered it accepted "only when it is subjected to verification and scrutiny by others in the field. . . . " Dr. Swan's reanalyses were excluded because they "do not comply with this standard; they were unpublished, not subject to the normal peer review process."[6] The opinion concluded with a quote from Peter Huber's book, *Galileo's Revenge: Junk Science in the Courtroom*: "[t]he best test of certainty we have is good science—the science of publication, replication, and verification, the science of consensus and peer review."[7]

The Supreme Court granted certiorari on the question whether the Ninth Circuit was right to rely on *Frye*, or whether *Frye*'s admissibility standard had been superseded by the Federal Rules of Evidence, in particular by Rules 402 and 702.[8] In a partially unanimous decision written by Justice Blackmun, the Court vacated the Ninth Circuit decision, holding that, given the "Rules' permissive backdrop," *Frye*'s "austere standard" had been replaced. The case was remanded to reconsider the admissibility of the Swan reanalyses.

Over a partial dissent by Chief Justice Rehnquist (which Justice Stevens joined), Justice Blackmun went on to offer some "general observations" on how the lower courts should consider "purportedly scientific evidence."[9] To decide whether the proffer is the kind of scientific knowledge that "will assist the trier of fact" as required by Rule 702, the court must make "a preliminary assessment of whether the reasoning or methodology underlying the testimony is scientifically valid and of whether that reasoning or methodology properly can be applied to the facts in issue." A nondefinitive checklist was provided:

(1) Whether the theory or technique can be (and has been) tested—a concept the Court referred to as falsifiability.
(2) Whether the theory or technique has been subjected to peer review and publication.
(3) The known or potential rate of error and the existence and maintenance of standards controlling the technique's operation.
(4) General acceptance in the scientific community.

The Court also noted that Federal Rule of Evidence 703 limits expert testimony on otherwise inadmissible hearsay to facts or data "of a type reasonably relied upon by experts in the particular field," that Rule 706 permits the court to choose an expert of its own, and that Rule 403 permits the exclusion of relevant evidence whose "probative value is substantially outweighed by the danger of unfair prejudice. . . . " Finally, the Court emphasized that courts retain their powers under Federal Rules of Civil Procedure 50(a) and 56 to enter judgment as a matter of law when the evidence is insufficient to establish the plaintiff's case.

II. Points for Discussion

Is there a problem, what are its dimensions? *Frye* was premised on the notion that the evidence of a scientist-expert poses a special problem for the judicial system because its validity is difficult to evaluate and its apparent objectivity overwhelms lay jurors. In 1923, when *Frye* was decided, this perception was possibly correct. It is not so clear that it is correct today: most people likely to serve on juries received some science education in school. Moreover, the public is better acquainted with scientific materials now than in 1923: weather reports have been replaced by meteorological summaries; recipes come with complete nutritional analyses; computers are commonplace. Scientists' views have shifted on enough issues (for example, the safety of coffee and the advantages of weight loss) for most people to have developed a healthy skepticism of the insights of science.

Nonetheless, critics across the political spectrum have argued that the use of science in judicial decisionmaking continues to present special dangers. In the tort context, the claim is best exemplified by Peter Huber's book, cited by the Ninth Circuit. Huber and other tort reformers argue that the easy admissibility of evidence of questionable scientific value has imposed heavy costs on industry, which has been found liable (or settled) in cases where the prevailing view of the scientific community is that the evidence does not support the plaintiff's claim. The Bendectin question at issue in *Daubert* is one example; others include claims that trauma causes cancer, that spermicides cause birth defects, and that mistakes in delivery cause cerebral palsy.[10] Huber claims to be a scientific positivist, who believes that genuine scientists are in the business of discovering truths about how the world genuinely works. Even though the people whose testimony he opposes often hold traditional credentials,[11] Huber frames the *Daubert* issue in terms of finding a way to distinguish between the mathematicians, chemists, and astronomers he believes should be permitted to testify, and the cabalists, alchemists, and astrologers that he thinks have been allowed to testify based on (what he calls) a scientific relativist approach, which holds that "culture and context determine everything" and that therefore "anything goes."[12]

Other commentators, notably Dorothy Nelkin and Laurance Tancredi, have questioned the use of scientific evidence for other reasons. They claim that courts are often drawn to science because it provides easy, quick answers that are seemingly neutral and therefore not easily criticized. In their view, science in the courts is changing social norms, often in the absence of serious debate. Examples include the use of various brain-function tests such as Positron Emission Tomography (PET) scans instead of the M'Naghten Rule, which alters the concept of criminal responsibility; and use of DNA fingerprint evidence as dispositive proof of paternity instead of Lord Mansfield's rule, which alters the relative importance of nature and nurture in child custody determinations.[13] In some ways, these critics are relativists because they do believe that science is culturally driven. However, they are not relativists in Huber's sense, for they appear to agree with him that scientific research yields important insights into how the world works, insights that can be taken as true. Rather, their concern is that the questions scientists choose to explore are socially determined and that the larger society gives interpretive effect to what their research uncovers. They see the admission into evidence of even "good" science as potentially problematic, because it is often accorded significance beyond its point of demonstration.

Where are we now? On its surface, *Daubert* opens the courts to evidence formerly held inadmissible. *Frye*'s general acceptance test had long been criticized as creating a lag between the time that new understandings are achieved in science and the availability of these insights to the judicial process.[14] After all, general acceptance can take time. Overruling *Frye* presumably frees courts to admit information at the cutting edge of science. *Daubert* relied heavily on *United States v. Downing*,[15] a Third Circuit decision by Judge Edward Becker premised precisely on the fact that *Frye* is inconsistent with the spirit of the Federal Rules of Evidence, with their liberal "helpfulness" standard and flexible approach.

Another view is, however, possible. Despite the fact that the Court called *Frye* "austere" and characterized the Federal Rules as "permissive," the checklist the Court provides sets up a standard that is harder to meet than some applications of *Frye*. *Frye* was, as Judge Becker noted in

Downing, rather malleable. Many *Frye* courts required acceptance only within that part of the scientific community that could be expected to have experience with the work. So long as a "cottage industry" in a field developed, courts could find a community accepting the test.

Conversely, the *Daubert* factors are difficult for many—if not most—scientific work to meet. The fourth factor simply reimports *Frye* and its attendant problems.[16] The other factors also create substantial obstacles. The first relies on terminology—"falsifiability"—that many scientific disciplines do not expressly utilize. Some of the "hard" (natural) sciences such as physics and chemistry proceed by observation and explanation.[17] They do not use the social science technique of putting forth a falsifiable hypothesis which they then construct a controlled experiment to prove or disprove. Astronomers and epidemiologists lack the capacity to do controlled research—they must rely on observation. Theoretical physics, which deals with waves and particles too small and too fast to see, is not verifiable at all. In all of these disciplines, what "counts" as a good theory is one that is predictive. Of course, it could be that the Court meant predictivity when it said "falsifiability." But, as Justice Rehnquist pointed out in his dissent, the Court's meaning is not at all clear.[18] Moreover, predictivity is a criterion uniquely unsuited to courts, which must make decisions based on what is known now, not on how well a theory accommodates the findings of future experiments.

The Court's second criterion—peer review—is similarly problematic. Not all scientists publish all their work; publication can take a long time. Publication may depend on factors other than the intrinsic validity of the research, such as the stature of the authors and the extent to which the topic of the work is "in fashion" in academic circles. More important, in their own work scientists do not limit their thinking to things that have been peer-reviewed: only those very far out of the loop learn new findings from journal articles. Ironically, work is usually validated by scrutinizing the underlying raw data and the experimental methodology—exactly the kind of reanalysis that Dr. Swan conducted. Finally, cases of fraud and plagiarism demonstrate that peer review is not infallible.[19]

This aspect of *Daubert* can also be criticized for failing to distinguish between peer review of a theory or technique and peer review of its application in a particular case. A preference for peer review of the theory or technique (in this case, reanalysis) makes some sense, because it allows the court to take the scientific community's views on methodology into account. But requiring peer review of the specific application (here, Swan's paper) is extraordinarily limiting, especially for litigants whose specific cases have not attracted widespread interest among scientists.

The Court's third criterion, which refers to the maintenance of standards controlling the technique's operation, is troublesome for much the same reason as peer review. First, very new techniques need time to attract organizations to maintain standards. Techniques developed specifically to test plaintiff's claim are especially unlikely to have such support. Second, the existence of a standard-maintaining organization should not be as important as whether standards were, in fact, maintained when the technique was used to generate the data proffered in the case.

Although *Daubert* does not claim to contain an exhaustive list of factors to consider in deciding whether to admit evidence, certain omissions seem particularly surprising. Judge Becker's *Downing* decision, for example, spoke not only of the error rate, but also of the direction of error and whether it favors the proponent or the adversary of the evidence.[20] *Downing* also suggested other indicia of reliability: nonjudicial uses to which the technique is put, the existence of a specialized literature, the relationship between the technique and established modes of analysis, and the qualifications of the witness. The latter inquiry could be enlarged, as Margaret Berger has suggested, to include a look at the qualifications of the people opposed to use of the technique and the strength of their views.[21] Berger would also look to whether the expert witness is prepared to discuss uncertainties, and whether both sides have comparable access to the data.

Furthermore, *Downing* put a great deal of emphasis on the "fit" between the information sought to be introduced through scientific testimony and the actual issues in the case. Fit was not an issue in *Daubert*, but there are certainly cases where the scientific evidence introduced alters the ultimate issues in the case. The cases that Tancredi and Nelkin are concerned with, for example, are as much about fit as about reliability.[22]

Where does Daubert apply? The "fit" question brings up another issue: does *Daubert* apply to all uses of novel scientific evidence? Does it apply only in the toxic tort context in which it arose? To the criminal context in which *Frye* arose as well? Kenneth Chesebro has done an exhaustive survey of the *Frye* literature showing that the "general acceptance" standard it enunciated was used almost exclusively in criminal cases.[23] Chesebro concludes that the problems worrying Huber were not caused by jurisdictions having abandoned the *Frye* rule.

Of course, Chesebro's analysis cannot determine whether Huber's concerns, or the problems articulated by other critics of scientific evidence, can be *cured* by *Frye* or *Daubert*. That depends in part on the answer to the previous question—how strictly is *Daubert* to be interpreted? It will also depend on how flexibly it is interpreted—on how seriously lower courts take Justice Blackmun's statement that he is not setting out "a definitive checklist or test," and on whether they see the criteria that are enunciated as requirements that must be met in every case.

Some observers of the science problem take the position that different issues, and different disciplines, raise disparate concerns. In *Daubert*, for example, it was clear that if the statistical evidence was reliable, it was relevant to the causation issue. In some cases, the "fit" is not so easily determined. For example, no matter how accurate DNA tests are, the results of such tests are relevant to custody cases only if it is genetics that are dispositive of the question who should care for a child. Especially for older children, perhaps nurture is more important than nature. The relevant question is thus the extent to which the scientific findings are congruent with other social norms embedded in the law. Conversely, there may be cases where the fit is so very tight, the absence of some *Daubert* criteria should not prevent the utilization of a new technique in court.

Another aspect of the scope problem was noted in Justice Rehnquist's dissent: the Court does not indicate whether its general observations apply only to "scientific knowledge" or to other types of expert knowledge as well. Rule 702 speaks of "scientific, technical, or other specialized knowledge." Is there a difference between scientific and technical knowledge?

Daubert's relationship to substantive policies. Daubert is a good example of a claim often made by the so-called scientific relativists that debates over the admissibilty of scientific evidence can obscure core policy questions. Thus, the argument that epidemiological evidence is necessary to win a product liability case, when coupled with the requirement that there be consensus within the scientific community on the study proffered by the plaintiff, is really a claim that tort liability should be allocated only on the basis of fault, and then only when the fault is considered probable by an elite group of decisionmakers. That claim deserves to be parsed and debated directly.

One could, for example, certainly argue that allowing juries to decide cases on the basis of questionable evidence will, in effect, lower the burden of proof on the issue of fault; that this lower burden will impose high costs on research and development firms; and that these high costs will discourage innovation to the point where suboptimal levels occur. Casting the debate in such terms allows society to confront questions about the optimum level of innovation and how to achieve it. Similarly, rather than blindly imposing a high standard for admissibility that limits who can be found liable, it is worth thinking about whether tort liability should be based only on fault, or expanded to include other goals, such as risk spreading, deterrence, and allocating costs to the cheapest cost avoider.[24] In like manner, it is well worth considering whether society wants to defer to scientists as heavily as *Daubert* contemplates. The technical nature of the data makes deference seem desirable, but the data are not complete and they are often ambiguous. Are scientists more expert than lay people in dealing with uncertainty and ambiguity?

Centralization of scientific decisionmaking. As noted above, *Daubert's* emphasis on peer review and general acceptance accords to the scientific establishment a special role in the social order, a role that will grow if the trend favoring use of novel scientific evidence continues. Whether one views this as progress depends on whether one views science as apolitical, objective, and neutral. But *Daubert*'s thrust also raises another question, namely whether it makes sense to centralize decisionmaking in the hands of any one group. That is, there is a flavor in, for example, the Bendectin-generated literature that *Daubert* should be decided in favor of the manufacturer because Merrell Dow won so many previous cases. It is as if it is a pity that plaintiffs are not issue-precluded by these prior cases or by the fact that the health care establishment has already converged on the decision that Bendectin does not cause birth defects.[25] This claim can be examined in two ways.

First, is the convergence story an accurate picture of science? While the notion of a scientific community building toward consensus has some truth to it, it represents only part of the story. Sociologists like Thomas Kuhn distinguish between periods of "normal" and "extraordinary" science.[26] During periods of normal science, most scientists spend their time solving problems that are raised by the prevailing theories and paradigms in their field. They rarely replicate (or falsify) earlier work because doing the necessary experiments is costly and unlikely to earn them the recognition achieved by publishing new and original research. Moreover, the thrust of research in normal periods is to *reconcile* empirical observations to the theories with the prevailing view—with the theories to which the researchers (and the dominant scientists in the field) are already intellectually committed. Eventually, however, these theories become so distorted by attempts to reconcile new observations, that a revolution occurs. It is during these extraordinary periods that old ideas and work are reviewed with critical skepticism and fresh ideas are proposed. Eventually, a new paradigm emerges—although for a time, only the younger scientists accept it while older scientists continue to defend the earlier view. The scientific community eventually does coalesce around the new paradigm, but it can take a generation to do so.[27]

It is important to see that in neither period is the consensus-building mechanism of science very useful in determining the significance that courts should accord to scientific evidence. During the normal phases, scientists tend to ignore or explain away observations that fail to fit the prevailing wisdom. A litigant who is challenging the results of that wisdom is not likely to find a community that will support the proof she offers. During the extraordinary periods, however, everything is up for reexamination and reexplication. At such a time, it makes no sense to defer to scientists since they too are in disagreement. Indeed, it would violate both the letter and the spirit of res judicata law to ascribe certainty to any particular view: the spirit because the law generally does not give to the decision of any decisionmaker more effect than that decisionmaker would give it itself,[28] and the letter because our current understanding of due process is that every litigant gets its own day in court.[29]

Second, even if the *Daubert* view is correct, even if the scientific community is identifiable enough for *Daubert* to apply easily, even if science is apolitical, objective, neutral, and wholly benevolent, concentrating decisionmaking in the hands of the scientific community is worrisome. Individual scientists are not accountable to the public for the way they set their research agendas, nor are there mechanisms to require funding organizations (including government) to favor particular research projects. Women, for example, have only recently begun to realize how little work has been done on health care issues of unique concern to them. Tort litigation can be viewed as establishing a market for research results—that is a mechanism to register demand for, and procure supply of, research on topics of public concern.[30] Indeed, tort reformers such as Sheila Birnbaum criticize use of a strict liability standard in product cases precisely because it is not as good as a negligence standard in encouraging firms to conduct safety research.[31] Before litigation is slowed by giving special deference to the scientific community, alternative mechanisms for consumers of research to influence the supply of this product need to be developed.

Notes

1. 113 S. Ct. 2786 (1993).
2. For a full analysis of these cases, see Joseph Sanders, *From Science to Evidence: The Testimony on Causation in the Bendectin Cases*, 46 Stan. L. Rev. 1 (1993).
3. 951 F.2d 1128 (9th Cir. 1991).
4. 293 F. 1013 (D.C. Cir. 1923).
5. *Id.* at 1014. *Frye* held inadmissible expert testimony based on the forerunner of the modern polygraph.
6. 951 F.2d 1129, 1130 (1991).
7. Peter Huber, Galileo's Revenge: Junk Science in the Courtroom 228 (1991).
8. Fed. R. Evid. 402 provides: "All relevant evidence is admissible. . . . " Fed. R. Evid. 702 provides: "If scientific, technical, or other specialized knowledge will assist the trier of fact to understand the evidence or to determine a fact in issue, a witness qualifed as an expert. . . . may testify thereto in the form of an opinion or otherwise."
9. *Daubert*, 113 U.S. at 2796.
10. In addition to *Galileo's Revenge*, Huber has written on this issue in Huber, *Junk Science in the Courtroom*, 26 Val. L. Rev. 724 (1992), and Huber, *Medical Experts and the Ghost of Galileo*, 54 L. & Contemp. Probs. 119 (1991).
11. For example, Dr. Swan, the statistician in the Daubert case, holds a Ph.D. from, and a faculty appointment at, the University of California at Berkeley. She is chief of the section of the California Department of Health and Services that determines causes of birth defects, and she has consulted for the World Health Organization, the Food and Drug Administration, and the National Institutes of Health. *Daubert*, 113 S.Ct. at 2792 n.2.

12. Huber, *supra* note 10, 54 L. & Contemp. Probs. at 119, 122-23.
13. Dorothy Nelkin & Lawrence Tancredi, Dangerous Diagnostics 136-41, 155-58 (1989); Rochelle Dreyfuss & Dorothy Nelkin, *The Jurisprudence of Genetics*, 45 Vand. L. Rev. 313 (1992).
14. "Society need not tolerate homicide until there develops a body of medical literature about some particular lethal agent." *Coppolino v. State,* 223 So.2d 68, 75 (Fla. App. 1968)(concurring opinion), cited in Giannelli, *Frye v. United States*, 99 F.R.D. 188 (1983).
15. 753 F.2d 1224 (3d Cir. 1985).
16. In his comprehensive article, *The Admissibility of Novel Scientific Evidence:* Frye v. United States, *a Half-Century Later*, 80 Colum. L. Rev. 1197 (1980), Paul Giannelli noted the following problems: identifying the appropriate field that must accept the procedure, deciding which features of the technique or theory must be accepted, establishing general acceptance, deciding where *Frye* applies, determining the scope of appellate review, and deciding whether the information generated by the technique or theory is relevant to the issues in the case.
17. See, e.g., R. Feynman, R. Leighton & M. Sands, The Feynman Lectures in Physics 2-1 (1963).
18. "I am at a loss to know what is meant when it is said that the scientific status of a theory depends on its 'falsifiability.'" *Daubert*, 113 S.Ct. at 2800.
19. See, e.g., *Bill Would Set Fraud Guidelines for Scientific Publications*, 242 Science 187 (1988).
20. Consider, for example, the question of admitting evidence from an identification test, such as DNA fingerprinting, which demonstrates that the defendant committed the crime. If this test is known for many false negatives, but few false positives, it may be more probative than a test with a lower error rate, but which has more false positives than false negatives.
21. Margaret Berger, *Symposium on Science and the Rules of Evidence*, 99 F.R.D. 187, 231 (1983).
22. Nelkin & Tancredi, *supra* note 13, at 37-43.
23. Kenneth Chesebro, *Galileo's Retort: Peter Huber's Junk Scholarship*, 42 Am. U.L. Rev. 1637, 1693-94 (1993).
24. To be sure, Huber has entered the debate on these issues as well, see e.g., Peter Huber, The Legal Revolution and Its Consequences (1988); Peter Huber, *Safety and the Second Best: The Hazards of Public Risk Management in the Courts*, 85 Colum. L. Rev. 277 (1985).
25. See, e.g., Huber, *supra* note 10, 26 Val. L. Rev. at 724. See also Green, *Expert Witnesses and Sufficiency of Evidence in Toxic Substances Litigation: The Legacy of Agent Orange and Bendectin Litigation*, 86 Nw. U.L. Rev. 643, 679 (1992)("some courts' opinions suggest substantial reliance on these prior decisions and their determinations as the basis for concluding that plaintiffs have no case because of a dearth of causation evidence"). Green notes that courts were also heavily influenced by the conclusion of a review panel of experts convened by the Food and Drug Administration that "available data do not demonstrate an association between birth defects and Bendectin." Department of Health and Human Services News, No. P80-45 (Oct. 7, 1980).
26. See, e.g., T. S. Kuhn, The Structure of Scientific Revolution (1962). See also Rebecca Eisenberg, *Patents and the Progress of Science: Exclusive Rights and*

Experimental Use, 56 U. Chi. L. Rev. 1017 (1989)(discussing how scientists work); Black, *A Unified Theory of Scientific Evidence*, 54 Ford. L. Rev. 595 (1988).

27. Kuhn, *supra* note 26, at 77-80, 90. See also Ian I. Mitroff, The Subjective Side of Science 61-73 (1974); Barber, *Resistence of Science to Scientific Discovery*, 134 Science 596 (1961). Cf. Michael J. Mulkay, The Social Process of Innovation: A Study of the Sociology of Science 34-45 (1972)(noting the influence of new fields in redirecting theory).
28. See, e.g., Restatement (Second) of Judgments §26(b); cf. *Marrese v. American Academy of Orthopaedic Surgeons,* 470 U.S. 373 (1985).
29. *Martin v. Wilks,* 490 U.S. 755 (1989).
30. Kenneth Chesebro, for instance, has documented the relationship between litigation and research on a variety of products, such as tobacco and lead. See *supra* note 23 at 1680-85. Recent litigation on the safety of silicone-filled breast implants are a current example of the phenomenon. Chesebro also notes that reexamination of Bendectin through litigation was preceded by publicity surrounding other drugs marketed by Merrell, notably Thalidomide and MER/29, both of which turned out to pose serious health risks. *Id.* at 1672-73.
31. Sheila Birnbaum, *Unmasking the Test for Design Defect: From Negligence [to Warranty] to Strict Liability to Negligence*, 33 Vand. L. Rev. 551, 645 (1980)(also discussing the effect of changing the basis for tort liability from fault to risk-spreading).

A Panel Discussion of *Daubert v. Merrell Dow*

Moderated by Arthur R. Miller*

LINDA SILBERMAN: Arthur Miller was my Procedure teacher when I was a law student at the University of Michigan some 28 years ago. He left Michigan for Harvard where he was also Dean Sexton's Civil Procedure teacher, which I guess might be some evidence of the inspiration and mentor he has been for so many who were his students. To many of the judges, of course, Arthur is best known as a name author of the leading practice and procedure treatise, Wright, Miller, Cooper & Kane. And to anyone interested in civil justice reform, his recently completed tenure as chief reporter of the ALI Complex Litigation Study is noteworthy. The lay public knows Arthur from his various media appearances, as he has tried, I think more than anyone, to translate law from the technical world in which we as professionals see it to a way that can be comprehended by an ordinary individual. In similar roundtable format, Arthur has taken on a whole host of issues in law, ethics, journalism, and politics–leading discussions with experts in these fields. As busy as he is, Arthur has been a wonderful friend of the law school and of IJA, and he has come in the summers to help us with the Appellate Judges' Seminar. And he's joined us for one of those discussions today, this time on the role of scientific evidence in the courtroom.

We have also a wonderful group of experts to talk with Arthur. First, *Judge Edward Becker* of the U.S. Court of Appeals for the Third Circuit, whose approach to the problem of scientific evidence is relied upon by

---

*Bruce Bromley Professor of Law, Harvard University Law School.

the Supreme Court in the *Daubert* case. Judge Becker serves on the Long Range Planning Committee of the Judicial Conference. He's been a great friend to IJA, participating in our summer seminars and helping us plan our programs.

Professor Margaret Berger of the Brooklyn Law School is the reporter to the newly created Advisory Committee on the Federal Rules of Evidence. Professor Berger is also co-author, with Judge Jack Weinstein, of the leading evidence treatise. And she wrote the *amicus* brief of the Carnegie Commission in the *Daubert* case.

Sheila Birnbaum is a partner at Skadden, Arps, my former colleague, and a former law professor here at NYU. She is now practicing the subjects she used to teach–products liability, toxic torts, and insurance coverage litigation.

Kenneth Chesebro, a graduate of the Harvard Law School, is a specialist in appellate and constitutional litigation. He was lead counsel for the plaintiff in the *Daubert* case in the Supreme Court.

Rochelle Dreyfuss is a professor of law at NYU. Professor Dreyfuss is a former scientist herself at Ciba-Geigy. She teaches civil procedure, patents, and issues of science and law, and she has prepared an outline of many of the issues raised by *Daubert*, which you have in your materials.

Dr. Leon Gordis is a professor and epidemiologist at the Johns Hopkins School of Medicine. He's also chair of the committee on access to research data of the Society for Epidemiological Research.

Peter Huber, a senior fellow at the Manhattan Institute, is both a lawyer and a scientist. He was an associate professor at MIT before he went to law school. He's the author of numerous books, including *Galileo's Revenge: Junk Science in the Courtroom*, which has attracted extensive commentary and helped focus attention on the issue of scientific evidence in the courts.

Paul Marsden, a partner at Dixon, Carlson & Campillo, has broad litigation experience in legal malpractice and pharmaceutical product defense. He was attorney for the defendant Merrell Dow in California. So we have everybody here who played a role in the *Daubert* case.

Richard Meserve is a partner at Covington & Burling and a Ph.D physicist himself. Mr. Meserve's practice involves issues of substantial technical content, such as environmental and toxic tort litigation and nuclear licensing. He was on the brief of the National Academy of Sciences.

Dorothy Nelkin holds a University Professorship at NYU, where she's a professor of sociology but also teaches in the law school. She is the author of numerous books, including *Controversy: The Politics of Technical Decision*, and her research focuses on controversial areas of science, technology and medicine and the relationship of science to public policy.

Mel Weiss, name partner at Milberg, Weiss, is a securities, trial, and appellate lawyer of national renown.

Our reporter over there, *Margaret Farrell*, teaches at Cardozo Law School in the fields of health care and law and medicine. Professor Farrell has just completed a year long fellowship at the Federal Judicial Center, where she prepared for judges a manual on science and technology dealing with the reliability of different types of scientific evidence.

Judge Becker asked me earlier, Arthur, whether you had the Marquis of Queensberry rules for this discussion. So I'll turn it over to you.

ARTHUR MILLER: Thank you, Linda. It's always a pleasure to be at NYU, as an old New Yorker. Sometimes I think I spend more time here than I do in Cambridge, but that's because faculty meetings are so much fun up there.

What are we going to do? Well, several of the panelists asked me that a few minutes ago. You see, we have not met. The next two hours will be completely spontaneous. Nothing is rehearsed. Where we are going, I don't think we know. But we'll look back at 4:00 p.m. and see where we've been. I've told the panelists that I'd like this to just be a bull session about scientific evidence, particularly the aftermath and the future, now that we have *Daubert*. And they've been invited to speak anytime they feel like speaking. There are microphones strewn about in this room, and the room isn't so big that if anyone in the audience wants to participate and speak he or she should hesitate to join us. Indeed, you're really invited to join us so that we have sort of a bull session of the whole, so to speak. So, please, join in whenever you hear something particularly offensive.

Now, I'm a procedurelist, supposedly— at least Linda keeps reminding me that I was her teacher. And John, I think, would just as soon forget about that, now that he controls the casebook he was taught from. I'm not an evidence type. So I start this discussion with a very benign question, which I'll ask Ken Chesebro. Who won?

KEN CHESEBRO: We did.

ARTHUR MILLER: You did. Why?

KEN CHESEBRO: Because the 9th Circuit threw out the case, affirming summary judgment on the ground that the *Frye* rule had not been met, and we got cert and had it unanimously reversed.

ARTHUR MILLER: Hmm. That sounds very legalistic to me. Everybody knew the *Frye* rule was dead. So isn't that sort of a Pyrrhic victory?

KEN CHESEBRO: Well, seven days before *Daubert* came down, the 7th Circuit said, "There's a lot of dispute about this *Frye* rule, but we love it and we intend to keep on using it." So I think it's only in retrospect— once Merrell Dow and the Solicitor General abandoned *Frye* because the arguments were simply too weak to support it—that everybody says it's a non-event when the Supreme Court overrules a judge-made evidence rule that's been followed for 70 years. But the more important. . . .

ARTHUR MILLER: You feel defensive about that, I sense. People are saying, "Ken, you are the biggest non-event of the year," huh?

KEN CHESEBRO: Basically, yeah. I think it gives you some perspective if you think about the lay of the land a year before the *Daubert* ruling. The more important holding in *Daubert*, frankly, and I guess it's not a holding, is the court's statement that the subject of Rule 702 is the scientific validity of the methodology and the principles relied upon by the expert in addressing a question for the jury. And the focus is solely on the experts' methodology and not on the conclusions that they generate. And that's a distinction that Bert Black laid out in a 100-page article in 1988, his seminal article in the Fordham Law Review,[1] where he said you've got to look at the scientific reasoning process and have a unified theory that recognizes that we have questions about the validity of the methodology that an expert uses, and then you have to look at the reliability of the conclusions that are generated by applying that methodology. And that was the distinction that the *Christophersen* en banc panel focused on in analyzing evidence,[2] and it's the distinction the Court analyzed in coming to that final conclusion—that we want to look at the methodology under 702, but not at the conclusion.

ARTHUR MILLER: Paul, do you think he's telling us a straight story?

PAUL MARSTEN: Look, if you're asking who won, I know it's a rude thing in the company of lawyers, but there are two clients here, one is Jason Daubert, the other is Merrell Dow Pharmaceuticals. And so far as I know, no check has changed hands yet, and I will show how reckless and irresponsible I am by saying that I don't expect any check will change hands. I don't think Jason Daubert is going to get paid. We don't know that yet. So far only lawyers have won in this case, but when the reckoning comes down, I think Merrell Dow will win this case.[3]

ARTHUR MILLER: Well, do you want to try that now?

MAN: Well, I'd be delighted to. With apologies to Ken, he didn't finish his statement from last night where he said that he may have won 9 to 0, but Merrell Dow may have won 7 to 2. I suspect that at the end of the day, we'll find that although *Frye* no longer defines the test, those who favor having judges act as gatekeepers to prohibit the admission of unreliable scientific evidence will prove to be victorious. And I think, for example, if you take a yellow highlighter and compare the briefs on the Merrell Dow side and on the Daubert side with the opinion, you'll find a lot more highlighting of the Merrell Dow briefs than of Ken's excellent work.

ARTHUR MILLER: This is wonderful. This is like Rashoman. Three speakers, each with a different perspective, not only on who won, but on how you measure who won. With one saying no check has passed, one using a yellow highlighter to see how many words the court took from which briefs. . . . What do you think, Dick? You were one of the supposed neutrals.

RICHARD MESERVE: Well, I think in the narrowest technical sense the petitioner got a 9-0 decision. But if the test is whether the Court adopted the legal principle that each of the parties was striving to attain, one would conclude that the respondent won the case. I thought at the time, and still believe, that the petitioners were swinging for the fence by arguing that the sole question for a federal judge is whether a given witness is an expert, and once he is recognized as an expert there are no restraints on the opinions that he or she can offer. The Court very clearly held that the trial judge has an obligation not only to screen as to whether somebody is an expert, but also to examine whether the opinion itself is admissible. And I think that issue, which was the core issue to my clients, was clearly resolved in favor of the respondent Merrell Dow.

ARTHUR MILLER: Sheila?

SHEILA BIRNBAUM: Well, having read most of the briefs but not having been in the lawsuit, I don't have to worry about who won. But I think. . . .

ARTHUR MILLER: Are you asserting that you're neutral?

SHEILA BIRNBAUM: No. But I think the decision is going to be used mostly by defendant-manufacturers because it does something that's quite important, especially in the federal courts. It has brought the issue to the fore and made the judge as gatekeeper. We are going to see *Daubert* hearings, we're going to see *Daubert* in limine motions, we're going to be seeing *Daubert* summary judgment motions. This case is going to have enormous ramifications in the litigation of a whole host of cases, and it is going to be used mainly by defendants to try to keep what Peter Huber has always called junk science out. And now they have a great deal of ammunition to do that based on *Daubert*.

ARTHUR MILLER: Margaret, you, I know, are neutral on this.

MARGARET BERGER: I did write a brief that I thought was neutral. I think the great thing about *Daubert* is that it swept away the cliché of the *Frye* opinion, which I always thought was so popular because it was written like a cliché, though it had very little substance behind it. Looking at the cases, I could never find any appreciable difference between courts that said they were following *Frye* and courts that said they weren't. They simply attached the appropriate label when they were done and repeated the clichés from *Frye*. What's useful now is that we have a new starting point, and I think it's too early to see really how that will be developed completely, but I think there are real problems.

ARTHUR MILLER: Well, how would you describe the starting point?

MARGARET BERGER: Well, actually. . . .

ARTHUR MILLER: The word "gatekeeper" has been used twice now.

MARGARET BERGER: Yes. I would say that, although this is an opinion that talks about rules of evidence throughout and is seen as an evidentiary opinion. This will ultimately have to turn into much more of a procedural and substantive opinion. I think it is unworkable unless we figure out procedural mechanisms to help courts make these determinations; I think it will depend on some preliminary procedural mechanisms. And I think ultimately the appellate courts will have to develop substantive rules of law about what sufficiency means in categories of case.

ARTHUR MILLER: Now Judge, loosely speaking, you're Father *Daubert*, because your Third Circuit opinion was certainly instrumental in the court's thinking. What do you make of this? Did they do you justice? You know who "they" are.

JUDGE EDWARD BECKER: They paid me a compliment by essentially adopting the rationale of *Downing*.[4] But taking off from the previous discussion, I don't think we're starting from scratch. And I don't think (unlike the Phillies being in the World Series) that it's a great big deal, because we've essentially had this regime in the Third Circuit since January of 1985, when *Downing* came down. Most of what I've read subscribes to the "Chicken Little" theory—that the sky is falling and all of this junk science is now going to get in. That's what most of the literature has said. This afternoon we've heard the other view. In terms of our experience in the Third Circuit, it has not caused that many ripples. First of all, even though *Daubert* will be cited in all of these cases—because in any case involving expert opinion it's the lead case—it's only going to be in a very small percentage of cases that it'll make any difference. I surveyed the district judges in the Third Circuit and asked, "have you ever had these kinds of problems?" Most of them said no. It's been in the toxic tort cases, since it arises whenever you've got epidemiological problems as to toxicity and causal relations between chemical agents and various injuries. But that's about it. And even in those cases, the Chicken Little theory should be disproven by the district judge's opinion in *DeLuca*, which is a carbon copy of *Daubert*.[5] We remanded the case to District Judge Garrett Brown of New Jersey, because he didn't follow the *Downing* procedures—that is, he didn't have an in limine hearing, develop evidence on scientific reliability, and make findings. The lawyers then did their homework; the judge did his homework, and he filed a lengthy opinion with about 60 or 70 findings of fact, basically applying the *Downing* standards (which are essentially the same as the *Daubert* standards). He found that the expert opinion lacked scientific reliability and threw it out, and the Third Circuit affirmed that opinion.[6] So that, it seems to me, may justify Mr. Marsten's confidence as to what will happen in *Daubert* itself. I don't know. But the short of it is that we have a regime which puts the lawyers and the judges to the test, which says develop a record, have an in limine hearing on reliability. The judge will then make findings, and it will go from there. The world hasn't come to an end.

ARTHUR MILLER: I love that. It's no big deal, huh? Not like the Phillies being in the World Series. Just proving once again that life is perspective. Because if you're from Atlanta, it is a very big deal. Professor Nelkin, do you think it's a big deal?

DOROTHY NELKIN: Well, I was particularly interested in this case's calling attention to the increasingly complex relationship between science and law. And I was particularly struck, even amused, by the effort to import the peer review system from the arena of science into the legal arena, particularly at a time when peer review is under attack within the scientific community. Just the other day someone said that PR stands not for peer review but for public relations. So that peer review, which is understood at this point not to be the talisman of truth within science, but a kind of convention, is now looked on as a kind of talisman of truth in the legal arena. And that's the dimension that interests me.

ARTHUR MILLER: Are you saying that to some degree the two disciplines (treating law and science as if they are two disciplines, though we know that they are actually hundreds of disciplines) are still talking past each other?

DOROTHY NELKIN: I think that they're talking past each other in certain respects. To look to science to resolve certain problems overlooks that there are many issues that come before the courts on which science really has nothing to say. For example, a lot of the toxic torts deal with fetal harm. There's been a ban on fetal research for eight or nine years now. Scientists know very little about it, although I'm sure you could find scientific experts to testify. So there's a lot for which science really has no relevance to the court. And also science doesn't deal very well with issues if there's really genuine uncertainty; it's not a solution. So I like the *Daubert* decision in the sense that it places more responsibility on judges as gatekeepers.

ARTHUR MILLER: To be judges.

DOROTHY NELKIN: To be judges.

ARTHUR MILLER: And Dr. Gordis, how do you react?

LEON GORDIS: Well, first of all, let me say that I'm the token scientist here, or at least one of them. So it's a minority opinion in this august body. But I'm glad to be here. I'm more optimistic about the peer review system. Let me say that there is no better system, at the moment, that I know of for evaluating science, whether it's in research proposals or published results. And until we have something better, I think it's the one we have to use. And I don't think it's inappropriate for courts to consider it among other factors. I think there are areas where science may have less to contribute. But to me the critical issue is, in those areas where science has something to contribute, how do you use the evidence and how do you make that evaluation? That's going to be done by judges, and it seems to me that an important issue is how can we equip judges to be better able to handle scientific evidence? I've had the pleasurable experience now of teaching epidemiology to federal judges on several occasions. And I think it is possible to introduce the basic concepts of scientific methodology to a group of judges who are motivated because they're dealing with toxic tort decisions or other relevant areas. And perhaps with the formalization of this in the Supreme Court ruling—making it so explicit in terms of the role of the judges—perhaps we have to address further what specific steps should be taken for providing educational opportunities for judges to better equip them to carry out their responsibilities.

ARTHUR MILLER: I sense you're optimistic.

LEON GORDIS: Always.

ARTHUR MILLER: Always. You're not a wee bit concerned that this has just a touch of brain surgery self-taught. Unleash judges, God bless them, on the scientific method and they'll have it screwed up in a week, won't they?

LEON GORDIS: Well, as a non-lawyer, non-judge, let me say that when I look at the content, I mean, there are basically four components that were articulated for the role of the judges. Peer review still plays a role. General acceptability plays a role. I think it's not so explicitly stated as an all-or-nothing issue, and it is left to a subjective decision on the part of the judges. But I think it's a reasonable approach. What I guess is particularly gratifying to me is that the Supreme Court did not take what might have been an easy approach and hinge things on statistical significance. Statistical significance is one of the great misinterpretations of the legal system, and I think too much weight is put on that in deciding the adequacy of scientific evidence. That might have been an easy crutch, and so I was delighted to see that it was not used.

ARTHUR MILLER: Rochelle, the judge says it's not a big deal. Margaret, whose job with the evidence committee means that she's going to bear some of the burden of developing procedures, suggests that we've got to do a lot here. What's your take on the impact of this case?

ROCHELLE DREYFUSS: Well, the judge touched on another point that I think worth thinking about: how far is *Daubert* going to go? What kinds of cases is it going to apply to? I think in the toxic tort area it is kind of a straightforward application, and having the judge act as gatekeeper seems to me to be a very valid way to go about it. I don't like juries in general and taking a little bit more away from them is a good thing, just to touch on part of yesterday's conversation. But I do think that it's possible that this nifty little test, which can be stated so nicely, and for which there'll be wonderful procedures that Margaret will soon write, might start worming its way into other areas and might be applied to other kinds of cases where I'm not so sure that I'll be happy about its application.

ARTHUR MILLER: Since we're just talking generally at the front end of this discussion, give us some sense of the dimension, of these other areas that you have in the back of your head.

ROCHELLE DREYFUSS: Well, in this particular area the question was, did Bendectin harm this child? What kind of evidence could we possibly have on that issue? Medical evidence. And so it seems quite right that you would look at the best medical evidence you have, and this would be the way in which to decide the question of causation. But there are lots of other kinds of cases in which one might have scientific evidence, but it might not be so clear that that is really the linchpin of how the question ought to be decided. Questions about whether criminal responsibility should be placed upon somebody when that person claims to have brain dysfunction, for example. It's quite easy to look at tests for brain dysfunction, apply a *Daubert* analysis and say, "Wow, admissible evidence," without asking the question, "Wait a minute? Do we think that brain disfunction is a sign that somebody shouldn't be criminally responsible for the deeds that have been committed?" Scientific existence is being used, for example, in paternity cases—I think this is even a rather non-controversial use of scientific evidence. We determine whether somebody is the child's biological father, and then we turn around and say, "Well, that's the father" in cases in which the child might have been living with some other man whom that child considered to be his father. And suddenly that father is no longer the real father, the other father is the real father. These are situations in which we have a scientific way to think about the problem, the relationship between a child and its parent. We have a scientific way to think about the relationship between a person's activity and their mental capacity. But that might not be completely congruent with the way that the law thinks about it. And I'm afraid that *Daubert* might mask other questions that the legal system would normally ask.

MARGARET BERGER: Actually, I don't agree, because I think that one of the things *Daubert* does by cutting off admissibility from sufficiency is to refocus attention on the fact that the rule of law that governs the case is not necessarily the same as what might lead something to be an item of evidence. And I think that in the toxic tort cases too, the question of medical evidence really does not necessarily answer the basic question of whom does our system want to compensate.

ROCHELLE DREYFUSS: Yeah, I actually think that's true too. I think in some ways *Daubert* is a good example of that, and it's a question of allocating the burden in a situation in which we don't know the right answer. Simply admitting the evidence isn't really the way to do that. That's true. I can see the two thoughts.

ARTHUR MILLER: I sense in Rochelle's earlier remark that she's fearful of an abdication, a policy abdication—that under the mask of the scientific method and scientific evidence we'll stop asking who should be the father and just say "the science tells us that X is the father." Is that really a risk? Do you think these able-bodied judges are just going to look at Dr. Gordis and say, "you decide."

LEON GORDIS: No way. Never in a million years.

ARTHUR MILLER: Never in a million years?

LEON GORDIS: Absolutely not. I don't think there's any risk that there'll be an abdication of the basic decision making. The question is, what's going to be the foundation on which that decision is made? In *Daubert*, the issue is, does this drug cause this phenomenon, both generally and in this particular case? And the consequence of answering that question then leads to the decision. But the answer to the question is not the decision. I think it's very unlikely that the phenomenon of *Daubert* is going to start to drive scientific judgments down the throat of the law, but rather it's going to give the law a basis for delimiting the area in which a specious suit will be able to have other broader implications. I did want to mention, though, talking about the ambit of what *Daubert* is going to apply to, that it's been cited about 50 plus times since then, including by Judge Joiner who was sitting by designation on a Court of Appeals. I have yet to see it used to authorize the admission of evidence, at least in the kind of cases we've been talking about. The most interesting application of it was in the criminal prosecution of John Gotti, where they actually permitted an organized crime family expert to testify, including about the role of his lawyer, Mr. Cutler. And just as an aside, there's this great exchange between Gotti and Cutler, where Gotti is expletive deleting him about his attorney's fees and saying, "You're plucking me for these dah-dah-dah attorney's fees." Then the organized crime family expert came in and testified on the relationship between the capos and the lieutenants and it was very interesting to then see that, "okay, I mean, you laid the foundation about how this person knows this." And they cite *Daubert* as authority for it. That really surprised me. In the other cases, the toxic tort and pharmaceutical liability cases, I note, true to my prediction, that *Daubert* has so far been used to exclude some evidence on very important public policy issues, like the liability of manufacturers for childhood vaccines (which has been an issue that the Clinton Administration addressed at the front end of their discussion of health care reform).

ARTHUR MILLER: Mel, if I know anything about you, I would guess that something Rochelle said probably hit a raw nerve, namely, that any time you can take something away from a jury that's a good thing. In other words, to Rochelle, the only good jury is a dead jury. And I know you don't think that way.

MEL WEISS: I made a list of winners and losers. I'll just read it to you. The first winners are the plaintiffs, because the pendulum stops swinging against them, at least that was my perception. The second winner is the defense bar because they get to charge a lot of hourly fees in bringing these issues before the bench. And, of course, the plaintiff's attorney is usually working on a contingency so the statement before that the lawyers won is only half true. The third winners are the scientific experts who are going to get a lot of money for testifying. On the loser side is the jury system. That was the first one I had on my list. And, of course, that depends upon the persuasion of the judge. But I see an erosion of the role of the jury as the trier of fact, not only in this field, but in my primary field, the securities field. The plaintiff with an individual claim is a loser, because the cost of this kind of procedure is going to be enormous. Before, you had one issue, and it was basically whether this was the majority view in the medical field. Now you have to cover all bases: there's all kinds of different tests that the court's going to look at, so you have to hire multiple experts just to get the issue resolved. The judicial system is a big loser, because the judges are going to be horribly burdened with this gatekeeper task. And the final and best loser, is Peter Huber of the Manhattan Institute, because they wanted to kill us dead and they didn't.

PETER HUBER: Could I, at least as Peter Huber and not perhaps for the Manhattan Institute, say that I have a wife who is six months pregnant at the moment, and I have certain sort of intimate familiarity with morning sickness, perhaps more so than many people in this room. I think there are a lot of other losers, and I'd just like to extend the list. While I think Merrell Dow will not pay—after all, *DeLuca* has already been decided two or three times and once in the post-*Daubert* environment. If the Third Circuit is going to do that, I think the Ninth will find a way. We'll see, I mean, I could be wrong. But at the same time, I think it is essentially inconceivable that Merrell Dow will ever bring back a morning sickness drug to the U.S. market. No manufacturer with any assets at all will *ever* market a morning sickness drug again in the United States—at least not in the foreseeable future, I will say two decades. It just will not happen. And this is regardless of what the FDA says about the drug, regardless of how much the drug may be used anywhere else in the world. It will not be marketed in the United States. I'm willing to make these predictions. I can be proved wildly wrong and declared a loser yet again. I hope I will be since I plan to have more kids. But the fact is, there's still something badly wrong with our system if my statement is right. I'd be very interested to hear the plaintiff's lawyer flatly make a prediction on *Daubert*. I seem to be the only one who's willing to talk about Jason Daubert. And, secondly, assuming that Merrell Dow wins and wins and wins, as it has been winning, will anybody ever market such a drug again in this country? I think the fairly confident answer is that they won't, which tells us that there's something wrong with a legal system that simply cannot give a yes answer regardless of what evidence may be out there.

SHEILA BIRNBAUM: Just in response to Mel, it's not going to be any more expensive for plaintiffs who've needed these same experts and have already had to respond to defendants experts in front of juries rather than at a preliminary stage. In fact, if *Daubert* works as it should work, some of these decisions will be made earlier rather than later because they will be made on summary judgment motions, where a court can have a hearing. Now, yes, I think you're right, in fact, that fewer of these cases will go to the jury if the judges play their gatekeeper role and the science is like in Bendectin cases. It's fascinating when you look at Bendectin, the first big case that was tried was a scientific trial. And when the case was tried before Judge Rubin, you had six experts for the plaintiff, and six experts for the defendant. No "victims," no children who were deformed were in the courtroom. And on the question whether Bendectin could cause certain birth defects, the jury found for the defendant. When these same cases were tried one-on-one in other jurisdictions, such as Washington, D.C., there were verdicts of $25 million of compensatory and $75 million for punitive damages. They were all reversed by circuit courts, which said you can't find for plaintiffs under these circumstances, with 30 or 40 epidemiological studies that all show the same thing (no causal connection) against the testimony of a doctor who is relying on something that is scientifically weak. So the question is, should those cases still be in the court system and should the judges be playing this gatekeeper role? Some of us think they should.

MAN: I agree with Sheila that the system will work more efficiently and that you won't have endless mini-trials delving into all the evidence, but for a different reason. What happened in the D.C. circuit after that multi-district action, was that you had the *Richardson* case.[7] You had a trial, where all the experts used the same methodology: they looked at the animal in vivo and in vitro data, the chemical structure data, and the 30 or so, then it was 20, epidemiology studies. And the plaintiffs' experts looked at it and said, "The fact that you can't prove with 95% certainty from the epidemiology alone doesn't mean that Bendectin is safe. And we look at all the data, and we think it causes birth defects." And then you have a differential diagnosis about the particular plaintiff. But on the issue of general causation, they looked at all the data, and they thought that the animal data was pretty powerful and that the epidemiology didn't do much. The defense experts said, "No, no, we draw the conclusion that Bendectin is safe." So you had different conclusions from the same evidence, using the same conceivably valid methodology. And what happened was the trial judge decided that he agreed with the defense experts and disagreed with the those of plaintiffs. And on appeal that ruling was explained by the D.C. Circuit based on Rule 703. Rule 703 talks about reasonable reliance upon data. As the Supreme Court said in *Daubert*, Rule 703 lets the expert refer to hearsay sources without having to admit those hearsay sources in a laborious process. So what the D.C. Circuit did was to transform Rule 703, which is just an efficiency device for permitting the use of hearsay, into a rule that said, "Let's look at the conclusion of the expert and decide if it's reasonable for the expert to draw a conclusion that Bendectin is harmful from this data." And the thing is, the Court has said that you don't look at the ultimate conclusion of the experts—the same thing that the en banc Fifth Circuit said in *Christophersen* in holding that the nature of an expert's conclusion is generally irrelevant even if it is controversial or unique. Now the Court has said very clearly that if you have qualified experts that are relying on methodologies that, after a fact finding process, the judge determines are valid in general, then it's basically a matter of the sufficiency of the evidence. That's the way I see it. And I think that what caused all these endless pre-trial proceedings was the idea that judges should look at the weight of the ultimate conclusion to decide if it's a "misvote," which was a little unusual. And that whole process has played itself out. There'll be some new issues, of course.

ARTHUR MILLER: You want to respond to that?

MARGARET BERGER: Yes. I think that one has to remember what the Third Circuit *DeLuca* case looked like when it went back to the district court, which had a hearing on methodology and discovered that there were real methodological problems with some of the things the experts were testifying to.

MAN: Absolutely. Definitely. With one of the experts, correct.

MARGARET BERGER: Well, two of the experts, because one of the experts was relying on figures supplied by the first expert, and the first expert couldn't remember quite how he got to those figures- - which at times turned out to have been taken from preliminary studies, the authors of which had changed their minds in their final studies though the numbers hadn't been changed. I mean, there was a whole series of things. Now I think the difference between that and the D.C. trial, and what is so important about *Daubert*, is that now you have findings of fact from a judge looking at this as a preliminary matter on a summary judgment motion, whereas when you have a trial you get a jury with a general verdict at the end. If in a future case like Bendectin you had specific findings of fact from a judge, then I assume that when the next case comes up in another circuit, in another district, even in a state court, the judge could say to the expert, "Have you corrected these numbers? Now that you have substituted the correct numbers, what is the conclusion?" In other words, I'm not sure that you would have these cases go on and on the way they did in the Bendectin litigation. And therefore, I think we really may be at a different stage.

JUDGE JANE R. ROTH: I would like to voice the opinion that nothing has changed. Before *Daubert* if someone had asked me, "What is general acceptance?," I would have scratched my head and I would have said, "Well, has anything been published about this? Is there any peer review? Are there tests? Is there a predictable error rate? Are there maintainable standards?" Now you look at *Daubert* and that's what *Daubert* says. So *Daubert* has simply taken general acceptance, turned it inside out, and called it by another name. District court judges have been gatekeepers for years. When I was a district court judge, I said on a number of occasions, "this expert can't testify," or "this expert can testify about A but not B." I think the world is as it has been except the Dauberts have another chance, and that is the sum and substance of what happened.

MAN: Although I agree with almost everything that you said, from the standpoint of a defense lawyer one important difference is that, in the federal courts, many practitioners feel that once you get the letters after the name of a particular witness you don't have much more to evaluate. And that, I think, is a very positive result of this opinion. I agree with you: I think if there is any district court judge here who said that he or she did not feel like a gatekeeper, we would be quite surprised, because they rule on objections and overrule them and sustain them every hour of every trial. But now we have a very clear articulation that their job is to evaluate not only credentials but also methodology, and from the perspective of a member of the defense bar, that is a very encouraging aspect of the *Daubert* case.

ARTHUR MILLER: Well, if you put together the remarks of the two judges who have spoken, the least you can say about *Daubert* is that it's a codification of existing practice.

WOMAN: For some judges.

ARTHUR MILLER: For some judges.

MAN: Right, for some.

ARTHUR MILLER: And a wake-up lesson for the remaining judges?

PAUL CARRINGTON: I wanted first to report that there are amendments to the civil rules presently pending that fit this pattern to some degree, because what the Civil Rules Committee had in mind was a possible revision of Rule 702, but it also proposed revisions of Rule 16 and 26 that were designed to give the court an earlier opportunity to make rulings about the appropriateness of scientific and technical information. The Civil Rules Committee was also thinking about another dimension of this that the panel hasn't touched on, and I thought I might just mention it to see if anybody wished to speak to it. The Civil Rules Committee was not merely concerned with the reliability of scientific evidence, but also with its elaboration beyond the point at which it was efficient or just or appropriate given the expense to the parties and sometimes to the court. We were acquainted with some very long trials that were very long because of elaborate scientific testimony that in hindsight at least made us ask, "Why did we spend all that time listening to all that testimony when it really didn't matter very much?" And the Committee was concerned that, on occasion, elaborate scientific presentations are employed as a tactical device for wearing down the other side and imposing costs on adversaries. It was the belief of the Civil Rules Committee that district judges ought to accept some responsibility for that, not paramount perhaps, but at the margins, at least, it is appropriate for a district judge to say, "We're not going to spend two weeks inquiring into a particular scientific issue that's really not very important and ought not to affect the decision, at least not enough to go into it for two weeks worth." And I wonder if any members of the panel have any reaction to that kind of responsibility on the part of the court—to protect itself and protect the parties from getting overburdened with scientific and technical information?

MEL WEISS: Arthur, if I can just interject here because, you know, I have the *Stringfellow* litigation. It's my only excursion into this field away from the securities area. And when I hear people say it doesn't cost a lot of money to have one of these hearings, well, we had a *Frye* hearing in a state court in California in a case with 4,000 plaintiffs, not a class action. And we spent millions on that *Frye* hearing, between the plaintiffs and the defendants. A big part of it was on the plaintiffs' side, and the defendants took every opportunity, picking up on the last statement, to bring issues before the court for preliminary determination on scientific evidence. They wanted to wear the plaintiffs down, to make it costly for us, to find out what was in our heads and what was in our experts' heads prematurely, you know, out of the ordinary order of things in a complex litigation. It depends on the judge on whether they get away with it. And I'm afraid that this decision is going to open up the door for judges who have a bias against plaintiffs' cases to permit this tactic and make it extremely costly for us and maybe just grind us into the ground and to extract a settlement that's really much too low.

WOMAN: Mel, that was a case with 4,000 plaintiffs in it. I mean, isn't that what the defendant is supposed to be doing? I'm sure you're trying to extract from the defendants a whole lot of money by the fact that you've got 4,000 plaintiffs. Isn't that what the court's supposed to do? Listen to the scientific evidence if there is legitimate grounds to put the science in question?

MEL WEISS: But you just said if there's legitimate grounds, and what I'm suggesting is that this becomes a litigation tactic that becomes very, very expensive. And I think it's wrong to say that it's not expensive or that it's not any more expensive when you set the *Daubert* test against what judges were doing before, because *Daubert* opens the door up to all kinds of different considerations. The court went out of its way to say, "These aren't the only things you can look at. There are other things you can look at." Well, how many other things are you going to look at and what are the defendants going to dredge up for the court to look at in virtually every case—big and small? And what are the judges going to have to deal with?

ROCHELLE DREYFUSS: That's why I think Professor Carrington's point is a good one, because there is a question that *Daubert* mentions but doesn't address very explicitly, and that's the question of the relationship between what the science is going to prove and what the case is actually about. I think there probably are cases in which the scientific evidence is not going to prove very much, or the scientific evidence is pretty even on both sides. And rather than have a parade of experts either in a *Daubert* hearing or in front of the jury itself, one might instead say, "The science is pretty even, what's the burden of proof in this case?" What do we do when we deal with a case in which there is true uncertainty about the question of causation? And there might be ways in which, instead of looking at whether we're going to admit all of this evidence, we say, "Look, the scientists are in equipoise. There's some on this side, there's some on that side. Shouldn't we be dealing with these cases in a rather different way?" Or is the science question truly the question that's really at issue in this particular case? Sometimes I'm not sure it is.

JUDGE BECKER: Well, I think that *Daubert* did address that in applying the so-called fit requirement.

WOMAN: No, I think that's a very important requirement.

JUDGE BECKER: It is an important requirement, and I think it was addressed. But let's posit that *Daubert*'s going to apply in all kinds of cases and there are going to be great big cases where you're going to have great big hearings. I believe that I probably had the longest *Daubert*-type hearing ever in the *Japanese Electronics* case,[8] where I had six weeks of hearings morning, noon, and night on the admissability of the economics expert. . . .

ARTHUR MILLER: I hadn't realized it ended.

JUDGE BECKER: But most cases are not going to be like that. And in terms of the burden on the judge, bear in mind that busy judges are going to deal with this the same way they've been dealing with these things for years. A lot of times there's not going to be a formal hearing. It's going to be done by affidavits, by offers of proof, by stipulations, by introductions of learned treatises, all of which will be summed up in memoranda. Now, as an appellate judge, I'm not going to tell you that that stuff doesn't take an awful lot of time to read. It does. But we're talking *in terrorem* here, and across the board it's not going to be a burden in every case. If Mel Weiss has got 4,000 plaintiffs, well, a judge gets a case like that once or maybe twice in a lifetime, and it's going to require a great expenditure of time. But there aren't so many cases like that.

ARTHUR MILLER: Let me just get a point of information. Ed Cooper is sitting out there. He owns the Civil Rules Committee right now. Do you have a footnote on what Brother Carrington said before? Is there anything going on inside the Civil Committee that bears on this?

ED COOPER: Nothing in addition.

ARTHUR MILLER: Terse as always, Ed. Justice Neely?

JUSTICE NEELY: This is not my traditional balm, but I think it important to recognize something that we haven't mentioned here. And I feel a sense of moral obligation to mention it, given what I see going on, particularly in the federal courts, but also in some state courts. This *Daubert* decision is extraordinarily dangerous as it relates to criminal law. I was really outraged at the John Gotti example. The rules of evidence are driven primarily—driven with regard to hearsay, with regard to expert testimony—by the desire of the plaintiff's bar to get the issue to the jury without some Republican-appointed, federal gatekeeping judge to keep them from redistributing the wealth. Now, basically, the defendant's bar, politically, with the exception of Victor Schwartz, isn't worth a bowl of warm spit. The defendant's bar gets paid regardless—win, lose, or draw—and so the defendant's bar is not active *politically*. You can get a product liability bill through the Senate because Senators require large amounts of money, which is the one thing the defendant's bar can deliver. But you will never get it out of committee in the House, because House members have to deal with the shock troops of the political process, the plaintiff's bar, out there in the neighborhoods. You know what I mean? The plaintiffs' lawyers are storefront, and they've got real friends. The defense bar is on the 87th story of the World Trade Center, walking around with blown dry hairdos and three-piece suits singing "How Great Thou Art" to one another. So the plaintiff's bar has driven the federal rules of evidence, and particularly the state adoption of the federal rules of evidence. There is no such thing as a criminal defense bar. Criminals are scum bags who don't have enough money to hire anybody. Right? It's all court appointed. You can't find anybody. I realize that in New York you have a few white collar criminal lawyers—you have people like Murray Janus and Richmond, you have some fine criminal defense lawyers. But they are as rare as hen's teeth. It's the bottom 20% of the bar. It's public defenders who've got an 85 person caseload, or it's court appointed lawyers. They have no political organization, no political clout, and nobody gives a damn. And these days the federal courts have decided, in an incredible reaction to the way the Warren Court handled procedural matters, that we're going to treat criminal defendants like meat on the way to dressing and processing. With very few exceptions, it is darn hard in federal court for anybody to hear the words "not guilty" pass anybody's lips, right? The probation officers and the United States Attorney determine the sentencing, the sentencing guidelines make it impossible for anybody who doesn't have an ironclad defense not to plead guilty. The whole system is a set-up, and this expert evidence rule is the final cap to all of that. When you start bringing in witch doctors to throw bones in the criminal process you are really doing something terrible. In West Virginia, and I've finally come to my point, we distinguish with regard to the expert evidence rule. Basically, we have the federal rules, but we do not apply the same rules to civil cases and criminal cases, because we know how to get out of transsubstance or whatever the hell that word was this morning. When you want to screw a defendant in a civil case you just say "we're going to screw the defendant in a civil case" without creating a rule that has to apply to everybody from the beginning of time and in every conceivable case. And I hope that the rest of you—other judges who are sitting on courts of last resort—do the same thing. This *Daubert* thing is a very, very dangerous rule to put into criminal cases because suddenly you're going to have the witch doctors from Zululand throwing bones in your court saying John Gotti was guilty.

MAN: You know, Justice Neely, the irony of your comment is that the criminal defense bar, particularly in assailing DNA evidence, has actually had a lot more impact than most of us lay people who read about DNA identification would expect. And, in fact, the government, the federal prosecutor's office, has often shot itself in the foot by over-trying cases to create bad law. In the use of DNA, consider the *United States v. Jackobitz* case,[9] which was up at the same time that Ken's petition on *Daubert* was up there. That was a case in which you didn't need an iota of evidence, but the greedy U.S. attorney went and put the evidence in and raised a whole slew of review problems in the Second Circuit. So I think that the *Daubert* rule, in fact, might actually take a big hit at the method, and I think the criminal defense bar is to be complimented, although I agree generally that lack of resources in the criminal defense bar makes this an unequal fight.

JUSTICE NEELY: Yeah, it's very hard. Again, states like California and Illinois and New York are big enough to have a very small, but extraordinarily high quality core of serious defense people who are available, among other things, to help kids. But in West Virginia, with the exception of one or two guys who do federal tax fraud cases, there really is no expert criminal defense bar. In Virginia there are probably five or six, and Virginia is a pretty big state.

JUDGE STEPHEN WILLIAMS: I have a question about the scope of review of the gatekeeper's function. *Daubert* gives district judges the sort of multi-factor, close-grained issue that normally leads to a highly deferential standard of review, like clearly erroneous or abuse of discretion. With all those factors, it's almost impossible to develop uniformity across cases, and it's hopeless for the courts of appeals to try to do so. On the other hand, it seems to me that in many respects this issue is one that calls overwhelmingly for uniformity across cases—take the Bendectin cases, for example. And that, obviously, suggests the importance of a fairly intrusive appellate review. So one aspect of the question is, what are the arguments in terms of the level of review? Second, if I'm right that there is tension between these competing things, won't it at some point be necessary for the rules to shakedown to a comparatively small number of tests, perhaps safe harbors on either side, where courts of appeals will develop rules that will introduce some kind of predictability, and, above all, uniformity across cases?

ARTHUR MILLER: Let me hold responses now to that first question with regard to the scope of review. Justice Neely is probably the only man I know who can make the word gatekeeper sound like a dirty name. What do you think the scope of review should be, Judge Becker?

JUDGE BECKER: I think, for the most part, the scope of review is going to be deferential. There are going to be subsidiary findings that will be subject to clearly erroneous review. Insofar as the ultimate findings are concerned, if you can call them that, the Supreme Court construing Rule 52(a) says that that's also deferential review. We have a common law system which is laden with indeterminacy, and we've lived with this for years, and I think we'll continue to live with it. I think that unless you're involved with questions of the adequacy of the procedures followed by the district judge, unless you're dealing with misapplication of the standard of *Daubert*, the review is largely going to be deferential.

ARTHUR MILLER: But what about the point just made, that that is going to leave you at sea because it will not produce uniformity or predictability?

JUDGE BECKER: Well, I talked about the indeterminacy of the common law system. I think that's built into our system—something we live with and something that induces what Hubert Will taught me in New Judge School is the highest form of justice: a freely negotiated settlement between the parties.

ARTHUR MILLER: Freely negotiated. Let me play devil's advocate one level further. If it is true that *Daubert*, in effect, creates a multi-faceted inquiry on the question of admissability, doesn't it create a situation in which the amount of discretion goes up because of the variety of factors that can motivate a particular decision?

JUDGE BECKER: Sure. The answer is yes. And I should add in this respect that I don't think the *Daubert* factors were intended to be exhaustive. I think the Court assumes that there can be a lot of other factors. I would agree with you that, to that extent, the level of discretion goes up. But the trial judge's decision—if the decision is to exclude the evidence and this leads to summary judgment—is going to be a much higher quality decision because of the rigor that is required. As I understand *Daubert*, it requires the development of a rigorous record, and rigorous findings by the trial judge. And, therefore, if I may use the term reliability in another sense, I think that the trial judge's decision is going to be more reliable because of that imported rigor.

ARTHUR MILLER: Could I impose on you, Judge Higginbotham, to react as an appellate judge to what the future may be for your court in terms of scope of review?

JUDGE HIGGINBOTHAM: Well, I agree with Eddie that the enumeration of factors is plainly going to cause a closer examination by an appellate court of the trial court decision. And I have only one footnote to what he said. I think that in certain substantive areas there may be more interest in the particular case, perhaps ideologically driven, that may lead some judges to examine the gatekeeping function more closely. The appellate courts abdicated routine matters of evidence a long time ago: everything became subject to abuse of discretion review, which always sort of baffled me. Most of the federal appellate courts just don't come to grips very often with these kind of rulings any more. But with the high profile tort litigation, you may have some closer examinations.

And so the litany and the explanations may be the same, but the examination may in actuality be a little more rigid and stringent. With that one footnote, I agree completely with what Eddie has said: deferential review.

ARTHUR MILLER: Given Justice Neely's concern about the criminal side of the equation, where the stakes are arguably higher and the resource allocation is more disparate, is scope of review the same on the criminal side as on civil side?

JUDGE HIGGINBOTHAM: Well, I think the same reality I was just describing operates. On the criminal side, I think appellate judges are more exacting because it is a criminal case. Can you see that articulated in the opinions directly? Perhaps not. But I think you have some legal principles that produce a more exacting review. When you start to bring in confrontation problems and other concerns for the rights of criminal defendants, I think you can justify a closer review. The reality is that there is more stringent appellate review on the criminal side. And I think at the trial court level you'll get closer examination of these issues. I don't really see a change in the trial court practice that people are concerned with. I think the proposed Rules Committee's rules are largely validating practices that already exist out there. The truth of the matter is that pre-trial examination of expert witnesses has been going on for years, as Eddie mentioned earlier in talking about the *Japanese Electronics* case. The standing orders of many district courts across the country insisted on disclosure of expert testimony. With regard to the criminal side, a parallel to that, we've seen the phenomenon arise of a pre-trial procedure on conspiracy. We have long been concerned about "subject to connection" admissions, where we would take the prosecutor's word that the state would tie in a conspirator somewhere down the line, and three weeks into trial it still hadn't been done. In response, some courts will create a pre-trial procedure and tell the prosecutor, "you articulate where that is." So there we see on the criminal side the judicial creation of a pre-trial examination of a matter of evidence to resolve a problem that I don't think is worlds apart from what we're dealing with here. I see no real problem in terms of rule creation. I think we're already doing it. I think the equipment is in place. And I think that's what you'll see happening.

ARTHUR MILLER: Any other reaction on appellate review?

ROCHELLE DREYFUSS: Just one point: uniformity probably has a special meaning in this area since presumably the science changes and more things are known and new scientists come up with new kinds of studies, which they do in light of the ones that were introduced in previous cases. So in some sense uniformity is going to be something that you're not going to have as much of in this area no matter how you try and slice it.

MAN: But that's a change from case to case that people can understand. It's a problem, though, when district judges come out simultaneously in different directions on what appears to an ordinary mortal to be exactly the same issue, and I think it's somewhat more disturbing when judges are purporting to evaluate scientific reliability than when juries come out with disparate verdicts.

ARTHUR MILLER: Having heard at least partial opinions of the third and fifth circuits, do you want to pursue your second question?

MAN: Oh, well, I'd certainly invite speculation on it. It was simply the question of whether the tension that I, at least, see will lead to some kind of formalization of the *Daubert* inquiry such that if you have A, B, and C it's in; if you lack D, E, and F it's out, and then there's some intermediate range of cases where it's up for grabs.

ARTHUR MILLER: I see a lot of heads shaking on the horizontal.

MAN: I think we will see some heuristics evolve. I mean, you have to get down to specifics here. It's been commonplace for a treating physician to talk not only about what ails the person he treated but also about what caused the ailment. Now there's no scientific methodology that says examine one case and declaim about causality. There just is no methodology. I think—and Ken or others can contradict me on the scientific propositions—but I think we can get heuristic on these points: 30 million women have used a drug; not many scientists say look at rats instead. They'd say look at the epidemiological data. And I think if you begin peeling things off into fairly specific narrow issues—like is extrapolating from rats to women reliable, at least in the context of something that's been tested on women directly, and so on—I think we will see these evolving. Curiously, if nothing much has changed with *Daubert*, it's striking how uniform the federal courts have been on Bendectin. There's no federal court at the appellate level that has approved a Bendectin verdict. I expect, I will predict yet again, that we will be able to say that 10 years from now. There has been one state court that seems to have upheld a Bendectin verdict—the District of Columbia, and perhaps Texas is still open—but no federal court has yet approved one.

ARTHUR MILLER: Eleanor.

ELEANOR FOX: Yes, I want to turn to a question that Professor Dreyfuss raised a while ago, and I would like to hear discussion from the panel on it. If the gatekeeper admits both sides' scientific evidence, Rochelle said there may come a time when the scientific evidence looks like it is in equipoise. The jury has to make a decision. The jury can decide, yes, the Bendectin does tend to cause limb deformity, and might be able also to decide, yes, it did cause it in this child. But the jury may also be able to decide the contrary. Is there anything illegitimate about such an open system, where the jury decides and nobody ever knows for sure whether causation in fact existed? Is there a problem with our all-or-nothing causation principle in tort law? Should there be any kind of probability verdict?

WOMAN: I must say, I feel the same way about whether the traffic light was red or green. I truly do not see the difference. There is no "truth" out there. And I think one of the great problems with scientific evidence is that somehow we think that there is a different level of certainty, of truth, than actually exists. Your example bothers me no more than a jury saying, "We've now decided that, you know, five years ago this was the fact even though we've had witnesses testifying both ways."

ARTHUR MILLER: You mean, you're prepared to let juries speculate on things that are in equipoise?

WOMAN: Yeah, I do not agree with Rochelle.

MAN: You have problems in any toxic tort case of both the general and the particular. The science may be, as you say, in equipoise on the general issue. I don't think it is with Bendectin, but in the abstract, science may be in equipoise on the general issue of whether or not a substance can cause an event or a condition. That may be in very strong dispute. But then another issue that must get litigated—not unlike whether the light was red or green or whether you were sober or not—is whether the substance caused the condition in this particular individual. Now, in Bendectin, because of the way it's gone, the defense has been able to cut cases off at the *general* condition. But of course there was a lot of debate, if you actually look at the record, on whether the *particular* was true. And, in fact, there have been some cases, the case involving Dr. Geier with DPT vaccine, where essentially all he said was "based upon my professional judgment this child's encephalopathy is a product of her vaccination." And the only testability was from this earlobe to the next earlobe in Dr. Geier. But that's how you could have equipoise and still have controversy as to the particular case.

ROCHELLE DREYFUSS: See, no, I think it's different. Eleanor is thinking of cases in which there is general scientific agreement that sometimes some people get the disease from this problem. And the question *is* the particular question: Did *this* person get it? So there's a 10% increase in disease X among people who've had a particular vaccine. And that is different from the red light or the green light, I think. Because we know that some people are going to get it. What percentage? It's below 50%, so you can *never* prove by a preponderance of the evidence that this particular person got it. And yet we do know that some people get it. And for that, I think, current tort law just doesn't work very well. And my concern about *Daubert* is that it will obscure those kinds of cases. Because I think we need a different solution for those cases. You want the manufacturer to internalize the costs of the diseases that were caused by the drug, and it never internalizes those costs because no individual person can ever prove that his or her disease was caused by it. So it's when we know the general but not the specific that the question arises.

SHEILA BIRNBAUM: Rochelle, it's much more complex than that.

ROCHELLE DREYFUSS: Of course it is.

SHEILA BIRNBAUM: With almost every one of these probabilities or possibilities, when you get to the individual case and you're talking about diseases that are commonplace and can be caused by a multitude of things, the issues that you're raising go to legislative questions of who should pay what to whom. In some instances, we have the legislature coming into the vaccine situation, and in others we have medical device legislation that is going to provide preemption on almost all medical devices that get approved by the FDA. We are making some of these decisions on a legislative basis. But what Eleanor's question raises, I think, is the most complex of all these issues. In many toxic tort cases, we don't have any science really, at least not any science that scientists would accept, as to whether X causes Y. And we won't have it maybe for years. I mean, Judge Weinstein in the *Agent Orange* decision clearly said when he threw out all the opt-out cases, "at this point we have some epidemiological evidence, we have some animal tests, but the evidence doesn't meet the test that it's more probable than not that anybody's injuries were caused by exposure to a dioxin." We have dioxin cases all over the country still. Courts are continually deciding whether the evidence now meets the test. So the real issue is not a case like Bendectin. Bendectin is a fairly easy case, at least as I see it, because there's overwhelming epidemiological evidence in Bendectin. The really hard cases for the judiciary are when we've got all this soft science, and all this non-science, and all these continuing things that we're beginning to learn about. We can now test for dioxin in parts per quadrillion. So we're litigating cases where the question is, does dioxin at that level cause the injury that that plaintiff is alleging? Breast cancer and lung cancer, common diseases caused by all kinds of things, present the kind of hard issues that courts are going to be confronted with every day after *Daubert*.

WOMAN: In the area I work in, geneticists are testifying on genetic predisposition, and you have companies, defending themselves on the ground that a client who committed suicide was genetically predisposed. I mean, the level of understanding in that area! But this is an increasing issue in law. It goes back to what Ronald Dworkin said at lunch. Genetic defenses are beginning to enter the debate, and that's an even more exaggerated form of the same thing Sheila's talking about.

ARTHUR MILLER: At the risk of offending the two people stating that, let me just pursue it. (By the way, those of you who are waiting for a break, there will be none. There is coffee at the back, and you all know where the bathrooms are. But we're going to proceed here even if we're alone until about 4:00 p.m. So just enjoy yourself.) Suppose you have a situation in which you do not have the kind of science that you've arguably got in Bendectin. And you look at the *Daubert* factors and whatever other factors one might think of—you look at falsifiability, you look at peer review, you look at standards, you look at general acceptability—and, by God, there's damn near a vacuum, as I gather is the case in a great deal of the universe of science. Science just hasn't gotten around to this. What do you want us to do, Doc?

LEON GORDIS: Well, fund more science, of course. In the absence of adequate scientific evidence, I think it's important to distinguish between cases where we don't have scientific knowledge but we could obtain it in year or two, and cases where it's just not possible to obtain the data. For example, leaving out the biological markers that we've just referred to in connection with dioxin, at the time of Judge Weinstein's actions there was no way of distinguishing between exposed and non- exposed individuals in Vietnam. There were no records. It was a very problematic situation. Even now it's a question of how we interpret the biological markers. But at that time, it was a situation in which we didn't have evidence to demonstrate conclusively that exposed workers had increased risks. And the outcomes that were being looked at, reproductive hazards, congenital malformations and the like, were very common ones. So the question became the societal one, where the courts have to play a role in deciding how you are going to allocate responsibility or whether you are going to disregard the claims of these plaintiffs on the assumption that you don't have enough evidence. But to me, again, as someone outside the judicial system, the picture is different if it's possible to get data, to do a study within six months or a year, or if it's a situation where the old records don't exist and we just can't get the information. We then have to make a value judgment on societal values.

ARTHUR MILLER: Would you be offended if the system said, as it occasionally must, "we realize there's pretty much of a vacuum out there, but we're in business to decide cases, so let's roll the dice with the jury on the basis of what we've got?"

LEON GORDIS: Well, I'm not easily offended. If you ask me would I be concerned about the integrity of science, I don't think courts are going to affect the integrity of science. If we're talking about the judicial process, that's a different set of questions. I would argue as a scientist that if it is feasible within a reasonable period of time to get relevant answers, then perhaps the courts ought to step back for a few months or a year and say, "Let's get the study" or "let's commission someone to get the data and conclusions." If it's not feasible, then I think the courts have to face the decision on whether to compensate or not and at what levels.

JUDGE BECKER: Well, I don't suggest that it would operate in a vacuum. We do have to remember that Justice Blackman in *Daubert* did refer to the overall liberal construction rule, that is, that the federal rules of evidence should be liberally construed. So that may give us some guidance at least in a close situation.

ARTHUR MILLER: Now, Peter, doesn't that bother you?

PETER HUBER: I'm still puzzled by the question. Take cellular phones, for example, and assume that Larry King and one other plaintiff think they cause brain tumors. They may, but if there's a complete absence of science, who's at your *Daubert* hearing? If there's no science you've got nobody to qualify. So this should be very easy.

JUDGE BECKER: You can always use Rule 706 and appoint an expert. That will solve the problem.

PETER HUBER: How can you qualify an expert?

JUDGE BECKER: Oh. You can't.

PETER HUBER: If we're assuming that there's no science out there. The difficult case arises when there's some fringe science, or proto-science, or novel science out there. And to pick back up on a point that was made before, I think *Daubert* actually does open up one area and change things sharply from what they were before. If you can make an honest case—"look, this is brand new, this is hot off the presses, we've just completed this study and, by golly, cellular phones really are causing brain cancer"—I think *Daubert* is then a pretty liberal decision. Whereas clearly, under the literal language of the old *Frye* rule, you couldn't have gotten that in. So one does see a change. But the case where there is a vacuum is not the problem. Nor, I might add, is the case where the science is in equipoise: you know, a respectable school here says there's global warming, a respectable school here says there isn't. That's an easy case too. The experts on both sides are going to get in. This is let-it-all-in, like it or not, we're going to the jury. The difficult cases, I think, are the 90-10 cases.

ARTHUR MILLER: The partial vacuum.

PETER HUBER: Well, no, the vacuum on one side of the courtroom. Where you've got everybody sitting on one side of the ship, then *Daubert* makes a difference. Then you say this ship isn't leaving port, at least, that's what you should be saying.

MEL WEISS: You know, Arthur, plaintiff's lawyers face a lot of risk in bringing actions that have no foundation or no reasonable basis, and they have to do a fair amount of investigation before they get involved in these suits, because they are very expensive. Take this toxic waste dump case that I had, the issue really comes down to whether there is evidence of exposure and causation. You see, what happens is, you have these Superfund laws and they have these big clean ups and you get hysterical communities living in close proximity to these places. And if you examine the people who come to you, you see a much higher incidence of different kinds of maladies, whether they be rashes or running eyes, and then you find a higher percentage of cancers. And these people are really in need of something. So you try to bring the cases on a reasonable basis. You try to find the evidence and an expert who will support some causation argument, and you get into these things because—I'm talking as a local lawyer—because people you know are involved. Doctors have been treating people and giving them advice, saying "you probably have some condition that was causally connected from your exposure to this waste." There's an overflow, it ran by the school, the kids were exposed to it. There are a lot of social aspects to this that you can't just ignore, and the courts have to understand that. It's not as simple as just laws of evidence and such a cold, calculated approach to things. After all, the state created a very dangerous condition. They created a dump site that leaked all over the place. Then they let industrial waste dumpers come in and put this poison right on top of a hill overhanging a community of people who lived exposed to that for 20 years until it was closed. Then when they closed it, they put an aeration system around it and sprayed it into the air. Now, these are things that happen. But when you get to the science part, the expert part, it's not too difficult for the defendants (it's usually a large group of lawyers representing the state, representing all kinds of big industrial dumpers) to come in with an army of experts to attack everything you're trying to demonstrate that caused injury to your clients. The costs become astronomic. And if you talk to them about trying to settle the case, baloney, forget about it, they're going to go all out war against you, because there are insurance problems and this or that problem; they always find some rationalization for not resolving this. And I'm not so sure that *Daubert* is going to help much. I think that maybe the judges should make that the point in a case to really interject themselves and try to get settlements. And I think that this could really be a benefit of the whole thing, if judges use the *Daubert* hearing as a good settlement juncture.

MAN: But demonstrating things that aren't true should be very expensive. I mean, it should be extremely costly.

MEL WEISS: Well, what do you mean by not true? I broke out in a horrible rash this summer. I could have been exposed to one thing for one minute and my doctor said that this rash could explode all over my body. You say it's not true. I mean, are you telling me that living next to poisons that are being excreted into the atmosphere day in and day out has no chance of injuring people?

MAN: No, I'm saying that if they can so easily line up reams of experts and you can't find a single one, maybe that's telling you something.

MEL WEISS: No, we have experts. Of course, we. . . .

MAN: Well, then you'll survive *Daubert* if you've got a legitimate case.

MEL WEISS: But the cost of these hearings, these *Frye*-type hearings, now it's going to be *Daubert*-type hearings, are astronomical.

WOMAN: Mel, just one question. The amount of money changing hands from one body of people to another body of people is fairly astronomical as well. I mean, what was the total settlement in your case?

MEL WEISS: I got $96 million before the trial against the state. We just finished an 8-month trial with a mixed verdict. The case against the state still has 3,983 plaintiffs to go. We'll probably settle it. But do you know what they spent defending it? They could have settled it at a much earlier stage for a lot less than they spent defending it. But there's a lot of factors that go into why they spent that money, mostly insurance company decisions, as well as defense lawyers trying to make a good buck.

ARTHUR MILLER: Margaret?

MARGARET BERGER: I think the rules of evidence are wonderful, but they can't cure a situation like that. I mean, no matter what they are they cannot deal with those kinds of problems. But I do think that what Judge Becker said before—that district judges are going to have to scrutinize these questions more carefully and will, therefore, perhaps look at them from the beginning—does mean that some of the scientific issues will be put into some kind of a hierarchy, as is done sometimes with regard to discovery issues. What I mean is that the judge may say earlier, "first let's hear a little about this exposure problem and exactly what evidence there is of exposure and levels of exposure before we go onto the causation problem."

MEL WEISS: And what is the burden of proof at that stage? Is it a predominance burden? Does the judge find. . . .

MARGARET BERGER: Yes, if it is a Rule 104(a) problem, as the Supreme Court has said, then I assume it is a preponderance of the evidence standard.

MEL WEISS: Well, that's where you're going to have a lot of problems.

MAN: I'm not sure I buy this cost argument either. It seems to me that when you're dealing with these kinds of cases you're going to be fighting over the experts, either at the *Daubert* hearing before the trial has really started, or as a collateral matter at trial that's going to confuse the jury. And you're going to have all the same expenses in terms of preparing to deal with the matter.

MEL WEISS: You have it twice, three times, four times.

MAN: Well, there is a good prospect that the case will be simplified. The case will be simplified because you've had the *Daubert* hearing and, in fact, it may facilitate settlement because each side will see the strength of the other side's expert testimony. It seems to me that there are lots of efficiencies that could be achieved by this process and, in fact, I think that's the aim.

ROBERT CONASON: It becomes another discovery procedure, an additional one, unless the defendant prevails. So in every semi-technical case, defendants are getting additional discovery: first they take the deposition of the expert as they do now. Then you have a hearing in court, and if it's admitted you have the trial, which unquestionably increases the cost. It's another discovery phase whether or not the defendants sincerely believe they can exclude the evidence. They now have two depositions of the expert. It has to increase cost.

ARTHUR MILLER: I just wanted to even up the left and the right side of the V. I didn't want Mel swinging out there by himself. I better get to these two people lest they come down with phlebitis and say I caused it.

MAN: This is a good way of staying awake, Arthur.

MAN: Justice Neely made the point that the *Daubert* rule will "do in" defendants in criminal cases. As Gershwin said, "It ain't necessarily so." In *Downing*, the Third Circuit had to deal with an application by a defendant for an expert on eye witness testimony. I assure you this was not something the government wanted. And it was a legitimate effort on the part of the defense to inject reasonable doubt into the process. I had occasion, and I hasten to add that the case is over at all levels, to accept the teachings of *Downing* in an organized crime case, a situation involving a pick axe in the back of a gentleman's neck on a glorious night in New Jersey. An application was made by the defense with the same idea. So it works both ways. And for those who are interested in the criminal process, read *Downing*. It's instructive, and I don't think *Daubert* really changes the situation in that regard.

MAN: My reaction to Justice Neely's point, and to Mel's point, is that I don't think it's relevant to be worried about criminal defendants or toxic tort plaintiffs or the fact that when millions of dollars are at stake defendants will use every procedural alternative available. I think the Court took cert because Congress was clear about one thing in 1975: it wanted uniform rules, nationwide, in criminal and civil cases. And it was pretty clear that having the *Frye* rule out there, which is almost always used in criminal cases, could not be squared with the rule Congress laid out, Rule 402, saying that all relevant evidence is admissible unless it's specifically excluded under a given rule. And that was the linchpin. If you want a special rule in a given area, you're talking about substantive law revision or amendment of the federal rules. But I think if you have uniform rules, as the court has clarified them, then you have to follow them. But one argument that the Court didn't have to face, is that Rule 402 prohibits using the supervisory power to throw evidence out because it's unfair, because Rule 402 says if it's relevant you have to admit it. And that seems to preclude judges from playing fairness games, even though in some cases there might be a compelling reason to do so. So I just don't see that the subject matter debate raised by Justice Neely, which may seem well founded in some cases, is relevant to what these rules mean and how they have to be applied.

ARTHUR MILLER: Steve?

PROFESSOR STEVE BURBANK: To what extent, Professor Nelkin, do you think that judges are equipped to perform the role that *Daubert* gives them? I tend to see the case as raising the question of whether power over the admissability of evidence has been transferred from the scientific community to judges, as a superficial view of *Frye* would have it, and also perhaps a superficial view of *Daubert*. Are judges capable of taking a more sophisticated view of the scientific process than was suggested by your colleague, our only scientist who talks about the integrity of science? Or are they likely to have their eyes glaze over and to fail to recognize the contingencies of the scientific process?

DOROTHY NELKIN: Well, I certainly think that judges are capable of understanding what is good evidence and what is not under terms that are very reasonable for the courts. And what I see, at least in the things I'm involved in, is a tremendous amount of activity in the legal community to learn about scientific issues. But there is also a tendency for courts to look at science as a kind of easy way to resolve ambiguities. There is a myth of scientific neutrality that pervades the society generally, of which judges are a part. There's a seductiveness to the apparent predictability that comes from science. And science is used as a means of credibility. My own introduction to this issue came when I was holed up in Little Rock, Arkansas, as an expert witness in the creationism trial, where for three weeks the court had a parade of scientific experts debating the origin of life. And all of a sudden I became aware, strikingly aware, as somebody mentioned, that science was being used as a means of credibility to an extraordinary extent, well beyond what I think science can really provide for the courts.

JUDGE BECKER: If I can get a little nutsy-boltsy and pick up on something that Ken Chesebro said a bit earlier, I foresee a problem that relates to the underlying data and arises out of a circuit split between the Third, Fifth and Seventh circuits on the one hand, and some other circuits on the other. If we can talk for a few minutes about the underlying data, as opposed to the scientific methodology, Rule 703 says that hearsay may be considered by the expert "so long as it of a type reasonably relied upon by experts in the field." Now the three circuits that I've mentioned said that the person who identifies what is reasonable is not the judge, but the experts. In these three circuits, the rule is that if the experts think, or an expert arguably thinks, that it's reasonable, then the expert may rely on it. Now query whether reliance on unreliable data is a flaw in methodology. If you're in a circuit which says that the expert is the judge of what is reasonably relied upon the court may be stuck with that expert's opinion and may not be at liberty to disregard it under *Daubert* principles, which focus on methodology.

ARTHUR MILLER: That's a great example of the control issue. Who has control? Steve, don't disappear. Are you offended by that?

STEVE BURBANK: Am I offended by a rule that says the experts get to judge? Absolutely, because I think you must filter questions that the scientific process resolves in one way through the values of the legal system.

JUDGE BECKER: Well, that's what I said in *Japanese Electronics*, and I got reversed by the Third Circuit (before I was on it). But there's a split in the circuits, and I would hope that the advisory committee for which Professor Berger is the reporter will address that. I think there is a serious tension and a problem. I agree with Professor Burbank.

MARGARET BERGER: I must say that I wondered when reading the *Daubert* opinion whether there was a discussion of this in the Court that the Justices left unresolved. Because if you look, the majority is talking about Rule 702 throughout. But if you look at page 2799, the dissent says something that is either a typo or an uncorrected piece of opinion where things got chopped. In the last full paragraph on that page, the dissent says "this is not to say that such materials are not useful or even necessary in deciding how Rule 703 should be applied." The dissent is not talking about 702, which is what the majority opinion is about. And, as I said, either this is a typo, or at some point there were opinions that addressed whether the case could be analyzed under Rule 703, since there were certainly briefs filed suggesting that the issue of what the expert could reasonably rely upon was in the case as well.

ARTHUR MILLER: Bob?

MAN: I'm not sure I understand Judge Becker correctly, but if I did, he seemed to be saying that if only one expert appears and says, "what I relied upon is accepted in the scientific community," the trial judge is bound by that. If that's what he meant, I think that runs counter to a number of things that have been said, including some said by the Supreme Court, that the trial judge and appellate court are not bound by what a couple of experts selected by the party in a case have to say. The trial judge's obligation, and the appellate court's obligation, is to go beyond that—and Judge Becker agrees with that, I think, because he has said some things in some of his appellate opinions that support the proposition that courts have an obligation to beyond what the experts selected by the parties have to say.

JUDGE BECKER: Well, obviously, the ultimate admissibility question isn't determined by a prima facie showing. It's a 104(a) problem, not a 104(b) problem of conditional relevancy. But there is, I think, a tension between these decisions and *Daubert*. I'm agreeing with you, but I think that it has to be resolved.

WOMAN: I know the federal judiciary is talking more about the role of federal courts in appointing experts, and this may be an area where we see judges saying, "I'm not sure. I can't understand the scientist. I have the plaintiff's expert and the defendant's expert. They're both telling me something else. I need some help. I need my own expert." I think we may see some of that.

JUDGE KEETON: At this point I come back to the question that Judge Williams put, which I don't think has been satisfactorily answered. If we have cases all around the country on essentially one scientific issue, and the trial judges appoint their own experts and they get different advice and reach different decisions, what do we do? Do we just relax and say, "Oh, well, that's the litigation process." I'm disturbed by that.

MAN: I think that's addressed in the rules themselves and you've written on this, I think. Rule 201 says that judges can take judicial notice of adjudicated facts if they're not reasonably susceptible to disagreement. Now, the Fifth Circuit wouldn't even take judicial notice that asbestos causes cancer, because there's a problem if you start using an expansive concept of judicial notice to wipe out trials and not even hear evidence. But short of being able to take judicial notice, both admissibility and the factual issue itself have to be determined based on the record. I think Judge Becker was getting at the question of when might a judge say that, although all the experts on one side say that what they're doing is reasonably relied upon, he or she can still reach outside to see if that's true. And I think it's largely an issue of judicial notice.

JUDGE KEETON: Judicial notice is no help there, because judicial notice applies only to things that cannot reasonably be disputed. When we have experts around who are giving us different advice, we cannot take judicial notice of either view because they're in conflict with each other. What do we do?

MEL WEISS: Why doesn't that issue go to the jury? I don't understand why that issue doesn't go to the jury.

JUDGE KEETON: So we are willing to tolerate different answers to a single question on which members of the scientific community have disputes and just relax and say "alright."

MAN: I think actually—one good example—someone mentioned Judge Rubin in the mass trial. Yet, after that was done and 800 plaintiffs lost, the Sixth Circuit said that it could have gone either way. The evidence was admissible. The jury could have gone for the plaintiffs. They didn't. Judge Rubin allowed another trial to go forward and refused to grant summary judgment saying, "It's a jury issue. Sure, they lost first time around, but they can come out differently in a different case." And that seems to be a price of our individualized system of adjudication. It's a very difficult problem. I know a lot of people are worried about it.

ARTHUR MILLER: Wait a second, we're letting Judge Keeton off way too easily. I know you were a torts teacher. You were *my* torts teacher. You used to play those games in '55-'56. You tell us what you think should happen in that situation.

JUDGE KEETON: I think the judges, both trial and appellate, ought to be free to go outside the record and get all the information they can get from whatever source instead of being of bound to decide the case based solely on what the advocates bring to their attention through hired guns.

ARTHUR MILLER: Without the independent expert?

JUDGE KEETON: That's the first question. And I think, secondly, that the notion that *Daubert* says appellate courts should be as deferential to the trial judge's decision as this panel seems to think is wrong, because having appellate courts review non-deferentially gives us at least the possibility of getting the same answer to all the different cases that are being decided around the country. So, right or wrong, at least it doesn't look like justice is being administered by a roll of the dice depending on who the trial judge happens to be.

ARTHUR MILLER: But it's only a possibility.

JUDGE KEETON: One more point. It has been said here that nothing has changed. Maybe I'm looking at this from the perspective of a working trial judge, but I think *a lot* has changed. I have been given by *Daubert*, a lot more power, that I didn't ask for, and a lot more work, that I didn't ask for. That's a real change.

ROCHELLE DREYFUSS: My pediatrician once told me that my son needed some minor surgery, and I didn't want him to have it and I said, "Well, I'd like a second opinion." And the doctor said, "Well, go get one." And I said, "Could you give me a recommendation?" And he said, "Well, do you want your son to have the surgery or do you want your son not to have the surgery? I could get you either opinion." So it's true, a judge can usually go outside and get some expert to help her understand what's going on in the trial. But to just give judges the right to choose the expert that they want is to give judges the right to choose the decision in the ultimate case—at least in cases in which the scientific community is in disarray.

JUDGE KEETON: I'm in 100% agreement with you, and that's why I think we should not give this power to trial judges. If we're going to give it to somebody in the judicial system, give it to the courts of higher resort so that we'll have some chance of having a single answer.

MAN: There are other candidates, I mean, the FDA has reviewed Bendectin in horribly long length, and I think I'm the first to mention that today. Bendectin is still approved by the FDA. You have regulatory agencies everywhere else in the world, and they actually convene scientific panels and do everything that *Daubert* set out. We could give greater preemptive effect to those.

MARGARET BERGER: Yeah, but maybe we could use a more concrete example. I think there's one floating around at this very moment, which is whether asbestos can cause colon cancer. The highest court of New Jersey has upheld verdicts for plaintiffs finding colon cancer caused by asbestos. And Judge Sweet, in just the last few weeks, in the Southern District, reviewed the literature and decided that he just didn't see enough of an increased risk. So he refused to allow a judgment for the plaintiff. Now I think those cases really raise two kinds of issues. One is the evidentiary issue of what kind of studies should you admit and which experts will be allowed to testify? But then I think you get to the kind of substantive law issue that an appellate court is going to have to decide. It is really a question of tort law and compensation and no longer just a question of what kind of evidence do we have out there. And I think that those are two very different kinds of issues.

ARTHUR MILLER: Dr. Gordis has been a very gentle person we like.

LEON GORDIS: Thank you. I would like to comment as a scientist on some of the issues relating to expert witnesses and science. A statement was made earlier in the afternoon that science doesn't deal well with uncertainty or something along those lines. I would argue that science deals very well with uncertainty, but the legal system doesn't. The legal system wants a yes or no answer. Science thrives on uncertainty. When we do studies we are producing the probability estimate of a certain finding, with the recognition that this finding may change over time. So there is a problem of reconciling the role of the scientist with the role of the courts, because I think you – speaking globally of the legal system – can't handle that. It's not science's problem with handling uncertainty, it's your problem in handling science. Now Professor Nelkin referred to the lack of neutrality of science. Certainly there are many scientists who are not neutral. There are people who will be riding the circuits as plaintiffs' witnesses in a certain category of cases. But there's a distinction to be drawn between bias and neutrality, or biaslessness and neutrality. Each of us as individual human beings, whether we're scientists, lawyers, judges, or anything, has biases. And we bring that to bear whether we're doing science or law. But with all my biases, I can be neutral on issues in which I don't have a vested interest. I could review the methodology applied in the Bendectin case, for example, and give a pretty detached assessment using whatever expertise I have about whether the methodology is sound or not. Because I'm not in the pay of anybody and I don't think I have an axe to grind. You may disagree with me. Maybe my expertise isn't enough. But I don't think it's a question of lack of neutrality. It may be my own biases about how strict a constructionist to be about use of data. But I think we ought to draw that distinction, because I think there are expert witnesses who are neutral. Let's face it, the fact is that the legal system has not taken advantage of the vast majority of scientists and academicians. There's a tremendous barrier, a big gulf, between the legal system and the academicians. I can tell you that, in general, my colleagues don't want to be involved with you. It's a very serious point. They don't want to be impeached in court. They find it embarrassing and humiliating. It doesn't advance them in the academic system. There are no brownie points. It's not publications. It's not increased salary or rank. They don't get any reward for it in the academic system. Yet we have hundreds and thousands of scientists and academicians who have biases, but are neutral and could provide their expertise in the legal system if we devise a way and build bridges to educate them about what it is you want in the legal system, what they can offer you, and how there can be a common language between the two. And I think the witness hired by the courts or by the judge has the potential to do this, where the motivation issue may be a little bit clearer than when the expert is hired by the plaintiff or the defendant. I would just like to close by pointing out that there are examples of reviews, of consensus conferences carried out by scientifically reputable organizations dealing with controversial topics and trying to find the most reasonable position for the present time.

NIH does this all the time, without an axe to grind. And I recommend that we attempt to have reciprocal educational programs. There's been a lot of concern about educating lawyers in science. There's been very little concern about educating scientists in law. And I think we need it in both directions if we don't want to be having the same discussions five years from now. There ought to be some demonstration projects that try to do that.

MAN: One problem I see with the consensus building sort of procedure, especially sitting in an appellate court, is that I don't think it's really within our purview to say, "this is the scientific fact." That's why I disagree with Judge Keeton. One court may take one view, another court another view, and at a later time the same court may take a still different view. I don't think it's for courts to say what is scientific fact when there's a dispute in the scientific community. What we can do is say what the result should be in a particular case. We can ask, what is the proof in that case? What experts have come forward in that case? And, given that, what is the just end result? There's a verdict, and it's affirmed or it's reversed for that case. Later time, different proof, different advance in science, so you can have a different result. The New Jersey case that was mentioned before, that was a series of cases, and I had one of them. And as it came up, we had the proof and there were epidemiological studies showing 1.1, 1.3, 1.5—nothing over 2, where you could come in and just draw the line. So we had to decide, what are we going to do with it? And the expert witness came in and said, "Well, I know it's only a 1.2, 1.3 factor, but in this case I examined the plaintiff. I eliminated other causative factors for the colon cancer, and I think that in this particular situation, it is more likely than not that ingestion of asbestos affected the particular cells and caused the cancer, etc." And it was Dr. Doane who said this, and she was listened to. The jury returned the verdict. Now to say in this case that asbestos ingestion could cause colon cancer doesn't mean that in a later case someone's going to say asbestos ingestion can't cause or didn't cause colon cancer, as the case may be. I don't see anything wrong with that. It's what the justice system does. It's what we do when we decide things on a case-by-case basis, and I don't really think we have to throw up our hands and say, "Isn't it terrible? Look at the inconsistencies." There are inconsistencies all the time.

MAN: I agree that we don't have to throw up our hands, because it's our job to adjudicate particular problems. But I've been struck at all three sessions here by how we've stepped back from our role as lawyers and asked "is this a good thing?" It's interesting when you realize, as Peter said, that what I (obviously from a biased perspective) think is a marvelous product is not available for women now. When the DPT litigation started, the shot was about five and a half bucks a pop; it's now about $42 a pop, and very large segments of our population—mostly disadvantaged—no longer have that vaccine available. As a result, there has been a dramatic increase in some neighborhoods in whooping cough, which children under six months don't survive.

MAN: We had federal legislation that cured that.

MAN: True, true, but if we see the problem in just the narrow context of our particular profession, I fear that ultimately we're going to become the laughing stock of the public. Because we're not recognizing the broader impact of the fact that we only look at that narrow little window. There are, I would say, scores of companies that have graced the Chapter 11 courts of this country, not employing people any more, with destroyed capital, with no shareholder value, a lot because of what has come from our pens. And I'm not always certain that we're cognizant of the power that we yield, even though I agree with you entirely that our paradigm is to look at the box and adjudicate the facts in those boxes.

MEL WEISS: But companies are coming from all over the world to do business in the United States. They have in the past, they continue to do so, and they will in the future. They love to do business here. They buy into our justice system, our civil justice system, because they like it, because there's some degree of accountability, and they like to compete on that basis. And if you go and teach what we do to people outside our country, like I did this summer at the Salzburg seminars, you find that they love the access to courts that our people have and they want it for their countries. If you read the newspaper clippings, you see that in Japan they're talking about bringing more litigation there, because they can't stand the horrible way that their people live, the corruption, the fact that they're captive to a bunch of monopolists and oligopolists. We don't have that in this country, and we should be proud of it. And if a couple of products get shut down because they may be injurious to the public, so be it. If those manufacturers thought the products were really that good and really that safe, they'd find a profitable way to market them. Make no mistake about it. These are not shrinking violets. They know how to make profit.

MAN: I'm intrigued by the discussion about court appointed experts, and the legislative branch seems to have gotten involved to some extent. You have a significant body of data regarding exposure to asbestos in the industrial context, and then a big dispute about whether asbestos in buildings causes a problem. And you have litigation around the country on that. So Congress set up something called the Health Effects Institute. And Archibald Cox of Harvard chaired the Institute, which was supposed to take an unbiased look at the issue. And they studied it for several years and came up with the conclusion that there was no credible epidemiological evidence of hazard to building occupants from the presence of asbestos in products. Yet it seems to me that courts are not sure what to do with that sort of evidence. Is that something that should simply be left to the experts, or is there room in this process for an instruction from the court that a study of that sort has some special significance in the process?

MAN: I'm very unpersuaded by the idea of appointing independent experts. I've been doing this for 18 years, and I've never seen one appointed. I'd be interested to see a show of hands of how many of the trial court judges have appointed them. I think they're extraordinarily rare. The danger is that the central thing that makes these verdicts acceptable is that the litigants have ownership because they've clashed with the other side. There wouldn't be any ownership of the scientific conclusion with an independent expert, and so I'm frankly suspicious. I say that, moreover, notwithstanding the fact that this model worked well in Canada, an independent expert was hired by the Canadian government to evaluate the scientific evidence on Bendectin and came to the same conclusion. Ironically, he's the person who did the affidavit upon which the *Daubert* motion for summary judgment was met. So you have a very complicated problem.

ARTHUR MILLER: Let me test what you just said. The FJC study does say that court appointed experts are rare. Could we have a show of hands, your names will not be taken, of any judge in the room who has appointed an expert? That doesn't strike me as being that rare. Now, is this a contextual thing? What made you appoint, Charlie?

MAN: I didn't know about the issue and I needed help.

ARTHUR MILLER: So this was remedial reading for you? Bob, have you ever appointed an expert?

MAN: Only when the parties agreed to it to get a case settled. Really not in this context.

ARTHUR MILLER: Okay. Because I know you've had a lot of technical litigation lately. Judge?

MAN: In general, in equity cases. Many times I've had situations in which I would appoint them and found the case settled with the return of the expert's report. Where it didn't, it was a great help. And, in fact, in matrimonial cases it's common practice to appoint both county experts and psychological experts. Where the court appoints them, it's very good.

MAN: You do see them, I guess, in appraisals and in special master accounting problems sometimes.

MAN: Even though I have an engineering background, I felt I couldn't handle some issues and had someone from the University of Texas come out to New Jersey and help.

ARTHUR MILLER: Anyone had a bad experience with a court appointed expert? Something to watch out for, worry about?

MAN: I've been told that in our trial courts in New Jersey, when judges deciding matrimonial cases appoint experts, the experts try to figure out what the judge wants to hear and tell the judge what the judge wants so that they can get hired the next time. This is probably the fault of the judge for not seeing this.

ARTHUR MILLER: Just an observation: the sort of pre-*Daubert* and immediately post-*Daubert* literature, unscientifically read by me, almost universally supports the court appointed expert. Now I just put that out as a datum. I also link it to Dr. Gordis, because the science community to the judge is a natural linkage to the court appointed expert. All right. Time permits only these last two folk. Go ahead.

MAN: I want to address the issue of whether or not scientists are neutral, and I might take issue with Dr. Gordis. Certainly it would be the case that if we looked at the biobehavioral areas of science, *i.e.,* psychiatry, there are tremendous ideological presuppositions with the construction of research designs and studies, let alone the ways in which those research designs are ultimately interpreted. But even in the more biologically oriented fields like internal medicine, we have seen in studies, for example, of treatments for angina, that ideology fuels the ways in which scientists actually develop their studies and come to their conclusions about the appropriateness of treatments. Ergo, I would take the same position as Dorothy Nelkin on this, that science is not neutral, especially in the biomedical and biobehavioral areas.

MAN: In the FJC study, about 20% of the judges indicated that they had appointed an expert in some context. And we asked judges if they found this to be a satisfactory experience. They were uniformly enthusiastic about it. We also asked judges why they used the device so infrequently, because about half the judges had used it only once. And they said it's a procedure to be used only in a very rare circumstance, a circumstance where the information is difficult to discern and the parties aren't providing the information that's necessary for the judge to reach a reasoned and principled decision. Even those judges who were successful in using court appointed experts find it to be a very limited prescription. So I think in the end court appointed experts will continue to be rare, and these issues will always be back in the judges laps.

MAN: I think court appointed experts are also always at a disadvantage because they don't have the support of either litigant for their preparation.

I leaned over here and asked Mel if he had ever been in a case with one, and not only did he say no, but he looked a little derisively and said, "I'd tear 'em to shreds." And probably he would, because the court appointed expert would come in completely unprepared for those of you who are trial lawyers, would come in completely unprepared in the sense of "get ready for Mel, here comes this big steamroller who's about to make you very thin."

ARTHUR MILLER: Somehow I think, that from the lawyer's perspective, the notion of the court appointed expert poses a virility problem. It's 4:00. We promised management and the bus company that we would be done. My thanks to the panel.

Notes

1. Black, *A Unified Theory of Scientific Evidence*, 56 Fordham L. Rev. 595 (1988).
2. *Christophersen v. Allied-Signal Corp.*, 939 F.2d 1106 (5th Cir. 1991).
3. This prediction proved to be on the money, so to speak, as the Ninth Circuit reaffirmed its previous decision on remand from the Supreme Court. See 1995 WL 1736 (9th Cir. Jan. 4, 1995).
4. *United States v. Downing,* 753 F.2d 1224 (3d Cir. 1985).
5. *DeLuca v. Merrell Dow Pharmaceuticals,* 911 F.2d 942 (3d Cir. 1990).
6. *DeLuca v. Merrell Dow Pharmaceuticals,* 791 F. Supp. 1042 (D.N.J. 1992), *aff'd without opinion*, 6 F.3d 778 (3d Cir. 1993).
7. *Richardson v. Richardson-Merrell, Inc.*, 857 F.2d 823 (D.C. Cir. 1988).
8. *In re Japanese Elec. Prods. Antitrust Litig.*, 513 F. Supp. 1100 (E.D. Pa. 1981), *rev'd*, 723 F.2d 288 (3d Cir. 1983), *rev'd sub nom.*, *Matsushita Elec. Indus. Co. v. Zenith Radio Corp.*, 475 U.S. 574 (1986).
9. 955 F.2d 786 (2d Cir. 1992).

Daubert v. Merrell Dow Pharmaceuticals: Experts Testify on Expert Testimony

Margaret G. Farrell*

When the Supreme Court handed down its 1993 decision in *Daubert v. Merrell Dow Pharmaceuticals,*[1] the first case in which it considered the admissibility of scientific expert testimony, both sides claimed victory.[2] On the one hand, plaintiffs, who asserted that Merrell Dow's drug Bendectin had caused their birth defects, cheered the reversal of a judgment which had excluded the testimony of plaintiffs' experts. On the other hand, Merrell Dow congratulated itself for the fact that the Court had adopted much of its argument that scientific experts must base their testimony on reliable and valid scientific methodology. The case was remanded to determine whether plaintiffs' expert testimony met the Court's new standards.

Six months later, a panel of eleven prominent judges, scholars and practitioners still could not agree on either who had won or what the Supreme Court's decision will mean for the administration of justice. Reading the full transcript of the panel's proceedings makes clear that there was strong disagreement among the panel members about the fundamental premises of the decision. On one level, their discussion is about the procedural and substantive consequences of the *Daubert* decision—the timing and nature of the pleadings, hearings, and evidence now necessary to establish the admissibility of scientific testimony, and the different substantive outcomes these procedures may produce. On another level, their deliberation is about the incongruence between legal and scientific understandings of fact; the struggle to define judicial authority vis-a-vis juries, scientists, and lawgivers; and *Daubert*'s effect on

*Professor of Law, Widener University School of Law.

the integrity and legitimacy of the adversary system. We learn from the panelists' efforts to come to grips with the nature of their disagreements what the issues really are in *Daubert* and what further research scholars and the Institute of Judicial Administration might fruitfully undertake to further explore its consequences and implications.

This report begins by describing the panel's discussion of the practical effects of *Daubert* on the work of the federal courts and the outcomes of cases. The report then summarizes the panel's deliberations in terms of three overarching concerns that run through them, before suggesting what kind of research might usefully be undertaken to resolve some of the issues posed. While the Daubert decision is part of an effort to develop a law of science (legal rules govering the use of scientific evidence), we might take its deference to the scientific method seriously enough to consider the development of a science of law—a more empirical study of the effect of legal rules.

I. The Daubert Decision

Before considering the panel's discussion of *Daubert*, we should make sure we understand the case itself. (Readers who are already familiar with this story may want to skip this brief recounting and turn to the next section.) Two children born with limb defects sued Merrell Dow Pharmaceuticals, the manufacturer of Bendectin, an anti-nausea drug ingested by their mothers during pregnancy which the plaintiffs claimed caused their defects.[3] In response to the defendant's summary judgment motion, plaintiffs submitted the affidavits of eight experts who had reviewed animal, cellular, and chemical studies, and reanalyzed epidemiological studies, and had concluded that Bendectin caused their deformities.

Despite these affidavits, the trial court granted the defendant's motion, holding that the animal, cellular, and chemical studies relied on by the plaintiffs' experts were inadmissible because there was available a wealth of human epidemiological studies of the effects of Bendectin.[4] The human epidemiological studies relied on by plaintiffs' experts were not admissible, however, because they were reanalyses of previously published studies that had found no statistically significant association between Bendectin and birth defects. The district court refused to admit expert testimony based on reanalysis absent a showing that the reanalyzed studies had been published in peer-reviewed journals. Accordingly, the court held that plaintiff's evidence was "insufficient to take the matter to a jury."[5]

The district court judgment was affirmed by the Ninth Circuit Court of Appeals, which held that in order to be admissible, plaintiffs' experts' testimony must be based on a scientific technique that is "generally accepted" as reliable by the relevant scientific community citing *Frye v. United States*.[6] There had been no showing in the district court that reanalysis was such a technique. Because of sharp division among the circuit courts regarding the proper standard for admitting expert testimony, the Supreme Court granted certiorari.

The Supreme Court was thus asked to decide whether expert opinion testimony not found by the lower court to have been accepted by the relevant scientific community could nevertheless be admissible under the Federal Rules of Evidence. While it did not exactly disapprove of *Frye*, the Supreme Court unanimously held that its 1923 common law rule was replaced in 1975 by Federal Rule of Evidence 702.[7] According to the Court, Rule 702, which permits the admission of testimony based on "scientific knowledge," requires only that such testimony meet a "standard of evidentiary reliability" or trustworthiness.[8] In a cryptic footnote, the Court declared that "evidentiary reliability will be based on scientific validity."[9] In text, Justice Blackmun set forth a flexible, non-exhaustive list of four factors that bear on the scientific validity of expert testimony for purposes of Rule 702. First, scientific knowledge is knowledge that can be and has been tested, *i.e.*, theories, principles, and reasoning that are falsifiable.[10] Second, because scrutiny by the scientific community is a component of good science, submission of the theory or technique in question to a peer reviewed journal is a relevant, but not dispositive, factor to consider in determining its validity.[11] Third, the known or potential error rate, as well as the standards governing operation of the techniques, should be considered.[12] And, finally, " 'explicit identification of a relevant scientific community and an express determination of a particular degree of acceptance within that community' " is a relevant and permissible, though not requisite, inquiry for a court to make in determining the validity, and hence the admissibility, of proffered scientific evidence.[13] Finding that the trial court had not applied the proper rule to determine the admissibility of plaintiffs' evidence, the Court vacated the judgment of the Ninth Circuit and remanded the case for further proceedings.

On remand, the Ninth Circuit panel decided not to send *Daubert* back to the District Court. Instead, the court of appeals reviewed the trial court record on summary judgment. It held that plaintiffs' expert evidence was not admissible under the standard established for Rule 702 by the Supreme Court because the testimony of plaintiffs' experts was neither reliable nor relevant and affirmed its judgment for Merrell Dow.[14]

II. The Practical Consequences of the Daubert Decision

A. The Effect on Procedure

The first question the IJA panel had to address was whether the *Daubert* decision really changed anything. Several panelists contended that it had not changed the standards for admitting scientific evidence very much from the general acceptance standard that was applied under *Frye*.[15] Professor Berger noted that, before *Daubert*, there was not much difference in the admission of scientific evidence in *Frye* and non-*Frye* jurisdictions, although different verbal formulations were used.[16] In apparent confirmation, Judge Becker, author of the 1985 *Downing* decision upon which *Daubert* was partially modeled, said that *Downing* had created few ripples: "The world hasn't come to an end." Judge Becker reminded the panel that the ruling had been applied in only a small number of cases, largely toxic torts.[17] Others found *Daubert* a greater departure from *Frye* and its progeny. Peter Huber maintained that *Daubert* was more liberal than *Frye*, because it would admit testimony regarding new scientific findings based on accepted methodologies, while Frye would have kept it out unless the findings were generally accepted in the relevant scientific community.[18] Perhaps the greatest effect of *Daubert* was to shift the focus from experts' conclusions to their methodology. As Ken Chesebro made clear, the Supreme Court in *Daubert* requires courts to evaluate the methodology upon which scientific evidence (or the scientific knowledge about which experts testify) is based—not the expert's conclusions.[19]

There was more general agreement that whatever *Daubert* did to the standard of admissibility, it created a need for new procedures. For one thing, the admissibility of proffered scientific testimony must now be established before trial at Rule 104(a) hearings, as suggested by Justice Blackmun, on the basis of oral testimony, stipulations, affidavits, and memoranda setting out learned treatises.[20] Second, such hearings and written submissions would be needed to create a record for appeal of the application of *Daubert*'s standards. Finally, the need to establish admissibility at the pre-trial stage is consistent with recent amendments to Civil Rules 16 and 26, which require parties to disclose during discovery the expert testimony they intend to offer at trial.[21] With respect to the last point, Judge Higginbotham noted that many district courts already have standing rules to this effect.[22]

Whether it is a matter of creating new discovery rules or applying old ones, attorney Mel Weiss asserted that applying the *Daubert* standards in pre-trial proceedings is going to impose enormous additional expense on the parties.[23] Before *Daubert*, the parties were required to present their expert witnesses for pre-trial depositions and at trial. Now they will have to present them for deposition before *Daubert* hearings, then again at *Daubert* hearings, and then yet again at the trial.[24] Several panelists, however, believed that pre-trial *Daubert* hearings will simplify the issues by permitting judges to put scientific issues in a hierarchy of importance and to reduce the overall costs by cutting short litigation based on inadmissible expert opinion.[25]

There was much debate over the degree of deference that appellate courts should give to a district court's gatekeeping determinations under

Daubert. Some panelists argued in favor of little deference so that appellate decisions can create uniformity in determinations about the admissibility of particular kinds of scientific evidence.[26] Others argued that because *Daubert* requires trial judges to consider an indeterminate number of factors before admitting scientific testimony, appellate courts will have to apply a highly deferential standard of review, such as clearly erroneous or abuse of discretion.[27] Either way, complying with *Daubert* will require a hearing, produce a record, and compel specific findings regarding the *Daubert* factors. In doing so, other panelists observed, it will impose greater rigor on the trial judges in a way that invites greater appellate scrutiny.[28] Thus, district court opinions should become more reliable after *Daubert*, if not more predictable or uniform.

Some panelists felt strongly that appellate review should not be formalized simply to provide predictability. Rather than build a body of precedent about what kind of scientific proof is necessary in certain cases—in the way that epidemiological evidence was required by some appellate courts in Bendectin cases—some panelists argued that appellate courts should confine themselves to the substantive tort question of legal responsibility and leave decisions about admissibility to district court discretion.[29] One consequence of the unpredictability that will be caused by *Daubert*'s indeterminacy was thought to be that it might foster settlements. As discussed below, one of the significant effects of process on substance in this area may be to favor private resolution of disputes that involve scientific evidence.

Some participants contended that, while a deferential standard of review might be appropriate in civil cases, in criminal cases a stricter standard should be and, in fact, is applied.[30] Others disagreed. They maintained that civil/criminal distinctions are inappropriate when the question is the validity and reliability of the same scientific evidence.

B. The Effect on Outcomes

Although the district court decision in the case does not make the distinction clear, we should remember that the issue in *Daubert* was the admissibility of expert testimony, not its sufficiency to support a judgment for plaintiffs on the merits.[31] As Professor Berger emphasized, the Supreme Court's distinction between admissibility and sufficiency should help us focus on substantive questions of law that must be decided apart from their scientific proof.[32] One panelist noted, scientific evidence about the likelihood that Agent Orange caused service men's injuries in Viet Nam does not answer the question of who ought to bear responsibility for them.[33]

While agreeing with that proposition, some participants felt that the change in standards for admissibility would have a significant effect on substantive outcomes. Peter Huber, for one, was quick to state his conviction that liberal admission of scientific expert testimony has led to the withdrawal of useful products from the market. Manufacturers stop making products like Bendectin because of the expense of defending them in litigation, even if defendants will ultimately win the law suits.[34] Speaking generally, Huber observed that *Daubert* will not affect the outcome of cases in which there is an absence of scientific evidence on one side of the case or where the scientific evidence is in equipoise and both parties' experts are permitted to testify. The problem arises where one relies on novel science or has only a little scientific evidence while there is considerable scientific evidence on the other side. Then *Daubert* makes a difference, Huber asserted, by providing a standard that would exclude the novel science or the minimal science.[35]

Several panelists felt that *Daubert* would effect outcomes not by changing the standards for admitting scientific evidence, but by obscuring the normative questions to be resolved. They worried that *Daubert* will be applied in many different kinds of cases—malpractice cases, paternity suits, criminal prosecutions, and so on—and that we will stop asking substantive questions about who should be compensated and who should bear responsibility, because we think we have scientific answers to questions about the causal relationship between events.[36]

In light of that concern, there was disagreement about whether the *Daubert* criteria should be used in criminal as well as civil cases. Justice Neely of the West Virginia Supreme Court of Appeals urged the use of different evidentiary rules in civil and criminal cases. He contended that, on the civil side, the plaintiffs bar is politically powerful and organized and fights to get scientific and other evidence before juries and away from judges in an effort to redistribute wealth through plaintiff verdicts. But whereas the civil defendants' bar may act as a counterweight of sorts, the criminal defense bar is weak and unorganized and cannot mount an effective battle to keep scientific or other evidence out of court. Justice Neely feared that liberal application of the *Daubert* standards would permit the introduction of questionable experts whose testimony would support criminal convictions.[37] Other panelists thought you could not predict the effect of *Daubert* in criminal cases so easily. They noted that in some criminal cases, like *Downing*, defendants would be able to introduce scientific expert witnesses to contest the prosecution's evidence.[38]

III. Some Theoretical Implications for the Administration of Justice

A. Incoherence in the Discourse Between Science and Law

The larger project of which *Daubert v. Merrell Dow* is but one part is the construction of a "law of science"—a body of law to determine how to use science for legal purposes.[39] The effort is to use information provided by persons who regard themselves as scientists to further the legal objective of assigning responsibility for human actions, usually past actions. This project is made all the more difficult by a lack of congruence between legal and scientific concepts of reality that leads the disciplines to talk past each other.[40] One of the panelist explained, there are situations in which we have a scientific way of thinking about a problem, like paternity, that might not be completely congruent with the way that the law thinks about it.[41]

As the *Daubert* panelists discussed different aspects of the case, they repeatedly encountered discrepancies between the myth of scientific certainty, which forms the basis for laws like Rule 702,[42] and the realization that science does not purport to provide certainty, but only make statements about probabilities. One panelist observed, "There is no 'truth' out there. And I think one of the great problems with scientific evidence is that somehow we think that there is a different level of certainty, of truth, than actually exists."[43] However, because law, and the adversarial nature of its dispute resolution function, seeks to provide an all or nothing answer, we have looked to science for a kind of certainty and predictability that it cannot provide.[44] Science can only give answers to questions in terms of probabilities and possibilities.[45] Indeed, Dr. Leon Gordis pointed out that it isn't science that fails to deal well with uncertainty, but law. Dr. Gordis observed that science thrives on uncertainty. The problem, as he saw it, is one of reconciling the role of the scientist with the role of the courts, not requiring them to play the same role.[46]

In a larger sense, the law asks science to provide not only certainty and predictability, but integrity as well. We expect science to provide neutral, unbiased answers to questions posed by law. The myth of scientific neutrality was seen by one panelist as pervading society generally—a myth seized upon by law to establish its own credibility.[47] One panelist felt that scientists could be neutral if they had no personal interest in the issues at stake, and he urged legal scholars and judges to help educate scientists about the law.[48] But others argued that scientists necessarily proceed on ideological presuppositions and that these determine scientific research designs and studies as well as how these studies are interpreted.[49] According to this view, these ideological premises make neutrality as impossible for scientists as it is for lawgivers.[50]

Some panelists wondered whether judges could appreciate the complex sociological factors that shape the scientific enterprize and the contingencies of the scientific process. Professor Stephen Burbank commented, "We have become aware of the socially constructed nature of scientific reality and of the intermingling of facts and values in disputes arising at the frontiers of science."[51] For instance, one panelist observed that peer review is seen in the scientific community as a convention, not a talisman of truth, and she was amused at the exalted status it has been givenin law.[52] Another was gratified that *Daubert* did not take the easy way out and fashion a legal rule for the admission of scientific evidence based on statistical significance—an approach that would entail borrowing an inappropriate scientific standard for legal ends.[53] Scientists have purposes of their own for generating information,[54] and those purposes may or may not be the purposes for which law seeks to use that information. Only by acknowledging the different epistemological premises underlying concepts of fact, causation, and truth can we have a rational discussion of the way in which knowledge generated for scientific purposes can be used for legal purposes. As one participant advised, "we must filter questions that the scientific process resolves in one way through the values of the legal system."[55]

B. The Threat to Judicial Power

The *Daubert* decision was seen by one participant as giving judges "a lot more power . . . and a lot more work."[56] Indeed, the question of judicial power came up repeatedly as panelists tried to assess the impact of *Daubert* on the authority of judges vis-a-vis juries, scientists, and lawgivers. The concern was with both the practicality and the legitimacy of assigning to generalist judges the task of evaluating the validity of scientific evidence. On the one hand, judges are jealous of their law-making prerogatives—which they exercise, in part, through the power to admit or exclude evidence. On the other hand, judges understand that they do not have the specialized knowledge needed to rationally evaluate the relevance, reliability, and trustworthiness of much of the technical information offered by scientific experts.

1. Vis-a-vis Juries

Panelists debated whether the new authority given judges by *Daubert* to exclude scientific opinion testimony from consideration by juries was a good or a bad thing. *Daubert* requires judges to determine, at an earlier stage of the proceedings and outside the jury's presence, not only whether a relevant scientific community finds proffered expert testimony methodologically reliable, but also whether the work is falsifiable, published in a peer-reviewed journal, and so on. As such, it gives judges authority to admit evidence that might have failed the *Frye* test and to exclude evidence that might have been admitted under *Frye*. This "gatekeeping" function was hailed by some panelists for giving judges long overdue power to prevent juries from considering unreliable scientific evidence.[57] Several panelists pointed out that no jury verdict in favor of plaintiffs in a Bendectin case has been sustained on appeal. If in the final analysis judges are going to determine liability anyway, they believed, it is better to let them do so at an earlier stage.[58]

Other panelists regretted that juries are the big losers after *Daubert*.[59] The question of jury power arises in cases where there is "soft" or weak science on one or both sides—cases like those involving dioxin, asbestos, colon cancer, and genetic predispositions.[60] If there is soft science on both sides, or the scientific evidence is otherwise in equipoise, why not let the jury decide? Or should the judge apply *Daubert* to keep the science away from the jury, leaving the dispute to be decided on the burden of proof? Some panelists thought the evidence should come in and juries should be allowed to decide.[61] As was pointed out in an early article by Professor Lawrence Tribe, civil trials are not only a search for historical truth, but also a kind of popularly approved, umpired game for the peaceful settlement of disputes in which juries bring intuition and a sense of community values to the ultimate disposition.[62] Others warned that admitting scientific evidence risks deluding juries into thinking that science can answer normative issues.[63]

2. Vis-a-Vis Scientists

The description above suggests that there was as much concern about surrendering policy decisions and law making responsibility to scientists as there was fear of leaving this responsibility with juries.[64] Abandonment of the *Frye* rule took admissibility determinations away from the scientific community and put them back into the courtroom. But, in doing so, *Daubert* makes generalist judges the evaluators of principles and methods they do not understand, presented to them in a language they do not speak. As Justice Rhenquist warned in dissent:

> [I] am at a loss to know what is meant when it is said that the status of a theory depends on its "falsifiability," and I suspect some [federal judges] will be too. I do not doubt that Rule 702 confides to the judge some gatekeeping responsibility in deciding questions of the admissibility of proffered expert testimony. But I do not think it imposes on them either the obligation or the authority to become amateur scientists in order to perform that role.[65]

Leon Gordis observed that, after *Daubert*, the "important issue is how can we equip judges to be better able to handle scientific evidence?"[66] In order to speak intelligently about the science involved, judges will have to enlist scientists as teachers and rely on expert witnesses. One panelist noted that there had been an increase in the number of judges trying to educate themselves about science in the courtroom, and Dr. Gordis called for specific steps to be taken to provide educational opportunities for judges to learn how to carry out their responsibilities.[67] For instance, The Federal Judicial Center has recently published a reference manual on scientific evidence that is intended to provide judges with basic knowledge about certain scientific disciplines.[68]

At the same time that panelists were concerned about relying exclusively on the parties' experts to educate themselves in the science of a case, they were also uncomfortable with use of so-called neutral experts. Should trial judges and appellate courts be bound by what a couple of experts selected by the parties have to say? Or would judges obtain a better understanding of science from a court-appointed expert acting under Rule 706.[69] While experts appointed under Rule 706 are usually presented as witnesses at trial—and given considerable deference by juries—courts have also used expert witnesses as confidential teachers and advisors.[70] But, as some panelists pointed out, if there is disagreement within the scientific community, the choice of such "neutral" experts will often determine the answer to whatever question is posed.[71] Put another way, the selection of a particular expert advisor, with a particular slant or opinion, determines the outcome before the scientific question is even considered by the court.

In addition, some panelists expressed concern that the relevant data and conclusions cannot be separated from the values that inform the expert's knowledge—scientific values that may not comport with judicial values. The very dependence of judges on scientists made the judges worry that implementing *Daubert* would require them to relinquish to scientific experts even more fundamental judicial responsibilities than was required by *Frye*. Arthur Miller sensed a fear "that under the mask of the scientific method and the scientific evidence," we will stop asking what "should" be and just accept what science tells us "is."[72] When scientific evidence is offered, the scientific questions may not be the questions legally at issue in the case, but they may be the ones that get tried.[73] By misapprehending the questions, judges and juries alike give scientists authority to frame social policy debate or even to provide the outcome. Even when scientific and legal questions are properly distinguished, judges are dependent on scientific expertise to evaluate the evidence, because they lack the intellectual tools necessary to discern the normative content of scientific knowledge.

C. Implications for the Legitimacy of Adversary Process

At bottom, the discussion about *Daubert* was a discussion about the legitimacy of the adversary process of which it is now a part.[74] The discussion had three themes: first, the fact that *Daubert* may require a departure from essential tenets of the adversary system; second, the unpredictability that may be created by the indeterminate standards provided in *Daubert*; and third, the lack of uniformity likely to result from the discretion granted by the decision to generalist judges. Both uniformity and predictability were viewed as in some sense essential to the legitimacy of the legal system. (For purposes of this essay, legitimacy means the ability of law to satisfy certain principles and values that transcend positive laws and thereby make it attractive to accept positive laws as rules one "ought" to obey.) Much of the legitimacy of particular procedural rules, in the sense of their broad acceptance, is derived from the extent to which they conform to traditional justice models. In our Anglo-American tradition, the adversary model has informed our understanding of justice for centuries. Procedural rules that depart from the model risk losing its legitimating grace. *Daubert* may risk just that.

In very general terms, the adversary model works on the premise that fact finding will be more accurate and legal reasoning sounder if persons whose interests are affected by the dispute take strongly opposing positions on fact and law and submit their dispute to a neutral decisionmaker authorized to award victory to one side or the other.[75] Procedural rules make the parties responsible for marshaling and presenting facts to a passive judge and lay jury. The judge is responsible for rendering a reasoned determination of particularized disputes based on the evidentiary record thus created. It is a process, in other words, that creates a polarized, zero sum game in which the only players are the parties and the judge acts as neutral umpire.

Several of the panelists sensed that *Daubert* may require significant departures from this model. Some felt strongly that the parties' dispute should be decided solely on a record created by the parties in accordance with the law's allocation of the burden of proof.[76] Others simply were not willing to let disputes over the validity of conclusions about scientific knowledge be decided in a battle of partisan experts: "This may be an area where we see judges saying, 'I'm not sure. I can't understand the scientist. I have the plaintiff's expert and the defendant's expert. They're both telling me something else. I need some help. I need my own expert.' "[77]

Thus, the panelists searched for ways to obtain needed scientific expertise other than by relying exclusively on the parties' experts. As discussed above, some panelists would look to court appointed experts under Rule 706.[78] Others registered the same concern voiced by many of the federal judges recently polled by the Federal Judicial Center about their use of court appointed experts: that court appointed experts depart too significantly from the adversary mode.[79]

There were also proposals to give more formal deference to the findings of administrative agencies, like the Food and Drug Administration,[80] National Institute of Health, or bodies created specially to consider particular scientific issues. As Judge Keeton advised, "I think the judges, both trial and appellate, ought to be free to go outside the record and get all the information they can get from whatever source instead of being bound to decide the case based solely on what the advocates bring to their attention through hired guns."[81] Still others wondered about making greater use of judicial notice, although judicial notice can be taken only of scientific facts that are not in dispute. All the panelists recognized that failure to rely exclusively on the testimony of party experts constitutes a departure from the classic adversary model.

Is reliance on expertise not provided by the parties consonant with our traditional justice system and the essential principles it embodies? One can argue, at least, that it is not. To the extent that *Daubert* forces our impartial, generalist judges to seek out scientific information from court appointed experts, administrative agencies, expert panels, and manuals on scientific evidence, it arguably departs from the adversary model to which we have traditionally accorded legitimacy. Indeed, it can be argued that *Daubert* moves us toward a more inquisitorial model, with an activist judge who takes responsibility for collecting and screening evidence as well as for finding facts.[82] In his controversial article on the West German system, Professor John Langbein described how a German court may on its own motion commission an expert to serve as an advisor rather than a witness. Advisors are selected from lists of experts designated by official licensing or quasi-public bodies authorized by government to identify experts.[83] Unlike special masters and court appointed experts in this country, court designated experts in Germany are paid by the losing party, and thus their determinations are given more credibility than the findings of party-paid experts in our adversary system. These advisors and the judge shape the development of scientific facts through a process of interrogatories, document procurement, and successive hearings in which the parties do not play a decisive role. Although the parties are permitted to comment orally and in writing on fact gathering prior to the court's decision, and may offer experts of their own, the parties cannot cross examine the court's experts nor easily appeal their findings. Protection from judicial abuse in the Continental model rests largely with the restraints of the German civil service system from which judges are selected. In contrast, our adversary system relies primarily on the right of the parties to participate in and control the fact finding process.

The Continental model may provide a more efficient way of obtaining scientific expertise, but it may work poorly here precisely because it deviates from the dominant American model of justice. As one panelist observed,

> The danger [with court appointed experts] is that the central thing that makes these verdicts acceptable is that the litigants have ownership because they've clashed with the other side. There wouldn't be any ownership of the scientific conclusion with an independent expert.[84]

The "acceptance" and "ownership" of verdicts in cases in which scientific facts are viewed as pivotal may simply not occur if the verdicts are based on facts elucidated from outside the adversary process—or worse, based on the conclusions of amateur judicial scientists, judicial notice, the advice of court-appointed experts, and deference to findings of agencies and other courts. A lack of legitimacy in this sense may be particularly troublesome in product liability and mass tort cases, because these are cases in which plaintiffs seek to shift the burden of their losses to others and spread the risk more broadly so that it will be borne by all consumers of the product that injured them. To the extent that judgments spreading or refusing to spread a risk of loss are seen as grounded outside our traditional justice system, they may not be accepted by the broad audience of consumers whose interests are affected. Such judgments may perpetuate rather than settle disputes, thus failing to discharge the justice system's most essential task. What is more, legitimacy may rest in large measure on the notion that the law is rationally impartial and provides like results in like cases. Yet many of the panelists worried that application of the *Daubert* factors by gatekeeping judges will produce lack of uniformity in admissibility determinations and case outcomes, and thus erode confidence in the judicial system.

Though not carefully distinguished from concerns about predictability, the problem of non-uniform judgments stems from the conviction that to be just, our legal process must do equity—must treat likes alike. After *Daubert*, impartiality may be difficult to perceive or demonstrate, because *Daubert* permits judges to take all, some, or none of the factors suggested by Justice Blackmun into account in evaluating the validity of scientific expert testimony. In addition, lack of uniformity may result from the fact that science changes over time,[85] that different court appointed experts will reach different conclusions,[86] and that parties' experts will offer different opinions in particular cases.[87] Some panelists believed that determinations on admissibility are less likely to be consistent after *Daubert*, and they argued that confidence in our justice system is eroded more when judges render inconsistent decisions than when juries do it.[88]

Accordingly, some panelists advocated strict appellate review to provide as much uniformity as possible,[89] while others argued that strict review is not possible if district courts exercise the discretion that *Daubert* grants them. There was, on the whole, considerable tolerance for whatever lack of uniformity reasonably results from *Daubert*'s indeterminacy.[90] No one is especially troubled when juries reach different determinations, and some panelists felt that we should be equally tolerant when judges do.

Though closely related to uniformity, the concern for predictability is more about efficiency than equity. Decisions by different judges in different judicial districts in the federal system need not be uniform to be predictable, but predictability is critical to the parties forming and acting upon reasonable expectations. The ability to predict legal results is thus necessary as a matter of efficiency, permitting parties to seek outcomes that the law permits them to achieve. In addition, predictability serves law's normative function of instructing people that they ought to conform their actions to a particular standard. When the applicability of a standard is unpredictable, how can conformity be demanded? Yet like uniformity, predictability is frustrated by the uncertain, discretionary principles adopted in *Daubert*. Some panelists, accordingly, decried the lack of predictability as a flaw in *Daubert*'s approach to the problem of scientific evidence. Others, like Judge Becker, pointed out that this kind of indeterminacy is inherent in a common law system—something we have tolerated well over the years.[91] Somewhat paradoxically, the indeterminacy of *Daubert* may be conducive to settling of disputes. If the parties are unable to predict how a court will resolve their case, they have a greater incentive not to risk a roll of the dice and instead to settle their differences by compromising.[92]

IV. Empiricism and Falsification: Bridging the Gap Between Legal Theory and Legal Practice

The panel's discussion of the practical and theoretical implications of the *Daubert* decision has made clear that we have only begun to develop a law of science—a jurisprudence for using scientific evidence in the administration of justice. Efforts like those of the Institute of Judicial Administration are laudable for attempting to bridge the gap between legal theory and practice by convening experts in both disciplines to discuss particular issues. But discussion and conceptual analysis may not be enough.

It is interesting to consider, for instance, whether members of the panel would have been permitted under *Daubert* to offer their expert opinions about the implications of the decision to a jury. The panelists are among the most talented and accomplished specialists in their fields and would certainly qualify as experts under Rule 702. In addition, their testimony is surely relevant under Rule 402, and the methodology upon which their opinions are based (conceptual analysis, logical reasoning, experience, and normative assertion) would likely be deemed acceptable by the relevant intellectual communities of which they are a part.

There are, however, several *Daubert* factors that the panel's experts do not meet. Most of their opinions on the decision have not been published in peer-reviewed journals. Legal academics, at least, seldom publish in journals reviewed by other professional scholars, but inexplicably consigning their work to student law reviews. The scientists on the panel publish more often in peer-reviewed journals, but seldom render opinions on the legal matters before the panel. The opinions of judges, of course, are periodically reviewed by higher courts and approved, as was Judge Becker's opinion in *Downing*.

More important, the methodology used by many of the panelists is not falsifiable. Practitioners, legal scholars, scientists and judges all base their opinions on close reading and analysis of authoritative sources—logical reasoning and judgments informed by a life-time of reading and experience. With the exception of judicial opinions, which can be "falsified" by being reversed by a superior court, the method used by legal scholars and practitioners does not provide for disproof. We do not test legal opinions in the crucible of empirical experience except in the most impressionistic way. They are, rather, refuted by other scholars and practitioners employing the same analytic and normative approach.

There is, moreover, no accepted error rate with regard to legal methodology. Yet according to Justice Blackmun, "the court should consider the known or potential rate of error . . . and the existence and maintenance of standards controlling the technique's operation."[93] Other fields have developed customary standards for acceptable error. In epidemiology, for instance, the standard is that there be no more than a five percent likelihood that findings are the result of chance.[94] There are no similar standards or customary error rates controlling the study of law.

Perhaps we can learn something from the scientific method that *Daubert* tells us to scrutinize. Perhaps we can develop a science of law as well as a law of science.[95] I do not mean here to allude to the old and rightly discarded notion that "law is a science." I am, rather, suggesting that we make a greater effort to use empirical data to identify the procedural variables associated with the specific problem under investigation. The Jurimetrics Journal has long been dedicated to a more empirical study of the judicial process,[96] and some legal scholars (though certainly not many) use empirical methods to examine the legal process.[97]

In the case of the *Daubert*, it would be interesting to know, as the panel conjectured, whether the decision will make a difference in either the admission of evidence or the outcomes of cases. Did things actually change after the decision was rendered? To find out we might conduct retrospective studies of product liability cases decided before *Daubert*, comparing cases in which defendants were found liable with cases in which they were not to determine whether there were differences between circuits applying the *Frye* rule and those using *Downing* or some similar rule. Prospective studies would be more difficult to do, because *Daubert* now imposes a uniform rule on the federal courts. It might, however, be possible to identify two sets of similar products liability cases, one in the federal courts and one in states that do not follow *Daubert*. The results in these cases could be compared with respect to both the admission of scientific expert testimony and the outcomes. Obviously, many difficult issues must be resolved before we can carry out such studies. We must, for example, identify confounding and contributing variables and use regression analysis to control for those that are unimportant. Nevertheless, we might learn a lot in the process. At that point, the Institute's *Daubert* panel should be reconvened to ponder the results. But, a scientist, not a lawyer, should serve as reporter.

Notes

1. *Daubert v. Merrell Dow Pharmaceuticals, Inc.,* 113 S. Ct. 2786 (1993).
2. Barry J. Nace, *Reaction to Daubert*, 1 Shepard's Expert and Scientific Evidence Q. 51 (1993). Mr. Nace, attorney for Daubert and the other petitioners, describes his surprise, after the Supreme Court reversed a judgment against his clients, in reading Merrell Dow's News Release stating that "the United States Supreme Court, in a 7–2 opinion, today agreed with the legal position of Merrell Dow and the Solicitor General of the United States. . . . "
3. *Daubert v. Merrell Dow Pharmaceutical, Inc.,* 727 F. Supp. 570 (S.D. Cal. 1989).
4. *Id.* at 572, 575.
5. *Id.* at 576.
6. *Daubert v. Merrell Dow Pharmaceuticals, Inc.,* 951 F.2d 1128, 1129 (9th Cir. 1991).
7. *Daubert v. Merrell Dow Pharmaceuticals, Inc.,* 113 S. Ct. 2786, 2793 (1993).
8. *Id.* at 2795, n.9.
9. *Id.*
10. *Id.* at 2796 ("Scientific methodology today is based on generating hypotheses and testing them to see if they can be falsified. . . . ") Justice Blackmun cites the work of Karl Popper, who espoused deductive falsifiability as a hallmark of the scientific method. Popper conceived of scientific knowledge as growing gradually through an accumulation of information derived from the testing of new ideas which originate, not in logic or empiricism, but intuition. Karl Popper, Objective Knowledge 8–30 (1972). Falsification would eventually eliminate all wrong theories, and truth would be known through this process of elimination and consensus. Karl Popper, The Logic of Scientific Discovery 45 (rev. ed. 1968).
11. 113 S.Ct. at 2797. Justice Blackmun cites Sheila Jasanoff, The Fifth Branch: Scenic Advisors as Policy-makers 61–76 (1990), for the proposition that peer review and publication are not the *sine qua non* of admissibility.
12. 113 S.Ct. at 2797.
13. *Id.* (quoting *United States v. Downing,* 753 F.2d 1224, 1238 (3d Cir.1985)).
14. 63 U.S.L.W. 2420 (Jan. 4, 1995); 1995 WL 1736 (9th Cir. 1995). The Court of Appeals, per Judge Kozinski, understood *Daubert* to provide "illustrative factors rather than exhaustive ones" to decide whether an expert's testimony is based on sound scientific methodology:

    > [T]hough we are largely untrained in science and certainly no match for any of the witnesses whose testimony we are reviewing, it is our responsibility to determine whether those experts' proposed testimony amounts to "scientific knowledge," constitutes "good science" and was derived by the "scientific method."

    Slip op. at 5. The appeals court held that the expert testimony was not based on research conducted independent of the litigation, nor was it published in a peer reviewed journal. Therefore, it was not reliable under the flexible *Daubert* standard. In addition, the court found that the testimony plaintiffs' experts would have given was not relevant because the experts did not conclude that it was more likely than not that the plaintiffs' birth defects were caused by Bendectin, but only that there was some likelihood that they were. *Id.* at 8.

15. Judge Jane R. Roth, p. 187. [Citations to the panel discussion will state only the identity of the speaker, if known, and the page in this volume where the statement referred to may be found.]
16. Margaret Berger, p. 178.
17. Judge Edward Becker, p. 179.
18. Peter Huber, p. 199.
19. Kenneth Chesebro, p. 177; 113 S. Ct. at 2797.
20. Sheila Birnbaum, p. 178; Margaret Berger, pp. 186–87; Judge Becker, p. 190.
21. Paul Carrington, p. 188.
22. Judge Patrick Higginbotham, p. 194.
23. Melvyn Weiss, pp. 184, 188, 201.
24. This point was also made by Robert Conason, an attorney with Gair, Gair, Conason, Steigman and Mackauf, p. 202.
25. Sheila Birnbaum, p. 185.
26. Judge Robert E. Keeton, p. 206. See also John Monahan and Laurens Walker, *Social Authority: Obtaining, Evaluating and Establishing Social Science in Law*, 134 U. Pa. L. Rev. 477 (1986), and *Social Frameworks: A New Use of Social Science in Law*, 73 Va. L. Rev. 559 (1987), proposing that conclusions based on social science research be classified as "social authority" and treated in much the same way as legal precedents are treated under the common law.
27. Judge Stephen R. Williams, p. 192.
28. Judge Becker, p. 193; Judge Higginbotham, p. 193.
29. Margaret Berger, p. 207.
30. Judge Higginbotham, p. 194.
31. 727 F. Supp. 570 (S.D. Cal.1989).
32. Margaret Berger, p. 183.
33. Sheila Birnbaum, p. 197.
34. Peter Huber, pp. 184–85; see also pp. 209–10 for a discussion of the withdrawal of whooping cough vaccine from the market before Congressional legislation saved it by providing an indemnity mechanism for compensating losses due to adverse reactions.
35. Peter Huber, p. 199.
36. See, e.g., Rochelle Dreyfuss, p. 182.
37. Justice Neely, pp. 190–91.
38. In *Downing*, the defendant sought to introduce an expert in eye witness identification to refute the reliability of the prosecution's eye witness testimony. Judge Becker, p. 202.
39. In their opinion, concurring in part and dissenting in part, Justices Rehnquist and Stevens argued that the lower courts should be given an opportunity to develop a "law of science" free from the constricting science-based "factors" set out by Justice Blackmun in the majority opinion in *Daubert*. 113 S. Ct. at 2800. For a discussion of the need to educate generalist judges and lay juries in scientific and technical areas so they can render judgments that serve the purposes of our adversary justice system see E. Donald Elliott,

Toward Incentive-Based Procedure: Three Approaches for Regulating Scientific Evidence, 69 B.U.L. Rev. 487–89 (1989).

40. Arthur Miller, p. 180. For a discussion of the epistomological problems encountered in that project see Margaret G. Farrell, Daubert v. Merrell Dow Pharmaceuticals, Inc.: *Epistemology and Legal Process*, 15 Cardozo L. Rev. 2183 (1994).
41. Rochelle Dreyfuss, p. 182.
42. The Supreme Court's opinion in *Daubert* cites the Advisory Committee's Notes to the effect that, as a general rule, the common law excluded opinion testimony and insisted that a witness have first-hand knowledge or testify to a fact that can be and has been perceived by the senses. 113 S.Ct. at 2795 n.9. An exception was made for the opinion of experts testifying on the basis of scientific knowledge, because scientific knowledge was regarded as equally trustworthy—a sensory-based, empirical process of testing hypotheses about the world through observation and experimentation. 1 Charles T. McCormick et al., McCormick on Evidence §§10, 11 (John W. Strong, ed. 4th ed. 1992). See also Edward J. Imwinkelried, *The Next Step After Daubert: Developing a Similarly Epistemological Approach to Ensuring the Reliability of Nonscientific Expert Testimony*, 15 Cardozo L. Rev. 2271, 2277 (1994)("Lockean epistemology put the question in *Daubert*; and Newtonian science provided the answer.")
43. See p. 196.
44. See generally Troyen A. Brennen, *Casual Chains and Statistical Links: The Role of Scientific Uncertainty in Hazardous-Substance Litigation*, 73 Cornell L. Rev. 469, 480 (1988). In light of the impossibility of certainty, one panelist asked whether juries should be permitted to render probability verdicts, rather than an all-or-nothing determination. Eleanor Fox, p. pp. 195–96.
45. Rochelle Dreyfuss, pp. 182–83.
46. Leon Gordis, pp. 207–8.
47. Dorothy Nelkin, p. 203.
48. Leon Gordis, pp. 208–9. Dr. Gordis pointed out that currently there are few incentives for the vast majority of scientists and academicians to testify as expert witnesses. They get no professional "brownie points" and risk the embarrassment of impeachment and cross examination. He added:

    > [W]e have hundreds and thousands of scientists and academicians who have biases, but are neutral and could provide their expertise in the legal system if we devise a way and if we build bridges to educate them on what it is you want in the legal system, what they can offer you, and how there can be a common language between the two.

49. P. 209.
50. See Richard Tarnas, The Passion of the Western Mind 359 (1991):

    > Because induction can never render certain general laws, and because scientific knowledge is a product of human interpretative structures that are themselves relative, variable and creatively employed, and finally because the act of observation in some sense produces the objective reality science attempts to explicate, the truths of science are neither absolute nor unequivocally objective.

See also Peter H. Schuck, *Multi-Culturalism Redux: Science, Law, and Politics*, 11 Yale L. & Pol'y Rev. 1 (1993), for a discussion of some implications of the cultural conflicts that divide the legal, scientific, and political communities.

51. See also Sheila Jasanoff, The Fifth Branch: Science Advisors as Policymakers, vii (1990); Thomas F. Gieryn, *Boundary-Work and the Demarcation of Science from Non-Science: Strains and Interests in the Professional Ideologies of Scientists*, 48 Am. Soc. Rev. 781 (1983); and Sheila Jasanoff, *What Judges Should Know About the Sociology of Science*, 32 Jurimetrics J. 345 (1992).
52. Dorothy Nelkin, p. 180. Dr. Gordis disagreed, arguing that there is no better system for evaluating science at the moment.
53. Leon Gordis, p. 181. For a discussion of the use of statistical significance as a standard for the admissibility of evidence of causation see *DeLuca v. Merrell Dow Pharmaceuticals, Inc.*, 911 F.2d 941, 947 (3d Cir. 1990); Kenneth Rothman, Modern Epidemiology 117 (1986); Farrell, *supra* note 40.
54. As Justice Blackmun acknowledged, "there are important differences between the quest for truth in the courtroom and the quest for truth in the laboratory." 113 S. Ct. at 2798. Others have observed that the scientific enterprise can be regarded as descriptive, positive, and predictive—an effort to describe what is and what will be in the future. J. Bronowski, The Common Sense of Science 69 (1978). In contrast, law can be regarded as prescriptive and normative—an effort to describe what ought to be. The goal of science is truth; the goal of law is justice.
55. Stephen Burbank, p. 204.
56. Judge Keeton, p. 206.
57. Rochelle Dreyfuss, p. 182.
58. Sheila Birnbaum, p. 185.
59. Mel Weiss, p. 184.
60. Sheila Birnbaum, p. 197.
61. Eleanor Fox, p. 195.
62. Laurence H. Tribe, *Trial by Mathematics: Precision and Ritual in the Legal Process*, 84 Harv. L. Rev. 1329, 1376 (1971).
63. Rochelle Dreyfus, p. 189.
64. Arthur Miller, pp. 183–84.
65. 113 S. Ct. at 2800 (Rehnquist, C.J., concurring in part and dissenting in part.)
66. Leon Gordis, p. 181. For a discussion of the problem of educating judges and juries in scientific methodology see The Evolving Role of Statistical Assessments as Evidence in the Courts 176–81 (Stephen F. Feinberg, ed. 1988).
67. Leon Gordis, p.181.
68. Fed. Jud. Ctr., Reference Manual on Scientific Evidence (1994).
69. Arthur Miller, pp. 211-12. See generally Joe S. Cecil & Thomas E. Willging, *Court-Appointed Experts: Defining the Role of Experts Appointed Under Federal Rule of Evidence* 706 (Fed. Jud. Ctr. 1993); Joe S. Cecil and Thomas E. Willging, *Scientific and Technological Evidence: Accepting Daubert's Invitation: Defining A Role for Court-Appointed Experts in Accessing Scientific Validity*, 43 Emory L.J. 995 (1994); Samuel R. Gross, *Expert Evidence*, 1991 Wis. L. Rev. 1113, 1220–31.

70. See, e.g., *Reilly v. United States,* 665 F. Supp. 976 (D.R.I. 1987), *aff'd in part,* 863 F.2d 149, 155–56 (1st Cir. 1988).
71. Rochelle Dreyfuss, p. 207.
72. Arthur Miller, p. 183.
73. Rochelle Dreyfuss, p. 189.
74. Legitimacy can be conceived of in two ways. First, we may think about positive legitimacy, or an authoritative declaration or performance of an act to which certain consequences attach. Second, legitimacy can consist of certain principles of morality to which legislative and judicial actions must conform before they can be classified as law. See generally George P. Fletcher, *Two Modes of Legal Thought*, 90 Yale L.J. 970, 974 (1981); H.L.A. Hart, The Concept of Law (1961).
75. See generally Lon L. Fuller, *The Forms and Limits of Adjudication*, 92 Harv. L. Rev. 353, 369 (1978).
76. See p. 205.
77. *Id.*
78. See text accompanying notes 69–71, *supra.*
79. Cecil & Willging, *supra* note 69.
80. See p. 207.
81. Judge Keeton, p. 206.
82. John H. Langbein, *The German Advantage in Civil Procedure*, 52 U. Chi. L. Rev. 823 (1985)(setting out the major features of the Continental fact-finding process, using the West German system as an example.) For a discussion of the Continental model and the use of special masters under Rule 53 of the Federal Rules of Civil Procedure to provide scientific and technical expertise, see Margaret G. Farrell, *Coping with Scientific Evidence, The Use of Special Masters*, 43 Emory L. J. 927, 986–92 (1994).
83. Langbein, *supra* note 82, at 828, 935.
84. See p. 211.
85. Rochelle Dreyfuss, p. 194.
86. Judge Keeton, p. 205.
87. See p. 209.
88. Judge Shepard, p. 195.
89. Judge Keeton, pp. 205, 207.
90. Judge Higgenbotham, p. 194.
91. Judge Becker, p. 193.
92. Melvyn Weiss, p. 200.
93. 113 S.Ct. at 2797.
94. Reference Manual on Scientific Evidence *supra* note 68, at 121, 151–56.
95. The phrase is offered with apologies to Justice Holmes, who authored an article entitled "Law in Science and Science in Law" in 12 Harv. L. Rev. 443 (1899) (mentioned in Holmes's letter of October 17, 1901 to Richard T. Ely, which was called to this reporter's attention by a source who wishes to remain nameless, though the reader cannot be blamed for wondering who but a descendant of the letter's recipient would be rummaging about in such correspondence).
96. See, e.g., Anthony Champagne et al., *An Empirical Examination of the Use of Expert Witnesses in American Courts*, 31 Jurimetrics J. 375 (1991);

Anthony Champagne et al., *Expert Witnesses in Courts: An Empirical Study*. 76 Juridicature 5 (1992).

97. See, e.g., Peter H. Schuck & Donald Elliott, *To the Chevron Station*, 1990 Duke L.J. 984; Peter H. Schuck & Donald Elliott, *Studying Administrative Law: A Methodology for, and Report on, New Empirical Research*, 42 Admin. L. Rev. 519 (1990). In a separate effort, Professor James William Hurst and others at the University of Wisconsin Law School fostered the development of an empirical methodology for investigating the impact of substantive legal rules and inspired many scholars in the law and society movement.

Substance and Form in Scientific Evidence: What *Daubert* Didn't Do

Samuel R. Gross*

On its face, *Daubert v. Merrell Dow Pharmaceuticals*[1] was about as easy a case as the Supreme Court gets. The plaintiffs claimed that their birth defects were caused by the anti-nausea drug Bendectin, which their mothers had used during their gestation. In response to a motion for summary judgment by the defendant, the plaintiffs presented affidavits of eight expert witnesses who offered their opinions—based on a variety of studies—that Bendectin was indeed the culprit. The federal district court that heard the motion granted summary judgment to the defendant, and the Ninth Circuit affirmed. Both lower courts held that critical portions of the plaintiffs' evidence were inadmissible, and that without that evidence the plaintiffs had not met their burden of producing sufficient evidence to present a genuine factual dispute. The first holding—that this expert evidence was inadmissible—was the sole issue in the Supreme Court.

The question is governed by Rule 702 of the Federal Rules of Evidence:

> If scientific, technical, or other specialized knowledge will assist the trier of fact to understand the evidence or to determine a fact in issue, a witness qualified as an expert by knowledge, skill, experience, training, or education, may testify thereto in the form of an opinion or otherwise.

---

*Professor, University of Michigan School of Law. This chapter has benefited from advice and comments by David Garabrandt, Heidi Feldman, Richard Friedman, Robert Harris and Richard Lempert, and from excellent research assistance from Nancy Laetham, Kristina Maritczac and Nancy Vettorello. The research was supported by the Cook Funds of the University of Michigan School of Law.

Was this a case in which scientific knowledge would "assist the trier of fact"? Certainly. Were the plaintiffs' witnesses qualified by "knowledge, skill, experience, training, or education" to testify as experts? That was uncontested. Were there any other requirements that these witnesses had to satisfy? Arguably—plausibly—the term "knowledge," *scientific* knowledge, implies that the experts' testimony must be based on scientific information—which it was. Arguably, also, their evidence was subject to the requirement in Rule 703 of the Federal Rules of Evidence that the information on which an expert opinion is based, if it is not itself admissible in evidence, must be "of a type reasonably relied upon by experts in the particular field in forming opinions or inferences upon the subject." Would a reasonable scientist who was assessing the possibility that a drug produces birth defects rely on the sort of information these experts used? That too was not in dispute; in fact, the defendant's experts used much of the same data themselves.

Why then did two lower courts erroneously exclude this evidence? Why was Supreme Court review necessary? Why did this case attract 22 briefs *amicus curiae* and an unusual amount of publicity, even by Supreme Court standards?

For the most part, the defendant in *Daubert*, the lower courts, and the *amici curiae*, were all concerned with issues other than whether this sort of evidence is admissible under the Federal Rules of Evidence. There were several additional questions hovering around the case, of greater or lesser importance and generality, and much of the debate and the anxiety were directed at these other questions: (1) Does Bendectin in fact cause birth defects in human beings? The scientific consensus on this question is that Bendectin probably does not cause birth defects, and that certainly there is no substantial evidence that it does. (2) Do juries answer such questions correctly? Many people contend that juries sometimes, perhaps frequently, make terrible mistakes in dealing with scientific issues in general, and with causation in toxic torts cases in particular. Juries have obviously been wrong on Bendectin at least several times, if for no other reason because they have reached inconsistent verdicts in different cases. (3) Is the danger of such errors—and the resulting risk of legal liability—wreaking havoc in the American pharmaceutical industry or in American manufacturing generally? Some people contend that product liability litigation based on bogus science is destroying our international competitiveness. (4) Can we do anything to help juries get scientific questions right? Perhaps some new rule of evidence or procedure would improve matters. (5) Should juries decide such issues at all? Does it make sense to entrust scientific questions to ad-hoc tribunals of lay people? And if not juries, who should do it? Judges? Medical or scientific experts? Administrative bodies?

These issues were not before the Supreme Court, but they might have been affected by its opinion. Supreme Court opinions often make law well beyond the specific questions at hand. In this case that seemed particularly likely, since the Court rarely addresses the problems of scientific evidence. It didn't happen.

The good news about *Daubert* is that the Supreme Court got it right. It understood the technical issue presented by the case, and it wrote about as useful an opinion as possible given the structure of the Federal Rules of Evidence. The bad news is that (as with most easy cases) the Court did little. Its decision is not likely to change practice much, and it will not have any major effect on the important side issues that generated most of the heat.

The problem with *Daubert* is that it deals with form rather than content, the admissibility rather than the sufficiency or accuracy of the scientific evidence. The underlying substantive question is simple: How strong is the evidence that Bendectin causes birth defects? On that factual issue as well *Daubert* was an easy case, but in the opposite (anti-plaintiff) direction. By the time the District Court issued its opinion there was a clear scientific consensus that Bendectin is safe, or in any event that there is no substantial evidence to the contrary.

The lower courts that have handled Bendectin cases *have* been influenced by the substance of the evidence, and their decisions have come to reflect the consensus among scientists. In recent years they have uniformly judged the evidence against Bendectin lacking, and have held for the defendant. But they have done so by subterfuge, claiming that the plaintiff's evidence is legally insufficient under the standard that applies to motions for summary judgment, or that it is inadmissible altogether. Neither rationale is consistent with the usual rules that apply to these procedural issues.

I have no quarrel with the courts' judgment in the Bendectin cases, but their methods are unfortunate. Instead of distorting procedural law they ought to say directly what they are really doing: ruling on the factual merits of a scientific claim. In an easy case—and *Daubert* certainly qualifies—this would amount to nothing more than an application of the well established doctrine of "legislative fact finding." On other scientific issues the evidence is often less one-sided, and the outcome less obvious. Even so, courts may do well to extend the practice of substantive judicial decision making to some harder scientific issues, provided they do it explicitly and with great care. In all cases, courts will do better by adding reliable scientific evidence from trustworthy sources than by excluding evidence they consider unreliable.

I. *Daubert* and the Bendectin Cases

Daubert was a late Bendectin cases. Bendectin is the brand name for an anti-nausea drug that was marketed by the Richardson-Merrell pharmaceutical company ("Merrell") from 1956 until 1983.[2] It was widely prescribed for morning sickness; in the 1960s and '70s Bendectin was taken by perhaps as many of 25% of all pregnant women in the United States.[3] In January 1977 a lawsuit was filed on behalf of David Mekdeci, who was born with missing and malformed fingers and a missing pectoral muscle. The suit alleged that these birth defects were caused by the Bendectin that was prescribed to his mother while she was carrying him. This was the first Bendectin case; it ended in 1981, after a retrial, with a defense verdict that was upheld on appeal.[4] Between 1980 and 1991 about 1,700 additional Bendectin cases were filed, some thirty trials were held, and several dozen decisions were published by state and federal courts.[5] By December 1991, however, when the Ninth Circuit issued its *Daubert* opinion, this spate of litigation was all but completely over.

The Bendectin cases, as a group, constitute one of several recent examples of mass toxic tort litigation. As mass toxic tort litigation goes, Bendectin is a neat and inviting subject for study, because the entire lifespan of the issue covered a mere dozen years. Asbestos litigation, by contrast, has been going on for decades, with no end in sight. Three inter-related reasons made it possible to dispose of the Bendectin claims with such relative dispatch. *First*, the alleged harm has a short latency; it is apparent at the birth of the plaintiff, which is necessarily within nine months of the use of the drug. For other toxic substances—asbestos, for example, or the drug DES[6]—ill effects may not be apparent until ten or twenty or fifty years after exposure. Therefore it was comparatively easy to identify potential plaintiffs quickly. *Second*, because of this short latency, the claim that Bendectin causes birth defects was also comparatively easy to examine; the studies can be completed in months rather than years or decades. As a result, and also because of the intense legal interest in the issue, Bendectin was studied with uncommon intensity.[7] *Third*, the clear conclusion from the large body of scientific evidence that had accumulated by the mid-1980's was that Bendectin does *not* cause birth defects.[8]

There is no need for an extensive history of the Bendectin litigation in this context. It is not important to the issues in *Daubert*, and a detailed and excellent description of the life cycle of this set of cases has been already published by Professor Joseph Sanders, on whose work this section is largely based.[9] A synopsis of the highlights, however, will be useful.

The next Bendectin trial (after *Mekdeci*) was *Oxendine v. Merrell Dow Pharmaceuticals*,[10] which was tried in the Superior Court for the District of Columbia in May 1983. In *Oxendine* the jury awarded the plaintiff $750,000, the trial judge entered a judgment notwithstanding the verdict in favor of the defendant, and the District of Columbia Court of Appeals reversed the j.n.o.v. and reinstated the jury's verdict. *Oxendine* remains the only Bendectin case in which a verdict against Merrell has been sustained on appeal. In the meantime, starting in February 1982, all Bendectin cases that were pending in federal courts were consolidated for pretrial discovery before Judge Carl A. Rubin of the Southern District of Ohio (the home district of Merrell). Eventually most of these cases—818 out of 1,186—were consolidated before Judge Rubin for trial as well as discovery.[11] Judge Rubin ordered a trifurcated joint trial, which began in February 1985. The first part was restricted to general causation: does Bendectin cause any birth defects in humans? A jury found that it does not, which ended the proceedings. In September 1985, Judge Rubin denied the plaintiffs' motions for j.n.o.v. or a new trial;[12] three years later the judgment for the defendant was upheld on appeal.[13]

There have been some 24 trials and retrials of Bendectin cases since the joint trial before Judge Rubin.[14] They have produced two hung juries, one mistrial, fourteen defense verdicts, and seven plaintiff's verdicts—of which five have been reversed and two are pending on appeal. In three of the reversals, a federal circuit court granted a j.n.o.v. to the defendant, or upheld a j.n.o.v. by the trial court, on the grounds that the plaintiff's expert evidence on the issue of general causation was either inadmissible or insufficient as a matter of law,[15] and in a fourth reversal a j.n.o.v. was remanded for reconsideration in light of *Daubert*.[16] By one route or another, several federal circuits in succession decided that on the existing state of the scientific evidence, Bendectin claims could not be maintained: the First Circuit and the D.C. Circuit in 1987,[17] the Fifth Circuit in 1989,[18] the Sixth Circuit in 1992.[19] As this pattern emerged, trial court judges became more willing to short-circuit the process by granting pre-trial motions for summary judgment on the same grounds.[20] Not surprisingly, trials became increasingly rare. There was one *Bendectin* trial in 1985 (in addition to the joint trial), seven in 1986, eleven in 1987, three in 1988, none in 1989, two in 1990, one in 1991 and none since.[21]

Initially, *Daubert* fit right into this pattern. Judge Earl Gilliam of the United States District Court for the Southern District of California granted a defense motion for summary judgment in November 1989.[22] Like other late Bendectin opinions, Judge Gilliam's consists primarily of a review of the evidence on general causation, in the context of earlier opinions on the same issue dealing with much the same evidence.

Briefly: There are four types of scientific studies that are commonly used to determine whether a substance has toxic consequences:[23] analyses of the chemical structure of the compound that focus on similarities between it and known toxins; *in vitro* tests that examine its effects on human or animal cells that are cultivated in the laboratory for this purpose; *in vivo* studies that test its effects on laboratory animals; and *epidemiological* studies that examine its effects on human beings. There is general agreement that epidemiological studies are the best and most informative, since only they provide direct evidence on the occurrence of pathologies in people. Unfortunately, epidemiological studies are also considerably slower and more expensive than *in vitro* or *in vivo* studies. Our advanced industrial economy produces thousands of potentially toxic substances; for many (perhaps most) there are *no* epidemiological studies at all. Bendectin is different. It has been heavily studied, for several reasons—because it's a regulated drug that required FDA approval before marketing, because the effect at issue is comparatively easy to test, and because of the interest generated by litigation. By 1985, thirty-seven epidemiological studies of the relationship between Bendectin and human birth defects had been published; in 1989 one more appeared.[24] In none of these studies did the researchers conclude that Bendectin is a teratogen, a substance that causes birth defects. In six the authors reported some relationship between the drug and one or more types of birth defects, but concluded that their evidence was insufficient to show causal connection. In the remaining thirty-two studies, they drew no conclusion about the teratogenic effects of Bendectin or affirmatively concluded that it has none.[25]

This state of the evidence was presented to Judge Gilliam in affidavits from expert witnesses submitted by Merrell in support of its motion for summary judgment. The plaintiffs responded with affidavits from eight experts of their own. The District Court held, in two stages, that the evidence offered by the plaintiffs was inadmissible. (1) Several experts concluded that Bendectin causes birth defects on the basis of their evaluations of its chemical structure, and on *in vitro* and *in vivo* studies. Judge Gilliam, following cases in other circuits, concluded that in the absence of "statistically significant epidemiological evidence" in support, such expert opinions were inadmissible because they "lack[] the sufficient foundation necessary under FRE 703"[26]—in other words, because experts in their fields would not "reasonably rely" on such data to reach a conclusion such as this. (2) One of the plaintiffs experts, however, also based his opinion on a reanalysis of previously published epidemiological data. Despite the fact that the expert claimed to have found a statistically significant relationship between Bendectin and birth defects, Judge Gilliam held that this evidence was "insufficient to take this matter to the jury"[27] because the claim was too vague, and because it was "never published or subjected to peer review."[28] Judge Gilliam seemed to say that this final expert opinion, like the others, was *inadmissible* under FRE 703, but he could also be read to mean that although it was admissible, it was insufficient to raise a question for the jury to decide.[29]

II. *Daubert* and the *Frye* Rule

A. The Ninth Circuit Opinion

The District Court opinion in *Daubert* was in line with the trend in Bendectin cases. Judge Gilliam granted summary judgment to the defendant on narrow grounds. His opinion could conceivably mean that statistically significant epidemiological evidence is required in every toxic tort case. Or it could simply mean that the evidence offered by the plaintiff was inadmissible *in this case* because, given the wealth of negative epidemiological data on Bendectin, no expert could reasonably conclude that Bendectin is a teratogen on the basis of the limited data these experts relied on. Either way, the impact of the opinion, like that of other trial-court and appellate opinions in Bendectin cases, was limited to one claim, or to a single class of claims. It did nothing to restrict the use of expert evidence in general.

The Ninth Circuit opinion in *Daubert* is a sharp departure from this pattern.[30] The court (in an opinion by Judge Alex Kozinski) begins its legal analysis by restating and relying on a general evidentiary rule, the rule that the Circuit Court for the District of Columbia announced in 1923 in *United States v. Frye*:[31] The issue in *Frye* was the admissibility of a "systolic blood pressure deception test," a primitive precursor of the modern polygraph. The District of Columbia Circuit laid down the standard:

> Just when a scientific principle or discovery crosses the line between the experimental and the demonstrable is difficult to define. Somewhere in this twilight the evidential force of the principle must be recognized . . . [but] the thing from which the deduction is made must be sufficiently established to have gained general acceptance in the particular field in which it belongs.[32]

Although the *Frye* rule had been a controversial element of American evidence law on expert evidence for nearly seventy years, it played essentially no role in the Bendectin litigation up to that point. *Frye* was cited only once in the half-dozen circuit court Bendectin opinions preceding *Daubert*: in *DeLuca v. Merrell-Dow Pharmaceuticals, Inc.*,[33] the Third Circuit noted that it had rejected the *Frye* test. This is hardly surprising. Whatever the cryptic "general acceptance" test means, its range was always understood to be restricted to the type of issue that was presented in *Frye* itself, the admissibility of *novel* scientific evidence. But there was nothing novel about the plaintiffs' expert evidence in *Daubert*, or any of the other Bendectin cases; on the contrary, both the data and the modes of analysis were tried and true, old hat. The problem was a different one – simply that it seemed quite clear that the plaintiffs' experts were *wrong*.

The Ninth Circuit begins its discussion of the evidence in *Daubert* by adopting a principle it derives from other circuit court Bendectin cases: "animal and chemical studies . . . [are] insufficient to establish a link between Bendectin and birth defects."[34] That leaves the reanalysis of published epidemiological studies as the plaintiffs' last hope. For that item, the court invokes the *Frye* standard,[35] with a twist. As a mode of scientific investigation, reanalysis of published data is neither novel nor controversial; but that is not enough:

> [T]he reanalysis of epidemiological studies is generally accepted by the scientific community only when it is subjected to verification and scrutiny by others in the field. . . . Plaintiffs' reanalyses do not comply with this standard: they were unpublished, not subjected to the normal peer review process, and generated solely for use in litigation.[36]

Does this mean that under the Ninth Circuit's interpretation of *Frye*, peer review and publication are general prerequisites for the admissibility of scientific evidence? The opinion doesn't quite say so, but a couple of passages do suggest that reading. The court says that to be admissible the evidence "must meet *all* of the essential requirements" "imposed by the scientific community," and it quotes a passage from a muckraking book on "junk science in the courtroom:"

> [T]he best test of certainty we have is good science – the science of publication, replication, and verification, the science of consensus and peer review.[37]

Judge Kozinski's opinion in *Daubert* is poorly reasoned and carelessly written. If it means what it seems to mean, it might have changed the use of scientific evidence in a big way. *Frye* said that evidence based on *novel* scientific *techniques* is inadmissible until the basic principles and technology have become "generally accepted." Kozinski suggests that every scientific *finding* that an expert witness relies on – and perhaps every *conclusion* the expert testifies to – must be "generally accepted," as demonstrated by publication in a peer-reviewed journal. This would have been a vast extension of *Frye*, and it would have been utterly unworkable.

Peer review is the procedure by which articles are evaluated for possible publication in scientific journals. It is an extremely useful institution for the purposes for which it was designed, but not as a test for admissibility in court. Given the Supreme Court decision in *Daubert*, I will mention only some of the objections to the peer-review version of *Frye*, and only in the briefest passing.[38]

(1) Peer review is not a substantive evaluation of the truth of the findings reported in the scientific research. The reviewers, however pos-

itive their evaluations, do not attest to the accuracy of the study; their assignment is simply to evaluate the appropriateness of the methodology, the completeness of the reporting, and the importance and novelty of the topic.

(2) Studies that are rejected for publication by peer review are not necessarily wrong or misleading. In fact, there are famous examples of articles that were turned down at first and went on the become classics in their fields, (and famous examples of published peer-reviewed nonsense).

(3) Peer review is a slow process that is designed for substantial works of original research. Most scientific testimony in court cases consists of specific applications of established principles. Such work is usually unsuitable for publication because it has little or no general scientific interest, and publication is often impractical because it must be completed and presented quickly to meet the timetable of litigation.

(4) Courts could not successfully apply a standard based on an editorial process with which they are so thoroughly unfamiliar. Worse, making peer review an issue in legal proceedings would have predictable and unfortunate effects on the operation of scientific journals. Judge Kozinski's opinion contains no definition of a "peer-reviewed journal." The world of science already includes a large and varied collection of publications that fit that description, ranging from those at the top that are extremely selective (e.g., The *New England Journal of Medicine*), to some at the bottom that are not so choosy. A peer review-based *Frye* test would create an incentive to send any research that might be the subject of testimony straight to the bottom, in order to avoid the danger of rejection. Worse, it might spark the creation of ersatz "peer reviewed journals." If they printed their purpose on the masthead—*The Annals of Impending Testimony* or the *Journal of Unpublishable Results*—they might be spotted. But more realistic ventures, with respectable shells and mixed purposes, would get by.

B. The Supreme Court Opinion

The Supreme Court used *Daubert* as a vehicle to review the viability of the *Frye* test, and to reject it.[39] Given that decision, it was unnecessary to consider the peculiar additions embroidered on to *Frye* by Judge Kozinski—extending *Frye* from scientific techniques to the conclusions of expert witnesses, and (apparently) equating "general acceptance" with peer review.[40]

Frye was widely followed by American courts, but never universally endorsed. For decades, it was the dominant authority on the admissibility of scientific evidence,[41] but by 1992 its heyday had passed. It was the rule in seven federal circuits,[42] four circuits had rejected it,[43] and the First Circuit—along with the Supreme Court—had not spoken on the issue.[44] Many state courts followed *Frye*, but some did not.[45] Almost all cases applying *Frye* were criminal prosecutions;[46] *Daubert* was only the third federal civil case to use this rule.[47] In the two decades before *Daubert*, *Frye* had been widely attacked as outmoded, unmanageable, and unduly restrictive.[48] Critics argued that the "general acceptance" test required judges to make decisions they were not competent to make, imposed an excessively high burden on the proponents of novel scientific evidence, excluded valuable information at the frontiers of knowledge, and produced arbitrary results depending on how a court defined the "field" in which the evidence had to attain acceptance. Moreover, since the adoption of the federal rules of evidence in 1975, the legal status of *Frye* (in federal courts at least) had been under a cloud. The petitioners in *Daubert*, and many evidence scholars before them, argued that *Frye* had been repealed by Rule 702. The Supreme Court agreed—correctly, I believe—and reversed.

The question turns on Federal Rule of Evidence 402, which states:

> All relevant evidence is admissible, except as otherwise provided by the Constitution of the United States, by Act of Congress, by these rules, or by other rules prescribed by the Supreme Court pursuant to statutory authority. Evidence which is not relevant is inadmissible.

In other words, Rule 402 abolishes common law objections to evidence. Since *Frye's* "general acceptance" test is not mentioned anywhere in the Federal Rules that govern expert evidence, *Frye* could only survive if it is a reasonable and useful interpretation of the relevant portion of Rule 702: "If scientific knowledge will assist the trier of fact . . . a witness qualified as an expert . . . may testify thereto. . . ."

Nothing about Rule 702 itself suggests that the unstated qualification "generally accepted" should be read into it. The best argument that could be made is that "general acceptance" is an implied quality of "scientific knowledge." This would have been a strained reading, unless the Court were willing to derive the insertion from the historical context: *Frye* was widely applied in 1975, and since the drafters of the Federal Rules of Evidence did not explicitly reject it, they must have endorsed it. In fact, the context suggests the opposite, since (as the Court noted in *Daubert*) it was the clear intention of the drafters to liberalize the use of expert testimony.[49] But the strongest arguments against *Frye* are not historical or textual but practical. A majority on the Court undoubtedly believes that federal courts have the authority to devise judge-made rules to fill in gaps, resolve ambiguities, and help provide consistency in the application of Federal Rules generally. They certainly do it themselves. But why *this* rule? It's arbitrary, it was not much good to begin with, by now its problems are famous, and *Daubert* presented a clear occasion to reconsider and reject it.

Having rejected *Frye*'s "general acceptance" test for scientific testimony, the Supreme Court proceeded to devise one of its own. Under Rule 702, the trial judge must decide two preliminary issues[50] in order to admit any scientific evidence:[51] "whether the expert is proposing to testify to (1) *scientific knowledge* that (2) will *assist the trier of fact* to understand or determine a fact in issue."[52] Or, to phrase it differently, judges must decide "whether the reasoning or methodology underlying the testimony is scientifically *valid* and whether that reasoning or methodology can be *properly applied* to the facts at issue."[53]

The Court recognizes that this is a "flexible" inquiry,[54] and that "many factors will bear on it."[55] It then goes on to list four that are likely to become the focus of future litigation: (1) Is the theory or technique testable, and has it been tested? If not, it probably does not qualify as science.[56] (2) Has the theory or technique "been subjected to peer review and publication"?[57] This ought to be "a relevant though not dispositive consideration in assessing the scientific validity" of the evidence.[58] (3) If the evidence concerns a particular scientific technique, what is its "known or potential rate of error"?[59] (4) Finally, "general" or "widespread" acceptance, while not a requirement, "can be an important factor in ruling particular evidence admissible. . . . "[60]

C. Did Frye *Matter?*

So *Frye* has been rejected; so what? At first blush, I'm tempted to say "Not much"—and that may prove to be so. *Frye* had two aspects. It embodied a recognition that courts must (in some manner) screen purportedly scientific evidence that is presented to them. That is an enduring and uncontroversial precedent. But *Frye* also announced a specific test for admissibility, the test that was rejected in *Daubert*. As a specific test, *Frye* may never have mattered nearly as much as all the fuss suggests.

As I've mentioned, several states never adopted *Frye*, and others explicitly rejected it within the past ten years.[61] Has practice in these states differed markedly from that in states that follow *Frye*? Not in any major way. For example, most states continue to exclude polygraph evidence—at least in the absence of a stipulation by the parties—regardless of whether they follow *Frye*.[62] Among the few state decisions admitting polygraph evidence without a stipulation, the two earliest were in New Mexico,[63] which followed *Frye*,[64] and Ohio,[65] which did not follow *Frye* and later explicitly rejected it.[66] Similarly, most federal court cases on polygraph evidence continued to exclude it, in *Frye* and non-*Frye* circuits alike, but some recent cases in both types of jurisdiction say that trial judges have discretion to admit polygraph evidence, at least at the request of a criminal defendant.[67] Or consider voiceprint identification evidence, which was in vogue in the 1960s and 70s,[68] but fell into disrepute after a committee appointed by the National Academy of Science found that the technique had no scientific basis.[69] In that case the admissibility of the evidence did bear *some* relationship to the test applied, since the admissibility of voice print evidence was the context in which a few courts rejected *Frye*.[70] Even so, admissibility could not be predicted from the local status of *Frye*, especially not among the more recent cases.[71] Finally, on the most hotly debated scientific evidence issue of the decade—the admissibility of DNA identification evidence—the courts are nearly unanimous in letting it in, regardless of the test they use.[72]

Daubert is not the first federal case that both rejects *Frye* and directs judges to screen scientific evidence by reference to a set of several factors. Eight years earlier, in *United States v. Downing*,[73] the Third Circuit produced its own alternative to the "general acceptance" test: a list of eight factors, several of which overlap with those later listed by the Supreme Court.[74] And yet, there is no particular reason to believe that practice in the Third Circuit with regard to scientific evidence has diverged from that in other circuits; Bendectin claims, for instance, have fared about as poorly there as elsewhere.[75]

It should not be much of a surprise that the formal test for admission of scientific evidence seems to make little difference. For one thing, the two types of tests are more similar than they may seem. *Daubert* and *Downing* both include "general acceptance" as a factor to be considered among others, and while *Frye* says that "general acceptance" is the only criterion, there is rarely direct evidence on this point, so judges must look for circumstantial indicia of "general acceptance"—including, conspicuously, reliability. As the Sixth Circuit put it:

> [W]e deem, general acceptance as being nearly synonymous with reliability. If a scientific process is reliable, or sufficiently accurate, courts may also deem it "generally accepted."[76]

More important, *Downing* and *Daubert* promise more than they can deliver. They avoid some of the arbitrary consequences (read: arbitrary exclusions) that may follow from mindless reliance on "general acceptance," if judges are knowledgeable and make good use of their new freedom in conducting the "flexible inquiries" that are now required—a significant if. *Frye* was criticized because the "general acceptance" of a principle or technique is a scientific issue that courts are not competent to evaluate. *Daubert* and *Downing* require them to make that same evaluation and a good deal more.

In most cases, of course, judges don't do any of this. They decide whether to admit scientific evidence not by determining global facts (is the polygraph a "generally accepted" test for deception?), nor by weighing factors pro and con (Testability?—yes; tested—yes; peer review—no; and so forth), but by referring to specific governing precedents: has DNA identification been admitted in this state? Has that decision been affirmed by the State Supreme Court? Ultimately, it seems, the major precedential decisions on which trial courts rely tend to converge on the same results, regardless of the test used.

Nonetheless, *Daubert* may have substantial impact after all. On its face, the Supreme Court's decision loosens the standard for admitting scientific evidence by overruling the restrictive test announced by the District of Columbia Circuit seventy years earlier. In theory, such a ruling could produce a sharp increase in the quantity of questionable scientific evidence that is admitted in federal courts. In practice, not only is such a shift unlikely, but the decision is more likely to cause a modest shift in the opposite direction. The *Daubert* opinion recognizes—no, celebrates—the role of the trial judge as a gatekeeper who screens scientific evidence on its way to the jury. The discretionary power of the trial court judge is broadcast at every turn. The Court removes any ambiguity that the decision is for the judge, not the jury.[77] It lists multiple statutory bases for decisions to exclude—Rule 702, Rule 703, and Rule 403, the catch-all provision that gives judges discretion to exclude relevant evidence if it is unduly confusing, wasteful or prejudicial.[78] The Court allows judges to base their decisions on a wide range of factors rather than on a single and apparently specific test,[79] and it explicitly recognizes and accepts the costs of giving them this power:

> We recognize that in practice, a gatekeeping role for the judge, no matter how flexible, inevitably on occasion will prevent the jury from learning of authentic insights and innovations. That, nevertheless, is the balance that is struck. . . .[80]

Paradoxically, the main effect of *Daubert* may be to embolden some judges to exclude more purportedly scientific evidence than they would have under the "inflexible" and "austere" *Frye* test[81] that *Daubert* rejects as unduly restrictive.[82]

III. What's Really at Stake?

As we have seen, the real claim in *Daubert* was not that the data or the method of the plaintiffs' experts were unacceptable, but that the conclusion they reached was false. This concern surfaces time and again in the lower court opinions in *Daubert*, in the Supreme Court briefs submitted by Merrell and its *amici*, and in other Bendectin cases. The First Circuit's opinion in *Lynch v. Merrell-National Laboratories Division of Richardson-Merrell* is a good illustration.[83] After brief review of the studies, the court concludes:

> [O]n the basis of the epidemiological evidence to date, Bendectin is as likely as aspirin to cause limb reduction [birth defects]. . . . The association of Bendectin with limb reduction is in the opinion of the health-care community an instance of popular delusion and error. . . .

A new study coming to a different conclusion and challenging the consensus would be admissible in evidence. Without such a study there is nothing on which expert opinion on Bendectin as a cause [of birth defects] may be based.[84]

In *Richardson v. Richardson-Merrell Inc.*,[85] the District of Columbia Circuit followed *Lynch*. In the process it had to distinguish an earlier toxic tort case, *Ferebee v. Chevron Chemical*,[86] in which it had affirmed a judgment based on evidence no stronger than that offered by the plaintiff in *Richardson*. The issue in *Ferebee* was whether exposure to the herbicide paraquat can cause pulmonary fibrosis. The evidence in support consisted of the opinions of two of the deceased plaintiff's treating physicians, who testified that they believed that had happened in this case. Apparently, no systematic studies of any sort were introduced, and even one of the plaintiff's experts concluded "that cases like Ferebee's were rare."[87] Chevron argued that this was not enough, but the court disagreed: "The short answer to Chevron's argument is that two expert witnesses refuted it and the jury was entitled to believe those experts."[88]

In *Richardson*, however, the D.C. Circuit explains that paraquat is one thing and Bendectin something else entirely. The relationship between paraquat and lung disease was untested, it stood "at the frontier of current medical and epidemiological inquiry."[89] With Bendectin, however,

> we are at the other end of the spectrum. . . . And far from a paucity of scientific information on the oft-asserted claim of causal relationship of Bendectin and birth defects, the drug has been extensively studied and a wealth of published epidemiological data has been amassed, none of which has concluded that the drug is teratogenic.[90]

Any ambiguity about the meaning of *Richardson* was removed in *Ealy v. Richardson-Merrell, Inc.*,[91] a later District of Columbia Circuit case following it:

> [A]n expert opinion that Bendectin is a human teratogen which caused the plaintiff's birth defects is without scientific foundation under Federal Rule of Evidence 703 in the face of "a wealth of published epidemiological data" to the contrary. . . . Accordingly such expert opinion is inadmissible.[92]

The underlying rule that emerges is simple: "expert opinion evidence that Bendectin causes birth defects is inadmissible because it is wrong." It's also an oxymoron. This cannot be a test for *admissibility*. A court could hardly apply such a test and then require the jury to answer the question: "Does Bendectin cause birth defects?" A court that employs this test is obviously using "admissibility" as a disguise to determine the merits of the claim; it has already decided that Bendectin does not cause birth defects. In *Daubert* itself, the Supreme Court (without citing *Lynch* or *Richardson*) disapproves this sort of evaluation: "The focus [of the judge's inquiry], of course, must be solely on principles and methodology, not on the conclusions they generate."[93]

Why use such an internally inconsistent rule? The impulse to find for the defendant in Bendectin cases is perfectly understandable: the evidence is overwhelmingly in its favor. What's more, since Merrell keeps facing the same evidence in case after case and winning (at trial or on appeal), it's also understandable that judges would want to short-circuit the process and rule for the defendant as a matter of law. But why not do it the obvious way—why not simply rule (on a motion for judgment as a matter of law) that the evidence against Bendectin, while admissible, is *insufficient* to create a genuine factual dispute? Two federal circuits have done just that: the Fifth Circuit in *Brock v. Merrell Dow Pharmaceuticals, Inc.*,[94] and the Sixth Circuit in *Turpin v. Merrell Dow Pharmaceuticals, Inc.*,[95] both on records similar to that in *Daubert*. But three other circuits—the First in *Lynch*, the District of Columbia in *Richardson* and *Ealy*, and the Ninth in *Daubert* itself—all relied on admissibility rather than sufficiency to achieve the same result.

A scientific question is never presented to the courts in the abstract. It comes up in the context of a particular dispute between specific parties that must end with a binding final judgment. In the process, all factual issues must somehow be resolved, even if essential questions cannot be answered with confidence. This is true for specific historical facts (Was the light red or green? Did the defendant see something that looked like a knife before he shot the deceased?) as least as often as it is for general scientific issues (Does Bendectin cause birth defects in human fetuses? Does non-ionizing radiation from electrical power lines and substations cause cancer?). But there are two differences. (1) The exact same scientific question can come up repeatedly, in dozens or in thousands of cases; similar patterns are rare for ordinary historical issues, and when they do occur (e.g., common factual issues in airline crash cases), the number of trials involved is likely to be comparatively small. (2) There is a well developed and highly successful method for investigating such questions—the scientific method—that it is at odds with the requirements of legal fact finding. Scientists are interested in truth, which is elusive; therefore they try to be comfortable with uncertainty. They work with hypotheses and theories that can be disproven but not directly proven. The most interesting and innovative scientific thinking is usually provisional, and even established scientific findings—in principle, *all* scientific findings—are subject to revision. Courts are happy to find truth, if they can, but (truth or no truth) they are required to decide cases by judgments that cannot normally be revised if better information becomes available.

All legal systems need some method or another for reaching final judgments on uncertain facts. In our system the archetypal procedure for doing so is trial by jury. In fact many legal disputes—probably most—are tried by judges without juries,[96] and some of those include tricky scientific questions. But the prominent cases with problematic scientific evidence seem to occur in categories that are generally tried by juries: criminal prosecutions and personal injury suits of one sort or another. As a result this issue has been framed in terms of fact finding by juries.

A jury is a one-time, ad-hoc, non-professional decision-making group. Juries are probably more unpredictable than other fact finders because each jury is constituted for one case only. A jury has no collective experience of its own to learn from, no track record for litigants to rely on, and almost no opportunity to learn from the experience of other juries. Juries are also delphic. They are never asked to justify or explain their decisions, or to describe the evidence on which they relied. A typical jury verdict consists of very few words—the name of the winning side, and (if it's the plaintiff in a civil case) the amount of the judgment. In unusual cases, civil juries are sometimes asked to answer one or several factual interrogatories; for example, the jury in the consolidated Bendectin trial answered "no" to the question: "Have the plaintiffs established by a preponderance of the evidence that ingestion of Bendectin at therapeutic doses during the period of fetal organogenesis is the proximate cause of human birth defects?"[97] But even this unusual procedure makes the jury's judgment only slightly less opaque.

Finally, and most important, jury decisions are substantively unreviewable. This is an overstatement, but only a slight one. Judges do occasionally grant motions for new trial or for judgment notwithstanding the verdict, but these are limited restraints. They are infrequently exercised, and they require the judge to decide that the jury's final verdict is unreasonable or inconsistent with the evidence. There is no procedure for a court to review the quality of a jury's reasoning or the accuracy of the factual premises on which it relied, since these intermediate steps are neither recorded nor expressed, and the jurors themselves are not allowed to "impeach their verdict" by telling the court how it was reached.[98] Indeed, it is hard to avoid the impression that on the whole judges not only accept the fact that jury verdicts are impenetrable, they relish it. Faced with what looks like an unanswerable question—does paraquat cause pulmonary fibrosis?—they seem happy to say: "Given the conflicting evidence, the jury was entitled to find. . . . " Or, to put it unkindly: "Following a proper ceremony, the question was put to the oracle. . . . " This argument sells. It's not exactly a religion, but the jury may be the most popular and trusted institution we use to exercise governmental authority.

Judges, of course, are not mindless jury fans. Quite the contrary. They worry that juries are too readily confused, too easily swayed by passions, too willing to ignore fixed rules of law out of sympathy or anger. Much of the elaborate common law of evidence is based on this systemic mistrust of juries. Some judges also complain that juries are unsuitable for "complex" cases, especially those that depend on expert and technical evidence[99] – although it's not at all obvious that judges themselves handle such cases better. Finally, juries cost a lot. It is expensive, in both cash and opportunity costs, to run trials in the dramatic, over-prepared, do-or-die, one-time continuous performance mode that is required by this awkward fact finder.

These are general characteristics of juries. There is also a particular problem that looms large in the context of Bendectin and other toxic tort cases: Juries tend to be *inconsistent* in the sense that different juries reach different judgments on the identical issue. This has been shown repeatedly by experimental studies of juries[100] – but it is also necessarily true of *jurors* and of individual decision makers, including judges. Indeed, jury research shows that the collective process of deliberation reduces interpersonal variation in judgment.[101] If each case presented a new issue, juries might have no disadvantage in this respect over judges or any other type of tribunal, or they might be better. But when the same issue is tried repeatedly jury decision making suffers by comparison not because juries are stupid but because they are ephemeral. The jurors in a Bendectin case are unlikely to be influenced by the decisions of other juries dealing with the identical issue for the simple reason that they won't know about them. The judgments of other juries are inadmissible as evidence that what those juries found is true – that would be hearsay and inadmissible opinion evidence – and (in the usual case) there will be no other jury issue on which those judgements are relevant. Equally important, jurors will typically have no information about other similar cases through informal channels.

A judge, however, will know. Many of the earlier decisions (or appeals from them) are published in case reports. The judge may have seen them on her own, heard about them from colleagues, or even read about them in a law review article; if not they will be brought to her attention in motions to dismiss or for summary judgment, or informally in pre-trial discussions of motions, dates, and possible settlements. Trial judges, therefore, are able to make their findings consistent from case to case, if they want to. If they don't want to, consistency can be more easily achieved on review. Appellate judges may be more willing to reverse the verdict of other judges than those of juries, and they certainly have more to work with, since judges must justify their decisions with written findings of fact and conclusions of law.

In the Bendectin cases, most juries came to the correct conclusion, assuming (as I do throughout) that Bendectin is not in fact a teratogen. Of 22 jury trials that produced verdicts, the defendant won 14, for an overall success rate of 64%. (There were also 2 hung juries and one mistrial.)[102] But that also means that juries were wrong in 36% of the cases, and wrong in the face of overwhelming scientific evidence for the defense. It is tempting to conclude that judges would have done better, but it's not obvious that they are any more skillful than juries at evaluating evidence of this sort. For example, *Wells v. Ortho Pharmaceutical Co.*[103] was another product liability law suit in which the plaintiff claimed that her birth defects were caused by a product that her mother used during the plaintiff's gestation. The product in *Wells* was orthogynol spermicidal jelly, a popular contraceptive that is widely used in the United States in conjunction with diaphragms. As with Bendectin, the epidemiological evidence in *Wells* was strong and one-sided: several studies had shown that orthogynol spermicidal jelly is not a teratogen.[104] *Wells* was tried without a jury, and despite this evidence the judge awarded the plaintiff a judgment of $5.1 million.[105] *Wells* was the first orthogynol trial. (In the only other case of which I am aware, the defendant won a motion for summary judgment.[106]) If the Bendectin litigation had consisted of 25 first trials, the outcomes may have been roughly the same whether tried by judges or by juries.

There was, of course, only one first trial, which was retried, followed by a second, followed by the consolidated trial in the Southern District of Ohio, and so forth. By the end of 1985 the defendant had won 3 of the 4 cases that had been completed, including the consolidated trial. At that point the emerging pattern could have become a *de facto* trial-court rule, if juries had no role in the remaining cases. In any new Bendectin case, everybody—including the trier of fact—would know in advance that Merrell had already won repeatedly on the same issue and the same evidence. To rule against Merrell would seem both unfair and inefficient, and (since appellate courts could be expected to feel the same way) would court reversal. As it happened Merrell won both of the Bendectin bench trials that went to verdict after 1986 (the only bench trials in the entire set), but only 11 of the 17 jury trials.[107]

(Merrell's attorneys did make this point, as best they could. For example, in *DeLuca v. Merrell Dow Pharmaceuticals*,[108] the Third Circuit comments that the defendant's "apparent litigation strategy . . . was to emphasize that 'in all material respects, the instant case is identical to the cases where summary judgment has been granted in Merrell Dow's favor.' "[109] This was no doubt an excellent plan even, as in *DeLuca*, in the context of a motion for summary judgment; it would have succeeded more readily if the argument could have been addressed to a judge with plenary power to weigh the evidence.)

The only way to achieve consistency in a set of cases of this sort is to take them away from juries. The most effective method is to bar the underlying claim, procedurally (by a statute of limitations, by some form of immunity, or whatever) or substantively (by holding that there is no cause of action for these injuries against this defendant)—if there is some legal basis for doing so. In the case of Benedectin, there appears to have been none. If that's not possible, the courts will be forced to dismiss any suits that are filed on one of the two available evidentiary grounds: by holding that the evidence is *insufficient* as a matter of law, or by holding that it is *inadmissible*. As the Bendectin cases illustrate, courts do not like to admit evidence and say it's insufficient. Instead, they will go to unfortunate lengths to find that essential parts are inadmissable, and then say that there's not enough left to go to the jury.

The basic problem seems to be that judges do not want to look as though they are abrogating the role of the jury as trier of fact. The legal sufficiency of evidence is, technically, a question of law, but it looks and sounds like a judgment on the weight of the evidence—it *is* a judgment on the weight of the evidence, only an extreme one. This is particularly true for expert evidence, since traditionally courts have held that the testimony of any qualified expert is sufficient to sustain a verdict on any issue on which she testified.

Expert testimony is admitted in evidence as an exception to the usual rules limiting opinion evidence and restricting witnesses to facts within their personal knowledge. In effect, such evidence is an exception to a basic division of functions in common-law trials: witnesses *present* information, jurors *evaluate* it. *Expert* witnesses *evaluate* facts as well as present them; indeed, that is often their main function.[110] Frequently they testify to evaluations—expert conclusions—that are identical to those the jury must make,[111] and yet we consider this *evidence*. It is hard to say that the testimony of a witness who speaks in such terms—"the plaintiff is diabetic" or "Bendectin causes birth defects"—is admissible but insufficient to support a finding of fact that simply restates the testimony. That would amount to saying: "The jurors may hear and consider this witness—in fact they are required to do so—but they are also required to disbelieve her."

Evidence is often said to be either circumstantial or direct. Circumstantial evidence of a fact at issue is evidence which (if believed) supports an inference that the fact exists. Testimony that there were bootprints in the snow (to choose a traditional cliche) is circumstantial evidence that a person has walked by, since the conclusion depends on the (extremely plausible) inference that the prints were made by a walking person. Direct evidence is evidence which, if believed, directly proves the fact at issue, with no intervening inference—for example, testimony from a witness who claims to have seen a person crossing the snowy field. McCormick explains how the issue of sufficiency differs in the context of these two types of evidence: "Generally no difficulty occurs where the evidence is direct. Except in rare cases, it is sufficient, though given by one witness only, however negligible a human being she may be. But if the evidence is circumstantial, forensic disputes often arise as to its sufficiency. . . ."[112]

Strictly speaking, expert opinion testimony is neither direct nor circumstantial evidence in the usual sense of these terms. It is a *judgment* about facts that the expert has considered. However, an expert opinion on causation in a Bendectin case *sounds* very much like direct evidence: the opinion, if believed, resolves the issue at stake with no additional steps. As a consequence, the testimony of a single expert—"however negligible"—is often given the same dignity (for the purpose of rulings on the sufficiency of evidence) as the testimony of a lone eyewitness. A case from the California court of appeals illustrates this link:

> The testimony of a medical witness in answer to hypothetical questions based on the facts in the record is sufficient to support a finding contrary to the testimony of other medical experts who have seen and examined the patient. The testimony of one credible witness, if believed, is sufficient to support a finding of the court.[113]

In the context of toxic tort litigation, this classic position was restated by the District of Columbia Circuit in *Ferebee*:

> [I]f experts are willing to testify that such a link exists [between long term exposure to paraquat and pulmonary fibrosis] it is for the jury to decide whether to credit their testimony.[114]

But, of course, if the court finds the expert evidence *inadmissible*, the jury never faces this task.[115]

In short, the nature of expert testimony invites substantive judicial review. Since expert witnesses are allowed to pronounce judgment on the central issues in dispute—a prerogative we otherwise reserve to juries and judges—it is natural that the courts sometimes intervene to evaluate the quality of their evidence. Our rules of practice, however, drive judges who do so to pretend that they are acting on a question of procedure, namely, admissibility.

Unfortunately attempts to use admissibility to achieve consistency in toxic tort litigation do not work, at least not if the attempt resembles anything like a true rule of evidence. On the one hand, a court can get specific and say, as the District of Columbia Circuit has said, that "an expert opinion that Bendectin is a human teratogen . . . is inadmissible."[116] But it is unprincipled to pretend that this is really an evidentiary ruling. Rulings on objections to evidence are supposed to be made on the basis of categorical criteria—testimony is hearsay because it repeats an out-of-court statement and is offered to prove the truth of that statement; a document is not privileged because it was not written as a communication to an attorney; and so forth. To be sure, many evidentiary rulings require the court to consider the item in question in the context of other evidence. (This is particularly true for objections that evidence is irrelevant in the absence of other evidence of a necessary precondition,[117] or that the probative value of evidence is substantially outweighed by the danger of confusion and prejudice.[118]) But it takes judicial chutzpah to decide the central factual issue of a case, grant summary judgment, and call it a ruling on admissibility.

A court could try to achieve the same result by devising a genuine rule of exclusion. But the tool does not fit the task. Admissibility, like liability, is an either/or proposition. Not surprisingly, courts that do this try to define evidentiary requirements that have the same dichotomous quality: general acceptance, statistical significance, peer review. At first blush, this seems appropriate: a technique or a finding either is or is not generally accepted, or statistically significant, or whatever, so a court can easily say whether it is or is not admissible. In practice, these rules break down, one after the other.

The worst problem with such rules is the misuse of scientific concepts. Scientists do not use general acceptance or peer review as preconditions for *considering* information, and most no longer use statistical significance for that purpose, if they ever did. Peer review[119] and tests of statistical significance[120] were designed for other purposes, and general acceptance is not a scientific criterion for anything. Sometimes the most informative findings on an issue will be not statistically significant (perhaps because of a limited number of observations), or not published, or not generally recognized.

In addition, the major virtue of these rules turns out to be illusory: In practice, they are not easy to apply after all. Statistical significance looks like a readily determinable attribute, but in fact it can become quite tricky. For example, in many situations an expert (or a lawyer) can select (or manipulate) the data that are subjected to this statistical test—as the use of meta analysis in the Bendectin cases illustrates. Peer review looks like a straightforward issue—did it take place or didn't it?—but that may be true only so long as peer review does not have determinative forensic significance. If peer review became a general requirement for admissibility, it would also become distorted and problematic, and courts might be forced to settle disputes over whose peers and which journals are good enough to count. And general acceptance, of course, is a notoriously slippery concept, even as applied to theories and techniques. You can't see it; you have to infer it from whatever evidence you can gather about the field assuming that the field is somehow well defined. An attempt to determine the general acceptance of a particular scientific conclusion quickly becomes an inquiry into its truth—which, again, cannot be a method of determining the admissibility of evidence of the truth of that very same conclusion.

Finally, creating a rule of admissibility in order to resolve a substantive problem breeds new problems in future cases. It may satisfy the needs of the moment to say that the expert's opinion is inadmissible because there is no epidemiological research, no statistically significant finding, or no peer reviewed study. But will this test work in the next case up? Should we have to go through a plenary trial in a Bendectin case (or five of them) just because a plaintiff produces evidence of a statistically significant finding in a single epidemiological study of uncertain quality that was published in a "peer reviewed" journal of extremely modest distinction? Should we dismiss outright a case like *Ferebee*, or a stronger case, in which the available evidence consistently suggests that the substance in question did cause the plaintiff's pathology, because no epidemiological studies have yet been completed?

IV. What to Do?

A. Easy Cases

Daubert was an easy case in more senses than one. Not only was the legal issue before the Court a clear call, but so was the underlying factual dispute as well. By 1993 just about everybody agreed that Bendectin is not a human teratogen, or at least that there is no substantial evidence that it is. This consensus is reflected in the decisions of most juries that tried Bendectin cases, and in the actions (if not always words) of almost all judges who presided over and reviewed those trials. The final problem was, and is, merely procedural: how to dispose of the remaining cases efficiently and consistently.

The simple straightforward way to do so would be to redefine the question of causation—does Bendectin cause birth defects?—as one of "law" (to be decided by the judge) rather "fact" (to be decided by the jury). At first blush, this sounds like cheating. How can this be anything other than a question of fact? But courts constantly resolve factual questions in the process of deciding "legal" issues, from "was the statement made under a belief in impending death?"[121] to "is this the sort of evidence on which experts in the field reasonably rely in reaching conclusions on such matters?"[122] The issue is whether *this* factual question is for juries to decide or for judges; the category in which it is placed, "factual" or "legal," is simply a label we attach to that assignment. In this case, there is a strong argument that it should be given to judges.

To be sure, the question of causation in a tort case is one we normally submit to juries. But not always. A plaintiff who claimed that the defendant caused his ulcer by witchcraft would not get far, nor would a defendant who admitted exposing the plaintiff to staphylococcus but denied that bacteria cause illness. Either case would present a traditional context for judicial notice that the claims are wrong, since contrary propositions are widely regarded as indisputable. Unfortunately, the case for Bendectin is less clearcut. Even given the lopsided pattern of epidemiological findings, the claim that Bendectin is a human teratogen is hardly "indisputably" false—although one could argue that it is indisputable that the available evidence is inadequate to prove that claim by any standard.

In other contexts, courts frequently make similar factual decisions without requiring anything like indisputability. When a court decides that five-member juries function less well than six-member juries,[123] or (applying *Daubert*) that DNA profiling is a reliable technique for determining the identity of a suspect in a criminal case,[124] it is making a factual determination on a debatable question as a step in the process of announcing a "rule of law." In 1942, Professor Kenneth C. Davis named this age-old process "legislative fact finding,"[125] and the name has stuck. Legislative fact finding is often described as a species of judicial notice,[126] which makes some sense, since under both procedures the court makes factual decisions and is not restricted to the record in doing so. But, as Professor Davis wrote, the role of the common law judge requires more latitude than the traditional restrictions on judicial notice permit:

> [J]udge made law would stop growing if judges, in thinking about questions of law and policy, were forbidden to take into account the facts they believe, as distinguished from facts that which are "clearly . . . within the domain of the indisputable."[127]

Judging from published opinions, legislative fact finding must be something like sex: judges do it all the time, but rarely talk about it in public. Most if not all decisions that announce significant innovations in legal doctrine include factual premises that are open to dispute, and typically these premises rest at least in part on extra-judicial information. But very few opinions actually mention this embarrassing activity by name, and those that do generally keep the references to the margins—in a footnote,[128] in a concurring or a dissenting opinion,[129] describing what some other court has done in some other case.[130] The reason, I suppose, is that the name smacks of judicial legislation, which is a political taboo. In any event, this shyness makes it possible to overlook the fact that the practice (like sex) is essential, widespread, and accepted.

The real issue is not whether legislative fact-finding by courts is legitimate, but when and where. That question requires a comparison with the competing procedure, adjudicative fact finding on the records by the trier of fact:

> When a court or agency finds facts concerning the immediate parties—who did what, where, when, how, and with what motive or intent—the court or agency is performing an adjudicative function, and the facts are conveniently called adjudicative facts. . . .
>
> Stated in other terms, adjudicative facts are those to which the law applies in the process of adjudication. They are the facts that normally go to the jury in the process of adjudication. They relate to the parties, their activities, their properties, their businesses.[131]

By contrast:

> Legislative facts are those which help the tribunal to determine the content of a law and policy and to exercise its discretion in determining what course of action to take. Legislative facts are ordinarily general and do not concern the immediate parties.[132]

Many issues can be neatly classified by this dichotomy. How fast was the bus going?—Adjudicative. Are buses subject to the speed limit for automobiles or that for trucks?—Legislative. Did the defendant know that it was wrong to kill the deceased?—Adjudicative. What is the test for legal insanity?—Legislative. Unfortunately, the main issue at stake in the Bendectin cases—is this drug a teratogen?—falls between these two stools. The factual issue is not one that concerns the immediate parties—"who did what, where, when, how, and with what motive or intent"—but it does look like the type of issue that normally goes to the jury. Is it the sort of fact that helps judges "determine the content of law"? Maybe, but that merely begs the question. The issue at stake—causation in a tort case—is one we ordinarily submit to juries; but that doesn't mean that we are required to do so in this context.

Courts are not reluctant to base findings of legislative fact on scientific evidence. For example, several courts have held that the results of a blood-grouping test that purports to exclude paternity are conclusive. The only issues left for the jury are whether the test was properly conducted, and whether that was the finding:

> There should be no occasion for expert testimony in every case to prove the scientific validity of blood-grouping tests resulting in exclusion of paternity. The scientific opinion on that point is so general that courts may take judicial notice of it in filiation proceedings.[133]

And, of course, courts are perfectly comfortable making legislative findings of scientific fact when they decide that a scientific technique has gained general acceptance or is sufficiently reliable to warrant admission in evidence. For example, in *United States v. Jakobetz*,[134] after a detailed discussion of the scientific bases and techniques of DNA profiling, the Second Circuit held that "in future cases with a similar evidentiary issue, a court could properly take judicial notice of the general acceptability of the general theory and the use of these specific techniques."[135]

The evidence on the issue of general causation in the Bendectin cases is roughly the same type as the evidence in the DNA profiling or the blood-group paternity cases. The conclusion the courts might reach, however, is not so similar. In the cases on DNA profiling, the courts have found that the technique is sufficiently reliable to be admissible. This is a traditional, old-fashioned evidentiary ruling that opens the door to a category of evidence. In the absence of other information, the outcome of a particular case cannot be predicted from such a ruling; the

DNA evidence could help prove a defendant's identity as the criminal, or it could help prove his innocence, or it could be indeterminant. The decisions on blood tests in paternity cases are closer to a legislative finding that Bendectin does not cause birth defects. The statement "a drug cleared by 30 epidemiological studies did not cause the plaintiff's birth defects" does sound quite a bit like the statement "a man cleared by blood tests is not the father of the infant in this case." In fact, the former statement is more sweeping. It is one thing to decide that a blood test (or any other item of scientific evidence) has determinative weight on an issue; the jury still has to find that this particular man was cleared by a properly conducted test. It is another matter to conclude that the universe of available evidence will not support a claim. To do that is to abolish a cause of action in an entire set of cases, without regard to the position of any individual party.

In an article on the use of science in the courts published nearly thirty years ago, Professor Harold Korn wrote:

> The effect of characterizing a determination as "legal" is to place it within the court's sphere of influence and to acknowledge that the determination has the capacity for authoritative assimilation into the legal system as transmissible doctrine.[136]

Judges, according to Korn, engage in a "ceaseless search for consistency and predictability in the legal order."[137] They achieve this consistency by a form of forensic manifest destiny; to quote Thayer, a jury question "is likely to be absorbed by the judge, 'whenever a rule about it can be laid down.' "[138]

The Bendectin cases cry out for absorption into transmissible legal doctrine. And in fact, that has taken place. The unmistakable meaning of the last decade of Bendectin litigation is this: *No claim that Bendectin caused a birth defect will be considered*. This is a rule of law. The rule could be changed in the unlikely event that some surprising new research undermines the factual premises on which it is based, but that is not unusual. What is slightly more unusual is that the courts are reluctant to own up to what they have done.

The two Circuit Courts that held the evidence against Merrell insufficient as a matter of law were fairly explicit about what they were doing. The normal standard for decision will not support their decisions—the plaintiffs' expert evidence, considered in isolation, *is* legally sufficient to go the a jury—but these are not *normal* cases. The essence of the problem is the generality of the main issue. The Sixth Circuit:

> The cases are variations on a theme, somewhat like an orchestra which travels to different music halls, substituting musicians from time to time but playing essentially the same repertoire.[139]

The Fifth Circuit:

> [I]n mass torts the same issue is often presented over and over to juries in different cases, and juries often split both ways on the issue. . . . Appellate courts, if they take the lead in resolving those questions . . . can reduce some of the uncertainty which can tend to produce a sub-optimal amount of new drug development.[140]

Both Circuits were also careful to limit their rulings to Bendectin cases. The basis for the decisions is the plaintiffs' failure to present epidemiological evidence that Bendectin is a teratogen; however, "we do not hold that epidemiological proof is a necessary element in all toxic tort cases,"[141] and "[w]e do not mean to intimate that animal studies lack merit or power when it comes to predicting outcomes in humans."[142] It is only in the context of this record, with all the negative epidemiological studies, that such a failure is fatal. These courts did not quite say "we have weighed the evidence on both sides, and find as a matter of law that Bendectin is not a teratogen," but they came close,[143] and their meaning is clear.

Even this level of explicitness goes against the grain. Summary judgment is only supposed to be granted when the losing party has failed to present sufficient evidence to sustain a verdict, not when it has presented substantial evidence but the opposition has presented an overwhelming rebuttal.[144] At least, that's the rule when summary judgment is ordered on the "facts," because of insufficient evidence, rather than on the "law"—and this one looks like a decision on the "facts." So courts retreat to the safer ground of ruling on admissibility.

There was a strong push in that direction in the Fifth Circuit. In *Brock*, a suggestion for a rehearing en banc was rejected by a vote to 8 to 6, and the dissenters made clear that they were more concerned about the rationale for the panel's opinion than the outcome: "It strikes me that the issue in this case revolves around the admissibility of the expert testimony. . . . the panel [however] chooses to accept the admissibility of the testimony and to quarrel with its effect."[145] Admissibility, of course, was the basis for decision in the First, Ninth, and District of Columbia Circuits, the other three federal appellate courts that have explicitly closed the door on Bendectin suits. As far as this set of cases is concerned, the effect is same. The route would be shorter, however, and the law of torts and of evidence would be clearer,[146] if judges recognized what they were doing and said it.

B. Hard Cases

Litigation favors hard cases. Truly easy issues are not likely to be disputed at all, and if a disputed question *becomes* easy—e.g., Bendectin—the courts tend to weed out the cases that depend on it, by one means or another. They are replaced by a steady stream of new cases, raising questions that are not so easy—at least not yet. It's for these hard cases that the evidentiary and substantive rules governing scientific evidence matter most.

Hard cases are not all equally hard. Some depend on issues that have been the subject of a great deal of scientific research—enough to make legislative fact finding possible, even though the conclusion is not foregone. A prime example is Judge Weinstein's famous opinion in *In re "Agent Orange" Product Liability Litigation*.[147] The cases decided by this opinion were claims by Vietnam veterans against various chemical companies, alleging that they had been injured by exposure to dioxin, a toxic contaminant of the herbicide "Agent Orange" which had been manufactured by those companies and widely used in the Vietnam war. The vast majority of the Agent Orange claims were included in a class-action settlement, engineered by Judge Weinstein.[148] However, 281 plaintiffs elected to opt out of this class action. These remaining "opt-out" cases were dismissed by Judge Weinstein, who granted the defendants' motion for summary judgment on the ground that the plaintiffs had presented insufficient evidence that their injuries had been caused by exposure to Agent Orange.[149] A lot has been written about Judge Weinstein's opinion in the opt-out cases.[150] I will add very little to that body of writing—only my own general conclusion that parts of the opinion are hard to defend, but that Judge Weinstein's basic judgment was correct. The plaintiffs could not prove that exposure to Agent Orange had harmed them, although the research was not as one-sided as the Bendectin studies. The Agent Orange opt-out opinion encouraged other courts to take similar action in other toxic tort cases, not least in the Bendectin cases. In *Brock*, for example, the Fifth Circuit saw itself as following Judge Weinstein's lead:

> We are not without precedent in our approach to this problem. The case before us parallel's in many respects the recently conducted Agent Orange Litigation.[151]

A more recent toxic tort case, however, provides a better example of a comparatively hard case in which legislative fact finding may still be appropriate.

In *In re Joint Eastern and Southern District Asbestos Litigation* (the "Joint Asbestos" case),[152] the central issue was whether a deceased sheet metal worker's colon cancer had been caused by workplace exposure to asbestos. After a jury returned a $4,510,000 verdict against several defendants, Judge Sweet of the Southern District of New York granted the defendants' motion for j.n.o.v. on the ground that the plaintiff had presented insufficient evidence of causation. Judge Sweet (who cites the Agent Orange opt-out opinion and various Bendectin cases profusely) appears to have excluded no scientific evidence at trial. Instead, he claims to apply the usual standard for deciding a motion for a judgment as a matter of law: "[T]he sufficiency of the Plaintiff's epidemiological evidence must be determined by analyzing that evidence on its face and without weighing the evidence against it."[153] His published opinion belies that claim. In a twelve-page discussion of the epidemiological and clinical evidence, the judge goes back and forth from the plaintiff's case, to the defendants' case, to the published literature, comparing and criticizing.[154] A fair reading of the opinion leaves no doubt that his conclusion—"the Plaintiff's epidemiological evidence fails to support the claim that exposure to asbestos causes colon cancer"[155]—is based on a detailed analysis of the entire record, on both sides.

The record on which Judge Sweet based his opinion is extensive. "During the course of the trial, approximately 45 epidemiological studies and surveys of studies were discussed by the parties' experts. . . ."[156] Judging from the opinion, most of these studies show no association between asbestos and colon cancer, but a few do seem to show a comparatively weak correlation. Given these studies, Judge Sweet's conclusion sounds right: exposure to asbestos may increase the likelihood of developing cancer of the colon, but the effect (if there is one) is too small to justify a conclusion that any individual's cancer was more likely than not caused by asbestos.

Exposure to asbestos is a common problem in the United States, and colon cancer is a common cause of death. Inevitably, the possible causal relationship between these two events has become a recurring issue in litigation.[157] In that context—and given a sufficiently well developed scientific basis—legislative fact finding is a sensible way to handle the issue. That does not mean it's easy. Judge Sweet's opinion, like Judge Weinstein's Agent Orange opt-out opinion, clearly reflects long study and careful attention to abstruse technical issues. Most judges would probably never try to reach reasoned scientific judgments in cases where many studies find no causal relationship, but (unlike Bendectin) a few seem to go the other way. And just as well. It should only be done with great care.[158] Judge Sweet seem to have done well, but without a great deal of expert knowledge, there's no sure way to tell. The real test, of course, is time.[159] In any event, if judges do write opinions like these it would be better if they would say what they mean. If it is appropriate for the courts to make substantive scientific judgments on liability as a matter of law, they should not muddy the waters by pretending merely to apply procedural and evidentiary rules.

C. Harder Cases

The great majority of scientific issues that are presented in litigation are not even remotely suitable for legislative fact finding. This is true, of course, for legions of cases where the critical issue is the evaluation of one person or a unique occurrence. It is also true of the issue of general causation in many toxic tort cases. *Vann v. City of Woodhaven*[160] — which is described in detail by Professor Troyen A. Brennan[161] — is a good example. The plaintiffs in *Vann* were the parents of a 12 year old boy who died of aplastic anemia; they claimed that the disease was caused by exposure to a pesticide, Pratt 505K, which the defendant had sprayed to kill mosquitos. Various chemical companies that manufactured the ingredients of Pratt 505K were joined as third-party defendants. Since there were no epidemiological studies of Pratt 505K or its constituents, the plaintiffs' experts relied on less telling evidence: case reports, structural similarities between the chemicals involved and others that were known to be toxic, in vitro studies and animal studies. The defense experts denied that these were valid bases for reaching a conclusion on causation.[162] The jury, ultimately, found for the defense.

There was no evidentiary basis for excluding the plaintiffs' evidence in *Vann*. It was, in fact "standard toxicological evidence."[163] At the same time, there was no scientific basis for deciding whether or not Pratt 505K causes aplastic anemia: the available evidence was sufficient to pose the question, but not to answer it. Worse yet (from a scientific point of view) the problem is too uncommon to ever justify the time and expense it would take to find out. Courts could resolve this type of difficulty by requiring epidemiological evidence in every toxic tort case. But that requirement would virtually foreclose an entire class of cases — individual claims of uncommon types of injuries from exposure to allegedly toxic substances. "There are over 100,000 synthetic chemical used in the United States. Only a very small fraction have been subject to epidemiological investigation."[164] Short of such a drastic step, the only solution is to let the trier of fact — the jury — decide the merits of the competing scientific claims.

In other words, there is no procedural short cut. In *Vann*, and in many thousands of other law suits, courts must resolve scientific or technical disputes, the significance of which is limited to the case at hand or to a small set of related incidents. The issue may be the toxicity of a pesticide, or the safety of a highway exit ramp, or the cause of an individual's brain tumor, or the interpretation of fiber-match evidence. Ultimately such questions are resolved by that notorious embarrassment of adversarial fact finding, the battle of the experts.

Criticisms of this method are legion. They have been stated, forcefully, for well over a hundred years.[165] I will not even attempt to summarize them in this paper. For present purposes, Professor Brennan's comment on the evidence in *Vann* will suffice:

> Plaintiffs had every incentive to emphasize the importance of case studies. Defense witnesses in turn had the same incentives to deny the importance of animals studies and short-term tests. Thus, the court never heard an even-handed account of toxicology.[166]

The common solution proposed for this problem is to call non-partisan court-appointed experts to testify in addition to the parties' witnesses.[167] I have written about this issue in detail elsewhere;[168] I will merely state my main conclusions: Court appointment of expert witnesses is a widely praised widely available procedure that is almost never used. The best hope for improving our use of scientific evidence, and of expert evidence in general, is to devise procedures that succeed in encouraging judges to make wider use of this option.

Non-partisan experts might be as useful in cases in which courts engage in legislative fact finding as they would be in trials. The ultimate judgment on Bendectin was clear, but it might have been reached more easily and quickly if some judge along the line—or several judges—had appointed a qualified epidemiologist to provide a non-partisan appraisal of the evidence. Apparently that never happened.[169] In harder cases, the value of non-partisan expertise is greater. While Judge Weinstein may have done an excellent job in the Agent Orange opt-out case, his method, as Professor Schuck has pointed out, was chancy. Despite all his hard work, "he remained self-taught and incompletely informed, lacking the intuition and finely honed technical judgment of the experienced scientist."[170] Wouldn't his judgment have been safer if he had appointed an experienced scientist to advise him?[171]

The same applies to a determination of the "general acceptance" or the "validity" of a scientific theory or technique as the basis for a ruling on the admissibility under *Frye* or *Daubert*. *Christopherson v. Allied Signal Corp.*[172]—yet another toxic tort case—is a good example. The plaintiff in *Christopherson* claimed that her deceased husband contracted small-cell colon cancer—a rare disease—as a result of work-place exposure to nickel and cadmium. In the absence of epidemiological evidence, the plaintiff's expert—Dr. Miller—based his conclusion on the following reasoning: Nickel and cadmium are known to cause small-cell carcinomas in other sites in the human body, especially the lungs. Small-cell carcinomas have the same histology—that is, they appear to be made up of the same cells—regardless of their location. Therefore, it is likely that these metals also cause small-cell carcinomas in the colon, and—given the evidence on exposure and on other possible causes—it is likely that they did so in this individual.

The trial court granted the defendant's motion for summary judgment, concluding, among other things:

> Dr. Miller's conclusion that a small cell carcinoma of the lung is likely to be associated with a small cell carcinoma located elsewhere in the body is "without precedent in cancer epidemiology and is not scientifically correct."[173]

The Fifth Circuit, en banc, held that "[t]his finding of what is a scientifically correct conclusion is not for the district court."[174] Nonetheless, the court affirmed (over a bitter dissent[175]) on the ground that this impermissible judgment amounted to an implicit finding that Dr. Miller's methodology failed *Frye's* general acceptance test. The same result could just as easily have been reached under *Daubert* if the district court, or the Fifth Circuit, had concluded that Dr. Miler's reasoning was not scientifically valid.

Was the district court judge right? The only evidence before him were affidavits from partisan experts; faced with a conflict he "simply chose sides in this battle of the experts"[176] and accepted the defendants' theory of science. On what basis? Was it because there were several defense experts but only one for the plaintiff? Or because the defense experts had flashier credentials, or wrote better prose? Or was it because the judge understood the scientific issues and accurately chose the correct position?

As a matter of science, the judge in *Christopherson* may have made the right choice,[177] but the process by which he reached his decision hardly inspires confidence. Judges, no less than jurors, do get such questions wrong.[178] If a judge is going to "usurp[ ] the role of the jury in evaluating the evidence"[179] on a difficult scientific issue, he ought to have some basis for his conclusion beyond the statements of experts hired by the winning side. Of course, if non-partisan expert evidence *were* available, the temptation to take the issue from the jury in the first place would have been greatly reduced.[180]

One last note. Critics of the use of court-appointed experts—almost invariably, trial lawyers—argue that this procedure increases the power of judges alarmingly: "Trial by jury . . . becomes no more than an empty illusion, a shibboleth, to which lip service is paid while its destruction is endorsed."[181] I doubt if this argument impresses many judges, but for one reason or another they do go along with the conclusion: they almost never appoint expert witnesses. But this hardly represents a conservative position on the power of judges. They won't seek independent expert advice, but they will exclude the core of a party's case on the basis of their lay assessment of its scientific merit. They won't appoint non-partisan experts to provide information to their jurors, but they will dismiss an entire class of claims as unsound. At least in the context of toxic torts, we have come to accept judicial responses to scientific problems that are both more drastic than the appointment of a witness, and less effective. Whatever the issue—admissibility or sufficiency or liability—the solution to the problem of troublesome scientific evidence is more information, not less, but from a trustworthy source.

Appendix

In the text I predict that if *Daubert* has any systematic effect on the treatment of scientific evidence, it will encourage courts to exclude more often than they had done under *Frye*. It's too early to reach any solid conclusion, but the first year-and-a-half's worth of federal cases applying *Daubert* are consistent with that prediction.

For the most part, these post-*Daubert* decisions are unsurprising. There has been a shift, conspicuously in the types of the cases that raise questions concerning scientific evidence. Cases applying *Frye* were usually criminal—until the last several years almost exclusively so (see *supra* note 46 and accompanying text)—but most of the cases applying *Daubert* are civil. Moreover, there are signs of instability among the civil cases, especially on appeal. In this respect, *Daubert* seems to have accelerated a trend that was already underway.

Criminal Cases

Among reported decisions in federal criminal cases, *Daubert* has changed almost nothing. The best defined subgroup consists of cases on the admissibility of DNA identification evidence. Like all appellate opinions on point, they let it in. *United States v. Martinez*, 3 F.3d 1191, 1198 (8th Cir. 1993); *United States v. Bonds*, 12 F.3d 540, 554 (6th Cir. 1993); *United States v. Chischilly*, 30 F.3d 1144, 1156 (9th Cir. 1994); *United States v. Davis*, 40 F.3d 1069, 1075 (10th Cir. 1994); *Gov't of the Virgin Islands v. Penn*, 838 F.Supp. 1054, 1073 (D. Virg. Is. 1993). Another set of non-path breaking cases deal with a variety of chemical tests in drug prosecutions. As before *Daubert*, their admission, too, is upheld on appeal. *United States v. Bynum*, 3 F.3d 769, 773 (4th Cir. 1993)(chromatographic analysis is admissible to show that three samples of crack cocaine came from the same batch); *United States v. McCaskey*, 9 F.3d 368, 380 (5th Cir. 1993)(evidence of Fourier Transform Infrared Spectrophotometer test for cocaine base admissible at sentencing hearing); *United States v. Muldrow*, 19 F.3d 1332, 1337 (10th Cir. 1994)(testimony by forensic chemist on tests to identify cocaine admissible); *United States v. Harris*, No. 93–5943, 1994 U.S. App. LEXIS 20145 at *5 (4th Cir. 1994)(evidence of field test for cocaine admissible). Cf. *United States v. Lee*, 25 F.3d 997, 999 (11th Cir. 1994)(remand to determine the admissibility under *Daubert* of trace evidence of narcotics collected via the Sentor and Ionscan machines).

Although *Daubert* speaks directly only to the admissibility of expert *scientific* evidence, several cases cite the standards announced in *Daubert* as the basis for approving admission of other types of expert testimony: *United States v. Markum*, 4 F.3d 891, 896 (10th Cir. 1993)(expert testimony by fire chief that fire was caused by arson); *United States v. Locascio*, 6 F.3d 924, 938–939 (2nd Cir. 1993)(expert testimony by a police officer on the workings of the underworld); *United States v. Muldrow*, *supra* 19 F.3d at 1337–1338 (police officer's testimony on whether possession of one kilo of cocaine would be for personal use or distribution); *United States v. Johnson*, 28 F.3d 1487, 1497 (8th Cir. 1994)(expert testimony by unindicted coconspirator on gang structure and drug trafficking). See also *United States v. Sepulveda*, 15 F.3d 1161, 1183 (1st Cir. 1993)(trial court's exclusion of *improper* expert opinion testimony by a police commander on defendant's roles in cocaine trafficking organization did not necessitate a mistrial). None of these decisions would likely have been different two years earlier.

Various types of expert scientific evidence that have traditionally been considered unreliable were still excluded after *Daubert*, at least when offered by criminal defendants: polygraph evidence, *United States v. Black*, 831 F. Supp. 120, 122 (E.D.N.Y. 1993); forensic anthropology in a robbery case that turned on identification, *United States v. Dorsey*, 45 F.3d 809, 814–816 (4th Cir. 1995); evidence that the defendant in an attempted extortion case had had "dependant personality disorder," *United States v. Marsh*, 26 F.3d 1496, 1502–1503 (9th Cir. 1994); and expert voice identification, *United States v. Jones*, 24 F.3d 1177, 1180 (9th Cir. 1994)(although the witness was allowed to give *lay* opinion evidence on the same issue). By contrast, the admission of testimony by a prosecution expert on a photogrammetry process for calculating the height of an individual from surveillance photographs was affirmed, on the basis of the trial court's finding that the calculations were neither novel nor controversial. *United States v. Quinn*, 18 F.3d 1461, 1465 (9th Cir. 1994).

The only post-*Daubert* criminal cases that were remanded on appeal dealt with expert evidence on the reliability of eyewitness identification testimony. In *United States v. Amador-Galvan*, 9 F.3d 1414, 1418 (9th Cir. 1993), the Ninth Circuit remanded for a trial-court determination on whether the evidence qualified for admission under *Daubert*. And in *United States v. Minnis*, No. 93–50330, 1994 U.S. App. LEXIS 14727 at *4 (9th Cir. 1994), the same court followed *Amador-Galvan* and ordered a similar evidentiary hearing. Between these two decisions, in *United States v. Rincon*, 28 F.3d 921, 923 (9th Cir. 1994), the Ninth Circuit affirmed the decision of a different district court that such evidence was inadmissible under the same standard. It's hard to see any trend here—in *Rincon* the court emphasized that it was not setting a general rule, and that other litigants may meet the criteria for admission for similar evidence. *Daubert* seems to have been an occasion for the Ninth Circuit to make the undramatic statement that at least in some types of cases, trial judges are required to *consider* admitting expert evidence on eyewitness identifications, but having done so in the approved manner they can admit or exclude the evidence as they please.

Civil Cases

A sizeable minority of the civil post-*Daubert* cases concern medical evidence. Two are Bendectin cases: *Elkins v. Richardson-Merrell, Inc.*, 8 F.3d 1068, 1071 (6th Cir. 1993) in which the Sixth Circuit followed *Turpin*, *supra* note 20, and held the plaintiff's evidence admissible but legally insufficient; and *Daubert* itself on remand, 43 F.3d 1311 (9th Cir. 1995), in which the Ninth circuit held the same evidence inadmissible under the new standard. See *supra* note 60. In both *Elkins* and *Daubert* the plaintiff claimed that the defendants' affidavits were inadmissible under *Daubert*; in both the circuit court responded that this argument misconstrued the defendant's burden on summary judgment.

Most of the rest of the medical-evidence cases involve other toxic tort claims, and in most of these the scientific evidence was excluded or its exclusion was upheld: *Porter v. Whitehall Laboratories*, 9 F.3d 607, 616 (7th Cir. 1993)(summary judgment to defendant ibuprofen manufacturers affirmed); *O'Conner v. Commonwealth Edison Co.*, 13 F.3d 1090, 1107 (7th Cir. 1994)(summary judgment affirmed in radiation exposure case); *Claar v. Burlington N. R.R. Co.*, 29 F.3d 499, 503 (9th Cir. 1994)(summary judgment for defendant affirmed on complaint alleging various injuries from exposure to various chemicals); *Sorensen v. Shaklee Corp.*, 31 F.3d 638, 650 (8th Cir. 1994)(summary judgment for defendant in case alleging that plaintiffs' birth defects were caused by their parents' consumption of alfalfa health food tablets affirmed); *Bradley v. Brown*, 42 F.3d 434, 438 (7th Cir. 1994)(exclusion at bench trial of evidence on Multiple Chemical Sensitivity); *Hayes v. Raytheon Co.*, No. 92–4004, 1994 U.S. App. LEXIS 8415 at *17, (7th Cir. 1994)(summary judgment for defendant upheld in case alleging that video display terminals caused cervical cancer); *Chikovsky v. Ortho Pharmaceutical Corp.*, 832 F.Supp. 341, 346 (S.D. Fla. 1993)(summary judgment to manufacturer of acne medication Retin-A in birth defect case). See also *Wheat v. Pfizer, Inc.*, 31 F.3d 340, 343 (5th Cir. 1994)(dictum that testimony linking defendant's drug to plaintiff's hepatitis would be inadmissible under *Daubert*; summary judgment for defendant affirmed on other grounds). On the other hand, in a few post-*Daubert* federal toxic tort cases, the scientific evidence was admitted at trial or on appeal: *Cantrell v. GAF Corp.*, 999 F.2d 1007, 1014 (6th Cir. 1993)(admission of evidence linking laryngeal cancer to asbestos affirmed); *Glaser v. Thompson Medical Co., Inc.*, 32 F.3d 969, 975 (6th Cir. 1994)(exclusion of evidence that Dexatrim can cause hypertension and summary judgment for defendant reversed); *Hopkins v. Dow Corning Corp.*, 33 F.3d 1116, 1125 (9th Cir. 1994)(admission of plaintiff's expert evidence affirmed in breast implant case).

As a group, the post-*Daubert* toxic tort cases suggest that (at least in this context) federal judges are, if anything, more willing than before to scrutinize and exclude scientific evidence that they see as weak—e.g., evidence that is based on "common sense" with no published support, *Chikovsky, supra.*, 823 F.Supp. at 345–46, or evidence from a witness who represents a "lone voice" in the scientific community, *O'Conner, supra.*, 13 F.3d at 1105–1106. The two non-toxic tort medical-evidence cases add little. Both are medical malpractice cases, and in both the admission of the disputed testimony was affirmed: *Cella v. United States*, 998 F.2d 418, 425 (7th Cir. 1993)(plaintiff's medical expert allowed to testify to cause of polymyositis); *Carroll v. Morgan*, 17 F.3d 787, 790 (5th Cir.), *reh'g denied* 26 F.3d 1117 (1994)(defendant's expert cardiologist allowed to testify to cause of death).

The non-medical post-*Daubert* civil cases are an extremely assorted group. In most the court excluded or approved the exclusion of testimony by experts whose qualifications or data were questionable: *Joy v. Bell Helicopter Textron, Inc.*, 999 F.2d 549, 569 (D.C. Cir. 1993)(economist's testimony on future earning capacity of deceased plaintiff if he had survived); *Frymire-Brinati v. KPMG Peat Marwick*, 2 F.3d 183, 186 (7th Cir. 1993)(accountant's valuation of investments as worthless); *Rosado v. Deters*, 5 F.3d 119, 124 (5th Cir. 1993)(accident reconstructionist's tesimony about motorcycle accident); *Wilson v. City of Chicago*, 6 F.3d 1233, 1238 (7th Cir. 1993)(pathologist's testimony that plaintiff's story of electroshock torture was credible); *Marcel v. Placid Oil Co.*, 11 F.3d 563, 567 (5th Cir. 1994)(economist's testimony on life expectancy of oil rig workers); *Berry v. City of Detroit*, 25 F.3d 1324, 1354 (6th Cir. 1994)(expert testimony that failure to discipline police officers caused defendant officer to shoot plaintiff); *Habecker v. Clark Equip. Co.*, 36 F.3d 278, 290 (3d Cir. 1994)(expert testimony on simulation on forklift accident); *American and Foreign Ins. Co. v. General Elec. Co.*, 45 F.3d 135, 139 (6th Cir. 1995)(affidavit of engineer regarding design of circuit breaker); *Stanczyk v. Black and Decker, Inc.*, 836 F. Supp. 565, 568 (N.D. Ill. 1993)(feasibility of safer rotary saw design); *McLendon v. Georgia Kaolin Co.*, 841 F.Supp. 415, 418–419 (M.D. Ga. 1994)(geologist's testimony on Kaolin deposits); *Israel Travel Advisory Serv., Inc. v. Israel Identity Tours, Inc.*, No. 92 C 2379, 1993 U.S. Dist. LEXIS 13749 at *5, 1993 WL 387346 at *6 (N.D. Ill. 1993)(economic testimony on damages to a business); *Liu v. Korean Air Lines Co.*, No. 84 Civ. 0690 (PLN), U.S. Dist. LEXIS 16233, at *1–11, 1993 WL 478343 at *1–10 (S.D.N.Y. 1993)(economist's testimony on future earnings of deceased plaintiff, expert restricted but not excluded); *Doe v. Tag, Inc.*, No. 92 C 7661, 1993 U.S. Dist. LEXIS 16356, at *3–7, 1993 WL 484212 at *3–7 (N.D. Ill. 1993)(expert testimony by social workers and economist excluded, but evidence from MD's admitted, in civil child abuse case).

On the other side, however, there are several cases in which evidence on similar issues was admitted, or its exclusion was reversed on appeal: *Petruzzi's IGA Supermarkets, Inc. v. Darling-Delaware Co.*, 998 F.2d 1224, 1240–1241 (3d. Cir. 1993)(affidavits by economists in antitrust case); *United States v. Deccarett*, 6 F.3d 37, 58 (2d Cir. 1993)(expert testimony by DEA agent on money laundering, in civil forfeiture case); *Iacobelli Constr., Inc. v. County of Monroe*, 32 F.3d 19, 24–25 (2nd Cir. 1994)(affidavits by experts on underground construction in contract case); *Pioneer Hi-Bred Int'l v. Holden Found. Seeds, Inc.*, 35 F.3d 1226, 1229 (8th Cir.

1994)(electrophoresis, liquid chromatography, and growout testing in suit alleging misappropriation of the genetic make-up of seed corn); *Auvil v. CBS "60 Minutes"*, 836 F. Supp. 741, 741 (E.D. Wash. 1993)(evidence on toxicity of apples treated with daminozide).

There is a clear pattern across this entire set of civil post-*Daubert* cases. Almost all the action involves plaintiffs' witnesses. For example, seven of these cases report trial-court decisions: *Chikovsky, McLendon, Liu, Stanczyk, Israel Travel Advisory Service, Doe* and *Auvil*. As one might expect, all but one (*Auvil*) are cases in which purportedly scientific evidence was excluded (although in two of those, *Liu* and *Doe*, some such evidence was admitted as well). What's less predictable and more striking is that in every case in which evidence was excluded it was offered by a plaintiff, while in the only reported trial court opinion in which the scientific evidence was admitted it was offered by the defendant.

The largest well-defined cluster of appellate opinions consists of six toxic tort cases in which the plaintiffs' scientific evidence was excluded in the trial court, and the resulting summary judgment for the defendant was affirmed: *Porter, O'Conner, Hayes, Sorenson, Claer*, and *Daubert* on remand. If the original Ninth Circuit opinion in *Daubert* was written in part to encourage trial courts to clamp down on plaintiffs' experts in toxic tort cases, its reversal by the Supreme Court opinion has not stopped federal judges from doing just that. There are no post-*Daubert* cases of any sort that involve summary judgment for the plaintiff.

There are eleven opinions in this set that affirm judgments after trial: six for plaintiffs and five for defendants. With two exceptions, *Marcel* and *Carroll*, these cases are similar in a telling way: they all concern *plaintiffs' witnesses*. (Indeed, *Marcel, Carroll* and *Auvil* are the only three civil post-*Daubert* cases that involve defense witnesses, regardless of the issue or the outcome.) When a plaintiff's judgment is affirmed, the circuit court opinion upholds the district court's decision to *admit* the plaintiff's scientific evidence (*Pioneer Hi-Bred Int'l, Daccarett, Cantrell, Hopkins, Cella*); when a defense judgment is affirmed, the appellate court affirms the decision to *exclude* the plaintiff's evidence (*Habecker, Rosado, American and Foreign Ins. Co., Chicovsky*).

The most interesting pattern of all shows up in the seven cases in which trial courts were reversed. They fall into two groups: four cases in which a jury *verdict* for the plaintiff was reversed because of improper *admission* of scientific evidence (*Frymire-Brinati, Wilson, Berry, Joy*), and three in which *summary* judgment for the defendant was reversed because of improper *exclusion* of plaintiff's expert affidavits (*Glasser, Iacobelli Construction, Petruzzi's IGA Supermarkets*). In other words, sometimes the trial courts are too lax and let plaintiffs introduce scientific evidence that should be kept out; when that happens, judgments may have to be reversed. Other times they go too far in the other direction and exclude evidence too quickly, on summary judgment; then cases have to be sent back to do things the right way. One way or another, judging from these early reversals under *Daubert*, the issue of the moment is what to do about scientific experts who testify for plaintiffs.

Notes

1. 113 S. Ct. 2786 (1993).
2. The name and the corporate identity of the manufacturer of Bendectin both changed a couple of times between 1956 and 1983, and a couple more times since. Joseph Sanders, *The Bendectin Litigation: A Case Study in the Life Cycle of Mass Torts*, 43 Hastings L.J. 301, 311–12 (1992). Following Sanders's lead, I will refer to the company throughout this article simply as "Merrell."
3. Michael D. Green, *Expert Witnesses and Sufficiency of Evidence in Toxic Substances Litigation: The Legacy of Agent Orange and Bendectin Litigation*, 86 Nw. U.L. Rev. 643, 661 (1992).
4. *Mekdeci v. Merrell Nat'l Lab.*, 711 F.2d 1510 (11th Cir. 1983).
5. Sanders, *supra* note 2, at 396–401, 410–418; Sanders, *From Science to Evidence: The Testimony on Causation in the Bendectin Cases*, 46 Stan. L. Rev. 1, 4–8 (1993).
6. See Michael D. Green, *The Paradox of Statutes of Limitations in Toxic Substances Litigation*, 76 Calif.L.Rev. 965, 973 (1988) (asbestos); *Sindell v. Abbot Labs.*, 26 Cal.3d 588, 594, 607 P.2d 924, 925 (1980) (DES).
7. Sanders, *supra* note 2, at 331–348.
8. *Id.* at 347–48.
9. Sanders, *supra* note 2. See also Sanders, *supra* note 5; Green, *supra* note 3.
10. See 506 A.2d 1100,1113 (D.C. App., 1986), *appeal after remand* 563 A.2d 330 (D.C. App. 1989), *cert. denied*, 493 U.S. 1074 (1990), *appeal after remand* 593 A.2d 1023 (D.C. App. 1991).
11. See *In re Richardson-Merrell, Inc. "Bendectin" Products Liability Litigation*, 624 F.Supp 1212, 1216 (S.D. Ohio, 1985).
12. *Id.*
13. *In re Bendectin Litigation*, 857 F.2d 290 (6th Cir. 1988).
14. Sanders, *supra* note 5, at 6. I have excluded three European trials listed by Sanders and included one more recent trial: *Blum v. Merrell Dow Pharmaceuticals, Inc.*, Pa. Ct. Common Pleas, Phila. County No. 1C27 (discussed in Products Liability Daily, June 21, 1994, p.3).
15. *Richardson v. Richardson-Merrell, Inc.*, 857 F.2d 823 (D.C. Cir. 1987), *cert. denied*, 493 U.S. 882 (1989); *Brock v. Merrell Dow Pharmaceuticals*, 874 F.2d 307 (5th Cir.), *modified* 884 F.2d 166 (5th Cir. 1989), *cert. denied*, 494 U.S. 1046 (1990); *Ealy v. Richardson-Merrell, Inc.*, 987 F.2d 1159 (D.C. Cir.), *cert. denied*, 498 U.S. 950 (1990).
16. *Raynor v. Richardson-Merrell, Inc.*, No. 93–7109, 1993 U.S. App. LEXIS 35818 (D.C. Cir. 1993).
17. *Lynch v. Merrell Dow Laboratories*, 838 F.2d 1190 (1st Cir. 1987); *Richardson*, *supra* note 15.

18. *Brock*, *supra* note 16.
19. *Turpin v. Merrell Dow Pharmaceuticals,* 959 F.2d 1349 (6th Cir. 1992).
20. E.g., *Hull v. Merrell Dow Pharmaceuticals,* 700 F.Supp. 28 (S.D. Fla. 1988); *Daubert v. Merrell Dow Pharmaceuticals,* 727 F.Supp. 570 (S.D. Cal. 1989), *aff'd*, 951 F.2d 1128 (9th Cir. 1991); *Turpin v. Merrell Dow Pharmaceuticals,* 736 F.Supp. 737 (E.D. Ken. 1990), *aff'd*, 959 F.2d 1349 (6th Cir. 1992); *DeLuca v. Merrell Dow Pharmaceuticals,* 131 F.R.D. 71 (D.N.J. 1990), *rev'd*, 911 F.2d 942 (3d Cir. 1990), *summ. judgment granted on remand*, 791 F.Supp. 1042 (D.N.J. 1992), *aff'd without opinion*, 6 F.3d 778 (3rd Cir. 1993); *Lee v. Richardson Merrell,* 772 F.Supp. 1027 (W.D. Tenn. 1991), *aff'd*, 1992 U.S.App. LEXIS 8478 (6th Cir. 1992).
21. Sanders, *supra* note 5, at 6.
22. *Daubert*, *supra* note 20.
23. Sanders, *supra* note 2, at 321–331; Green, *supra* note 3, at 644–658.
24. Sanders, *supra* note 2, at 395.
25. *Id*. at 430.
26. *Daubert*, 727 F.Supp. at 575.
27. *Id*. at 576.
28. *Id*. at 575.
29. Judge Gilliam also disposed peremptorily of another expert's "unsupported allegation" that the data of a single published study show a statistically significant teratogenic link. *Id*. at 576.
30. 951 F.2d 1128 (9th Cir. 1991).
31. 293 F. 1013, 1014 (D.C. Cir. 1923).
32. *Id*. at 1014.
33. 911 F.2d 941, 955 (3rd Cir. 1990).
34. 951 F.2d at 1130.
35. As applied by the Ninth Circuit in *United States v. Solomon,* 753 F.2d 1522, 1626 (9th Cir. 1985) (cited in *Daubert*, 951 F.2d at 1129–30).
36. 951 F.2d at 1131.
37. 951 F.2d at 1131 (quoting Peter Huber, Galileo's Revenge: Junk Science in the Courtroom 228 (1991)).
38. The issue is discussed in detail in several briefs *amicus curiae* that were filed in *Daubert* by organizations and individuals with deep experience in the process of scientific peer review: Brief *Amici Curiae* of Physicians, Scientists and Historians of Science in Support of Petitioners; Brief *Amici Curiae* of American Society of Law, Medicine and Ethics, *et al.*, in Support of Petitioners; Brief *Amici Curiae* of Daryl E. Chubin, *et al.*, in Support of Petitioners; Brief of the Carnegie Commission on Science, Technology, and Government as *Amici Curiae* in Support of Neither Party; Brief of the New England Journal of Medicine, *et al.*, as *Amici Curiae* in Support of Respondent; Brief of the American Medical Association, *et al.*, as *Amici Curiae* in Support of Respondents; Brief *Amicus Curiae* of the American College of Legal Medicine in Support of the Respondent; Brief of *Amici Curiae* of Nicolaas Bloembergen, *et al.*, in Support of Respondents; Brief *Amicus Curiae* of Professor Alvan Feinstein in Support of Respondent; Brief for the American Association for the Advancement of Science, *et al.*, as *Amici Curiae* in Support of Respondent. Significantly, while several *amici*

wrote in favor of peer review in general, none endorsed it as an all-purpose test for the admissibility of scientific evidence.

39. 113 S. Ct. 2786 (1993).
40. The Court also sidestepped another argument by the Petitioners: that *Frye*, as a federal judge-made rule could not, under *Erie R. v. Tompkins,* 304 U.S. 64 (1938), be applied in a federal diversity law suit (such as *Daubert*). 113 S. Ct. at 2794 n.6. This issue had not surfaced before *Daubert*, no doubt because *Frye* had been applied almost exclusively in criminal cases. See *infra* note 46 and accompanying text.
41. See Edward J. Imwinkelreid, *The Standard for Admitting Scientific Evidence: A Critique From the Perspective of Juror Psychology*, 28 Vill. L. Rev. 554, 556–57 (1982–83): "*Frye* was not only the majority view among American courts; it was the almost universal view, with the overwhelming majority of federal and state courts following it. Indeed, at one point in the mid-1970's, *Frye* seemed to be the controlling test in at least forty-five states." See also Note, *Changing the Standards for the Admissibility of Novel Scientific Evidence: State v. Williams*, 40 Ohio St. L.J. 757, 769 (1979).
42. See, e.g., *Daubert v. Merrell Dow Pharmaceuticals, Inc.*, 951 F.2d 1128 (9th Cir. 1991); *Christophersen v. Allied-Signal Corp.*, 939 F.2d 1106, 1110–1111, 1115–1116 (5th Cir. 1991) (en banc), *cert. denied*, 112 S.Ct. 1280 (1992); *United States v. Smith,* 869 F.2d 348 351 (7th Cir. 1989); *United States v. Shorter,* 809 F.2d 54, 59–60 (D.C. Cir.), *cert. denied,* 484 U.S. 817 (1987); *United States v. Metzger,* 778 F.2d 1195, 1203 (6th Cir. 1985), *cert. denied,* 477 U.S. 906 (1986); *United States v. Smith,* 776 F.2d 892, 898 (10th Cir. 1985); *United States v. Alexander,* 526 F.2d 161, 163–164 (8th Cir. 1975).
43. See, e.g., *United States v. Williams,* 583 F.2d 1194 (2d Cir. 1978); *United States v. Piccinonna,* 885 F.2d 1529, 1536–1537 (11th Cir. 1989); *United States v. Downing,* 753 F.2d 1224, 1237–1240 (3d Cir. 1985); *United States v. Baller,* 519 F.2d 463, 465–466 (4th Cir.), *cert. denied*, 423 U.S. 1019 (1975).
44. In *deVries v. St. Paul Five and Marine Insurance Company,* 716 F.2d 939, 945 (1st Cir. 1983), the First Circuit cited *Frye* with approval, but on the narrow issue of the unreliability of polygraph tests.
45. The status of *Frye* in state courts was always a tricky issue, since many state followed *Frye* with modifications or limitations, and some adopted a "general acceptance" test without citing *Frye*. See Paul C. Giannelli, *The Admissibility of Novel Scientific Evidence:* Frye v. United States, *A Half-Century Later*, 80 Colum. L. Rev. 1197, 1128–29 (1980). In *Daubert*, the States of Texas, Montana, Idaho, and South Dakota stated in a brief *amicus curiae* that *Frye* had been rejected—at least as an exclusive test—in 25 states; for 18 of the 25 states they list, the opinion cited is from 1987 or later. Brief *Amici Curiae* of the States of Texas, *et al.*, in Support of Petitioners, at 6–7.
46. See id.; Paul C. Giannelli, *"Junk Science": The Criminal Cases*, 84 J. Crim. L. & Criminology 105 111 (1993).
47. The two earlier cases were *Barrel of Fun, Inc. v. State Farm Fire and Cas. Co.,* 739 F.2d 1028, 1031 (5th Cir. 1984); and *Christophersen v. Allied Signal Corp.,* 939 F.2d 1106, 1115–16 (5th Cir. 1991) (per curiam) (en banc).
48. See, e.g., Giannelli, *supra* note 45, and authorities cited therein at 1206 n. 59; Hanson, *James Alphonso Frye is Sixty-Five Years Old; Should He Retire?*, 16 W. St. U.L.Rev. 357 (1989).

49. 113 S. Ct. at 794. Nor does Rule 703 help preserve the *Frye* test. Rule 703 permits an expert to rely on *inadmissible* evidence if it is "of a type reasonably relied upon by experts in the particular field in forming opinions or inferences upon the subject." It does nothing to limit the *admissible* bases for expert opinion evidence. Assuming that "reasonable reliance" is equivalent to "general acceptance," this rule would permit an expert witness to rely on a systolic blood pressure deception test as the basis for an opinion on a witness's credibility (assuming the evidence was otherwise admissible) if she had performed it herself (and could therefore testify from personal knowledge), but not if an associate conducted the test and informed her of the results (which would be hearsay)—unless the test were "of a type reasonably relied upon," etc. Obviously, this is *not* the *Frye* test.
50. The procedure that governs these preliminary judicial findings is described in Federal Rule of Evidence 104(a).
51. The rejected *Frye* test (as we have noted) was limited to evidence of *novel* scientific principles and techniques. Rule 702 is not, and therefore neither is the Court's interpretation of that rule. However, the Court recognizes that for "well established propositions" it will be easy to satisfy these requirements, and some may be subject to judicial notice. 113 S. Ct. at 2796 n.11.
52. *Id.* at 2796 (footnote omitted) (emphasis added).
53. *Id.* (emphasis added).
54. *Id.* at 2797.
55. *Id.*
56. *Id.*
57. *Id.*
58. *Id.*
59. *Id.*
60. *Id.* On remand from the Supreme Court, the Ninth Circuit reaffirmed its earlier judgment. *Daubert v. Merrell Dow Pharmaceuticals,* 43 F.3d 1311 (9th Cir. 1995). The court (in another opinion by Judge Kozinski) found the plaintiffs' evidence inadmissible under the Supreme Court opinion in *Daubert,* in part because there was insufficient evidence to support a finding that it constituted reliable "scientific knowledge," *id.* at 1316–21, and in part because in the absence of any claim that Bendectin more than doubled the risk of limb-reduction birth defects, the evidence could not show that it "caused" the plaintiffs' injuries by the standard that applies under California law, and therefore the evidence would not "assist the trier of fact," *id.* at 1321–22.
61. See *supra* note 45 and accompanying text.
62. Cleary et al., McCormick on Evidence §206 at 912–14 (4th ed. 1992).
63. *State v. Dorsey,* 88 N.M. 184, 539 P.2d 204 (1975).
64. *State v. Lindemuth,* 56 N.M. 257, 243 P.2d 325 (1952); see also *Montoya v. Metropolitan Court,* 98 N.M. 616, 651 P.2d 1260 (1982), *overruled, State v. Alberico,* 116 N.M. 156, 861 P.2d 192 (1993).
65. *State v. Sims,* 52 Ohio Misc. 31, 369 N.E.2d 24 (1977), *overruled sub silentio, State v. Souel,* 53 Ohio St.2d 123, 372 N.E.2d 1318 (1978).
66. *State v. Williams,* 446 N.E.2d 444, 446–48 (Ohio 1983).
67. Anno., *Modern Status of Rule Relating to Admission of Results of Lie Detector (Polygraph) Test in Federal Criminal Trials*, 43 ALR Fed 68, and supp.

68. See Margaret A. Berger, *Novel Forensic Evidence: The Need for Court-Appointed Experts after Daubert*, 1 Shepard's Expert & Scientific Evid. Q. 487, 488 (1994).
69. Committee on Evaluation of Sound Spectrograms, National Research Council, On The Theory and Practice of Voice Identification (1979).
70. *State v. Williams,* 388 A.2d 500 (Me. 1978); *United States v. Williams,* 583 F.2d 1194 (2d Cir. 1978); *State v. Williams,* 446 N.E.2d 444, 446–48 (Ohio 1983).
71. Anno., *Admissibility and Weight of Voiceprint Evidence*, 97 ALR 3d 294, and supp.; Berger, *supra* note 68, at 488.
72. Anno., *Admissibility of DNA Identification Evidence*, 84 ALR 4th 313, and supp. Courts are divided, however, on the admissibility of inferential evidence based on estimates of the frequency of various DNA types in relevant human populations. Compare, e.g., *State v. Vandebogart,* 136 N.H. 365, 616 A.2d 484, 494 (1992) (excluding population frequency estimates under *Frye*), with United States v. Yee, 134 F.R.D. 161, 210 (N.D. Ohio 1991) (admitting such evidence, also under *Frye*). See generally Berger, *supra* note 68, at 489–90; William C. Thompson & Susan Ford, *DNA Testing: Acceptance are Weight of the New Genetic Identity Tests*, 75 Va. L. Rev. 45 (1989).
73. 753 F.2d 1224 (3rd Cir. 1985).
74. The *Downing* factors are: (1) the "degree of acceptance" of the technique or theory in the relevant scientific community; (2) the "novelty" of technique or theory, and (3) "the existence of a specialized literature" dealing with it, both which bear on (4) the extent to which it "has been exposed to critical scientific scrutiny"; (5) "the qualifications and professional status" of the witnesses offering the evidence; (6) "the non-judicial uses to which the scientific technique are put"; (7) the "frequency with which the technique leads to erroneous results"; and (8) "the type of error" it produces. *Id.* at 1238–39. The Court in *Daubert* gave qualified approval to the *Downing* test, and to various other tests for admissibility proposed by commentators: "all these versions may have some merit, although we express no opinion regarding any of their particular details." 113 S. Ct. at 2797 n.12.
75. See *DeLuca*, *supra* note 20.
76. *United States v. Franks,* 511 F.2d 25, 33 (6th Cir. 1975).
77. 113 S. Ct. at 2796 n. 10 and accompanying text.
78. *Id.* at 2797–98.
79. *Id.* at 2796–97.
80. *Id.* at 2798–99.
81. *Id.* at 2794.
82. It's too early to say for sure, but the first batch of federal cases applying *Daubert* is consistent with this prediction. See Appendix for a summary of such cases through early 1995.
83. 830 F.2d 1190 (1st Cir. 1987).
84. *Id.* at 1194 (citation omitted).
85. 857 F.2d 823 (D.C. Cir. 1988).
86. 736 F.2d 1529 (D.C. Cir. 1984).
87. *Id.* at 1535.
88. *Id.* at 1535.
89. *Id.* at 1534.

90. 857 F.2d at 832.
91. 897 F.2d 1159 (D.C. Cir. 1990).
92. *Id.* at 1160 (citation to *Richardson v. Richardson-Merrell,* 857 F.2d 823 (D.C. Cir. 1989) omitted).
93. 113 S.Ct. at 2797.
94. 874 F.2d 307 (5th Cir. 1989).
95. 959 F.2d 1349 (6th Cir. 1992).
96. Kevin Clermont & Theodore Eisenberg, *Trial by Jury or Judge: Transcending Empiricism*, 77 Cornell L. Rev. 1124, 1127 n.7 (1992).
97. *In re Richardson-Merrell*, 624 F.Supp. at 1268.
98. E.g., Federal Rule of Evidence 606(b).
99. E.g., *In re Japanese Electronic Products Antitrust Litigation,* 631 F.2d 1069, 1086 (3rd Cir. 1980); Warren Burger, *The Use of Lay Jurors in Complicated Civil Cases*, Remarks to the Conference of State Chief Justices 3–5 (Aug. 7, 1979); Goodman, Greene & Loftus, *What Confuses Jurors in Complex Cases: Judges and Jurors Outline the Problem*, Trial, Nov. 1988 at 65. But see In re United States Fin. Sec. Litig., 609 F.2d 411, 429–30 (9th Cir. 1979). See generally Richard O. Lempert, *Civil Juries and Complex Cases: Lets Not Rush to Judgment*, 80 Mich. L. Rev. 68 (1981); Joe S. Cecil, Valerie P. Hans and Elizabeth C. Wiggins, *Citizen Comprehension of Difficult Issues: Lessons From Civil Jury Trials*, 40 Am. U.L. Rev. 727 (1991); Richard Lempert, *Civil Juries and Complex Cases: Taking Stock after Twelve Years*, in Robert E. Litan, Ed. Verdict, Assessing the Civil Jury System, 181–247 (The Brookings Institution 1993).
100. E.g., Reid Hastie, Steven Penrod & Nancy Penington, Inside the Jury (1983), *The Effects of Death Qualification on Jurors' Predisposition to Convict and on the Quality of Deliberation*, 8 L. & Hum. Beh. 53 (1984).
101. Phoebe C. Ellsworth, *Are Twelve Heads Better Than One?*, 52 L. & Contemp. Probs. 205 (1989).
102. Sanders, *supra* note 5, at 6.
103. 615 F.Supp. 262 (N.D. Ga. 1985), *aff'd and modified in part*, 788 F.2d 741 (11th Cir. 1986).
104. Samuel R. Gross, *Expert Evidence*, 1991 Wisc. L. Rev. 1113, 1121–24.
105. Wells, 615 F.Supp. at 298. The judgment was reduced on appeal to $4.7 million. 788 F.2d at 747.
106. *Smith v. Ortho Pharmaceutical Corporation,* 770 F.Supp. 1561 (N.D. Ga.1991).
107. Sanders, *supra* note 5, at 6 (omitting European cases).
108. 911 F.2d 941 (3rd Cir. 1990).
109. *Id.* at 944 (quoting Appellant's Brief at 38).
110. See Gross, *supra* note 104, at 1153–58.
111. Federal Rule of Evidence 704(a), for example, specifically permits expert testimony that "embraces an ultimate issue to be decided by the trier of fact." (Except for some statements about the mental state of criminal defendants, which are not permitted by Rule 704(b).)
112. McCormick, *supra* note 62, §338 at 434 (footnote omitted). The "rare case" cited is instructive: *Scott v. Hansen,* 228 Iowa 37, 289 N.W. 710 (1990), in which a witness testified that he saw a cow hit by a car, after which the cow

"flew pretty near thirty feet without touching the pavement at all; and then she hit the pavement and bounced better than five feet. . . ." *Id.* at 712.

113. *Gimbel v. Laramie,* 181 Cal. App.2d 77, 80, 5 Cal. Rptr. 88, 90 (1960) (citations omitted).
114. *Ferebee*, *supra* note 86, 736 F.2d at 1534.
115. In Federal diversity cases, treating the problem of questionable scientific evidence as an issue of admissibility has another consequence that judges may like: it enables them to avoid the requirement of *Erie R.R. v. Tompkins,* 304 U.S. 64 (1938), that in diversity cases federal courts apply the substantive law of the states in which they sit. In *Richardson*, the plaintiffs argued that *Erie* meant that the Federal Courts for the District of Columbia were obliged to follow the holding of the District of Columbia Court of Appeals in *Oxendine v. Merrell-Dow Pharmaceuticals, Inc.,* 563 A.2d 330 (D.C. 1989), reversing a j.n.o.v. in a Bendectin case and reinstating the jury's verdict for the plaintiff. The Circuit Court replied: "[T]he *Erie* doctrine applies to *substantive*, not *procedural*, law. . . . [I]t is clear that *Erie* does not affect the federal courts' application of the Federal Rules of Evidence. . . . Because the admissibility of testimony . . . is the crux of our decision in this case . . . the Richardsons' argument must be rejected." See also *Ealy v. Richardson-Merrell, Inc.,* 897 F.2d 1159, 1163 (D.C. Cir. 1990).
116. *Ealy*, 897 F.2d at 1160.
117. See, e.g., Federal Rule of Evidence 104(b).
118. See, e.g., Federal Rule of Evidence 104.
119. See *supra* note 38 and accompanying text.
120. See, e.g., David H. Kaye, *Is Proof of Statistical Significance Relevant?*, 61 Wash. L. Rev. 1333 (1986).
121. See Federal Rule of Evidence 804(b)(2).
122. See Federal Rule of Evidence 703.
123. *Ballew v. Georgia,* 435 U.S. 223 (1978).
124. *U.S. v. Martinez,* 3 F.3d 1191 (8th Cir. 1993).
125. Kenneth C. Davis, *An Approach to Problems of Evidence in the Administrative Process*, 55 Harv. L. Rev. 364 (1942).
126. E.g., Advisory Committee's Note to Federal Rule of Evidence 201(a).
127. Kenneth C. Davis, *A System of Judicial Notice Based on Fairness and Convenience*, in Perspectives of Law 69, 82 (1964).
128. *Lockhart v. McCree,* 476 U.S. 162, 166 n.3 (1986); *Dunagin v. City of Oxford, Miss.,* 718 F.2d 738, 748 n.3 (5th Cir. 1983).
129. *In re Asbestos Litigation,* 829 F.2d 1233, 1245–51 (Becker, J., concurring) (3rd Cir. 1987); *id.* at 1256–60 (Hunter, J., dissenting).
130. *Id.*, 829 F.2d at 1233, 1245–51, 1256–60 (interpreting *Beshada v. Johns-Manville Products Corp.,* 90 N.J. 191, 447 A.2d 539 (1982)). But see *Democratic Party v. Nat. Conservative P.A. Committee,* 578 F.Supp. 797, 830–31 (E.D. Pa. 1983), *modified sub. nom., Fed. Election Comm. v. Nat. Conservative P.A. Committee,* 470 U.S. 480 (1985).
131. Kenneth C. Davis, Administrative Law Treatise 353 (1978).
132. Kenneth C. Davis, *Judicial Notice*, 55 Colum. L. Rev. 945, 952 (1955).
133. Commissioner of Welfare *ex rel. Tyler v. Costonio,* 277 App. Div. 90. 92, 97 N.Y.S.2d 804, 806 (1st Dep't 1950) (Shientag, J., concurring). See also *Jordan v. Mace,* 144 Me. 351, 69 A.2d 760 (1949).

134. 955 F.2d 786 (2d Cir. 1992).
135. *Id.* at 799–800.
136. Harold L. Korn, *Law, Fact and Science in the Courts*, 66 Colum. L. Rev. 1080, 1102 (1966).
137. *Id.* at 1105.
138. James Bradley Thayer, *A Preliminary Treatise on Evidence at the Common Law* 249 (1898) (quoting Lord Mansfield in Tindfal v. Brown, 1 T.R. 167, 168, 99 Eng. Rep. 1033, 1034 (K.B. 1786)).
139. *Turpin*, note 20, 959 F.2d at 1351.
140. *Brock*, 874 F.2d at 310 (footnotes omitted).
141. *Id.* at 313.
142. *Turpin*, 959 F.2d at 1360.
143. E.g., "*In light of the evidence presented*, we are convinced that the Brocks did not present sufficient evidence regarding causation to allow a trier of fact to make a reasonable inference that Bendectin caused Rachel Brock's limb reduction defect." *Brock*, 874 F.2d at 315 (emphasis added). "Dr. Palmer [a plaintiff's expert] does not . . . take issue with his peers and explain the grounds for his differences." *Turpin*, 959 F.2d at 1360.
144. See, e.g., Jack H. Friedenthal, *Cases on Summary Judgment: Has There Been a Material Change in Standards?*, 63 Notre Dame L. Rev. 770, 781 (1988).
145. *Brock*, 884 F.2d at 169 (Higginbotham, J., concurring in the dissent); see also *id.* at 168 (Reavley, J., dissenting).
146. Thus, for example, some courts have interpreted *Brock* as setting a general requirement of statistically significant epidemiological evidence for any toxic tort case. E.g., *Thomas v. Hoffman-La Roche,* 731 F.Supp. 224, 228 (N.D. Miss. 1989), *aff'd*, 949 F.2d 806 (5th Cir. 1992); Porter v. Whitehall Labs, Inc., 791 F.Supp. 1335, 1347 (S.D. Ind. 1992).
147. 611 F. Supp.1223 (E.D.N.Y. 1985), *aff'd on other grounds*, 818 F.2d 187 (2nd Cir. 1987), *cert. denied*, 487 U.S. 1234 (1988).
148. See Peter H. Schuck, Agent Orange on Trial, Mass Toxic Disasters in the Courts 143–167 (1986).
149. 611 F. Supp. 1223. Judge Weinstein also granted summary judgment on the ground that the plaintiffs could not, in any event, prove *which* defendant might have harmed them, 611 F. Supp. at 1263, and on the "government contract defense." *Id.* at 1263–64. The Second Circuit affirmed on this last ground. 818 F.2d at 194.
150. E.g., Schuck, *supra* note 148; Green, *supra* note 3; Charles Nesson, *Agent Orange Meets the Blue Bus: Factfinding at the Frontiers of Knowledge*, 66 B.U.L. Rev. 521 (1986).
151. 874 F.2d at 310 (citation omitted).
152. 827 F. Supp. 1014 (S.D.N.Y. 1993).
153. *Id.* at 1050.
154. *Id.* at 1038–50.
155. *Id.* at 1050.
156. *Id.* at 1038.
157. See *Washington v. Armstrong World Indus.,* 839 F.2d 1121 (5th Cir. 1988); *Landrigan v. Celotex Corp.,* 127 N.J. 404, 605 A.2d 1079 (1992); *Caterinicchio v. Pittsburgh Corning Corp.,* 127 N.J. 428, 605 A.2d 1092 (1992). The *Joint Asbestos Case* itself concerns a single claim out of a group of 16 that were

initially jointly prosecuted. See *In re Joint E. and S. Dist. Asbestos Litig.,* 758 F.Supp. 199.200 (S.D.N.Y. 1991).

158. See Schuck, *supra* note 148 at 239. ("Weinstein personally read an enormous amount of the technical literature on toxicology, statistics, and other relevant disciplines. . . . Were all judges as incisive as Weinstein, there might be much to be said for this intervention.")
159. A very recent study found that exposure to one of two common types of asbestos – amphibole, but not serpentine – "may be associated with colorectal cancer," but this association appears relatively weak and might be caused by "misdiagnosis of lung cancer or other types of cancer in reported causes of death." David M. Homa, David H. Garabrant, & Brenda W. Gillespie, *A Meta-Analysis of Colorectal Cancer and Asbestos Exposure*, Am. J. Epidemiology (forthcoming). This is not likely to be the last word on the subject.
160. No. 84 425 091 NI (Wayne County Cir. Ct. Mich. June 12, 1988).
161. Troyen A. Brennan, *Helping Courts with Toxic Torts: Some Proposals Regarding Alternative Methods for Presenting and Assessing Scientific Evidence in Common Law Courts*, 51 U. Pitt. L. Rev. 1, 44–48 (1989).
162. *Id.* at 45–46.
163. *Id.* at 46.
164. *Id.* at 47, n. 197.
165. E.g., Emory Washburn, *Testimony of Experts*, 1 Am. L. Rev. 45, 48–49 (1866); *Rutherford v. Morris,* 77 Ill. 397, 405 (1875); Learned Hand, *Historical and Practical Considerations Regarding Expert Testimony*, 15 Harv. L. Rev. 40 (1901); Mason Ladd, *Expert Testimony*, 5 Vand. L. Rev. 414 (1952); Jack B. Weinstein, *Improving Expert Testimony*, 20 U. Rich. L. Rev. 473 (1986).
166. Brennan, *supra* note 161, at 48.
167. *Id.*; see also Washburn, *supra* note 165; Hand, *supra* note 165.
168. Gross, *supra* note 104, at 1187–1208, 1220–30.
169. Needless to say, experts would have been useful to the jurors for in those Bendectin cases that went to trial. For example, Joseph Sanders has published a fascinating description of the jury deliberations in one Bendectin trial, *Havner v. Merrell Dow Pharmaceuticals,* Texas Dist. Ct., 214th Fud. Dist. (1991), based on post-deliberation interviews with several jurors. He found a "strong tendency [for the jurors] to conclude that [scientific] opinion is evenly divided" on whether Bendectin is a teratogen. Joseph A. Sanders, *Jury Deliberation in a Complex Case: Havner v. Merrell Dow Pharmaceuticals*, 16 Justice Sys. J. 45, 64 (1993). Any court-appointed expert would have disabused the jury of that mistake; and yet the defense, which would clearly have benefited, apparently did not seek the appointment of such an expert. Their failure to do so was no aberration. Trial lawyers hardly ever ask to have experts appointed, whether they are likely to gain or lose from such an appointment. See generally Gross, *supra* note 104, at 1198–1200.
170. Schuck, *supra* note 148, at 239.
171. Various commentators have suggested more radical proposals for dealing with scientific issues in mass-tort cases – e.g., the creation of a "Science Court," James A. Martin, *The Proposed "Science Court,"* 75 Mich. L. Rev. 1058 (1977), or a "Science Board" that, among other functions, would appoint panels to resolve important recurring issues. Brennan, *supra* note 161, at 62–71. These might be worthy suggestions, but they require legislative innovations. Almost all American jurisdictions already permit judges to appoint non-partisan

expert witnesses in any type of case, on motion of a party or on their own motion. See, e.g., Federal Rule of Evidence 706.

172. 902 F.2d 302 (5th Cir. 1990), *superseded en banc*, 939 F.2d 1106 (1991).

173. 939 F.2d at 1116. The quotation is from an affidavit submitted by a defense expert; apparently, it is taken out of context. See 902 F.2d at 366 n.3.

174. 939 F.2d at 1116.

175. *Id.* at 1124–34 (Reavely, J., dissenting). See also *Id.* at 1119–20 (Clark, C.J., concurring); 902 F.2d 362 (panel opinion of Reavely, J., reversing).

176. 902 F.2d at 366.

177. As it happens, I believe the district court *was* right—but only because I have checked with a non-partisan expert on my own, an Associate Professor of Occupational Medicine at a major university who is an expert on cancer epidemiology. He confirmed that there is no epidemiological evidence linking nickel or cadmium and colon cancer of any sort, and that small-cell colon cancer is rare, but he dismissed the argument that the fact that a substance produces small-cell carcinomas in one organ means its likely to do the same in other organs: "There's no evidence of that. That's just not the way it works." Conversation between the author and Dr. David H. Garabrant, M.D., M.P.H., Associate Professor of Occupational Medicine, University of Michigan Medical School and School of Public Health, 12/12/93. Needless to say, I do not mean to suggest that this informal consultation is a model for the use non-partisan experts in litigation. And for any purpose, if more depended on the issue, I would want more detailed information and explanation—but from the same type of source.

178. *Wells* is a clear example.

179. *Christopherson*, 902 F.2d at 366.

180. Court-appointed experts may promote speed and efficiency, as well as accuracy and consistency, since their presence might encourage the parties to settle. Thus, for example, a study by the Federal Judicial Center found that in most of the rare occasions in which court-appointed experts have been used, their main function is to facilitate settlement rather than testify at trial. Joseph Cecil & Thomas A. Willging, *Defining a Role for Court-Appointed Experts*, 4 Fed. Jud. Ctr., Directions 6 (Aug. 1992).

181. Elwood S. Levy, *Impartial Medical Testimony—Revisited*, 34 Temp. L.Q. 416, 425 (1961).

Scientific Validity, Admissibility, and Mass Torts After *Daubert*[*]

Joseph Sanders[**]

I. Introduction

The death of *Frye v. United States*,[1] is no longer greatly exaggerated.[2] *Frye* finally met its federal court demise in 1993.[3] In *Daubert v. Merrell Dow Pharmaceuticals, Inc.*,[4] the Supreme Court did what commentators[5] had long recommended and declared that the "*Frye* test" did not survive the adoption of the Federal Rules of Evidence.[6] The *Frye* test had declared inadmissible novel expert testimony that was not "generally accepted" as reliable in the relevant scientific community.[7] Commentators criticized *Frye* both for its unidimensional approach[8] and for being too malleable to be useful.[9] In *Daubert*, the Supreme Court held that Federal Rule 702 superseded *Frye* and rejected the approach followed by a majority of courts.[10] Not only does *Daubert* mark the end of a long controversy over

---

*This article was previously published in 78 Minnesota L. Rev. 1387 (1994). We are grateful to the author and publishers for permission to reprint it.

**Professor of Law, University of Houston Law School. Work on this paper was supported by the University of Houston, Environmental Liability Law Program. I wish to thank Roger Park for encouraging me to write this article and the editors at the Minnesota Law Review for their careful editing. Special thanks are due to Linda Gordon Hestor who contributed significantly to the quality of the finished product. Space limitations precluded our plans for a longer, jointly-authored article.

Frye's viability after the Federal Rules,[11] it also marks the end of debate on *Frye*'s merits as the primary device for controlling expert scientific testimony.[12]

The timing of *Frye*'s rejection is of greater interest than the event itself. The Federal Rulcs of Evidence have been in place for nearly 20 years and, for most of that period, the circuits have disagreed about whether the Rules incorporated *Frye*. Yet only now has the Supreme Court taken the time to resolve the issue. One important reason for the Court's recent interest is a new sense of urgency concerning the increasing use of scientific expert testimony and the role judges should play in monitoring and controlling such testimony. The emerging belief that an increase in "junk science" in the courtroom[13] requires greater judicial vigilance in admitting expert opinion has fueled this sense of urgency.[14] For example, the Judicial Conference Advisory Committee on Civil Rules, intending to curtail the use of expert testimony, recently proposed a change to Federal Rule 702 that would allow expert testimony only if it is "reasonably reliable and will substantially assist the factfinder."[15]

These developments were not lost on the Supreme Court. After dispensing with the *Frye* rule, the Court outlined the trial judge's gate keeping role.[16] The Court's discussion raises two primary questions addressed in this Article: what approach should courts employ in assessing the admissibility of expert scientific opinion and, given this approach, how restrictive should courts be in allowing expert opinion into evidence?

Part II reviews *Daubert*'s approach to admissibility. This Article argues that the concept of scientific validity lies at the heart of the Court's approach to admissibility. By taking this approach, the Court has invited judges to dispense with surrogate measures of scientific validity and to investigate the issue directly.[17] Even though scientific validity is central to the Court's approach, the Court failed to sufficiently develop the concept in its opinion. Part III argues that this deficiency principally stems from the Court's failure to recognize that scientific validity has multiple meanings and is always a matter of degree. This Part illustrates this deficiency by sketching out four different threats to the validity of scientific research.

Although the *Daubert* Court devoted significant attention to how courts should approach the admissibility of scientific evidence, it largely failed to define how restrictive courts should be.[18] The Court failed to offer any realistic examples to clarify what it means to call an expert's methodology, data, or reasoning invalid.[19] Rather, the Court offered little more than the general observation that courts should judge the admissibility of scientific evidence on the basis of scientific principles of reliability and validity. In this regard, *Daubert* suffers from an ailment frequently attributed to *Frye*: it provides little guidance on how to apply Rule 703 in actual cases. The wide variation in the way the courts have applied Rules 702 and 703 in the past does little to clarify the issue.[20] Despite the Supreme

Court's silence, however, the degree to which a court may aggressively act to keep an expert's proffered testimony from the jury presents the critical issue surrounding admissibility.[21]

This Article approaches this issue in the light of scientific evidence concerning the drug Bendectin. Some of the most restrictive admissibility determinations in recent years, including *Daubert* itself, have occurred in cases involving this drug.[22] Part IV reviews several Bendectin cases in which the court excluded the plaintiff's expert testimony and re-examines these rulings under a scientific validity standard. It inquires whether this standard can support the Bendectin rulings or, to put the question differently, whether the plaintiff's proffered testimony in those cases was so invalid that a court could reasonably exclude it on that basis? This Part concludes that most of the restrictive rulings are questionable under a scientific validity standard.

Despite the fact that a scientific validity standard does not justify such restrictive rulings, courts nonetheless have expressed a willingness to restrict scientific evidence in this manner. Part V provides two explanations for the judicial propensity to exclude scientific evidence: courts want to achieve judicial efficiency and to improve jury decision making by shielding juries from marginal science. The first objective is especially salient in mass tort cases or any situation in which the same expert testimony is repeatedly presented.[23] The second objective is relevant in all cases, including mass torts, that involve a complex body of scientific data. Although these are reasonable objectives, restrictive admissibility rulings should not be the primary means of achieving them. Several factors make restrictive evidentiary rulings especially ill-suited devices for controlling the flow of information to juries. First, achieving consistency across different types of cases is very difficult if not impossible. Second, and more importantly, marginal science is not the primary reason juries encounter substantial difficulty with scientific evidence. Rather, the primary source of difficulty is the way in which the legal process presents scientific evidence to the jury. Part VI recognizes that restrictive admissibility rulings do little to solve this problem and proposes some alternatives that will assist the fact finder in understanding and weighing scientific testimony in complex cases.

II. The *Daubert* Opinion

Jason Daubert and Eric Schuler both suffer from limb reduction birth defects. They sued Merrell Dow, the manufacturer of Bendectin, claiming that the morning-sickness drug, which their mothers ingested during pregnancy, caused their defects.[24] The trial judge granted the defendant's motion for summary judgment.[25] The trial court based its holding on several grounds. First, the court held that only epidemiological evidence is relevant to the question of whether Bendectin is a teratogen[26] and that the published epidemiological research contains no studies that demonstrate a statistically significant association between Bendectin and birth defects.[27] Moreover, the court found that the plaintiff's expert reanalyses of existing data, which purported to reveal a significant relationship, were insufficient to satisfy their burden of coming forward with statistically significant epidemiological evidence.[28] Thus, the court concluded that the strongest inference a jury could draw from the evidence was "that Bendectin could possibly have caused plaintiff's injuries," which was insufficient to avoid the defendant's motion for summary judgment.[29]

On appeal, the Ninth Circuit affirmed in a two page opinion.[30] Basing its analysis on *Frye*, the Ninth Circuit held the plaintiff's expert testimony inadmissible because its underlying methodology diverged substantially from the procedures and techniques generally accepted in the field.[31]

The Supreme Court granted certiorari, primarily to announce *Frye*'s demise.[32] Noting the sharp division among the circuits as to Frye's continued vitality, the Court held that the Federal Rules of Evidence superseded the *Frye* test.[33] The Court grounded its analysis in the language of Federal Rule 702 which reads as follows:

> If scientific, technical, or other specialized knowledge will assist the trier of fact to understand the evidence or to determine a fact in issue, a witness qualified as an expert by knowledge, skill, expertise, training, or education, may testify thereto in the form of an opinion or otherwise.[34]

The Court noted that the text of the rule did not preserve the general acceptance standard, nor did its legislative history make any mention of *Frye*. The Court thus concluded that a rigid "general acceptance" standard would be contrary to the thrust of the Federal Rules which were intended to lower barriers to expert opinion testimony.[35]

Daubert is an incomplete opinion. The Court granted certiorari primarily to announce *Frye*'s death and the ensuing discussion of what standard should replace *Frye* is sketchy at best. Although the Court was quite explicit that Rule 702 does not incorporate *Frye*, it was far less clear about what Rule 702 does require.[36] The Court began by holding that Rule 702 modifies Rule 402's directive to admit all relevant evidence.[37] This holding rejected the argument that Rule 702 speaks only to the expert's credentials and that a court may admit all evidence consistent with Rules 401, 403, and 703 if presented by a qualified expert.[38] Rather, the Court held that Rule 702 requires reliability as well as relevance; evidence which is relevant but unreliable is inadmissible.[39] This interpretation of Rule 702, however, raises a fundamental question: What constitutes reliability? Importantly, the Court turned to science to answer that question: To be reliable, the offering party must have acquired the evidence through the "methods and procedures of science."[40]

In this context, evidentiary reliability is very similar to "scientific validity."[41] Although *Daubert* did not offer a systematic presentation of what scientists mean when they use this term, it did describe some broad parameters relevant to the validity inquiry. The Court emphasized that the 702 inquiry should be a flexible one and that the factors set forth in other opinions[42] and the legal literature[43] may prove valuable in determining whether scientific testimony is reliable. The trial judge should determine whether proffered evidence is scientifically valid by examining the reasoning and methodology underlying the expert's testimony and the "fit" between the testimony and the factual issue presented to the judge or jury.[44] Generally, the expert's theory must be both testable and falsifiable.[45] The unreliability of a procedure and its potential rate of error[46] may likewise merit exclusion.[47]

Moreover, the trial court may consider a number of secondary, surrogate indicia of reliability. These include whether the theory or technique has been subject to peer review,[48] whether the results have been published[49] and, in a partial resurrection of the *Frye* test, whether the expert's methods and reasoning enjoy general acceptance in a relevant scientific community.[50] Unlike the *Frye* test, however, which determines the value of science primarily through the surrogate of general acceptance,[51] the *Daubert* surrogates are secondary to a direct analysis of the testimony's scientific validity.

Finally, the Court also noted that Rule 702 does not stand alone. Rule 703 provides that a court may admit expert scientific opinion only if the facts or data are "of a type reasonably relied upon by experts in the particular field in forming opinions or inferences on the subject."[52] Rule 706 allows the court to appoint its own expert when necessary.[53] Finally, the court may employ Rule 403 to exclude expert testimony when its prejudicial effect or potential to confuse or mislead the jury substantially outweighs its probative value.[54]

In sum, *Daubert* clearly ended *Frye*'s reign in the federal courts. Rules 702 and 703 superseded *Frye* and supplanted its "general acceptance" standard. Unfortunately, *Daubert* was far less clear about precisely what these rules, especially Rule 702, require. At the core of the Court's analysis of admissibility under Rule 702, however, is the idea of scientific validity. The next section attempts to remedy *Daubert*'s failure to define this term.

III. The Varieties of Scientific Validity

Daubert's references to validity pose two primary problems: the Court used the term as if it encompassed a unitary concept with a single meaning; and the Court implied that validity must be either present or absent and not a matter of degree.[55] Validity, however, is a complex concept with multiple dimensions. For example, Cook and Campbell have identified four basic types of validity: statistical conclusion validity, internal validity, construct validity, and external validity.[56] Each may be threatened to various degrees and in a number of ways.

A. Statistical Conclusion Validity

Statistical conclusion validity is an important consideration with all quantitative data. The typical threats to statistical conclusion validity have been widely discussed.[57] When researchers observe a co-variation between two variables, they may wish to conclude, based on a statistical analysis, that the variables are causally related. Tests of significance guard against the danger that researchers will conclude that a relationship exists when it does not. Typically, tests of statistical significance test the null hypothesis that no relationship exists between two variables–that the relationship observed could be the result of chance.[58] Unless a relationship is statistically significant, the null hypothesis will not be rejected.[59] These tests, therefore, guard against Type I errors, a validity threat that occurs when one concludes that a relationship exists when, in fact, none does.[60] Thus, a researcher may reject a causal interpretation of an apparent relationship that is not statistically significant.

Recent interest has focused on the problem which arises when researchers attempt to assess causation with respect to rare events such as limb reduction birth defects.[61] Whenever a study has a relatively small number of subjects, statistical tests will fail to detect a significant difference unless the relationship is quite strong. This may cause a Type II error, which occurs when one accepts the null hypothesis as true when it is actually false. This threat to validity is one of low statistical power.[62] Researchers can employ a number of techniques to guard against this threat, including meta-analysis which increases the number of cases by combining the results of several studies.[63]

Two other threats to statistical conclusion validity deserve special mention. First, there is the error rate problem. Researchers engaged in a fishing expedition, sifting through a large number of correlations in search of significant relationships, will inevitably find some. For example, if one concludes that a relationship is significant if there is less than one chance in twenty (Alpha = .05) that it would occur if the null hypothesis is correct, a study of sixty relationships will produce three significant correlations even if no true causal relationships exist.[64] The unreliability of measurement techniques pose the second threat. Epidemiological research depends on determining whether individuals have or have not been exposed to a toxic substance and whether or not they suffer from some adverse effect. Coding errors occur when researchers treat individuals who were not exposed as having been exposed and those exposed as not exposed, or the researcher misdiagnoses the individuals. Unreliable coding threatens validity by inflating error variance and attenuating true relationships.[65]

B. Internal Validity

Statistical conclusion validity presents a special case of internal validity, which Cook and Campbell define as "the approximate validation with which we infer that a relationship between two variables is causal or that the absence of a relationship implies the absence of cause."[66] Threats to internal validity usually can be thought of as specification errors. Specification errors occur when the researcher fails to consider a factor that mediates the observed effect between two variables, either because it explains changes in both the "cause" and the "effect" or intervenes between the "cause" and the "effect" and acts independently on the "effect."[67] Among the threats to internal validity Cook and Campbell discuss are history (the threat that an observed effect may be due to an event that takes place between two points of measurement when this event is not the treatment under investigation),[68] testing (the threat that an effect may be due to the number of times responses are measured),[69] and selection (a threat that groups being compared are composed of different types of individuals and, therefore, that observed differences are due to factors other than the treatment under investigation).[70] A basic advantage of experimental research is its ability to control for many selection effects by randomly assigning individuals to treatments.[71] Of course in many situations, such as investigating the effect of toxic substances on individuals, human experiments are impossible. In such cases, the researcher can attempt to control selection threats by carefully matching cases and controls in case-control studies.[72]

C. Construct Validity

The third broad type of validity is construct validity. Confounding operations intended to represent one particular cause or effect construct with some other construct usually threaten construct validity.[73] What one investigator may interpret as evidence of a causal relationship between constructs A and B, another investigator may interpret as a relationship between constructs X and B or even X and Y.[74] There are several sources of construct invalidity. One, experimenter expectancy, occurs when the experimenter anticipates a certain outcome.[75] Another, evaluation apprehension, arises when the subject wishes to please the investigator.[76] Finally, hypothesis-guessing may threaten construct validity when the subject attempts to guess the hypothesis being tested and adjust his or her answers accordingly.[77] For example, drug testing experiments often present construct validity concerns because any observed effect between the drug and a therapeutic effect may be due, not to the chemical action of the drug, but rather to the psychological expectation that the pill will have a beneficial effect.[78]

Another source of construct invalidity is the confounding of constructs and levels of constructs.[79] One might conclude that A does not cause B when the test involves very low levels of A. At higher levels of A, however, the researcher might uncover a relationship.[80] In an attempt to avoid this threat, laboratory animal studies routinely expose animals to suspect drugs at more than one dose level.[81]

A similar threat arises whenever one has but a single operationalization of the cause or the effect: a mono-operation bias.[82] Early animal studies failed to detect the teratogenetic effects of Thalidomide, in part because they used species unaffected by the drug.[83] Even when there are multiple operationalizations, the use of a single method to measure a relationship threatens validity.[84] Wherever possible, researchers should employ multiple methods.

Assessing construct validity is frequently a question of convergence and divergence across measures. One is much more likely to believe that a cause and effect relationship exists when different measurements and methods *converge* to produce the same result.[85] Similarly, researchers are more likely to believe that a cause and effect relationship of a particular type exists if there is a *divergence* between measures and manipulations of related but distinct constructs.[86]

D. External Validity

Finally, there is external validity. Just as statistical conclusion validity is a special type of internal validity, construct validity is a type of external validity. External validity involves the ability to generalize conclusions to *particular* persons, settings and times and to *types* of persons, settings and times.[87] Cook and Campbell list three basic threats to external validity,[88] each of which can be expressed in terms of an interaction between a treatment and some other factor. First, the potential interaction between selection and treatment poses a threat to external validity.[89] If a study uncovers a cause and effect relationship, the researcher must determine to which categories of individuals the relationship can be generalized. For example, if a study includes only men as subjects, the researcher must determine whether the results can be generalized to women. Other examples involve the ability to generalize across race, ethnicity, and class. Other, more subtle threats to generalization may pose special problems in the courtroom. For instance, jurors may rely upon the persuasiveness of experts as an indicator of the merits of their position. Litigants select testifying experts in part for their persuasiveness and, therefore, the assumption that a causal relationship exists between persuasiveness and correctness may be unwarranted for the *type* of expert that appears as a witness in court.[90]

The interaction between setting and treatment creates a second threat. A researcher may not be able to generalize studies done in one setting to other settings. All laboratory studies are vulnerable to this threat.[91] Even well crafted experiments that do their best to increase external validity cannot insure that their results can be transferred from the laboratory. Some laboratory studies suffer from multiple threats to external validity. For example, some laboratory studies of jury decision making involve college sophomores rather than actual jurors.[92] The subjects read a written fact pattern and each individual "juror" renders his or her own decision, instead of the "jury" issuing a collective decision after deliberation.[93] Likewise, laboratory animal studies encounter difficulty in extrapolating across both dose rates and species.[94] Courts have frequently focused on threats to external validity when refusing to admit expert testimony.[95] This brief review of validity's different facets indicates some of the ways in which conclusions about causation may be in error. Statistical conclusion validity and other types of internal validity concentrate on the danger of Type I or Type II errors, drawing false positive or false negative conclusions about causation. Statistical conclusion validity deals with threats to internal validity caused by random error, the possibility that an observed relationship could be due to chance. Other threats to internal validity are due to the possible existence of bias through factors that systematically affect the value of the means of variables.[96] Construct validity and other types of external validity concentrate on the danger of generalization. The principal threat stems from the possible existence of an undetected interaction.[97] With respect to construct validity the danger is that an effect can be obtained using one measure, such as individual juror judgments, and a different effect using a different measure, such as collective jury judgments. The risk of undetected interaction effects is even easier to see with respect to other threats to external validity, such as the interaction between selection and treatment.[98] In each case, a relationship observed in one circumstance may not apply in a different circumstance. The next section employs these categories of scientific validity to discuss specific admissibility rulings in Bendectin cases.

IV. Restrictive Admissibility Rulings in the Bendectin Cases

Bendectin has become a very important product, primarily because it has precipitated a reanalysis of the judiciary's proper role in assessing the admissibility of scientific evidence. For nearly a decade, trial and appellate courts have wrestled with the admissibility of plaintiffs' expert testimony that Bendectin is a teratogen.[99] This section investigates whether *Daubert*'s scientific validity analysis can explain and justify the Bendectin cases' restrictive admissibility rulings and whether the excluded testimony in those cases was so invalid that the courts properly excluded it. The Article addresses this question in the context of two specific themes that have arisen in Bendectin litigation: the primacy of epidemiology, and the exclusion of testimony based on a reanalysis of published epidemiological results.

A. The Primacy of Epidemiology

1. Evidence of a Causal Relationship

Bendectin is a substance that is not obviously harmful.[100] It does not produce a signature disease and no generally accepted biological theory exist about how it produces its alleged effect. Moreover, the correlation between the product and the plaintiffs' injuries is not strong. The evidence as to the causal relationship between the drug and birth defects comes in five basic types: structure-activity, *in vitro* research, animal studies, epidemiology, and secular trend analysis.[101]

Structure-activity. Substances with similar chemical structures may have similar effects on the human body. Bendectin contains doxylamine succinate, an antihistamine acting as an antinauseant.[102] Some antihistamines are known teratogens and plaintiff experts point to this structural similarity.[103]

In vitro. *In vitro* research involves exposing cells or organs maintained in a culture to a substance.[104] One study indicates that Bendectin inhibits certain limb bud cell differentiation[105] and another suggests that Bendectin may be a weak DNA damaging agent.[106]

Animal studies. *In vivo* studies examine the effects of a substance on animals. Researchers have conducted Bendectin animal studies on chicks, rats, rabbits, and primates.[107] As plaintiff experts note, some studies report a relationship between Bendectin or one of its ingredients and a teratogenic effect. For example, one primate study found that the drug caused a delay in the closure of the ventricular septa.[108] On the other hand, several studies have failed to find a correlation between Bendectin and birth defects.[109]

Epidemiology. Epidemiological studies compare the incidence of birth defects among those exposed to and those not exposed to a substance. There are two general ways of making such comparisons: cohort studies and case-control studies.[110] Cohort studies compare the incidence of defects among groups of persons exposed to the substance and groups of persons not exposed.[111] Case-control studies match a group of persons who have the injury in question with another group that does not have that injury.[112] The studies then compare exposure rates for the two groups. Nearly 40 published epidemiological studies discuss Bendectin.[113] In no individual study did the authors conclude that Bendectin is a teratogen. In six studies, however, the authors found at least one significant correlation between Bendectin use and some injury and concluded that, although a single study alone is insufficient to support an attribution of causation, an effect might exist.[114] In the remaining 33 studies the authors either drew no conclusion or concluded that no statistical relationship existed.[115]

Secular trend. Secular trend data, which is similar to epidemiology, compares the total reported incidence of various types of birth defects with the volume of Bendectin sales and prescriptions. This method investigates whether increases or reductions in birth defects paralleled the rapid increase in Bendectin prescriptions in the 1970s or the precipitous drop in prescriptions in the early 1980s.

In recent years defense experts have concentrated their testimony on the epidemiological and secular trend evidence. As to the epidemiological data, Bendectin defendants have argued that, taken as a group, the studies indicate that Bendectin is not teratogenic.[116] They have also reviewed secular trend evidence that indicates no significant decrease in birth defects after Bendectin manufacturers withdrew the product from the market.[117] Plaintiff experts, on the other hand, have devoted substantial attention to structure-activity, *in vitro*, and animal studies, as well as to reanalyses of epidemiological data.[118]

2. Problems with Non-Epidemiological Evidence

Structure-activity, *in vitro*, and animal studies each pose substantial validity questions. Most problematic, perhaps, is the structure-activity evidence. Although research exists linking antihistamines to teratogenic injuries, several factors undermine its validity.[119] First, even minor changes in molecular structure can alter a substance's effect.[120] The metabolic process stands as an unknown intervening variable between the original chemical structure and the adverse effect. Thus, structure-activity data presents a problem of internal validity.

In vitro evidence is superior to structure-activity evidence because it does investigate the effect of the Bendectin ingredients. *In vitro* evidence suffers, however, from the same internal validity problem confronting structure-activity data because the relevant chemical compound does not go through the metabolic process before affecting the culture.[121] Moreover, the confounding of constructs and levels of constructs threatens this type of evidence. For example, the study which found that Bendectin inhibited cell differentiation employed a unit of measure called the teratogenic potential.[122] The authors observed an effect for Bendectin at a dose of .05 mg/ml.[123] Caffeine produces a similar effect at 2.3 mg/ml and vitamin A does so at .000013 mg/ml.[124] It is difficult to translate such dosages in *in vitro* studies to the doses humans actually experience.

Because animal studies require ingestion of a drug, they do not confront all of the threats to internal validity that structure-activity and in vitro studies face. They do, however, confront external validity threats. Some of the threats result inevitably from reasonable tradeoffs designed to avoid threats to internal validity. Among these tradeoffs, dose rates pose the most important problem. Researchers usually give animals a substance at a dose rate much higher than humans would ingest.[125] Several compelling reasons merit this practice. Animal research is expensive and time consuming. Many substances that are suspected of causing harm do so in only in a small percentage of organisms exposed at a rate similar to that found in the environment.[126] Subjecting the animals to dose rates no greater than typical environmental rates would require a very large N to avoid a high probability of a Type II error. Thus, in order to guard against threats to statistical conclusion validity, researchers increase the dose so that a larger percentage of animals will react adversely.[127] This closage, however, creates a significant threat to external validity. The high doses create the potential for construct validity problems similar to those presented in in vitro tests: confounding constructs with levels of constructs. At sufficiently high dose levels almost all substances are teratogenic.[128] Moreover, in the case of suspected teratogens, very high animal dose rates begin to poison the mother and cause fetal injuries as the byproduct of maternal toxicity and not the substance's teratogenic effect.[129]

Even at more modest dose rates, extrapolation difficulties pose significant threats to external validity. Assuming a positive result in an animal study, toxicologists must then extrapolate a predicted effect at a dose level humans actually experience. No single agreed upon model for this extrapolation exists and competing models produce different predictions.[130] Nor is dose rate the only necessary adjustment. There must also be an adjustment for the fact that species are of different sizes and mature and age at different rates. Again, there is no agreed upon formula for this adjustment, and different scaling factors lead to different estimates of human effects.[131]

One reason toxicologists tolerate the threat to external validity posed by high dose rates is that most animal studies are designed to be part of the regulatory process rather than part of proof of causation in litigation. When testing a new drug the critical question is whether a teratogenic effect might arise in humans even though it is not observed in animals. The crucial error to avoid is a Type II error. When litigants take these studies to the courtroom, however, the central question becomes whether a known effect in a test animal is probative of whether a human effect exists at a much lower dose rate. Although it is quite rare for a known human teratogen to fail to cause birth defects in at least some animals,[132] it is more likely that a substance for which there is no evidence of human teratogenicity will produce an effect in some animal species.[133]

3. Court Attitudes Towards Non-Epidemiological Data

The validity threats facing non-epidemiological data have caused several courts to refuse to allow Bendectin plaintiffs to introduce this type of evidence or prevail thereon.[134] Courts have reached this conclusion by a number of different paths. One group has directed verdicts or ordered summary judgment for the defendant without ruling on the admissibility of the plaintiff's non-epidemiology experts.[135] These are properly characterized as sufficiency rulings; the court concludes that the plaintiff cannot survive a directed verdict or a summary judgment motion because the causal proof cannot sustain a verdict for the plaintiff. For example, in *Brock v. Merrell Dow*, the Fifth Circuit held that the plaintiff could not prevail without epidemiological evidence of a statistically significant relationship between Bendectin and the plaintiff's limb reduction defect.[136] Because the opinion followed a jury trial, the Fifth Circuit did not need to rule on the admissibility of the plaintiff's non-epidemiological evidence.[137] In *Turpin v. Merrell Dow Pharmaceuticals, Inc.*,[138] however, the Sixth Circuit affirmed the trial court's grant of summary judgment for the defendant and held that the plaintiff's proffered testimony was insufficient to sustain a verdict.[139]

Another group of courts simply holds that non-epidemiological evidence is inadmissible.[140] Some, such as the Ninth Circuit in *Daubert*, reach this result under the *Frye* test.[141] More relevant in the post-*Frye* environment, however, are those cases which excluded the plaintiff's testimony under Federal Rule 702 or 703.[142] In *Lynch v. Merrell-National Laboratories*, [143] one of the earliest opinions to take this position, the trial court entered summary judgment for the defendant after concluding that testimony on human teratogenicity based on structure-activity, *in vitro*, or animal studies was not of the "type reasonably relied upon by experts in the particular field" and therefore inadmissible. [144]

A similar analysis can be found in *Richardson v. Richardson-Merrell, Inc.*:

> These three types of studies then–chemical, *in vitro*, and *in vivo*–cannot furnish a sufficient foundation for a conclusion that Bendectin caused the birth defects at issue in this case. Studies of this kind, singly or in combination, are not capable of proving causation in human beings in the face of the overwhelming body of contradictory epidemiological evidence.[145]

The key to *Richardson* is its comparative analysis. The court essentially held that structure-activity, *in vitro* and animal studies cannot form a sufficient foundation when substantial epidemiological evidence exists.[146]

Similar language can be found in the district court opinions in *Lee v. Richardson-Merrell, Inc.*,[147] and *Turpin v. Merrell Dow Pharmaceuticals, Inc.*,[148] both of which excluded non-epidemiological evidence.

Whether such non-epidemiological evidence should be excluded under a scientific validity standard turns on how precisely one poses the issue. If one asks whether, standing alone, structure-activity, in vitro and animal studies should be excluded, the answer depends on which type of evidence is under consideration. Inevitably, validity is a matter of degree. All types of non-epidemiological evidence suffer from some external validity problems when used to address whether Bendectin is a human teratogen at normal dose levels. The animal studies data, however, confronts far fewer problems and have some strengths vis-a-vis epidemiological studies. If the only evidence available to a "first plaintiff"[149] expert is an animal study indicating a teratogenic effect on mice exposed to Bendectin at a dose rate one order of magnitude greater than a human dose, it is difficult to see why this should not be admissible. The question becomes more difficult when the only evidence is an *in vitro* study indicating DNA damage to cells exposed to Bendectin. In an extreme case, where the only available evidence is a structure-activity study relating some antihistamines to birth defects, the threats to internal and external validity may indeed be so large that the evidence cannot form the basis of an expert opinion that Bendectin is a teratogen. Thus, judging each type of evidence on its own, a court might reasonably exclude an expert's conclusion that Bendectin is a teratogen if it is based solely on structure-activity evidence, but might admit an opinion based on animal studies.

The courts that have excluded non-epidemiological data in the Bendectin cases have not approached the problem in this way. They have not independently assessed the admissibility of each type of evidence as if it were the only available evidence and they been hesitant to conclude that plaintiffs can never reach a jury without epidemiological evidence. Instead, they have carved out an exception for Bendectin cases because of the rich epidemiological data available.[150] Whether the admissibility of one type of evidence should vary depending on the existence of other evidence poses an interesting, but different, question. More precisely, should the admissibility of non-epidemiological evidence turn on the existence of epidemiological evidence? Applying a validity analysis under Rule 702, the answer is no. Under that standard, if the threats to internal and external validity do not render a piece of evidence unreliable, that evidence does not become unreliable simply because better data is available.

The Bendectin courts, however, have not relied on Rule 702 as the basis of their opinions. Rather, most have found the evidence inadmissible under Rule 703 and held that non-epidemiological findings are not the type of evidence relied upon by experts in the field.[151] The propriety of this approach depends on the structure of the plaintiff's entire case.

An everyday example illustrates this point. When the only evidence whether a dog walked across the front lawn last night is the report of three eyewitnesses who say they saw no dog, this constitutes the best evidence available and is admissible. When, on the other hand, it snowed during the night, the presence of dog tracks across the lawn greatly diminishes the value of the eyewitness testimony. Similarly, when animal studies supply the only available evidence that a substance causes harm, teratology experts may reasonably rely on this finding. When a large and rich body of epidemiological data exists, however, experts may cease to rely on the animal study as the primary basis of their opinion about whether the substance is a teratogen. Nevertheless, an independent Rule 702 validity analysis indicates why courts should refuse to conclude that non-epidemiological evidence is inadmissible even when a large body of epidemiological data exists.

One could argue, under Rule 703, that it would be inappropriate to form one's opinion about whether Bendectin is a teratogen based entirely on non-epidemiological evidence. Something like a "best scientific evidence" rule might render an opinion based solely on such evidence inadmissible.[152] This does not mean, however, that the best alternative is to base an opinion solely on the epidemiological evidence. On the contrary, from a scientific validity perspective it would be preferable to form one's opinion about Bendectin based on all of the available evidence: epidemiological, animal studies, in vitro and perhaps even structure-activity. This conclusion focuses on questions of construct validity. Any single operation–any single study–is threatened by a potential mono-operation bias.[153] Cook and Campbell note: "Since single operations both under represent constructs and contain irrelevancies, construct validity will be lower in single exemplar research than in research where each construct is multiple operationalized in order to triangulate on the referent."[154] Thus, confounders or other irrelevancies, may affect the results of a single epidemiological study. Multiple studies provide greater certainty that the observed relationships does in fact represent the concepts under investigation.

Even multiple epidemiological replications suffer from mono-method bias. "[W]hen all the manipulations are presented in the same way, or all the measures use the same means of recording responses, then the method is itself an irrelevancy whose influence cannot be dissociated from the influence of the target construct."[155] As a method, epidemiology has many strengths, but it also has weaknesses. Because it is not an experimental method, it inevitably suffers from some internal validity problems. On the other hand, because animal studies are experiments, it is relatively more certain that the substance experimentally manipulated caused any observed effect. Each type of evidence addresses some of the weaknesses of the other. The whole is greater than the sum of the parts.

Bendectin plaintiffs have never argued that epidemiological data should be disregarded. On the contrary, plaintiff experts who are prepared to testify that more likely than not Bendectin caused the plaintiff's birth defect, have based their conclusion on all available evidence, including animal studies and epidemiological research.[156] Excluding non-epidemiological evidence because better, epidemiological evidence exists is erroneous under a scientific validity standard. Within the context of a scientific validity discussion, the admissibility of such evidence is not contingent upon the existence of other, arguably better evidence. Likewise, exclusion under Rule 703 conflicts with common scientific understandings of construct validity and mono-method bias.

B. The Exclusion of the Reanalysis of Epidemiological Studies

Plaintiff efforts to produce a prima facie case of causation have never depended entirely on non-epidemiological evidence. Throughout, Bendectin plaintiffs have offered epidemiological evidence in the form of a reanalysis of existing epidemiological studies.[157] Epidemiological studies have typically escaped the criticism that they are so invalid as to be inadmissible. Nevertheless, plaintiff experts usually design the reanalyses to correct for alleged threats to the validity of results reported in published epidemiological research.[158] They have focused on threats to statistical conclusion validity, primarily stemming from unreliable measurement and the relatively small Ns of many studies.[159] The most serious measurement threat derives from the fact that many of the studies were unable to determine exactly when the expectant mothers took Bendectin. For example, limb reduction defects occur when the limbs are first forming, a period that lasts approximately two weeks.[160] If researchers included women who took Bendectin after this period among the exposed group, the study will underestimate any effect.[161] The effect of changes in defining exposure can be dramatic.[162] The existence of doxylamine succinate in products such as Unisom adds another potential source of bias.[163] Unless researchers ask women whether they took such products during pregnancy, they may code certain women as unexposed who in fact ingested Bendectin's most suspect ingredient. As in the case of misclassification due to time of ingestion, coding errors will underestimate any effect.

In addition, because limb reduction defects, which underlie many Bendectin claims, are rare events, the number of individuals who suffer from a given defect and whose mothers took Bendectin is relatively small. As a consequence, there is a substantial risk of making a Type II error due to low statistical power. For example, five cohort studies which report limb reduction injuries together contain only eleven such cases.[164] One way to increase statistical power is to conduct case-control studies that purposefully pick as cases individuals who exhibit the injury under investigation.[165] Four published case-control studies include limb reduction defects with a total N of 312 cases, 61 of whom had mothers who were exposed to the drug.[166] Only two of the studies had Ns sufficiently large to afford a 50% chance of detecting a relative risk of two or smaller.[167] In fact, except for one case-control study,[168] the total data on limb reduction defects is quite limited.[169]

Plaintiff experts Shanna Swan and Alan Done have criticized the published studies for all of these reasons and challenged the statistical conclusion validity of their results.[170] They have also recoded and reanalyzed the data in some studies. Are such reanalyses so invalid that they should be excluded under Rule 702? The proffered testimony of Dr. Swan and Dr. Done supply two examples of plaintiff efforts to reanalyze the epidemiological evidence and provide a framework for addressing this question.

1. The Testimony of Dr. Swan

The first example involves Dr. Shanna Swan's reanalysis of the Center for Disease Control epidemiological data published by Cordero.[171] A fundamental threat to the internal validity of epidemiological research is recall bias.[172] Mothers bearing children with a birth defect may sift through their pre-natal experience in search of an explanation for the injury. As a consequence, in case-control studies employing a control group of healthy babies, the case mothers will remember more drug exposures which produces a biased result. Researchers can try to alleviate this threat in several ways. One alternative is to examine the prescription records of the mother's physician. Epidemiologists at the Center for Disease Control employed another particularly innovative method in analyzing data from the Metropolitan Atlanta Congenital Defects Program.[173] The investigators divided the data into categories of birth defects and then examined the rate of first-trimester Bendectin exposure for each defect.[174] They compared these "cases" to a control group composed of infants with birth defects other than the one being evaluated.[175] Because all children in the study, both cases and controls, suffered from some birth defect, the study minimized recall bias.[176] As the authors noted, this technique would not allow them to detect an effect if a substance under investigation uniformly increased the risk of all types of defects investigated.[177] The authors discounted this possibility, however, noting that known human and animal teratogens cause specific birth defects or patterns of defects.[178]

Dr. Swan argued that, if Bendectin causes more than one kind of birth defect, this technique would underestimate its teratogenic effects because Bendectin exposure would cause some of the control group defects and the resulting analysis would underestimate the drug's effect.[179] Dr. Swan re-read interview forms from the study and corrected what she perceived to be coding errors in drug use or date of exposure.[180] Then, in order to avoid a control group of children with defects potentially caused by Bendectin exposure, she chose as a control only those children afflicted with Down's Syndrome and other known genetic disorders.[181] Dr. Swan reasoned that, because researchers know that drug exposure does not cause these injuries, diagnostic bias would not attenuate the results.[182] Using this new control group, her reanalysis produced a significant correlation between Bendectin and limb reduction defects.[183]

Measured by a validity standard, Dr. Swan's use of a different control group seems reasonable. It attempted to achieve some of what the CDC investigators hoped to achieve by using a control group comprised of children with defects while also controlling for a separate threat to internal validity arising from the "misdiagnosis" of the control group. There is, however, an additional factor to consider. As the First Circuit observed in *Lynch v. Merrell Dow Pharmaceuticals, Inc.*, the Odds Ratio between Bendectin exposure and Down's Syndrome in the Atlanta sample was 0.57–children suffering from Down's Syndrome were *less* likely to have been exposed to Bendectin than children suffering from other defects.[184] Cordero's study prominently reported this result and Dr. Swan must have known this when she chose to use children with genetic defects as the control group. A comparison between the Down's Syndrome children and children with most other defects will produce an Odds Ratio substantially in excess of 1.0.[185] The First Circuit referred to this when it dismissed Swan's analysis:

> As far as appears from what is in the record, Swan made no allowance for the possibility that the very fact of having such a severe genetic deficiency as Down's Syndrome might operate to make other rare deficiencies such as limb reduction less likely to occur in the control group–that is, that the combination of Down's syndrome and another major misfortune might be extremely unusual. Without accounting for this possible skewing of the control group, Swan's basis for her comparative conclusion is not apparent.[186]

The court provided no authority to support its assertion and the Cordero Study's data supplies no evidence for this proposition. The study does not imply that Down's Syndrome is a prophylactic against other types of defects; that conclusion would require a comparison of Down's Syndrome children and all other children for the existence of an additional defect. Absent some authority that Down's Syndrome has this effect, the court's assertion is little more than unsubstantiated hypothesis, hardly the type of validity threat that merited rejecting Dr. Swan's testimony.

This does not mean that Dr. Swan's analysis is preferable to that of Cordero and his colleagues. In fact, there are at least three reasons why their analysis is superior. First, Dr. Swan's analysis creates a greater likelihood of recall bias. Because the parents of a Down's Syndrome child know that the defect has genetic origins, they are less likely to search through their pre-natal experience for possible chemical causes of the injury. In addition, the incidence of morning sickness among mothers carrying children with Down's Syndrome is unknown. If the incidence is lower than other mothers experienced, Down's Syndrome mothers would presumably be less likely to take any morning sickness medication which would make Down's Syndrome children an inappropriate control. Finally, the control group was inappropriate because Dr. Swan knew the result she would obtain before she conducted her reanalysis. Because Dr. Swan knew before she began that her comparison would produce a positive correlation between Bendectin use and limb reduction defects, the analysis could not test this hypothesis; it could not produce a negative answer. The possibility of a Type II error was zero and the possibility of a Type I error was essentially unknowable. Perhaps this lies at the heart of the First Circuit's rejection of her analysis. Although it is particularly troublesome when an investigator preparing an analysis for litigation knows *a priori* that the results will support the client's position, it does not necessarily follow that a court should exclude such testimony. The problem with Dr. Swan's testimony arose because she completed the reanalysis for the purposes of litigation; she was not testing a research hypothesis. To exclude her testimony on this ground, however, would condemn many, if not most reanalyses of existing data by experts hired for litigation.

2. The Testimony of Dr. Done

The second example is Dr. Done's proffered testimony in *DeLuca v. Merrell Dow Pharmaceuticals, Inc.*[187] When the case first appeared before him, Judge Brown entered summary judgment for the defendant.[188] He first affirmed a Magistrate's order excluding all *in vitro* and *in vivo* studies.[189] He then held that the plaintiff's expert testimony on epidemiology was inadmissible because it lacked the requisite Rule 703 foundation.[190]

The Third Circuit reversed, first noting that the primary difference between Dr. Done and the opposing epidemiologists was that Dr. Done subscribed to the approach advocated by Professor Kenneth Rothman,[191] which deemphasizes traditional significance testing in favor of reporting relative risks and confidence intervals surrounding estimates of relative risk.[192] The court held that without a record-supported, factual finding that the data Dr. Done used was not of the type reasonably relied upon by experts in epidemiology, Rule 703 did not bar his testimony.[193] Because Dr. Done used data from the same published epidemiological studies the defense relied on, the court expressed serious doubts that such a finding would be possible.[194] Turning to Rule 702, the court noted that the admissibility of Dr. Done's analysis was susceptible of judicial notice to the extent he based it on traditional epidemiological methodology.[195] Because the existing record was insufficient to make this decision, the court remanded and invited the trial judge to conduct hearings and obtain expert assistance in determining whether the evidence was sufficiently reliable to be admissible.[196] Finally, the Third Circuit specifically refused to decide whether epidemiological proof is inadmissible unless the data allow one to reject the null hypothesis at a .05 level of statistical significance, leaving the question for the trial court on remand.[197] It did note, however, that the trial court should not focus solely upon tests of significance but rather should assess "all the risks of error posed by the proffered evidence."[198]

In many respects the Third Circuit's analysis in DeLuca exhibits the best understanding of validity issues of all the Bendectin opinions. The court's appreciation for the importance of both Type I and Type II errors, and its recognition of the existence of multiple threats to validity stand in sharp contrast to the analyses in *Lynch* and *Brock*. This very understanding, however, made it difficult for the court to announce any specific admissibility guidelines and it left those issues to the trial court.[199]

Judge Brown proceeded to hold a five day hearing followed by extensive post-hearing submissions.[200] The parties offered written direct testimony and oral cross examination of eight expert witnesses.[201] Based on this record the judge made 120 separate findings of fact and 41 conclusions of law.[202]

Judge Brown first contrasted the lack of a statistically significant relationship between Bendectin ingestion and limb reduction defects in the published literature with Dr. Done's conclusion that reanalysis demonstrated a relationship.[203] The parties did not dispute that Dr. Done's underlying data were of a type reasonably relied upon by experts in epidemiology.[204] They did dispute, however, the validity of Dr. Done's calculations and the manner in which he presented his ultimate results, what Judge Brown characterized as "the methodology employed by Dr. Done."[205] Addressing this methodology, Judge Brown noted occasions in which Dr. Done included data that he arguably should have omitted,[206] other occasions where he excluded data that he should have included,[207] and still other occasions where he selectively reported data.[208] The judge noted that Dr. Done's reanalysis did not give greater weight to studies with larger number of exposed defects, the studies with the greatest power.[209] Dr. Done also failed to weight studies based on their design or control for other sources of bias.[210] Dr. Done did not attempt to reach a quantitative conclusion based on his reevaluation of the data, either by way of pooled data or a meta analysis.[211] Finally, the Judge noted a number of ways in which Dr. Done's presentation was misleading.[212]

The judge then proceeded to hold Dr. Done's testimony inadmissible under both Rules 702 and 703.[213] He followed a five part Rule 702 analysis which considered: the novelty of the technique; the existence of a specialized literature; the expert's qualifications; the non-judicial uses to which the scientific techniques are put; and the frequency with which the technique leads to erroneous results.[214] With respect to each element, Judge Brown found Dr. Done's testimony to be wanting.[215] Although the judge did not discuss scientific validity in making his 702 ruling, the opinion can be translated into this language. Statistical conclusion validity posed the biggest threat to Dr. Done's findings. The thrust of his analysis was that, although individual studies fail to produce a statistically significant relationship between Bendectin and limb reduction defects, an analysis of all the data together do reveal a relationship. Unfortunately, Dr. Done selected his 106 "data sets" in a manner that made it difficult to assess the relative likelihood of Type I and Type II errors. One gets the sense that Dr. Done engaged in a fishing expedition, sifting through large number of correlations in search of significant relationships. Moreover, the reanalyses contained measurement errors due to unreliable coding, incorrect calculations or both.

The judge also held the testimony inadmissible under Rule 703, concluding that experts in the field would not use the data Dr. Done relied on in rendering an opinion.[216] Again, the judge presented a detailed, particularistic analysis. Epidemiological studies are, of course, of a type reasonably relied upon by experts in the field. Dr. Done's recalculations, however, produced "new data" that "has not and cannot in many instances be replicated by other experts in the field or even be explained."[217] Because Dr. Done's testimony was inadmissible under Rules 702 and 703, the plaintiffs could not meet their burden of proof on the issue of causality and the court granted the defendant's summary judgment motion.[218]

The testimony Dr. Done proffered in DeLuca presents a particularly difficult case. From a validity point of view it is tempting to agree with the judge's conclusion. At several points the judge implied that the basic flaw in Done's analyses was that neither defense nor plaintiff experts were able to replicate a number of Dr. Done's conclusions.[219] This inability to replicate the data, however, does not present a problem if one can trace Dr. Done's methods with sufficient specificity to attempt a replication. Under these circumstances Dr. Done's conclusions would be falsifiable and, in this core sense, scientific.[220] Because a substantial number of Dr. Done's conclusions were falsifiable, however, Judge Brown was able to demonstrate how they were in error. Indeed, it is this detailed demonstration of error that gives power to the opinion. The court did not question epidemiology as a valid methodology. Rather, the judge challenged Dr. Done's particular recalculations and the "new data" these suspect recalculations generated. At this level of analysis the court found Dr. Done's testimony to be flawed largely because it was not a neutral rendition of the epidemiological evidence concerning Bendectin. The judge depicted Dr. Done as a "party witness" who designed his analysis to advance his employer's case. Less apparent, however, is whether Dr. Done's testimony was significantly different from that of experts in other cases and whether this level of analysis casts doubt on the admissibility of a great deal of expert testimony.

This question is unlikely to be answered any time soon. Although the Third Circuit demonstrated particular concern for the dangers of devising a special rule for Bendectin cases, Judge Brown did just this on remand. The judge noted that ordinarily the inclusion and exclusion of certain data is a matter for the battle of the experts but in this case, Dr. Done's plaintiff-leanings, combined with the errors and uncertainties in his calculations, threatened to confuse the jury.[221] It is hard to imagine that this consideration would carry as much weight if the scientific evidence is not fully developed and, therefore, the errors in the expert's analysis are not so obvious. Likewise, the importance the trial court placed on the fact that Dr. Done had not published his work in a peer review journal was inevitably influenced by the existence of a large body of published research on Bendectin. The lack of publication would not weigh so heavily if there were very little published research.[222] Most important, such a detailed analysis of an expert's proferred testimony is unlikely to occur in more than that handful of cases in which the courts have become particularly concerned with issues of judicial efficiency and jury confusion.

3. Summary

The rejection of epidemiological evidence in *Lynch* and *DeLuca* again indicates the uncertain nature of admissibility determinations under a *Daubert*-like analysis. The proffered testimony of both Drs. Done and Swan presented validity problems. Scientific validity, however, encompasses a complex set of concepts and is always a matter of degree. It is difficult to pinpoint exactly why the courts found that this testimony was so invalid as to be inadmissible. Dr. Done's situation is particularly instructive. Even were one to conclude that the trial judge's opinion fairly reflects Dr. Done's proffered testimony, this at best supports excluding 50%, 60% or perhaps even 80% of his testimony on scientific validity grounds. It does not, however, fairly support the exclusion of all Dr. Done's testimony. Importantly, neither *Lynch* nor *DeLuca* made clear why the problems with the proffered testimony did not go to weight rather than admissibility. A full understanding of these opinions lies beyond questions of scientific validity and even beyond questions of admissibility.

V. Reasons for Restrictive Admissibility Rulings

Why have courts been so willing to make restrictive admissibility rulings in Bendectin cases? In part, the answer can be found in the objectives courts attempt to achieve by restricting the scope of admissible scientific testimony and in the special problems mass torts pose. There are at least two reasons to restrict the admissibility of scientific evidence. First, restricting this evidence fosters judicial efficiency. If a party's scientific arguments are without merit, excluding them minimizes the expenditure of resources required to resolve the issue and husbands scarce judicial resources for the resolution of closer questions.[223] A second reason to restrict this testimony is that juries[224] will likely be unable to distinguish between reliable and unreliable evidence.[225] Although juries may be good factfinders with respect to lay testimony, some argue that their lack of specialized knowledge renders them incapable of assessing the merits of expert testimony.[226] Restrictions on admissibility reduce the probability that "a credulous jury will now and again transform scientific dust into gold."[227]

These considerations apply with special force to mass torts, such as the Bendectin litigation. The many congregations[228] of substance-related mass torts[229] that have emerged over the last decade and a half are a new phenomenon of the tort system. The size and scope of these cases have placed enormous pressures on the judicial process and judges have reacted by seeking out new, efficient ways to dispose of them. A first step toward this goal is procedural rationing. Courts have used class actions under Rule 23 of the Federal Rules of Civil Procedure,[230] consolidation under the Multi-District Litigation Act,[231] and consolidation of cases for trial under Rule 42 of the Federal Rules of Civil Procedure[232] in the Bendectin cases and other mass torts. Courts have likewise engaged in substantive rationing.[233] In situations such as asbestos exposure, the courts, reasonably confident that many plaintiffs have valid claims, have frustrated defendants' efforts to tie up the legal system by relitigating previously tried issues[234] or demanding a separate trial for each claimant.[235] Conversely, in the Bendectin cases, the courts became increasingly certain that plaintiffs did not have valid claims and sought to prevent separate trials for those individual plaintiffs who had not litigated their claims in a 1985 consolidated trial in the Southern District of Ohio.[236] Admissibility rulings provided one of the few devices available to achieve the goal of non-suiting these plaintiffs.

Likewise, concern about the jury's ability to understand scientific evidence is particularly salient in mass tort cases. Here, as in any lawsuit where multiple juries try similar facts, an inability to understand the evidence may produce inconsistent results. In most situations inconsistent verdicts can be explained in terms of unique facts presented in one case and not another. In mass tort cases, however, the outcome frequently turns on questions of general causation and inconsistencies are not easily hidden.[237] Concerns about jury inconsistency echoes through the Bendectin cases, including *Lynch*[238] and *Brock*.[239] Inconsistency may, of course, reflect the fact that a trial poses a particularly close fact pattern and that reasonable juries may differ about the correct outcome. If so, over time jury verdicts should produce outcomes that reflect the underlying strength of the parties' case.[240]The verdicts will define the expected value of a case and, if that value is low enough, past verdicts will deter future claimants.[241] Faced with this type of inconsistency, courts might wish to facilitate settlements but would not necessarily want to interfere with the trial process.

Inconsistency may reflect a more fundamental problem, however: that an unacceptable percentage of juries are reaching "incorrect" verdicts and, therefore, the verdicts as a group do not reflect the merits of the issue. Some Bendectin opinions evidence a belief that jury verdicts for the plaintiff were erroneous.[242] The restrictive admissibility opinions reflect a judicial belief that, left alone, too many juries will reach an incorrect outcome. Judges[243] and others[244] are particularly suspicious of the jury's ability to arrive at a correct decision in trials involving the expert presentation of complex technological and scientific questions, trials that typify much of mass tort litigation. The outcome of the Bendectin trials do little to alleviate this concern. Of the twenty jury trials that have reached a verdict on the merits, eight resulted in a plaintiff victory.[245] This 40% success rate mirrors the overall success rate in product liability cases.[246] Thus, the one-sided nature of the scientific evidence has not resulted in a perceptible tilt in favor of Bendectin defendants. Restrictive admissibility determinations may be interpreted as a response to these "incorrect" verdicts. They are, from this point of view, an ad hoc method of jury control.

The twin objectives of achieving an efficient use of judicial resources in mass tort cases and assisting the jury in understanding scientific evidence are meritorious goals. Restrictive admissibility rulings, however, are a flawed means to these objectives. With respect to the efficiency goal, the courts have attempted to achieve with admissibility rulings what they should be achieving with sufficiency rulings. Indeed, several of the Bendectin opinions employed a sufficiency analysis. The *Brock* court had a relatively easy task because it had a full transcript on which to rule. The courts in *Lynch* and *DeLuca* did not enjoy this luxury. Instead, they encountered expert witnesses prepared to testify that Bendectin more likely than not caused the plaintiff's injury. If these courts admitted even part of the proffered testimony, the plaintiff would be able to present a prima facie case on causation, making summary judgment for the defendant inappropriate. Therefore, excluding all of the plaintiff's causation evidence was a necessary prerequisite to ruling for the defendant as a matter of law. In *every* Bendectin opinion that excluded the plaintiff's expert testimony on causation, the court ultimately entered a judgment for the defendant.

This need to find all of the plaintiff's causation testimony inadmissible helps to explain the restrictive rulings in the Bendectin cases. The courts, persuaded that the plaintiffs had insufficient evidence to prevail on the merits, sought to avoid still another trial that might result in a verdict for the plaintiff and require them to enter a j.n.o.v., as in *Richardson*,[247] *Brock*,[248] and *Ealy*.[249] Efficiency considerations, therefore, play an important role in these rulings.

Using admissibility rulings in this way has several drawbacks. The Bendectin admissibility decisions confuse an already blurry line between admissibility and sufficiency.[250] Sufficiency necessarily entails a decision about the entire body of the party's case. Perhaps in a *Frye*-world admissibility might be thought to raise a similar question: whether a significant part of the scientific community believes that the case presents an arguable scientific issue. After *Daubert*, however, admissibility is best described as a decision about individual pieces of scientific evidence, a conception ill-suited to the global assessment of the science supporting a party's position.

Moreover, as others have observed,[251] the Bendectin cases are unique in a number of ways including the existence of an unusually rich body of epidemiological data, an extensive legal record produced by hundreds of cases and thirty trials and, perhaps most fundamentally, a relatively one sided body of scientific evidence. Admissibility criteria created to dispense with Bendectin cases may present problems in other areas where the science is neither as well developed nor its weight as one sided.[252] Perhaps this is inevitable when courts bend the rules of evidence to foster efficiency. If 80% of a party's expert testimony can be excluded, a court will be very reluctant to admit the last 20% and allow a trial on the merits. The court will find reasons to exclude the remaining 20% which may undermine a sophisticated approach to the question of scientific validity. Moreover, admissibility decisions that require a hearing and briefing as extensive as Judge Brown's in *DeLuca* erode efficiency gains.[253]

Although this Article opposes the use of admissibility rulings to non-suit plaintiffs in order to achieve efficiency goals, it does recognize that mature congregations, such as the Bendectin cases, do pose special problems for the courts and society. Special solutions should be developed but they should focus on the problem at hand: the repeated litigation of the same issue in a mature congregation of cases.[254] Along these lines, Professor Berger has suggested several ways to deal with this issue.[255]

VI. The Juror's Problem and Alternative Solutions

Restrictive admissibility rules are also an inappropriate solution to the problems juries have with complex scientific arguments in mass tort cases. A problem does exist, however. A mounting body of evidence supports the position that jurors do have a difficult time understanding and assessing expert scientific testimony. For example, the American Bar Association Section on Litigation commissioned a Special Committee to study jury comprehension in complex cases.[256] The Committee studied four complex cases in the areas of sexual harassment, antitrust, arson-related insurance fraud, and misappropriation of trade secrets. The scientific evidence was particularly difficult in the trade secrets case[257] and jurors reported that they had trouble understanding the facts. The authors of the report concluded the following:

> [A]lthough one plaintiffs' attorney suggested that jurors would not need to understand the chemical processes in dispute to decide this case, it seems apparent that some ability to comprehend and evaluate the technical information was in fact, imperative.
>
> It is not clear that jurors—even those employed as engineers who had completed college courses in chemistry—had that ability. Even these jurors felt overwhelmed by the technical nature of the evidence. Less educated jurors suggested that they were completely "out of their league."[258]

The jury also had difficulty applying the facts to the jury instructions to determine whether the facts established the claims.[259]

The fact that 40% of the juries that reached the merits of the Bendectin cases found for the plaintiff is not inconsistent with the jury's experience in the trade secret case. Interviews with jurors in one Bendectin trial indicated that they also had difficulty understanding the scientific evidence.[260] A detailed analysis of six Bendectin trial transcripts indicated some of the reasons jurors have difficulty with the scientific evidence. Most importantly, the trial structure itself makes it very difficult to weigh evidence and, at least within the tort context, to separate the scientific analysis of causation from other elements of the tort.[261] Many factors contribute to produce this result.[262] The parties typically employ experts whose objectivity is therefore suspect. Although both plaintiff and defense experts may testify concerning exactly the same scientific studies and findings, the structure of trials separates their testimony, sometimes by many days. Frequently, a roughly equal number of experts from each side testify on each scientific issue, producing a perception that real conflict exists within the scientific community on nearly all questions.[263] Because the parties focus on the science that they believe best supports their position, the jury is likely to conclude that all types of scientific evidence are equally probative to the issue in dispute.[264]

Ironically, the problem courts have attempted to correct through restrictive admissibility rulings is, in part, a product of the Rules of Evidence themselves. For example, under Rule 703 experts may base their opinion on facts or data of a type reasonably relied upon by experts in the particular field in forming opinions on a subject. Any published articles the expert relied on would ordinarily be hearsay unless admitted under some exception such as the Learned Treatises exception. Even when admitted under this exception, however, "the statements may be read into evidence but may not be received as exhibits."[265] As a consequence, the jury does not have the ability independently to examine and assess statements those works contain. Rather, it must view them through the filter of party advocacy, a filter that makes it very difficult to assess the weight of scientific opinion on an issue.

All of these difficulties reflect a more general problem with the presentation of scientific evidence. Much of what goes on at trial in America is a process of deconstructing science. As Peter Schuck has noted, law and science are in some ways competing cultures, each with its own set of central values, incentives, techniques, biases and orientations.[266] Although science and law share a wide range of cultural values, differences do exist. The core values of these two cultures reflect these differences. Whereas science's central value is truth, law's central value, at least in its judicial manifestation, is justice.[267] Law does not pursue justice as an abstract ideal, however, but in a context that acknowledges the existence of competing views of what constitutes a just outcome and allows these competing views to contend for supremacy within an adversarial trial. The differences between the two cultures create tensions and contests for dominance.[268] In the courtroom, the battle frequently involves attacking the scientific culture itself by focusing on its biases, its implicit assumptions, and the many ways it inevitably fails to live up to its own ideals of rigorous methodology and objectivity.[269]

As Sheila Jasanoff has noted, scientific discoveries, like other types of knowledge, are premised on underlying assumptions and conventions that remain in the background until controversy erupts.[270] The assumptions include both experimental and interpretative conventions. In ordinary scientific conversations these assumptions lie in the background and scientists speak of things as being true or false. Because scientific knowledge, like other forms of knowledge, is constructed by a community of individuals, it can be deconstructed, pulled apart by questioning each assumption, each shared understanding, and each indeterminacy that inevitably infects even the most artfully crafted research. Indeed, many of the admissibility battles discussed in this Article reflect exactly this type of deconstruction and it is important to note that both plaintiffs and defendants, motivated by a lawsuit, actively participate in this process. The adversarial trial is particularly well suited to such an effort, which, in this context, is its greatest weakness:

> Adversarial process is indeed a wonderful instrument for deconstructing "facts," for exposing contingencies and hidden assumptions that underlie scientific claims, and thereby preventing an uncritical acceptance of alleged truths. The adversary process is much less ef-

fective, however, in reconstructing the communally held beliefs that reasonably pass for truth in science. Cross-examination, in particular, unduly privileges skepticism over consensus. It skews the picture of science that is presented to the legal factfinder and created an impression of conflict even where little or no disagreement exists in practice.[271]

From this perspective the problem confronting the courts involves more than simply assessing the validity of a particular fact, method, or conclusion. Rather, the court must find a balance between the pursuit of justice in an environment of adversarial legalism and respect for science's culture, values and assumptions. If the heart of the problem confronting juries is that the law so successfully deconstructs scientific findings that juries find it very difficult to assess the relative merits of any position and ultimately begin to discount the value of scientific "truth" for the resolution of the problem posed to them,[272] restricting the evidence they hear is a problematic cure. This cure runs the inevitable risk of balancing the excessively skeptical environment that ordinary methods create with an uncritical determination that there is good science and bad science, that the two can be distinguished, that the trial judge can capably make this distinction, and that the court can protect the jury by the excluding the bad.

Undoubtedly, admissibility decisions have a role to play in excluding marginal "science" from the courtroom.[273] There are, however, superior alternatives available in most situations. These alternatives directly confront the problems that arise from the undervaluation of "normal" scientific understandings when litigants introduce science through traditional adversarial processes.[274] They include the use of court-appointed experts and expert panels, the bifurcation of trials in order to try causal questions separate from breach of duty questions, and the potential use of specialized science courts and blue ribbon juries.[275] Each of these alternatives would either reduce the perception that science is mostly conflict with little consensus or reduce the degree to which the central scientific value of truth is pitted against the core legal value of justice.[276]

Conclusion

Mass torts continue their relentless assault on our common law tort system. They have forced us to rethink accepted methods of proving causation, the appropriate measure of damages and even the system's fundamental commitment to an individualized trial of each plaintiff's case.[277] Many mass torts create a pair of problems for the court system. They consume judicial resources and pose complex scientific questions that frequently confuse juries. The increased use of expert scientific witnesses that has accompanied the rise of mass torts has prompted charges that many of these witnesses are introducing "junk science." The Supreme Court crafted its decision in *Daubert* against this background. From a narrow perspective, *Daubert* simply resolved a longstanding issue in the law of evidence by holding that the Federal Rules of Evidence superseded *Frye*. From a wider perspective, the opinion represents an attempt to define, or perhaps redefine, the relationship between science and the law.

The American legal system, both in its judicial and regulatory capacities, has constructed a set of structures that facilitate attacks on science and undermine trust in the judgment of the scientific community.[278] In one sense *Daubert* attempted to redefine this relationship. By placing the concept of scientific validity at the center of admissibility decisions, *Daubert* invoked scientific understandings of what constitutes good and bad science. The Court recognized that for science to be useful the law must attend to more than the scientist's conclusion. The legal system must, to some degree, be attentive to the scientific method itself. It must interpret scientific conclusions in the context of the methods and culture which precipitated them.

This very change, however, reveals the degree to which many restrictive rulings in the Bendectin cases cannot be justified from the perspective of scientific validity. These opinions are better explained in terms of two other goals: achieving the efficient resolution of mass torts and responding to the perceived inability of juries to understand and apply complex scientific analyses. The Ninth Circuit's *Daubert* opinion is an example of this response. It is not surprising that the judiciary has reached for whatever tools are readily at hand in an attempt to deal with these problems. This Article has argued that restrictive admissibility rulings are not the best way to achieve these objectives. Restrictive admissibility rulings do resolve the problems created by the repeated litigation of the same factual question. They do so, however, at the cost of confusing the issues of sufficiency and admissibility and of casting a shadow of uncertainty over whether similar rules may be applied in other circumstances. To the degree courts do require more efficient ways of resolving individual cases in mature mass torts, they should develop sufficiency rules specific to this need.

The problem of jury comprehension of complex scientific arguments presents a more complex issue. Sometimes parties do attempt to introduce testimony so lacking in validity that exclusion is appropriate because the testimony threatens to cloud the issue and confuse the jury. Even with respect to Bendectin litigation, however, an area that some have pointed to as an example of "junk science,"[279] it is difficult to justify the exclusion of the plaintiff's entire case on scientific validity grounds. More importantly, marginal science is not the primary source of jury difficulties with complex scientific arguments. The heart of that problem lies not in the arguments of expert witnesses but rather in the structures and

processes of adversarial adjudication that systematically disadvantage the cultural values of science. It is there that we should seek a remedy.

Notes

1. 293 F. 1013 (D.C. Cir. 1923).
2. Commentators have announced *Frye*'s death on numerous occasions. See 3 Jack B. Weinstein & Margaret A. Berger, Weinstein's Evidence ¶702(3), at 702–36 (1993); 22 Charles A. Wright & Kenneth W. Graham, Jr., Federal Practice and Procedure §5168, at 86–91 (1978). Others have argued that *Frye* did survive the Federal Rules. See 1 David W. Louisell & Christopher B. Mueller, Federal Evidence §105, at 818 (1977).
3. *Frye*'s continued vitality in state courts remains unclear. In an early state case considering the issue, the Arizona Supreme Court sidestepped the question by stating "we are not bound by the United States Supreme Court's non-constitutional construction of the Federal Rules of Evidence when we construe the Arizona Rules of Evidence." *State v. Bible,* 858 P.2d 1152, 1183 (Ariz. 1993)(en banc). For a valuable summary of state and federal law with respect to *Frye*'s status, see Roger S. Hanson, *James Alphonzo Frye is Sixty-Five Years Old; Should He Retire?*, 16 W. St. U. L. Rev. 357, 372–90 (1989).
4. 113 S. Ct. 2786 (1993).
5. See Paul C. Gianelli, *The Admissibility of Novel Scientific Evidence:* Frye v. United States *a Half-Century Later*, 80 Colum. L. Rev. 1197, 1245–50 (1980); Mark McCormick, *Scientific Evidence: Defining a New Approach to Admissibility*, 67 Iowa L. Rev. 879 (1982).
6. In so holding, the Supreme Court stated:

   > The drafting history makes no mention of *Frye*, and a rigid "general acceptance" requirement would be at odds with the "liberal thrust" of the Federal Rules and their "general approach of relaxing the traditional barriers to 'opinion' testimony. . . . " Given the Rules' permissive backdrop and their inclusion of a specific rule on expert testimony that does not mention "general acceptance," the assertion that the Rules somehow assimilated *Frye* is unconvincing. *Frye* made "general acceptance" the exclusive test for admitting expert scientific testimony. That austere standard, absent from and incompatible with the Federal Rules of Evidence, should not be applied in federal trials.

   Daubert, 113 S. Ct. at 2794.
7. The D.C. Circuit reasoned as follows:

   > Just when a scientific principle or discovery crosses the line between the experimental and demonstrable stages is difficult to define. Somewhere in this twilight zone the evidential force of the principle must be recognized, and while courts will go a long way in

> admitting expert testimony deduced from a well-recognized scientific principle or discovery, the thing from which the deduction is made must be sufficiently established to have gained general acceptance in the particular field in which it belongs.

Frye, 293 F. at 1014. Over the next fifty years, many jurisdictions adopted the *Frye* rule. See Edward Cleary, McCormick on Evidence 606 (3d ed. 1984).

8. See Andre A. Moenssens, *Admissibility of Scientific Evidence–An Alternative to the Frye Rule*, 25 Wm. & Mary L. Rev. 545, 559–64 (1984).
9. The "general acceptance" test can be strictly applied to exclude all but widely accepted, mainstream scientific principles and techniques. See, e.g., *United States v. Zeiger*, 350 F. Supp. 685, 688 (D.D.C.), *rev'd*, 475 F.2d 1280 (D.C. Cir. 1972) (per curiam). Other courts have applied the test very liberally, however, prompting some observers to conclude that these judges often do little more than rely upon the opinion of a few experts. Gianelli, *supra* note 5, at 1209–11. As Gianelli notes, identifying the appropriate field within which general acceptance must be achieved can be problematic because almost all scientific techniques have received general acceptance in some narrowly defined field. *Id.* at 1211 n.95. In addition, it is not always clear what facets of the proffered testimony or underlying methodology must be "generally accepted." See Steven J. Grossman & Christopher K. Gagne, *Science and Scientific Evidence II*, 25 Conn. L. Rev. 1053, 1055–57 (1993); see also *United States v. Shorter*, 809 F.2d 54 (D.C. Cir.) (discussing expert testimony concerning compulsive gambling disorders), *cert. denied*, 484 U.S. 817 (1987).
10. *Daubert*, 113 S. Ct. 2786 (1993); see Paul C. Gianelli & Edward J. Imwinkelried, Scientific Evidence §1–5, at 8–13 (1993); see also *U.S. v. Smith*, 869 F.2d 348, 350 (7th Cir. 1989) (affirming the continued use of the *Frye* text).
11. See Edward R. Becker & Aviva Orenstein, *The Federal Rules of Evidence After Sixteen Years–the Effect of "Plain Meaning" Jurisprudence, the Need for an Advisory Committee on the Rules of Evidence, and Suggestions for Selective Revision of the Rules*, 60 Geo. Wash. L. Rev. 857, 876–85 (1992); Margaret A. Berger, *A Relevant Approach to Novel Scientific Evidence*, 26 Jurimetics J. 245, 246 (1986); Bert Black, *A Unified Theory of Scientific Evidence*, 56 Fordham L. Review 595, 625–58 (1988); Ronald L. Carlson, *Policing the Bases of Modern Expert Testimony*, 39 Vand. L. Rev. 577, 582 n.17 (1986); Paul C. Giannelli, *Scientific Evidence: A Proposed Amendment to Federal Rule 702*, 26 Jurimetrics J. 260, 263–64 (1986); Hanson, *supra* note 3, at 357; Edward J. Imwinkelried, *The "Bases" of Expert Testimony: The Syllogistic Structure of Scientific Testimony*, 67 N.C. L. Rev. 1, 5–7 (1988); Frederick B. Lacey, *Scientific Evidence*, 24 Jurimetrics J. 254, 266 (1984); Frederic I. Lederer, *Resolving the Frye Dilemma–A Reliability Approach*, 26 Jurimetrics J. 240, 240 (1986); Moenssens, *supra* note 8, at 545; James E. Storrs, *Frye v. U.S. Restructured and Revitalized: A Proposal to Amend Federal Rule 702*, 26 Jurimetrics J. 249, 250–52 (1986). The Rules' failure to clarify the standard for admitting novel scientific evidence, once called "the greatest single oversight in the Rules," precipitated this extensive literature. Becker & Orenstein, *supra*, at 877.
12. See David Bernstein, *Out of the Fryeing Pan and into the Fire: The Expert*

Witness Problem in Toxic Tort Litigation, 10 Rev. Litig. 117 (1990); John D. Borders, *Fit to be Fryed:* Frye v. United States *and the Admissibility of Novel Scientific Evidence*, 77 Ky. L.J. 849 (1989); Gianelli, *supra* note 5; Frederick A. Bechtold, Note, *The Admissibility of Scientific Evidence? DNA Print Identification*, 19 Stetson L. Rev. 245 (1989); Dirk Eshleman, Note, *Different Standards and Conflicting Results: A Re-Evaluation of the Frye Test for Admitting Novel Scientific Evidence in Light of Decisions Involving Spectrographic Evidence Introduction*, 5 Rev. Litig. 327 (1986).

13. Peter Huber, *Galileo's Revenge: Junk Science in the Courtroom* 6 (1991) [hereinafter Huber, *Galileo's Revenge*]; Peter Huber, Liability: The Legal Revolution and Its Consequences 43–44 (1988); Peter Huber, *Junk Science in the Courtroom*, 26 Val. U. Law Rev. 723 (1992); see Kunzweil et. al, The Environmental Expert After *Rubanick* and *Christophersen:* Beware the Jabberwock! 1 (1991); Jeffrey K. Sherwood, *In Re* Paoli Railroad: *The Third Circuit Punts to the "Coffincorner,"* Toxics L. Rep., Nov. 14, 1990, at 773, 781 (criticizing the Third Circuit's approach giving plaintiffs' experts leeway in valuing non-tangible injuries).

14. See *Chaulk v. Volkswagen of America, Inc.* 808 F.2d 639, 644 (7th Cir. 1986); *Stoleson v. United States,* 708 F.2d 1217, 1222 (7th Cir. 1983); E. Donald Elliott, *Toward Incentive-Based Procedure: Three Approaches for Regulating Scientific Evidence*, 69 B.U. L. Rev. 487, 489–93 (1989); Barry M. Epstein & Marc S. Klein, *The Use and Abuse of Expert Testimony in Product Liability Actions*, 17 Seton Hall L. Rev. 656, 656–59 (1987); Michael S. McCarthy, Note, *"Helpful" or "Reasonably Reliable?:" Analyzing the Expert Witness's Methodology Under Federal Rules of Evidence 702 and 703*, 77 Cornell L. Rev. 350 (1992); see also John Langbein, *The German Advantage in Civil Procedure*, 52 U. Chi. L. Rev. 823, 835 (1985) (noting that judges select and commission expert witnesses in German trials); Jack B. Weinstein, *Improving Expert Testimony*, 20 U. Rich. L. Rev. 473, 482 (1986) (observing that the Federal Rules allow parties to use expert testimony "to obfuscate what would otherwise be a simple case"). But see Peter Bell, *Strict Scrutiny of Scientific Evidence: A Bad Idea Whose Time Has Come*, Product Safety & Liability Rep., Jan. 17, 1992, at 79.

15. The proposed rule would read, in relevant part:

> Testimony providing scientific, technical, or other specialized information, in the form of an opinion or otherwise, may be permitted only if (1) the information is reasonably reliable and will substantially assist the trier of fact to understand the evidence or to determine a fact in issue and (2) the witness is qualified as an expert by knowledge, skill, experience, training, or education to provide such testimony.

Comm. on Rules of Practice and Procedure of the Judicial Conference of the United States, Preliminary Draft of Proposed Amendments to the Federal Rules of Civil Procedure and Federal Rules of Evidence 83 (1991) (emphasis omitted). With respect to these changes, the committee noted:

> [T]he revision requires that expert testimony be "reasonably reliable" and "substantially assist" the fact-finder. The rule does not

> mandate a return to the strictures of *Frye v. United States*, 293 F.2d [sic] 1013 (D.C. Cir., 1923) (requiring general acceptance of the scientific premises on which the testimony is based). However, the court is called upon to reject testimony that is based upon premises lacking any significant support and acceptance within the scientific community or that otherwise would be only marginally helpful to the fact-finder.

Id. at 84. For a critique of the proposed change, see Jack B. Weinstein, *Rule 702 of the Federal Rules of Evidence is Sound; It Should Not Be Amended*, 138 F.R.D. 631 (1991). The Judicial Conference Committee has deferred action and referred the issue to the new Advisory Committee on the Federal Rules of Evidence. Summary of the Report of the Committee on Rules of Practice and Procedure 11–12 (1992).

16. *Daubert*, 113 S. Ct. at 2795–98.
17. See Bert Black et. al, *Science and the Law in the Wake of* Daubert: *The Supreme Court Launches a New Search for Scientific Knowledge*, 72 Tex. L. Rev. (forthcoming 1994) (manuscript at 29–30, on file with author).
18. The *Daubert* Court did reject the argument that relevancy alone should govern the admissibility of scientific evidence. 113 S. Ct. at 2795.
19. The Court's unenlightening example concluded that a purported relationship between the existence of a full moon and the probability that an individual was unusually likely to have behaved irrationally would not satisfy its scientific validity standard. *Id.* at 2796.
20. See Bernstein, *supra* note 12, at 133–35; Eshleman, *supra* note 12, at 328–31. For example, the District of Columbia Circuit adopted a very passive stance in *Ferebee v. Chevron Chem. Co.,* 736 F.2d 1529 (D.C. Cir.), *cert. denied*, 469 U.S. 1062 (1984). The plaintiff claimed that exposure to paraquat, a herbicide, caused his lung disease. *Id.* at 1532. Two of the plaintiff's treating physicians proffered expert testimony on the causality issue. *Id.* at 1533. They based their opinion that paraquat exposure caused the plaintiff's disease on clinical observations of the plaintiff and the fact that one expert had identified other "similar" cases. *Id.* The court did not examine the scientific validity of this testimony, allowing the experts to testify and affirming a jury verdict for the plaintiff, noting that: "On questions such as these, which stand at the frontier of current medical and epidemiological inquiry, if experts are willing to testify that such a link exists, it is for the jury to decide whether to credit such testimony." *Id.* at 1534–39. The *Ferebee* court's description of the evidence as a "classic battle of the experts, a battle in which the jury must decide the victor," has been cited frequently. *Id.* at 1535. For a discussion of the *Ferebee* opinion, see Troyen A. Brennan, *Causal Chains and Statistical Links: The Role of Scientific Uncertainty in Hazardous Substance Litigation*, 73 Cornell L. Rev. 469, 496–97 (1988).

    The District of Columbia Circuit, however, assumed a more aggressive stance in *Richardson v. Richardson-Merrell, Inc.*, affirming a trial court's grant of summary judgment for the defendant:

> The question whether Bendectin causes limb reduction defects is scientific in nature, and it is to the scientific community that the law must look for the answer. For this reason, expert witnesses are

> indispensable in a case such as this. But that is not to say that the court's hands are inexorable tied, or that it must accept uncritically any sort of opinion espoused by an expert merely because his credentials render him qualified to testify.

857 F.2d 823, 829 (D.C. Cir. 1988), *cert. denied*, 493 U.S. 882 (1989). The court held that the expert testimony lacked an adequate foundation and was therefore inadmissible under Rule 703, distinguishing *Ferebee* on the ground that a greater body of scientific evidence existed concerning Bendectin. *Id.* at 832. It is not obvious why this distinction, even if true, should lead to the conclusion that the plaintiff's evidence lacked an adequate foundation in *Richardson* but not in *Ferebee*.

Divergent views can also be found at the trial level. Compare, for example, *Wells v. Ortho Pharmaceutical Corp.*, 615 F. Supp. 262 (N.D. Ga. 1985) (following a passive approach comparable to *Ferebee*), *aff'd*, 788 F.2d 741 (11th Cir.) (reducing damages), *cert. denied*, 479 U.S. 850 (1986), with *In re* "Agent Orange" *Products Liability Litigation*, 597 F. Supp. 740 (E.D.N.Y. 1984) (following a more restrictive approach comparable to *Richardson*), *aff'd*, 818 F.2d 145 (2d Cir. 1987).

21. Black et. al., *supra* note 17, at 49.
22. See, e.g., *Richardson*, 857 F.2d at 829 (addressing the issue of whether Benedictin causes limit reduction defects).
23. For example, in the area of eyewitness identification, expert testimony rarely deals with the specifics of a given trial. Thus, experts proffer essentially the same testimony from case to case. See Roger Elliott, *Expert Testimony About Eyewitness Identification: A Critique*, 17 Law & Human Behavior 423, 423 (1993); Joseph Sanders, *Expert Witnesses in Eyewitness Facial Identification Cases*, 17 Tex. Tech L. Rev. 1409, 1409–10 (1986). Appellate courts have increasingly affirmed the exclusion of such testimony. See, e.g., *United States v. Harris,* 995 F.2d 532, 534 (4th Cir. 1993); *United States v. Curry,* 977 F.2d 1042, 1051–52 (7th Cir. 1992), *cert. denied*, 113 S. Ct. 1357 (1993). But see, e.g., *United States v. Stevens,* 935 F.2d 1380, 1400 (3rd Cir. 1991) (reversing a decision excluding expert testimony); *Campbell v. People,* 814 P.2d 1, 8 (Colo. 1991) (also reversing a decision excluding expert testimony).
24. *Daubert v. Merrell Dow Pharmaceuticals, Inc.*, 727 F. Supp. 570, 571 (S.D. Cal. 1989), *aff'd*, 951 F.2d 1128 (9th Cir. 1991), *vacated*, 113 S. Ct. 2786 (1993). The *Daubert* and *Schuller* cases are among 1,700 or so cases brought against Merrell Dow claiming that Bendectin causes birth defects. See Joseph Sanders, *The Bendectin Litigation: A Case Study in the Life Cycle of Mass Torts*, 43 Hastings L.J. 301, 359–62 (1992) [hereinafter Sanders, *The Bendectin Litigation*].
25. *Daubert*, 727 F. Supp. at 576. *Daubert* is but one of many Bendectin cases resolved at the summary judgment stage. See Joseph Sanders, *From Science to Evidence: the Testimony on Causation in the Bendectin Cases*, 46 Stan. L. Rev. 1, 11, n.35 (1993) [hereinafter Sanders, *From Science to Evidence*].
26. *Daubert*, 727 F. Supp. at 575. The court explained that all other evidence lacks a sufficient foundation under Federal Rule of Evidence 703. *Id.* A teratogen is a substance that causes birth defects.
27. *Id.* The court was incorrect on this point. See *infra* note 114 and accompanying

text (noting six studies finding a correlation between Bendectin use and injury).

28. *Daubert*, 727 F. Supp. at 575.
29. *Id.* at 576.
30. *Daubert v. Merrell Dow Pharmaceuticals, Inc.*, 951 F.2d 1128 (9th Cir. 1991), *vacated*, 113 S. Ct. 2786 (1993).
31. *Id.* at 1129–31.
32. 113 S. Ct. 320 (1992). The Court's refusal to grant certiorari in two other Bendectin cases, which also resulted in summary judgment for the defendant, reveals its purpose. See *Turpin v. Merrell Dow Pharmaceuticals, Inc.*, 113 S. Ct. 84 (1992) (denying petition for writ of certiorari); *Lee v. Richardson-Merrell, Inc.*, 113 S. Ct. 192 (1992) (same). The Ninth Circuit's exclusive reliance on *Frye* represents the primary distinction between these cases and *Daubert*.
33. *Daubert v. Merrell Dow Pharmaceuticals, Inc.*, 113 S. Ct. 2786, 2792–93 (1993).
34. Fed. R. Evid. 702.
35. *Daubert*, 113 S. Ct. at 2794 (citing *Beech Aircraft Corp. v. Rainey*, 488 U.S. 153, 169 (1988)).
36. *Daubert*'s record offered little on which to base a discussion of what standard should succeed *Frye*. For this reason, Judge Weinstein argued that the Court erred in granting certiorari to *Daubert* and that a better choice would have been *Christophersen v. Allied Signal Corp.*, 939 F.2d 1106 (5th Cir. 1991), *cert. denied*, 112 S. Ct. 1280 (1992); see Prod. Safety & Liability Rep. (BNA) 10 (Apr. 12, 1993).
37. *Daubert*, 113 S. Ct. at 2795.
38. See Prod. Safety & Liab. Rep. (BNA) 12–30 (Apr. 26, 1993).
39. *Daubert*, 113 S. Ct. at 2795. The Court may have borrowed this analysis from the Advisory Committee's proposed change in the language of Rule 702. See *supra* note 15.
40. *Daubert*, 113 S. Ct. at 2795.
41. *Id.* at 2795 n.9. Bert Black has proposed a modification of Rule 702 that would require scientific evidence to be based on "scientifically valid reasoning" in order to be admissible. Black, *supra* note 11, at 611.
42. *Daubert*, 113 S. Ct. at 2797. Specifically, the Court referred to the analysis in *United States v. Downing*, 753 F.2d 1224 (3d Cir. 1985). In *Downing*, the Third Circuit held that the admissibility of scientific testimony on the accuracy of eyewitness identification was "not automatic but conditional." 753 F.2d at 1226. In order to be admissible, evidence must survive the trial court's preliminary inquiry. In an *in limine* proceeding, the judge should balance: (1) the reliability of the scientific principles the expert employed; against (2) the likelihood that the evidence may overwhelm or mislead the jury. *Id.* In addition, the trial court should examine the "fit" between the proffered scientific testimony and the contested issues in the case. *Id.* at 1226. For a discussion of *Downing* by Judge Becker, its author, see Becker & Orenstein, *supra* note 11, at 881.

    The court in *Christophersen v. Allied-Signal Corp.* set out a similar test for admissibility. 939 F.2d 1106 (5th Cir. 1991) (en banc), *cert. denied*, 112 S. Ct. 1280 (1992). In *Christopherson* the Fifth Circuit, sitting *en banc*, sustained the trial judge's grant of summary judgment to the defendant. *Id.* at 1116. The plaintiff had argued that exposure to nickel/cadmium caused her husband's fatal colon cancer. *Id.* at 1108. The *en banc* opinion established a four factor test of admissibility:

> (1) Whether the witness is qualified to express an expert opinion [under Rule 702];
>
> (2) whether the facts upon which the expert relies are the same type as are relied upon by other experts in the field[, as Rule 703 requires];
>
> (3) whether in reaching his conclusion the expert used a well-founded methodology [under *Frye*]; and
>
> (4) assuming the expert's testimony has passed Rules 702, 703, and the *Frye* test, whether . . . the testimony's potential for unfair prejudice substantially outweighs its probative value [under Rule 403].

Id. at 1110. The court noted that these four factors "lend themselves to sequential application." *Id.* For a further discussion of the *Christopherson* case, see Bruce James, *Fryed Expert Witnesses: The 5th Circuit Takes Charge of Scientific Testimony*, 12 Rev. Litig. 171, 188 (1992).

43. *Daubert*, 113 S. Ct. at 2797 n.12. The court cites 3 Weinstein & Berger, Weinstein's Evidence ¶702[03], at 702–41, 702–42 and Mark McCormick, *Scientific Evidence: Defining a New Approach to Admissibility*, 67 Iowa L. Rev. 879, 911–912 (1982), both of which appear to have been taken from Black, *supra* note 11, at 642, n.258. Weinstein & Berger list seven factors that a court may use in assessing scientific evidence: (1) the technique's general acceptance in the field; (2) the expert's qualifications and stature; (3) the use which has been made of the technique; (4) the potential rate of error; (5) the existence of a specialized literature; (6) the novelty of the invention; and (7) the extent to which the technique relies on the expert's subjective interpretation. Weinstein & Berger, *supra* note 2, ¶702[03], at 702–41, 702–42, *quoted in* Black, *supra* note 11, at 642. Black also summarized eleven factors set forth by McCormick: (1) the technique's potential error rate; (2) the existence and maintenance of standards governing its use; (3) the presence of safeguards in the technique's characteristics; (4) analogy to other scientific techniques whose results are admissible; (5) the extent to which scientists in the relevant field have accepted the technique; (6) the nature and breadth of the inference adduced; (7) the clarity and simplicity with which the technique can be described and its results explained; (8) the extent to which the courts and jury can verify the basic data; (9) the availability of other experts to test and evaluate the technique; (10) the evidence's probative significance in the circumstances of the case; and (11) the care with which the expert employed the technique. Black, *supra* note 11, at 642 n.258 (quoting McCormick, *supra* note 5, at 911–912).

44. "An additional consideration under Rule 702—and another aspect of relevancy —is whether expert testimony proffered in the case is sufficiently tied to the facts of the case that it will aid the jury in resolving a factual dispute." *United States v. Downing,* 753 F.2d 1224, 1242 (3d Cir. 1985). In *Daubert*, the Supreme Court did not directly relate its discussion of "fit" to questions of validity. Nevertheless, it seems reasonable to apply that concept in this context. A particular piece of research may support one conclusion

and not another. This is frequently a question of external validity. See *infra* part III.D.

45. *Daubert*, 113 S. Ct. at 2796.
46. *Id.* at 2796–97 (citing *United States v. Smith,* 869 F.2d 348, 353–354 (7th Cir. 1989)).
47. The Court noted, almost in passing, that the "focus, of course, must be solely on principles and methodology, not the conclusions that they generate." *Id.* at 2797. This statement will likely generate a good deal of controversy. Bendectin plaintiffs have already picked up on this point and argued that their expert testimony should not be excluded under *Daubert* when its methodology is sound and the defense only objects to the expert's conclusion. See *BENDECTIN: Plaintiffs seek rehearing after CA 3 Affirms Defense Judgment*, Prod. Safety & Liab. Rep. (BNA) 2 (Sept. 1, 1993).
48. *Daubert*, 133 S. Ct. at 2797.
49. *Id.*
50. *Id.*
51. See Black, *supra* note 11, at 629.
52. *Daubert*, 113 S. Ct. at 2797. The full text of Rule 703 reads:

> The facts or data in the particular case upon which an expert bases an opinion or inference may be those perceived or made known to the expert at or before the hearing. If of a type reasonably relied upon by experts in a particular field in forming opinions or inferences upon the subject, the facts or data need not be admissible in evidence.

Fed. R. Evid. 703.

There has been confusion concerning the relationship of Rules 702 and 703. See, e.g., *Zenith Radio Corporation v. Matsushita Elect. Indus., Inc.*, 505 F. Supp. 1313, 1318 (E.D. Pa. 1980) (discussing the general relationship among rules 702, 703 and 704), *aff'd in part, rev'd in part*, 723 F.2d 238 (3d Cir. 1983), *rev'd*, 475 U.S. 574 (1986). Professor Imwinkelried has proposed that courts use Rule 702 to regulate the expert's major premise—the principles and theories upon which the expert bases its opinion, and that courts use Rule 703 to address the expert's minor premise—how the principles and theories apply to the facts and data in the case at hand. See Imwinkelried, *supra* note 11, at 14–16, 16–19. When the expert's testimony follows this major premise-minor premise format, Professor Imwinkelried's analysis may prove especially useful. Expert testimony, however, is not always easily broken into these two categories. See David Faigman, *Struggling to Stop the Flood of Unreliable Expert Testimony*, 76 Minn. L. Rev. 877, 886 (1992).

53. See Joe S. Cecil & Thomas Willging, Court Appointed Experts: Defining the Role of Experts Appointed Under Federal Rule of Evidence 706 (1993).
54. The full text of Rule 403 reads: "Although relevant, evidence may be excluded if its probative value is substantially outweighed by the danger of unfair prejudice, confusion of the issues, or misleading the jury, or by considerations of undue delay, waste of time, or needless presentation of cumulative evidence." Fed. R. Evid. 403.
55. *Daubert v. Merrell Dow Pharmaceuticals, Inc.,* 113 S. Ct. 2786, 2795, n.9 (1993).

56. Thomas D. Cook & Donald T. Campbell, Quasi-Experimentation: Design and Analysis Issues for Field Testing 37–39 (1979). The authors do not claim that this list is exhaustive. *Id.*
57. See, e.g., Michael D. Green, *Expert Witnesses and Sufficieny of Evidence in Toxic Substances Cases: The Legacy of Agent Orange and Bendectin Litigation*, 86 Nw. U.L. Rev. 643, 682–94 (1992); Sanders, *The Bendectin Litigation*, *supra* note 24, at 342–45.
58. Frederick Williams, Reasoning With Statistics: How to Read Research 54 (3d ed. 1986).
59. By convention, the null hypothesis will not be rejected unless the probability that chance caused a result is less than one in 20 (Alpha = .05) or, occasionally, less than one in 100 (Alpha = .01). *Id.* at 59.
60. Williams, *supra* note 58, at 65–67.
61. Green, *supra* note 57, at 653.
62. Power is a function of the study's sample size, the size of the effect one wishes to detect, and the significance criterion used to guard against Type I error. Jacob Cohen, Statistical Power Analysis for the Behavioral Sciences 14 (2d ed. 1988).
63. See generally Frederic Marc Wolf, Meta-Analysis: Quantitative Methods for Research Synthesis (1986) (basic text on meta-analysis); Thomas R. Einarson et al., *A Method for Meta-Analysis of Epidemiological Studies*, 22 Drug Intelligence & Clinical Pharmacy 813, 813–23 (1988) (applying meta-analysis to Benedictin studies).
64. Thoughtful investigators assess their findings in light of this threat to validity. For example, Shiono and Klebanoff examined births in Northern California for 58 categories of birth defects. Patricia Shiono & Mark Klebanoff, *Bendectin and Human Congenital Malformations*, 40 Teratology 151, 152–55 (1989). Bendectin ingestion was significantly related to three types of defects: lung defects, microcephaly (small head size) and cataracts. *Id.* at 152. The authors noted that three significant relationships out of 58 are "exactly the number of significant relationships that would have been expected by chance" when using 95% confidence intervals, and concluded that the three associations "are unlikely to be causal." *Id.* at 155.
65. Plaintiff experts in Bendectin cases typically recode data in an attempt to increase reliability. See *infra* part IV.B (discussing reanalyses of epidemological data, in particular, those of plaintiff experts Dr. Swan and Dr. Done).
66. Cook & Campbell, *supra* note 56, at 37.
67. See *id.* at 50.
68. *Id.* at 51. Bendectin defendants often introduce evidence indicating that a measurable decrease in birth defects did not accompany rapid withdrawal of the drug from the market between 1981 and 1983. See *infra* note 117 and accompanying text. Discovery of a new teratogenic substance, introduced into the environment over this same period, would constitute a history threat to the validity of the conclusion that Bendectin does not cause birth defects.
69. Cook & Campbell, *supra* note 56, at 52. For example, a prior opportunity to identify a suspect in a lineup may affect the courtroom identification of the suspect.
70. *Id.* at 53. Selection effects take many different forms and often interact with other threats to internal validity. One example of a potential selection

effect in Bendectin research derives from the fact that morning sickness is a weak indicator that the fetus is healthy. See Margaret Weigel & Ronald Weigel, *Nausea & Vomiting in Pregnancy and Pregnancy Outcome*, 96 British J. Obstetrics & Gynecology 1312 (1989). Thus, women who took Bendectin were more likely to have a healthy baby than women who did not. But see Anne Kricker et al., *Congenital Limb Deficiencies: Maternal Factors in Pregnancy*, 26 Australia-New Zealand J. Obstetrics & Gynecology 272 (1986) (study concluding that "vomiting of [sic] pregnancy was associated with an increased risk of longitudinal limb reduction defects").

71. Cook & Campbell, *supra* note 56, at 55.
72. Even experimental designs cannot control for all threats to internal validity. For example, experiments cannot entirely control for differential mortality in treatment groups. Differential mortality obscures the interpretation of other results because the remaining individuals in the two groups may no longer be comparable on average. Cook & Campbell, *supra* note 56, at 57. This difference may be attributable to the treatment itself, such as when animals die from very large doses of a substance. See, e.g., Rochelle W. Tyl et al., *Developmental Toxicity Evaluation of Bendectin in CD Rats*, 37 Teratology 539, 540 (1988) (noting high "maternal mortality" in certain rat groups given Bendectin).
73. Cook & Campbell, *supra* note 56, at 59.
74. *Id.*
75. *Id.* at 67.
76. *Id.*
77. *Id.* at 66.
78. *Id.* at 61. In an effort to increase construct validity, scientists have designed methods such as placebo controls and double blind designs. *Id.* In a double blind design, neither the subject nor the researcher knows who is receiving the treatment and who is receiving the placebo. *E.g.*, A.G. Hendrickx et al., *Evaluation of Bendectin Embryotoxicity in Non-human Primates: Double-Blind Study in Cynomolgus Monkeys*, 32 Teratology 191 (1985).
79. Cook & Campbell, *supra* note 56, at 67.
80. *Id.*
81. Sanders, *The Bendectin Litigation*, *supra* note 24, at 323.
82. Cook & Campbell, *supra* note 56, at 65.
83. Thalidomide is not a teratogen in all animal species. See Max Sherman & Steven Strauss, *Thalidomide: A Twenty-Five Year Perspective*, 41 Food Drug Cosm. L.J. 458, 461 (1986) (noting that Thalidomide is not a teratogen in rats, mice or hampsters).
84. Cook & Campbell, *supra* note 56, at 66.
85. This is known as convergent validity. *Id.* at 61.
86. This is sometimes called discriminant validity. *Id.*
87. *Id.* at 71.
88. *Id.* at 73–74.
89. *Id.* at 73.
90. Samuel R. Gross, *Expert Evidence*, 1991 Wis. L. Rev. 1113, 1134 (1991).
91. Cook & Campbell, *supra* note 56, at 74.
92. Reid Hastie et al., Inside the Jury 40 (1983).
93. *Id.*

94. See *infra* notes 125–131 and accompanying text.
95. For example, several courts, like the *Daubert* trial court, have resisted the introduction of expert opinion based on animal studies because of concerns about external validity. See *infra* text accompanying notes 125–29 (discussing the external validity problem posed by animal studies); *infra* text accompanying notes 134–48 (discussing courts' refusal to allow non-epidemiological evidence such as animal studies).
96. Cook & Campbell, *supra* note 56, at 80.
97. *Id.* at 81.
98. *Id.* at 74.
99. A list of all reported Bendectin opinions through 1991 can be found in Sanders, *The Bendectin Litigation*, *supra* note 24, at 410–18.
100. See Louis Lasagna & Sheila R. Shulman, *Bendectin and the Language of Causation, in* Phantom Risk: Scientific Inference and the Law 100, 100–01 (Kenneth R. Foster et al. eds., 1993). Other mass exposures that currently fit into this category include exposure to Agent Orange, PCBs, certain toxic waste dumps, breast implants, and electro-magnetic fields.
101. Joseph Sanders, *The Jury Deliberations in a Complex Case:* Havner v. Merrell Dow Pharmaceuticals, Inc., 16 Just. Sys. J. 45, 52–53 (1993) [hereinafter Sanders, *Jury Deliberation*].
102. Sanders, *The Bendectin Litigation*, *supra* note 24, at 317.
103. *DeLuca v. Merrell Dow Pharmaceuticals, Inc.*, 911 F.2d 941, 946 n.8 (3d Cir. 1990).
104. See, e.g., Stuart Freeman et al., *Post-implantation Embryo Culture for Studies of Teratogenesis, in* Biochemical Toxicology: A Practical Approach 83 (K. Snell & B. Mullock eds. 1987) (assessing studies of teratogenesis).
105. John R. Hassell & Elizabeth A. Horigan, *Chondrogenesis: A Model Developmental System for Measuring Teratogenic Potential of Compounds*, 2 Teratogenesis, Carcinogenesis, & Mutagenesis 325, 325–27 (1982).
106. John D. Budroe et al., *A Study of the Potential Genotoxicity of Methapyrilene and Related Antihistamines using the Hepatocyte/DNA Repair Assay*, 135 Mutation Res. 131, 135–36 (1984).
107. Sanders, *The Bendectin Litigation*, *supra* note 24, at 394.
108. A.G. Hendrickx et al., *Evaluation of Bendectin Embryotoxicity in Non-human Primates: Ventricular Septal Defects in Prenatal Macaques and Baboon*, 32 Teratology 179, 179–89 (1985); A.G. Hendrickx et al., *supra* note 78, at 194.
109. For a list of the published animal studies, see Sanders, *The Bendectin Litigation*, *supra* note 24, at 403.
110. Leon Gordis, *Estimating Risk and Inferring Causality in Epidemiology, in* Epidemiology and Health Risk Assessment 51, 52 (Leon Gordis ed. 1988).
111. *Id.*
112. *Id.*
113. For a list of published epidemiological studies through 1991, see Sanders, *The Bendectin Litigation*, *supra* note 24, at 404–06.
114. Pamela Aselton et al., *Pyloric Stenosis and Maternal Bendectin Exposure*, 120 Am. J. Epidemiology 251 (1984); Jose F. Cordero et al., *Is Bendectin a Teratogen?*, 245 JAMA 2307 (1981); Brenda Eskenazi & Michael B. Bracken, *Bendectin (Debendox) as a Risk Factor for Pyloric Stenosis*, 144 Am. J. Obstetrics & Gynecology 919 (1982); G.T. Gibson et al., *Congenital Anomalies*

in Relation to the Use of Doxylamine/Dicyclomine and other Antenatal Factors: An Ongoing Prospective Study, 1981 Med. J. Austl. 410 (1981); J. Golding et al., *Maternal Anti-nauseants and Clefts of Lip and Palate*, 1983 Human Toxicology 63 (1983); Kenneth J. Rothman et al., *Exogenous Hormones and Other Drug Exposures of Children with Congenital Heart Disease*, 109 Am. J. Epidemiology 433, 435 (1979).

115. Sanders, *The Bendectin Litigation, supra* note 24, at 395.

116. Einarson, Leeder & Koren included 17 studies in a meta-analysis examining whether first-trimester Bendectin ingestion caused any birth defect. See Einarson et al., *supra* note 63. The overall odds ratio was 1.01, $c^2 2 = 0.05$, $p = 0.815$. They also conducted separate meta-analyses for cohort and case control studies. For cohort studies ($N = 12$) the ratio was 0.95, $c^2 = 0.66$, $p = 0.418$. For case control ($N = 5$) studies the ratio was 1.27, $c^2 = 2.71$, $p = 0.10$. *Id.* at 819–20. The authors concluded that these meta-analyses confirm previous subjective analyses that Bendectin is not associated with human teratogenic outcomes. *Id.* at 822; see also Leslie J. Sheffield & Ron Batagol, *The Creation of Therapeutic Orphans–Or, What Have We Learnt From the Debendox Fiasco?*, 143 Med. J. Austl. 143, 144–45 (1985) (noting "great uniformity" in studies "finding no teratogenic effect of Debendox").

The odds ratio is the cross product in a 2×2 table. In a cohort study examining exposed and unexposed individuals, the odds ratio is the ratio of the odds of injury if the person was exposed, to the odds of injury if the person was not exposed.

Odds Ratio in a Cohort Study

	Injured	Not Injured	
Exposed	a	b	$\frac{a}{b=ad}$
Not Exposed	c	d	$\frac{c}{d=bc}$

In a case-control study comparing injured subjects to "controls" without the injury, the odds ratio is the ratio of the odds that the injured subjects suffered exposure to the odds that the controls suffered exposure.

Odds Ratio in a Case-control Study

	Cases (With Injury)	Controls (Without Injury)	
History of Exposure	a	b	$\frac{a}{c=ad}$
No History of Exposure	c	d	$\frac{c}{d=bc}$

For example, if one conducted a case-control study with the following results a=60, b=40, c=40, d=60, the odds ratio would be (60*60)/(40*40) = 3600/1600 = 2.75. See Harold Kahn, An Introduction to Epidemiologic Methods 38–45 (1983).

117. Robert L. Brent, *Bendectin and Interventricular Septal Defects*, 32 Teratology 317, 317 (1985); see D.W.G. Harron et al., *Debendox and Congenital Malformations in Northern Ireland*, 281 Brit. Med. J. 1379, 1381 (1980).

118. Sanders, *From Science to Evidence, supra* note 25, at 43–44.

119. C.T.G. King et al., *Antihistamines and Teratogenicity in the Rat*, 147 J. Pharmacology & Experimental Therapeutics 391, 395 (1965).

120. Green, *supra* note 57, at 658.
121. O.P. Flint, *An In Vitro Test for Teratogens Using Cultures of Rat Embryo Cells, reprinted in* In Vitro Methods in Toxicology 339, 354 (C.K. Atterwill & C.E. Steele eds. 1987).
122. Hassell & Horigan, *supra* note 105, at 327, 330.
123. *Id.* at 330.
124. *Id.* The authors do not express an opinion about whether Bendectin is dangerous to humans when taken in normal therapeutic doses. *Id.* at 330–31.
125. Michael D. Hogan & David G. Hoel, *Extrapolation to Man, reprinted in* Principles & Methods of Toxicology 879, 879–80 (Wallace Hayes ed., 2d ed. 1989).
126. Jack L. Landan & W. Hugh O'Riordan, *Of Mice and Men: The Admissibility of Animal Studies to Prove Causation in Toxic Tort Litigation*, 25 Idaho L. Rev. 521, 537 (1988–89).
127. Even with high dose rates, the relatively small number of animals in some experiments may create a threat to statistical conclusion validity when searching for a weak causal link.
128. Thomas H. Shepard, *Human Teratogenicity*, 33 Advances in Pediatrics 225, 227 (1986).
129. See Tyl et al., *supra* note 72, at 549.
130. For example, varying statistical models for extrapolating carcinogenic effects produce different results when the laboratory dose rate is substantially greater than the environmental dose rate. OSHA Generic Cancer Policy, 45 Fed. Reg. 5002, 5184–85 (1980); David S. Salsburg, *Statistics and Toxicology: An Overview, in* Scientific Considerations in Monitoring and Evaluating Toxicological Research 123, 130–31 (Edward Gralla ed., 1981).
131. See James P. Leape, *Quantitative Risk Assessment in Regulation of Environmental Carcinogens*, 4 Harv. Envtl. L. Rev. 86, 98–99 (1980). Comparisons of risk estimates of cancer based on extrapolations from animal data with actual human epidemiological data indicate that only half the substances examined yielded accurate estimates. Landau & O'Riordan, *supra* note 126, at 548 (indicating that many estimates err by factors of 10 or more).
132. Ian C.T. Nisbet & Nathan J. Karch, Chemical Hazards to Human Reproduction 98–99 (1983).
133. A 1980 FDA study reported that of 165 compounds with no reported human teratologic effects, only 28% appeared negative in all animal species tested. 45 Fed. Reg. 69,816, 69,823 (1980); Nisbet & Karch, *supra* note 132, at 105. For explanations of how and why effects in humans differ from various animal species, see Edward J. Calabrese, Principles of Animal Extrapolation 237–38 (1983); Gary P. Carlson, *Factors Modifying Toxicity,* in Toxic Substances and Human Risk: Principles of Data Interpretation 47, 49 (R. Tardiff & J. Rodricks eds., 1987). One example is reported in *Turpin v. Merrell Dow Pharmaceuticals, Inc.,* 959 F.2d 1349, 1359 n.4 (6th Cir. 1992), *cert. denied,* 113 S. Ct. 84 (1992). Several animal studies have found that cortisone causes severe cleft palate birth defects in several animal species, but not in humans. Alfred M. Bongiovanni & Arthur J. McPadden, *Steroids During Pregnancy and Possible Fetal Consequences*, 11 Fertility & Sterility 181, 184–85 (1960). It may be, of course, that some chemicals with no apparent carcinogenic or

teratogenic effect are not in fact completely harmless because of significant limits on the ability of epidemiological studies to detect small risks.

134. See *Daubert v. Merrell Dow Pharmaceuticals, Inc.*, 727 F. Supp. 570, 575 (S.D. Cal. 1989), *aff'd*, 951 F.2d 1128 (9th Cir. 1991), *vacated*, 113 S. Ct. 2786 (1993).
135. See, e.g., *Brock v. Merrell Dow Pharmaceuticals, Inc.*, 874 F.2d 307, 311–13 (5th Cir. 1989), *cert. denied*, 494 U.S. 1046 (1990).
136. *Id.* at 313.
137. *Id.* at 313–15; see *Merrell Dow Pharmaceuticals, Inc. v. Havner,* No. 13–92–540-CV, 1994 WL 86436 (Tex. Ct. App. March 17, 1994).
138. 959 F.2d 1349 (6th Cir.), *cert. denied*, 113 S. Ct. 84 (1992).
139. *Id.* at 1360–61. The court refused to conclude that animal studies could never form the basis of an opinion that a substance is a human teratogen, only that the plaintiff's animal studies could not. *Id.* at 1360. The *Turpin* district court excluded much of the plaintiff's evidence under Rule 703 but held in the alternative that, even if admissible as a matter of law, the evidence could not support a verdict for the plaintiff. *Turpin v. Merrell Dow Pharmaceuticals, Inc.*, 736 F. Supp. 737, 744 (E.D. Ky. 1990); see also *Elkins v. Richardson-Merrell, Inc.*, 8 F.3d 1068 (6th Cir. 1993) (affirming grant of summary judgement for defendant by relying on *Turpin*), *cert. denied*, 62 USLW 3618 (1994).
140. See, e.g., *Richardson v. Richardson-Merrell, Inc.*, 857 F.2d 823 (D.C. Cir. 1988), *cert. denied*, 493 U.S. 882 (1989).
141. *Daubert v. Merrell Dow Pharmaceuticals, Inc.*, 951 F.2d 1128 (9th Cir. 1991), *vacated*, 113 S. Ct. 2786 (1993).
142. An important non-Bendectin case with a similar ruling is In re "Agent Orange" Products Liability Litigation, 611 F. Supp. 1223 (E.D.N.Y. 1985), *aff'd*, 818 F.2d 145 (2d Cir. 1987), *cert. denied*, 487 U.S. 1234 (1988). There, Judge Weinstein refused to allow the plaintiff's experts to base their opinion on animal studies, primarily because of external validity concerns:

> The many studies on animal exposure to Agent Orange, even plaintiffs' expert concedes, are not persuasive in this lawsuit. . . . There is no evidence that plaintiffs were exposed to the far higher concentrations involved in both the animal and industrial exposure studies. *Cf. In re* "Agent Orange" Product Liability Litigation, 597 F. Supp. 740, 782 (E.D.N.Y.1984). The animal studies are not helpful in the instant case because they involve different biological species. They are of so little probative force and are so potentially misleading as to be inadmissible. See Fed. R. Evid. 401–403. They cannot be an acceptable predicate for an opinion under Rule 703.

In re "Agent Orange", 611 F.Supp. at 1241; see *In re Paoli Railroad Yard PCB Litigation,* Nos. 86–2229, 1992 U.S. Dist. LEXIS 16287, at *15 (E.D. Pa. Oct. 21, 1992) (holding that animal studies are of limited reliability when attempting to apply their results to humans).

143. 646 F. Supp. 856 (D. Mass. 1986), *aff'd*, 830 F.2d 1190 (1st Cir. 1987).
144. *Id.* at 866–67. The court noted the following: "None of the animal studies submitted by the plaintiffs provide evidence of teratogenicity at doses comparable to the human therapeutic dose of Bendectin. These animal studies are therefore lacking in probative value and must be found inadmissible. . . .

For similar reasons, this Court must reject the plaintiffs' proffered evidence of in vitro studies and studies of analogous chemical structures as a basis for the plaintiffs' experts testimony. . . . This Court also cannot find, pursuant to Rule 703, that such studies are 'of a type reasonably relied upon by experts in the particular field.' Dr. John Hassell, the author of one such *in vitro* study, has expressly recognized that neither his technique nor any other *in vitro* system has yet been validated as an accurate predictor of teratogenicity in animals or humans. . . . Thus, a careful review of the material before this Court indicates that the only relevant, probative, and non-misleading evidence on the issue of Bendectin's role in the causation of birth defects are the controlled observations of human beings, documented in more than 25 published epidemiological studies." *Id.*

145. 857 F.2d 823 (D.C. Cir. 1988).
146. In situations where there is not a substantial body of epidemiological data, however, courts have been more accepting of animal study data. See, e.g., *Marder v. G.D. Searle & Co.*, 630 F. Supp. 1087, 1094 (D. Md. 1986), *aff'd sub nom.*, *Wheelahan v. G.D. Searle & Co.*, 814 F.2d 655 (4th Cir. 1987).
147. 772 F. Supp. 1027, 1029–33 (W.D. Tenn. 1991), *aff'd*, 961 F.2d 1577 (6th Cir.), *cert. denied*, 113 S. Ct. 197 (1992).
148. 736 F. Supp. 737, 739–44 (E.D. Ky. 1990). The courts in *Lee* and *Turpin* employed a test developed in *United States v. Green,* 548 F.2d 1261 (6th Cir. 1977) and *United States v. Kozminski,* 821 F.2d 1186 (6th Cir. 1987), *aff'd*, 487 U.S. 931 (1988). The *Green* court set forth a four-prong test for admissibility: (1) a qualified expert must be offered; (2) the expert must testify on a proper subject; (3) the expert must testify in conformity with a generally accepted explanatory theory; and (4) the probative value of the testimony must outweigh any prejudicial effect. *Green*, 548 F.2d at 1268. *Kozminski* further refined the third element by requiring that the explanatory theory must have: (a) received at least some exposure within the scientific peerage to which it belongs; (b) been subjected to peer evaluation to determine its scientific validity and reliability; and (c) achieved general acceptance within the scientific community to which it belongs. *Kozminski*, 821 F.2d at 1201.
149. A "first plaintiff" is the first individual to claim that a toxic substance causes injury. This individual must frequently litigate on an undeveloped scientific record. See Sanders, *The Bendectin Litigation*, *supra* note 24, at 349.
150. See *Richardson v. Richardson-Merrell, Inc.*, 857 F.2d 823 (D.C. Cir. 1988). At least two courts have refused to adopt this unique approach in Bendectin cases. In *Longmore v. Merrell Dow Pharmaceuticals, Inc.*, the court concluded as follows:

> Animal studies are generally relied upon by experts determining the link between a drug and birth defects and the same is true for chemical analysis. While the Court will leave open the question of the admissibility of particular studies during the trial of this matter, the Court cannot now preclude all such studies under Rule 703.

737 F. Supp. 1117, 1121 (D. Idaho 1990). In *In Re Bendectin Products Liability Litigation*, Judge Rubin, the trial judge who presided over the 1985 Multidistrict Litigation Bendectin Trial in Ohio, also refused to hold non-epidemiological evidence inadmissible under Rule 703, noting the following:

> The division in the scientific community over whether epidemio-

> logical studies should be relied upon exclusively necessitates the inescapable conclusion that experts may reasonably rely upon other types of data when forming an opinion as to the teratogenicity of Bendectin. A contrary finding is unjustifiable without a pronouncement in this circuit that, as a matter of law, epidemiological studies are the sole basis upon which an expert may reasonably rely when forming an opinion on a drug's teratogenicity.

732 F. Supp. 744, 749 (E.D. Mich. 1990) (citations omitted).

151. See, e.g., *Richardson*, 857 F.2d at 829–32.
152. See Green, *supra* note 57, at 676 (noting that the probity of toxicology evidence, especially animal studies, varies inversely with the quality of the epidemiological evidence).
153. Cook & Campbell, *supra* note 56, at 65.
154. *Id.*
155. *Id.* at 66.
156. See, e.g., *Oxendine v. Merrell Dow Pharmaceuticals, Inc.*, 506 A.2d 1100, 1104–08 (D.C. Cir. 1986).
157. See Testimony of Dr. Shanna Helen Swan, morning session, Sept. 19, 1991, at 43–64, *Havner v. Merrell Dow Pharmaceuticals, Inc.*, No. 88-3915-F (Tex. Dist. Ct., 214th Jud. Dist., March 17, 1994) (on file with the author).
158. *Id.*
159. *Id.*
160. Green, *supra* note 57, at 650.
161. When it is unknown whether the mother ingested the drug during organogenesis, the study will mistakenly categorize women who took the drug too late in their pregnancy for it to cause a defect as women exposed to Bendectin. These women should be counted as "controls," women not exposed to the drug. The precise consequences of this misclassification are difficult to assess. For "negative cases"—women whose children do not have defects—the misclassification underestimates the drug's teratogenic. For "positive cases," however, the misclassification overestimates the teratogenic effect. Overall, such misclassification introduces an error term that will attenuate any effect that does exist. See Green, *supra* note 57, at 650 n.32.
162. See *id.* at 650.
163. Physician's Desk Reference 2642 (1994).
164. See Jon Powell, *How to Tell the Truth With Statistics: A New Statistical Approach to Analyzing the Bendectin Epidemiological Data in the Aftermath of* Daubert v. Merrell Dow Pharmaceuticals, 31 Hous. L. Rev. 1221 (1994). These studies together have an N of nearly 97,000 and yet they contain only 113 total limb reduction defects. *Id.*
165. In contingency table analyses typical of epidemiological research, the frequency of exposure in the population (the percentage of pregnant women using Bendectin) and the incidence of the effect (the frequency of limb reductions) both affect the study's power. See generally James J. Schlesselman, Case-Control Studies: Design, Conduct, Analysis (1982). In cohort studies the frequency of an effect in any given study sample approximates the frequency in the population from which the sample was drawn. When the effect is very rare one needs very large samples to avoid Type II errors. In case-control studies the incidence of the effect is set at an artificially

high level because researchers purposefully pick cases that exhibit the injury. Thus, when the incidence of an effect is rare in the population, case-control studies are much more powerful than cohort studies. See Carl F. Craynor, Regulating Toxic Substances: A Philosophy of Science and the Law 36 (1993); Kahn, *supra* note 116, at 54.

166. See Powell, *supra* note 164, at 58.

167. *Id.* at 61. This assumes an Alpha of .05 and a two tailed test of significance. *Id.*

168. Janet McCredie et al., *The Innocent Bystander: Doxylamine/Dicyclomine, Pyridoxine and Congenital Limb Defects*, 140 Med. J. Austl. 525 (1984).

169. Pooling and meta analysis combine data from several studies, producing a larger N and, *ceteris paribus*, greater statistical power. See generally Einarson et al., *supra* note 63 (presenting a step-by-step method for conducting a meta-analysis of epidemiological data); Wolf, *supra* note 63 (basic text on meta-analysis). Even these techniques cannot completely rule out the possibility that Bendectin is a weak teratogen. Powell performed meta analyses on studies with limb reduction data. See Powell, *supra* note 164. In a meta analysis of case-control studies, the Odds Ratio was 1.1, with a Chi Square of .2, p. < .65, and a 95% confidence interval of 0.56–2.17. A meta analysis of cohort studies generated an Odds Ratio of .89, with a Chi Square of .03, p. < .86 and a 95% confidence interval of 0.20–4.02. A meta analysis combining all studies generated an Odds Ratio of 1.05, with a Chi Square of .06, p. < .81, and a 95% confidence interval of 0.42–2.62. *Id.* at 78. Plaintiff experts have criticized these techniques, in part because they may treat all included studies as if they were of equal quality. See Testimony of Dr. Shanna Helen Swan, morning session, Sept. 19, 1991, at 39ff, *Havner v. Merrell-Dow Pharmaceuticals, Inc.*, No. 88–3915-F (Tex. Dist. Ct., 214th Jud. Dist., March 17, 1994) (on file with the author).

The limited number of limb defects in the epidemiological literature raises the issue of whether the relationship between Bendectin use and other types of defects is relevant to the question of whether Bendectin causes limb reduction defects. This, of course, is a question of external validity. Bendectin plaintiffs and defendants have, from time to time, been on both sides of this issue. See Sanders, *From Science to Evidence*, *supra* note 25, at 26.

170. See, e.g., Testimony of Dr. Shanna Helen Swan, morning session, Sept. 19, 1991 at 1–81, *Havner v. Merrell-Dow Pharmaceuticals, Inc.*, No. 88–3915-F (Tex. Dist. Ct., 214th Jud. Dist., March 17, 1994) (on file with the author).

171. Cordero et al., *supra* note 114, at 2307.

172. Recall bias is just one of many potential sources of bias that threaten the internal validity of epidemiological studies. Other important sources of bias are: publication bias—only studies that uncover significant results are published; and the existence of confounders that interact with the drug in question to produce injury. See Green, *supra* note 57, at 649–51; David L. Sackett, *Bias in Analytic Research*, 32 J. Chronic Diseases 51, 51 (1979).

173. Cordero et al., *supra* note 114, at 2307–09.

174. *Id.* at 2307.

175. *Id.*

176. *Id.* at 2310.

177. *Id.*
178. *Id.*
179. *Lynch v. Merrell-Nat'l Lab., Inc.*, 830 F.2d 1190, 1194 (1st Cir. 1987).
180. *Id.* at 1195.
181. *Id.*
182. *Id.*
183. *Id.*
184. *Id.* at 1195. The study coded approximately 6% (10 of 166) of the Down's Syndrome children as exposed to Bendectin. In the entire sample, approximately 9.5% (117 of 1,231) of the children were exposed. Cordero et al., *supra* note 114, at 2308, tbl. 2.
185. The Cordero study reported a 1.18 Odds Ratio for limb reductions. *Id.* Using only the data reported in the study and, using the Downs Syndrome children as the controls, the Odds Ratio for limb reductions is approximately 2.3 (14*156)/(10*115). See id.
186. *Lynch*, 830 F.2d at 1195.
187. 131 F.R.D. 71 (D. N.J. 1989), *rev'd*, 911 F.2d 941 (3d Cir. 1990), *on remand*, 791 F. Supp. 1042 (D. N.J. 1992), *aff'd*, 6 F.3d 778 (3d Cir. 1993), *cert. denied*, 114 S. Ct. 691 (1994).
188. *Id.* at 74.
189. See *DeLuca v. Merrell Dow Pharmaceuticals, Inc.*, 791 F. Supp. 1042, 1045 (D. N.J. 1992), *aff'd*, 6 F.3d 778 (3d Cir. 1993), *cert. denied*, 114 S. Ct. 691 (1994). The plaintiff did not challenge this portion of the ruling. *Id.* at 1045, 1047 n.8.
190. *DeLuca*, 131 F.R.D. at 74.
191. See Kenneth Rothman, Modern Epidemiology (1986); *Amicus Curiae* Brief for Kenneth Rothman et al. in Support of Petitioners, *Daubert v. Merrell Dow*, 113 S. Ct. 2786 (1993).
192. *DeLuca v. Merrell Dow Pharmaceuticals, Inc.*, 911 F.2d 941, 946–49 (3d. Cir. 1990), *on remand*, 791 F. Supp. 1042 (D. N.J. 1992), *aff'd*, 6 F.3d 778 (3d Cir. 1993), *cert. denied*, 114 S. Ct. 691 (1994).
193. *Id.* at 953.191 *Id.*
194. *Id.* at 954.
195. *Id.* at 955–56.
196. *Id.* The defendant had urged this position. *Id.* at 954. The statistical significance requirement was, of course, at the heart of the Fifth Circuit's opinion in *Brock v. Merrell Dow Pharmaceuticals, Inc.*, 874 F.2d 307, *modified*, 884 F.2d 166 (5th Cir. 1989), *cert. denied*, 494 U.S. 1046 (1990). Recall, however, that *Brock* employed a sufficiency and not an admissibility analysis. See Brock, 874 F.2d at 311–15.
197. *DeLuca*, 911 F.2d at 955.
198. *Id.* at 959.
199. *DeLuca*, 791 F. Supp. at 1044.
200. *Id.*
201. *Id.* at 1044–59.
202. *Id.* at 1059.
203. *Id.* at 1045–46.
204. *Id.* at 1047 n.10.
205. *Id.*

206. *Id*. Judge Brown then proceeded to examine Dr. Done's calculations and presentation in considerable detail. He compared Dr. Done's calculations of relative risks with those of the defense experts and Dr. Shanna Swan, the plaintiff's other expert witness. On several occasions, he noted that Dr. Swan's analysis contravened Dr. Done's. *Id.* at 1047–49.

207. *Id.* at 1050.

208. *Id.* at 1051.

209. *Id.* at 1051.

210. *Id.* at 1051–52.

211. *DeLuca*, 791 F. Supp. at 1052.

212. *Id.* at 1053. "Dr. Done's statement that 70% of his data sets have an upper confidence level above 2.0 is misleading without the corresponding information that 94% have lower confidence limits below 2.0 and only 30% of his data sets have a relative risk greater than 2.0." *Id.* In Dr. Done's analysis, a "data set" is a reported risk ratio between Bendectin use and a defect. Some studies appear several times in Dr. Done's analysis because he reports relationships for more than one type of defect. Other studies appear only once. There were a total of 106 data sets, all apparently given equal weight in constructing statements such as the one quoted above. *Id.* at 1052.

Judge Brown also noted that: "Although Dr. Done stated in his report that '92%' of the studies are compatible with an increase, he did not mention in his report that the studies were also compatible with a decrease (a proposition which he readily admits)." *Id.* at 1053 (citations omitted).

213. *Id.* at 1059.

214. *Id.* at 1056.

215. *Id.*

216. *Id.* at 1059.

217. *DeLuca*, 791 F. Supp. at 1059.

218. *Id.*

219. *Id.* at 1048, 1059.

220. See Black et al., *supra* note 17, at 68–70.

221. *DeLuca*, 791 F. Supp. at 1058.

222. Most debate over the peer review process concerns its ability to monitor the scientific validity of reported findings. See, e.g., Thomas S. Burack, *Of Reliable Science: Scientific Peer Review, Federal Regulatory Agencies, and the Courts*, 7 Va. J. Nat. Resources L. 27 (1987). In this regard, the value of peer review is frequently overrated, as any academic who has been a reviewer can attest. Less frequently noted is that publication in a reputable peer review journal imposes a style of discourse that encourages a relatively conservative, dispassionate, and neutral presentation rarely found in trial testimony. Peer reviewed, published articles are less likely to overstate or understate the value of a particular finding or use causal language to describe their results. See Dan L. Burk, *When Scientists Act Like Lawyers: The Problem of Adversary Science*, 33 Jurimetrics J. 363, 368 (1993); Robert Rosenthal & Peter David Blanck, *Science and Ethics in Conducting, Analyzing, and Reporting Social Science Research: Implications for Social Scientists, Judges, and Lawyers*, 68 Ind. L.J. 1209, 1212 (1993).

223. See Sanders, *The Bendectin Litigation*, *supra* note 24, at 301.

224. On the question of whether the judge or jury is a better factfinder, see Phoebe C. Ellsworth, *Are Twelve Heads Better Than One?*, 52 Law & Contemp. Probs. 205, 217–18 (1989); Richard Lempert, *Civil Juries and Complex Cases: Taking Stock after Twelve Years, in* Verdict: Assessing the Civil Jury System 181 (Robert Litan ed., 1993); Robert MacCoun, *Inside the Black Box What Empirical Research Tells Us About Decisionmaking by Civil Juries, in* Verdict: Assessing the Civil Jury System 137 (Robert Litan ed., 1993); Sanders, *From Science to Evidence, supra* note 25, at 82.
225. "The principal argument for reviewing expert testimony is the concern over jurors' ability to discount unreliable expert testimony appropriately." Faigman, *supra* note 52, at 881.
226. See generally Huber, *Galileo's Revenge, supra* note 13.
227. *Id.*; see *The Evolving Role of Statistical Assessments as Evidence in the Courts* 150 (Stephen E. Fienberg ed., 1989) [hereinafter *The Evolving Role*]. In *Turpin v. Merrell Dow Pharmaceuticals, Inc.*, the court cited jury confusion as one of the reasons for closely reviewing scientific evidence. 959 F.2d 1349, 1352 (6th Cir. 1992), *cert. denied*, 113 S. Ct. 84 (1992).
228. On the concept of case congregations, see Marc Galanter, *Case Congregations and Their Careers*, 24 Law & Soc'y Rev. 371 (1990); Sanders, *The Bendectin Litigation*, *supra* note 24, at 307.
229. Substance-related mass torts should be distinguished from mass torts generated by a single event such as an airplane crash.
230. Fed. R. Civ. P. 23; see Richard A. Chesley & Kathleen Woods Kolodgy, *Mass Exposure Torts: An Efficient Solution to a Complex Problem*, 54 U. Cin. L. Rev. 467, 490–96 (1985); Linda S. Mullenix, *Class Resolution of the Mass-Tort Case: A Proposed Federal Procedure Act*, 64 Tex. L. Rev. 1039, 1043 (1986).
231. Multi-District Litigation Act, 28 U.S.C. §1407 (1988). For discussions of consolidation of multi-district litigation, see David F. Herr, Multidistrict Litigation: Handling Cases Before the Judicial Panel on Multidistrict Litigation (1986); Cornelius J. Moynihan, Jr., *Multiple Products Liability Suits and Their Collateral Estoppel Aspects*, 73 Mass. L. Rev. 83 (1988); Blake M. Rhodes, *The Judicial Panel on Multidistrict Litigation: Time For Rethinking*, 140 U. Pa. L. Rev. 711 (1991); Joan Steinman, *Law of the Case: A Judicial Puzzle in Consolidated and Transferred Cases and in Multidistrict Litigation*, 135 U. Pa. L. Rev. 595, 622–26 (1987).
232. Fed. R. Civ. P. 42. See generally Linda S. Mullenix, *Beyond Consolidation: Postaggregative Procedure in Asbestos Mass Tort Litigation*, 32 Wm. & Mary L. Rev. 475, 500 (1991).
233. For a thoughtful early discussion of these and other devices designed to deal with mass torts, see Jack B. Weinstein, *Preliminary Reflections on the Law's Reaction to Disasters*, 11 Colum. J. Envtl. L. 1 (1986). Courts continue to explore different means of rationing law in mass tort cases. Recent initiatives include attempts to create mandatory limited fund class actions, (see *In re Joint Eastern and Southern Dist. Asbestos Litig.*, 14 F.3d 726, 728 (2d Cir. 1993)), the settlement of claims of future plaintiffs, (see *Carlough. v. Amchem Products, Inc.*, 5 F.3d 707, 710 (3d Cir. 1993); *$4.75 Billion Settlement Proposed for Silicone Breast Implant Cases*, Prod. Safety & Liab. Rep. (BNA) 1 (September 14, 1993) (settlement of all existing and future breast implant cases)) and the use of the All Writs Act to prohibit some claimants from

bringing claims in state courts (see *In Re* "Agent Orange" Product Liability Litig., 996 F.2d 1425, 1431 (2d Cir. 1993), *cert. denied*, 114 S. Ct. 1125 (1994)). All these means share a common feature: they deny individual claimants the right to a separate, individualized trial of their cause of action.

234. Offensive collateral estoppel has proven to be an unsuccessful device to achieve the goal of improving efficiency in mass tort cases. Michael D. Green, *The Inability of Offensive Collateral Estoppel to Fulfill It's Promise: An Examination of Estoppel in Asbestos Litigation*, 70 Iowa L. Rev. 141, 186–87, 207–12 (1984) [hereinafter Green, *Offensive Collateral*]; see *Setter v. A.H. Robins Co.*, 748 F.2d 1328, 1330 (8th Cir. 1984); *Hardy v. Johns-Manville Sales Corp.*, 681 F.2d 334, 340–41 (5th Cir. 1982). Other tactics have been more successful. In *Beshada v. Johns-Manville Products Corp.*, the New Jersey Supreme Court ruled that the defendant could not raise a state-of-the-art defense in an asbestos products liability action. 447 A.2d 539, 542 (1982). Although the court quickly retreated from this position in *Feldman v. Lederle Laboratories*, it did not overturn *Beshada*, but restricted it to "the circumstances giving rise to its holding." 479 A.2d 374, 387–88 (1984). One interpretation of this statement is that, after a substantial amount of asbestos litigation, the *Beshada* court engaged in substantive rationing by refusing to allow the defense to use an argument that had failed repeatedly in the past. See *In Re Asbestos Litigation,* 829 F.2d 1233, 1243–44 (3d Cir. 1987), *cert. denied*, 485 U.S. 1029 (1988).

235. See *Cimino v. Raymark Indus., Inc.,* 751 F. Supp. 649, 651–52, 662 (E.D. Tex. 1990) (rejecting an individual-by-individual approach to damage awards in a class action suit); Deborah Hensler, *Resolving Mass Toxic Torts: Myths and Realities*, 1989 U. Ill. L. Rev. 89, 90, 103–04 (1989) (discussing the development of aggregation in mass claims).

236. *In Re* Richardson-Merrell, Inc. "Bendectin" Products Liability Litig., 624 F. Supp. 1212, 1250 (S.D. Ohio, 1985), *aff'd sub nom.*, *In Re* Bendectin Litig., 857 F.2d 290 (6th Cir. 1988), *cert. denied*, 488 U.S. 1006 (1989).

237. See, e.g., Green, *Offensive Collateral*, *supra* note 234, at 215–20 (discussing concerns of inconsistent jury verdicts). Professor Green gives an example of jury inconsistency in a mass tort case where five separate juries heard the same evidence on questions common to five asbestos cases tried simultaneously in the same courtroom against twelve defendants in 1982. *Id.* at 221–22. In response to special interrogatories the juries disagreed about whether some or all of the products were defectively designed and marketed; whether asbestos exposure was the sole cause of mesothelioma; whether the defendant, Johns-Manville, was grossly negligent; and the date on which the defendant should have foreseen the dangers associated with work-place asbestos exposure. *Id.* at 222. As to this latter determination, the jury answers ranged from 1935 to 1965. *Id.* at 222–23, 228–35.

238. *Lynch v. Merrell-Nat'l Lab.,* 646 F. Supp. 856, 861–62 (D. Mass. 1986), *aff'd*, 830 F.2d 1190 (1st Cir. 1987).

239. *Brock v. Merrell Dow Pharmaceuticals, Inc.,* 874 F.2d 307, 310 (5th Cir.) (noting that inconsistent jury verdicts suggest that appellate courts should resolve such questions), *modified*, 884 F.2d 166 (5th Cir. 1989), *cert. denied*, 494 U.S. 1064 (1990); see *Turpin v. Merrell Dow Pharmaceuticals, Inc.,* 959 F.2d 1349, 1349 (6th Cir. 1992), *cert. denied*, 113 S. Ct. 84 (1992); *DeLuca*

v. Merrell Dow Pharmaceuticals, Inc., 911 F.2d 941, 951–52 (3d Cir. 1990), *aff'd*, 6 F.3d 778 (3d Cir. 1993), *cert. denied*, 114 S. Ct. 691 (1994).

240. A question related to verdict consistency is damages consistency. Once the defendant's liability has been adjudicated or conceded, one intriguing solution to damage inconsistency is to average damage awards from a representative sample of cases chosen for trial and apply this result to untried cases. The court in *Cimino v. Raymark Industries* adopted this approach. 751 F. Supp. 649, 664–65 (E.D. Tex. 1990). This solution greatly reduces transaction costs, produces a better estimate of the plaintiffs' "true" damages than any individual verdict, and promotes fairness between different plaintiffs. See Glen O. Robinson & Kenneth S. Abraham, *Collective Justice in Tort Law*, 78 Va. L. Rev. 1481, 1490–96 (1992); Michael J. Saks & Peter David Blanck, *Justice Improved: The Unrecognized Benefits of Aggregation and Sampling in the Trial of Mass Torts*, 44 Stan. L. Rev. 815, 815 (1992).

241. See Galanter, *supra* note 228, at 388–93; Francis McGovern, *Toward a Functional Approach for Managing Complex Litigation*, 53 U. Chi. L. Rev. 440, 478–83 (1986).

242. In *Brock v. Merrell Dow Pharmaceuticals, Inc.*, for example, the court was concerned that inconsistent verdicts would over-deter defendants and thus hinder the development of new drugs. 874 F.2d 307, 310, *modified*, 884 F.2d 166 (5th Cir. 1989), *cert. denied*, 494 U.S. 1046 (1990); see Alan Golanski, *Judicial Scrutiny of Expert Testimony in Environmental Tort Litigation*, 9 Pace Envtl. L. Rev. 399, 465 (1992).

243. See *In re Japanese Electronic Products Antitrust Litig.*, 631 F.2d 1069, 1084–85 (3d Cir. 1980) (due process considerations may create a complex case exception to the right to a jury trial).

244. William V. Luneberg & Mark Nordenberg, *Specially Qualified Juries and Expert Nonjury Tribunals: Alternatives for Coping with the Complexities of Modern Civil Litigation*, 67 Va. L. Rev. 887 (1981); see Lempert, *supra* note 224.

245. Sanders, *From Science to Evidence*, *supra* note 25, at 9.

246. *Id.* at 5 n.16.

247. *Richardson v. Richardson-Merrell, Inc.*, 857 F.2d 823 (D.C. Cir. 1988), *cert. denied*, 493 U.S. 882 (1989).

248. *Brock v. Merrell Dow Pharmaceuticals, Inc.*, 874 F.2d 307 (5th Cir.), *modified*, 884 F.2d 166 (5th Cir. 1989), *cert. denied*, 494 U.S. 1046 (1990).

249. *Ealy v. Richardson-Merrell, Inc.*, 897 F.2d 159 (D.C. Cir.), *cert. denied*, 498 U.S. 950 (1990).

250. See Susan R. Poulter, *Science and Toxic Torts: Is there a Rational Solution to the Problem of Causation?*, 7 High Tech. L.J. 189, 193–94 (1992).

251. Green, *supra* note 57, at 677.

252. This risk exists for incautious sufficiency decisions as well. The best example of this is *Brock*'s requirement that plaintiffs present statistically significant epidemiological evidence of a relationship between Bendectin use and their injury. *Brock*, 874 F.2d at 313–15.

253. Although there may be relatively few efficiency gains in a particular case, especially where *DeLuca*-like hearings are required, the restrictive admissibility rulings may have a chilling effect across the entire congregation of

cases and cause plaintiffs to postpone or forego litigation that enjoys a slim chance of success.

254. One possibility would be to define certain bodies of knowledge as "social framework" information and allow the court to instruct the jury on this framework as the court instructs the jury on the "legal framework," it should use in deciding the case. See Laurens Walker & John Monahan, *Social Frameworks: A New Use of Social Science in Law*, 73 Va. L. Rev. 559 (1987).
255. See Margaret A. Berger, *Procedural Paradigms for Applying the* Daubert *Text*, 78 Minn. L. Rev. 1345 (1994).
256. Special Committee on Jury Comprehension, Jury Comprehension in Complex Cases i-ii (1989) [hereinafter Jury Comprehension]. The Committee engaged Elizabeth Loftus, Jane Goodman and Edith Green to conduct the study. *Id.*
257. This judgment is based on Richard O. Lempert's article, *Civil Juries and Complex Cases: Taking Stock after Twelve Years*. See Lempert, *supra* note 224. Lempert examined thirteen complex cases and rated each on a three point difficulty scale: low, moderate, and high. *Id.* at 185–90. The trade secret case and two others were scored high. *Id.* at 185–90, tbl. 6.1.
258. Jury Comprehension, *supra* note 256, at 103.
259. *Id.* at 54. Jurors in other complex cases have similar problems when the science is difficult to understand. See Sanders, *Jury Deliberation*, *supra* note 101, at 49–51.
260. *Id.* at 45.
261. Sanders, *From Science to Evidence*, *supra* note 25, at 61.
262. For a valuable discussion of the shortcomings of present methods of introducing expert testimony, see Samuel Gross, *Expert Evidence*, 1991 Wis. L. Rev. 1113 (1991).
263. Sanders, *From Science to Evidence*, *supra* note 25, at 40.
264. For example, several jurors interviewed from the *Havner* Bendectin trial perceived the epidemiological evidence to be no more probative than animal studies or *in vitro* studies on the question of whether the drug is a teratogen. Sanders, *Jury Deliberation*, *supra* note 101, at 62.
265. Fed. R. Evid. 803(18).
266. Peter Schuck, *Multi-Culturalism Redux: Science, Law and Politics*, 11 Yale L. & Pol'y Rev. 1 (1993) (discussing the differing cultures of science, law and politics).
267. *Id.* at 21; see Sheila Jasanoff, *What Judges Should Know About the Sociology of Science*, 32 Jurimetrics J. 345, 354 (1992) (making the same distinction).
268. "[E]xpert testimony can be perceived to be a challenge to certain fundamental concepts implicit in the structure of trials in the common law tradition, which calls into question whether the common law mode of trial prevalent in the United States can accommodate expert testimony without substantial change."

     Ronald J. Allen & Joseph S. Miller, *The Common Law Theory of Experts: Deference or Education?*, 87 Nw. U. L. Rev. 1131, 1131 (1993).
269. Schuck, *supra* note 266, at 18.
270. Jasanoff, *supra* note 267, at 347–48.
271. *Id.* at 353–54.
272. The Special Committee of the ABA Section of Litigation concluded that jurors are not too impressed with experts and dismiss many of them as

hired guns. Jury Comprehension, *supra* note 256, at 40. Other research reflects similar attitudes. See Neil Vidmar, *Assessing the Impact of Statistical Evidence, A Social Science Perspective, in* The Evolving Role, *supra* note 227, at 296–97. The perception that experts overwhelm jurors simply because they are experts is unfounded. As a juror in an asbestos case reported: "The expert testimony was not a real factor in our decision, except in the very backhanded sense that it lent medical credence to any result." Jane Goodman et al., *What Confuses Jurors in Complex Cases*, Trial, Nov. 1985, at 65, 68.

273. Jasanoff has noted that much, if not all, of what passes for clinical ecology may be excluded because it violates basic canons of science. Jasanoff, *supra* note 267, at 355.

274. Of course, the term "normal" is itself difficult to describe. At its core, however, may reside the idea of an "empiricist repertoire," the conversations scientists hold when they are not attacking each other's accounts of reality. Jasanoff, *supra* note 267, at 348. See generally G. Nigel Gilbert & Michael J. Mulkay, *Opening Pandora's Box: A Sociological Analysis of Scientist's Discourse* (1984). "Normal" science may occasionally cease to exist in an area where science itself becomes so politicized that the scientific community divides into camps that constantly attack the other side's account of reality. Revealingly, this sometimes occurs when the law "captures" an area of science and uses it to resolve very controversial disputes. See Eleanor P. Wolf, Trial and Error: The Detroit School Segregation Case 335 n.34 (1981).

275. See Sanders, *From Science to Evidence*, *supra* note 25, at 67–82.

276. Specifically, the bifurcation of trials serves this end. It minimizes the parties' ability to construct presentations that invite the factfinder to trade a weak case of causation off against a stronger case of negligence. Sanders, *From Science to Evidence*, *supra* note 25, at 52. Some oppose bifurcation because it promotes "truth" over "justice." See *In re Beverly Hills Fire Litigation,* 695 F.2d 207, 217 (6th Cir. 1982), *cert. denied*, 461 U.S. 929 (1983); Roger Trangsrud, *Mass Trials in Mass Tort Cases: A Dissent*, 1989 U. Ill. L. Rev. 69, 80–82 (1989).

277. Robert L. Rabin, *Some Thoughts on the Efficacy of a Mass Toxics Administrative Compensation Scheme*, 52 Md. L. Rev. 951 (1993); Robinson & Abraham, *supra* note 240, at 1481–83.

278. See Sheila Jasanoff, *Acceptable Evidence in a Pluralistic Society, in* Acceptable Evidence: Science and Values in Risk Management 29 (Deborah G. Mayo & Rachelle D. Hollander eds., 1991) (comparing British and American regulatory approaches to risk).

279. Huber, *Galileo's Revenge, supra* note 13, ch. 7. But see Kenneth J. Chesebro, *Galileo's Retort: Peter Huber's Junk Scholarship*, 42 Am. U. L. Rev. 1637 (1993) (criticizing Huber's conclusions).

Part III
Post-Trial:
Improving Jury Decisionmaking

The civil jury is surely the most unusual feature of the American justice system. A few other nations rely on lay deliberation in criminal cases or use semi-professional, non-lawyer participants in legal decision making. But no other nation places so much responsibility in the hands of ordinary citizens chosen for no other reason than that they are ordinary citizens.

If the jury is our most distinctive institution, it may also be our most beleagured. Criticism has flowed freely for decades, replete with calls to abolish or dramatically scale back the right to trial by jury.[1] Jurors, we are told, do not decide on the basis of facts. They are moved by the eloquence (or not) of counsel. They are swayed by unfair biases and irrational prejudices. They lack perspective and routinely render verdicts that are disproportionate and excessively harsh. They are incapable of handling complicated evidence. And so on. Of course, the jury is not without defenders, and each of these criticisms has been answered by proponents of lay deliberation and the common sense of the common man or woman.

Back in the 1970s and 80s, the hot issue was whether juries should be permitted to decide complex cases. The papers were full of stories about high profile cases like the breakup of Ma Bell and the IBM antitrust litigation, and this, naturally, led critics to question the appropriateness of letting untrained lay persons decide the fate of an industry.[2] Today, such cases have been eclipsed by new and different problems. With the emergence of the mass tort, critics and reformers of the jury have turned their attention to the problem of excessive verdicts. Punitive damages receive the most attention, of course, including considerable scrutiny from the Supreme Court.[3] But commentators have also focused on other elements of "soft" damages, like awards for pain and suffering.[4]

Choosing a dollar amount as punishment or to compensate pain and suffering is necessarily a matter of judgment. It calls for instinct and intuition as well as evaluation, for subjective impressions as much as objective interpretation. As such, it involves the exercise of an especially broad discretion, which raises all the strongest objections to (and justifications for) the use of juries.

Complaints notwithstanding, the jury obviously is not about to be abolished. The question thus becomes: is there a problem with jury awards, and, if so, what can or should we do about it? The articles in this section explore these issues. They focus specifically on the problem of damages for pain and suffering, as it seems most useful to examine the general question of jury control in the context of a particular problem. But the approaches and analyses in the articles, as well as their proposals for reform, may be equally applicable in other contexts, like punitive damages.

Certainly there seems to be a problem. Jurors asked to award damages for pain and suffering receive little or no useful guidance from the court, but are merely told to choose what they deem an appropriate amount based on their collective conscience. Not surprisingly, as Oscar Chase explains in the article that begins this Part, numerous studies have found disparities in the resulting awards that seem difficult to justify. To date, the only legislative response has been to impose caps on damages, a solution that has found favor in a number of states and is currently being debated in Congress.[5] But, as Judyth Pendell and John Evancho explain in their contribution to the discussion, dollar caps present a slew of problems and disadvantages: they are arbitrary, they discriminate unfairly against young and severely injured claimants, and they afford juries no guidance. There is even evidence suggesting that they may not be all that effective in limiting awards. Professors Baldus, MacQueen, and Woodworth point out that caps also fail to address the problem of inadequate jury awards and do nothing about problems of inconsistency and arbitrariness among awards below the cap.

Rather than simply cutting awards off at some arbitrary point, a different–and better–solution might be to improve the process by which damages are assessed. Problems of variability and excessiveness may, for example, be due to the jurors' lack of information. Under present law, information about verdicts in other cases is inadmissible. Appellate courts may examine such cases on review to determine whether a particular verdict is excessive, but jurors are denied the information. Such an approach is ironic, to say the least. We ask people who have never before made such a decision to value a harm, and we ask them to do it in a vacuum–with no sense of what awards in the past have looked like or what other juries have done when faced with similar problems. We ask jurors to act as the voice of the community while depriving them of access to what the community thinks.

The articles by Oscar Chase and by Judyth Pendell and John Evancho propose to remedy this situation by giving jurors information about verdicts in prior cases. Such a proposal raises a host of difficult questions: Which verdicts should be presented and precisely what information about those verdicts should be included? Should jurors get detailed descriptions of all aspects of prior cases or only a barebones presentation of the most salient features? In what form should the data be presented? How should it be introduced at trial, and by whom? What instructions should the jury receive with the data? What should the effect be in subsequent review proceedings (both at the trial level and on appeal)?

Beyond questions of form and procedure lurk a variety of methodological issues: How will the data be gathered, and by whom? Can a data base be compiled and maintained at a cost that makes the effort worthwhile? Is it possible to make comparisons in a way that is fair and not misleading? Can we test the data for reliability? Can we trust jurors to use it properly?

The Chase and Pendell/Evancho articles each deal with both sorts of questions, though they differ in emphasis. Dean Chase concentrates on procedure, and his paper includes a detailed proposal for presenting such evidence to jurors, including a model instruction and many other essential details. Pendell and Evancho focus more on methodological problems, having conducted a careful study to test whether providing jurors with information about verdicts in comparable cases is feasible. Both Chase and Pendell/Evancho concentrate on New York, where data collection is relatively easy because juries are required to return verdicts that distinguish between different elements of damages and because a high precentage of the results are compiled and reported in a New York Jury Verdict Reporter. But while implementing a proposal along the lines suggested by these writers may be easiest in a state like New York, their studies suggest that implementation would not be much more difficult in other states.

Dean Chase proposes to inform jurors, in personal injury actions in which non-pecuniary damages are sought, of the range of awards made by other juries in the same state during a contemporaneous time period. The information would be provided in a chart constructed to allow comparison with similar cases in which damages were recovered (a sample chart is included in his paper). The chart would be described by the court in its instructions, and counsel would be free to comment on it during summation. The chart would be available to the jury during its deliberations. The jurors would not be bound by the information they receive, but could instead use it to inform their impression of what a "reasonable" award might be.

Pendell and Evancho set out to test the claim that such a proposal is infeasible or would require the creation of an elaborate (and expensive) data collection agency. They explore the possibility of providing the jurors with information based on what is available in the New York Jury Verdict Reporter, which reports how much of a total award was attributable to each component of the damages sought. Using a modification of the "injury severity scale" created by the National Association of Insurance Commissioners, they reviewed 1,843 cases decided between 1981 and 1992 in which damages were awarded for pain and suffering. The integrity of their categorization was tested and confirmed by a panel of physicians from the Harvard Medical School. Pendell and Evancho conclude that this information is sufficient to aid jurors and that it can be compiled and presented in a cost-efficient manner.

Reform along the lines suggested by Chase or Pendell and Evancho could easily be adopted. It could be utilized by judges deciding individual cases, though it would obviously be more convenient and less expensive to make this change by rule or, better still, by legislation. Yet some observers will find these proposals too radical a departure from the traditional conception of the jury's function, which is to make an individualized assessment of harm based solely on the facts of the particular case. For such critics, Professors Baldus, MacQueen, and Woodworth offer a different alternative: to strengthen the traditional judicial function of additur and remittitur review by providing similar information to judges.

As these commentators point out, courts in a number of jurisdictions, and especially federal courts sitting in diversity, have long engaged in some form of "comparative review." They do so, however, based on incomplete information, using an unnecessarily impressionistic methodology. Hence, Baldus, MacQueen, and Woodworth propose to strengthen additur/remittitur review by providing judges with better information and a more sophisticated method for making comparisons. They base their recommendations on a research project in which 461 cases from 20 states were examined to test the feasibility of what they call "enhanced additur/remittitur review."

While similar in broad outline to the Chase and Pendell/Evancho proposals, Professor Baldus and his co-authors capitalize on one distinct advantage of their approach: because the information will be presented to judges for review in post-trial proceedings, the nature of the review can be considerably more demanding. They recommend both a "qualitative" and a "quantitative" review method. Qualitative review entails identifying the characteristics of a case that are most salient to measuring pain and suffering, identifying a group of cases that share these characteristics, and comparing the relative level of the non-pecuniary harms and the damages awarded. To aid judges in this task, the authors have developed a system for making rudimentary qualitative comparisons.

This kind of qualitative comparison resembles what many courts already do. And while urging courts to perform this sort of analysis more frequently, Baldus, MacQueen, and Woodworth propose to enhance the process with a more rigorous form of quantitative comparison. This entails, among other things, adjusting previous awards for inflation, constructing a rank ordering of the cases, and revising the awards to reflect differences in the level of compensable harms. This last step is the most difficult and controversial one, so the authors ran a study to show that such comparisons were both feasible and reliable; the results reported in their paper are promising.

Proposals like these seem desirable. How can anyone oppose more informed decision making? Yet, as with all such changes, things are more complicated than they seem. The principal papers are thus followed by comments from three critics, each approaching the debate from a different angle. Gary Schwartz, a Professor of Law at UCLA, draws our attention to a number of subtle ways in which these proposals may be more difficult to implement than they seem; he proposes instead using a fixed schedule of damages for pain and suffering. Victor Schwartz, a member of the defense bar, asks us to consider whether so much solicitude for pain and suffering awards is even justified. Such awards, he maintains, are not an essential component of tort recover, but are a relatively recent innovation, driven by the financial interests of plaintiffs' attorneys. If damages for pain and suffering are difficult to implement and supervise, he suggests, perhaps we should consider abolishing them.

Paul Rheingold offers the opposite perspective, speaking (in his words) as "the plaintiff's lawyer on the panel." Rheingold argues that awards for pain and suffering do serve an important purpose in the tort system, both as compensation for wrong and as a deterrent. The system may not be perfect, he continues, but have the proponents of reform really made a case for changing it? Drawing on his experience in the courts, he argues that the present system of adversarial justice, combined with existing review of verdicts that are too low or too high, works well–or, at least, well enough. Plaintiffs who lie or exaggerate are exposed through cross-examination, and trial or appellate courts invariably scale down excessive awards. "The revisionists have a burden of proof," he concludes, "that I don't think they've met."

Professor Mark Geistfeld concludes this section with a brief report on the discussion that took place after the panel presentation. The central themes of these papers were sharpened and refined, with particular attention paid to the prospects for reform.

Notes

1. See, e.g., Jerome Frank, Law and the Modern Mind 180–81 (1930); Peck, *Do Juries Delay Justice?*, 18 F.R.D. 455 (1956); Burger, *Thinking the Unthinkable*, 31 Loyola L. Rev. 205 (1985).
2. See, e.g., Jorde, *The Seventh Amendment Right to Jury Trial of Antitrust Issues*, 69 Calif. L. Rev. 1 (1981); Kane, *Civil Jury Trial: The Case for Reasoned Iconoclasm*, 28 Hastings L. Rev. 1 (1976); Lempert, *Civil Juries and Complex Cases: Let's Not Rush to Judgment*, 80 Mich. L. Rev. 68 (1981).
3. See, e.g., Rustsad & Koenig, *The Historical Continuity of Punitive Damages Awards: Reforming the Tort Reformers*, 42 Am. U. L. Rev. 1269 (1993); Schwartz, *Mass Torts and Punitive Damages: A Comment*, 39 Vill. L. Rev. 415 (1994); Riggs, *Constitutionalizing Punitive Damages: The Limits of Due Process*, 52 Ohio St. L.J. 859 (1991). The Supreme Court has decided three significant punitive damages cases since 1989, see Browning-Ferris Indus. v. Kelco Disposal, Inc., 492 U.S. 257 (1989); Pacific Mutual Life Ins. Co; v. Haslip, 499 U.S. 1 (1991); TXO Prod. Corp. v. Alliance Resources Corp., 113 S. Ct. 2711 (1993), and it has granted certiorari to hear a fourth case during the 1995 Term, BMW of North America, Inc. v. Gore, No. 94–896.
4. See, e.g., American Bar Association, Report of the Action Commission to Improve the Tort Liability System 10–15 (1987); American Law Institute, Enterprise Responsibility for Personal Injury 199–230 (1991); Blumstein, Bovbjerg & Sloan, *Beyond Tort Reform: Developing Better Tools for Assessing Damages for Personal Injury*, 8 Yale J. Reg. 171 (1991); Bovbjerg, Sloan, & Blumstein, *Public Policy: Valuing Life and Limb in Tort: Scheduling "Pain and Suffering"*, 83 Nw. U.L. Rev. 908 (1989); Leebron, *Final Moments: Damages for Pain and Suffering Prior to Death*, 64 N.Y.U. L. Rev. 256 (1989); Schnapper, *Judges Against Juries*, 1989 Wisc. L. Rev. 237.
5. See, e.g., W. Va. Code §55–7B-8; Wash. Rev. Code §4.56.250; H.R. 956, 104th Cong., 1st Sess. §203(a) (1995).

Helping Jurors Determine Pain and Suffering Awards*

Oscar G. Chase**

Introduction

The process by which pain and suffering damages are awarded in the United States has been aptly called "procedurally simple but analytically impenetrable."[1] As the same author goes on to say, "The law provides no guidance, in terms of any benchmark, standard figure, or method of analysis, to aid the jury in the process of determining an appropriate award."[2] This state of affairs has prompted the attention of several commentators who have criticized the existing regime and suggested a variety of thoughtful proposals to improve the situation.[3] In addition to describing the problem and some of the suggested solutions in the literature, I will present a new proposal.

---

*A version of this article was previously published in 23 Hofstra L. Rev. 763 (1995), and we thank the Hofstra Law Review for permission to reprint it.

**Professor of Law and Vice Dean, New York University School of Law. I appreciate the valuable research assistance of Gail Balcerzak, John F. Brown, Arlo M. Chase, Kevin L. Mintzer, and Shari L. Rosenblum. I thank the Institute of Judicial Administration and Aetna Life and Casualty for providing financial assistance for this article. Helpful comments have been provided by Samuel Estreicher, Mark Geistfeld, Lewis Kornhauser, David W. Leebron, Burt Neuborne, Linda Silberman and Peter Tillers. All the views expressed in this paper are my own, and I am responsible for any errors it contains.

Apart from those who would dispense with non-pecuniary damages entirely, all of the suggestions of which I am aware (including my own) seek to enhance analytic coherence. But all do so at the price of procedural simplicity, and most would restrict the scope of the jury's authority. If reform is to be done at all, the question how must be answered by setting procedural loss against analytic gain. The proposal offered here preserves the power of the jury, enhances the jurors' ability to make an informed decision, and eschews procedural complexity.

I. The Current Regime, Its Defects, and Its Costs

Non-pecuniary damages have been criticized for different flaws by different observers. Most basic is the claim that they are without justification and should be abolished.[4] Other opponents of pain and suffering awards would cap them at some maximum dollar level, an argument that has found favor with some state legislatures.[5] These attacks on the substance of pain and suffering law are not the focus of this paper. They should, however, remind us that failure to mediate the deficiencies—the analytic impenetrability—of the current regime may be used by opponents of full tort recoveries as a justification for baby-and-bath water solutions.[6]

A less fundamental but still trenchant criticism goes to the standardless nature of the jury's task. Reviewing courts[7] are free (as jurors are not) to use information about prior awards in similar cases, but they too are hampered by lack of information and of commonly accepted principle.

An inescapable reality of the pain and suffering conundrum is that tort law requires the monetization of a "product" for which there is no market and therefore no market price. This largely explains the lamented fact that the jurors who must undertake the monetization are given no "absolute" standard by which to do it. There is none to give them. Each juror must bring or create his or her own standard in the courtroom.[8] Proposals for legislatively enacted mandatory schedules do not solve this problem. Although they might moderate the related problem of variation among awards, they merely shift the locus of responsibility to do the impossible and find the right level of compensation.

Consider the situation of a juror asked to find the right amount of money with which to compensate a plaintiff for suffering endured at the hands of the defendant. Our juror will have heard the plaintiff's testimony about the nature and severity of the suffering and perhaps observed something of its source (as, for example, if the plaintiff is paraplegic). He or she will have heard expert testimony about the severity and likely duration of the pain, perhaps seen a video tape of the plaintiff's distressful daily regimen, and will have been exhorted to be generous by the plaintiff's lawyer and reasonable by the defendant's. The typical jury charge on the issue gives no real guidance at all. In New York, the Pattern Jury Instructions, although not binding on courts, are commonly used. They prescribe these instructions:

> PJI 2:280. DAMAGES–PERSONAL INJURY–INJURY AND PAIN AND SUFFERING
>
> If you decide for the plaintiff on the question of liability you must include in your verdict an award of money for the injury you find that plaintiff (decedent) suffered and for conscious pain and suffering caused by defendant.
>
> Conscious pain and suffering means pain and suffering of which there was some level of awareness by plaintiff (decedent).
>
> Plaintiff is entitled to recover a sum of money which will justly and fairly compensate (him, her) for the injury and for the conscious pain and suffering to date.[9]

Another standard source, Jury Instructions on Damages in Tort Actions, is interesting for its effort to provide more specifics:

> SECTION 6–17 PHYSICAL PAIN AND SUFFERING–PAST AND FUTURE
>
> In assessing damages, if you have occasion to do so, the law allows you to award to plaintiff a sum that will reasonably compensate him/her for any past physical pain, as well as pain that is reasonably certain to be suffered in the future as a result of the defendant's wrongdoing.
>
> There are no objective guidelines by which you can measure the money equivalent of this element of injury; the only real measuring stick, if it can be so described, is your collective enlightened conscience. You should consider all the evidence bearing on the nature of the injuries, the certainty of future pain, the severity and the likely duration thereof.
>
> In this difficult task of putting a money figure on an aspect of injury that does not readily lend itself to an evaluation in terms of money, you should try to be as objective, calm, and dispassionate as the situation will permit, and not be unduly swayed by considerations of sympathy.[10]

In the attempt to give the jury some guidance, these instructions may introduce still greater confusion. What is a "collective enlightened conscience"? How much sympathy does it take to be "unduly swayed"? If there are no "objective guidelines," how should one proceed? What tools can one use? The open-ended quality of the jurors' task leads to three sorts of criticism of the process: that it introduces unwarranted variations in result and is therefore unpredictable; that it allows jurors to use inappropriate criteria; and that it diminishes public confidence in the legal system because of the apparently arbitrary nature of the process. Each of these is discussed in turn below.

A. Unacceptable Variations in Jury Awards

Both anecdotal and empirical evidence indicate that the disparity between awards for pain and suffering among apparently similar cases defies rational explanation. Bovbjerg, Sloan and Blumstein compiled a data base of 898 cases drawn from jury verdict reports in Florida and Kansas City.[11] They found that total compensation awarded varies with the severity of injury, but that this factor explained only two-fifths of the magnitude of variation.[12] Their data "reveals that variation in awards is enormous. Within an individual severity level, the highest valuation can be scores of times larger than the lowest."[13] They find, nonetheless, that "the current system works rationally and fairly in an aggregate sense."[14] That is, "the fairness between separate categories of injury is rather good. The main problem is the absence of 'horizontal' equity—the extent of variation within a single category."[15] And, as might be expected, "The distribution of awards for non-economic loss shows even wider dispersion than the distribution for total awards. . . . Thus, awards for pain and suffering and other intangible losses may be unreasonably inconsistent within the relatively discrete and unambiguous categories for injury severity."[16]

A similar conclusion was reached by David Leebron on the basis of his study of pain and suffering awards in 256 wrongful death cases.[17] By limiting his analysis to death cases he was able to eliminate much of the variation among fact patterns that might explain award variations. He concludes that "[a]s currently applied . . . the jury system, coupled with deferential judicial review, produces an unacceptable degree of variation in the awards."[18] A more recent survey of wrongful death awards supports Leebron's conclusion. Aaron J. Broder reported on the non-pecuniary damages awarded to victims of the Korean Air Line disaster, finding that the ten awards made by January, 1994, ranged from zero to $1.4 million.[19] Since the victims all died in virtually the same circumstances, such variations can be exlained only by arguably irrelevant factors such as the venue, the skill of the attorney, or (most probably) the predilection of the trier of fact in each case.

Variability is a problem primarily because it undermines the legal system's claim that like cases will be treated alike. The promise of equal justice under law is an important justification for our legal system. Variability is also said to create instrumental defects, i.e., it makes it harder to settle cases, thus adding unnecessary transaction costs to the tort system and delaying payment to needy plaintiffs.[20] Unpredictability also leads to inefficiencies in the form too many or too few precautions taken by affected industries and insurers.[21]

B. Jurors' Resort to Inappropriate Criteria

Deprived of any standard but their "collective enlightened conscience,"[22] it would be surprising if jurors, consciously or not, did not sometimes employ criteria for decision making that the formal legal system regards as inappropriate. This can be a more serious problem than juror whimsy, depending on the criterion applied.

There is disturbing evidence that some jurors are affected by the race of the litigants. In their study of verdicts in Cook County, Illinois, Chin and Peterson report that "race seemed to have a pervasive influence on the outcomes" of civil jury trials.[23] After adjusting for case types, injuries, and characteristics of other parties, black plaintiffs and defendants lost more often than other parties. When black plaintiffs did win, they recovered only seventy-four per cent of what other plaintiffs got for the same injury. (The authors do not report whether the latter figure was controlled for income levels of the plaintiffs.) On the other hand, awards against black defendants were ten per cent less than against other defendants.

Other investigators have found that the plaintiff's gender is influential on awards. A study using mock jurors found a propensity to award greater economic damages to female plaintiffs suing for a man's wrongful death than the reverse.[24] Leebron's data on pain and suffering awards in wrongful death cases also indicated that awards for male victims were less than those for female victims.[25] At a minimum, further investigation of the impact of race and gender is warranted, for the evidence we have only begins to suggest the dimensions of the problem. It suggests, however, that we are right to worry about the degree to which our standardless system allows bias to play a role.

The "deep pocket" effect has been another source of concern. Chin and Peterson found that corporations and government agencies were more likely to be found liable than individuals and that higher damages were assessed against them.[26] These findings were corroborated in another study using data gathered from twenty-seven states.[27] This need not suggest an anti-institution bias or an exercise in wealth redistribution. It may be that jurors conclude that corporations have more ability to act rationally than individuals and so should be held to a higher level of responsibility. But whatever the explanation, it seems that some jurors are bringing an inappropriate element into the damages deliberation.

Media coverage of jury verdicts and the tort "crisis" may also improperly affect actual jury behavior. One would expect the media to report only exceptional cases. To test this proposition we surveyed the personal injury awards reported in two New York newspapers over a six year period and compared the verdicts reported to the median and average actual verdicts during the same period. As predicted, the verdicts reported in the media exceeded the median actual verdict geometrically. The results are reported in Tables IA, IB, and II.

Table IA
N.Y. Times Personal Injury Award Reports
(All awards in millions of dollars)

Year	#	High	Low	Avg	Med
1988	16	25.0	.75	7.6	7.0
1989	16	200.0	.5	20.5	5.5
1990	13	15.1	.15	7.7	7.6
1991	17	30.7	.4	12.8	2.8
1992	19	127.0	.225	15.9	4.3
1993	14	163.9	1.0	25.3	10.1

Table IB
N.Y. Newsday Personal Injury Award Reports
(All awards in millions of dollars)

Year	#	High	Low	Avg	Med
1988	11	25.0	.75	6.7	4.75
1989	14	61.6	.02	9.8	4.6
1990	15	76.1	.12	11.5	6.1
1991	22	127.0	.4	9.2	1.5
1992	8	30.0	.5	6.2	2.4
1993	29	163.9	1.0	23.4	5.4

Tables IA and IB employ the following methodology:

If an award was reported in the same paper on more than one occasion, it was included in the data more than once if the reports appeared at least one week apart. This procedure was justified for two reasons. First, it is likely that a reader would recall an article referring to an award that had previously been reported if it was within one week. Second, higher awards tended to receive attention in a newspaper over the subsequent few days following every mention within the first week as a separate story would overly emphasize extremely large awards.

Only in cases where a defendent was found liable are included; no-liability findings were not recorded. Two reports are included in which multiple plaintiffs shared one award; the total award was recorded in the table as one award on the premise that a reader would recall the whole amount, not the average received by many plaintiffs. The two cases are an award of $30,700,000 reported by the New York Times on January 15, 1991, and an award of $7,150,000 reported in New York Newsday on December 16, 1988. If a jury award was subsequently reduced by a trial judge or an appellate court and the reduction was reported by the same newspaper, the lower figure reported at the later date was the only number recorded. If the adjustment was not reported in the same paper, the original jury award was recorded. Lastly, only personal injury cases, where pain and suffering damages could have been awarded, were included in the study.

Table II
Personal Injury Verdicts: 1988–1992
(Amounts in actual dollars)

	Year	Average	Median	Cases
A. Statewide (New York State)				
	1988	$882,940	$200,000	374
	1989	$1,107,381	$200,000	443
	1990	$1,086,383	$227,066	467
	1991	$851,128	$190,000	387
	1992	$964,553	$250,000	417
B. Metropolitan New York				
	1988	$967,432	$248,212	306
	1989	$1,138,104	$250,000	335
	1990	$1,121,312	$263,897	332
	1991	$954,996	$225,000	253
	1992	$1,034,039	$274,000	294
C. All other counties (Upstate)				
	1988	$374,180	$85,000	68
	1989	$300,378	$139,338	108
	1990	$858,097	$150,000	135
	1991	$490,385	$124,530	134
	1992	$637,546	$125,000	123

Only cases where plaintiffs recovered are included, not defense verdicts. Only personal injury cases are covered, and only jury verdicts are included. Figures courtesy of New York Jury Verdict Reporter.

To the extent that future jurors base their decisions on knowledge of past awards gained from the media, at least two possible problems arise. Jurors may tend to over-compensate because they have an unrealistic sense of the allowable range of recoveries. Alternatively, jurors may under-compensate because of their dislike for the "windfall" aspect of some very large awards.[28]

At least some players in the tort system apparently believe that mass media can affect verdicts: Institutions with major stakes in the outcomes produced by the tort system have used advertising to attempt to influence aggregate jury verdicts by stating the case for moderation.[29]

In short, jurors bring some information about levels of compensation actually made in tort cases with them when they arrive at the courthouse, but it is not very reliable information. It is wildly inflated.

C. Costs to the Justice System

Standardless pain and suffering verdicts may add to the cost of tort litigation not only by adding difficulties to the settlement process, but also by making deliberation in cases that are tried more protracted. Juries may (and this is conjectural) have difficulty agreeing on the right range when there is no guidance, and their unwitting departure from limits that courts think are appropriate undoubtedly adds to the frequency with which judges must review their verdicts.

Reviewing courts may at least turn to reported decisions to determine what other courts and juries have done with like cases. While not all courts engage in such an examination, the practice is well-established in some jurisdictions.[30] Yet courts that are willing to undertake a comparative review are ill-informed about the vast majority of cases because aggregate trends are not available to them. The cost here is not only the inefficiency of having each court undertake its own search for relevant data in reviewing each award, but the perhaps larger cost to the integrity of the system because it is hard to understand why judicial awards are more principled than jury verdicts when the process used to reach the decision is just as handicapped by ignorance, even if not to the same degree.[31]

II. Previously Proposed Solutions

The ABA Action Commission to Improve the Tort Liability System made three recommendations directed to pain and suffering damages. First, trial and appellate courts should make greater use of additur and remittitur to set aside verdicts that are "clearly disproportionate to community expectations," but there should not be ceilings on pain and suffering damages.[32] Second, one or more "tort award commissions" should be established to gather and report information that would be useful in "the framing of jury instructions, the exercise of the power of additur and remittitur, and the process of settling cases."[33] Third, "[o]ptions should be explored to provide more guidance to the jury on the appropriate range of damages to be awarded for pain and suffering in a particular case."[34] No specific method of providing juries with the desired guidance was endorsed, but the Comment states that some members would have the trial judge suggest a non-binding range of high and low awards. The Comment also notes that the data gathered by the proposed tort award commission could be useful in developing the guidelines.

As will become apparent, my own proposal attempts to put flesh on the bones of the Commission's recommendation.

The ALI Reporters' Study on Enterprise Liability for Personal Injury also recommends against mandatory ceilings for pain and suffering damages.[35] It instead suggests adoption of a threshold of serious injury that would have to be met before pain and suffering damages could be obtained.[36] The Study found that minor injuries tend to be overcompensated, so a floor would eliminate this problem, while freeing money for more serious injury victims.[37] The Study also recommends the development of "[m]eaningful guidelines" to aid juries in assessing pain and suffering damages.[38] "The guidelines should be based on a scale of inflation-adjusted damage amounts attached to a number of disability profiles that range in severity from the relatively moderate to the gravest injuries." The discussion of the guidelines indicates that the authors of the study held somewhat differing views about the degree to which the guidelines should be binding on the jury.[39] The proposal presented below adopts a non-binding approach.

In their chapter in this volume, Baldus, MacQueen and Woodworth focus less on guiding the jury than on making judicial review of jury verdicts more rational. They recommend using prior approved awards, inflation and other variables to construct a systematic method of review.

Bovbjerg, Sloan and Blumstein have proposed four specific methods of controlling jury unpredictability. One suggestion is to create an award matrix.[40] Each plaintiff's injury would be classified by severity level and plaintiff's age. The resulting "cells" of the matrix would be keyed to values for pain and suffering. The values would be obtained by averaging previous awards for similar injuries to similar plaintiffs. Juries would be free to determine the cell into which each case fell, but would have to award the exact amount indicated. A second proposal is to use standardized injury scenarios with associated dollar values.[41] The jury would be provided with a few relevant scenarios and instructed to determine which most closely approximates the plaintiff's situation and to base their pain and suffering award on it. The third alternative is "a set of floors and ceilings bounding jury awards at both the high and low ends of valuation."[42] The categories would be constructed from prior award averages, using age and severity levels. In a separate article, the same authors present a fourth alternative.[43] It would also provide aggregations of previous awards to the jury. Jurors would have to explain awards that fell in the top or lowest quartile of the range. Unexplained outliers would be presumed improper by reviewing courts.

Common to all four of these proposals is the development of a data bank of prior awards in the jurisdiction.[44]

III. An Information-Oriented Proposal

The various proposals discussed above differ primarily in the degree of flexibility they preserve for the jury. My own proposal is oriented toward preserving jury autonomy more strongly than most of the others. It assumes that providing jurors with more information about prior awards

Figure 1
Prior Pain and Suffering Awards in New York State for Persons in the Age Bracket N–N During Years 1989–1994, Keyed to Level of Severity of the Most Significant Injury

Injury Severity Level	Median Award	Highest Award	Lowest Award
1. Emotional only; fright, no physical damage			
2. Temporary insignificant; lacerations, contusions, minor scars			
3. Temporary minor; infection, fracture			
4. Temporary major; burns, brain damage, surgical material left in patient			
5. Permanent minor; loss of fingers, loss or damage to organs, non-disabling injuries			
6. Permanent significant; deafness, loss of limb, loss of eye, loss of one kidney or lung			
7. Permanent major; paraplegia, blindness, loss of two limbs, brain damage			
8. Permanent grave; quadriplegia, severe brain damage, lifelong care or fatal prognosis			
9. [Death*]			

* It would be better not to provide awards from wrongful death cases to jurors considering non-death cases, since the considerations are very different and the figures could lead to confusion.

will make their verdicts more rational. Thus, less control of jurors will be required. Some might see this as a first reform—to be followed by more drastic measures if problems persist. This proposal takes seriously the invitation of the ABA Commission to explore methods for providing more guidance to jurors.

I propose to inform jurors in all personal injury actions in which non-pecuniary damages are sought of the range of awards made by other

Figure 1 *(continued)*

←

Instruction to jurors: The conditions following each severity category in the are merely cxamplcs. They are intended to help you determine the severity level of the injuries suffered by the plaintiff. The awards reported on the chart inform you of the range of awards made for pain and suffering in other New York State cases for the indicated level of severity of injury during the past five years. All figures reflect only awards reached after a trial and any appeal. The median number is the mid-point of all reported cases. In other words, in half of the cases the award was higher than the median and in half it was lower.

You are not bound by the range of awards reported here. These awards are provided to help you, the representatives of the community, as you determine the right amount of money that should be awarded to the plaintiff to compensate [him/her] for pain and suffering. If you believe that some aspect of the plaintiff's injuries or suffering justifies a higher or lower award than was previously made for other plaintiffs who suffered the same severity level of injury, you may award that greater or lesser amount. After you determine the severity level, fill in the answer to the following special verdicts.

1. We find that the most significant injury suffered by the plaintiff falls in severity level __.
2. We find that the plaintiff's award for pain and suffering is $__.

juries in the same state for such damages during a contemporaneous time period.[45] The information would be provided in a chart constructed to allow comparison with roughly similar cases in which plaintiffs' verdicts were recovered.[46] The chart would be described by the court in its instructions, and counsel would be free to comment on it during summation. The chart would be available to the jury during deliberation, along with appropriate instructions on its purpose and related special verdicts. The jurors would not be bound by the information they receive. Presumably they would use it to form a general impression of a "reasonable" award.

More specifically, the chart would grid the median, high, and low sums awarded (after any judicial reduction or reversal) for each of the severity levels on the widely-accepted nine-point injury severity scale for persons in the plaintiff's age bracket.[47] The jury would be instructed to determine the injury severity level of the most significant injury suffered by the plaintiff due to the defendant's culpable conduct and to report this as a separate itemized verdict.[48] The jury would then be asked

Figure 2
Previous Pain and Suffering Awards in New York State During Years 1980–1987, Keyed to Level of Severity of the Most Significant Injury

Injury Severity Level	Median Award	Highest Award	Lowest Award
9. [Death*]	$70,000	$200,000	$50

* Jurors would be given award information at severity 1–8 levels in each case that did not involve death. In death cases they would get only the award information for death cases. The reason is that in all other categories other than death, the jurors' fact finding duties include choice of a severity level; no such issue arises in death cases. In death cases it would be needlessly confusing for the jurors to be given award reports for other severity levels. In non-death cases, the awards given in death cases are irrelevant. I am grateful to Mark Geistfeld for his contribution on this point.

to determine the award for pain and suffering as a separate item of damages.

A sample chart with model instructions (but without dollar amounts) is presented in Figure 1. Numbers are not included because the damage awards by severity category have not yet been calculated.

A rough idea of what the figures might looke like for one injury level can be constructed using Leebron's data for wrongful death cases, which include all the wrongful death cases he could find using the West Reporter System and "other means."[49] I constructed the grid in Figure 2 from the thirteen New York cases reported by Leebron in which an award for pain and suffering was made and survived judicial review. Because his data did not capture ages, I report all cases without regard to the victim's age.

If this proposal is adopted, determinations are likely to be more consistent with those in which similar facts were at issue. One can never be sure how jurors will use a chart such as that presented in Figures 1 and 2, but it is reasonable to expect them to try to develop a collective sense of the relative nature of the decedent's suffering by considering its length, intensity, and the person's level of consciousness (all of which will no doubt have been brought out at trial and discussed in summation). Jurors moved by what they conclude was extreme suffering by the plaintiff will probably return a verdict at or even above the highest award on the chart, but they are unlikely to return a verdict that is multiples higher or lower.

Because the jurors will be able to engage in a more informed deliberative process, they will be somewhat discouraged from relying on factors the formal legal system regards as extraneous, such as the race or gender of the plaintiff, the deep pocket of the defendant, or the context in which the injury occurred (*e.g.*, auto accident versus medical malpractice). Jurors will be less inclined to rely on an impressionistic sense of what the right level of damages should be as garnered from casual reading of newspaper articles or insurance company advertising campaigns. I expect that jurors making damage determinations under the proposed system will also develop more respect for the litigation process because of the more informed way in which they participate in it.

Other major actors in the personal injury litigation will also have access to improved information. The parties will be able to make a better informed assessment of the value of the case. Whether or not this leads to an increase in settlements, it could lead to more rational decision-making about whether to settle.

Courts confronted with attacks on verdicts, whether on appeal or in post-trial motions, should have more confidence in the jury's result because it will have been based on better information. Even a verdict that departs from the norm awarded for such injuries should be entitled to greater weight than at present, because in the absence of an indication of extraneous factors the higher verdict presumably reflects the jurors' collective sense that there was something anomalous about the case. Alternatively, a court would seem to have absolutely no reason to tamper with an award that falls within the high-low range. Thus, my proposal would strengthen our commitment to the ideal of the jury as the finder of facts. Courts that conclude that for some reason additur or remittitur is indicated will have a better sense of the appropriate degree of change in the light of the full range of experience in the jurisdiction, rather than having to rely entirely on the few (perhaps atypical) cases that were the subject of a published appellate opinion.

Publication of the tables on which the proposed grid would be constructed would likely also be useful to insurers in rate-making and to policy makers in evaluating the health of the personal injury compensation system.[50]

The proposal presented here could be adopted in any jurisdiction that has or will develop the necessary data base. Like others who have addressed the problem, I conclude that development of better data is a key ingredient in bringing more predictability to the system. I urge this proposal to the special attention of New York policy makers. New York already has the material to construct a suitable data base in the New York Jury Verdict Reporter.[51] This data base can include non-pecuniary damages as a separate item of recovery because New York already requires itemized verdicts in all personal injury actions; jurors must make a separate finding of the "pain and suffering" award.[52] New York is also suitable because its courts (like those of some other jurisdictions) have recognized the value of prior verdicts and judicial decisions as guides for deciding whether to set aside or affirm jury damage verdicts.[53] It is hard to see why courts, but not jurors, construing the reasonableness of an award should have access to information about awards in similar cases.

In some respects, the proposed grid has strengths and weaknesses that are analogous to a jury aid that is already used in New York and elsewhere, the standard mortality tables. Based on aggregate data that change over time, these tables are not a valid predictor for discrete subsamples or for any individuals, but they are nonetheless often admitted into evidence or even made subjects of judicial notice.[54] Cautionary instructions are deemed sufficient to prevent the jury from undue reliance on them.[55]

In addition, current New York practice makes its courts peculiarly susceptible to erratic verdicts: a six-person jury is prescribed in civil cases and only five-sixths need agree to return a verdict.[56] Adoption of my proposal in New York would, however, allow that state to serve as a "laboratory" in which the approach could be tested and evaluated.

I close by highlighting several respects in which my proposal rests on policy choices that are different from those made by others. As discussed earlier, I recommend the retention of non-pecuniary damages, and I reject flat caps. Beyond that, the key decisional points in this strategy are:

A. Preservation of Jury Control Over the Award for Non-Pecuniary Damages

My proposal involves no new direct restrictions on powers currently enjoyed by the jury. Jurors would simply be better informed than they are now. I am unpersuaded that a fixed schedule of non-pecuniary damages is a wiser course. Proponents of such an approach have not satisfactorily resolved the problems of individual, temporal, and jurisdictional variables. For example, the ALI study of Enterprise Responsibility for Personal Injury found some features of mandatory schedules attractive, but ultimately concluded that "idiosyncratic cases" would best be resolved by juries and that juries should have authority to exceed even the top award on the scale.[57] Moreover, even if indexed for inflation, binding schedules do not allow juries in the aggregate to reflect a sea-change in community thinking about how compensation for personal injury. We know from experience that such changes do take place, and the jury system has been a good way to allow their expression.

Even my proposal raises the possibility of an indirect impact on jury awards, because trial and appellate courts would also be better informed of prior awards and so might be tempted to overturn verdicts that depart even slightly from past patterns. This is not a necessary outcome. Departures from the norms represented by the grid may (appropriately) attract attention from the court, but the review should take into account whatever legitimate factors may have moved the jury and allow its verdict to stand if justified.

B. The Use of a Relatively Simplified Grid

I do not recommend fine-tuning injury types along the lines suggested by Baldus, MacQueen and Woodworth. They claim that to identify personal injury cases that are similar, it is necessary ideally to identify cases in which the *location* and *type* of injury are the same. Injuries to different limbs present different symptoms and require different treatments; such differences may, in turn, produce different functional outcomes. Classification, they urge, requires that we take into account "all factors that may bear on the level of the plaintiff's pain, suffering, and loss of enjoyment of life."

This point is undoubtedly correct. It is also true that an injury to my leg (I'm an avid, if geriatric, softball player) is not the same as an injury to that of a hypothetical chess hobbyist.[58] And it is the case that not all leg injuries (or even amputations) are the same in the respects mentioned by Baldus, MacQueen and Woodworth. The more one strives for close comparability, the more factors one must introduce in the grid. *Reductio ad absurdum* takes us back to the present regime of totally individualized jury awards and impressionistic judicial controls: No two plaintiffs are ever the same. The hard question, once one departs from the present approach, is to determine the right level of categorization.

In part the answer depends on which decisional body must deal with the distinctions. The Baldus, MacQueen and Woodworth approach has more to commend it if (as in their study) it is recommended for use by the judiciary in an enhanced additur/remittitur review. By aptitude and training, judges are better able to assimilate and use a complex set of facts. I fear that the more complex the aids presented to a jury, the more likely they are to confuse rather than clarify. As the list of factors grows, the temptation to ignore them grows too.

The use to be made of the grid also bears on the level of detail desirable. In a system of binding schedules it is more appropriate to fine-tune the categories, whereas more inclusive categories can be tolerated with a discretionary approach like that presented here. The assumption is that, given the freedom to do so, jurors will take the relevant differences into account even if they are not scheduled.

Increasing the complexity of any proposal based on classifications, whether binding or not, would seem to increase transaction costs at two points. A decisional body engaged in constructing the system will necessarily find its task more onerous as the lines needed to draw the complete picture are multiplied. Too, the jurors who employ the system may find it more difficult to agree on a series of mini-decisions than to pick an appropriate amount from within a general range.

The simplified grid implicitly rejects the use of injury "scenarios" beyond the brief examples included in the injury severity scale. Detailed scenarios keyed to recommended (or required) awards would be difficult to construct because of the myriad differences in real-world fact patterns. Assigning values would also be very controversial—it would defy principled solution. The start-up costs would be compounded by the difficulties jurors would likely encounter in digesting and applying the scenarios to the case at hand.

My suggested use of age and severity of injury as the only factors in the grid has empirical support. Bovbjerg and his colleagues report:

> We investigated the influence of [various] factors empirically for their influence on past patterns of awards for non-economic loss. . . . This analysis shows that the severity of injury is the strongest correlate of amount, with the age of the victim next. Body part alone is not as predictive of non-economic damages as injury severity. Moreover, it is not possible to use body part in the same regression as severity because it is too closely correlated with the nine-point severity scale.[59]

Their last point is especially telling given my proposal to use the nine-point scale. Adding body part to the matrix would be a kind of double counting.

To be sure, collapsing all injuries, including death, into nine categories introduces a wide range within each category. Some courts that engage in review of jury verdicts by making comparisons with other verdicts have restricted the comparison to similar type as well as similar degree of injury. For example, in *Wendell v. Supermarkets General Corp.*,[60] the plaintiff was a 54-year old woman who sustained two herniated discs, impingement of the spinal cord, and compression of the nerve to the shoulder and the arm. She was awarded $15,000 for past pain and suffering, and $15,000 for future pain and suffering. The trial court ordered a new trial unless the defendant stipulated to $75,000 for past pain and suffering and $100,000 for future pain and suffering. The Appellate Division held that the amount of damages for future pain and suffering deviated from what would be considered reasonable compensation in "similar circumstances,"[61] citing five cases: *Reed v. Harter Chair Corp.*,[62] *Dioria v. Scala*,[63] *Lamot v. Gondek*,[64] *Bottone v. New York Telephone Co.*,[65] and *Hughes v. Peters*.[66] Each of these cases involved a severe back injury, as did *Wendell*. That is the only similarity, however, as the plaintiffs in these cases differ by sex, age, and the manner in which the injury occurred. Awards for pain and suffering in the five ranged (after review) from $16,500 to $330,000. The *Wendell* court apparently felt comfortable with a figure somewhere in between, albeit on the low end.

The *Wendell* injury is in category 5 on the nine point scale, "permanent minor" injury.[67] But so too is the injury in *Leon v. J&M Peppe Realty Corp.*[68] The plaintiff there was a 26-year old man who suffered partial amputation of the three middle fingers of his left (non-dominant) hand, a 50–65% disability. He was initially awarded $1,600,000 for past and future pain and suffering, but the trial court ordered the verdict set aside unless the plaintiff stipulated to a reduction for future pain and suffering from $1,500,000 to $750,000; the $100,000 award for past pain and suffering was allowed to stand. The Appellate Division ruled that the reduced award was not out of line with recent awards upheld by the appellate courts, citing *Dauria v. City of New York*,[69] and *Stiles v. Batavia Atomic Horseshoes, Inc.*,[70] both cases involving amputations. In *Dauria*, the loss of two toes was held to justify an award of $1,800,000 in pain and suffering damages. In *Stiles*, the loss of three fingers of the right hand plus permanent deformity of the left was at issue; the court affirmed a total verdict (general plus non-pecuniary damages) of $1,705,000. The plaintiffs in all these cases are within the same age group, but there is no indication whether the court chose them for comparison for this reason or whether this occurred purely by chance. Thus, the *Stiles* court was comfortable comparing one plaintiff with a partial hand amputation and serious injuries to both hands to another plaintiff with a toe amputation.

Under the nine point grid, the grouping would be even broader. Both the *Stiles*-type injury (amputation) and the *Wendell*-type injury (permanent back pain) would apparently fall into the same category, with a resultant spread of awards from $16,500 to $1.8 million. A legitimate criticism is that such a range provides very little guidance. On the other hand, the median (approximately $300,000) would be useful as a starting point, and the jury could use the verbal description of the category to decide whether the particular case to be decided fit in the high or low end.

Another issue concerns the use of state-wide figures as opposed to smaller geographic units. Intra-state geographical differences in award patterns are probably nowhere as pronounced as in New York.[71] These aggregate differentiations probably survive even appellate review. It is very unusual for any of the four departments that make up the Appellate Division of the New York Supreme Court to look at cases from another department in any area of law, and the jurisdiction of these departments is geographically based. To lump awards for the entire state on the grid, regardless of the venue of the action is arguably unfair—especially if, as some claim, geographic variations reflect differences in the wealth of the respective communities. On the other hand, variations can also be seen as an aspect of the irrationality of the current system. In a mobile society in which the prices of major goods are determined nationally, why should the wealth of a locality determine the rate at which pain is compensated? Are not regional variations sufficiently accounted for in awards for lost income and future medical expenses? My proposal offers a workable compromise: A state-wide grid gives jurors in each locale a more cosmopolitan awareness, but since they remain free to find the right number on (or off) the grid, we leave room for strong local tendencies to reassert themselves.

Conclusion

The proposed grid could become law in one of three ways. A rule-making body such as the Judicial Conference, or in New York, the Chief Administrator of the Courts could promulgate a grid and revise it annually. Enabling legislation is therefore not necessary, though it is also a possibility.

Alternatively, a grid could be developed by counsel, placed into evidence through expert testimony, and then included in the charge. It was this process that eventually led to the general acceptance of the mortality tables. This could present a problem of potentially competing grids and battles between experts over which is more accurate. Legislative or administrative adoption (after full opportunity for the interested public to comment) is therefore far preferable.

However adopted, the proposed grid or some variant would help rationalize the process by which pain and suffering damages are awarded and would do so without substantive impact and with only modest procedural cost.

Notes

1. David W. Leebron, *Final Moments: Damages for Pain and Suffering Prior to Death*, 64 N.Y.U. L. Rev. 256, 265 (1989).
2. *Id.*
3. A partial listing includes ABA, Report of the Action Commission to Improve the Tort Liability System 10–15 (1987); 2 ALI Reporters' Study, Enterprise Responsibility for Personal Injury 199–230 (1991); James F. Blumstein, Randall R. Bovbjerg & Frank A. Sloan, *Beyond Tort Reform: Developing Better Tools for Assessing Damages for Personal Injury*, 8 Yale J. Reg. 171 (1991)[hereafter cited as Blumstein]; Randall R. Bovbjerg, Frank A. Sloan, & James F. Blumstein, *Public Policy: Valuing Life and Limb in Tort: Scheduling "Pain and Suffering,"* 83 Nw. U.L. Rev. 908 (1989)[hereafter cited as Bovbjerg]; Leebron, *supra* note 1; Eric Schnapper, *Judges Against Juries*, 1989 Wisc. L. Rev. 237.
4. See, e.g., ALI Report, *supra* note 3, at 204–17 (reviewing the arguments for and against pain and suffering damages, and, while finding the case for them "uneasy," recommending that they be retained); *id.*, Recommendation No. 1, at 229.

5. For discussion of the $250,000 cap adopted in California and the indexed cap adopted in the State of Washington, see *id.* of 218. The ALI Reporters questioned the use of caps because (i) unless indexed, they inexorably force a decline in tort recoveries when measured in constant dollars; (ii) they arbitrarily prevent full pain and suffering recoveries by the most severely injured persons, while allowing full recovery to others; and (iii) they do not eliminate the large variations in pain and suffering awards that have been the source of much of the criticism of them. *Id.*
6. See ALI Report, *supra* note 3, at 218: "We believe that the cap model has far more vices than virtues, and the fact that state legislatures have been so ready to impose such caps should give pause to those who assert that statutory tort reform reflects a fair and balanced appraisal of the interests of both actors and victims."
7. A trial or appellate court may set aside a damage award that is found to be too high or low. See Fleming James, Geoffrey Hazard and John Leubsdorf, Civil Procedure at 394–404 (4th ed. 1992).
8. Valuation must depend to some extent on the juror's economic circumstances and tolerance for pain. I had occasion to conduct a thought experiment on valuing pain and suffering while writing this article. I became ill with a non-threatening but very discomforting malady. After three days of what seemed like endless suffering, I asked myself how much money I would demand for each additional day of the illness, assuming I could make such a demand. I concluded that it would take at least $50,000 per day, but that the amount would escalate as the days wore on. I then asked myself what I would pay to reduce my illness by one day. The figure was closer to $1,000. Finally, I should confess, when I was able to get the prescription drug ordered by my physician, I complained about the price (about $25). How much was my suffering worth? I could not give a coherent answer.
9. New York Pattern Jury Instructions—Civil 534 (2d ed. Supp. 1995).
10. Other jurisdictions use similar language:

SECTION 1.3 INTRODUCTION TO DAMAGES
(Personal Injury—No Punitive Damages Sought)

In considering the issue of Plaintiff's damages, you are instructed that you should assess the amount you find to be justified by a preponderance of the evidence as full, just, and reasonable compensation for all of the Plaintiff's damages, no more and no less.

. . . .

You should consider the following elements of damage, to the extent you find them proved by a preponderance of the evidence, and no others. . . .

. . . .

SECTION 2.1 PERSONAL INJURY AND PROPERTY DAMAGE CASES
(Bodily Injury, Pain and Suffering, Disability, Disfigurement, Loss of Capacity for the Enjoyment of Life)

Any bodily injury sustained by the Plaintiff and any resulting pain and suffering . . . experienced in the past (or to be experienced in the future). No evidence of the value of such intangible things as mental or physical pain and suffering has been or need be introduced. In that respect it is not value you are trying to determine, but an amount that will fairly compensate the Plaintiff for the damages he has suffered. There is no exact standard for fixing the compensation to be awarded on account of such elements of damage. Any such award should be fair and just in the light of the evidence.

Committee on Pattern Jury Instructions, District Judges Assoc., Eleventh Circuit, Pattern Jury Instructions: Civil Cases 164, 166 (1990) (alteration in orginal).

SECTION 15.2 COMPENSATORY DAMAGES

If you find that the defendant is liable to the plaintiff, then you must determine an amount that is fair compensation for all of the plaintiff's damages. . . . The purpose of compensatory damages is to make the plaintiff whole—that is, to compensate the plaintiff for the damage that the plaintiff has suffered. . . .

. . . . If you decide to award compensatory damages, you should be guided by dispassionate common sense. Computing damages may be difficult, but you must not let that difficulty lead you to engage in arbitrary guesswork. On the other hand, the law does not require that the plaintiff prove the amount of his losses with mathematical precision, but only with as much definiteness and accuracy as the circumstances permit.

You must use sound discretion in fixing an award of damages, drawing reasonable inferences where you find them appropriate from the facts and circumstances in evidence.

You should consider the following elements of damage, to the extent you find them proved by a preponderance of the evidence. . . .

SECTION 15.4 INJURY/PAIN/DISABILITY/DISFIGUREMENT/LOSS OF CAPACITY FOR ENJOYMENT OF LIFE

You may award damages for any bodily injury that the plaintiff sustained and any pain and suffering . . . that the plaintiff experienced in the past (or will experience in the future) as a result of the bodily injury. No evidence of the value of intangible things, such as mental or physical pain and suffering, has been or need be introduced. You are not trying to determine value, but an amount that will fairly compensate the plaintiff for the damages he has suffered. There is no exact standard for fixing the compensation to be awarded for these elements of damage. Any award that you make should be fair in the light of the evidence.

U.S. Fifth Circuit District Judges Assoc., Pattern Jury Instructions: Civil Cases 168–69, 172 (1994) (alteration in original).

11. Bovbjerg, *supra* note 3, at 921 (Table 2).
12. *Id.* at 921.
13. *Id.* at 923 (footnote omitted). The "injury severity level" used by the authors for analysis of the data is the nine-point scale "conventionally used for evaluating malpractice insurance cases." *Id.* at 920. They reproduce this scale at *id.*, Table 1. They found that it is the "best available single predictor of award amount." *Id.* The same scale was used to analyze jury verdicts by Stephen Daniels & Joanne Martin, *Don't Kill the Messenger 'Till You Read the Message: Products Liability Verdicts in Six California Counties, 1970- 1990*, 16 Justice Sys. J. 69, 95 (1993).
14. Bovbjerg, *supra* note 3, at 924.
15. *Id.*
16. *Id.* at 936–38.
17. Leebron, *supra* note 1, at 324–25.

18. *Id*. Using the "further rarification" of death by drowning cases, Leebron reports a range of jury verdicts from zero to $137,000 before appellate review and $4,360 to $52,800 after appellate review. See *id*. at 297–298
19. Aaron J. Broder, Judges, Juries and Verdict Awards, New York Law Journal, January 3, 1994, at 3. All but one of the awards for non-pecuniary damages were jury verdicts. The one award by a judge was for $1 million.
20. There is some controversy about whether uncertainty increases or decreases the likelihood of settlement. See studies cited and discussed by Bovbjerg, *supra* note 3, at 926, n.92. Pendell, speaking from an insurer's perspective, asserts that "there is little doubt that predictability greatly facilitates settlement by narrowing the gap between plaintiffs' and defendants' judgments about their probability of success at trial and the likely size of the award." Judyth W. Pendell, *Enhancing Juror Effectiveness: An Insurer's Perspective*, 52 L. & Contemp. Probs. 311, 312 (1989).
21. Bovbjerg, *supra* note 3, at 925.
22. See *supra* note 10 and accompanying text.
23. Audrey Chin & Mark A. Peterson, Deep Pockets, Empty Pockets viii (1985).
24. Jane Goodman, Elizabeth Loftus, Marian Miller & Edith Greene, *Money, Sex and Death: Gender Bias in Wrongful Death Bias Awards*, 25 L. & Soc'y. Rev. 263 (1991).
25. Leebron, *supra* note 1, at 306.
26. Chin & Peterson, *supra* note 23, at v. See also Valerie P. Hans & William S. Lofquist, *Jurors' Judgments of Business Liability in Tort Cases: Implication for the Litigation Explosion Debate*, 26 L. & Soc'y. Rev. 85, 87 (1992) (collecting studies).
27. Brian Ostrom, David Rottman & Roger Hanson, *What Are Tort Awards Really Like? The Untold Story from the State Courts*, L. & Policy 79, 93 (January 1992): "The central conclusion to emerge from our model of verdicts in tort cases is that the size of the plaintiff's award is related most closely to litigant status rather than type of trial, the area of tort law, the length of time to disposition, or the locale."
28. "Jurors themselves are affected and influenced by other juries' decisions in a number of ways. The jurors we interviewed appeared to be quite cognizant of other civil juries, real and apocryphal. Their concerns about deep pockets, the litigation crisis, and the integrity of plaintiffs were implicitly and explicitly linked to the presumed excesses of antecedent juries.." Hans & Lofquist, *supra* note 26, at 111–112.
29. See examples and discussion in Stephen Daniels, *The Question of Jury Competence and the Politics of Civil Justice Reform: Symbols, Rhetoric, and Agenda Building*, 52 L. & Contemp. Probs. 269 (1989).
30. See the discussion in the chapter of this volume written by David Baldus, John MacQueen, and George Woodworth *infra* at 368–77.
31. The problem of incoherent judicial review of jury verdicts is addressed in depth by Baldus et al., *supra* note 32. See also Schnapper, *supra* note 3.
32. See *supra* note 3, Recommendation No. 2, at 13.
33. *Id.*, Recommendation No. 3, at 14–15.
34. *Id.*, Recommendation No.4, at 15.
35. See *supra* note 3, at 218–20.
36. *Id.*, Recommendation 2, at 218–21, 230.

37. *Id.* at 220–21.
38. *Id.*, Recommendation 3, at 221–27, 230.
39. *Id.* at 221–29.
40. See Bovbjerg, *supra* note 3, at 939–53.
41. *Id.* at 953–56.
42. *Id.* at 959–60.
43. Blumstein, *supra* note 3.
44. Bovbjerg, *supra* note 3, at 960.
45. Of course, the idea of providing information to jurors about previous awards has been suggested by others as well. See, e.g., ABA Report, *supra* note 3, at 15; ALI Report, *supra* note 3, at 230; Leebron, *supra* note 1, at 322–23. I am grateful to John Evancho and Judyth W. Pendell for directing my attention to this literature and to the use of the grid or chart as an aid to jurors.
46. The authority responsible for constructing the actual chart and the process for using it are discussed below.
47. The scale replicates the nine-point severity of injury scale discussed at note 13, *supra*.
48. This itemized verdict would aid a reviewing court in determining the jury's reasons for reaching the pain and suffering award and facilitate future statistical evaluation.
49. Leebron, *supra* note 1, at 291, n. 139. The 256 cases are listed in *id.*, Appendix A, at 326–42. Only officially reported cases are included.
50. The value of improved information about jury verdicts has been recognized by other commentators. See text accompanying notes 30–44.
51. This reporter, published monthly, collects and reports approximately 90% of all jury verdicts in personal injury cases tried to verdict in the metropolitan New York area, and 75% of all such verdicts in the remaining counties of the state. The results of post-verdict motions are also reported. So far as I am aware, however, appellate reversals of previously reported verdicts are not. Documented submissions by attorneys for the litigants are used as the prime source for the awards reported. Interview with Russell F. Moran, Editor, New York Jury Verdict Reporter (Aug. 3, 1993).

    Appellate decisions affecting awards would have to be added to the base to make it usable under my proposal. Further, the injuries described for each case by the New York Jury Verdict Reporter would have to be coded to the nine point severity scale proposed for my grid. Expansion of the percentage of reported cases to one-hundred would be desirable, though this is not, in my view, a precondition to the utility of the data because of the large size of the reported sample and the apparently random nature of the cases reported.
52. N.Y. Civ. Prac. L. & R. §4111(f)(McKinney 1994); see also *id.* §4213(b)(same obligation imposed on the judge when an action has been tried without a jury).
53. See *Senko v. Fonda,* 384 N.Y.S.2d 849, 851–52 (2d Dep't 1976). See also, e.g., *Martell v. Boardwalk Enterprises, Inc.*, 748 F.2d 740 (2d Cir. 1984); *Wendell v. Supermarkets General Corp.*, 189 A.D.2d 1063, 592 N.Y.S.2d 895 (3d Dep't 1993)(citing five other cases, all involving back injuries that, like the case under review, were likely to be permanent). See discussion *infra* text accompanying notes 65–75.

54. See, for example, New York Pattern Jury Instructions:

> If you find that any of Plaintiff's injuries are permanent, you must make such allowances in your verdict as you think that circumstance warrants, taking into consideration the period of time that has elapsed from the date of the injury to the present time and the period of time Plaintiff can be expected to live. In this connection it is pointed out to you that Plaintiff can be expected to live for ___ more years, that is, until age ___, according to the most recent life expectancy tables published by the United States government.

1 New York Pattern Jury Instructions—Civil 632 (2d ed. 1974) (Supp. 1995).

In *Vicksburg & Meridian Railroad Co. v. Putnam,* 118 U.S. 545, 554–55 (1866), the Supreme Court held that the plaintiff was entitled to recover for pain and suffering and loss of future income, and that life and annuity tables are competent evidence to assist the jury in making such an estimate. The Court relied on decisions in *Phillips v. London & Southwestern Railway,* 4 Q.B.D. 406, 5 Q.B.D. 78 (1879), and *Rowley v. London & Northwestern Railway,* 8 L.R. Ex. 221 (1873).

In *Phillips*, the English court stated that while there was no precise rule as to the measure of damages, the jury must take a reasonable view of all facts and circumstances when awarding damages, including the life expectancy of the plaintiff. *Phillips*, 4 Q.P.D. at 407. *Rowley* involved an action under Lord Campbell's Act (the English wrongful death statute). The trial judge admitted the testimony of an accountant who gave an estimate of the probable duration of the life of the deceased based upon the mortality rates collected in the Carlisle Tables. The Court of Exchequer held that the admission of such evidence was appropriate in a wrongful death action. The award of damages in a wrongful death action depends upon the ability of the jury to ascertain the probable duration of life at a given age, therefore it is material to know what the average duration of life is at that age. *Rowley*, 8 L.R. Ex. at 226. There is no better means of showing probable duration of life than "by proving the practice of life insurance companies, who learn it by experience." *Id.*

In *People v. Security Life Ins.,* 78 N.Y. 114 (1879), the New York Court of Appeals held that mortality tables are built on the long and varied experience of the insurance business and are therefore sufficiently reliable in the absence of something better to guide the courts in calculating the average life span of an individual. New York courts may take judicial notice of mortality tables with the qualification that the tables are based on average life span and that therefore the jury must also account for the particular plaintiff's health, constitution, habits, and manner of living. See, e.g. *McKenna v. McGoldrick,* 27 N.Y.S.2d 58, 262 (App. Div. 1941); *Giambrone v. Israel America Line,* 208 N.Y.S.2d 215, 26 Misc.2d 593 (1961).

55. See, e.g., the Eleventh Circuit's Pattern Jury Instructions:

> SECTION 4.1 MORTALITY TABLES–ACTUARIAL EVIDENCE
>
> If a preponderance of the evidence shows that the Plaintiff has been permanently injured, you may consider his life expectancy. The mortality tables received in evidence may be considered in determining how long the claimant may be expected to live. Bear in mind, however, that life expectancy as shown by mortality tables

is merely an estimate of the average remaining life of all persons in the United States of a given age and sex having average health and ordinary exposure to danger of persons in that group. So, such tables are not binding on you but be considered together with the other evidence in the case bearing on the Plaintiff's own health, age, occupation and physical condition, before and after the injury, in determining the probable length of his life.

Committee on Pattern Jury Instructions, District Judge Assoc., Eleventh Circuit, Pattern Jury Instructions: Civil Cases 177 (1990).

56. There is evidence that six-person juries produce greater variation in awards than twelve-person juries. Leebron, *supra* note 1 (citing Han Zeisel, . . . *And Then There Were None: The Diminution of the Federal Jury*, 38 U. Chi. L. Rev. 710, 716–17 (1971)). This problem is likely to be exacerbated if only five jurors need agree on the verdict.
57. See ALI Report, *supra* note 3, at 226–27.
58. The ALI Report, *supra* note 3, at 225, makes the same point by comparing a chess player with an amateur pianist.
59. Bovbjerg, *supra* note 3, at 941.
60. 189 A.D.2d 1063, 592 N.Y.S.2d 895 (3d Dept. 1993).
61. *Id.* at 896.
62. 185 A.D.2d 547, 586 N.Y.S.2d 401 (3d Dept. 1992).
63. 183 A.D.2d 1065, 583 N.Y.S. 2d 654 (3d Dept. 1992).
64. 163 A.D.2d 678, 558 N.Y.S.2d 284 (3d Dept. 1990)
65. 110 A.D.2d 922, 487 N.Y.S.2d 170, *leave to appeal denied*, 65 N.Y.2d 610, 494 N.Y.S.2d 1026, 484 N.E.2d 1053 (1985).
66. 167 A.D.2d 687, 563 N.Y.S.2d 269 (3d. Dept. 1990).
67. See *supra*, text accompanying note 50.
68. 596 N.Y.S.2d 380 (1st Dept. 1993).
69. 178 A.D.2d 289, 577 N.Y.S.2d 64, *leave to appeal denied*, 80 N.Y.2d 751, 587 N.Y.S.2d 287, 599 N.E.2d 691 (1991).
70. 174 A.D.2d 287, 579 N.Y.S.2d 790 (1st Dept. 1991), *rev'd on other grounds*, 81 N.Y.2d 950, 613 N.E.2d 572, 597 N.Y.S.2d 666 (1993).
71. See Stephen Daniel & Joanne Martin, *Jury Verdicts and the "Crisis" in Civil Justice*, 11 Justice Sys. J. 321 (1986) (reporting significant difference between metropolitan New York and the rest of the state). See also *supra* Table II. No personal injury practitioner familiar with the state would be surprised.

Toward Experimenting with Juror Guidance in Valuing Pain and Suffering Damages: Building on a Decade of Verdicts in New York State

Judyth W. Pendell*
John R. Evancho**

I. Introduction

Juries receive very little guidance when charged with the task of valuing pain and suffering damages; jury instructions are vague and nonspecific. Jurors typically are told to apply their "enlightened conscience" in selecting a monetary figure they consider to be fair.[1] Yet, jurors lack a framework within which they can confidently make that judgment.[2] There is no common, widely shared understanding of the monetary value of various degrees and types of pain and suffering which jurors can invoke to arrive at a "fair" award.

Not surprisingly, prior empirical research has indicated that pain and suffering awards by juries for injuries of comparable severity vary considerably. [3] This variability suggests that awards are apt to be unfair to some parties.[4] Since differences in the size of pain and suffering awards are based on the idiosyncratic, uninformed predilections of jurors, it is inevitable that the jury awards result in windfalls for some and inadequate awards for others.[5] This raises serious equity issues for both plaintiffs and

*Vice President, Law and Regulatory Affairs, Aetna Life and Casualty Company.
**Attorney, Law and Regulatory Affairs, Aetna Life and Casualty Company.
The authors express their appreciation to Brendan Ahearn, Shyrel Bauby, Mary Ellen Evancho, Sarah Kanwit, Carolyn Killian, Debra Koczon, Michael Topodas and members of Corporate Actuarial, Aetna Life and Casualty Company.

defendants. The defendant who is required to pay an excessive award should be as much a concern to society as the plaintiff whose recovery is inadequate. The costs of the tort system are ultimately passed back to society in the form of higher prices for products and services.[6] Further, the respect for and confidence in courts is diminished when they fail to effect just outcomes.

The problem is not solved through additur and remittitur. Such changes in awards generally occur only when the court finds egregious error,[7] and the standard for appellate review is the very high threshold of abuse of discretion.[8] Consequently, court imposed alterations in juror awards of pain and suffering damages are not common.

The absence of predictability in the size of pain and suffering awards can have a significant effect on the timing of settlement. For those cases destined to settle early, settlement is greatly facilitated by the parties' ability to arrive at comparable valuations of the case. The uncertainty over the likely jury award for pain and suffering in a given case interjects a wild card into the valuation process, which can prolong settlement. This raises the costs of litigation and, in those instances where the plaintiff will recover, lengthens the time until he or she receives compensation.

This paper explores reforms which might respond to these issues in several ways. Part II reports on and discusses the landscape of reforms that have been proposed. Part III offers a proposal designed to move the discussion about how to provide guidance to jurors forward by suggesting a possible experiment. Part IV presents data that report a decade of pain and suffering awards in New York state, data that could provide the foundation for experimentation with juror guidance.

II. Proposed Options for Reform

Several commentators have noted the variability of awards of damages for pain and suffering and have offered proposals to address the issue. Recommended reforms vary from eliminating to capping to scheduling damages for pain and suffering.

Some scholars have advocated abolishing damages for pain and suffering. Jeffrey O'Connell, for example, noting that "[p]ayment for pain and suffering has, for years, served substantially to pay claimants' lawyers,"[9] has suggested eliminating damages for pain and suffering in exchange for requiring a defendant to pay a plaintiff's attorney's fees in the event the plaintiff is awarded damages for personal injury.[10] Among the advantages of this proposal, according to Professor O'Connell, are "candor and openness,"[11] as well as the fact that "the amount of payment for attorneys' fees will be settled between experienced parties on both sides—claimants' lawyers and insurers, rather than experienced claimants' lawyers and inexperienced claimants."[12]

Many state legislatures have considered, and some have enacted, fixed monetary caps on damages for pain and suffering. Most limits now in effect are the result of state legislation enacted in response to the medical malpractice crisis of the mid-1970s and the liability insurance crisis of the mid-1980s.[13] Caps on damages for pain and suffering have taken the form of flat figures[14] as well as multiples of other awarded amounts.[15] Although limits on damages for pain and suffering may have some superficial appeal, there is some evidence suggesting that caps are ineffective in limiting awards in certain circumstances;[16] that they afford juries no guidance in most cases;[17] that they have suffered numerous successful constitutional challenges;[18] and that they unfairly discriminate against young and severely injured plaintiffs.[19]

Some proposals for reforming awards of damages for pain and suffering call for giving greater guidance to judges and juries. A commission of the American Bar Association, for instance, has specifically advocated "provid[ing] more guidance to the jury on the appropriate range of damages to be awarded for pain and suffering in a particular case."[20] The commission cited "the need for greater uniformity in the award of damages."[21] Although some members of the commission expressed concern about the means and extent of guiding a jury, other members specifically recommended "hav[ing] the trial judge suggest an advisory but non-binding range of high and low awards for pain and suffering on the basis of experience in prior similar cases (and after the liability issue has been tried)."[22]

Researchers at the University of Iowa have proposed a unique model for "comparative" additur or remittitur review on the part of trial judges in cases involving damages for pain and suffering (or punitive damages)—that is, "the explicit use of a comparative analysis of approved awards in similar cases to inform the court's judgment concerning the appropriate quantum of damages" for pain and suffering.[23] "Comparative" additur or remittitur review, as the researchers use the term, may be both qualitative and quantitative.

The qualitative methodology consists of (1) identifying the characteristics of a particular case that may affect the award of damages for pain and suffering, including the severity and duration of pain and suffering; (2) finding a group of cases from the same jurisdiction for comparison; and (3) analyzing the characteristics of the case in light of the cases used for purposes of comparison.[24] The researchers take as an example the decision of a federal appellate court in New York involving the traumatic loss by a boy of his left arm in a jet ski accident.[25] The court relied on a "comparative" analysis of seven other cases involving either amputation or loss of function of either an arm or a leg.[26]

The quantitative methodology includes not only adjusting for inflation, but also ranking the cases used for comparison in terms of the level of pain and suffering experienced by the plaintiff and placing a particular case in the ranking;[27] adjusting the damages for pain and suffering in the case to reflect an estimate of what would have been awarded and approved in each of the cases used for comparison had the level of pain and suffering been the same as the level in the case under consideration;[28] and generating "a range of reasonableness" from the ranked cases and adjusted awards for pain and suffering.[29] The researchers explain:

> [A]pproved actual awards in the comparison cases that are "near neighbors" to the review case may suggest an upper and lower award limit for it. Similarly, the listing of adjusted awards in the comparison cases, especially among the cases with the most comparable levels of compensable harm [in cases involving damages for pain and suffering] or punishment justification [in cases involving punitive damages], provide additional evidence of the range of expected awards in cases that are comparable to the review case. That distribution of awards may also suggest upper and lower limits. Or, in the alternative, the court may determine that a deviation of 10%, 20%, or 50% beyond the high or low end of these distributions may be a reasonable means of accommodating changing community standards. The specifications of a range of reasonableness in this manner may provide a principled base for adjusting the review case award to its proper level.[30]

Other commentators have proposed "scheduling" damages for pain and suffering in one way or another. Randall Bovbjerg, Frank Sloan, and James Blumstein, for example, have suggested several models of "scheduling."[31] One model consists of a matrix to be used by a jury to calculate damages for pain and suffering.[32] The matrix would rely on the objective factors of the age of the plaintiff and the severity of his or her injury; other characteristics of the plaintiff and the defendant, such as race, gender, and occupation, are to be ignored.[33] The values provided to the jury by the matrix would be based on prior jury awards, as adjusted by trial and appellate courts. The jury would be instructed that it is to award the exact amount indicated in the matrix, adjusted only for the comparative negligence of the plaintiff. A state may modify the matrix so that it indicated a range of values instead of a specific amount. The state may also implement some administrative process for considering unusual cases, allowing the plaintiff to apply to an agency with the authority to supplement awards.

Another model consists of "scenarios" of injuries, with the value of pain and suffering for each injury, to be provided to a jury.[34] The jury would receive a range of scenarios, representing less severe to more severe injuries.[35] The values associated with the scenarios would be "benchmarks" for the jury to use in determining damages for pain and suffering. Two examples of scenarios are provided, one "neutral," the other "more colorful." The former is: "Permanent minor injury (level five). Life expectancy 25 years. Mild persistent pain, usually controlled with aspirin. Unable to engage in more than light housework."[36] The latter is: "Plaintiff Peters has completely and permanently lost the use of her left arm. Her life expectancy is 25 years, according to standard life insurance tables. Her arm throbs painfully most of the time, but the pain can usually be controlled with aspirin. She cannot do more than light housework."[37]

Another model consists of flexible ranges, derived from a matrix or from values accompanying scenarios of injuries, in place of caps on damages for pain and suffering.[38] The ranges would reflect the age of a plaintiff and the severity of his or her injury. Each range would include a floor as well as a ceiling.

These same commentators have also suggested the development and implementation of what they call a "common law" of damages.[39] This proposal has three aspects. First, a jury would be required to provide specific information as to its determination of the severity of the injury of the plaintiff and the damages to compensate for his or her injury.[40] Second, decisions about damages would be reported to and recorded by an agency; such information would be made available to the judge or jury or both.[41] Third, awards in the middle range of the distribution of damages would be deemed "presumptively valid."[42] The result would be that

> where valuations in a case differ significantly from prior results, tort valuations should be subject to both a burden of explanation by the jury and heightened review by the court. For extreme awards (for example, those in the top or the bottom quartile), juries should identify specific factors that justify the variation. An unexplained outlier should constitute a prima facie case for either remittitur or additur by the trial judge or an appellate holding of inadequacy or excessiveness of the judgment.[43]

Professor Peter Schuck, in his comment on the proposed "common law" of damages,[44] mentions that such a scheme would enhance equity in the awarding of damages for pain and suffering; improve additur and remittitur, as well as appellate review; encourage settlement; reduce litigation and insurance costs; strengthen deterrence; and promote the insurability of risks.[45] But he also expresses reservations. Specifically, he is concerned that the "similar cases" necessary for scheduling damages may be difficult to determine, especially if only the age of a plaintiff and the severity of his or her injury are to be considered. He maintains that, while it may be possible to generate "more refined criteria of similarity" in theory, issues of cost, feasibility, and reliability may make the development of better criteria impossible in reality.[46]

Professor Schuck also notes that basing damages in a case on prior awards may be problematic. The system of reporting and recording awards of damages may not be very comprehensive, especially in light of the fact that the vast majority of cases settle and the cases that proceed to trial are "systematically different" from the cases that are settled.[47] He is also concerned that using prior awards may simply "impound and then compound what [the authors] themselves characterize as the distortions of the past, thereby projecting those distortions into the future."[48]

In addition, Professor Schuck indicates that requiring that a jury to be specific in its findings would lead to more "lawyering,"[49] longer deliberations on the part of the jury, and, more often than now, a hung jury. He also notes that requiring special verdicts in which the jury explains or justifies its decision "invites appeals and reversals" on such issues as the "formulation of the questions and the provision of answers."[50]

Frederick Levin has advocated a unique form of scheduling damages for pain and suffering, namely, adapting the concept of criminal sentencing guidelines in force in several states to awards of damages for pain and suffering.[51] He argues that the former are transferable to the latter because, in both contexts, judges and juries have almost unlimited discretion and almost no guidance in exercising that discretion.[52]

Implementation of Levin's proposal would happen in three phases. First, a governmental agency would establish and promulgate guidelines for awarding damages for pain and suffering. The agency would choose between "descriptive" and "prescriptive" guidelines.[53] The former reflect past practice; the latter are intended to promote a particular objective of public policy. Levin contends that guidelines for damages for pain and suffering ought to be "descriptive," in order to be "representative of community values."[54]

> The primary compensatory function of pain and suffering damages is to express society's view of the gravity of the dignatory harm wrongfully inflicted upon the victim. To the extent that the guidelines rely upon judgments made by actual jurors as opposed to judgments made by legislators or guidelines commission members, the guidelines will more likely reflect community sentiment concerning the monetary value of particular pain and suffering injuries.[55]

Levin would base the descriptive guidelines on a multiple linear regression analysis of the factors considered most important in awarding damages for pain and suffering. Such a statistical analysis would reduce the effects of "extralegal" factors, such as gender and race. That is, even if gender and race proved to be statistically relevant, such factors could be disregarded as a matter of public policy in the development of guidelines.[56]

Second, juries would be provided with the guidelines for damages for pain and suffering and would be instructed to consult the guidelines and determine which cell, within the appropriate matrix, best describes the case before it. The jury should be informed that the dollar figure listed at that point represents the presumptive award. If the jury determines that the best match possible under the under the grid inadequately describes the case before it, it should consider departing from the presumptive award in either direction. Because departures are important for "fine-tuning" the guidelines, it is important, at least initially, that juries be allowed to depart from the guidelines at will.[57]

Third, awards of damages for pain and suffering would be reported to the appropriate agency, which would include the information in a database. The agency would issue updated guidelines as new awards were entered in the database. In time, as the database comes to include more and more cases and so better reflects "jury sentiment," courts would be expected to enforce the values in the guidelines as presumptive awards.

Once a jury determined that a particular grid cell best described the case before it, a presumption would arise that the cell adequately describes the case before the jury. The trial judge would have the authority to order remittitur, additur, or a new trial on damages based on the jury s improper departure from the presumptive award.[58]

III. Advancing the Debate

The only reform that has been adopted in any jurisdiction, or for that matter, offered to decision making bodies for possible enactment is the one that many find least attractive from a public policy standpoint: dollar-caps on pain and suffering. Other reforms under discussion have some attractive features. Scheduling, for example, has the potential to provide equity and predictability without penalty to the most seriously injured.[59] Providing jurors with guidance by profiling large numbers of cases allows jurors to tap into a "community standard" to determine what is appropriate compensation for pain and suffering. The yardstick for valuing pain and suffering should not be that of one person, or six or twelve people, but of the community.[60] Providing jurors with information about how a significant number of other juries value pain and suffering in comparable cases not only might produce much better outcomes in terms of equity and predictability, but arguably could ease and shorten jury deliberations.

The reforms under discussion have drawbacks as well. Creating special agencies to collect and report data to establish the basis for schedules could be an expensive add-on to judicial budgets, already inadequate in many states. Using handpicked individual cases for data (as opposed to using schedules based on aggregated data) raises the spectre of endless disputes over whether particular individual cases are appropriate for comparison. Any reform that would require legislative enactment faces a future of protracted political debate, possibly never to be enacted.

Ideally, it would be possible to experiment with a scheduling process that provided guidance to jurors and allowed them to tap into the "community standard" for valuing pain and suffering damages at little cost to the courts. There is, in fact, a natural laboratory for such an experiment in New York State. For some time jurors have been asked to complete jury interrogatories and indicate on the record the amount of the pain and suffering award.[61] Reliable jury verdict reporters have been capturing this information together with other basic case characteristics. The data in these verdict reporters could be utilized relatively simply and inexpensively to create schedules. No doubt jury verdict reporters would rise to the market opportunity, moreover, and make customized data available to the courts should they have a need for the service.

We decided to accept the challenge and test whether the data needed to create such schedules could be collected and sorted into severity of injury categories with a reasonably modest commitment of resources. All pain and suffering awards in New York State between 1981 and 1992 are presented in the next section in injury severity categories. That section includes a detailed description of the process of data collection and analysis that resulted in the charts in that section.

It should be emphasized that the charts in Part IV are not intended to be presented in a form that courts would provide to juries. The charts lead one to focus on the high awards, since there is a more detailed breakout of the higher awards. This was done to clarify the significant disparity found, in most cases, between the median award and mean award.[62]

We believe that in whatever precise form the data are presented to jurors, the information should be simple and straightforward, and it should be very clear to jurors how the data were developed. This would be particularly important if the data were provided on an advisory basis only, with jurors free to use or disregard the information. We even resist any further sorting of the data beyond injury severity. First, no other characteristic consistently affects the degree of pain and suffering in the same direction. Age, for example, can exacerbate pain and suffering in the case of a long term injury, where a younger plaintiff suffers longer than an older plaintiff; but it can also lessen the extent of the pain (e.g., with fractures, a younger plaintiff may heal much more quickly and experience less discomfort). Second, further sorting would reduce the size of each comparison group and weaken the extent to which the groupings could be said to be representative of "community standards." Third, we believe there is a good alternative to further sorting, one that preserves jury discretion: If jurors were given the range of awards for comparable injuries and then told that mitigating and aggravating factors may affect the degree of pain and suffering and given examples of factors they could consider (as well as factors they should not consider), jurors then could structure a process for deciding approximately where on the continuum of prior awards the case before them belongs.

Before an experiment to provide jurors with information about prior awards can go forward, several decisions must be made. What is the appropriate geographic scope of the data to be aggregated and presented to the jury? The data in this report include all verdicts throughout New York in both state and federal courts. Should these data be broken down to acknowledge regional differences that now exist?[63] Should outliers be rejected from the data to enhance statistical validity?[64] Should the information be solely advisory, or should jurors be required to stay within the range presented, or perhaps provide justification for moving outside the range? Should the jury be required to disclose which injury categories they chose (both long and short term)? Should they be required to justify their choice? And what effect would disclosure have on any post trial procedures? Last, how should the effect of the use of advisory data be evaluated?

IV. Empirical Study of Damages for Pain and Suffering in New York State from 1981 to 1992

In an effort to discern whether "scheduling" damages for pain and suffering is feasible without onerous new procedures to acquire and transmit information about awards, the Civil Justice Reform unit of the Law and Regulatory Affairs Division at Aetna Life & Casualty undertook to create a computerized database of jury awards. The database contains all 1,843 civil jury verdicts that included an award of damages for pain and suffering published in *The New York Jury Verdict Reporter* between 1981 and 1992.[65] The cases encompass decisions in all the counties and federal judicial districts in the state.[66]

Information about cases[67] was manually entered from the jury verdict reporters into the database.[68] The data was verified by two reviewers working independently, and the entries for awards of damages were adjusted for the effects of inflation, using the Consumer Price Index.

The study relies on categories of severity of injury developed by the National Association of Insurance Commissioners (NAIC) in the context of medical malpractice insurance cases.[69] The NAIC scale has been adopted for official insurance reporting of closed malpractice claims in New York[70] and has been cited by numerous scholars and researchers.[71] One commentator has described the categories of the NAIC scale as "intuitively appealing,"[72] and notes that "the scale works well in practice."[73] The NAIC scale consists of three categories of temporary injuries and four categories of permanent injuries, as well as categories for emotional trauma and death. The NAIC scale included examples of injuries in each of the three temporary and four permanent categories.

Because the words "temporary" and "permanent" are misnomers when applied to specific injuries,[74] we substituted the terms "short-term" and "long-term," respectively. For purposes of the study, "short-term" is

Chart 1

EMOTIONAL ONLY

SHORT-TERM MINOR INJURY

- laceration
- contusion
- dizziness
- fatigue
- headaches
- minor scar
- rash
- inflammation
- stiffness
- vertigo

SHORT-TERM SIGNIFICANT INJURY

- infection
- back injury not requiring surgery
- bone dislocation not requiring surgery
- dental injury not requiring cutting of soft tissue
- incontinence
- knee injury not requiring surgery
- neck injury not requiring surgery
- fracture
- mild nerve damage to organ not requiring surgery
- mild temporary damage to organ no requiring surgery
- "tailbone" injury not requiring surgery
- temporomandibular joint ("TMJ") syndrome

SHORT-TERM MAJOR INJURY

- burns
- amputation
- back injury requiring surgery
- injury requiring body cast
- bone dislocation requiring surgery
- cancer
- temporary colostomy
- concussion
- dental injury requiring cutting of soft tissue
- eye injury
- head trauma
- heart attack
- hip injury
- brain damage
- injury requiring jaw wiring
- knee injury requiring surgery
- lead poisoning
- meningitis
- neck injury requiring surgery
- nerve damage requiring surgery
- temporary damage to organ requiring surgery
- temporary paralysis
- stroke
- improperly performed surgery
- unnecessary surgery

defined as up to two years in duration, and "long-term" means longer than two years. Because many disputes took more than two years to come to trial, if the plaintiff continued to suffer from the effects of an injury at trial, the injury would, of course, be considered "long-term." Finally, the terminology used to designate the NAIC categories was changed slightly for the sake of clarity and consistency.[75] Chart 1 illustrates the range of severity of injury by category.

Chart 1 (Continued)

LONG-TERM MINOR INJURY

- loss of finger(s)
- arthritis
- back injury
- burns
- carpal tunnel syndrome
- dizziness
- loss of one ear
- eye injury
- fatigue
- headaches
- partial hearing loss
- hip injury
- incontinence
- joint replacement
- damage to organ
- knee injury
- knee replacement
- limp
- neck injury
- nerve damage
- restriction of movement
- sexual dysfunction
- loss of sense of smell
- stiffness
- loss of sense of taste
- loss of toe(s)
- ulcer
- vertigo

LONG-TERM SIGNIFICANT INJURY

- deafness
- loss of one limb
- loss of one eye
- amnesia
- peripheral blindness
- "claw hand"
- "club foot"
- limited cognitive deficit
- colostomy
- epilepsy
- Erb's palsy
- loss of one kidney
- loss of one lung
- degloving injury
- hip replacement
- hysterectomy
- Parkinson's disease
- chronic lead poisoning
- loss of voice
- injury requiring wheelchair

LONG-TERM MAJOR INJURY

- blindness
- brain damage
- cancer
- loss of ability to absorb food
- heart attack
- loss of two limbs
- paraplegia
- quadriparesis
- stroke

LONG-TERM GRAVE INJURY

- quadriplegia
- severe brain damage

with lifelong care or fatal prognosis

- HIV infection

DEATH

Because the range of injuries in the cases from *The New York Jury Verdict Reporter* is larger than the few examples furnished by the NAIC for each category, it was necessary to add and analogize other injuries to the examples. In the "short-term significant" category, for instance, a "knee injury not requiring surgery" was analogized to a "fracture" (the latter example being specified by the NAIC) even if the "knee injury" was not actually a "fracture."[76] The injuries in italics in Chart 1 were taken from the NAIC scale; those not italicized are modifications or additions.

Because plaintiffs commonly suffer multiple injuries or differing effects from the same injury, the categories of severity of injury are combined to form groupings.[77] For example, suppose a plaintiff broke his or her leg and the broken leg does not require surgery but does cause a slight, permanent, limp. The severity of injury grouping would then be "short-term significant/long-term minor": short-term significant because of the broken bone, and long-term minor because of the limp. If the plaintiff broke his or her leg, but the broken bone requires surgery and causes a slight, but permanent limp, then the severity of injury grouping would be "short-term major/long-term minor." If the plaintiff were required to undergo amputation of the leg because of severe infection or other complication, the severity of injury grouping would be "short-term major/long-term significant": short-term major because of the amputation itself, long-term significant because of the amputated leg. The category or categories of severity of injury in every case were selected and coded initially by John Evancho working alone and using the adapted NAIC scale. Because Evancho lacks medical training, he used common sense to determine the appropriate category or categories, in much the same way that lay jurors would approach the task. The validity of his choices was then tested by a panel of three physicians from the Harvard Medical School and Massachusetts General Hospital, headed by the chief cardiac anesthesiologist at the hospital. The physicians performed an independent review of 150 cases generated at random from the computerized database. Although two of the doctors were studying to become anesthesiologists, one had extensive experience in obstetrics, the specialty involved in an substantial number of medical malpractice cases, and the other had been a practitioner of family medicine. Each of the 150 cases was examined by two physicians, and differences were discussed in detail by Evancho and member of the panel. For injuries to teeth and surrounding tissue, less formal consultations with a staff dentist and staff periodontist at Aetna were conducted. Both the physicians at Harvard and the dentists at Aetna confirmed that Evancho's initial choices were, for the most part, the same choices they themselves would have made. The categories of severity of both medical and dental injuries were then refined based on these discussions, and all cases were again reviewed by Evancho for accuracy and consistency.

The results of the study are reported in Charts 2–13 below.

Charts 2 and 3

Comparison of Means and Medians of Jury Awards for Pain and Suffering in New York State from 1981 to 1992 by Severity Grouping

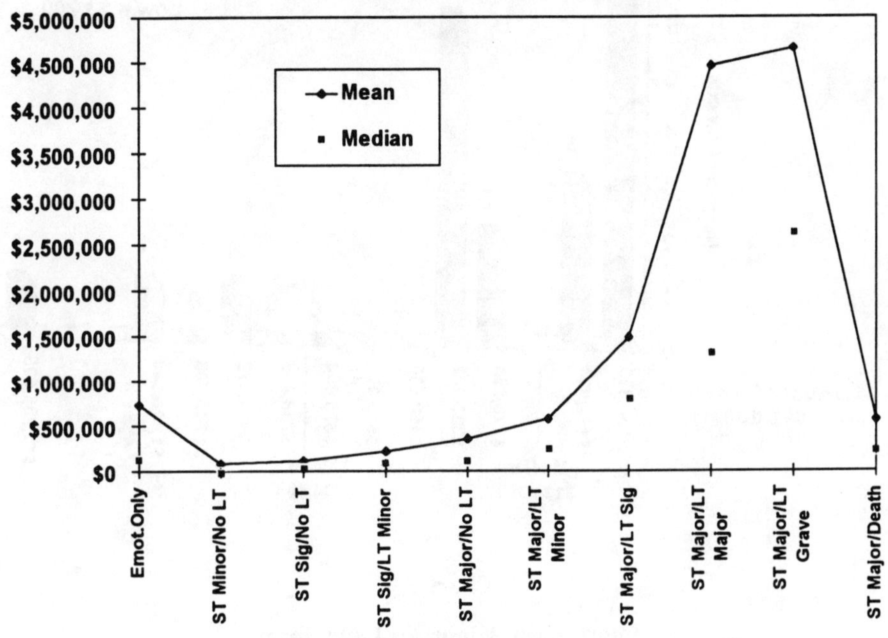

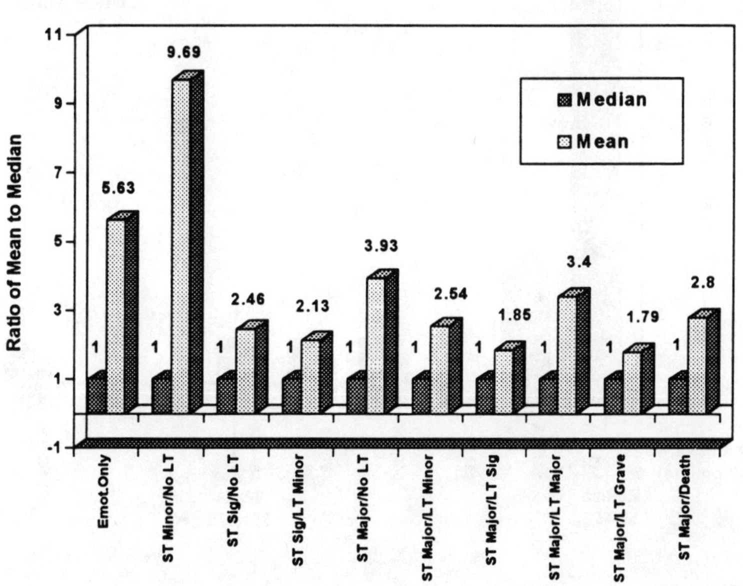

Chart 4

Emotional Only

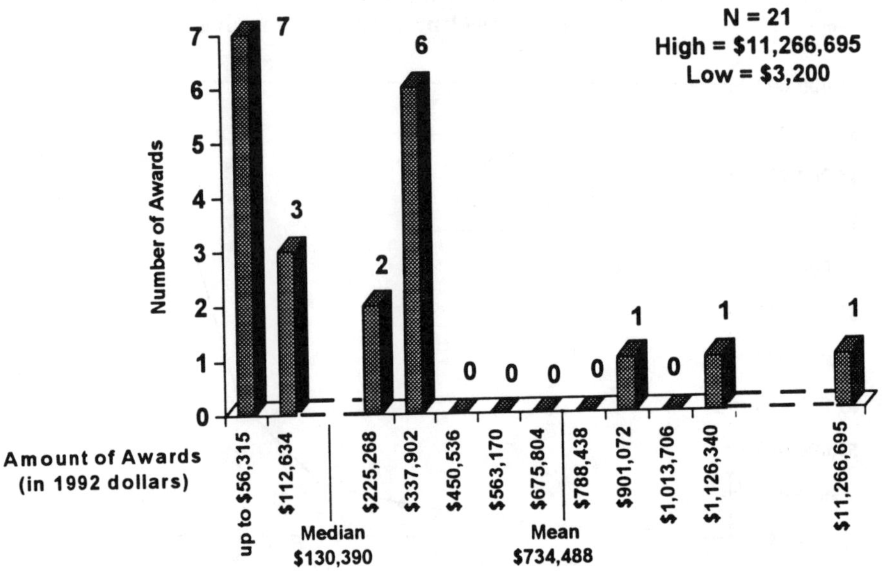

Chart 5

Short Term Minor/No Long Term

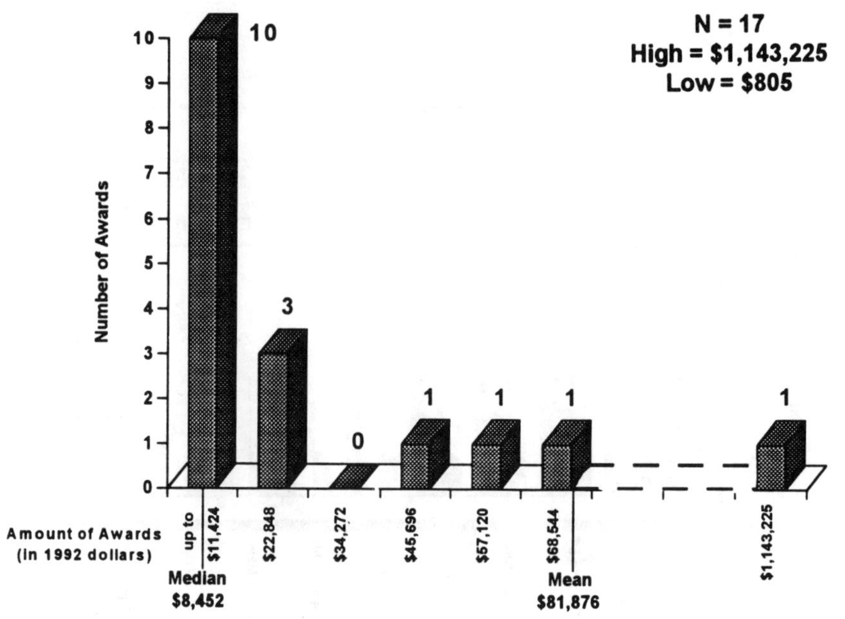

Chart 6

Short Term Significant/No Long Term

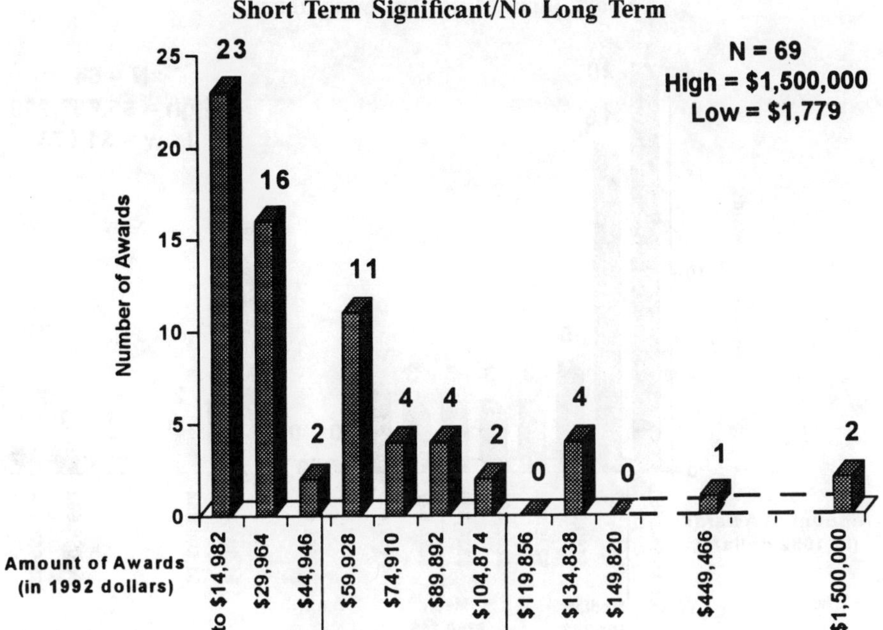

Short Term Significant/Long Term Minor

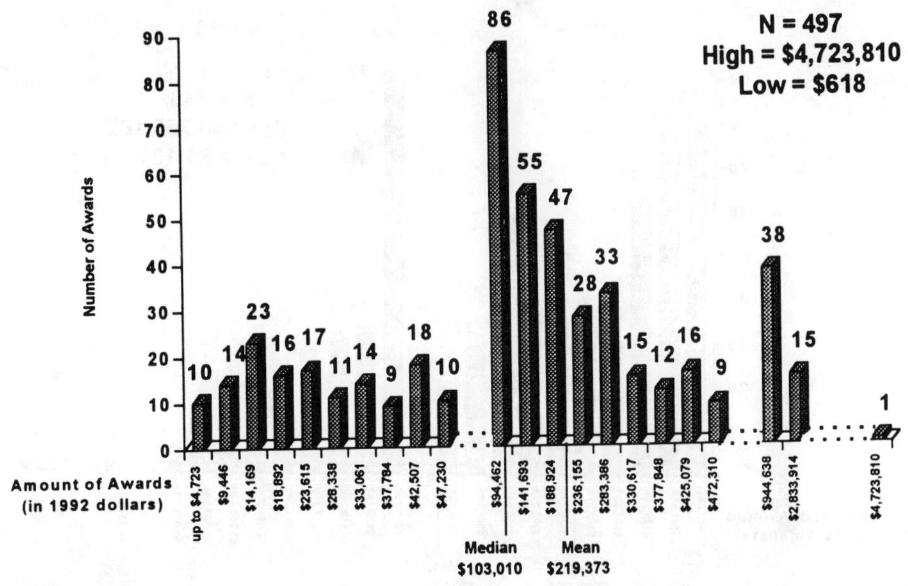

Chart 8

Short Term Major/No Long Term

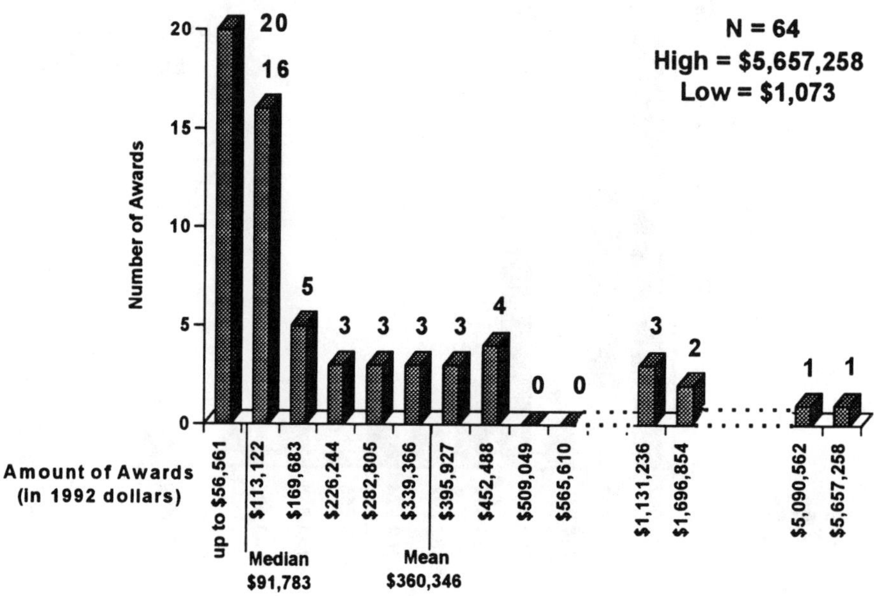

Chart 9

Short Term Major/Long Term Minor

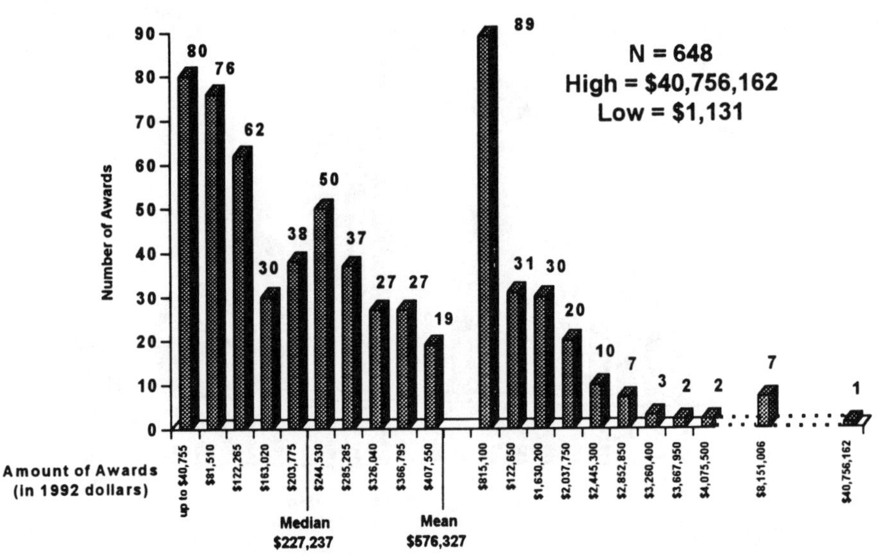

Chart 10

Short Term Major/Long Term Significant

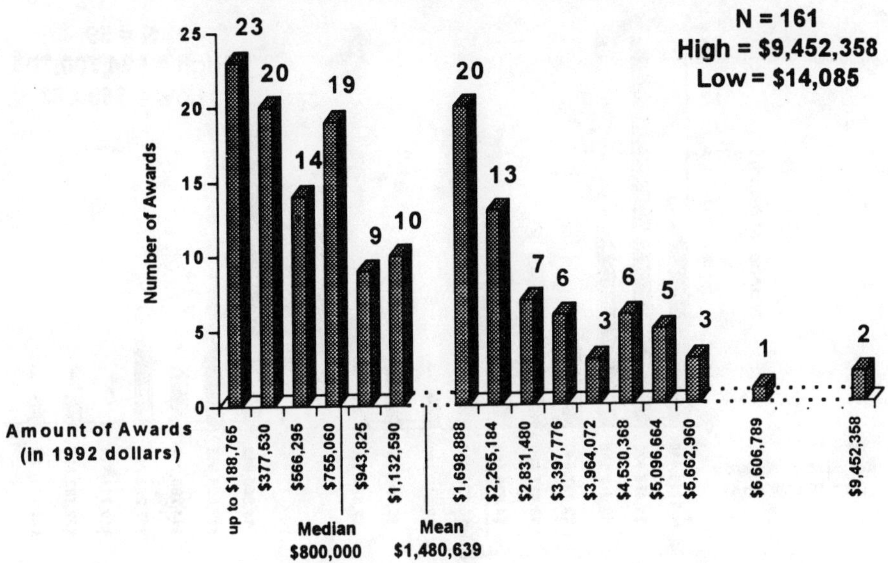

Chart 11

Short Term Major/Long Term Major

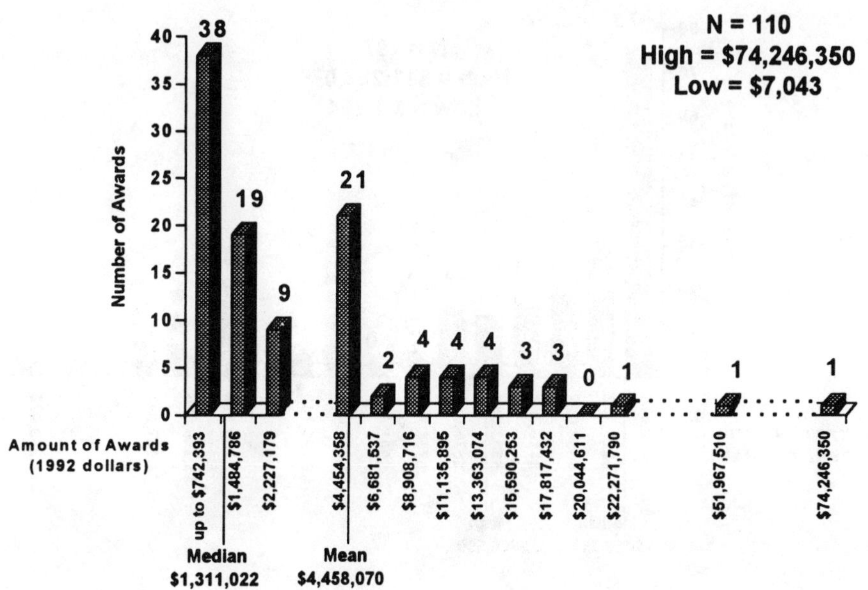

Chart 12

Short Term Major/Long Term Grave

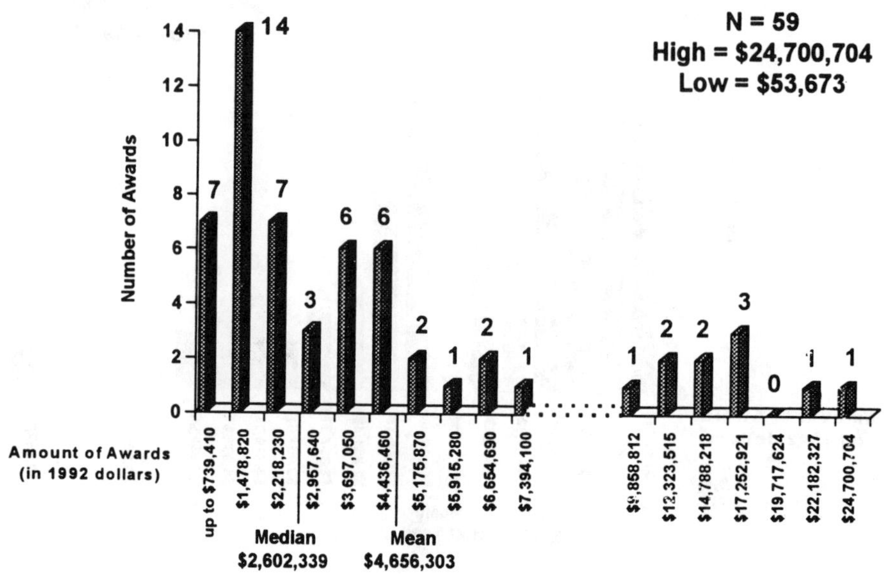

Chart 13

Short Term Major/Death

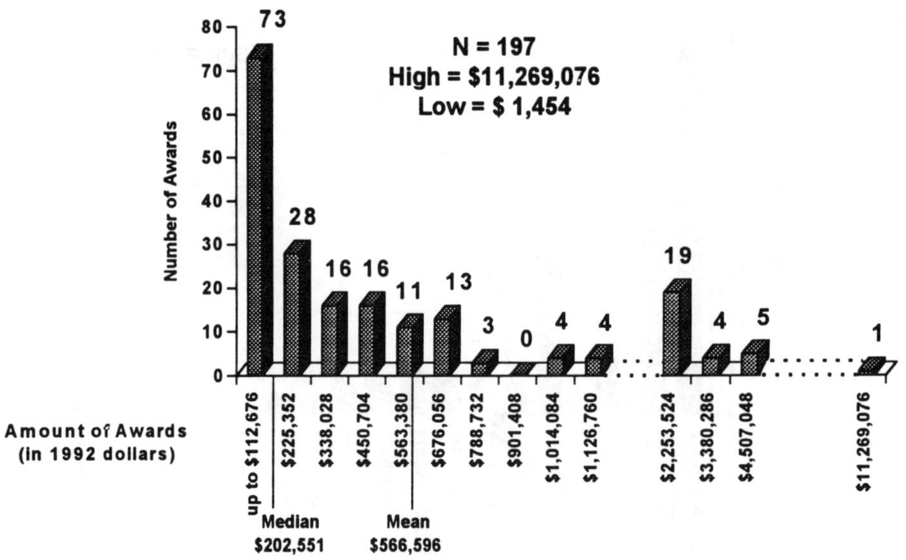

Notes

1. 2 American Law Institute, *Enterprise Responsibility for Personal Injury* 199, 202 (1991).
2. James F. Blumstein et al., *Beyond Tort Reform: Developing Better Tools Assessing Damages for Personal Injury*, 8 Yale J. Reg. 171, 174 (1990).
3. *Id.* at 173.
4. Frederick S. Levin, *Pain and Suffering Guidelines: A Cure for Damages Measurement "Anomie"*, 22 U. Mich J.L. Ref. 303, 308 (1989); *see also* Stanley Ingber, *Rethinking Intangible Injuries: A Focus on Remedy*, 73 Cal. L. Rev. 772, 778–79 (1985) ("without some basis for calculating loss, damage awards are apt in many cases to be unfair to one or the other of the parties. But no such standards have been developed. Juries are left with nothing but their consciences to guide them. Consequently, wide variations in monetary awards result.")
5. Levin, *supra* note 4, at 307 ("Presently, pain and suffering awards say little about the degree of plaintiff's suffering or how society values it. The message is so muddled that the award has scarcely any meaning at all.")
6. Jury awards for pain and suffering in personal injury cases may be costing consumers more than $7 billion above what they would be willing to pay. John E. Calfee & Clifford Winston, *The Consumer Welfare Effect of Liability for Pain and Suffering: An Exploratory Analysis*, in 1 Brookings Papers on Economic Activity: Microeconomic 133 (1993).
7. See Randall R. Bovbjerg et al., *Valuing Life and Limb in Tort: Scheduling "Pain and Suffering,"* 83 Nw. U. L. Rev. 908, 915-16 (1989).
8. Blumstein et al., *supra* note 2, at 173.
9. Jeffrey O'Connell, *A Proposal to Abolish Defendants' Payment for Pain and Suffering in Return for Payment of Claimants' Attorneys' Fees*, 1981 U. Ill. L. Rev. 333, 351.
10. *Id.*; see also Gregory A. Hicks, *Statutory Damage Caps Are an Incomplete Reform: A Proposal for Attorney Fee Shifting in Tort Actions*, 49 La. L. Rev. 763 (1989).
11. O'Connell, *supra* note 9, at 352.
12. *Id.*
13. Marco de Sae Silva, *Constitutional Challenges to Washington's Limit on Noneconomic Damages in Cases of Personal Injury and Death*, 63 Wash. L. Rev. 653, 654-55 (1988). The United States House of Representatives has recently enacted a cap of $250,000 in health care liability actions in a federal or state court. H.R. 956, 104th Cong., 1st Sess. §203(a)(1995).
14. E.g., W. Va. Code §55-7B-8 (Michie 1994) ("In any medical professional liability action brought against a health care provider, the maximum amount recoverable as damages for noneconomic loss shall not exceed one million dollars and the jury may be so instructed.")
15. E.g., Wash. Rev. Code §4.56.250 (1988) ("In no action seeking damages for personal injury or death may a claimant recover a judgment for noneconomic damages exceeding an amount determined by multiplying 0.43 by the average annual wage and by the life expectancy of the person incurring noneconomic damages.") (held unconstitutional in *Sofie v. Fibreboard Corp.*, 771 P.2d 711 (Wash.) (en banc), *modified in other respects*, 780 P.2d 260 (1989)).

16. See William P. Gronfein & Eleanor D. Kinney, *Controlling Large Malpractice Claims: The Unexpected Impact of Damage Caps*, 16 J. Health Pol., Pol'y & L. 441 (1991).
17. Bovbjerg et al., *supra* note 7, at 959.
18. E.g., *Fein v. Permanente Medical Group,* 211 Cal. Rptr. 368, 382, *appeal dismissed*, 474 U.S. 892 (1985) (substantive due process); *Arneson v. Olson,* 270 N.W.2d 125, 129 (N.D. 1978) (equal protection); *Boyd v. Bulala,* 647 F. Supp. 781, 788 (W.D. Va. 1986) (right to trial by jury), *aff'd in part and rev'd in part,* 877 F.2d 1191 (4th Cir. 1989); *Wright v. Cent. DuPage Hosp.*, 347 N.E.2d 736, 743 (Ill. 1976) (special legislation); *Prendergast v. Nelson,* 256 N.W.2d 657, 668-69 (Neb. 1977) (special privilege); *Smith v. Dep't of Ins.*, 507 So.2d 1080, 1087 (Fla. 1987) (right of access to courts).
19. Report of ABA Action Comm'n to Improve the Tort Liab. Sys. 11-12 (1987); Bovbjerg et al., *supra* note 7, at 957-58.
20. ABA Action Comm'n to Improve the Tort Liab. Sys., *supra* note 19, at 15.
21. *Id.*
22. *Id.*
23. David Baldus et al., *Improving Judicial Oversight of Jury Damage Assessments: A Proposal for the Comparative Additur/Remittitur Review of Awards for Nonpecuniary Harms and Punitive Damages* 80 Iowa L. Rev. (1995) (forthcoming). A shorter version of the same proposal is presented *infra* this volume.
24. *Id.*
25. *Martell v. Boardwalk Enters., Inc.*, 748 F.2d 740 (2d Cir. 1984).
26. *Id.* at 750-55.
27. Baldus et al., *supra* note 23.
28. *Id.*
29. *Id.*
30. *Id.*
31. Bovbjerg et al., *supra* note 7, at 938-60.
32. *Id.* at 938-53.
33. *Id.* at 944 ("[A]ll personal characteristics of plaintiffs (other than age) and defendants are irrelevant to levels of non-economic damage under the matrix; sex, race, occupation, and income are ignored as classifying factors regardless of their current impact in the 'real world.'")
34. *Id.* at 953-56.
35. *Id.* at 953 ("The scenarios would resemble the legal 'hypotheticals' so beloved by law professors, but would focus on the circumstances of injury, rather than on the law.")
36. *Id.* at 954-55.
37. *Id.* at 955.'
38. *Id.* at 956-60.
39. Blumstein et al., *supra* note 2, at 177-78.
40. *Id.* at 178.
41. *Id.*
42. *Id.* at 178-79.
43. *Id.* at 179 (footnotes omitted).
44. Peter H. Schuck, *Scheduled Damages and Insurance Contracts for Future Services: A Comment on Blumstein, Bovbjerg, and Sloan*, 8 Yale J. on Reg. 213 (1990).

45. *Id.* at 217.'
46. *Id.* at 217-18.
47. *Id.* at 218.
48. *Id.*; Levin, *supra* note 4, at 304.
49. See Levin, *supra* note 4, at 323 ("[G]uidelines encourage the lawyers to argue about the aspects of the case that distinguish it from the typical case described in the guidelines. The arguments should focus on factors that either aggravate or mitigate the degree of injury, and call for a greater or lesser award.")
50. Schuck, *supra* note 44, at 219.
51. Levin, *supra* note 4, at 311-19.
52. *Id.* at 312-13.
53. *Id.* at 313.
54. *Id.* at 315.
55. *Id.*
56. *Id.* at 322.
57. *Id.* at 318 (footnotes omitted).
58. *Id.* at 319.
59. Empirical research on the ratio of economic recovery to economic loss in tort law has consistently found overcompensation of modest losses and undercompensation of large ones. See Stephen J. Carroll & James S. KaKalik, *No-Fault Approaches to Compensating Auto Accident Victims*, 60 J. Risk & Ins. 265, 278- 279 (1993); Elizabeth M. King & James P. Smith, Economics, Loss and Compensation in Aviation Accidents 68 (1988).
60. Levin *supra* note 4, at 307-10.
61. Several other jurisdictions also require some itemization of damage awards. See, e.g., Alaska Stat. §09.17.040 (1991); Fla. Stat. Ann. §768.77 (West 1995); Iowa Code Ann. §668.3(8) (West 1987); Kan. Stat. Ann. §§60-249a, 60-1903, 60- 19a01, 60-19a02 (1994); Md. Code Ann. Cts. & Jud. Proc. §11-109 (Supp. 1994); Mass. Gen. Laws Ann. ch. 231, §60F (West Supp. 1995) (health care malpractice awards); and V.I. Code Ann. tit. 27, §166ib (1993) (health care malpractice awards).
62. The authors have not analyzed the data since the objective of this paper is to focus on the process of collecting and sorting the data, not on the substantive characteristics of the data that were uncovered.
63. Our study reveals, for example, that the mean award in Bronx County is over five times the mean award in the rural counties.
64. See Blumstein et al., *supra* note 2, at 181-84.
65. The *New York Jury Verdict Reporter* is issued weekly by the Moran Publishing Company of Islip, New York. Researchers at the Institute for Civil Justice at RAND indicated that, of various jury verdict reporters available, *The New York Jury Verdict Reporter* is among the most complete and most accurate. *The New York Jury Verdict Reporter* contains details about a case, such as the actions of a physician in a medical malpractice case or the driving conditions in an automobile accident case; information about the parties, such as their age, gender, and occupation; and the components of an award, including damages for past and future lost wages, past and future medical expenses, and past and future pain and suffering. Capturing such information is possible because juries in New York State are required to complete

detailed interrogatories. See N.Y. Civ. Prac. L. & R. §4111(d) (McKinney 1995). Several commentators have noted that any regime of "scheduling" damages for pain and suffering is dependent on the use of some form of special verdict. *See, e.g.*, Bovbjerg et al., *supra* note 7, at 962.

66. The database also includes cases from the New York Court of Claims, which has jurisdiction in lawsuits against a governmental entity. N.Y. Jud. Law §9 (McKinney 1995). Court of Claims cases, are not included in the study, however, because they are bench trials. *Id.* §1.

67. The database includes the following fields: the verdict date; the length of the trial; the location of the court; the age, gender, occupation, and employment status of the plaintiff; the type of defendant, that is, whether the defendant was an individual, a corporation, a not-for-profit organization, or a governmental agency; the age, gender, occupation, and employment status of the defendant, if an individual; the type of tort; the severity of short-term injury; the severity of long-term injury; the total damages awarded; damages for past and future pain and suffering; damages for past and future medical expenses; damages for past and future lost wages; punitive damages; the effects of comparative negligence; and the effects of additur and remittitur. The study analyzes damages for pain and suffering, severity of injury, and the effects of geography on damages for pain and suffering; future articles will examine information in the other database fields.

68. In entering damages in the database, including damages for pain and suffering, various rules of thumb had to be used. Concerning damages in general, if the total award in a case was not equal to the sum of the components, the components were assumed to be accurate and the sum of the components was presumed to be the correct total. Also, awards for loss of consortium were not entered because they are derivative, that is, they are intended to compensate an individual other than the physically or emotionally injured plaintiff; however, awards for loss of parental support were included because such awards are often an aspect of lost wages, that is, the portion of the adult plaintiff's income needed for the support of his or her child or children. Third, accrued pre-judgment interest was included in the award, but reduction to present value was not. For the awarding of pre-judgment interest, see N.Y. Civ. Prac. L. & R. §§5001–21 (McKinney 1995). Regarding damages for pain and suffering, in conformity with *McDougald v. Garber*, 538 N.Y.S.2d 937 (N.Y. 1989), and its progeny, damages for loss of enjoyment of life, mental anguish, emotional distress, and permanency of injury were included as part of damages for pain and suffering. In order to facilitate analysis of trends and patterns, such damages were included even if awarded before *McDougald* was decided. Concerning medical expenses, the following costs were included as part of an award for medical expenses: costs of physicians, physical therapists, and nurses; costs of physical and occupational rehabilitation; costs of facilitation of a disability lifestyle; costs of custodial care; and costs of cosmetic surgery. An award for the costs of housekeeping was not included in medical expenses, but was entered as part of the total award.

69. See National Ass'n of Ins. Comm'rs, Malpractice Claims: Final Compilation (1980).

70. See U.S. Gen. Accounting Office, Medical Malpractice: Characteristics of

Claims Closed in 1984 (1987).

71. See, e.g., Bovbjerg et al., *supra* note 7, at 921.
72. *Id.* at 920.
73. *Id.* at 920.
74. For example, the effects of some injuries may be long in duration, but not permanent.
75. Thus, "temporary insignificant," "temporary minor," and "temporary major," in the NAIC scale became "short- term minor," "short-term significant," and "short-term major," respectively, in order to align with the "permanent" or "long- term" categories of "minor," "significant," and "major." There is no "temporary" or "short-term" category to correspond with the "permanent" or "long-term" "grave" category or with the categories of emotional injury only or death.
76. The study uses everyday terms like "tailbone" rather than "coccyx," both for the sake of simplicity and because popular words and phrases are more commonly used by *The New York Jury Verdict Reporter*.
77. In classifying the severity of injury, it was necessary to make two assumptions. First, an injury which caused the death of a plaintiff within two years after the injury is presumed to be a "short-term major injury." Second, the following injuries were presumed to result in long-term injury, so long as the plaintiff presented any evidence to that effect, unless the jury specifically decided that the plaintiff suffered no residual injury: back, neck, and hip injuries; bone dislocations and fractures requiring surgery, such as the insertion of pins or rods; and severe burns.

Additur/Remittitur Review: An Empirically Based Methodology for the Comparative Review of General Damages Awards for Pain, Suffering, and Loss of Enjoyment of Life

David C. Baldus
John C. MacQueen
George Woodworth*

I. Introduction

This paper presents selected findings[1] from a research project designed to test the feasibility of empirically-based methods for conducting additur/remittitur review of (a) general damages awarded as compensation for nonpecuniary harms (pain, suffering, and loss of enjoyment of life), and (b) punitive damages.[2] In this paper we limit our discussion to additur/remittitur review of general damages.[3]

To test the feasibility of the methodology proposed here, we conducted an empirical study of 461 cases in which injured children from 20 states were awarded damages for personal injuries.[4] In the course of this study, we conducted for each case a simulated proportionality analysis of the type that could underlie a comparative additur/remittitur review.

We start with four assumptions about personal injury damage awards in the American tort system. First, a reasonable level of consistency in the damages awarded for nonpecuniary harms among similarly situated plaintiffs is desirable. Second, it is appropriate for trial and appellate courts to provide oversight of jury damage awards through additur/remittitur or a similar process of review. Third, the absence of objective standards to guide the exercise of jury discretion is a source of inconsistency and arbitrariness in the quantum of awards for pain, suffering, and loss of

*Professors of Law, Medicine, and Statistics (respectively), University of Iowa.

enjoyment of life; jurors are typically instructed merely to consider all the evidence and set the level of damages they consider fair and reasonable. Fourth, there is no consensus about the frequency with which juries return excessive and inadequate awards. Members of the legal profession, especially trial judges and personal injury lawyers, express little concern about the issue, while the medical profession and the public generally perceive a more serious problem.

Our proposal builds upon the law's traditional procedure for dealing with the problem of excessive and inadequate damages awards–additur/remittitur review–which empowers a court to consider a post trial claim that an award of damages, is either excessive or inadequate. Our research suggests that, as traditionally applied, additur and remittitur review is often ineffective. Indeed, the results of traditional forms of additur/remittitur review are often perceived to be as arbitrary as the underlying pattern of awards the process is designed to correct. The principal problem with the traditional approach to additur/remittitur review is that it is also based on a subjective standard, i.e., does the award shock the conscience of the court or appear to be unreasonable?

For some years, however, a minority of courts have conducted what is known as comparative additur/remittitur review, which in a number of respects is similar to the approach we are suggesting. Such courts look for guidance from awards in other cases and treat those awards as a form of precedent. Specifically, the reviewing court, whether a trial or appellate court, will look to jury awards in other comparable cases that have been (a) approved by another court (trial or appellate) as not excessive or inadequate, or (b) acquiesced in by the parties under circumstances suggesting that both parties considered the award reasonable. The following New York intermediate appellate court opinion summarizes the rationale:

> It is true that the amount of [compensatory] damages to be awarded for personal injuries is primarily a question of fact for the jury. However, where the verdict of a jury is contrary to the weight of the evidence, or where it is excessive or inadequate, the trial court is vested with the power, and has the duty, to set it aside and order a new trial. The exercise of this power rests in sound judicial discretion, based upon a careful consideration of the evidence. . . . Where the exercise of discretion is at issue, certain standards of uniformity should be adhered to.
>
> This is not to say that the amount of damages awarded or sustained in cases involving similar injuries are in any way binding upon the courts in the exercise of their discretion. However, prior verdicts may guide and enlighten the court and in a sense, may constrain it. "A long course of practice, numerous verdicts rendered year after

year, orders made by trial justices approving or disapproving them, decisions on the subject by appellate courts, furnish to the judicial mind some indication of the consensus of opinion of jurors and courts as to the proper relation between the character of the injury and the amount of compensation awarded." It was observed in one early opinion: "Long observation of the action of juries in cases of [similar] personal injury . . . affords a clue to the judgment of ordinary men as to the compensation that should be made for pain and suffering; and where a verdict is much above or much below the average, it is fair to infer, unless the case presents extraordinary features, that passion, partiality, prejudice, or some other improper motive has led the jury astray."[5]

The comparative method of remittitur review is most commonly used in diversity cases by federal courts striving to maintain consistency between the pattern of general damage awards in federal and state courts.[6] It is also frequently used in New York state courts.[7]

The system of comparative additur/remittitur review that we present in this paper represents a move toward *bureaucratic justice,* because it departs from the conception that every tort claim is unique and that completely individualized damage assessments must be made within the sole discretion of the fact finder. Because the core of the proposed procedure contemplates the use of prior damage awards to inform the exercise of judicial discretion in additur/remittitur review, it involves the application of an external standard, a practice distinctly characteristic of bureaucratic systems like worker's compensation. Comparative review also relies on aggregation and averaging, another feature of bureaucratic justice because its controlling standards are partially inferred from the pattern of awards in similar cases. It further shares with systems like worker's compensation the feature of floors and caps for defined categories of cases. It is, however, distinguishable from workers compensation in that it involves an individualized review of each award on the basis of all relevant case characteristics, as contrasted with the more limited number of case characteristics deemed salient by a worker's compensation payment schedule.

The methodology we propose is an alternative to the use of legislative caps, which limit the amount of damages that can be awarded for pain, suffering, and loss of enjoyment of life. These caps generally impose an upper limit of $250,000–$500,000. We oppose legislative caps for three reasons. First, they are arbitrary because there is no principled way to determine the appropriate level. Second, they are inequitable because seriously injured plaintiffs bear almost the exclusive burden of the caps. Third, caps are inefficient because they fail to address at all questions of inconsistency and arbitrariness among the pattern of awards below the cap level. Caps also totally ignore the question of inadequate jury awards. In fact, caps are largely irrelevant to the issue of arbitrariness. They are designed primarily to limit the absolute value of damages paid and to reduce the cost of insurance premiums.

In the balance of this paper we argue that comparative additur/remittitur review is a potentially useful procedure that represents an improvement over the traditional subjective approach and avoids the most conspicuous inequities associated with the use of legislative caps. We argue further that current comparative review practice can be improved without undue cost or complexity through methodological enhancements and modifications that can make it more objective and principled. Finally, we argue that the comparative review process can be strengthened through improved and expanded case reporting practices.

In short, we suggest that the key to a stronger system of additur/remittitur review is the use of a comparative approach, employing enhanced methodology and better data. The principal focus of our research was on these two methodological concerns. In that regard, the overriding question was whether courts today have the capacity (a) to identify groups of cases that are "comparable" in terms of pain, suffering, and loss of enjoyment of life, and (b) to use that information to inform their decisions in a manageable and trustworthy manner.

II. Contemporary Comparative Remittitur Practice in the Federal Courts

Because our proposal builds upon contemporary practice in the federal courts, we consider it useful to describe a state of the art application of the procedure in a federal court.[8] The example is *Martell v. Boardwalk Enterprises*,[9] summarized in part A of Table 1. Martell, a 16-year-old boy, was involved in a violent collision with a motorboat while driving a jet ski on Lake Erie. The impact traumatically amputated his non-dominant arm, and he suffered a series of other physical and psychological injuries. A jury award of two million dollars for his pain, suffering, and loss of enjoyment of life was approved as reasonable by the trial court, but reduced on appeal to $1.2 million in an opinion by Judge Kearse of the Second Circuit Court of Appeals.

The comparative methodology applied by Judge Kearse had two parts. First, she identified four cases decided in New York state courts (listed as "Very Severe Injury Cases" in Table 1) with awards approved by a trial or appellate court, that were comparable to Martell's, i.e., damages in the range of $1 to $2 million. She noted that each of these cases involved a much more serious injury than Martell's, specifically, quadriplegia, paraplegia, or extensive burns with massive scarring and disfigurement. Because the severity of Martell's injuries did not come close to those cases, she concluded his award was excessive.

Table 1
Cases Used in the *Martell* Remittitur Review

Name	Yr. of Award	Accident/Injury	Comparison Cost Approved General Damages Award (in 000s of dollars)
A. Review case			
Martell[1] ($2.0 million award reduced to $1.2 million	1983	16-year-old girl suffered loss of nondominant left arm in jet ski accident. Emotional problems, but adjusting. Continued involvement in football, skiing, squash, and sailing.	
B. Single limb injury cases			
1. *Kusisto*[2]	1975[a]	Plaintiff, a teenager, suffered kidney and bladder contusions, fractures of spinal process, and amputation of left leg at mid-thigh when his motorcycle was hit by a car. Unable to perform activities requiring mobility because stump tolerates little pressure. Continued pain and discomfort.	400[b]
2. *Kraft*[3]	1976[a]	Adult plaintiff involved in grinding wheel explosion, six operations, leg ultimately amputated	255[b]
3. *Dubicki*[4]	1978	Working as a cable splicer, adult plaintiff was involved in an accident with a motorist which resulted in a broken leg and groin injury. Plaintiff underwent several operations, which resulted in the complete loss of the use of his leg and the threat of possible future amputation.	810[b]
4. *Prata*[5]	1976	Railroad explosive of chemicals and sand blew off adult plaintiff's hand. Fitted with prosthesis and employable with some continued pain.	700

[1] 748 F2d 740 (2d Cir. 1984)
[2] 382 N.Y.S.2d 146 (N.Y. App. Div. 1976)
[3] 395 N.Y.S.2d 542 (N.Y. App. Div. 1977)
[4] 407 N.Y.S.2d 66 (N.Y. App. Div. 1978)
[5] 420 N.Y.S.2d 276 (N.Y. App. Div. 1979)
[a] Year of award estimated as year before appellate opinion.
[b] This was an unitemized general verdict that included an unknown proportion of the award as compensation for special damages, e.g., medical expenses or impaired earning capacity.

Table 1 (Continued)

5. *Terry*[6]	1979	Teenage plaintiff hit by boulder on left shoulder. Left arm withered and useless. Continued serious pain for life.	400
6. *Le Bel*[7]	1982[a]	Injury suffered when limousine slid into plaintiff and crushed leg between the limousine and another car. Destroyed bone, nerve, and connective tissue of leg. Recurrent infection and five hospitalizations of up to four months. Amputation of leg above knee is inevitable.	800[b]
7. *Novell*[8]	1983[a]	While lifting cable from eleventh to twenty-third floor, left leg of adult male plaintiff was caught in hoist rope and severly injured.	631[c]
C. Very severe injury cases			
1. *Caprara*[9]	1978[a]	Steering locked and car crashed, leaving adult plaintiff a quadriplegic.	2,000[b]
2. *Tabone*[10]	1981[a]	Grenade exploded in plaintiff's hand, setting him on fire. Hospitalized for 72 days, 2nd and 3rd degree burns over 35% of his body including face, neck, arms, and chest. Severe disfigurement. Loss of 2 fingers and 2 fingertips. Inability to use hands for $1\frac{1}{2}$ years, requiring help in eating, dressing, and other daily activities.	2,000
3. *Rush*[11]	1982	2nd and 3rd degree burns over 42% of body. Disfigurement, pain and suffering from burns and skin grafts. Still able to attend to own needs and be an employed, active member of society.	1,500
4. *Poulos*[12]	1981[a]	Motorcyle accident left 16-year-old plaintiff a paraplegic.	1,000

[6] 435 N.Y.S.2d 389 (N.Y. App. Div. 1981)
[7] 461 N.Y.S.2d 474 (N.Y. App. Div. 1983)
[8] 476 N.Y.S.2d 241 (N.Y. Tr. Div. 1984)
[9] 423 N.Y.S.2d 694 (N.Y. App. Div. 1979)
[10] 456 N.Y.S.2d 950 (N.Y. Ct. Cl. 1982)
[11] 461 N.Y.S.2d 559 (N.Y. App. Div. 1983)
[12] 472 N.Y.S.2d 3 (N.Y. App. Div. 1984)
[c] This was an unitemized general verdict, but the opinion included sufficient detail to estimate the proportions of the award intended to compensate for pain, suffering, and loss of enjoyment of life.

Her next and more difficult task was to identify the appropriate amount for Martell. It is one thing to say his award is too high. But what is the "right" amount? For that purpose she turned to a series of seven single-limb amputation cases, also approved by New York Courts, summarized in part B of Table 1. Her methodology here was straightforward. She briefly described the seven cases and reported the awards in them, which ranged from $255,000 in *Kraft* (#2) to $810,000 in *Dubicki* (#3). From there she moved directly to her order conditionally reducing the award from $2 million to $1.2 million. Or put more accurately, Martell was given two options: accept a reduced general damages award of $1.2 million, or face a new trial on damages. She offered no explanation of why the $1.2 million figure followed from the awards in the seven comparison cases.

Given the opaqueness of this analysis, one might ask why we consider it state of the art methodology. There are two reasons. First, Judge Kearse based her analysis on a manageable number of reasonably comparable comparison cases that she identified by name, a detail omitted by some courts. Second, she provided at least minimal information about the facts of the comparison cases bearing on the level of nonpecuniary harm, another important detail overlooked by some courts applying the method.

In spite of the strengths of Judge Kearse's analysis and the comparative approach widely used in the federal courts, we believe that with enhancement, an empirically based comparative approach can be even more objective, principled, and trustworthy.

III. Enhanced Methodology for Comparative Additur/Remittitur Review

The comparative model of additur/remittitur review involves both qualitative and quantitative components, which we summarize in Table 2.

In the review process, quite different resources might be available to the trial and appellate judges involved.[10] At one end of the spectrum, we contemplate a trial judge with no analytic resources available beyond his or her experience and judgment, a judge whose access to a data base is limited to the cases presented by counsel for the parties. We believe that our proposals offer a way to make the analysis of even such an informal data base more systematic and principled. At the other end of the spectrum, we contemplate a system in which the trial court and the parties have access to a state-wide data base of cases with rich information concerning the injuries and measures of compensable harm involved. Under this scenario, the basic analytic approach is the same, but the results are likely to be more accurate because of the enhanced resources.

Table 2

The Comparative Review Model: A Summary

A. The Qualitative Methodology
   1. Identify the characteristics of the review case that may properly affect the level of damages.
   2. Identify a group of comparable comparison cases.
   3. Conduct a qualitative comparative analysis.

B. The Quantitative Methodology
   1. Adjust the comparison case awards to account for the effects of inflation.
   2. Rank order the review case and the comparison cases by their respective levels of nonpecuniary harm, with the actual awards indicated (rank order method), and/or
   3. Adjust the awards in the comparison cases by estimating the award that would likely have been returned and approved in each, if it had had the same level of compensatory harm as the review case (adjusted award method).
   4. Estimate a range of reasonableness for the review case on the basis of the actual and/or hypothetical awards produced in steps 2 and/or 3 above.

C. The Outcomes
   1. Determination of excessiveness or inadequacy.
   2. Conditional enhancement or reduction of the review case award.

A. Qualitative Methods

Although it is desirable to use comparison cases that are nearly identical to the case being reviewed, it is clearly not necessary in order to conduct a meaningful comparative review.[11] Indeed, a principle finding of our research is that a court needs only a group of cases reasonably comparable to the review case in terms of the level of compensable, nonpecuniary harm.[12]

The qualitative methodology tracks the approach used by Judge Kearse in *Martell*. The first step, indicated under A-1 in Table 2, is to identify the characteristics of the review case that may properly affect the plaintiff's level of pain, suffering, and loss of enjoyment of life. While this seems like a straightforward point of departure, it is not uncommon for a court to give scant attention to many of the vital details that bear on the level of nonpecuniary harm in the review case. The second step is to identify a group of comparison cases that are reasonably comparable to the review case. Under current practice, most courts are limited in making this inquiry to cases published in reporter systems or to unreported cases produced by counsel. That is a defect in our current system that impairs the effectiveness of such reviews, which we mention briefly in Part V below.

The third step is to conduct a qualitative analysis of each comparison case. For that purpose, we developed a system that permits rudimentary qualitative comparisons. For each comparison case it calls for a judgment of whether the level of nonpecuniary harms is much less (ML), somewhat less (SL), equal (E), somewhat more (SM), or much more (MM) severe than the level of harm in the review case. A less systematic approach at this stage of the review simply involves a statement of the relevant facts of each comparison case, as was done in *Martell.* Moreover, as *Martell* illustrates, a court can move directly from the results of such a qualitative analysis to the outcomes of the review process, which are shown in item C of Table 2.

B. Quantitative Methods

It has been argued that a qualitative, intuitive analysis that moves directly from a review of comparison cases to a final order, a la *Martell*, is as rigorous and systematic a method as the subject matter will allow. Because of the subjective nature of the phenomena involved in the review of general damages (e.g., pain and suffering), we are told that a more systematic and quantitative mode of analysis would give a false or misleading impression of the reliability and validity of the review process. An alternative view is that the subject matter, although subjective, does lend itself to a more systematic and quantitative method of analysis. The legal system routinely relies on quantified assessments of similar phenomena—for example, quantified jury determinations of comparative fault in negligence cases, and quantified judicial fines and prison terms in criminal sentencing. In medicine, quantitative assessments of the equivalent of pain, suffering, and loss of enjoyment of life routinely provide the basis for treatment decisions (e.g., hip replacement) and assessments of the effectiveness of medical treatments. Our work on this project suggests that the use of the following four quantitative methods—which we illustrate in a reanalysis of *Martell*—can make the case matching process more objective, principled, and accurate, regardless of whether the results of such an analysis are reported by the reviewing court. Even if these procedures are not formally applied by a court, a conceptual understanding of their logic can increase a judge's ability to conduct an additur/remittitur review, whether done comparatively or in a more traditional, subjective manner.

1. Inflation Adjustment

The first possible quantitative enhancement involves adjusting the awards in the comparison cases upward to reflect the effects of inflation. Specifically, the comparison case awards are set to the inflated dollar value they would likely have had on the date of the award in the review case.[13] Only a few courts applying the comparative method have made such adjustments.[14] It is, however, a straightforward procedure.[15]

Adjustments for inflation permit a court to go back further in time to identify comparison cases without serious concern that the validity of the analysis will be significantly threatened by the changing value of the dollar. Since *the Martell* verdict was assessed in 1983, we adjusted its comparison case awards to 1983 values. In some of the earliest *Martell* comparison cases shown in Table 1, for example *Kusisto* (#1), the award increased from $400,000 to $740,000; in more recent cases like *LeBel* (#6), the increase was small, from $800,000 to $826,000.

2. Rank Order Method

Another possible enhancement is to construct a comparative rank ordering of the review and comparison cases. The cases are ordered in terms of the overall level of pain, suffering, and loss of enjoyment of life. The steps in this process are summarized in Table 3. Rank ordering builds upon the five-level qualitative ranking method described above, which classified the cases from much less (ML) to much more (MM) severe than the review case. Specifically, the rank order method involves additional case sorting within each of these five possible levels.

Table 3

Rank Order Method: Creating a List of Actual Awards in Comparison Cases That Have Been Rank Ordered

1. Evaluate the review and comparison cases in terms of their comparative levels of pain, suffering, and loss of enjoyment of life.
2. Rank order the cases in terms of the level of compensable nonpecuniary harms.
3. Make a list of actual awards in the cases that are most comparable to the review case and place the review case within the distribution.

Table 4 illustrates for the *Martell* case how the rank order method evolves from the qualitative classifications. Column C orders the comparison cases Judge Kearse used in her analysis into four of the five possible levels described above. With the rank order method, our law student raters produced the more refined sorting shown in Column B – producing a range from *Novell* as the least aggravated case, to *Tabone* the most aggravated, with *Martell* positioned as the third-least aggravated. These data shift our focus to the near neighbors of *Martell*, from an award of $446,000 in *Kraft* to an award of $1,069,000 in *Pratta*. These awards provide important evidence of the size of awards that are likely to be made and approved in cases like *Martell* over the long run.

The validity of this ranking procedure depends on the capacity of the court to order cases in terms of their levels of compensable harm. As noted above, the vehicle for testing our proposed methodology was

Table 4
Rank Order Method: *Martell* Reanalysis

A Case Name	B Estimated Level of Nonpecuniary Harm: Rank Order From Low to High	C Comparison Case Harm Level Compared to *Martell*	D General Damages Award in Thousands of '83 Dollars
Novell	1	SL	631
Terry	2	SL	549
Martell	**3**	–	**2000**
Kraft	4	E	446
Prata	5	SM	1069
Le Bel	6	SM	826
Kusisto	7	SM	740
Dubicki	8	SM	1332
Rush	9	MM	1548
Caprara	10	MM	3054
Poulos	11	MM	1000
Tabone	12	MM	2191

an empirical study of 461 seriously injured children, selected from nine injury categories (e.g., burns, amputation, lacerations, paralysis, etc.). Within each of these nine subgroups, law student raters ranked the cases. The results showed an acceptable degree of reliability and validity when compared with the reliability and validity of similar evaluations in medical science (for example, in studies measuring the reaction of a patient to a parent's death, dysfunctional personal behavior, and responses to treatment for low back pain).[16] This research therefore gives us confidence in the capacity of courts to conduct similar analyses. We also found that the ranking process disciplined the comparative analysis and highlighted issues that would have been overlooked in a more intuitive analysis.[17]

3. Adjusted Award Method

A third possible enhancement involves adjusting the damages awards in the comparison cases to reflect, for each, an estimate of the size of the damages award that would have been returned and approved in each of those cases if the level of compensable harm had been the same as in the review case. Put differently, the results of the adjustment procedure constitute an estimate of the size of awards that would have been returned and approved by the jury and by the court in each comparison case

Table 5

Adjusted Award Method: Creating a List of Adjusted Awards in Comparison Cases

1. Rank order all cases in terms of their levels of compensable harm.
2. Without knowledge of the actual awards, score each case in terms of their relative levels of compensable nonpecuniary harms over a maximum range of 0 to 100 (the most severe case score is 100, but the least severe case score need not be 0). "RHS" is the review case harm score, "CHS" is the comparison case harm score.
3. For each comparison case, calculate an award adjustment ratio (R) that reflects the degree to which the level of compensable harm in each comparison case differs from the review case. Specifically, divide the comparison case harm score (CHS) by the review case harm score (RHS), i.e., CHS/RHS to obtain the ratio (R).
4. Adjust the comparison case award by dividing the original award by R. The adjusted award is an estimate of the award the jury in the comparison would have returned had its salient features been the same as the review case.

had they also been called upon to assess and review a general damages award in the review case. The steps in this process are summarized in Table 5.

This adjustment process is analogous to the procedure used by real estate appraisers applying the comparative sales method of property valuation.[18] In that process, the actual sales price in each "comparable" comparison property is adjusted to estimate the price it would have brought in the market if it were identical to the appraisal property. The range of these adjusted sales prices provides the principal basis for the appraiser's final valuation of the appraisal property.[19]

In an additur/remittitur review, a comparable adjustment of awards in the comparison cases calls for a quantitative estimate of the degree of compensable harm in each comparison case vis a vis the review case, and an adjustment of the award in the comparison cases to reflect differences between the review case and each comparison case in terms of the level of compensable harm. The final judgments concerning the level of compensable harm in each case may be based on a close analysis of the facts of the cases and on more narrowly focused direct measures of pain, suffering, and loss of enjoyment of life. Assume, for example, that the compensable harm score for the review case is 50, the harm score for a comparison case is 25, and the award in the comparison case is $100,000. This suggests that if the jury in the comparison case had also been asked to assess damages in the review case, its award would have been twice as high as it was in the comparison case. Accordingly, the $100,000 award in the comparison case would be adjusted upward by a factor of 2 to $200,000 to reflect the two times higher level of compensable harm in

Table 6

Illustration of Adjusted Award Method: *Martell* Reanalysis

A	B	C	D
	Review Case	Comparison Cases	
Steps	*Martell*	*Le Bel*	*Tabone*
1. Estimated Compensible Harm Level Rank Order	3	6	12
2. Estimated Compensible Harm Score	30 (RHS)	40 (CHS)	100 (CHS)
3. Comparison Case Award Adjustment Ratio (R): (CHS/RHS)		1.33	3.33
4. Comparison Case Award Adjustment			
a. Comparison case award in 1983 dollars		$826,000	$2,191,000
b. Adjusted Award: (row 4a/R)		$621,000	$658,00

the review case. The end result of this analysis is a listing, or range, of hypothetical adjusted awards for each comparison case. As a group, these awards are further evidence of the range of awards that can be expected in cases comparable to the review case.

Table 6 illustrates the use of the adjusted award method in a reanalysis of *Martell.* The data presented in Table 6 are strictly for the purposes of illustrating the arithmetic that underlies the procedure. Row 1 indicates the rank order numbers reported earlier, in column B of Table 4, with *Martell* the least severe, *LeBel* somewhat more severe, and *Tabone* the most severe.

Row 2 reports the "compensatory harm score" our raters estimated for each case. We started by scoring the most serious case (*Tabone*) at 100. The rater then asked how *LeBel* and *Martell* compare with *Tabone*. Row 2 reflects the raters' initial judgment that Martell's harms were 30% of Tabone's, and LeBel's were 40% of Tabone's. The rater then examined the 10 percentage point difference between the *Martell* and *LeBel* scores to see if the difference seemed coherent given the harms in the two cases or whether it was necessary to reconsider the initial judgments.

Once a rater settles on the compensatory harm scores for all the cases in the analysis, adjusting the comparison case damage awards

Table 7
Adusted Award Method: *Martell* Reanalysis

A Case Name	B Compensable Harm Score	C General Damages Award in Thousands of '83 Dollars	D Comparison Case Adjusted Award in Thousands of '83 Dollars
Novell	20	631	942
Terry	25	549	661
Martell	**30**	**2000**	—
Kraft	32	446	417
Prata	35	1069	914
Le Bel	40	826	621
Kusisto	45	740	493
Dubicki	50	1332	798
Rush	90	1548	516
Caprara	92	3054	995
Poulos	95	1000	315
Tabone	100	2191	658

is straightforward. As shown in row 3, the rater calculates for each comparison case the ratio of the "comparison case harm score" (CHS) to the "review case harm score" (RHS), i.e., CHS/RHS. For *LeBel,* this ratio is 1.33 (40/30), while the ratio for *Tabone* is 3.33 (100/30). In the final step, the rater divides the original comparison case awards in row 4a by the adjustment ratio in row 3 to obtain the final adjusted awards in row 4b.[20]

Table 7 lists the adjusted awards for all of the cases used in Judge Kearse's analysis. Column B presents in rank order the compensatory harm score for each case. Column C reports the inflation-adjusted general damages award for each comparison case. And column D reports the adjusted awards for each case, which range from a low of $417,000 in *Kraft* to a high of $995,000 in *Caprara.* These data provide additional evidence of the likely range of awards one would expect to see over the long run in cases like *Martell.*

People skeptical about the ability of lawyers to rank order cases are even more skeptical about the ability of lawyers to quantify the fine-grained differences called for in the rank order method. We asked law student raters not only to rank order the 461 cases in our study, but also to assign each a compensatory harm score. Using those scores, we conducted reliability/validity studies, and we are satisfied that the process can be conducted with acceptable levels of reliability and validity. As noted above, we base this judgment on an assessment of the levels

Table 8

Actual and Adjusted Comparison Case Damage Awards: *Martell* Reanalysis (in Thousands of 1983 Dollars

A. Actual Damage Awards in the Single Limb Cases Listed in Order of the Estimated Level of Compensable Harm (rank order method)

631	549	**2000**	446	1069	826	740	1332
(Novell)	*(Terry)*	**(Martell)**	*(Kraft)*	*(Prata)*	*(Le Bel)*	*(Kusisto)*	*(Dubicki)*

B. Adjusted Damage Awards For Single Limb Case Comparison Cases Listed in Order of the Estimated Level of Compensable Harm (adjusted award method)

942	661		417	914	621	493	798
(Novell)	*(Terry)*	**(Martell)**	*(Kraft)*	*(Prata)*	*(Le Bel)*	*(Kusisto)*	*(Dubicki)*

C. Adjusted Damage Awards for Severe Injury Cases Listed in order of Estimated Level of Compensable Harm (adjusted award method)

516	995	315	658
(Rush)	*(Caprara)*	*(Poulos)*	*(Tabone)*

of reliability/validity reported in the literature when similar judgments are made in medical contexts. Specifically, our results showed levels of reliability and validity that were comparable to or better than the results reported in those contexts.[21]

4. The Range of Reasonableness

The two lists of awards produced with the rank order and adjusted award methods provide a factual basis for assessing a range of reasonableness for awards in cases comparable to the review case. In a remittitur review, approved *actual* awards in "near neighbor" comparison cases suggest one upper award limit. Similarly, the listing of *adjusted* awards in comparison cases, especially among the cases with the levels of compensable harm closest to the review case, suggest another upper limit. For example, the results of the *Martell* reanalysis reported in Table 8 suggest an upper limit of $1,069,000 (*Prata*) in the actual awards among *Martell's* near neighbors (Part A).[22] The list of adjusted awards suggests an upper limit of $942,000 (*Novell*) among the single limb cases (Part B), and of $995,000 (*Capara*) among the very severe injury cases (Part C).

But should this evidence of prior high awards prescribe the top limit allowable for future awards? Community values change, and historically we have seen an upward trend in the awards assessed and approved by the courts and acquiesced in by the parties. In apparent recognition of the need to accommodate changing community values, federal courts in particular have been quite gtolerant in allowing upward deviations from prior historical highs of as much as 20%, 30% even 40%, although these deviations are generally approved without explanation or discussion. We agree that deviations should be expected and allowed in setting the upper and lower limits of the range of reasonableness. We also believe that explicit attention to the issue would enhance the legitimacy of the procedure.

For purposes of illustration, how could the data in Table 8 be used to define the appropriate "range of reasonableness"? We select 10% as an appropriate and more conservative deviation factor than what we have seen recently in the federal courts. We start with the three historically high awards referred to above (expressed now in thousands of dollars)–$1,069 (*Prata*), $942 (*Novell*), and $995 (*Caprara*)–yielding an average of $1,002. If we allow a 10% upward deviation from this figure, the upper limit would round to $1.1 million. If in deference to the exercise of jury discretion, we use the top award ($1,069) to set the upper limit and also allow a 10% upward deviation, it would round to $1.2 million–exactly the figure approved by Judge Kearse.[23]

C. Procedure

As we envision the comparative review process in its simplest form, the parties would initially bring the comparison cases to the court's attention.[24] The trial court would select from these candidates (and other cases uncovered through its own research) the cases it deems most appropriate.[25] Depending upon the analytic method adopted by the court, counsel would also present arguments about comparative levels of compensable harm among all the cases involved. These suggested findings would focus the issues for the trial judge and provide the foundation for a final judgment concerning the proper adjusted award, if the court uses a strictly qualitative approach, or a ranking and scoring of cases in terms of levels of compensable harm if the court also uses a quantified approach. Table 9 summarizes what we consider to be the principal differences between the comparative approach as currently applied in the courts and the enhanced comparative methodology presented in this report.

IV. Pros and Cons of Enhanced Comparative Review

The principal argument of this study is that contemporary American courts possess the capacity to engage competently in an enhanced version of comparative additur/remittitur review at reasonable cost. We also believe that the procedure has distinct strengths in comparison to legislative caps, the largely subjective traditional approach, or no review at all. First, it provides a more factual and objective foundation to control and bring into line both high and low outlying verdicts. The approach provides a

Table 9

Differences Between the Current Comparative Approach and an Enhanced Comparative Approach

1. More systematic qualitative case comparisons.
2. Adjustment of comparison case awards to account for the effects of inflation.
3. More explicit measurement of levels of compensable harm (rank order method).
4. Quantification of levels of compensable harm (adjusted award method).
5. More explicit explanation and justification of case matching procedures and results.
6. More explicit specification and justification of the range of reasonableness.
7. An expanded data base with more reported cases containing better information relevant to the quantum of damages.

series of caps and floors, for all injury types, that do not unfairly burden plaintiffs with serious injuries. The method thus addresses issues of horizontal equity between similarly-situated cases across the range of injuries from most to least severe. Second, to the extent that it is informed by an analysis of prior approved jury awards, the method better reflects the overall values of the community than do either the legislative judgments that set cap levels or the subjective judgments of judges applying the traditional approach to additur/remittitur review.[26] Third, it can provide a more secure basis for informing settlement negotiations.

Finally, we believe that the experience of the federal courts in this country suggests that the comparative additur/remittitur review can be conducted without undue complexity. The experience of the English courts also supports this conclusion.[27]

There is, however, another side to this story, part of which we have already addressed. The first counterargument is (a) that for a series of methodological and practical reasons, the system we propose cannot produce reliable and consistent results; and (b) that application of the method would result in unacceptable levels of complexity, uncertainty, and cost. The second argument is that such a review system is unnecessary. The third argument is that even if the system could achieve its goal of ensuring reasonable levels of consistency at acceptable levels of complexity, uncertainty, and cost, its application would conflict with other principles underlying our tort system that are more important than preventing inconsistency. Each of these arguments suggests that either limited judicial review with the traditional subjective methodology or no review at all is preferable to the comparative approach.

The first argument commences on methodological grounds. Critics assert that courts lack the capacity to identify, in a reliable and valid way, comparable cases and to draw helpful guidance from them. In a nutshell, the argument is that because all cases are "unique," the search for comparable or similar cases is inherently flawed; the "nature and extent" of pain and suffering "is seldom, if ever, alike in any two cases."[28] These "differences in the details of the harms and the circumstances" of plaintiffs "inevitably make a comparison of the verdicts difficult if not impossible."[29] Second, the inherently subjective basis of awards for pain and suffering confounds the measurement and quantification required for a coherent proportionality review; there simply are no standards to measure the subjects at issue or to convert them into dollar amounts.[30] In response, we believe that the analysis described in Part III of this paper establishes that a comparative analysis does not require "identical" comparison cases, and that cases can be accurately compared in terms of their nonpecuniary harm levels,[31] much as criminal defendants are compared and rated in terms of levels of criminal culpability.

It is further argued that comparative procedures place inappropriate normative weight on the decisions of other juries, litigants (when they acquiesce in awards[32]), and judges (when they approve awards). Do we know that these earlier decisions are "correct"? Of course not. Indeed, there is no "correct" general damages award for any nonpecuniary harm. Rather, the test is the impact of an award on the general level of consistency among similar cases. Toward that end, the methods we propose are designed to identify the range of awards we are likely to see in the long run among cases that are comparable to the review case.[33]

Next, it is argued that the effects of inflation fatally undercut the comparability of verdicts awarded and approved in different years. While it is true that preference should be given to recent comparison cases, the risk of using earlier comparison cases to enlarge the pool of comparable cases can be substantially reduced by adjusting the awards in the earlier cases for inflation.[34]

A more significant criticism is that the data base currently available to many courts is inadequate to support a viable system of comparative review. The continuing widespread use of general verdicts (which do not distinguish between damages for economic and noneconomic harms) requires speculation about the amount of damages intended by the jury as compensation for nonpecuniary as contrasted to economic harms. Another problem is that the reported decisions used as comparison cases are probably unrepresentative of all damage awards approved by courts or acquiesced in by the parties in comparable cases. Moreover, the reported facts in these cases bearing on the level of nonpecuniary harm are often sparse or nonexistent. These are real problems, and they do limit the capacity of many systems to support an effective system of comparative review. But these problems can be significantly ameliorated, and in the final section of this paper we describe practical steps that can be taken in that direction.

The application of the comparative approach has also been criticized as no less arbitrary and unprincipled than the traditional approach. First, the comparison of cases can be easily manipulated. Second, the factual basis and justification for distinctions between cases is often not reported. Third, the facts of comparison cases that underlie the comparative analysis are often not reported.[35] Fourth, the standards used to prescribe the range of acceptable awards are often not reported. There is force to these arguments with respect to some applications of the comparative approach. We have sought to demonstrate, however, that with full reporting of both the facts of the comparison cases and the rationale for their inclusion in the analysis (together with the weight they are given), a coherent, principled system is possible. This is also true with respect to the standards used to describe the range of reasonableness.

There is also an argument that even if comparative additur/remittitur worked as intended, it is unnecessary and inappropriate. One claim is that inconsistency in jury awards is not a problem or that the current system addresses it satisfactorily. Unfortunately, the data to determine the degree of arbitrariness and inconsistency in the current system do not exist. There is, however, a strong sense among the public and the medical profession that there is a serious problem with the current system to which it is not responding well. Our view is that whatever the scope of the problem may be, if it is to be corrected through judicial intervention, the comparative approach is the most effective way of maintaining a reasonable level of consistency in a principled and objective manner.

A more fundamental claim is that the system of comparative additur/remittitur we present in this paper is an unacceptable move toward "bureaucratic justice"; specifically it represents a departure from the conception that every tort is unique and the belief that damage assessments should be totally individualized and within the sole discretion of the fact finder. According to this view, the comparative approach represents an "undue encroachment" on the traditional exercise of jury discretion.

The jury discretion argument appears to reflect different concerns. One may be a belief that jury awards should be immune from regulation by any external standard, whether from additur/remittitur review in any form or from legislative caps. If so, the claim runs against a long tradition of concern in tort law about grossly excessive and inadequate damage awards. The jury discretion argument may also reflect a belief that the subjective standard applied in traditional additur/remittitur review is preferable to the objective standard applied in a comparative review. We fail to see, however, how the judge-made "shock the conscience" standard is more legitimate than a standard driven by prior jury awards. We also fail to see how the traditional approach when it is applied represents any less of an encroachment on the exercise of jury discretion.[36]

To be sure, the overall pattern of jury awards driving the comparative approach is tempered by judicial review. If the trend of awards in comparable cases rises or falls, however, the judicially applied range of reasonableness should take that movement into account. But what if judges applying the comparative system are not, in fact, guided by the underlying pattern of jury awards? What if, instead, they set the approved damage level based on political and economic considerations and use the comparative approach as a subterfuge to legitimate their exercise of discretion? Such a system would, of course, be no more legitimate than the traditional "shock the conscience" approach. But we believe that if data were available on both the underlying jury awards and the amounts approved by the court, any such use of the system would become apparent.

A related jury discretion argument focuses on the *magnitude* of the encroachment. Even though driven by prior jury verdicts, the procedure can produce significant reductions in jury awards. For example, Judge Kearse conditionally lowered the *Martell* award by 40% ($800,000/$2,000,000). Among the eleven New York comparison cases cited in *Martell*, three of the original jury awards were approved by the New York courts, one was increased, and six were cut. The resulting cuts in those six jury awards ranged from $110,000 to $6,769,000, averaging $1,708,000. The sole additur was $250,000, raising a $150,000 award to $400,000. Overall for the seven adjusted awards, the original total awards of $23,279,000 were reduced 43% to $13,279,000.

Reductions of this magnitude are obviously a disappointment to the affected plaintiffs and their lawyers. But are they appropriate? Our reanalysis of *Martell* suggests that Judge Kease's decision put the *Martell* award roughly in line with the trend of decisions in the New York courts. The principle of reasonable consistency, therefore, supports her decision, as does the objective of keeping federal awards in diversity cases in line with state court awards.

But what do we actually know about the underlying New York decisions? The reported New York comparison cases provide very little detail on the level of non-pecuniary harm involved, and in several cases the amount of the jury award intended as compensation for nonpecuniary harms is not known with certainty.[37] Moreover, we do not know the extent to which the approved awards in the New York cases actually reflect the underlying pattern of jury awards as contrasted with the assessments of New York judges about the award levels they consider politically and economically acceptable.

Encroachment on the exercise of jury discretion is of particular concern when an appellate court which has not heard the evidence in the case conducts a de novo review that gives little or no deference to the trial court. This was the situation in *Martell*, as well as among the six *Martell* comparison cases with a remittitur, all of which were ordered on appeal after a jury award had been approved by the trial court.

Because trial judges have heard all the testimony and evidence in the review case, they are better situated than appellate judges to determine the level of nonpecuniary harm suffered by the plaintiff. For that reason the results of a trial court's comparative review should receive the same level of deference as other trial court findings of fact, provided the trial court provides a comparative analysis to support its finding. In that regard, trial judges may have less access than appellate judges to records and data on comparison cases. When an appellate court does undertake review, due deference to jury discretion may suggest tolerance for a greater deviation beyond the upper or lower limits than is suggested by the historic pattern of awards in comparable cases. Indeed, such a policy of deference may well explain the routine willingness of federal appellate courts in remittitur reviews to tolerate substantial deviations from the historic pattern of prior high awards in similar cases.

Another argument is that a system of comparative review will compromise the traditional jury decisionmaking function in two ways. First, it is asserted that a judge's review of a jury award will diminish the significance of the facts of the case that underlay the jury's award. This argument misconceives the role of the reviewing judge. If she conscientiously and thoroughly compares the relevant facts of the review cases with the relevant facts of the comparison cases, the judge will necessarily consider all the facts of the case that affected the level of nonpecuniary harm and were the predicate of the jury's award.

The second argument is that by taking into account jury awards assessed and approved in other cases, the reviewing judge inappropriately bases her decision on information that was not before the jury. (Juries currently receive no information about awards assessed in earlier cases.) This argument has some appeal, since the jury's verdict might have been altered on the basis of such information. However, the argument overlooks the fact that the judge is making a *legal* determination of whether the evidence of nonpecuniary harm is sufficient to sustain the jury's verdict. In other cases involving evidentiary legal issues, judges also seek guidance through comparative reference to earlier cases. For example, when a defendant claims the evidence will not support a jury's finding of liability, judges commonly examine the strength of the evidence in earlier decided cases to inform their legal judgment of whether the jury's verdict is supported by the evidence.[38] In such cases, the court's reference to the external standard provided by earlier decisions is recognized as inherent in the law/judge versus fact/jury dichotomy in the common law.

Finally, it has been suggested that the comparative approach will unreasonably encourage both the use of additur/remittitur and appeals. These claims raise empirical issues on which we have limited data. The experience in England, whose system most closely approximates what we are proposing,[39] generates few additur/remittitur claims and few appeals on damages issues. On the contrary, the English system increases certainty about what a case is worth, and in the opinion of English barristers for both plaintiffs and defendants, the comparative approach to additur/remittitur review encourages settlement both before and after trial. As noted above, however, the English courts have a more well-developed tradition of reporting facts bearing on the level of nonpecuniary harm, which facilitates comparative review.

In the reported cases from jurisdictions that use the comparative approach in this country (New York and the federal courts), we do see greater use of additur/remittitur review at trial and on appeal than elsewhere. However, we lack sufficient data to determine whether these systems are better off as a result in terms of the level of consistency in their general damages awards.

V. Data Base Enhancement

Whatever analytic methods a court applies, the effectiveness of its review depends on the quality of the data base from which comparison cases are drawn. One issue concerns the representativeness of the potential comparison cases. A second issue concerns the quantity and quality of the relevant information available for those cases. On both points, the data bases currently available have definite limitations.

First, the pool of cases from which comparison cases are selected is usually limited to reported trial and appellate decisions. The awards reported in these cases are not generally perceived to be representative of the entire universe of trial court awards.

The issue concerning the information available on the cases has two dimensions. The first is the widespread use of "general" compensatory damages verdicts that do not itemize the amount of the award for nonpecuniary harms such as pain, suffering, and loss of enjoyment of life, as contrasted to the amount of the verdict awarded for economic harms such as impaired earning capacity. When the review case has only a general verdict, the trial court conducting a review has at least had the benefit of having heard the testimony and is in a position to make a reasonable estimate of the levels of general and special damages in the general verdict. But when the comparison cases have only a general verdict, they are of no use at all or call for speculation on the basis of a cold record often containing very little information. In *Martell*, for example, 8 of the 11 comparison cases had general verdicts. Moreover, in the 461 cases in our children's study, only about 25% involved an itemized verdict or sufficient data on the economic losses to permit a reasonable estimate of the general damages actually awarded.

A second dimension of the information problem is the frequent sparseness of facts in the reported comparison cases relating to the quantum of damages actually awarded. For example, in *Martell*, several of the opinions from the comparison cases used by the court described the plaintiff's injuries in too little detail to support a thorough comparative analysis of the pain, suffering, and loss of enjoyment of life involved in the cases.

We recommend three policies to improve the existing state and federal data bases:

1. Itemize compensatory damages awards to specify the allocation between pecuniary and nonpecuniary harms.
2. Encourage judges to include in their opinions reasonable detail on the facts of the case that bear on the quantum of damages awarded, even when the size of the award is not at issue.
3. For all cases involving damage awards, (a) increase the frequency with which intermediate appellate court opinions are published, and (b) authorize and encourage the publication of trial court opinions in cases that are not appealed.

VI. Conclusion

The results of this study indicate that comparative additur/remittitur review has the potential to control excessive and inadequate general and punitive damage awards and to maintain a reasonable level of consistency among awards in similar cases. Our findings suggest that this can be accomplished in a reasonably objective and principled manner through:

1. the use of a comparative review methodology,
2. more systematic and fully explained comparative review and case reporting practices,
3. the use of rudimentary quantitative methods, and
4. the enhancement of existing data bases and long term development of statewide data bases.

Our research further suggests that progress in this direction can be made at tolerable levels of cost and complexity. We also believe that an enhanced system of comparative review would represent an improvement over more traditional methods of additur/remittitur review. Finally, it would avoid the limitations and inequities currently associated with the use of legislative caps or with no review at all.

Notes

1. A more detailed presentation of our findings and proposed methodology, including an application of the method to awards for punitive damages

is presented in David Baldus et al., *Improving Judicial Oversight of Jury Damage Assessments: A Proposal for the Comparative Additur/Remittitur Review of Awards for Nonpecuniary Harms and Punitive Damages*, 80 Iowa L. Rev. (1995) (forthcoming) [hereinafter *Improving Judicial Oversight*]. This paper is an abbreviated version of the Final Report submitted to our funding agencies–the State Justice Institute and the Bureau of Maternal and Child Health and Resources Development (SJI-87–11X-D-068 & MCH-197054)–under the same title as the forthcoming Iowa Law Review article. We had an advisory panel, consisting of a state trial judge, a state supreme court justice, a group of doctors, plaintiff and defense counsel, an insurance company representative, a court administrator, and a handful of academics. We met with this group twice in 1993 to present our ideas.

2. Additur/remittitur review is the common law procedure that empowers both trial and appellate courts to order conditionally a reduction (remittitur) or an increase (additur) in a jury award it considers to be excessive or inadequate. If the party defending the jury's award agrees to the increase or decrease suggested by the court, the original award will be so modified. If the party defending the original award refuses to accept the adjusted award, the court may order a new trial, usually limited to damages. Counsel for the parties in additur/remittitur may suggest the level to which the challenged award should be set. In the absence of consent to an additur/remittitur order by the affected party, trial and appellate courts lack the authority to increase or decrease jury damage assessments. On additur/remittitur review generally, see Francis X. Busch, *Remittiturs and Additurs in Personal Injury and Wrongful Death Cases*, 12 Def. L.J. 521 (1963)[hereinafter Busch]; Leo Carlin, *Remittiturs and Additurs*, 49 W. Va. L.Q. 1 (1942)[hereinafter Carlin]; Fleming James, Jr., *Remedies for Excessiveness or Inadequacy of Verdicts*, 1 Duq. L. Rev. 143 (1963)[hereinafter James]; Thomas R. Newman, *Damages: A Call for Meaningful Precedents*, 3 Pace L. Rev. 605 (1983)[hereinafter Newman]; Irene D. Sann, *Remittitur (and Additur) in the Federal Courts: An Evaluation with Suggested Alternatives*, 38 Case W. Res. L. Rev. 157 (1987)[hereinafter Sann]; Eric Schnapper, *Judges Against Juries—Appellate Review of Federal Civil Jury Verdicts*, 1989 Wis. L. Rev. 237, 320–24, 327–36, 340–47, 353–57 [hereinafter Schnapper]; Note, *Appealability of Judgments Entered Pursuant to Remittiturs in Federal Courts*, 1975 Duke L.J. 1150; Note, *Constitutional Law—Right to Jury Trial—Judicial Use of Additurs in Correcting Insufficient Damage Verdicts*, 21 Va. L. Rev. 666 (1935); Comment, *Correction of Damage Verdicts by Remittitur and Additur*, 44 Yale L.J. 318 (1934); Richard Kinder, Comment, *Appellate Remittitur*, 33 Mo. L. Rev. 637 (1968); Barbara Lerner, Comment, *Remittitur Review: Constitutionality and Efficiency in Liquidated and Unliquidated Damage Cases*, 43 U. Chi. L. Rev. 376 (1976)[hereinafter *Remittitur Review*]; Michael A. Newsome, Comment, *Additur and Remittitur in Federal and State Courts: An Anomaly?*, 3 Cumberland L. Rev. 150 (1972); S.T. Rayburn, Comment, *Statutory Authorization of Additur and Remittitur*, 43 Miss. L.J. 107 (1972); Note, *Remittitur of Jury Verdicts in Iowa*, 48 Iowa L. Rev. 649 (1963); Comment, *Remittitur Practice in Alabama*, 34 Ala. L. Rev. 275 (1983); Irene Sann, Note, *Remittitur Practice in the Federal Courts*, 76 Colum. L. Rev. 299 (1976); William H. Wagner, Note, *Procedures to Lessen Remittitur's Intrusion on the Seventh Amendment Right to Jury Trial*,

1979 Wash. U.L.Q. 639.

3. The comparative approach has much less applicability to damage awards for economic losses, such as medical expense and impaired earning capacity. The reason is that the market already provides external standards. For example, the market price for labor and medical services that can be used to evaluate the reasonableness of such awards.
4. We focused our study on injured children to establish comparability in terms of the injured plaintiff's age and to draw on the expertise of Dr. MacQueen, who has treated and studied severely injured children for more than 40 years.
5. *Senko v. Fonda,* 384 N.Y.S.2d 849, 851–52 (N.Y. App. Div. 1976)(citations omitted).
6. See Schnapper, *supra* note 2.
7. See Newman, *supra* note 2.
8. We are not suggesting that all federal courts use the comparative method. The Supreme Court has never addressed the issue, nor is it required by the federal rules. Nevertheless, a great number of federal courts use the comparative approach to remittitur review. Federal courts are not permitted to conduct additur review.
9. 748 F.2d 740 (2d Cir. 1984).
10. See, e.g., Louis Harris and Assoc., Inc., *Judges' Opinions on Procedural Issues: A Survey of State and Federal Trial Judges Who Spend At Least Half Their Time On General Civil Cases, Oct-Dec 1987*, 69 B.U.L. Rev. 731, 760–62 (1989) (stating that in 1987 one-quarter of state judges were without a full time secretary, one-half were without a law clerk, and one-third had no access to word processing facilities).
11. As we explain below, factually identical comparison cases are no more essential to the conduct of a coherent additur/remittitur review than are factually identical "comparables" essential to the conduct of a comparative appraisal of a parcel of real estate. The important point in both processes is that the difference between the review case and each comparison case is noted and accounted for in the court's or the appraiser's final assessment. See *infra* note 19 and accompanying text.
12. There is relatively little variation among states on the factors that bear on the quantum of general damages. Marilyn Minzer et al., Damages in Tort Actions chs. 4, 8 (1993).
13. For detail on sources of cost of living data and the methodology available to make such calculations, see *Improving Judicial Oversight*, *supra* note 1.
14. See, e.g., *Precopio v. Detroit Dept. of Trans.,* 330 N.W.2d 802, 809 (Mich. 1982); *Monroe v. Leonard,* 308 N.Y.S.2d 933, 935 (N.Y. Civ. Ct. 1969).
15. One complication is that medical cost inflation is higher than general cost inflation. Therefore, to the extent that pain and suffering awards are tied to medical expenses and lost earnings, exclusive reliance on the general consumer price index may underestimate the actual degree of inflation.
16. Discussion of and data on the reliability and validity of the rank order and adjusted award methodology described in the next section are presented in Appendix H to *Improving Judicial Oversight*, *supra* note 1.
17. For example, close case matching in one simulated review sharpened an issue regarding the weight that should be placed on a small permanent scar

on a girl's cheek compared to the weight that should be placed on a boy's permanent, but mild limp.

18. See Byrl N. Boyce & William N. Kinnard, Jr., Appraising Real Property 167–202 (1984)[hereinafter *Appraising Real Property*]; American Institute of Real Estate Appraisers, The Appraisal of Real Estate 274–92 (6th ed. 1977) [hereinafter *Appraisal of Real Estate*].

19. There are several reasons why real estate appraisal methodology provides a useful model for comparative additur/remittitur review. First, each inquiry focuses on "the state of mind of the public." Philip Nichols, The Law of Eminent Domain 212 (P. Rohan ed., 3d ed. 1991)[hereinafter Nichols]. In the appraisal context, the focus is on the market behavior of purchasers, which reflects the value citizens place on property, while in the additur/remittitur context, the focus is on jury verdicts, which reflect community judgments of the value of nonpecuniary harms and the amount of punishment highly culpable defendants deserve. Second, in each context, the ultimate inference concerning the public's state of mind is based on both actual and hypothetical distributions of outcomes (prices versus jury awards) that one would expect if the comparison cases had possessed all the basic and pertinent characteristics of the review case or property. In the real estate context, the appraiser starts with actual sales prices and then estimates a series of hypothetical prices based on a comparison of each comparison case with the property being valued. Cases may be matched on as many as twenty items that vary considerably in terms of their objectivity, e.g., age, number of bedrooms, quality of construction, design, and appeal. For some of these items, a specific dollar adjustment may be estimated or the characteristic is merely noted as a basis for the final price adjustment for the comparison cases. In the additur/remittitur context, the court starts with actual awards in comparison cases, from which it can also develop a list of hypothetical jury awards based on a comparison of each comparison case with the review case. The ultimate inferences in the two processes differ, of course. In the valuation context, the appraiser uses the distribution of actual and hypothetical sales prices to identify a single measure of value, while in the additur/remittitur context, the lists of actual and hypothetical awards provides a basis for specifying a range of reasonable awards and ultimately assessing the excessiveness or inadequacy of the damages award under review.|hb Third, the methodological requirements in both contexts are similar. The first requirement is access to a data base from which a reasonable sample of comparison cases (sales/verdicts) can be selected for use in the analysis. The second is the availability of sufficiently complete and valid information on the comparison cases to conduct a reliable comparative analysis. The third requirement is a reasonably reliable method to adjust the prices and verdicts in the comparison cases to reflect the differences between them and the appraisal case or the review case. In the appraisal context, for example, the price of a comparison property involving 4 bedrooms and 3 baths might be adjusted to permit a valid comparison with an appraisal property that has only 2 bedrooms and 1 bath. In the context of additur/remittitur review, the verdict of a comparison case involving second degree burns with scarring on the face might be adjusted to allow a comparison with a review case involving similar burns and scars that are less severe because they are on the plaintiff's arms

or legs. Real estate appraisal and comparative additur/remittitur review have another thing in common. In both, the empirical results of the comparative analysis require substantial interpretation. The valuation assessed for a parcel of real property is based ultimately on the appraiser's experience, knowledge of the market, and sound judgment. Similarly in an additur/remittitur review, the court's estimation of likely awards in cases similar to the review case and its judgment of whether the review case award are too high or low is based ultimately on the court's knowledge of jury behavior, experience, and sound judgment.

20. $826,000/1.33 = $621,000 for *LeBel*; $2,191,000/3.33 = $658,000 for *Tabone*.
21. *Supra* note 16 and accompanying text.
22. We discount the $1,332,000 award in *Dubicki* as being substantially out of line with its near neighbors *LeBel* and *Kusisto*, which involved only slightly less severe injuries. In the course of a comparative analysis it is not unusual to observe that one or more earlier approved awards represent a significant departure from the norm for comparable cases. Such awards may be disregarded or further adjusted if there is some basis for doing so. The former situation may exist if there are systematic differences between awards in urban and rural places, e.g., the differences between award levels in upstate New York and metropolitan New York City. If the analysis includes comparison cases that were acquiesced in by the parties and not approved by a court, further adjustment of the award, or exclusion of the case from the analysis, may be appropriate. This would be the case if it appears to the reviewing court that the acquiescence of the parties in the award may substantially reflect a compromise driven by concerns about liability issues rather than a consensus about the reasonableness of the award amount. See *infra* note 32. All of the comparison cases used in *Martell* had been approved by a trial or appellate court.
23. We did another reanalysis of *Martell* using cases from around the country. The results using a 10% deviation factor were almost identical.
24. We support the current comparative review practice of limiting the comparison cases to officially reported cases in which the damages award was approved by the court or acquiesced in by the parties. To open the door to unreported comparison cases, e.g., in jury verdict reporters or other legal news-like sources could create several problems. First, it could raise accuracy issues requiring hearings. Second, it would create even greater incentives than currently exist for lawyers to publish a biased sample of their cases in jury verdict reporters. Third, it would likely advantage repeat players, such as insurance companies, large defendants, and lawyers in large data networks. Fourth, a "published cases only" rule will create pressures in the system to increase the proportion of cases involving personal injuries and punitive damages that are officially "published" by the judicial system. See *infra* Section V for a discussion of policies that would increase the case reporting rates. We are grateful to Michael Green for his suggestions on this issue.
25. In a jurisdiction with more resources, the court itself could access a full state-maintained data base to supplement the cases suggested by the parties.
26. *See* Prentice H. Marshall, *A View from the Bench: Practical Perspectives on Juries*, 1990 U. Chi. Legal Forum 147, 158 ("[I]t is appropriate for the jury

to assess the harm allegedly inflicted on the plaintiff in light of the values of the community in which it occurred. Jurors do just that.")

27. The English experience with their equivalent to additur/remittitur review also suggests that most of the current problems with the comparative approach in this country are manageable. A principal distinction between the two systems is that the English do not use juries. A judge, with knowledge of the permissible ranges for different injury types, sets the awards in the first instance. As a result, there is less initial variability in the trial court awards. Another important difference is that the English review process operates under much stricter guidelines than we see in American courts applying the comparative approach. Finally, because English trial judges (a) explicitly itemize their awards as between general and special damages, and (b) describe the relevant facts of the case bearing on damages in rich detail, their courts have much better information with which to conduct comparative analyses.

Proportionality arguments in the English system are developed within the context of damages guidelines, known collectively as a "tariff," that are adopted by the Court of Appeals to establish presumptive general damages awards for "various common kinds of injuries." *Housecroft v. Burnett,* [1986] 1 All E.R. 332, 336. The guidelines are based in part on the trend of awards in similar cases but heavily reflect the normative judgments of Court of Appeals judges. They take into account the special features of individual cases in a particular injury category, which may make the nonpecuniary harm suffered "greater or less than the general run of cases" involving injuries of the same kind. *Id.* at 336. Over time, the appellate courts create "brackets" or ranges for given injury categories through their review of trial court damages awards. For example, in 1985 the Court of Appeals set 75,000 pounds as the presumptive award for "an average case of tetraplegia," which was deemed to exist when the "injured person is not in physical pain, is fully aware of the disability, has an expectation of life of 25 years or more, powers of speech, sight, and hearing are present, and needs help with bodily functions." *Id.* at 338, 340. The factors that operate to increase the award above the average figure are physical pain and a diminution in the power of speech, sight, or hearing. The factors that operate to reduce the award are lack of awareness of the condition and a reduction in expectation of life.

Similar guidelines provide the standards by which the English trial courts set their damages awards. Striving for "even-handed justice," the first sub-goal of the English appellate courts is to keep the guidelines "simple and easy to apply although broad enough to permit allowances" for special circumstances. The second sub-goal is to provide a sufficient degree of predictability so that potential litigants will "very broadly" know the value of a claim if 100% liability is established. *Id.* at 336.

The tariff system is believed to enhance the consistency of English damage awards. However, because the English appellate system is decentralized (the Court of Appeals operates in three judge panels), guidelines have not been set for many injuries, and adjustments for inflation, which require further appellate court action, are often years out of date. Although English practitioners appear generally content with their system, especially with the influence of damages precedent on the quantum of damages awarded, they also complain that the guidelines sometimes lack internal consistency; that precedents, especially in cases with small awards, are not adjusted for inflation; and that the published cases whose awards are available as precedent are not a representative sample. Interviews with Richard Metheun, Barrister, London, England (June 30, 1988), and Anthony Brisco and John Maher, Barristers, New Castle, England (June 28, 1988).

28. *Cabler v. L.V. Hart, Inc.,* 164 S.E.2d 574, 577 (S.C. 1968).
29. Schnapper, *supra* note 2, at 330.
30. *Id.* at 340; Busch, *supra* note 2, at 543–44 (stating there is "no rule of measurement" for pain and suffering).
31. See *supra* note 11 and accompanying text.
32. The parties' acquiescence in an award may provide useful evidence of their belief in its reasonableness. However, such acquiescence is less authoritative than a judicial decision approving the award, and for this reason approved awards are favored. (The use of awards in which the parties acquiesce increases the number of comparison cases when the number of comparable cases involving approved awards is small.) The reason for this preference is that the acquiescence of the parties and their failure to appeal may also reflect judgments about their prospects of success on appeal on liability issues that have nothing to do with the reasonableness of the jury award. Similarly, the weight given to an unappealed jury verdict can be discounted if the parties settle post-trial for a substantially different amount than the jury verdict and the agreed amount appears primarily to reflect a compromise on damages reflecting the plaintiff's concern about liability issues. It follows, therefore, that when the parties acquiesce in or agree to a general damages award, the weight given in a comparative review should be influenced by evidence of the extent to which the acquiescence or agreement reflects a judgment about the reasonableness of the award rather than a compromise driven by concerns about liability issues.
33. For reasons we discussed *supra* note 22, the method may require adjusting or discounting awards in factually comparable comparison cases if these appear to deviate arbitrarily from the norm.
34. See *supra* notes 13–15 and accompanying text.
35. See, e.g., Newman, *supra* note 2, at 609 (commenting on New York's comparative review system: "Meaningful settlement negotiations cannot take place unless there is some commonly understood and agreed upon basis whereby all interested parties can assess how the appellate division might be expected to react to the facts of their case"); Sann, *supra* note 2, at 208 ("The reader is left to guess at the court's analysis").
36. Critics of any form of additur/remittitur review may prefer the traditional approach on the pragmatic ground that because of its widely perceived inadequacies, the traditional approach is less likely to be used by judges than the comparative approach.
37. In this regard, the general application of the comparative approach in the New York courts has been properly criticized by Newman, *supra* note 2 at 609, who gives the impression that the results of remittitur review in New York are as arbitrary as one would expect under the traditional "subjective" approach.
38. See, e.g., *Farthing v. City of Shawnee,* 39 F.3d 1131, 1139–40 (10th Cir. 1994)

(appellate court sustained defendant's motion for summary judgment on the basis of an explicit comparison of the evidence in the review case with evidence in an earlier case which sustained a defendant's motion for a directed verdict); *Futrell v. J.I. Case*, 38 F.3d 342, 346–50 & n.2 (7th Cir. 1994) (appellate court reversing a JNOV that had overturned a plaintiff's verdict explicitly compared the strength of evidence in the review case with the evidence in two earlier cases with weaker evidence in which a JNOV had been sustained).

39. See *supra* note 27.

Proposals for Reforming Pain and Suffering Awards

Gary T. Schwartz*

The papers by David Baldus (and his colleagues) and by Oscar Chase each accept as a given the rightness of substantial awards for pain and suffering in tort cases. My comment will likewise assume that substantial pain and suffering awards make good policy sense. Each of the papers expresses concern about the variability of awards for pain and suffering as they are entered by individual juries. Here, too, I accept for the sake of discussion the appropriateness of this concern.

How then do the two papers seek to solve the problem they identify? The Baldus paper sets forth what I will call the "Iowa plan." That plan would leave undisturbed the current processes by which juries reach their decisions on the amount of pain and suffering damages. The plan would, however, strengthen the practices of remittitur and additur—which permit judges at both the trial and appellate level to review juries' pain and suffering awards. Under the Iowa plan, the parties to the immediate litigation, and also the reviewing judge or judges, would search out the awards for pain and suffering in recent "officially reported cases" within the particular jurisdiction that seem to involve the same basic injury type.[1] The reviewing judge would then rely primarily on this base of data as he exercises his traditional authority of remittitur and additur in the immediate case. The improved data base would enable judges to exercise their authority both more frequently and more rationally.[2]

The Chase paper sets forth what will here be called the "New York plan." That plan likewise calls for the gathering of information on

*Professor, University of California at Los Angeles School of Law.

comparative verdicts. Under this plan, however, the verdicts are simply those that juries have entered; there is no requirement that the case be officially reported.[3] Moreover, the information on prior verdicts would be turned over not to the judge but rather to the jury. That is, the jury would be given a chart of relativcly recent jury awards within the particular state. The word "chart" here is potentially misleading. The jury would be provided with only three pieces of data: the low award, the high award, and the median award for the particular category of injury.[4] Under the New York plan, the jury would not be strictly bound by this (limited) chart. Nevertheless, the jury would be invited by the judge to take the chart significantly into account as it develops its own award for pain and suffering.

As I consider the Iowa and New York plans, I can express my general preference for the latter. As noted, the Iowa plan would preserve the existing system of jury decision-making. Under that system, prior jury awards for pain and suffering are not binding on the jury in the immediate case. Indeed, those awards are deemed entirely irrelevant: the jury is not even allowed to receive information as to what those prior awards have been. Rather, the jury is required to base its award solely on the evidence in the particular case. That evidence will typically consist of the victim's own testimony, as he describes the extent of the pain he has suffered. Also, in jurisdictions that allow plaintiff's counsel to advance a "per diem" argument, the plaintiff will often submit to the jury a diary he has kept, in which he has recorded on a daily basis the pain he experiences. Moreover, plaintiffs' counsel increasingly provide juries with "day in the life" videos, which seek to document the indignities that the plaintiff suffers and likewise the extent to which the plaintiff has incurred the loss of ordinary life enjoyments.[5] In evaluating all of this evidence, the jury considers the arguments of counsel, and eventually consults its own collective common sense.

This is how the jury currently reaches its decision on pain and suffering. Under the Iowa plan, that jury decision would then be reviewed by trial and appellate courts. In conducting their reviews, the judges would primarily consider awards in prior cases that are deemed comparable. Moreover, in placing great weight on these comparable awards, the reviewing judges would inevitably be led to downplay the testimony and other evidence offered in the individual case. The very notion that prior cases can be deemed comparable would tend to undermine the plaintiff's claim that his own case (and his own injury) should be deemed unique.

A procedure such as this strikes me as very unsatisfactory. On the one hand, the evidence that the jury had been told should control its decision is evidence that the reviewing judges will essentially deemphasize. On the other hand, the evidence on which those judges will primarily rely in reversing a jury's verdict is evidence that the jurors themselves were not even permitted to consider. In our civil justice system, it is routine for jury awards to be set aside for a lack of substantial evidence in the record as a whole. It seems extremely strange to encourage, indeed, to require reviewing judges to set aside the jury's award on the basis of evidence that has been formally excluded from the original record. For that matter, if this process seems irregular, it is also likely to be produce large numbers of appeals—for the process would increase the number of jury verdicts that could be appraised as vulnerable if an appeal is filed.

To be sure, the Iowa plan is by no means unprecedented. Even now, reviewing judges, in exercising their remittitur and additur authority, sometimes rely on officially recorded awards in prior cases that are seemingly similar. Yet, as the Baldus paper points out, under current practices judges frequently ignore such awards, relying instead on their own conscience and judgment in determining whether the verdict in the individual case is inappropriate. Certainly the Iowa plan, *both* by encouraging additur and remittitur *and* by requiring that these practices be conducted in a certain way, would convert a status quo that contains occasional irregularities into a new situation in which these irregularities would become commonplace. Absent a further effort at justification, this is a plan I cannot support.

As for the New York plan, it would gather information on all comparable verdicts within the particular jurisdiction; it would not limit itself to officially reported cases. But the primary difference between the New York and Iowa plans is that the New York plan would present the relevant data not to reviewing judges, but to the jury itself. The New York plan would then encourage the jury to take these prior awards significantly into account. In so doing, the plan would tend to render jury verdicts more rational, or at least more in line with verdicts that appellate courts are willing to support as they engage in their additur/remittitur practices. The improvement of the rationality of jury awards is a good thing in and of itself; moreover, by reducing the likelihood of successful appeals, the New York plan should reduce the number of appeals actually taken. Furthermore, in cases where juries do evidently deviate from the pattern of past verdicts, an appellate court would be in a better position to focus on the facts of the individual case so as to understand what might have prompted the jury's deviation. In this way, the New York plan would also render more rational the practice of additur/remittitur.

In all these respects, I find the New York plan attractive, at least at the general level. The problems arise when one considers the plan's details. Keep in mind that the chart called for by the plan would evidently present the jury with only three numbers: the high, low, and median award for the particular category of injuries. Granted, the jury would be instructed as to the meaning of "median," and therefore could appreciate how important the median figure is. Nevertheless, to present this particular package of information to the jury would foreseeably overemphasize in the jurors' minds the significance of both the high award and the low award. Almost by definition, each of these awards is something of an outlier. Yet under the New York plan, these awards would provide what psychologists call "anchors" for the jury. Put another way, providing the jury with only three numbers, two of which are the high and the low, would encourage juries to consider rendering an award that lies quite close to either that high or that low. To be sure, the problem here identified could be solved by amending the New York plan so as to provide the jury with a more extensive set of data: perhaps a density chart that shows the full array of awards that juries have come up with in recent cases.[6] Such a chart might well show the majority of awards clustering fairly close to the median.

The second problem with the New York plan is that the nine categories of injuries that it incorporates seem insufficiently homogeneous.[7] Consider, for example, the first category, which is defined in terms of "emotional only; fright, no physical damage." This category would evidently include the jury's award in an offensive battery case in which an angry defendant has lightly shoved the plaintiff. But the category would also include the emotional distress award granted to a mother who has observed her child being run down and killed by a negligent motorist. A $1000 award might well be generous in the first case; a $50,000 award might be quite appropriate in the second. Insofar as both of these cases would be lumped together in the category of "emotional only," the category seems too broad to serve as the basis for providing the new jury with relevant information.

Consider, for that matter, the sixth category, which focuses on "permanent significant" injuries, including "deafness, loss of limb, loss of one eye, loss of one kidney or lung." Assume here that tort law provides awards not only for actual pain and suffering, but also for deprivation of the ordinary enjoyments of life. Especially if this is so, the category of "permanent significant" injuries seems much too diffuse. So long as loss of life enjoyments is deemed compensable, one can easily say that the award of damages for nonmonetary harms in a lost kidney case should be less than the award in a case involving the loss of one eye; that latter award, in turn, should be less than the award in a case involving the loss of an arm or leg; and that award should be substantially less than the award in a case of deafness. To be sure, one can readily acknowledge the problem of added costs that are incurred as a program attempts to engage in the process of subcategorization. (Consider the recent experience with criminal sentencing guidelines.) Nevertheless, the categories relied on in the New York plan are so amorphous as to preclude endorsing that plan in its current form.

Here, too, the problem could be solved by appropriate modifications in the plan, though such modifications would concededly make the plan more costly to prepare and administer. Let me now, however, identify some problems with the New York plan that may well resist solution.

Consider a jury award for pain and suffering that seems unusually high. Because of its size, the award will likely be appealed by the defendant. Once an appeal is filed, the case may well be settled by the parties. Under the terms of the settlement, the defendant will agree to pay the plaintiff a sum of money that is significantly less than the jury's award; in exchange, the plaintiff secures protection against the real risk of having that award reversed or reduced by even a larger amount in the appeal itself. This settlement is, in essence, the final disposition of the case – a disposition that takes into account both the jury's original award and the substantial possibility that the award will be reduced on appeal. Yet the New York plan would factor only the jury's award into its data base, making no effort to acknowledge the actual disposition. To this extent, the plan would rely on information that is in a quite basic way inaccurate.

Return now to those verdicts originally entered by juries. As we know, the vast majority of all tort cases are settled; settlement has the advantages of economizing on the costs of litigation and accommodating the risk aversion of the parties. Indeed, the logic favoring settlement is so strong that one can regard those cases finally submitted to the jury as almost pathological—or at least exceptional. Admittedly, the exceptional feature of the cases that go to trial might concern the issue of liability rather than the quantum of damages. Even so, because so few cases do finally get submitted to juries and because these cases are probably in some sense abnormal, I am wary of any procedure that would allow some compilation of the cases' verdicts largely to control the disposition of later cases.

Furthermore, the assessment above has not yet taken into account the strategies that parties might adopt once the New York plan is itself approved and implemented. Consider a case that falls within Category X of the New York plan; and assume also that the parties appreciate that the facts of the case might lead the jury to make an especially high award for pain and suffering. Assume further that one of the parties—most likely the defendant (or its liability insurer)—is a "repeat player" in the tort system. As a repeat player, that party has a concern not only with the resolution of the individual case but also with its impact on subsequent litigation. This concern might give the defendant a special incentive to settle. Whether or not the amount of the settlement is disclosed, the fact that the case has been settled obviously prevents it from being considered by a jury. As a result, the settlement rules out the possibility of a very high jury verdict—a verdict which, once entered, would then be given extra impact by the New York plan. The settlement strategy employed by the defense thus deprives the New York plan of a datum that the plan would deem quite relevant. Try now another possibility. Assume that a case does go to trial, and results in a verdict that is *unexpectedly* high. Given that verdict, and given also the defendant's awareness of how the New York plan would give effect to that verdict in later cases, the defendant would face a special set of incentives as it considers the alternatives of appeal and settlement pending appeal. Knowing that a settlement would result in the inclusion of the original verdict in the chart callcd for by the New York plan, the defendant might decline a settlement offer that it would otherwise accept; it might insist on pursuing its appeal in the hopes of achieving a substantial formal reduction in the jury's verdict. In this way, the New York plan would inhibit settlements that both parties to the litigation would otherwise regard as within their interest.

As presented in the Chase paper, the New York plan thus fails to consider how its operation would affect the strategies of parties and lawyers as they select cases for trial and as they appeal cases that have already reached verdicts. And at this point the problems in question may be insoluble, for it is far from clear that the New York plan could be modified or amended in a way that would appropriately take the parties' strategic choices into account. To make essentially the same point in a somewhat different way, if the New York plan *is* modified in a way that acknowledges these foreseeable strategies, the modified plan will encourage lawyers to develop another set of strategies—which, once developed, will weaken the rationality of the plan even in its modified form.

To recap, I find the Iowa plan insupportable, while the New York plan seems promising yet vexing. This pair of assessments leads me to consider with more sympathy than the Baldus and Chase papers seem able to muster the idea of an actual schedule for pain and suffering damages. To be sure, developing such a schedule would encounter all the problems of categories and subcategories referred to above. Even so, as the Chase paper points out, informal schedules for pain and suffering damages have been implemented in what seems like a generally satisfactory way in England. Admittedly, in this country such a schedule would need to be established, or at least authorized, by a state legislature. In light of what we all have learned from the public choice literature, it would be foolish to assume that the legislature, in taking action, would necessarily be trying to achieve the public interest; it would be even more foolish to assume that legislative enactments would necessarily achieve the public interest.

Yet even acknowledging the inevitable distortions in any schedule for pain and suffering damages that an American jurisdiction might implement, there are major advantages in such a schedule that neither the Baldus nor the Chase paper attempts to identify. To explain that advantage, some background is needed. A 1974 article by Cornelius Peck conveyed to the community of law professors the new medical learning as to the nature of physical pain itself.[8] The older view was that pain could largely be understood as a matter of external stimuli that operate on the body. The newer understanding of pain emphasizes the role played by the victim's own internal system—a system that filters external stimuli and evaluates their significance.

There is an obvious lesson of this newer understanding. Anything that strengthens the individual's own internal system can, by doing so, reduce the actual pain the victim subjectively experiences. Yet the current tort regime does the very opposite: It weakens the victim's internal system by encouraging the victim to dwell on his pain, to wallow in it. The victim is encouraged to focus on his pain as he undergoes interviews and depositions and prepares his testimony for trial. Indeed, his lawyer may, as noted, encourage the victim to keep a diary in which he records the pain he has experienced on a daily basis. In recent years, I have spoken with the administrators of pain clinics in Southern California. They tell me that their clinics refuse to admit as patients anyone who has a tort claim pending. The reason for their refusal lies in the belief that so long as the prospective patient is thinking about the prospect of a legal recovery, he is in a poor position to learn to live with his pain, to overcome his pain, to attempt to put his pain behind him.

All of this suggests a tragic paradox in the current tort system. Certainly pain and suffering can be both very real and very significant. Tort law would, accordingly, fail in its efforts to achieve fairness and deterrence if it failed to take pain and suffering significantly into account as it develops the plaintiff's verdict. Yet the current tort system, in endeavoring to give appropriate recognition to the pain victims suffer, does so in a way that actually increases the amount of pain that victims experience. In commendably attempting to provide a response to a bad situation, the tort system thus makes that situation worse.

Nothing in the Iowa or New York plans recognizes this tragic paradox or offers anything that might resolve it. The Iowa plan would preserve the existing system by which the plaintiff presents evidence to the jury, though it would then subject the jury's award to increased post-verdict controls. Even under the New York plan, the plaintiff would have a major incentive to do the best possible job in presenting his pain and suffering evidence to the jury, and the jury would continue to take that evidence into account in reaching its verdict–in determining how to maneuver between "high" and "low" past verdicts and considering whether to exceed that high. A pain and suffering schedule would, by contrast, eliminate the need for any testimony from the victim as to his pain and suffering experience. Moreover, such a schedule would provide other important advantages. It would considerably simplify trials, by eliminating most of the evidence as to the victim's subjective pain. Furthermore, it would do an even better job than the Iowa and New York plans in rendering more predictable the results of litigation. This predictability would, in turn, render cases easier to settle.[9]

To be sure, a schedule for pain and suffering damages would lack "individualization." Trial lawyers fervently believe in the justice of individualization of this sort. I do not share this belief. Granted, the new learning on pain does emphasize both the reality of "pain thresholds" and the variation in these thresholds among individuals. Yet, as noted, in recognizing this reality and hence aiming at the goal of individualization, current practices tend to weaken rather than strengthen the pain thresholds of particular victims. Moreover, even if we concede the reality of variations in pain as subjectively experienced, we can also recognize that juries currently learn of the victim's individual pain only insofar as the victim offers testimony at trial. And the impact of this testimony on the jury may be more a matter of the victim's personality type than of the actual experience of pain that the victim has undergone. A more reserved plaintiff might be less effective in explaining his pain than a victim who is more gregarious and articulate. Moreover, much may depend on how the jury identifies with the plaintiff—and this raises all the bias problems that the Chase paper describes. From the defendant's perspective, a more general problem concerns the extreme subjectivity of the plaintiff's testimony as to pain and suffering. So long as the plaintiff avoids some serious gaffe, there is no evidence the defendant can offer that can clearly challenge or refute the plaintiff's own testimony. Any extended effort by the defense to cross-examine the plaintiff as to the extent of his suffering might lead the jury to perceive the defendant as callous.

On balance, then, a schedule for pain and suffering damages would provide major advantages; and the benefit of individualization associated with current tort practices seems illusory, or at least problematic. The development and implementation of such a schedule should be the focus of tort reform efforts.

Notes

1. There is no obvious way in which a case can be "officially reported" unless there has at least been some post-verdict ruling on the case by either the trial judge or an appellate court. Such a ruling might well address the size of the jury's damage award. If the ruling affirms the award, all the better; if the ruling reduces the award, this modified award is what the Iowa plan would take into account. Yet so long as the case is "officially reported," the Iowa plan would not require that the size of the jury's award actually receive post-verdict judicial consideration; it is enough if the award has been "acquiesced in" by the parties in their post-verdict motions.
2. The Iowa plan also contemplates providing the judge who is reviewing a punitive damage award with a chart providing information on prior punitive

damage awards in comparable cases. Cases would be deemed comparable by considering how the "justifications for punishment" apply to the cases' facts. These charts could then be taken into account by the judges in considering how to rule on motions for additur or remittitur. The task of determining which prior cases are comparable in light of the "justifications for punishment" seems extremely difficult. In any event, nothing in the Baldus paper explains how this task would be carried out. My Comment will therefore focus on that paper's treatment of pain and suffering damages. This is what the Baldus paper spends most of its time discussing.

3. Yet the plan's proposal does assume that some service is available within the state that regularly publishes jury verdicts.
4. Of course, in cases where there is controversy about what injuries the plaintiff has actually suffered, the jury would receive the three-piece data set for each of the injuries whose existence the jury might end up affirming.
5. Jurisdictions differ in terms of how they handle "lost life enjoyment" evidence.
6. Such a set of information is what the Iowa plan seems to contemplate.
7. A similar problem afflicts the Iowa plan.
8. Cornelius J. Peck, *Compensation for Pain: A Reappraisal in Light of New Medical Evidence*, 74 Mich. L. Rev. 1355 (1974). Later studies have confirmed this newer learning. See Gary T. Schwartz, *Waste, Fraud, and Abuse in Workers' Compensation: The Recent California Experience*, 52 Md. L. Rev. 983, 1001–02 (1993).
9. Mark Ramseyer and his co-author have shown how an informal damage schedule in auto cases in Japan results in an exceptionally high rate of settlement. J. Mark Ramseyer and Minoru Nakazato, *The Rational Litigant: Settlement Amounts and Verdict Rates in Japan*, 18 J. Legal Stud. 263 (1989).

Pain and Suffering Damages: What Are They and Can They Be Measured?

Victor E. Schwartz*

All of our speakers today have accepted a premise that is worth analysis: what is the public policy basis for pain and suffering damages, and are they truly immutable and not subject to change? If one looks back in the history of tort law, it is interesting to note that until the early 1950s pain and suffering damages were generally viewed as punitive in nature—to punish a defendant for the wrongfulness of his conduct. They did not have a strong compensatory component. At the time, tort law dealt almost entirely with *fault*; strict liability was rarely imposed. In that context, it is easy to understand why pain and suffering damages were viewed as a "fault measure."[1]

Apart from their fault focus, pain and suffering damages were small, especially when measured by today's standards. While we do not have extensive data from the 1950s, what data are available suggest that pain and suffering damage awards rarely exceeded economic losses.

Many persons can claim responsibility for dramatically changing the nature of pain and suffering damages. As everyone knows, today such damages are viewed as compensatory in nature, and they are substantial in size. A person who can take a great deal of credit for these fundamental changes is Melvin Belli. Beginning in the 1950s, Mr. Belli developed new evidentiary means to suggest that pain and suffering awards should be compensatory in nature and to increase their amount. Some of his earliest work shows how he achieved these goals.[2]

*Senior Partner, Crowell & Moring, Washington, D.C.

As awards began to focus on compensation and increase in amount, lawyers sought ways to provide a "measure" for something that, by definition, could not be measured. As the panelists on this topic have correctly observed, there is no "market" for pain and suffering damages, no market measure to tell us what amount is appropriate for a broken arm or any other harm.

In the 1950s, advocates of making the immeasurable measurable came from the plaintiffs' side. One method developed was the so-called "per diem" argument, which involved breaking down pain and suffering into days, hours, or even minutes; setting a value on each unit; and calculating the total number of units that pain and suffering have lasted and may be expected to last.

There is a certain amount of courtroom theatrics in this approach, since it poses an apparently reasonable or even insignificant figure and then multiplies it by an apparently "modest" factor to attain a potentially prodigious result. Consider, $.10 a minute becomes $52,560 a year, and $1 a minute becomes over half-a-million dollars. Many courts, even today, allow plaintiffs' lawyers to suggest this type of measurement to juries.

As the numbers or amounts awarded for pain and suffering grew, however, both neutral and defense oriented scholars attempted to put some limit on them. Some learned academics went back to basics and questioned whether "money really alleviates pain." For example, in the early 1970s, Professor Cornelius Peck of the University of Washington Law School conducted a legal/medical study and concluded that pain and suffering damages should be allowed only for pain that has a physiological basis.[3] Some twenty years later, the Brookings Institute considered the need for pain and suffering damages and concluded that they were not essential. One basis for the Brookings conclusion was that a very large survey of laypersons showed they would decline to pay a small premium increase in their health or accident insurance if that amount were used to insure them for "pain and suffering" damages.[4]

The fact that pain and suffering damages are not essential can also be seen in the fact that workers who are compensated through workers' compensation do not receive them. There has been no major demand from workers to change this fact. There are no pain and suffering damages under most so-called no fault compensation systems in automobiles either. Again, there has been no public outcry to change this fact. More broadly, in almost every country in the world, pain and suffering damages are either unavailable or insignificant in tort liability awards. There has been no showing that in such countries there has been a public demand for pain and suffering damages.

As I suggested at the beginning of my remarks, it is useful to step back from the data for a moment and appreciate that high compensatory pain and suffering awards are basically a product of the imagination and hard work of the plaintiffs' bar and its excellent representatives, like Melvin

Belli and my distinguished fellow panelist, Paul Rheingold. Indeed, the plaintiffs' bar has done such a good job in creating this phenomenon that almost all of us have come to accept pain and suffering awards as a fact and necessity of life. The truth is that they are not a "fact of life," but something generated by our own legal system, again, with special credit to the creative mind and spirit of the plaintiffs' bar.

The acceptance of pain and suffering damages has come so far that proposals to place limits on them are regarded as immoral or even heretical. I have watched my good colleague from the University of Virginia, Professor Jeffrey O'Connell, suffer slings and arrows for making suggestions of this kind. When a distinguished group of professors completed a five-year study of the tort system under the aegis of the American Law Institute and recommended that reasonable or rational limits can be placed on pain and suffering awards, their work was subject to extraordinary criticism by prominent plaintiffs' attorneys.

In our session here today, both Professor Baldus (and his co-authors) and Professor Chase attempt, in a most temperate way, to make suggestions about pain and suffering damages. They are not seeking to limit them, but to develop processes to make them more consistent. Professors Baldus and Chase are not calling for strict and automatic limits on pain and suffering damages, but a flow of greater information to judges and juries, information to help them form more rational judgments about how much is a reasonable award. While representatives of the plaintiffs' bar will argue against either of these suggestions, such contentions have an ironic ring: they suggest that juries should not be entitled to consider information that is available from the public record, specifically, what other juries have done with similar types of cases.

Mr. Rheingold of the plaintiffs' bar suggests that no tort case is really "similar" to another and that some of the categories used in the proposed systems contain a wide variety of different types of behavior. Juries can be made to appreciate those differences. In fact, a fundamental argument that plaintiffs' lawyers have relied upon in other contexts is that juries are great ciphers of generally relevant information; it should be left to the jury to consider and evaluate such information with help from an attorney's searching cross-examination.

Perhaps, on reflection, some of the leadership in the plaintiffs' bar will reconsider their absolute position against giving juries access to information about cognate pain and suffering awards from other cases. Both Professor Baldus's and Professor Chase's studies are trying to bring harmony to how our judicial system treats similar injuries.

While anyone can nit-pick the Baldus and Chase papers, one has to praise both for trying a new approach—sharing information that certainly fits within the broad standards of relevance utilized by courts today. One should appreciate that such information cannot supplant the need for some outside limit on pain and suffering damages; there is a need to develop a line beyond which a judgment becomes irrational. Judges and legislators must develop the limits, even though they may seem arbitrary; it is more arbitrary to allow pain and suffering awards to be totally unwieldy and unpredictable. I have tried to show that pain and suffering damages, while important, were created by human beings with strong economic incentives to do so. Human beings can also develop rational limits on them; pain and suffering damage law is not immutable to change.

Life's experience has taught me that all these ideas must ultimately pass muster in the political arena, sometimes the Congress, but usually state legislatures. This is especially true if the ideas are to be meaningful and have a practical impact. Even the temperate suggestions of Professors Baldus and Chase are unlikely to be accepted by the plaintiffs' bar and their advocates in the legislative arena. While no one can predict the outcome of such battles, it should be noted that throughout our society, excesses are being reduced; perhaps rationality can be brought into pain and suffering damages law. If this is to be accomplished, objective scholars can make a difference in an ever on-going political fray about what has become a highly political subject.

Notes

1. See O'Connell & Carpenter, *Payment for Pain and Suffering Throughout History*, 50 Insurance Couns. J. 411 (1983).
2. Melvin Belli, *The More Adequate Award* (1952).
3. See Cornelius Peck, *Compensation for Pain: A Reappraisal in Light of New Medical Evidence*, 72 Mich. L. Rev. 1355 (1974).
4. See The Brookings Institution, *Pain and Suffering Awards: How Much Are They Costing Customers?* (1993).

Improving Jury Decisionmaking: Is There Really a Problem?

Paul D. Rheingold*

I'm the plaintiff's lawyer on the panel, so you won't be surprised by my statement. Have the principal speakers really made the case for a problem? I don't think there is a problem with jury verdicts in the sense of inconsistency and arbitrariness permeating the pain and suffering system in New York State—or any other place we might look at in the country. I think there are occasional aberrations, and the question is, what system can best deal with the aberrations without unduly inhibiting the jury's role? I think most people who sit in a courtroom, whether judges or attorneys, see that most of the time verdicts are consistent with prior verdicts. I can guess what they're going to be. Judges can guess what they're going to be. And we're not far off usually—not always, but usually. We're skilled enough to know how to settle a case for an "eye out" or an "arm off," in the parlance of the courthouse. The process of settlement is not much interfered with by any fear of arbitrariness. The problem to address is the occasional aberration, a verdict too low or too high. (And we're here because of the too high ones; I haven't heard much concern expressed about verdicts that are too low.) But the way to solve that problem is through the judge's review power, which can be exercised without the kind of complex system suggested by Dave Baldus and his co-authors.

New York, as you know, has a statute—Civil Practice Law §5501(c)—that tells judges to look at comparable verdicts. The criticism, evidently, is that the judges are not very clear about how they do it. But they're

*Partner, Rheingold & McGowan, New York, NY.

clear enough. They talk about the highest amount previously sustained, they cite other cases (perhaps without a lot of discussion). And if we get a bellringer award now and then, we expect to see a cutback. Knowing that a remittitur is coming, moreover, influences us to settle the case in the first place. So I don't see anything in this system that interferes with lawyers settling cases. I'd like to see the statistics to see how many verdicts are truly outliers. And then I'd like to see, in New York State at least, what happened to those outliers. I bet 99 percent are cut back to a point comparable to what prior juries had done. True, verdicts go up over time—just like your health care costs go up, just like the cost of bread and everything else goes up.

With regard to a program that provides judges with extensive data, a sentencing guidelines-type approach, I think the fundamental problem is that no two cases are the same and you can give a judge data by which to compare verdicts only in the broadest sense. You can't get minute and pretend that there's some sort of scientific calculation to be made—that there's some way to compare "arm offs" when one's a kid and one's a man, or one lost a dominant hand and one the other hand, or one person has persevered and gone on with his life and become a lawyer or whatever and the other person has had his life destroyed. That's what the jury is there for: to listen to those different cases and see how much suffering there is. And people get caught if they exaggerate their injuries, because there are good defense attorneys who come forward to cross examine and because juries are alert to signs of malingering.

I think letting the jury have such guidelines is even more frightening. You can have a million instructions along the lines of "this is just evidence and you're free to disregard it if you want." But we all know that if we give the jurors numbers, they're going to follow the numbers rather than play their proper role—which is to be the conscience of the community and try to figure out from listening to the case what's a fair sum. And, of course, Gary Schwartz's suggestion that we determine pain and suffering damages with fixed schedules is the most frightening to the plaintiff's bar of all three.

So, folks, my message is: let the jury do it. The system has worked for a long time, and the revisionists have a burden of proof that I don't think they've met.

Improving Jury Decisionmaking: Damages for Pain and Suffering

Mark Geistfeld*

This summary describes the general discussion following the panel presentation in terms of the issues addressed rather than the order in which the discussion proceeded.

I. Is There a Problem That Requires Reform?

A number of participants questioned the premise that awards for pain and suffering reflect an unacceptable amount of variability for injuries of the same type. In their view, a comparative study that finds discrepancies across cases does not show that the system is irrational unless the comparison accounts for the individual characteristics in each case that are relevant to its outcome. Participants who felt that there is an undesirable degree of variability in these awards acknowledged that the categories currently used for comparison are too crude and imprecise to provide a definitive answer.

One participant noted that the problem of variability in pain and suffering awards may in fact be more pronounced than depicted in the Aetna study. The study includes only awards after remittitur, and since remittitur reduces the verdict, there must be even more variability in awards made prior to remittitur.

Another participant observed that it is an empirical question whether variability in pain and suffering awards reduces the likelihood of settlement. Consequently, it would be desirable to compare settlement rates

*Assistant Professor, New York University School of Law.

for cases that involve such awards with cases that do not. This participant thought that perhaps insurance companies or claims adjusters would be able to provide such data.

This participant then noted that in California, for cases involving a claim for pain and suffering damages, settlement negotiations typically proceed by taking medical costs, multiplying by three, and adding (for plaintiffs) or subtracting (for defendants) some amount to provide a settlement range. Another participant said that an insurance company used to rely on this approach in its settlement negotiations, but no longer does because it gives plaintiffs an incentive to overstate their medical costs.

One participant thought that the current system for awarding pain and suffering promotes settlements. Defendants often do not have an incentive to settle and would rather fight a "paper war" in an attempt to overwhelm the plaintiff. By asking the right questions about how settlement negotiations are proceeding, judges can re-balance the system by emphasizing the possibility that the defendant faces substantial pain and suffering damages. For this reason, this participant concluded that the variability in pain and suffering awards may provide judges with an effective tool for expediting settlements.

II. Comments on the Proposals

One participant stated that an insurance company currently uses a real-estate appraisal approach in estimating damages for pain and suffering. This approach derives an estimate by comparing the amount claimed to awards in two or three similar cases. This is a rational approach to the problem, in this participant's view, because pain and suffering is difficult to quantify and so the award should reflect community standards. Basing an individual award upon a larger number of cases provides a better estimate of community standards than does an award based solely upon the facts of one case.

A different participant observed that if there is a tort crisis that requires reform, the problem does not exist with outliers—the extreme awards—but instead with the average case—the mean. This participant thought that the proposals here do not appear to address the size of the average award.

Other participants also noted that the proposals made by the panelists are more likely to achieve consistency across cases than to reduce overall costs. Two participants stated that a more direct method for achieving a reduction in the average amount of damage awards for pain and suffering would be to take an award within each injury category and then scale that award downwards by a given percentage, for example, seventy-five percent of the scheduled award.

Participants observed that the concern about undesirable variability in pain and suffering awards is very similar to concerns about consistency in criminal sentencing that led to the enactment of the United States Sentencing Guidelines. They accordingly thought that we should look to the experience of courts with the Sentencing Guidelines to gain a sense of whether the proposals here would lead to more consistent outcomes without an undue increase in administrative costs.

Relatedly, participants noted that delay in resolving cases is one of the civil justice system's biggest problems. These participants expressed the concern that, not only do the proposals here not address that problem, but ultimately they may exacerbate it by increasing the length of trials or the frequency of appeals.

One participant observed that in developing the databases upon which any of the proposals rely, it is necessary to account for the effects of comparative fault, as the amount included in the database should not reflect any reductions stemming from the plaintiff's comparative fault. Another participant explained that this is why settlements should not be included in the database.

Participants expressed various concerns about whether the database relied upon for any of the proposals captures all of the information relevant to the award's determination. One participant questioned whether juries increase pain and suffering awards as the culpability of the defendant's conduct increases. If so, how could this be accounted for in the database? Another participant took the position that pain and suffering awards reflect community values. The data, accordingly, should be adjusted for differences across time and community. Merely adjusting for inflation is not sufficient in this regard. A different participant thought that in determining the pain and suffering damage award, the jury includes consideration of the defendant's ability to pay the award. This participant thus thought that the database should include information regarding the defendant's ability to pay.

Relatedly, another participant observed that the difficulty of defining injury categories in a manner that captures all the relevant aspects of the injury may lead judges or juries to disregard the schedule. This is because judges or jurors who do not believe that the injury categories are sufficiently analogous to the case at hand will be inclined to ignore the schedule in order to provide an award they feel is more appropriate for the injury before them. For example, prior to the enactment of the Sentencing Guidelines, the United States Court of Appeals for the Second Circuit adopted a program that provided sentencing judges with twenty-five different fact patterns and a proposed sentence for each fact pattern. The program failed, according to this participant, because sentencing judges perceived a lack of sufficiently close correspondence between the facts at hand and the hypothetical fact patterns underlying the proposed sentences.

Other participants expressed the concern that the proposals are flawed because they rely upon a database that does not have an independent source of accuracy or validity. If the underlying data are not legitimate, or are otherwise suspect because current standards for determining pain and suffering awards are inadequate, we must question whether it is appropriate to rationalize future awards on the basis of these prior suspect awards.

Another participant stated that policy reforms in this area ought to be constrained by the fact that we are operating in a data-poor environment. The norm for empirical research in this area is that the data do not exist. In assessing the desirability of reform proposals that rely upon the collection and distribution of data to jurors and courts, this participant concluded, we need to account for the limited resources and capabilities of most jurisdictions in this regard.

One participant thought that the problem with pain and suffering awards is much more fundamental than that depicted by the panel presentation: Because such damages often involve relatively large sums of money, there are a number of individuals profiting from the current system. Indeed, the pursuit of damages for pain and suffering has created a "growth industry" with a stake in the continued expansion of such awards. In this participant's view, unless and until we take the difficult step of stopping the growth of the pain and suffering "system," it will not be possible to deal with deserving cases in an appropriate manner.

III. Reporter's Summary of the Discussion

In many senses, the general discussion is representative of the current debate regarding reform of the civil justice system. Some observers advanced the view that there is no problem with respect to pain and suffering damages or that the costs of reform would exceed any benefits. Others opposed these proposals as too piecemeal, as missing the big picture. When attention was directed to the specific proposals discussed by the panel, the need for more data often became the focus of the discussion. Many thought that more information is needed to make the case that these proposals would be an improvement or to make them operational.

There is an element of truth to all these points. Whether the current approach of awarding damages for pain and suffering is in need of reform depends crucially upon one's views of the purposes that should be furthered by the civil-justice system. And even if we agree on purpose, which at present we do not, we are still left with the questions of where do we stand now, and where can and should we go? Getting the relevant data is crucial to answering these questions. As one participant aptly put it, at this point we are operating in a "data poor environment."

Nevertheless, in my view there is a well-defined method that could be implemented under current law and would enable juries to determine a defensible measure of pain and suffering damages. But that is another story.[1]

Notes

1. See Mark Geistfeld, *Placing a Price on Pain and Suffering: A Method for Helping Juries Determine Tort Damage for Nonmonetary Injuries,* 83 Cal. L. Rev. 773 (1995).

Contributors

Professor David C. Baldus
University of Iowa College of Law

Professor Oscar G. Chase
New York University School of Law

Professor Edward H. Cooper
University of Michigan School of Law

Professor Rochelle C. Dreyfuss
New York University School of Law

John R. Evancho
Attorney, Law and Regulatory Affairs
Aetna Life and Casualty Co., Inc.

Professor Margaret G. Farrell
Widener University School of Law

Professor Mark Geistfeld
New York University School of Law

Professor Samuel R. Gross
University of Michigan Law School

Honorable Patrick E. Higginbotham
United States Circuit Judge
United States Court of Appeals for the Fifth Circuit

Professor Lewis A. Kornhauser
New York University School of Law

Professor Larry Kramer
New York University School of Law

Dr. John C. MacQueen
Director, National Maternal & Child Health Resource Center
University of Iowa

Professor Arthur R. Miller
Harvard University Law School

Professor Geoffrey P. Miller
New York University School of Law

Judyth W. Pendell
Vice President, Law and Regulatory Affairs
Aetna Life and Casualty Co., Inc.

Professor Richard L. Revesz
New York University School of Law

Paul D. Rheingold, Esq.
Rheingold & McGowan, New York

Professor Joseph Sanders
University of Houston Law School

Robert N. Sayler, Esq.
Covington & Burling, Washington, D.C.

Professor Gary T. Schwartz
University of California at Los Angeles School of Law

Victor E. Schwartz, Esq.
Crowell & Moring, Washington, D.C.

Professor George Woodworth
Department of Statistics & Actuarial Science
University of Iowa

Index